P9-CLD-774

THE FAITH

of the

EARLY FATHERS

Volume One

A source-book of theological and historical passages from the Christian writings of the Pre-Nicene and Nicene eras

selected and translated

by

W. A. JURGENS

TH
08
JU-FA
VI

The Liturgical Press   *Collegeville, Minnesota*

Nihil obstat: John Eidenschink, O.S.B., J.C.D., *Censor deputatus. Imprimatur*: ✠ George H. Speltz, D.D., Bishop of St. Cloud, June 9, 1970.

Copyright © 1970, The Order of St. Benedict, Inc., Collegeville, Minnesota. Printed in the United States of America. ISBN 0–8146–0432–3.

All rights reserved under United States copyright law, and the International and Pan-American Conventions, including the right to reproduce this booklet, or parts thereof, in any form, by mimeograph, or other mechanical or electronic devices.

Dedicated to the Memory

of

JOSEPH J. MULLEN

A great seminary Rector

✦

He never really believed
that one man could teach another
— but for more than fifty years
he did it anyway

TABLE OF CONTENTS

FOREWORD

Today, it seems, one can write nothing without some reference to Vatican II — certainly not a book of patristic texts, and in the hands of some authors, not even a grocery list. The Second Ecumenical Council of the Vatican now belongs to history. While it was yet in session there were undoubtedly some, even very capable men, who honestly believed that it would take a place beside Pistoia, so many of whose doctrines it seemed, through poor reporting, to be emulating. It is now clear to all, however, that it must be accorded its rightful place beside Nicaea and the rest of the properly approved Ecumenical Councils.

It will now be almost universally recognized that the late Council suffered a great deal from poor reporting and worse public relations. At no time did newspaper accounts ever seem to stumble against the important fact that the Second Vatican Council was the logical historical development of the First. On July 18, 1870, it was formally declared in the presence of Pius IX and the Assembled Council Fathers that the Bishop of Rome, successor of Peter and vicar of Christ, rejoiced in the properly defined prerogative of infallibility. Italian nationalist troops were even then marching on Rome. The Fathers dispersed, expecting to meet again later. They never did. The Council remained unclosed, but had in fact ended. This left a great many open questions. What, in fact, was the position of local ordinaries, individually and collegially, in the face of an infallible monarch? This inevitable question would surely have been taken up in the intended later sessions of the First Vatican Council, had that Council been able to continue.

Collegiality was not a new question. Cyprian of Carthage already knew something of the problem, and indeed, he knew even the term *College of Bishops (e. g., in* § 576b, *below).* That Cyprian's concept of that college was something different from that of the Fathers of the Second Vatican Council, considering their different backgrounds and the developments in the area of papal authority in the intervening seventeen hundred years, can be in no way surprising. The question of the College of Bishops, precisely what it is and what its magisterial authority, is a question of the greatest antiquity, finally brought to ardent importance by the monumental definition of Papal Infallibility in the First Vatican Council, and then importunately dropped because of that Council's forced cessation due to political exigencies.

No student of history could ever have imagined that the Second Vatican Council would find it possible to ignore the question of collegiality. Nor did it. It is the function of a historian to know the past so that he may, insofar as it be within his feeble powers, regulate the present in such a way that he may reckon upon a future. If we might venture a humble prediction, we would suggest that future historians will see the question of episcopal collegiality as the most burning of all the issues treated by the Second Vatican Council.

If initially there were some who looked upon the proceedings of Vatican II with somewhat of a jaundiced eye, all must now admit the great importance of what has been done. The age in which we lived is a dead one, and it will not live again. Anyone equipped with even a modest faculty of memory would not want it back again.

We live in an age in which the role of the layman in the Church is a tremendously important task. If the layman is to be effective he must prepare himself adequately. No Catholic today can afford to be ignorant of the past: neither of his glorious heritage, nor of its occasional less glorious moments. Our book is published for a primary audience of theological students engaged directly in a theological course of studies; but its secondary audience is every interested layman.

In the early forties of the present century there began a revival of interest in patristic studies, which never quite bore its promised fruit. With the advent of Vatican II and its monumental re-assessments, that revival of patristic interest has been renewed; and while not positing a direct cause and effect relationship between the two, it is probably fair to say that the measure of Vatican II's successful effectiveness will be similar to the fate of the new revival of patristics. Should the former succeed, so also will the latter; and should the latter die on the vine as once before it died, so also will the former. With that thought, we commend not merely our book but even to a large extent the future development of the Church into the hands of the layman.

Patrology is usually defined as the study of the lives, doctrines, and writings of the Fathers of the Church.

The Church, we learned as children, has four marks by which it may be known. Coincidentally there are four marks also by which a writer is recognized as a Father of the Church: *a*) orthodox doctrine, *b*) sanctity of life, *c*) antiquity, and *d*) approval of the Church. Antiquity is easily decided. The patristic age, by common agreement, ends in the West with the death of St. Isidore of Seville in the year 636 A. D., and in the East with the death of St. John Damascene in 749 A. D. Unless one belong within the period proper to his locale, he cannot be called a Father. And it is perhaps worthwhile noting now that those whose antiquity is so great that they were in fact the immediate associates of the Apostles are called Apostolic Fathers.

The other three notes are less precise. To be regarded as a Father, one must have orthodox doctrine; but this does not exclude all doctrinal error. An occasional material heresy can be found even in the greater lights among the Fathers. It does imply, however, a devotion to orthodoxy and a faithful adherence to the orthodox Church.

Even sanctity of life must be taken in somewhat of a broad sense. St. Jerome had an abominable gift for invective; and it was probably his own lack of humility that brought him to accuse St. Basil, even be it justifiably, of pride. No doubt the early Church venerated many as saints who could never have escaped the telling barbs of a devil's advocate. But it was an infallible Church which initiated their veneration; and they are saints as certainly as those of a later time who attained the honors of the altar only after due canonical process. In general we may say that those to whom ecclesiastical tradition has accorded the title of saint fulfill the requirement of sanctity of life.

The last note of a Father, approval of the Church, is perhaps the most nebulous of all. It is not necessary that there be express approbation, but there need be only such approbation as can be deduced from ecclesiastical usage.

In actual practice, patrology does not confine itself to those who are, in the more technical sense of the term, Fathers of the Church. Rather, it includes virtually all Christian writings of the proper antiquity. Those authors who do indeed belong to the patristic age, but who lack one or more of the other notes, are called Ecclesiastical Writers. Thus the writings of heretics, like Arius, are included; and of schismatics, like Novatian. The writings of non-Christians, however, are excluded. That is why the works of Philo and Josephus, however valuable to the history of early Christianity their study may be, do not properly form a part of the subject matter of patrology; for their authors are Jews and, in the technical sense of a very unecumenical term, infidels.

It is a cliché of book introductions to say that the editor and publishers are confident that a work will fill a long felt need. Yet, in the present instance, it is not likely that all the humility of all the Fathers together could induce us to say otherwise, when we consider that for the past fifty years it has been customary to refer to passages from the Fathers and Ecclesiastical Writers by a conventional series of accepted numbers — the arbitrarily numbered passages of Rouët de Journel's *Enchiridion patristicum* — and that there are by this time literally thousands of theological and historical works which employ these conventional numbers, while there has not been until now a single work in English to provide a reference to such passages in the same numerical sequence. The format of the present work will be familiar to all who are acquainted with Rouët de Journel's *Enchiridion*. The plan is a simple one. In a nearly chronological sequence we quote such passages from the writings of the first three and one-half or four centuries of the Christian era, as have special theological and historical significance, and which are most frequently referred to by theological authors of the present day. The passages are numbered consecutively for reference. Marginal numbers refer to the *Doctrinal Index*, pp. 413-432, where will be found, again in numerical sequence for easy reference, the theological points in regard to which the passage is generally cited, along with the numbers of any other passages dealing with the same subject matter.

For example: a student, reading on page 220 of Volume IV, Tome 2, Part 1, of Ludwig

Lercher's *Institutiones theologiae dogmaticae,* will find that in respect to pre-Nicene testimonials to Christ's Eucharistic presence, he is referred to Clement of Alexandria's *Paedagogus,* R 408. This indicates to him that he will find the pertinent text from Clement's *Paedagogus* or *The Instructor of Children,* either in Latin or in Greek or in both, in § 408 of Rouët de Journel's *Enchiridion patristicum.* Now, for the first time in the fifty years in which these numbers have been in use, he has in his hands a book in which he will find, in § 408, an English translation of the passage in question. If the student will turn then to § 408 of the present book, he will find also certain marginal numbers appended there, *viz.* 877, 230, 416, 781, and 850. Each of these refers to a numbered statement in the *Doctrinal Index* of the present work, on which the matter of § 408 has some bearing. Turning to number 877 in the *Doctrinal Index,* he will find the statement: *The Eucharist was so instituted that it might be received in the manner of food, for the refreshment of the soul;* and appended thereto for the convenience of anyone inclined to further patristic investigation of the point are the numbers of other passages in our work dealing with the same matter: 7, 187, 362, 394i, 408, 410, 436a, and 707.

In no sense of the word, however, is our present work a translation of Rouët de Journel. We have made a thorough investigation of the theological textbooks in common use, in order to discover the patristic passages most frequently cited. From this study of existing works, we have made what is entirely our own selection of passages. Moreover, since the *Doctrinal Index* is eminently useful also when one wants to find patristic texts pertinent to particular doctrinal points, a method especially useful to the preacher, we have included also some few especially pregnant passages which have generally escaped the attention of the authors of textbooks.

In all, we have made our own selection of passages, including much that is in Rouët, much that is not in Rouët, and excluding a number of less useful passages although they are included in Rouët. In this last category of excluded passages are some which are simply repetitious, some which scholars now agree are really not pertinent to the theological point in which regard they were usually cited, and some which are now known to be spurious in respect to the author and period for which they were generally cited. We have taken care, at the same time, that any passage found both in Rouët and in the present work shall bear in both the same reference number. Omitted passages are simply skipped in the numerical sequence, while additional passages are given a number with an alphabetic subscript.

For example: Rouët's work opens with ten citations from the *Didache,* numbered, of course, from 1 through 10. Our work opens with thirteen citations from the *Didache,* numbered as follows: 1, 1a, 1b, 2, 3, 4, 5, 6, 7, 7a, 8, 9, and 10. Passages numbered 1a, 1b, and 7a are not found in Rouët. All the others are, and bear the same numbers as do the same passages in his work. Had we elected to omit the passages which Rouët numbers 6 and 7, our sequence of numbers would simply have skipped from 5 to 7a. Nor are the delimitations of similarly numbered passages necessarily the same. Rouët's passage number 1 includes only Ch. 1, Vs. 2-3 of the *Didache.* Our passage number 1 is Ch. 1, Vs. 1-6; but since it includes all that part which Rouët cites, we give it his number. In this way the numbers standard through half a century are preserved in order to avoid confusion and to increase the utility of the present work.

We have given very brief and more necessary notes in regard to the authors whose works are included, in regard to the state of preservation of the texts, in regard to authenticity of works, and in reference to the reliability of the best available editions. And we have felt it necessary to include also occasional footnotes of greater importance in respect to the interpretation of various passages and in regard to words of particularly interesting significance. It should be immediately evident, however, that the present work is in no way intended to substitute for the student's regular use of a standard manual, such as those of Altaner or Quasten.

Rouët included no notes whatever, and hence was able to cover the entire patristic period in his one volume, down to St. John Damascene in the 8th century. We have concluded our present work with the latter part of the 4th century: a logical division, since it embraces the entire pre-Nicene period along with what may be called the Nicene era, *i.e.,* the aftermath of

Nicaea, up to and including the Second Ecumenical Council, that of Constantinople of 381 A. D. The Cappadocians, though they fall within the last years of this same period, and the others down to St. John Damascene, belong to another age. We have thought it better to treat more adequately of a shorter period; and if our work is accepted as we hope it will be, a second volume will suffice to cover the second half of the patristic age. In any case, either book will be a complete work in itself, and entirely useful without the other.

All passages in the present work have been newly translated from the best critical editions. In almost every instance we have indicated two references to the original text: not only the current standard critical edition, which will frequently be the *Corpus christianorum;* the *Corpus scriptorum ecclesiasticorum latinorum,* familiarly known as the *Vienna Corpus;* the series *Die griechischen christlichen Schriftsteller der ersten [drei] Jahrhunderte,* familiarly known as the *Berlin Corpus;* or the *Corpus scriptorum christianorum orientalium;* but also, because it will be for many a convenience, reference is made to the proper place in Migne's *Patrologiae cursus completus, series latina* (PL) or to his *Patrologiae cursus completus, series graeca* (PG). In every instance we point out the edition which we regard as being the best or the present standard; and in every instance it is this which has served as the basis for our translating.

And while we frequently point out the inadequacy of the texts printed by Migne, which are mostly reprints of the work of the Maurists and other great editors of a century and more before even Migne's time, we must take this single occasion to note, as a general remark, that while Migne's actual texts are mostly superseded by more recent critical editions prepared in conformity with more modern and sounder principles of scholarship, still, the vast amount of erudite notes and instructive introductions in Migne makes his work even yet an indispensable tool for any who have not the older editions which he reprints.

W. A. JURGENS

Cleveland, Ohio
March, 1970

INDEX OF SELECTIONS

xviii

TABLE OF ABBREVIATIONS

AND OF LATIN TERMS

A.D. = year or years [of the Lord].

ante = before.

apud = in, among, with.

aut = or [else].

ca. = *circa* = about.

Ch. = chapter.

Chs. = chapters.

CSEL = *Corpus scriptorum ecclesiasticorum latinorum.* Series of Latin texts of the Fathers, edited by the Wiener Akademie der Wissenschaften, 1866ff. Commonly called the *Vienna Corpus.*

CSCO = *Corpus scriptorum christianorum orientalium.* Series of the writings of the Fathers in the various oriental languages, each accompanied by a translation in a more commonly understood language. Publication began at Paris in 1903, and continues, now at Louvain. The corpus has seven sub-series: Syriac, Coptic, Arabic, Armenian, Georgian, and Ethiopic texts and translations; and *Subsidia*, embracing various monographs and linguistic treatises.

et postea = and afterwards.

fl. = *floruit* = flourished.

forte = perhaps.

GCS = *Die griechischen christlichen Schriftsteller der ersten [drei] Jahrhunderte.* Series of Greek texts of the Fathers, edited by the Preussische Akademie der Wissenschaften, 1897ff. Commonly called the *Berlin Corpus.*

inter = among, between.

nisi forte = or maybe.

paulo post = soon after.

PG = Abbé J. P. Migne, *Patrologiae cursus completus: Series graeca.* 161 volumes, Paris, 1857–1866. Greek texts with Latin translation.

PL = Abbé J. P. Migne, *Patrologiae cursus completus: Series latina.* 221 volumes, including 4 of indices, Paris, 1844–1855.

post = after.

postea = afterwards.

regn. = *regnavit* = reigned.

seu = or [also].

sive = or [also].

Vs. = verse.

VV. = verses.

The Faith of the Early Fathers

DIDACHE *or* TEACHING OF THE TWELVE APOSTLES [*ca. A. D.* 140]

The *Didache* was first published in 1883, following its discovery by Philotheos Bryennios, the metropolitan of Nicomedia, in the 11th century manuscript, *Codex Hierosolymitanus 1056.* Upon its publication, it was quickly observed that large parts of the work had previously been extant as quotations within other works, but had not been recognized for what they were. For example, almost all of the Greek text of the *Didache* was recoverable from the already well-known seventh book of the *Apostolic Constitutions,* originating in Syria in the 4th century. Since Bryennios' discovery of the complete text, numerous other finds have been made of fragmentary texts and translations of the *Didache,* and of a complete translation in Georgian. Fragments are now extant in Latin, Coptic, Ethiopic, and Syriac, along with the complete translation in Georgian, and, of course, the complete Greek text.

The best current scholarship on the *Didache* provides the following hypothesis: The part of the *Didache* comprising Ch. 1, VV. 1-3a and Chs. 2, V. 2 through the end of Ch. 6 is originally a Jewish work for the instruction of gentile proselytes to Judaism. This Jewish *Grundschrift,* possibly a work of Essene origin, may be referred to as the *Two Ways Document* or the *Urdidache.* In Syria not later than *A. D.* 160 and perhaps about *A. D.* 140, the *Two Ways Document* found entrance to Christian circles. The parts comprising Ch. 1, V. 3b through Ch. 2, V. 1, and Ch. 7, V. 1 to the end (Ch. 16, V. 8) were added by a Christian, thus producing the *Didache* as we have it now, a work for the instruction of catechumens.

A convenient edition, text and translation, is that of Kirsopp Lake, *The Apostolic Fathers,* Vol. 1, pp. 303-333, in the Loeb Classical Library series, London and New York, 1930. The best and most recent critical edition is Funk-Bihlmeyer-Schneemelcher, *Die apostolischen Väter, Vol. 1,* Tübingen 1956, pp. 1-9.

1

[1, 1]
There are two ways, one of life and one of death: and great is the difference between the two ways. [2] The way of life is this: first, you shall love God, who created you; second, your neighbor as yourself (1). Whatever you would not wish to be done to you, do not do to another (2). [3] The teaching of these words is this. Bless those who curse you, and pray for your enemies: fast for those who persecute you. For what kindness is it, if you love those who love you? Do not even the pagans do this? Love those who hate you, and you will not have an enemy.

[4] Abstain from carnal and bodily desires (3). If anyone strike you on the right cheek, turn the other to him, and you will be perfect. If anyone force you to go one mile, go two with him. If anyone take your cloak, give him also your tunic. If anyone take from you what is yours, do not demand its return, not even if you can (4). [5] Give to everyone who asks, and demand no return; for the Father wishes that a share of His own gifts be given to all (5).

Blessed is the man who gives according to the commandment; for he is without blame. Woe to him that takes. Yet, if he takes because he is in need, he is blameless; but if he be not in need, he shall give an account of the why and the wherefore of his taking. He will be put under constraint so that he may be examined closely as to what he did; and he will not come out from there until he has paid the last farthing (6). [6] But concerning this it is also said: Let your alms perspire in your hands, until you know to whom you are giving (7).

64
66

1a

[2, 1]

The second commandment of the teaching: [2] You shall not murder. You shall not commit adultery. You shall not seduce boys. You shall not commit fornication. You shall not steal. You shall not practice magic. You shall not use potions. You shall not procure abortion, nor destroy a new-born child. [3] You shall not covet your neighbor's goods. You shall not perjure yourself. You shall not bear false witness. You shall not speak evil. You shall not bear malice (8).

[4] You shall not be double-minded nor double-tongued; for a double tongue is the snare of death (9). [5] Your word shall not be false nor vain, but shall be fulfilled in deed. [6] You shall not be greedy, nor extortionate, nor a hypocrite, nor malicious, nor proud. You shall make no evil plan against your neighbor. [7] You shall not hate any man; but some you shall reprove, some you shall pray for, and some you shall love more than the breath of life that is in you.

969

1b

[4, 3]

You shall not make a schism. Rather, you shall make peace among those who are contending. Judge justly, and take no regard of the person when correcting transgressions (10). [4] Do not be of two minds, whether a thing shall be or shall not be.

420

2

[4, 13]

You shall not abandon the commandments of the Lord; but you shall keep what you have received, adding nothing to it nor taking anything away (11).

104

3

[4, 14]

Confess your offenses in church (12), and do not go up to your prayer with an evil conscience. This is the way of life.

916

4

[7, 1]

In regard to Baptism — baptize thus: After the foregoing instructions (13), baptize in the name of the Father, and of the Son, and of the Holy Spirit (14), in living water (15). [2] If you have no living water, then baptize in other water; and if you are not able in cold, then in warm. [3] If you have neither, pour water three times on the head, in the name of the Father, and of the Son, and of the Holy Spirit (16). [4] Before the Baptism, let the one baptizing and the one to be baptized fast, as also any others who are able. Command the one who is to be baptized to fast beforehand for one or two days.

820
826
822
823
824
825

5

[8, 1]
Do not let your fasts be with the hypocrites. They fast on Monday and Thursday; but you shall fast on Wednesday and Friday. [2] Do not pray as the hypocrites do (17), but as the Lord commanded in His gospel, you shall pray thus (18): Our Father who   64 art in heaven, hallowed be thy name. Thy kingdom come, thy will be done on earth, as   60 it is in heaven. Give us this day our daily bread, and forgive us our debts, as we also forgive our debtors. And lead us not into temptation, but deliver us from evil (19). For thine is the power and the glory forever (20). [3] Pray thus three times a day.

6

[9, 1]
In regard to the Eucharist — you shall give thanks thus (21): [2] First, in regard to the cup: — We give you thanks, our Father, for the holy vine of David your son, which   871 you have made known to us through Jesus your Son. Glory be to you forever. [3] In regard to the broken bread: — We give you thanks, our Father, for the life and knowl-   860 edge which you have made known to us through Jesus your Son. Glory be to you forever. [4] As this broken bread was scattered on the mountains, but brought together was   880 made one, so gather your Church from the ends of the earth into your kingdom. For   420 yours is the glory and the power through Jesus Christ forever. [5] Let no one eat or   404 drink of the Eucharist with you except those who have been baptized in the name of   874 the Lord; for it was in reference to this that the Lord said: "Do not give that which is holy to dogs (22)."

7

[10, 1]
After you have eaten your fill, give thanks thus: [2] We thank you, holy Father, for   877 your holy name, which you have caused to dwell in our hearts; and for the knowledge and faith and immortality which you have made known to us through Jesus your Son.   388 Glory be to you forever. [3] You, almighty Master, have created all things (23) for   466 your name's sake, and have given food and drink to men for their enjoyment, so that they might return thanks to you. Upon us, however, you have bestowed spiritual food and drink, and eternal life through your Servant. [4] Above all we give you thanks,   871 because you are mighty. Glory be to you forever.
[5] Remember, O Lord, your Church. Deliver it from every evil and perfect it in   420 your love. Gather it from the four winds (24), sanctified for your kingdom, which you   404 have prepared for it. For yours is the power and the glory forever. [6] Let grace come, and let this world pass away. Osanna to the God of David (25). If anyone is holy, let   875 him come; if anyone is not, let him repent. Marana Tha (26). Amen. [7] But allow prophets to give thanks (27) as they will.

7a

[11, 3]
In regard to apostles and prophets, act according to the doctrine of the gospel (28). [4] Let every apostle who comes to you be received as the Lord. [5] Do not, however,   60 allow him to stay more than one day, or, if needs be, two. If he remains for three days, he is a false prophet. [6] When an apostle goes forth, let him take only enough bread to

last until he reach his night's lodging. If he ask for money he is a false prophet. [7] You shall not test or examine any prophet who speaks in a spirit. Every sin shall be forgiven, but this sin shall not be forgiven (29). [8] Not everyone, however, who speaks in a spirit is a prophet, unless he have the behavior of the Lord. By his behavior, then, the false prophet and the true prophet shall be known.   64

8

[14, 1]

On the Lord's Day of the Lord (30) gather together, break bread and give thanks (31),   875
after confessing your transgressions so that your sacrifice may be pure. [2] Let no one   916
who has a quarrel with his neighbor join you until he is reconciled, lest your sacrifice be defiled (32). [3] For this is that which was proclaimed by the Lord: "In every place and time let there be offered to Me a clean sacrifice. For I am a Great King," says the   894
Lord, "and My name is wonderful among the gentiles (33)."

9

[15, 1]

Elect (34) for yourselves, therefore, bishops and deacons worthy of the Lord, humble   406
men and not lovers of money, truthful and proven; for they also serve you in the   441
ministry of the prophets and teachers. [2] Do not, therefore, despise them; for they   954
are your honorable men, together with the prophets and teachers. [3] Correct one another, not in anger but in peace, as you find it in the gospel (35); and let no one   60
speak with you who has done a wrong to his neighbor, nor let him hear, until he repents. [4] Your prayers and your alms and all your acts you shall perform as you find in the gospel of our Lord.

10

[16, 3]

In the last days, then, false prophets and corrupters will be multiplied. Sheep will be   1010
turned into wolves and charity will be turned into hate (36). [4] As lawlessness increases, men will hate one another and persecute and betray; and then will appear the deceiver of the world as a Son of God. He will work signs and wonders and the world will be given over into his hands. He will do such wicked deeds as have not been done since the world began (37). [5] Then will all created men come to the fire of judgment, and many will be scandalized and will be lost (38); but those who persevere in their faith, will be saved (39) out from under the accursed thing itself (40).

[6] And then will appear the signs of the truth (41). First, the sign spread out in the   64
heavens; second, the sign of the sound of the trumpet (42); and third, the resurrection   1011
of the dead. [7] Not the resurrection of all men, but, as it was said: "The Lord will come, and all His saints with Him (43)." Then the world will see the Lord coming on the clouds of heaven (44).

1. Deut. 6:5; Lev. 19:18; Sir. 7:30 [Septuagint]; Matt. 22:37-39; Mark 12:30-31.
2. Tob. 4:16. The rule is given in its positive form in Matt. 7:12 and in Luke 6:31.
3. 1 Pet. 2:11.
4. οὐδὲ γὰρ δύνασαι.
5. Matt. 5:44, 46-47; Luke 6:27-35.
6. Matt. 5:26. Farthing is an apt rendering of κοδράντην.
7. This last sentence (verse 6) has much the appearance of a marginal gloss which has slipped into the text.
8. Ex. 20:13-17; Deut. 5:17-21; Matt. 5:33; 19:18.
9. Prov. 14:27 [Septuagint]; also Prov. 21:6.
10. Deut. 1:16-17; Prov. 31:9.
11. Deut. 4:2; 12:32.
12. Sir. 4:26 [Septuagint].
13. ταῦτα πάντα προειπόντες.
14. Matt. 28:19.
15. The implication of ὕδωρ ζῶν is a flowing stream. The *other water* is that of a lake or pool, which might even be warm and less pure. The third alternative is infusion or pouring.
16. Matt. 28:19.
17. Matt. 6:5.
18. Matt. 6:9a.
19. Matt. 6:9b-13.
20. This is a concluding formula for liturgical prayer, first found in Syrian usage and afterwards in Byzantine, where *kingdom* is often inserted before *power and glory*. It is found in numerous scripture manuscripts, but not in those of greater authority. Since it was the normal prayer conclusion and was familiarly appended to the *Our Father*, its presence in various scripture manuscripts is easily explained as a copyist's error.
21. περὶ δὲ τῆς εὐχαριστίας οὕτως εὐχαριστήσατε. Chapters 9 and 10 are generally referred to as the Eucharistic section. Yet, no less an authority than Berthold Altaner [*Patrology*, pp. 52-53, where bibliographical references are given] holds it as more probable that they refer to the Agape. The latter view is based principally upon an interpolation in chapter 10, in a Coptic *Didache* fragment, once thought to refer to the consecration of chrism, but now interpreted as referring to the Agape. The testimony of an unauthentic interpolation strikes us as strange evidence against the seemingly very clear language of these prayers. Quasten's remark [*Patrology*, Vol. 1, p. 32], however strong it may be, seems much more to the point; for he says that to regard these two chapters as non-Eucharistic table prayers is untenable.
22. Matt. 7:6.
23. Wis. 1:14; Sir. 18:1; 24:8 [Septuagint]. See also Apoc. 4:11.
24. Matt. 24:31.
25. Matt. 21:9.
26. While its general import is clear enough, the precise meaning of this Aramaic eschatological term, anticipating the parousia, is not known, because the division of the letters is not certain. The *Codex Hierosolymitanus*, the only complete manuscript of the *Didache* in Greek, writes it as a single word: μαραναθά: but the Aramaic which it transliterates is two words, either *Maran Atha*, or *Marana Tha*. If we read *Maran Atha*, as the editors of the *Didache* [Schneemelcher's Funk-Bihlmeyer] would have it, the phrase means *the Lord is coming*. The same term occurs in 1 Cor. 16:22, where Nestle prefers *Marana Tha*. This latter reading is suggested also by the ἔρχου κύριε Ἰησοῦ at the conclusion of the Apocalypse. *Marana Tha*, the imperative, seems to us the more likely reading: and it is rendered: *Come thou, Our Lord!*
27. See. Matt. 10:40-42. It is frequently pointed out by modern authors that the *Didache* reflects a duplex hierarchy: bishops and deacons on the one hand, and apostles, prophets and teachers on the other. We question whether or not apostles, prophets and teachers really represent three distinct classes, or whether perhaps the terms are vaguely synonymous with each other. Prophets and teachers are spoken of in Ch. 15 (§ 9 below); whereas Ch. 11 (§ 7a below) speaks of apostles and prophets. Perhaps, then, apostles and teachers are more or less synonymous. Moreover, it seems clear in Ch. 11 that the terms apostles and prophets are being used interchangeably.
28. Matt. 10:40-42. See previous note.
29. Matt. 12:31. See, however, 1 Cor. 14:29; 1 John 4:1; and Apoc. 2:2.
30. Κατὰ κυριακὴν δὲ κυρίου . . . .. This redundancy in the Greek indicates that the term *Lord's Day* had already become a common usage for Sunday, so much so that it is now used as a distinct term apart from its root meaning.
31. εὐχαριστήσατε, which we render *give thanks*, might also be translated *celebrate the Eucharist*.
32. Matt. 5:23-24.
33. Mal. 1:11, 14.
34. χειροτονήσατε.
35. Matt. 5:22-26; 18:15-35.
36. See 2 Pet. 3:3; Matt. 24:10-12; 7:15.
37. See Apoc. 12:9; 2 John 1:7; Matt. 24:24; 2 Thess. 2:9.

38. Matt. 24:10.
39. Matt. 10:22; 24:13.
40. σωϑήσονται ὑπ᾽ αὐτοῦ τοῦ καταϑέματος – snatched from its very jaws, as it were.
41. Matt. 24:30.
42. Matt. 24:31, See also 1 Cor. 15:52 and 1 Thess. 4:16.
43. Zach. 14:5.
44. Matt. 24:30; 26:64.

ST. CLEMENT OF ROME, POPE [*fl. ca. A. D.* 80 (92 - 101?)]

The various early lists of the Bishops of Rome make Clement either the first, second, or third successor of St. Peter. The better evidence and that generally accepted would have him Peter's third successor, following after Anencletus (also called Cletus), who succeeded Linus. Dio Cassius' (*Hist. Rom.* 67, 14) identification of St. Clement of Rome with the martyred consul Titus Flavius Clemens, a member of the imperial family, must be discarded; and there is little or no probability to the opinion of Origen (*Comm. in Ioan.* 6, 36) and Eusebius (*Hist. Eccl.* 6, 3, 15), who identify Clement of Rome with the Clement who was a collaborator of St. Paul, and whom the Apostle mentions in his Epistle to the Philippians (4: 3).

To base Clement's title of Apostolic Father on his supposed association with St. Peter is at best somewhat tenuous. But whether or not he was Peter's convert, as the *Pseudo-Clementines* would have it; whether or not he was consecrated Peter's successor, and by Peter himself, as Tertullian would have it; still, he is an Apostolic Father, and the title is firmly his, simply by reason of the fact that he is a man of the apostolic age.

The traditional dates of Clement's pontificate, *A. D.*, 92 to *A. D.* 101, are unworthy of credence. Believing that there is good evidence for dating his sole extant authentic writing *ca. A. D.* 80, a work clearly written while he was Bishop of Rome, the present author dates Clement's pontificate accordingly.

LETTER TO THE CORINTHIANS [*ca. A. D.* 80 (96/98?)]

Generally referred to as the *First Letter to the Corinthians,* this is the sole extant authentic writing of Clement. (For the so-called *Second Letter of Clement,* see below, p. 42). The original Greek is preserved in its entirety in the same codex in which Bryennios discovered the *Didache.* The 5th-century Greek *Codex Alexandrinus* lacks only the section from Ch. 57 V. 6 to Ch. 64 V. 1. Translations in Syriac and Latin are extant in full; and only a few chapters are lacking to make a completely extant Coptic version.

In regard to the date of composition, there is an almost universal acceptance, for no good reason, of the date 96/98 A. D. This dating is based upon an acceptance of the years 92-101 A. D. as constituting the term of Clement's pontificate – dates which otherwise are taken seriously by no one! – and upon the opening words of the body of the letter: "Owing to the sudden and repeated calamities and misfortunes which have befallen us," which are taken as referring to the persecution under Domitian, in order to fit the obscurely-alluded-to events into the period 92-101A. D. However, that there was a persecution under Domitian is a supposed fact which rests upon very slim evidence, and is itself scarcely more than a conjecture.

The present author believes that there is better internal evidence for the dating of the work in its own Ch. 64, where the names of the legates who will carry the letter to Corinth are given: Claudius Ephebus and Valerius Vito. Such names can scarcely be otherwise explained than as belonging to freed slaves of the household of the Emperor Claudius († 54 A. D.) and his wife Valeria Messalina († 48 A. D.). Roman law prohibited the freeing of a slave under thirty years of age. It is evident, then, that the two men in question cannot have been born after *ca. A. D.* 20; and, if they were freed near the beginning of Claudius' reign, they must have been born not later than *ca. A. D.* 10. The letter notes that the emissaries have grown old in the faith; but if the letter be dated, as is customary, in 96/98 A. D., these emissaries must be something like 80 or 90 years of age — much *too* old to be sent running to Corinth with letters!

It is easier to believe that these men grown old in the faith were about 60 years of age, and that the letter was written *ca. A. D.* 80, in which case the sudden calamities referred to may well be a reference not to a dubious persecution, but to a natural disaster, like the eruption of Mount Vesuvius outside Naples in 79 A. D., which occasioned a great fire even in a city so far away as Rome, and was followed by a period of pestilence. In point of fact, the conditions in Rome in 79 A. D., occasioned by the eruption of Vesuvius, are a much more understandable explanation of the calamities which prevented passage to Corinth than is the supposed persecution of Domitian twenty years later. There are very few New Testament quotations in the work, and the martyrdoms of Peter and Paul are referred to as events of quite recent occurrence, — additional reasons for preferring an earlier date to a later.

A convenient source for the text, along with a translation, is Kirsopp Lake's *The Apostolic Fathers* (in the Loeb Classical Library series) Vol. 1, New York and London, 1930. The text of Migne, PG 1, 199-328, is entirely superseded, the best and most recent critical edition being that of Funk-Bihlmeyer-Schneemelcher, *Die apostolischen Väter, Vol. 1,* Tübingen 1956, pp. 35-70.

10a

(Address)

The Church of God which sojourns in Rome to the Church of God which sojourns in Corinth, to those who are called and sanctified by the will of God through our Lord Jesus Christ. Grace and peace from almighty God be multiplied unto you through Jesus Christ. [1, 1] Owing to the sudden and repeated calamities and misfortunes which have befallen us, we must acknowledge that we have been somewhat tardy in turning our attention to the matters in dispute among you, beloved; and especially that abominable and unholy sedition, alien and foreign to the elect of God, which a few rash and self-willed persons have inflamed to such madness that your venerable and illustrious name, worthy to be loved by all men, has been greatly defamed.

433

11

[5, 1]

But, to leave the examples of antiquity, let us come to the athletes who are closest to our own time. Consider the noble examples of our own generation. [2] Through jealousy and envy the greatest and most righteous pillars were persecuted, and they persevered even to death. [3] Let us set before our eyes the good Apostles: [4] Peter,

who through unwarranted jealousy suffered not one or two but many toils, and having   431
thus given testimony (1) went to the place of glory that was his due. [5] Through   88
jealousy and strife Paul showed the way to the prize for endurance. [6] Seven times
he was in chains, he was exiled, he was stoned; he became a herald in the East and in
the West, and he won splendid reknown through his faith. [7] He taught righteousness   404
to all the world, and after reaching the boundaries of the West (2) and giving his testimony before the rulers he passed from the world and was taken up to the holy place.
Thus he became our greatest example of perseverance.

[6, 1]
    To these men who lived such holy lives there must be added a multitude of
the elect, who suffered terrible indignities and tortures on account of jealousy, and who
became shining examples in our midst. [2] Because of jealousy women were persecuted,
Danaids and Dirces (3), suffering frightful and unholy indignities. Stalwart, they finished
the racecourse of the faith and received a noble reward, in spite of the weakness of their
sex.

<h3 style="text-align:center">12</h3>

[7, 4]
    Let us fix our gaze on the blood of Christ and know how precious it is to His Father,
because it was poured out for our salvation and brought the grace of repentance to the   370
whole world. [5] Let us look back over all the generations, and let us learn that in   386
generation after generation the Master has given a place of repentance (4) to all those   724
who have the will to turn to Him.

<h3 style="text-align:center">13</h3>

[24, 1]
    Let us consider, beloved, how the Master is continually proving to us that there will
be a future resurrection, of which He has made the Lord Jesus Christ the firstling, by   1011
raising Him from the dead (5). [2] Let us look, beloved, at the resurrection which is   84
taking place seasonally. [3] Day and night make known the resurrection to us. The
night sleeps, the day arises. [4] Consider the plants that grow. How and in what manner
does the sowing take place? [5] The sower went forth (6) and cast each of the seeds   65
onto the ground; and they fall to the ground, parched and bare, where they decay. Then
from their decay the greatness of the Master's providence raises them up, and from the
one grain more grow, and bring forth fruit.

<h3 style="text-align:center">13a</h3>

[25, 1]
    Let us consider the strange sign which takes place in eastern lands, that is, in the re-
gions near Arabia. [2] There is a bird called the phoenix. It is the only one of its kind,
and it lives for five hundred years. When the time for its dissolution in death approaches,
it makes for itself a sepulchre of frankincense and myrrh and the other aromatics, into
which, when the time is fulfilled, it enters and dies. [3] From its decaying flesh a worm
is born, which is nourished by the juices of the dead bird until it grows wings. Then,
when it is strong, it takes up that sepulchre in which are the bones of the bird of former
times, and carries them far from the land of Arabia to the city of Heliopolis in Egypt;
[4] and there, in the daytime, in the sight of all, it flies to the altar of the sun where it
places them; and then it starts back to its former home. [5] The priests then inspect
the records of the times and find that it has come at the completion of the five
hundredth year (7).

[26, 1]

    Do we, then, consider it a great and wonderful thing that the Creator (8) of the uni-   460
verse will bring about the resurrection of those who have served Him in holiness and in   1011
the confidence of good faith, when He demonstrates the greatness of His promise even   554
through a bird?

14

[27, 4]

    By the word of His majesty did He establish all things; and by His word He is able to   460
destroy them.

15

[31, 2]

    Why was our father Abraham blessed? Was it not because of his deeds of justice and   760
truth, wrought in faith?

16

[32, 4]

    We, therefore, who have been called by His will in Christ Jesus, are not justified by our-
selves, neither by our wisdom or understanding or piety, nor by the works we have wrought
in holiness of heart, but by the faith by which almighty God has justified all men from the   758
beginning: To whom be glory forever and ever. Amen.   [33, 1] What, then, shall we   759
do, brethren? Shall we cease from good works, and shall we put an end to love? May   760
the Master forbid that such should ever happen among us; rather, let us be eager to
perform every good work (9) earnestly and willingly.

17

[34, 5]

    Let our glorying and our confidence be in Him. Let us be subject to His will. Let us   480
consider the whole multitude of His angels, how they stand waiting to minister to His
will.

18

[36, 1]

    This is the way, beloved, in which we found our salvation, Jesus Christ, the High
Priest of our offerings, the defender and helper of our weakness. [2] Through Him we   380
fix our gaze on the heights of heaven; through Him we see the reflection of the fault-   388
less and lofty countenance of God; through Him the eyes of our heart were opened;   301
through Him our foolish and darkened understanding shoots up to the light; through
Him the Master willed that we should taste of deathless knowledge; who, being the   263
brightness of His majesty, is as much greater than the angels as the more glorious name   482
which He has inherited (10).

19

[40, 1]

Since, therefore, these things are clear to us, and we have looked into the depths of the divine knowledge, we ought to do in proper order all those things which the Master has commanded us to perform at appointed times. [2] He has commanded the offerings and services (11) to be celebrated, and not carelessly nor in disorder, but at fixed times and hours. [3] He has, moreover, by His supreme will, determined where and by whom He wants them to be carried out, so that all may be done in a holy manner, according to His good pleasure and acceptable to His will. [4] Those, then, who make their of- 898
ferings at the appointed times, are acceptable and blessed; for they follow the laws of 406
the Master and do not sin. [5] To the high priest, indeed, proper ministrations are 953
allotted, to the priests a proper place is appointed, and upon the levites their proper 954
services are imposed. The layman is bound by the ordinances for the laity (12). 951

19 a

[41, 1]

Let each of us, brethren, in his own rank, be well-pleasing to God and have a good conscience, not over-stepping the defined rules of his ministration – in dignity. [2] Not everywhere, brethren, are the continual sacrifices offered, whether of petitions or in 898
reparation for sins and trespasses, but only in Jerusalem; and even there, not in every place, but only in front of the inner temple on the altar of sacrifice; and the offering is first inspected for blemishes by the high priest and the ministers already mentioned. [3] Those, therefore, who do anything contrary to His will suffer the penalty of death. [4] You see, brethren: the greater the knowledge entrusted to us, the more severe is the risk we incur.

20

[42, 1]

The Apostles received the gospel for us from the Lord Jesus Christ; and Jesus Christ 60
was sent from God. [2] Christ, therefore, is from God, and the Apostles are from 401
Christ. Both of these orderly arrangements, then, are by God's will. [3] Receiving their instructions and being full of confidence on account of the resurrection of our Lord Jesus Christ, and confirmed in faith by the word of God, they went forth in the com- 230
plete assurance of the Holy Spirit, preaching the good news that the Kingdom of God is coming. [4] Through countryside and city they preached; and they appointed their earliest converts (13), testing them by the spirit, to be the bishops and deacons of 440
future believers. [5] Nor was this a novelty: for bishops and deacons had been written 406
about a long time earlier. Indeed, Scripture somewhere says: "I will set up their 954
bishops in righteousness and their deacons in faith (14)."

21

[44, 1]

Our Apostles knew through our Lord Jesus Christ that there would be strife for the office of bishop. [2] For this reason, therefore, having received perfect foreknowledge, 406
they appointed those who have already been mentioned, and afterwards added the further provision that, if they should die, other approved men should succeed to their ministry. [3] As for these, then, who were appointed by them, or who were after- 440
wards appointed by other illustrious men with the consent of the whole Church, and who have ministered to the flock of Christ without blame, humbly, peaceably and with dignity, and who have for many years received the commendations of all, we con-

sider it unjust that they be removed from the ministry.   433

[4] Our sin will not be small if we eject from the episcopate those who blamelessly and holily have offered its Sacrifices. [5] Blessed are those presbyters who have already   890 finished their course, and who have obtained a fruitful and perfect release; for they have now no fear that any shall transfer them from the place to which they are appointed. [6] For we see that in spite of their good service you have removed some from the ministry in which they served without blame.

22

[45, 1]

Brethren, be contentious and zealous for the things which lead to salvation! [2] You have studied the Holy Scriptures, which are true and are of the Holy Spirit. [3] You   20 well know that nothing unjust or fraudulent is written in them.   25

23

[46, 6]

Do we not have one God, one Christ, and one Spirit of Grace poured out upon us?   230 And is there not one calling in Christ (15)?

24

[46, 7]

Remember the words of our Lord Jesus. [8] For He said: "Woe to that man. It were good for him if he had not been born, rather than that he should scandalize one of My elect. It were better for him that a millstone should be hung on him and he be   65 cast into the sea, than that he should turn aside one of My elect (16)."

25

[47, 6]

Shameful, beloved, extremely shameful, and unworthy of your training in Christ, is the report that on account of one or two persons the well-established and ancient Church   433 of the Corinthians is in revolt against the presbyters. [7] And this report has come not   406 only to us, but even to those professing other faiths than ours (17), so that by your folly you heap blasphemies on the name of the Lord, and create a danger for yourselves.

26

[49, 2]

Who is able to explain the bond of the love of God?   [3] Who is equal to the telling   590 of the greatness of His beauty? [4] The height to which love lifts us is unutterable. [5] Love unites us to God. Love covers a multitude of sins (18). Love endures all   912 things, is long-suffering in everything. There is nothing vulgar in love, nothing haughty. Love makes no schism; love does not quarrel; love does everything in unity (19). In love were all the elect of God perfected; without love nothing is pleasing to God.   592 [6] In love did the Master take hold of us. For the sake of the love which he had for us did Jesus Christ our Lord, by the will of God, give His blood for us, His flesh for   370 our flesh, and His life for our lives.

26a

[51, 1]

For whatever our transgressions, and whatever we have done through the attacks of the adversary, let us pray that we may be forgiven. . . . [3] For it is good for a man to confess (20) his failings rather than to harden his heart.

120
916

26b

[53, 1]

You are versed and, indeed, you are well-versed, beloved, in the Sacred Scriptures; and you have studied the oracles of God (21).

20

27

[57, 1]

You, therefore, who laid the foundation of the rebellion, submit to the presbyters and be chastened to repentance, bending your knees in a spirit of humility (22).

433
910

28

[58, 2]

Accept our counsel, and you will have nothing to regret. For as God lives, and as the Lord Jesus Christ lives, and the Holy Spirit, and the faith and hope of the elect, as surely will he that humbly and with equanimity and without regret carries out the commandments and precepts given by God, be enrolled and chosen among the number of those who are being saved through Jesus Christ, through whom there is glory to Him forever and ever. Amen.

230

202

28a

[59, 1]

If anyone disobey the things which have been said by Him through us, let them know that they will involve themselves in transgression and in no small danger. [2] We, however, shall be innocent of this sin, and will pray with earnest entreaty and supplication that the Creator of all may keep unharmed the number of His elect, which has been counted up in the whole world, through His beloved Child Jesus Christ, through whom He has called us from darkness to light (23), and from ignorance to the full knowledge of the glory of His name.

433

202

29

[63, 2]

You will afford us joy and gladness if, being obedient to the things which we have written through the Holy Spirit, you will root out the wicked passion of jealousy, in accord with the plea for peace and concord which we have made in this letter.

433

29a

[64]

And now may the all-seeing God and Master of spirits (24) and Lord of all flesh, who 401
chose the Lord Jesus Christ, and us through Him to be a special people (25), give
to every soul that is called after His glorious and holy name, faith, fear, peace, patience
and long-suffering, self-control, purity and moderation, that they may be pleasing to
His name through our High Priest and Leader, Jesus Christ, through whom be to Him
glory and majesty, might and honor, both now and forever and ever. Amen.

1. οὕτω μαρτυρήσας – *having thus given testimony,* might also be translated *having thus endured martyrdom.*
2. In Romans 15:16 Paul writes of his intention to visit Spain. The present remark of Clement is sometimes taken as evidence that Paul did in fact go to Spain.
3. The daughters of Danaus were slain by unknown tortures; and Dirce was dragged to her death, tied to the horns of a bull. Such mythological references as these would not be lost on Clement's audience.
4. Wis. 12:10.
5. 1 Cor. 15:20.
6. Mark 4:3, and parallel passages.
7. The myth of the phoenix is well-known in antiquity. In the *De defectu oraculorum* Plutarch cites Hesiod's statement that crows live nine times as long as men, stags four times as long as crows, ravens three times as long as stags, a phoenix nine times as long as a raven, and the nymphs ten times as long as the phoenix. *(Apud* Thorndike, *History of Magic and Experimental Science,* Vol. 1, p. 207). The phoenix is known also to Philostratus, Horapollo, the *Book of Enoch* (Old Slavonic version), Herodatus, Ovid, Pliny the Elder, Tacitus, and doubtless many others. The best-known account of the phoenix in Christian literature is the *De ave phoenice,* uncertainly attributed to Lactantius.
8. ὁ δημιουργός.
9. Tit. 3:1.
10. Heb. 1:3-4.
11. προσφορὰς καὶ λειτουργίας.
12. ὁ λαϊκὸς ἄνθρωπος τοῖς λαϊκοῖς προστάγμασιν δέδεται. This is the first use of the word *layman* in Christian literature. Its use as an adjective rather than as a substantive probably indicates that it is not yet a common term.
13. τὰς ἀπαρχὰς αὐτῶν. Literally, *their first-fruits.*
14. Clement quotes the passage as: καταστήσω τοὺς ἐπισκόπους αὐτῶν ἐν δικαιοσύνῃ καὶ τοὺς διακόνους αὐτῶν ἐν πίστει. No doubt he has a very loose memory of Is. 60:17 which reads (in the Septuagint): καὶ δώσω τοὺς ἄρχοντάς σου ἐν εἰρήνῃ καὶ τοὺς ἐπισκόπους σου ἐν δικαιοσύνῃ.

15. See Eph. 4:4-6.
16. See Mark 9:42; 14:21; Luke 17:2; 22:22; Matt. 18:6; 26:24.
17. A more literal translation were: *but even to those inclined away from us.*
18. 1 Pet. 4:8.
19. 1 Cor. 13:4-7.
20. ἐξομολογεῖσθαι.
21. τὰ λόγια τοῦ θεοῦ.
22. κάμψαντες τὰ γόνατα τῆς καρδίας ὑμῶν means literally *bending the knees of your hearts* – but this is a very difficult thing to do in English.
23. Acts 26:18.
24. Num. 16:22; 27:16. See also Heb. 12:9.
25. Deut. 7:6; 14:2; 26:18; Ex. 19:5.

LETTER OF BARNABAS [*ca. A. D.* 70/79 or 117/132]

Not a letter at all, the so-called *Letter of Barnabas* is actually a theological
tract. It nowhere asserts that Barnabas is its author, and lays no claim to an
apostolic origin. From earliest times the work was attributed to the Apostle
Barnabas, the companion of Paul. However, its decided antipathy to everything Jewish, together with the markedly un-Pauline character of its teachings, makes such authorship utterly untenable. The work is probably of
Alexandrian origin. It is extant in its original Greek in the biblical *Codex
Sinaiticus* of the 4th century, where it is apparently included among the

works comprising the New Testament, but is placed after the Apocalypse; also in the same *Codex Hierosolymitanus* which houses the *Didache*. There are other Greek manuscripts of the Barnabas letter; and it is extant also in a 3rd-century Latin translation.

In regard to the date of composition: modern authors tend more and more to favor the period *A. D.* 117 / 132, and a later rather than an earlier date within the period. The earlier date, *A. D.* 70 / 79, presents its own peculiar difficulties; but on the other hand, if one attempt to date it in the period 117 / 132, and especially if a date late in that period be taken, the almost total lack of clear New Testament citations in the work must prove an embarassment.

The text as given in Migne, PG 2, 727-782, is superseded by numerous better editions, the most recent of which is Schneemelcher's Funk-Bihlmeyer, *Die apostolischen Väter,* Vol. 1, Tübingen 1956, pp. 10-34. A convenient source for the text, along with a translation, is Kirsopp Lake's *The Apostolic Fathers* (Loeb Classical Library), Vol. 1, London and New York, 1930.

31

[5, 5]

Moreover, my brethren, if the Lord endured suffering for our souls although He is the Lord of the whole world, to whom God said before the foundation of the world, "Let Us make man in Our image and likeness (1)," how, then, did He endure suffering at the hands of men? Learn this: — [6] The prophets, having the gift from Him, prophesied concerning Him; and since He must manifest Himself in the flesh (2), He suffered so that He might destroy death (3) and demonstrate the resurrection from the dead, [7] in order to fulfill the promise made to the fathers and personally to prepare for Himself the new people, and to show while He was on earth that He Himself will raise the dead and judge the risen.

[8] Besides, while teaching Israel and working such great signs and wonders, He preached to them and loved them greatly. [9] And when He chose His own Apostles, who were about to preach His gospel, He chose men who were the worst kind of sinners in order to show that He came not to call the righteous but sinners (4), — and then He showed Himself to be the Son of God. [10] If He had not come in the flesh, there would be no way in which men could be saved by beholding Him: for even when they look at the sun, the work of His hands and a thing destined to perish, are they able to gaze straight into its rays? [11] For this reason, then, the Son of Man came in the flesh: to fill to the brim the measure of the sins of those who persecuted His prophets to death.

374
233
347
300
363

392

60

65
301

32

[6, 11]

Since, then, He has renewed us by the forgiveness of sins, He has put a different stamp upon us (5), so that our souls might be like the souls of children, as they would be if He were creating us anew.

752

33

[7, 2]

If, then, the Son of God, being the Lord and destined to judge the living and the dead (6), suffered so that His being wounded might make us live, let us believe that the Son of God could not suffer, except for our sake. [3] Furthermore, when He was crucified He was given gall and sour wine to drink (7). Hear how the priests of the temple foretold this. A commandment was written: "Whoever does not fast the fast will be exterminated in death (8)." The Lord commanded this because He Himself was about to offer the vessel of His spirit as a sacrifice for our sins, so that the type established in Isaac, who was offered on the altar, might be fulfilled.

392
380
375

34

[11, 10]

What else does He say? "And there was a river flowing on the right, and beautiful trees grew beside it, and whoever shall eat of them shall live forever (9)." [11] In this way He says that we descend into the water full of sins and foulness, and we come up bearing fruit in our heart, having fear and hope in Jesus in the spirit.

820
824
836

35

[12, 9]

Moses, therefore, said to Jesus, the son of Nave, after giving him this name, when he sent him to spy out the land: "Take a book in your hands and write what the Lord says, that in the last days the Son of God will tear out by the roots the whole house of Amalec (10)." [10] Behold, here is Jesus again, not a son of man but the Son of God, revealed in the flesh by a type. Since they are going to say that the Christ is the son of David, David himself prophesies, fearing and understanding the error of sinners: "The Lord said to my Lord, sit at my right hand, until I make of your enemies a footstool for your feet (11)." [11] And again Isaias says as follows: "The Lord said to Christ my Lord, whose right hand I upheld, that the nations should obey Him: — and I will shatter the strength of kings (12)." See how David calls Him *Lord* and does not say *son* (13).

300
301

36

[16, 7]

Before we believed in God the habitation of our heart was corrupt and weak, like a temple truly built with hands, because it was full of idolatry and, through doing things contrary to God, it was a house of demons. [8] "But it shall be built in the name of the Lord (14)." Take care, now, that the temple of the Lord may be built gloriously. Learn in what way. When we received the remission of sins and set our hope in the Name, we were made new and were created again from the beginning. Now God truly dwells in us, in the habitation which we are. [9] How? His word of faith, His announcement of the promise, the wisdom of His ordinances, the commands of His teaching, Himself prophesying in us, Himself dwelling in us. Although we had been enslaved to death, He opens the door of the temple, that is, our mouth, for us, giving us repentance; and thus it is that he leads us into the incorruptible temple.

752
753

37

[19, 12]

You shall not make a schism; but you shall pacify and bring together those who are quarreling. You shall confess your sins (15). You shall not go up to pray in the consciousness of having done evil. This is the way of light (16).

916

1. Gen. 1:26.
2. See 1 Tim. 3:16.
3. See 2 Tim. 1:10.
4. Mark 2: 17.
5. ἐποίησεν ἡμᾶς ἄλλον τύπον.
6. 2 Tim. 4:1. See also 1 Pet. 4:5.
7. Matt. 27: 34.
8. See Lev. 23:29.
9. See Ezech. 47: 1-12.
10. See Exod. 17: 14, 16; and in the Septuagint, Jer. 43: 2, 14. Jesus, the son of Nave, is familiar to those who read the Vulgate and translations thereof as Josue, the son of Nun.
11. Ps. 109 [110] :1.
12. See Is. 45:1, which, however, reads not τῷ Χριστῷ μου κυρίῳ — to Christ my Lord, but τῷ χριστῷ μου Κύρῳ — to Cyrus my anointed.
13. Mark 12:37; Matt. 22:45; Luke 20:44.
14. See 2 Sam. 7:13.
15. ἐξομολογήσῃ ἐπὶ ἁμαρτίαις σου.
16. See the Didache, 4, 3 and 4, 14 (§ § 1b and 3, above).

ST. IGNATIUS OF ANTIOCH [† *ca. A. D.* 110]

St. Ignatius was the third bishop of Antioch, succeeding St. Evodius, who was the immediate successor of St. Peter. He is accounted an Apostolic Father by reason of his having been a hearer of the Apostle John. During the reign of the Emperor Trajan (98-117 A.D.), and probably about the year 110 A. D., he was sentenced to the beasts in the arena. On his journey from Antioch to Rome and martyrdom he wrote seven letters, his only extant authentic writings. Almost everything of the little that is known of him must be gleaned from these letters, addressed to the Christian communities at Ephesus, Magnesia, Tralles, Rome, Philadelphia, and Smyrna, and a personal one to Bishop Polycarp of Smyrna. The most important of the letters is that to the Romans; yet, all seven are veritable treasure houses for the history of dogma.

Chiefly because the letters present so clear a view of a hierarchical and monarchical Church, the authenticity of the letters was long questioned by protestant scholars. The genuinity of the letters has now, however, been long since vindicated by J. B Lightfoot, Adolph von Harnack, Theodore Zahn, and F. X. Funk; and their authenticity is now almost universally accepted.

The text of the letters, however, is preserved in three distinct forms, known as the *short recension,* the *long recension* and the *Syriac abridgment.* The long recension, extant in Greek and in Latin, was the first known, and was regarded as authentic until the 17th century, when the short recension was first published. It is now recognized that the long recension is an interpolated text, made in the fourth century. It is the so-called short recension, extant only in Greek, (which, of course, is the original language of the letters), that is now regarded as the authentic text. The Syriac abridgment apparently was made from a no longer extant Syriac translation of the short recension, *i.e.,* the original Greek text.

Numerous other letters purporting to belong to the same Ignatian corpus are spurious.

The Migne text, PG 5, 643-728 is no longer serviceable. Like the writings of the other Apostolic Fathers, a convenient edition for text and translation is Kirsopp Lake's *The Apostolic Fathers,* in the Loeb Classical Library edition. However, for the best available critical edition, scholars will consult Schneemelcher's Funk-Bihlmeyer, *Die apostolischen Väter,* Vol. 1, Tübingen 1956, pp. 82-113.

LETTER TO THE EPHESIANS [*ca. A. D.* 110]

37a

[*Address*]

Ignatius, also called Theophorus, to the Church at Ephesus in Asia, which is worthy of all felicitation, blessed as it is with greatness by the fullness of God the Father, predestined from eternity for a glory that is lasting and unchanging, united and chosen through true suffering by the will of the Father in Jesus Christ our God: abundant greeting in Jesus Christ and in blameless joy.

202

301

38

[3,2]

For Jesus Christ, our inseparable life, is the will of the Father, just as the bishops, who have been appointed throughout the world, are the will of Jesus Christ. [4, 1] It is fitting, therefore, that you should live in harmony with the will of the bishop — as, indeed, you do.

404

38a

[5, 3]

Let us be careful, then, if we would be submissive to God, not to oppose the bishop.   406

38b

[6, 1]

Furthermore, the more anyone observes that a bishop remains silent, the more he should stand in fear of him. For anyone whom the master of the house sends to manage his business ought to be received by us as we would receive him by whom he was sent. It is clear, then, that we must look upon the bishop as the Lord Himself.   401

39

[7, 2]

There is one Physician, who is both flesh and spirit, born and not born, who is God in man, true life in death, both from Mary and from God, first able to suffer and then unable to suffer, Jesus Christ our Lord.   310
    322

40

[9, 1]

I have learned, however, that certain persons from elsewhere, who have evil doctrine, have stayed with you; but you did not allow them to sow it among you, and you stopped your ears so that you would not receive what they sow. You are like stones for a temple of the Father, prepared for the edifice of God the Father, hoisted to the heights by the crane of Jesus Christ, which is the cross, using for a rope the Holy Spirit. Your faith is what pulls you up, and love is the road which leads you to God. [2] You are, then, wayfarers all, bearing God, bearing a temple, bearing Christ, bearing holy things, and in every respect decked out in the commandments of Jesus Christ.   230
    370
    754

41

[16, 1]

Do not err, my brethren: the corrupters of families will not inherit the Kingdom of God (1). [2] And if they who do these things according to the flesh suffer death, how much more if a man corrupt by evil teaching the faith of God, for the sake of which Jesus Christ was crucified? A man become so foul will depart into unquenchable fire; and so also will anyone who listens to him.   1030
    1032
    1034

42

[18, 2]

For our God, Jesus Christ, was conceived by Mary in accord with God's plan: of the seed of David, it is true, but also of the Holy Spirit. He was born and was baptized so that by His submission He might purify the water. [19, 1] The virginity of Mary, her giving birth, and also the death of the Lord, were hidden from the prince of this world:— three mysteries loudly proclaimed, but wrought in the silence of God.   301
    779
    781

43

[20, 2]

I will [send you further doctrinal explanations] especially if the Lord should reveal to me that all of you to a man, through grace derived from the Name, join in the   405

common meeting in one faith, and in Jesus Christ, who was of the family of David   302
according to the flesh (2), the Son of Man and the Son of God, so that you give ear to
the bishop and to the presbytery with an undivided mind, breaking one Bread, which is   879
the medicine of immortality, the antidote against death, enabling us to live forever in
Jesus Christ.

1. See 1 Cor. 6:9.
2. Rom. 1:3.

LETTER TO THE MAGNESIANS [*ca. A. D.* 110]

43a

[2]
   Now, therefore, it has been my privilege to see you in the person of your God-inspired   952
bishop, Damas; and in the persons of your worthy presbyters, Bassus and Apollonius;   406
and my fellow-servant, the deacon, Zotion. What a delight is his company! for he is   954
subject to the bishop as to the grace of God, and to the presbytery as to the law of Jesus
Christ.

43b

[3, 1]
   It becomes you not to presume on the youth of the bishop, but to show him all
reverence in consideration of the authority of God the Father: just as even the holy
presbyters, so I have heard, do not take advantage of his outwardly youthful appearance,
but yield to him in their godly prudence: yet, not to him, but to the Father of Jesus   953
Christ, the Bishop of all.

44

[6, 1]
   Take care to do all things in harmony with God, with the bishop presiding in the
place of God and with the presbyters in the place of the council of the Apostles, and   406
with the deacons, who are most dear to me, entrusted with the business (1) of Jesus   952
Christ, who was with the Father from the beginning and is at last made manifest.

45

[8, 1]
   Do not be led astray by other doctrines nor by old fables which are worthless (2).
For if we have been living until now according to Judaism, we must confess that we have
not received grace. [2] The prophets, who were men of God, lived according to Jesus   389
Christ. For that reason they were persecuted, inspired as they were by His grace to   302
convince the disobedient that there is one God, who manifested Himself through His   157
Son, Jesus Christ, who is His Word proceeding from silence, and who was in all respects   260
pleasing to Him that sent Him. [9, 1] If, then, those who walked in ancient customs   301
came to a new hope, no longer sabbathing but living by the Lord's Day, on which we   52
came to life through Him and through His death,—which some deny,—through which   370
mystery we received faith, through which also we suffer in order to be found to be   347
disciples of Jesus Christ, our only Teacher:—[2] how then will we be able to live without
Him of whom even the prophets were disciples in the Spirit, and to whom they looked   300
forward as their Teacher? For this reason, when He for whom they had waited in
righteousness came, He raised them from the dead.

46

[10, 3]

    It is absurd to have Jesus Christ on the lips and at the same time to practice Judaism.   52
Christianity did not base its faith on Judaism, but Judaism on Christianity, in which every
tongue believing in God is brought together.

47

[11]

    Do not think, my beloved, that I have heard of any among you practicing Judaism.
I say this, however, although I am less than you, because I wish to warn you not to fall
into the snare of false doctrine. Be convinced of the birth and of the passion and of the   80
resurrection, which took place during the time of the procuratorship of Pontius Pilate.   84
These things were truly and certainly done by Jesus Christ, our hope, from which may
none of you be turned aside.

47a

[13, 1]

    Take care, therefore, to be confirmed in the decrees of the Lord and of the Apostles,
in order that in everything you do, you may prosper (3) in body and in soul, in faith
and in love, in Son and in Father and in Spirit, in beginning and in end, together with   230
your most reverend bishop; and with that fittingly woven spiritual crown, the presbytery;   952
and with the deacons, men of God. [2] Be subject to the bishop and to one another, as   406
Jesus Christ was subject to the Father, and the Apostles were subject to Christ and to the
Father; so that there may be unity in both body and in spirit.   405

1. διακονίαν.
2. 1 Tim. 1:4; Tit. 1:14.
3. Ps. 1:3.

LETTER TO THE TRALLIANS [*ca. A. D.* 110]

48

[2, 1]

    Indeed, when you submit to the bishop as you would to Jesus Christ, it is clear to me
that you are living not in the manner of men but as Jesus Christ, who died for us, that   758
through faith in His death you might escape dying. [2] It is necessary, therefore,—and
such is your practice,—that you do nothing without the bishop, and that you be subject   951
also to the presbytery, as to the Apostles of Jesus Christ our hope, in whom we shall be   440
found, if we live in Him. [3] It is necessary also that the deacons, the dispensers of the   954
mysteries of Jesus Christ, be in every way pleasing to all men. For they are not the
deacons of food and drink, but servants of the Church of God. They must, therefore,
guard against blame as against fire.

49

[3, 1]

    In like manner let everyone respect the deacons as they would respect Jesus Christ,   952
and just as they respect the bishop as a type of the Father, and the presbyters as the   440

council of God and college of Apostles. Without these, it cannot be called a Church.   406
[2] I am confident that you accept this, for I have received the exemplar of your love   951
and have it with me in the person of your bishop. His very demeanor is a great lesson,
and his meekness is his strength. I believe that even the godless do respect him.

50

[7, 2]

    He that is within the sanctuary is pure; but he that is outside the sanctuary is not   406
pure. In other words, anyone who acts without the bishop and the presbytery and the   951
deacons does not have a clean conscience.   952

51

[9, 1]

    Turn a deaf ear, then, when anyone speaks to you apart from Jesus Christ, who was of   80
the family of David and of Mary, who was truly born, who ate and drank, was truly   310
persecuted under Pontius Pilate, was truly crucified and died in the sight of those in   311
heaven and on earth and in the underworld, [2] who also was truly raised from the dead
when His Father raised Him up. And in the same manner His Father will raise us up in   84
Christ Jesus, if we believe in Him without whom we have no hope.   1011

LETTER TO THE ROMANS [ca. A. D. 110]

52

[Address]

    Ignatius, also called Theophorus, to the Church that has found mercy in the greatness   434
of the Most High Father and in Jesus Christ, His only Son; to the Church beloved and
enlightened after the love of Jesus Christ, our God, by the will of Him that has willed
everything which is; to the Church also which holds the presidency in the place of the   301
country of the Romans (1), worthy of God, worthy of honor, worthy of blessing, worthy
of praise, worthy of success, worthy of sanctification, and, because you hold the presidency
of love, named after Christ and named after the Father: her therefore do I salute in the
name of Jesus Christ, the Son of the Father. To those who are united in flesh and in
spirit by every commandment of His, who are filled with the grace of God without
wavering, and who are filtered clear of every foreign stain, I wish an unalloyed joy in
Jesus Christ, our God.

53

[3, 1]

    You have envied no one; but others you have taught. I desire only that what you   434
have enjoined in your instructions may remain in force. [2] Only pray for me that I
may have strength both inward and outward; that I may not merely speak but have also
the will; that I may not only be called a Christian but may also be found to be one.   684
For if I be found to be one, then I can also be called one and be deemed faithful even
when I am no longer visible in the world.

53a

[4, 1]

    I am writing to all the Churches and I enjoin all, that I am dying willingly for God's
sake, if only you do not prevent it. I beg of you, do not do me an untimely kindness.   1040

Allow me to be eaten by the beasts, which are my way of reaching to God. I am God's wheat, and I am to be ground by the teeth of wild beasts, so that I may become the pure bread of Christ.

54

[4, 3]

Not as Peter and Paul did, do I command you. They were Apostles, and I am a convict.   432
They were free, and I even to the present time am a slave. Yet, if I suffer, I shall be the   1011
freedman of Jesus Christ, and in Him I shall rise up free. Now in chains, I am learning
to have no desires of my own.

54a

[7, 3]

I have no taste for corruptible food nor for the pleasures of this life. I desire the
Bread of God (2), which is the Flesh of Jesus Christ, who was of the seed of David (3);   851
and for drink I desire His Blood, which is love incorruptible.

54b

[8, 2]

By this short letter I beg you to believe me. Jesus Christ will make it clear to you
that I am speaking the truth. He is the mouth which cannot lie, by which the Father has   80
spoken truly.

55

[9, 1]

Remember in your prayers the Church in Syria which now, in place of me, has God   120
for its shepherd. Jesus Christ, along with your love, shall be its only bishop.

1. Much has been written of the strange phrase ἐν τόπῳ χωρίου 'Ρωμαίων, and various critics have made several attempts to correct or normalize the text. While not wishing to deprecate in any way the labors of text criticism, and with a full appreciation of the great value that such criticism does frequently have, the present author believes that in the instance at hand, the simplest view is probably still the best: the phrase is merely a pleonasm. For a good common-sense treatment of the several difficulties in the address of the *Letter to the Romans*, see the critical edition (and notes thereto) of Joseph A. Fischer, *Die apostolischen Väter*, Munich 1956, pp. 129-130.
2. John 6:33.
3. John 7:42; Rom. 1:3.

LETTER TO THE PHILADELPHIANS [*ca. A. D.* 110]

56

[3, 2]

Those, indeed, who belong to God and to Jesus Christ — they are with the bishop. And   420
those who repent and come to the unity of the Church — they too shall be of God, and will   440
be living according to Jesus Christ. [3] Do not err, my brethren: if anyone follow a
schismatic, he will not inherit the Kingdom of God (1). If any man walk about with   417
strange doctrine, he cannot lie down with the passion. [4, 1] Take care, then, to use one   851
Eucharist, so that whatever you do, you do according to God: for there is one Flesh of   880
our Lord Jesus Christ, and one cup in the union of His Blood; one altar, as there is one   406
bishop with the presbytery and my fellow servants, the deacons.

57

[5, 1]

My brethren, I am overflowing with love for you, and exceedingly joyful in watching over you. Yet, not I, but Jesus Christ; and in chains for His sake, I am the more fearful because I am not yet perfected. Your prayer, however, will make me perfect for God, so that I may win the lot which has mercifully fallen to me. I make the gospel my refuge, as it were the flesh of Jesus, and the Apostles as the presbytery of the Church. [2] The prophets also do we love, because they too have announced the gospel; and they hoped in Him and awaited Him. In Him and by their faith in Him they were saved, being united to Jesus Christ. They are saints worthy of love and worthy of admiration, approved by Jesus Christ and numbered together in the gospel of the common hope.

	60
	15
	300
	389
	758

58a

[7, 1]

I cried out while I was in your midst, I spoke with a loud voice, the voice of God: "Give heed to the bishop and the presbytery and the deacons." [2] Some suspected me of saying this because I had previous knowledge of the division which certain persons had caused; but He for whom I am in chains is my witness that I had no knowledge of this from any human being. It was the Spirit who kept preaching these words: "Do nothing without the bishop, keep your body as the temple of God, love unity, flee from divisions, be imitators of Jesus Christ, as He was imitator of the Father."(2)

	406
	952
	405

59

[8, 1]

I did my best as a man devoted to unity. But where there is division and anger, God does not dwell. The Lord, however, forgives all who repent, if their repentance leads to the unity of God and to the council of the bishop. I have faith in the grace of Jesus Christ; and He will remove from you every chain.

	901
	681

60

[8, 2]

I beseech you, therefore, do nothing in a spirit of division, but act according to Christian teaching (3). Indeed, I heard some men saying: "If I do not find it in the official records in the gospel I do not believe (4)." And when I made answer to them, "It is written!" they replied, "That is the point at issue." But to me, the official record is Jesus Christ; the inviolable record is His cross, His death, and His resurrection, and the faith which He brings about:—in these I desire to be justified by your prayers.

	60
	63

61

[9, 1]

Good, too, are the priests; but the high priest is better, to whom was entrusted the holy of holies; and to him alone were entrusted the secret things of God. He is the door (5) of the Father, through which enter Abraham and Isaac and Jacob and the Prophets and the Apostles and the Church. All these are joined in the unity of God. [2] But the gospel has something of a pre-eminence, in view of the coming (6) of the Savior, our Lord Jesus Christ, His passion, and the resurrection. The beloved Prophets had a message pointing to Him, but the Gospel is the imperishable fulfillment. All alike are good, if your faith is grounded in love.

	388
	389
	60
	81
	51
	15

1. 1 Cor. 6:9-10.
2. 1 Cor. 11:1.
3. κατὰ χριστομαθίαν.
4. The Greek of this line is ambiguous, and we have done the reader the noble service of preserving the ambiguity in English. The term *official records* might also be translated *original source* or *archives* or *ancient records*. The problem is simply this: Is the term intended to refer to the Old Testament or to the New? For clarification, our translation requires the insertion of a comma: but should the comma be placed after records or after gospel? If the former, the line means: "If I do not find it in the Old Testament, then I do not believe it when I find it in the New!" If the latter, it means: "If I do not find it written down in the Gospels, I do not believe it" — or perhaps: "If I do not find it in Scripture, I do not believe it!" The problem is clouded somewhat, although not really intensified, by the fact that there is uncertainty even as to the correct reading of the Greek term which we have translated *official records:* is it ᾽αρχείοις or ᾽αρχαίοις?

   Some have attempted to find the solution in the word itself; but this is a hopeless task. Ultimately, it must be admitted that either term can be taken in the sense of *official records,* and might refer either to the Old or to the New Testament; and either term can be taken in the sense of *ancient records,* referring only to the Old Testament. The present author considers that, in view of the context of the remark, it is more probable that the term refers to the Old Testament, and that it is a Judaizing tendency that is being combatted. The comma, in this view, belongs after *records.* The sense of the passage, then, is: "If I do not find it in the official records, *i.e.,* in the Old Testament, then I do not believe it when I find it in the Gospels."
5. John 10:9. One has the impression at first that Ignatius is calling Christ the High Priest. More careful consideration of the passage makes it clear, however, that by the term *high priest* he simply means to indicate the whole of the Old Testament period, which prepares for and makes possible the New Dispensation.
6. It is clear in the context that παρουσία in this instance refers simply to the already accomplished historical fact of Christ's gospel coming, His birth in Bethlehem, and is not the technical term for His second coming, which still we await.

LETTER TO THE SMYRNAEANS [*ca. A. D.* 110]

62

[1, 1]

I give glory to Jesus Christ, the God who has made you wise; for I have observed   405
that you are set in faith unshakable, as if nailed to the cross of our Lord Jesus Christ   552
in body and in soul; and that you are confirmed in love by the Blood of Christ, firmly   554
believing in regard to our Lord that He is truly of the family of David according to the   310
flesh (1), and God's Son by the will and power of God, truly born of a Virgin,   302
baptized by John so that all justice might be fulfilled by Him (2), [2] in the time of   311
Pontius Pilate and Herod the Tetrarch truly nailed in the flesh on our behalf, — and   383
we are of the fruit of His divinely blessed passion, — so that by means of His resurrection He might raise aloft a banner (3) for His saints and believers in every age, whether   402
among the Jews or among the gentiles, united in a single body in His Church (4).

63

[2]

He underwent all these sufferings for us, so that we might be saved; and He truly   347
suffered, just as He truly raised Himself, not as some unbelievers contend, when they say   310
that His passion was merely in appearance (5). It is they who exist only in appearance;
and as their notion, so shall it happen to them: they will be bodiless and ghost-like   1012
shapes. [3, 1] I know and believe that He was in the flesh even after the resurrection.
[2] And when He came to those with Peter He said to them: "Here, now, touch Me,   84
and see that I am not a bodiless ghost (6)." Immediately they touched Him and, because   66
of the merging of His flesh and spirit, they believed. For the same reason they despised
death and in fact were proven superior to death. [3] After His resurrection He ate and   88
drank with them (7) as a being of flesh, although He was united in spirit to the Father.

63a

[4, 1]

I warn (8) you, beloved, although I know that you are of one mind with me. Yet, I would guard you in advance against beasts in the shape of men, whom not only must you not receive, but, if it is possible, do not even meet them. Only pray for them so that they might repent, difficult though that be: yet, Jesus Christ, our true life, has the power to do even this. [2] If it was merely in appearance that these things were done by our Lord, then it is merely in appearance that I am a prisoner.

310

63b

[6, 1]

Let no one be deceived: even the heavenly beings and the angels in their glory, and rulers visible and invisible, — even for these there will be judgment, if they do not believe in the Blood of Christ.

480
486

64

[6, 2]

Take note of those who hold heterodox opinions on the grace of Jesus Christ which has come to us, and see how contrary their opinions are to the mind of God. For love they have no care, nor for the widow, nor for the orphan, nor for the distressed, nor for those in prison or freed from prison, nor for the hungry and thirsty. [7, 1] They abstain from the Eucharist and from prayer, because they do not confess that the Eucharist is the Flesh of our Savior Jesus Christ, Flesh which suffered for our sins and which the Father, in His goodness, raised up again. They who deny the gift of God (9) are perishing in their disputes. It would be better for them to have love, so that they might rise again. [2] It is right to shun such men, and not even to speak about them, — neither in public nor in private.

851

1012

65

[8, 1]

You must all follow the bishop as Jesus Christ follows the Father, and the presbytery as you would the Apostles. Reverence the deacons as you would the command of God. Let no one do anything of concern to the Church without the bishop. Let that be considered a valid Eucharist which is celebrated by the bishop, or by one whom he appoints. [2] Wherever the bishop appears, let the people be there; just as wherever Jesus Christ is, there is the Catholic Church (10). Nor is it permitted without the bishop either to **baptize** or to celebrate the agape; but whatever he approve, this too is pleasing to God, so that whatever is done will be secure and valid (11).

406
440

866

421
828

1. Rom. 1:3.
2. Matt. 3:15.
3. Is. 5:26; 11:12; 49:22; 62:10.
4. Eph. 2:16.
5. δοκεῖν. Ignatius is already combating docetism. Precisely the same phrase is found in his *Letter to the Trallians* 10, and with the same rather gruesome turn of humor: There are unbelievers who say that Christ had no real body, and that the passion, therefore, was only in appearance; but it is they who shall one day exist only as dis-embodied ghosts. Perhaps his notion of universal resurrection of men is somewhat faulty.
6. See Luke 24:39.
7. Acts 10:41.
8. His warning, as is clear from the next verse of the present passage, is against docetism.
9. John 4:10.
10. This is the earliest use of the term ἡ καθολικὴ ἐκκλησία. It is especially interesting that it is a man of Antioch who first writes the term *Catholic Church;* for it was also at Antioch, as we know from the Acts

of the Apostles (11:26), that the followers of Jesus were first called *Christians*.
11. See Heb. 6:19.

LETTER TO POLYCARP [*ca. A. D.* 110]

66

[3, 2]

Become more diligent than you are. Observe well the times. Look for Him that is
above seasons, timeless; invisible, yet, for our sakes, becoming visible; who cannot be   347
touched; who cannot suffer, yet, for our sakes, accepted suffering, and who on our   370
account endured everything.

67

[5, 1]

Flee from base practices (1), but preach more against them: Speak to my sisters that
they love the Lord, and be content with their husbands in body and in soul. In like
manner, exhort my brothers in the name of Jesus Christ to love their wives as the Lord   984
loved the Church (2). [2] If anyone is able to remain continent, to the honor of the
flesh of the Lord, let him so remain without boasting. If he boast about it, he is lost;
and if he be more esteemed than the bishop, he is ruined. It is proper for men and   972
women who wish to marry to be united with the consent of the bishop, so that their
marriage will be acceptable to the Lord, and not entered upon for the sake of lust. Let
all things be done for the honor of God.

68

[6, 2]

Be pleasing to Him whose soldiers you are, and whose pay you receive. May none of
you be found to be a deserter (3). Let your Baptism be your armament; your faith,
your helmet; your love, your spear; your endurance, your full suit of armor. Let your
works be as your deposited withholdings, so that you may receive the back-pay which has   770
accrued to you. Be long-suffering with one another and gentle, just as God is with you.
May I rejoice in you always.

1. Τὰς κακοτεχνίας φεῦγε. Of itself, the term is suggestive of the forbidden practice of magic; and this may
    in fact be its meaning. In the light of what follows, however, the *base practices* may refer to violations of
    marital chastity. Or, if the line be regarded as a conclusion to the preceding chapter, the *base practices* may
    be the schemings of dissatisfied slaves whose virtue is but a sham while they seek to have the Church buy
    their freedom. Or, afterall, it may be completely generic, of as broad a meaning as our English makes it
    appear to be.
2. Eph. 5:25.
3. Here and through the rest of the passage Ignatius' use of Latin terms of military significance is quite
    extraordinary: δεσέρτωρ = *desertor;* δεπόσιτα = *deposita;* and ἄκκεπτα = *accepta.* It is conjectured that
    he would have heard the latter two terms often enough among the soldiers who guarded him on this, his
    last journey, to Rome. A soldier received only a portion of his pay in cash at stated intervals, the rest,
    the *deposita,* being deposited for him in a kind of savings-bank attached to his military unit. This *deposita*
    was paid out to him in cash or land as an *accepta* when he left the army. In regard to the soldiers who are
    taking him in custody to Rome, in the *Letter to the Romans* 5, Ignatius refers to himself as "chained to ten
    leopards, that is, to a detachment of soldiers, who only grow worse in the face of kindness." The use of the
    term *ten leopards,* δέκα λεοπάρδοις, is challenging. Was it perhaps a kind of nickname for a certain
    regiment? The usage is especially strange when we consider that this is the first occurrence of the term
    leopard in Greek or Latin literature.

THE COLBERTINE MARTYRDOM OF SAINT IGNATIUS [4th/5th cent.]

The Colbertine Martyrdom, so-called after its presence in the *Codex Colbertinus,* a Paris manuscript of the 10th century, purports to be an eye-witness account; and it dates Ignatius' death on December 20, *A. D.* 107. The account is judged, however, to be a fabrication of the 4th or 5th century. The Migne text, PG 5, 979-988, is superseded by F. X. Funk's *Patres apostolici,* Vol. 2 (second edition, Diekamp), Tübingen 1913, pp. 276-287.

69

[2, 4]
    Trajan said, "And who is Theophorus?"
Ignatius replied, "He that has Christ in his breast." 301
Trajan said, "Do we, then, seem to you not to have the gods in our minds, even though we
    enjoy their assistance in fighting against our enemies?"
Ignatius said, "You err in giving the name 'gods' to the demons of heathen peoples. There
    is, in fact, but one God, who made heaven and earth and the sea and all that is in them (1);
    and one Christ Jesus, His only-begotten Son, whose friendship may I enjoy!" 302
[5] Trajan said, "Do you mean the One who was crucified under Pontius Pilate?"
Ignatius said, "I mean Him that impaled sin along with him who was its inventor, and who 374
    has given judgment against every malice of the devil, setting the devil under the feet of 494
    those who carry Himself in their heart."
[6] Trajan said, "Do you, then, bear Christ within you?"
Ignatius said, "Most certainly, for it is written, 'I will dwell and walk about among
    you (2).' "

70

[6, 5]
    Only the harder parts of his holy relics were left, and these were conveyed to Antioch 123
and wrapped in linen, as an inestimable treasure left to the holy Church, on account of
the grace which was in the martyr.

1. Ps. 145 [146]:6.
2. 2 Cor. 6:16; Lev. 26:12.

THE PSEUDO-IGNATIAN LETTER TO THE ANTIOCHIANS [*ca. A.D.* 400]

Among the several spurious letters of the Ignatian corpus is the *Letter to the Antiochians.* Such a letter he ought to have written; but even if he did, this is not it. The letter preserved under this title is a fabrication of about the year 400 A.D., probably stemming from Origenist circles. Migne's text is in PG 5, 897-910. The present selection, however, is translated from the better critical source, Funk's *Patres apostolici,* Vol. 2 (second edition, Diekamp), Tübingen 1913, p. 170.

70a

[12, 1]

I salute the holy presbytery. I salute the sacred deacons, and that person dear to me (1):   952
may I behold him, in the Holy Spirit, taking my place, when I have attained to Christ.
May my life be given for his. [2] I salute the subdeacons, the lectors, the cantors, the   955
porters, the grave-diggers, the exorcists, and the confessors (2). I salute the keepers of   956
the holy gates, the deaconesses in Christ. I salute the virgins betrothed to Christ, on   957
account of whom I rejoice in the Lord Jesus. I salute the people of the Lord, from the
last to the greatest, and all my sisters in the Lord (3).

1. τὸ ποθεινόν μοι ὄνομα.
2. Ἀσπάζομαι ὑποδιακόνους, ἀναγνώστας, ψάλτας, πυλωρούς, τοὺς κοπιῶντας, ἐπορκιστὰς (al. ἐξορκιστὰς),
    ὁμολογητάς.
3. Between the salute to the virgins and that to the people of God, the old Latin translation interposes a salute
    to "the most upstanding widows."

ST. POLYCARP OF SMYRNA [A. D. 69/70 − A. D. 155/156]

St. Polycarp, Bishop of Smyrna, is one of the Apostolic Fathers, having been a
hearer of the Apostle St. John; and he is the same Polycarp to whom one of the
seven Ignatian letters is addressed. He died a martyr's death at the age of eighty-six,
in the year 155 or 156 A. D.

[SECOND] LETTER TO THE PHILIPPIANS [ca. A. D. 135]

Of the several letters which Polycarp is known to have written, all that is extant
from his pen is the *Letter to the Philippians*. What is preserved, however, as a single
letter to the Philippians is actually two such letters. The first letter consists of Ch. 13
in the text tradition, and possibly also Ch. 14. It dates from between the time
immediately before St. Ignatius arrived in Rome (*ca.* 110 A. D.) and the end of
Trajan's reign (*A. D.* 118). Within even this short period, an earlier date is preferable
to a later; for the first letter of Polycarp to the Philippians is merely the covering note
for the Ignatian letters which Polycarp forwarded to the Philippians. The second letter,
consisting of chapter 1-12 in the text tradition, dates from *ca. A. D.* 135. Migne's
edition, PG 5, 1005-1016, is entirely superseded by Funk-Bihlmeyer-Schneemelcher,
Die apostolischen Väter, Vol. 1, Tübingen 1956, pp. 114-120. Those who have not the
latter available may find Kirsopp Lake's *The Apostolic Fathers* (Loeb Classical Library)
a convenience.

72

[3, 1]

These things, brethren, concerning righteousness, I write to you not at my own instance, but because you first invited me. [2] For neither can I nor anyone like me match the wisdom of the blessed and glorious Paul. When he was among you, face to face with the men of that time, he expounded the word of truth accurately and authoritatively; and when he was absent he wrote letters to you, the study of which will enable you to build yourselves up in the faith which was given to you:—[3] a faith which is the mother of us   541 all (1), when hope follows along and the love of God and Christ and neighbor goes before (2). If anyone be devoted to these, he has fulfilled the commandment of justice: for whoever has love is far from every sin.

73

[6, 1]

Let the presbyters be compassionate, merciful to all, bringing back those who have   925 wandered astray, visiting those who are sick, neglecting neither widow nor orphan nor the poor, but providing always what is good in the sight of God and of men (3). Let them refrain entirely from anger, respect of persons, and unjust judgment; let them be far from the love of money, not quick to believe evil of anyone, not hasty in judgment, knowing that we are all debtors in the matter of sin.

74

[7,1]

Everyone who does not confess that Jesus Christ has come in the flesh is an Antichrist (4); whoever does not confess the testimony of the cross, is of the devil;   370 and whoever perverts the sayings of the Lord for his own desires (5), and says that there   1011 is neither resurrection nor judgment, such a one is the first-born of Satan (6). [2] Let   1020 us, therefore, leave the foolishness and the false-teaching of the crowd, and turn back to the word which was delivered to us in the beginning.   102

75

[8, 1]

Let us, then, continue unceasingly in our hope (7) and in the Pledge of our justification,   370 that is, in Christ Jesus, who bore our sins in His own body on the tree (8), who did no sin, nor was guile found in His mouth (9); yet, for our sakes, that we might live in Him (10), He endured everything.

76

[12, 2]

Now may God and the Father of our Lord Jesus Christ, and the Eternal High Priest (11) Himself, Jesus Christ, the Son of God, build you up in faith and in truth, in   380 meekness perfect and without resentment, in patience and in long-suffering, in endurance, and in purity. May He set your lot and portion among His saints, — and ourselves along with you, and all others under heaven who in the future will believe in our Lord Jesus Christ, and in His Father, who raised Him from the dead (12).

1. Gal. 4:26.
2. 1 Cor. 13:13.
3. Prov. 3:4; Rom. 12:17; 2 Cor. 8:21.
4. 1 John 4:2-3; 2 John 1:7.

5. ἐπιϑυμίας usually implies *carnal* desires. The sense of the passage is probably 'whoever, disregarding the words of the Lord, gives way to lust, and denies that there will be reward or punishment in another life, ...'
6. According to Irenaeus (§ 212 below), this is what Polycarp called Marcion to his face.
7. 1 Tim. 1:1.
8. 1 Peter 2:24.
9. 1 Peter 2:22; Is. 53:9.
10. 1 Peter 2:24.
11. Heb. 6:20; 7:3; Ps. 109 [110]:4.
12. Gal. 1:1. See also Col. 2:12 and 1 Peter 1:21.

THE MARTYRDOM OF SAINT POLYCARP [*A. D.* 155/157]

The Martyrdom of Polycarp is the oldest extant detailed and authentic account of a martyrdom. In the form of a letter from the Church of Smyrna to the Christian community of Philomelium in Greater Phrygia, over the signature of an otherwise unknown Marcion, it is a most precious document, and even after eighteen hundred years it is a singularly implacable person who can read it without tears. The Migne text, PG 5, 1029-1046, is valuable only as a quick and convenient reference. Kirsopp Lake's edition in *The Apostolic Fathers* (Loeb Classical Library) is also a convenience, though reliable enough. The scholar will require Funk-Bihlmeyer-Schneemelcher, *Die apostolischen Väter,* Vol. 1, Tübingen 1956, pp. 120-132.

77

[*Address*]

The Church of God which sojourns (1) in Smyrna, to the Church of God which 404
sojourns in Philomelium, and to all the dioceses of the holy and Catholic Church in every 405
place: May mercy, peace, and love of God the Father and of our Lord Jesus Christ be
given you in abundance (2).

78

[2, 3]

Fixing their minds on the grace of Christ, [the martyrs] despised worldly tortures, and
purchased eternal life with but a single hour. To them, the fire of their cruel torturers
was cold. They kept before their eyes their escape from the eternal and unquenchable 1034
fire. With the eyes of their heart they looked up to the good things which are reserved 1032
for those who persevere, things which neither has ear heard nor eye seen nor has the 1045
heart of man conceived (3): but to them, no longer men but already angels, a glimpse
of these things was granted by the Lord.

79

[8, 1]

When finally [Polycarp] had finished his prayer, in which he remembered everyone 120
with whom he had ever been acquainted, the small and the great, the reknowned and the
unknown, and the whole Catholic Church throughout the world, and the moment of 421

departure had arrived, they seated him on an ass and led him into the city. It was a   404
great Sabbath.

79a
[9, 3]

When the Proconsul urged him and said, "Take the oath and I will release you; revile   672
Christ," Polycarp answered: "Eighty-six years I have served Him, and He has never done
me wrong. How, then, should I be able to blaspheme my King who has saved me?"

80
[14, 3]

[About to die in martyrdom, Polycarp looked up to heaven and prayed:] ". . . In
this way and for all things I do praise you, I do bless you, I do glorify you through the   230
eternal and heavenly High Priest, Jesus Christ, your beloved Child: through whom be   380
glory to you with Him and with the Holy Spirit, both now and through ages yet to
come. Amen."

80a
[16, 2]

And of the elect, he was one indeed, the wonderful martyr Polycarp, who in our days   202
was an apostolic and prophetic teacher, bishop of the Catholic Church in Smyrna. For   422
every word which came forth from his mouth was fulfilled and will be fulfilled.   421

81
[17, 3]

[Christ] we worship as the Son of God; but the martyrs we love as disciples and   301
imitators of the Lord; and rightly so, because of their unsurpassable devotion to their   342
own King and Teacher. With them may we also become companions and fellow   121
disciples. [18, 1] When the centurion saw the contentiousness caused by the Jews, he
confiscated the body (4), and, according to their custom, burned it. [2] Then, at last,   123
we took up his bones, more precious than costly gems and finer than gold, and put them
in a suitable place. [3] The Lord will permit us, when we are able, to assemble there in
joy and gladness; and to celebrate the birthday of his martyrdom, both in memory of
those who have already engaged in the contest, and for the practice and training of those
who have yet to fight.

81a
[19, 1]

So much, then, for the Blessed Polycarp. Although he was, together with those from
Philadelphia, the twelfth martyr in Smyrna, he alone is especially remembered by all, and
is spoken of in every place, even by the heathen. He was not only a famous teacher,
but also an outstanding witness, whose martyrdom all desire to imitate, because it was
so much in accord with the gospel of Christ. [2] By his endurance he overcame the unjust   60
ruler, and thus gained the imperishable crown. Now with the Apostles and all the just he
is glorifying God and the Father Almighty, and he is blessing our Lord Jesus Christ, the
Savior of our souls, the Helmsman of our bodies, and the Shepherd of the Catholic   421
Church throughout the world.   404

1. παροικοῦσα, *sojourning*, i.e., dwelling in a place as a stranger or pilgrim. The noun παροικία means a *sojourning;* and by the early part of the 4th century it was a well-established term for an ecclesiastical district of jurisdiction. From the Greek term is derived the late Latin *parochia*, seen also in such forms as *parachia, paruchia, parohhia, porrehia,* and now usually spelled *paroecia*, meaning a *parish,* and only rarely and very early, a *diocese.* The plural form occurs in the next line of the present passage; and I think we do no wrong in translating it *dioceses* rather than *sojournings.*
2. Jude 1:2.
3. 1 Cor. 2:9. See also Is. 64:4.
4. θεὶς αὐτὸν ἐν μέσῳ – literally, he *placed it in the midst.* It is simply the Greek counterpart of the Latin technical term *in medio ponere,* to lay something before the people. The Centurion withdrew the body from any individual claimants, confiscating it for the state; and then, of course, cremated it.

HERMAS [*fl. ca. A. D.* 140/155]

The *Muratorian Fragment* (below, § 268) is responsible for the information that Hermas, author of *The Shepherd,* was the brother of Pope St. Pius I (*regn. ca. A. D.* 140-155). From *The Shepherd* itself a few other items of curious information reveal themselves about Hermas, *e. g.,* he was a slave and afterwards a freedman; he had a farm on the highway between Rome and Cumae, but lost it in business reverses; his children apostatized and betrayed him in the persecutions; his wife had an unbridled tongue and was generally shrewish. In fact, we know many quite delightful things about him; but in the dry category of what often passes for useful information, we are, in Hermas' case, quite at a loss — which, perhaps, is no great loss at all.

THE SHEPHERD [*ca. A. D.* 140/155]

The Shepherd is a rather lengthy work belonging to the category of apocryphal apocalypses. The work consists of three large sections, the first divided into five chapters called *Visions,* the second into twelve chapters called *Mandates,* and the third into ten chapters called *Parables.* The work is important for its ethical concepts, and for its bearing upon the sacrament of Penance.

Accepting the statement of the anonymous author of the *Muratorian Fragment* that the work was written at Rome by Hermas, while his brother Pius was Bishop, *i. e.,* between *ca. A. D.* 140-155, a special problem is presented by a remark in Vis. 2, 4, 3 of *The Shepherd* (§ 82a below), wherein it is implied that Hermas is writing while Clement is still alive. That it is Clement of Rome who is referred to cannot be doubted. The difficulty is usually obviated by stating hypothetically that Hermas wrote some part of the work much earlier, only bringing it to completion during his brother's pontificate.

Even if we accept the usual late date for Clement's reign (92-101 A. D.), this gives us a span of 40 to 60 years for the writing of the work. Our having taken an earlier date for Clement's reign (*fl. ca. A. D.* 80) makes even more difficult what was

already an unlikely possibility. However, in a work obviously much fictionalized, or at any rate, of the apocalyptic and visionary genre, there seems to be no good reason why we cannot suppose that Hermas may simply have introduced the name of Clement for any number of hidden or symbolic reasons, perhaps only by way of implying that the vision was one which came to him in his youth, or perhaps by way of adding a semblance of antiquity to his work.

No single manuscript preserves the original Greek in its entirety; but by collating the various fragmentary Greek texts, all except a few sentences near the end can be set down in order. The complete text is extant in Latin and in Ethiopic, and there are additional small fragments of a Coptic and of a middle-Persian translation.

Migne's text, PG 2, 891-1012, is entirely superseded by Funk's in Vol. 1 of his *Patres apostolici,* Tübingen 1901.

81b

[Vis. 2, 2, 1]

After fifteen days during which I fasted and prayed much to the Lord, the knowledge of the writing was revealed to me. This is what was written: [2] "Your offspring, Hermas, have rejected God, have blasphemed the Lord, and have betrayed their parents in great wickedness. They are called 'betrayers of parents'; yet, their betrayal has profited them nothing. Instead, they have but added dissoluteness and a mixture of evils to their sins, and thus their crimes have been made complete. [3] But make these words known to all your children, and to your wife, who henceforth shall be as your sister. She does not restrain her tongue, in which she does evil; but when she hears these words, she will restrain it, and will obtain mercy.

[4] "After you have made known these words to them, which the Master commanded me to reveal to you, all the sins which they have committed in past times will be forgiven them. And all the saints who have sinned up to this day shall be forgiven, if they repent with their whole heart, and put double-mindedness out of their hearts. [5] The Master has sworn to His elect by His glory, that if, after this day which is fixed as a limit, they still commit sins, they will find no salvation. Repentance for the just has an end. The days of repentance are finished for all the saints; but for the heathen there is repentance until the last day."   907

81c

[Vis. 2, 2, 8]

For the Lord has sworn by His Son that those who have denied their Christ have been rejected from life — those, that is, who are about to deny Him in the days to come. To those, however, who have formerly denied Him, mercy has been granted by reason of His great compassion.   902

82

[Vis. 2, 4, 1]

While I slept, brethren, a revelation was made to me by a very handsome young man, who said to me, "Who do you think the old woman is, from whom you received the little book?" I said, "The Sibyl." "You are wrong," he said: "She is not." "Who is she, then?" I said. "The Church," he replied. So I said to him, "Why, then, is she old?" "Because," he replied, "she was created the first of all things. That is why she is old. It was for her sake that the world was established."   400

82a

[Vis. 2, 4, 3]
[Hermas recounts that the old woman who is the Church came to him in a vision and said:] "Therefore shall you write two little books and send one to Clement and one to Grapte. Clement shall then send it to the cities abroad, because that is his duty; and Grapte shall instruct the widows and the orphans. But you shall read it in this city along with the presbyters who are in charge of the Church."

435

83

[Vis. 3, 4, 1]
I answered and said to her: "Lady, this is a great and wonderful thing. But the six young men who are building, who are they, lady?"

"These are the holy angels of God, who were the first to be created, and to whom the Lord entrusted all of His creation, to increase it and to build it up, and to be masters of the whole of creation. Through them, therefore, the building of the tower will be completed."

480
481
492

[2] "But the others, who are bringing the stones:—who are they?"

"They also are holy angels of God; but these six are superior to them. The building of the tower, then, shall be completed; and all alike shall rejoice around the tower, and shall give glory to God, because the building of the tower was accomplished."

488

84

[Vis. 3, 5, 1]
[The lady, who is the Church, addressed herself to Hermas and said:] "Listen now concerning the stones which go into the building. The stones which are square and white and which fit neatly in place, these are the apostles and bishops and teachers and deacons who walked according to the majesty of God and who ministered to the elect of God in holiness and reverence, in the work of overseeing and teaching and in giving service. Some of them have fallen asleep and some are still alive. They always agreed among themselves and had peace among themselves and listened to one another; and that is why in the building of the tower they fit neatly into place."

405

954

85

[Mand. 1, 1]
Believe first of all that God is one, that He created all things and set them in order, and brought out of non-existence into existence everything that is (1), and that He contains all things while He Himself is uncontained.

460
461
154

86

[Mand. 4, 1, 4]
I said to [the shepherd], "Sir, permit me to ask you a few questions." "Speak," he said. "Sir," said I, "if someone have a wife faithful in the Lord, and he discover her in some adultery, does the husband sin if he cohabits with her?" [5] "So long as he is ignorant," he said, "he does not sin; but if the husband knows her sin, and the wife does not repent, but continues in her fornication, and the husband cohabits with her, he makes himself a partner to her sin and an accomplice in her adultery."

[6] "What then, sir," said I, "shall the husband do, if the wife continue in this disposition?" "Let him divorce her," he said, "and let the husband remain single. But if he divorce his wife and marry another, he too commits adultery (2)." [7] "If, then, sir," said I, "after the wife be divorced, she repent and wish to return to her own

974
975

husband, is she not to be received?" [8] "Indeed," he said, "if the husband does not
receive her, he sins and brings great sin upon himself. It is necessary, in fact, to
receive the sinner who repents; but not repeatedly, for the servants of God have only   907
one repentance. It is in view of repentance, then, that the husband is obliged not to
marry. And this is the practice enjoined on husband and wife alike.

[9] "Not only," he continued, "is it adultery if a man defile his flesh, but whoever
does such things as the heathen do also commits adultery. If, then, anyone continue
in such practices, and do not repent, leave him and do not cohabit with him; for
otherwise you will be a partaker in his sin. [10] It was enjoined on you, however, to
remain by yourselves, whether husband or wife, because of the fact that in such cases
repentance is possible."

86a

[Mand. 4, 2, 1]
And I asked [the shepherd] again, saying: "Since the Lord has accounted me worthy
to have you live with me always, permit yet a few more words of mine; for I have no
understanding and my heart has been hardened by my former deeds. Give me understanding; for I am very foolish, and I comprehend absolutely nothing." [2] He
answered me and said: "I preside," he said, "over repentance (3), and I give understanding to all who repent. Indeed," he said, "do you not realize that this very
repentance is understanding? To repent," he said, "is great understanding. For the   910
sinner understands that he has done wickedly before the Lord; and the deed which he
has done comes into his heart, and he repents and does wickedly no longer; rather, he
does good abundantly, and humbles his soul and puts it to the torture because it sinned.
You see, then, that repentance is great understanding."

87

[Mand. 4, 3, 1]
"Sir," I said, "I will continue to question you." "Speak," he replied. "I have heard,
sir," said I, "from some teachers, that there is no other repentance except that which took
place when we went down into the water and obtained the remission of our former sins."   836
[2] He said to me, "You have heard rightly, for so it is. One who has received remission
of sins ought never sin again, but live in purity. [3] Since, however, you inquire accurately
about everything, I will explain this also to you, without giving any inducement to those
who shall in the future believe, or to those who already believe in the Lord. Those who
already believe or who shall in the future believe have no repentance of sins; but they do
have the remission of their former sins. [4] The Lord appointed repentance, however, for
those who were called before these days; for the Lord knows the heart; and knowing all
things beforehand, He knew the weakness of man and the subtlety of the devil, who
desires to do wickedness to the servants of God, and desires to do them evil. [5] The   494
Lord, then, being compassionate, dealt kindly with His creation and established this
repentance; and the control of this repentance was given to me. [6] But I say to you,"
he declared, "after this great and holy calling, if a man be tempted by the devil and sin,
he has one repentance. But if he sin and repent repeatedly — repentance is of little   907
value to such a man, and with difficulty will he live." [7] I said to him, "I am made to
live again by hearing these things from you so accurately; for now I know that if I do not
again add to my sins, I shall be saved." "You shall be saved," he said, "and everyone who
will do these things."

88

[Mand. 4, 4, 1]

I asked [the shepherd] again, saying: "Sir, since you did bear with me once, explain this   979
also to me." "Speak," he said. "If, sir," I said, "a wife should die, or a husband as the
case may be, and the survivor marry, does the one who marries sin?" [2] "He does not
sin," he said: "but if he remain single he will gain for himself uncommon honor and great
glory with the Lord. But even if he marry, he does not sin. [3] At all events, preserve
purity and holiness, and you shall live to God."

89

[Par. 5, 6, 2]

"God planted the vineyard," [the shepherd] said: "that is, He created the people,   493
and gave them over to His Son. And the Son appointed the angels to guard over them;   492
and He Himself cleansed them of their sins, laboring much and undergoing much toil."   374

90

[Par. 8, 11, 3]

And [the shepherd] answered me and said: "As many," he said, "as repent with their   911
whole heart and purify themselves of all the wickedness mentioned before, and no longer
add anything to their former sins, — they shall receive from the Lord a healing for their
former sins, provided they are not double-minded in regard to these commandments; and
they shall live to God. But as many," he continued, "as add to their sins and live in the
lusts of this world — they shall condemn themselves to death."

91

[Par. 9, 1, 1]

After I had written the Mandates and the Parables of the shepherd, the angel of
repentance, he came to me and said to me: "I wish to explain to you what the Holy Spirit   237
showed you when He spoke to you in the form of the Church; for that Spirit is the Son   302
of God."

92

[Par. 9, 16, 2]

"They had need," [the shepherd] said, "to come up through the water, so that they   836
might be made alive; for they could not otherwise enter into the kingdom of God (4),   831
except by putting away the mortality of their former life. [3] These also, then, who had
fallen asleep, received the seal of the Son of God, and entered into the kingdom of God.
For," he said, "before a man bears the name of the Son of God, he is dead. But when he
receives the seal, he puts mortality aside and again receives life. [4] The seal, therefore, is   822
the water. They go down into the water dead, and come out of it alive."   824

93

[Par. 9, 17, 4]

[The shepherd said:] "All the nations which dwell under heaven, when they heard and   404
believed, were called by the name of the Son of God. When, therefore, they received the   405
seal, they had one understanding and one mind; and their faith became one, and one their   420
love; and they carried the spirits of the virgins along with the name; and that is why the
structure of the tower was in one splendid color like the sun (5)."

93a

[Par. 9, 26, 5]

[The shepherd continued:] "For these, then, there is repentance, if they be not found   902
to have denied from their hearts. But if someone is found to have denied from his heart,
I do not know whether or not he will be able to live. [6] Nor do I say that in these days
one can deny and receive repentance; for it is impossible for him to be saved, who shall
now deny His Lord. Yet, there seems to be repentance waiting for those who denied in
times past. If anyone, then, is about to repent, let him make haste before the tower is
completed: otherwise he will be done to death by the women (6)."

93b

[Par. 9, 31, 4]

[The shepherd, the angel of repentance, continued:] "But I say to all of you, as many
as have received the seal (7): maintain your innocence, bear no grudge, do not persist in   836
wickedness nor in the bitter memory of past offenses. Be of one spirit and put away
these wicked divisions. Remove them from your midst, so that the Master of the flock
may rejoice in His sheep. [5] He will rejoice if all be found whole. But if He find some   200
of them fallen away, woe to the shepherds. [6] And if the shepherds themselves be fallen
away, how shall they answer for the flock? That they have fallen away because of the
sheep? They will not be believed. It is beyond credibility that a shepherd should be
harmed by his sheep; and their punishment will be the greater because of their lie. I,
too, am a shepherd, and I have the gravest obligation to give an account for you."

1. Eph. 3:9; 2 Mach. 7:28.
2. Mark 10:11. See also Matt. 5:32; 19:9; Luke 16:18; and 1 Cor. 7:11.
3. ἡ μετάνοια.
4. John 3:5.
5. The seemingly rather cryptic remark about 'carrying the spirits of the virgins along with the name' is to be
   understood in the light of Par. 9, 13, 2: "These virgins are the powers of the Son of God. If you bear the
   name but do not bear His power, you will be bearing His name in vain." The identity of the virgins is
   discovered in Par. 9, 15, 2: "The first is Faith, the second is Continence, the third is Fortitude, and the
   fourth is Long-suffering. The others . . . are Simplicity, Innocence, Purity, Joyfulness, Truth, Understanding, Concord and Love. He that bears these names and the name of the Son of God will be able to
   enter the kingdom of heaven."
6. The tower which is in process of building is the Church, the building of which continues until the parousia;
   and the women here referred to are the women of black raiment (Par. 9, 15, 3), whose names are Unbelief,
   Impurity, Disobedience, and Deceit; and also, but of lesser power than these four: Grief, Wickedness,
   Licentiousness, Bitterness, Lying, Foolishness, Evil-speaking, and Hate. There is some reason to believe that
   the 9th Parable was added to the work after its completion, and perhaps by Hermas himself, when the
   parousia was delayed beyond his expectations, and the time for repentance was extended.
7. The seal, of course, is Baptism.

ST. PAPIAS [*fl. ca. A. D.* 130]

St. Papias was Bishop of Hierapolis in Asia Minor. According to Irenaeus (*Adv. Haer.* 5, 33, 4), he was not only a friend of Polycarp of Smyrna but also a hearer of the Apostle John; and it is on the strength of this remark of Irenaeus that Papias is generally regarded as an Apostolic Father. As Eusebius *(Hist. Eccl.* 3, 39, 2) points out, however, Papias himself makes it clear that he was a hearer not directly of the Apostles, but of acquaintances of the Apostles. Since the tendency today is to take a more restrictive view in the matter of who is to be called an Apostolic Father, it is probable that Papias ought to be deprived of the title.

EXPLANATION OF THE SAYINGS OF THE LORD [*ca. A. D.* 130]

Eusebius says of Papias that, "as is clear from his books, he was a man of very little intelligence." He says this, no doubt, because Papias was a chiliast. Eusebius accepts approvingly Irenaeus' testimony that the five books of the *Explanation* constitute the sole literary endeavor of Papias. Certainly no further writings of Papias have come to light; and as for the *Explanation,* even of this one work we possess only a few small fragments, mostly preserved as quotations within Eusebius.

The Migne text, PG 5, 1255-1262, is no longer serviceable. The best edition is still that of Funk-Bihlmeyer, now republished by Schneemelcher, *Die apostolischen Väter,* Vol. 1, Tübingen 1956, 133-140. The book, chapter, and verse numbers of the following passages refer to the place where the passage occurs in Eusebius' *History of the Church.*

FRAGMENTS IN EUSEBIUS, History of the Church, BK. 3, CH. 39

94

[3, 39, 1]

Of Papias there are five books in circulation, which bear the title Explanation of the Sayings of the Lord. *Irenaeus remarks on these as the only ones written by him, writing very much as follows: "These things, too, Papias, a man of ancient times, who was a hearer of John and a companion of Polycarp, attests in writing in the fourth of his books. He wrote five books." [2] So much for Irenaeus. Papias himself, however, in the introduction to his treatises, makes it clear that he was never a hearer or an eyewitness of the Apostles. He shows, in fact, by the language he uses, that he received the doctrines of the faith through acquaintances of the Apostles:*

[3] "I shall not hesitate to set down for you along with my interpretations whatever I learned well from the presbyters and recall clearly, being thoroughly confident of their truth. Unlike most people, I do not delight in those who talk a great deal, but in those who teach the truth; nor in those who relate the commandments of others, but in those who relate the commandments given by the Lord to the faith, and which are derived from Truth itself. [4] And then too, when anyone came along who had been a follower of the presbyters, I would inquire about the presbyters' discourses: what was said by Andrew, or by Peter, or by Philip, or by Thomas or James, or by John or Matthew, or by any other of the Lord's disciples; and what Aristion and the Presbyter John, the disciples of the Lord, say. It did not seem to me that I could get so much profit from the contents of books as from a living and abiding voice."

102

[5] *Here it is worth noting that he twice mentions the name of John: the first in connection with Peter and James and Matthew and the rest of the Apostles, clearly*

referring to the evangelist; but the other John he mentions after an interval, and groups him with others outside the number of the Apostles, placing Aristion before him; and he distinctly calls him a presbyter. [6] *In this way he makes it quite evident that their statement is true, who say that there were in Asia two persons of that name; and that there are in Ephesus two tombs, each of which even to the present time is called the tomb of John. It is important to take note of this: because if anyone would not prefer the first, then probably it was the second who saw the Revelation which bears the name of John* (1).

42

95

[3, 39, 14]

Papias also gives in his own writings other accounts of the words of the Lord on the authority of the above-mentioned Aristion, and the traditions of John the Presbyter. We refer the studious to these. For our present purpose we will only add to his already-quoted words a tradition which, contained in these sources, concerns that Mark who wrote the Gospel:— [15] "And the Presbyter said this also: 'When Mark became the interpreter of Peter, he wrote down accurately whatever he remembered, though not in order, of the words and deeds of the Lord. He was neither hearer nor follower of the Lord; but such he was afterwards, as I say, of Peter, who had no intention of giving a connected account of the sayings of the Lord, but adapted his instructions as was necessary. Mark, then, made no mistake, but wrote things down as he remembered them; and he made it his concern to omit nothing that he had heard nor to falsify anything therein (2).' " *Such, then, is the account concerning Mark, as given by Papias.*

65

[16] *In regard to Matthew, he says this:* "Matthew, indeed, composed (3) the sayings in the Hebrew language; and each one interpreted them to the best of his ability." *The same writer made use of testimonies from the First Epistle of John, and likewise from that of Peter. And he related another story about a woman accused of many sins, which is contained in the* Gospel of the Hebrews.

64
42

1. εἰκὸς γὰρ τὸν δεύτερον εἰ μή τις ἐθέλοι τὸν πρῶτον τὴν ἐπ' ὀνόματος φερομένην Ἰωάννου Ἀποκάλυψιν ἑωρακέναι. This line has sometimes been so badly misunderstood as to make it appear that Eusebius is declaring it as his own opinion that the Presbyter John is to be preferred to the Apostle-Evangelist John as the author of the Apocalypse. Whatever opinion one will himself hold in that matter, let Eusebius be rightly understood: his words make it clear enough that he regards John the Apostle, John the Evangelist, and John, the author of the Apocalypse as one and the same John; but then he adds that if anyone prefer to consider that the Apostle-Evangelist John is not the author of the Apocalypse, then, in this view, it is probable that the author of the Apocalypse is Presbyter John.

2. It is probable that Papias' remarks, as recounted by Eusebius, were intended as an explanation of the apparent chronological discrepancies in the Gospel account: and his explanation, then, is simply this, that Peter's preaching had not been a chronological exposition of our Lord's career, and Mark, in writing down what he remembered of Peter's catecheses, made no attempt to re-arrange the material in a chronological fashion. The Gospel is not at fault chronologically, because no chronology was intended. The evangelist writes not chronologically but kerygmatically.

3. There is manuscript evidence for either of two readings: συνετάξατο and συνεγράψατο. We have accepted the former,—which, in fact, is the better attested,—as being the less precise and therefore the safer term. It must be noted, however, that the difference between the two words is not great. The emphasis in the former is upon the act of compiling or composing the work; but it would generally imply also that it was written down. The latter term, in its etymology, would seem to put the emphasis upon the act of writing down the work which was composed; but it is in fact a technical term for the work of composition, and might not necessarily, by its use, demand that the work be actually written down, as distinct from oral composition.

Neither term, then, could be taken as an absolute testimony to the fact of Matthew's having *written* a Gospel, as distinguished from his having *composed* a kind of oral Gospel. The same license attends these words in English. A man may say, "I have composed a song"; and he means thereby that he has not only composed it, but has written it down on paper. It is not a question of stating only a part of what he has done, for the word may (or may not!) embrace both processes. Another man, without deception, may say, "I have written a song," when, without ever having set a note on paper, he has invented the song mentally, gotten it well-ordered in his mind, and may even be ready to perform it in public.

LETTER TO DIOGNETUS [*A. D.* 125/200]

The anonymous *Letter to Diognetus* is an apologetic work in the form of a letter to a high dignitary among the pagans, one Diognetus. While it may well be that the letter is addressed to a particular person, it may be taken as certain that Diognetus is a pseudonymn. We have no space in the present work to consider the multitude of theories in respect to the identity of the author, the identity of the addressee, and the date of composition; but we cannot ignore a certain one of the more recent proposals: In the 1940's P. Andriessen proposed and vigorously defended the opinion that the *Letter to Diognetus* is in fact the *Apology* of Quadratus, otherwise evidenced only by the well-known fragment in Eusebius [§ 109 below]. The Eusebian fragment is not found in the *Letter to Diognetus;* but Andriessen pointed out that there seems to be a gap in the letter between Ch. 7, Vs. 6 and Ch. 7, Vs. 7, where something very like the Eusebian Quadratus fragment might be expected. In Andriessen's theory, Diognetus is the emperor Hadrian, and the *Apology* or *Letter to Diognetus* was presented to him by Quadratus in the Easter season of the year 125 A. D.

His theory is attractive, fascinating, but not convincing. As recently as 1949 H. G. Meecham defended a date of *ca. A. D.* 150 for the letter; and in 1951 H. I. Marrou defended a date of *ca. A. D.* 200. The question is not settled. For a bibliography on the subject, see J. Quasten, *Patrology,* Vol. 1, 1950, pp. 252-253, along with the more recent articles noted by Fischer, *Die apostolischen Väter,* 1956, pp. 270-271. Migne's text, PG 2, 1167-1186, is entirely superseded by Funk-Bihlmeyer-Schneemelcher, *Die apostolischen Väter,* 1956, pp. 141-149.

96

[3, 1]

Next, I suppose, you are especially anxious to hear why we do not worship in the same   52 way as the Jews. [2] The Jews, indeed, by abstaining from the [Greek polytheistic] religion already discussed, may rightly claim that they worship the one God of the universe and regard Him as Master; but in offering Him this worship in a manner similar to that of those already treated, they are altogether mistaken. . . . [4, 1] Furthermore, I do [not] (1) suppose that you need to learn from me how ridiculous and unworthy of any argument are their scruples about food, their superstition about the Sabbath, their pride in circumcision, and their sham in fasting. [2] How can it be anything but unlawful to accept for the use of man and thus account as created well, only some of the things created by God, while rejecting others as being useless and superfluous? [3] And how can it be anything but impious to falsely accuse God of forbidding that a good deed be done on the Sabbath day?

97

[5, 1]

The difference between Christians and the rest of men is neither in country, nor in   86 language, nor in customs. . . . [5] They dwell in their own fatherlands, but as temporary inhabitants (2). They take part in all things as citizens, while enduring the hardships of foreigners. Every foreign place is their fatherland, and every fatherland is to them a foreign place. [6] Like all others, they marry and beget children; but they do not expose their offspring. [7] Their board they set for all, but not their bed. [8] Their lot is cast in the flesh; but they do not live for the flesh (3). [9] They pass their time on earth; but their citizenship is in heaven (4). [10] They obey the established laws, and in their private lives they surpass the laws.

[11] They love all men; and by all they are persecuted. [12] They are unknown, and they are condemned. They are put to death, and they gain life (5). [13] They are poor, but make many rich (6); they are destitute, but have an abundance of everything. [14]

They are dishonored, and in their dishonor they are made glorious. They are defamed, but they are vindicated. [15] They are reviled, and they bless (7); they are insulted, and they pay homage. [16] When they do good, they are punished as evil-doers; and when they are punished they rejoice as if brought to life. [17] They are made war upon as foreigners by the Jews, and they are persecuted by the Greeks; and yet, those who hate them are at a loss to state the cause of their hostility.

97a

[6, 1]

To put it briefly, what the soul is in the body, that the Christians are in the world. [2] The soul is spread through all parts of the body, and Christians through all the cities   404
of the world. [3] The soul dwells in the body, but it is not of the body; and Christians dwell in the world, though they are not of the world. [4] The soul is invisible, but it is   412
sheathed in a visible body. Christians are seen, for they are in the world; but their   413
religion remains invisible.

98

[7, 2]

It was truly the almighty, all-creating, and invisible God Himself who established   460
among men the Truth from heaven and the holy and incomprehensible Word, and set Him firmly in their hearts. Nor did he do this, contrary to what one might suppose, by sending to men some minister, or an angel or a ruler, or one of those in charge of earthly things, or one of those entrusted with the administration of heavenly things. No, He sent the very Designer and Creator of the universe Himself, through whom He had made the heavens, and by whom He had enclosed the sea within its own bounds;   284
whose mysteries all the elements of nature faithfully guard; from whom the sun received the schedule of its daily flight; whose command the moon obeys in lighting up the night; to whom the stars give heed in following the path of the moon; by whom all things were ordered and bounded and placed in subjection: the heavens and the things in the heavens, the earth and the things on the earth, the sea and the things in the sea; fire, air, and the abyss; the things in the heights, the things in the depths, the things between — yes, He it was that He sent to men.
[3] But did He send Him, as one might suppose, in despotism and fear and terror?   372
[4] Not so. Rather, in gentleness and meekness He sent Him, as a king sending a son.   301
He sent Him as King, He sent Him as God, He sent Him to men. He sent Him for saving   302
and persuading, but not for compelling. Compulsion, you see, is not an attribute of God.

98a

[8, 1]

Indeed, before [Christ] came, what man had any knowledge at all of what God is? [2] Or would you accept the vain and foolish statements of those specious philosophers, some of whom said that God is fire — the place to which they are heading they call God! —   1032
and some said water; and some, one of the other elements which were created by God.

99

[9, 2]

When our inquity was complete, and it had become perfectly clear that punishment   362
and death were its expected recompense, and the time came which God had appointed to show forth His kindliness and power (8), — Oh, the magnitude of the kindness and

love which God has for man! — He did not hate us nor reject us, nor yet remember our
evils. Rather, He was long-suffering, and He was patient with us. In His mercy He
Himself took up our sins and He Himself gave His own Son as a ransom for us, the Holy   370
for the wicked, the Innocent for the guilty, the Just for the unjust, the Incorruptible for
the corruptible, and the Immortal for the mortal.

[3] Indeed, what else could have covered over our sins except His righteousness?
[4] In whom was it possible for us, in view of our wickedness and impiety, to be
justified, except in the Son of God alone? [5] Oh, the sweet exchange! Oh, the
unfathomable accomplishment! Oh, the unexpected benefits! — that the wickedness of
the many should be hidden in the One who is just; and that the righteousness of the
One should justify the wicked many!

100

[10, 7]
When you know what is the true life, that of heaven; when you despise the merely
apparent death, which is temporal; when you fear the death which is real, and which
is reserved for those who will be condemned to the everlasting fire, the fire which will   1034
punish even to the end those who are delivered to it — then you will condemn the   1032
deceit and error of the world.

1. The sole manuscript, and that only of the high middle ages, perished in the shelling of Strasbourg on August
   24, 1870. Careful copies of it had several times been made, however; and it is quite certain that the
   negative was not in the manuscript. It is, however, an obviously valid emendation, and had already been
   supplied by Stephanus in the *editio princeps* (Paris, 1592).
2. We recall having seen the same sentiment carved in the lintel over the entrance to a farmhouse in
   Liechtenstein:
   > *Ein Herberg hier für kurze Zeit:*
   > *Die Heimat ist in Ewigkeit.*
3. 2 Cor. 10:3; Rom. 8:12-13.
4. Phil. 3:20.
5. 2 Cor. 6:9.
6. 2 Cor. 6:10.
7. 1 Cor. 4:12.
8. Tit. 3:4.

THE SO-CALLED SECOND LETTER OF CLEMENT OF ROME
TO THE CORINTHIANS [*ca. A. D.* 150]

The so-called *Second Letter of Clement to the Corinthians* is not an authentic work
of Clement, but is in fact an anonymous homily. Opinions differ as to the origin of
the work; but the more likely theory would seem to be that which makes it a homily
originating in the Church of Corinth. Preserved in the archives in Corinth along with
Clement's authentic letter (page 6 ff., above), it could easily have happened that it
was copied out along with Clement's *Letter to the Corinthians,* and given the label of
Second Letter. Similarity in penitential doctrine to that expounded in *The Shepherd*
of Hermas leads to the dating of the work as *ca. A. D.* 150. The work, then, is the
oldest extant Christian homily. The Migne text (PG 1, 329-348) is superseded by
numerous critical editions, and especially by Funk-Bihlmeyer-Schneemelcher, *Die
apostolischen Väter,* Vol. 1, Tübingen 1956, pp. 71-81.

101

[1, 1]

Brethren, we must think of Jesus Christ as God and as the Judge of the living and the dead (1).

301
392

102

[5, 5]

And know, brethren, that our stay in this world in the flesh is short and fleeting; but the promise of Christ is great and wonderful, and brings us rest in the kingdom which is to come and in life everlasting. . . . [6, 7] If, then, we do the will of Christ, we shall obtain rest; but if not, if we neglect His commandments, nothing will rescue us from eternal punishment.

1043

1034

103

[8, 2]

Let us, then, so long as we are in this world, repent whatever evils we have done in the flesh, so that we may be saved by the Lord while yet we have time for repentance. [3] For after we have departed from this world it will no longer be possible to confess, nor will there be then any opportunity to repent.

911

991

104

[9, 1]

Let none of you say that this flesh is not judged and does not rise again. [2] Just think: in what state were you saved, and in what state did you recover your sight, if not in the flesh? [3] We must, therefore, guard the flesh as a temple of God. [4] In like manner, as you were called in the flesh, so you shall come in the flesh. [5] If Christ, the Lord who saved us, though He was originally spirit, became flesh and in this state called us, so also shall we receive our reward in the flesh. [6] Let us, therefore, love one another, so that we may all come into the kingdom of God.

1013

105

[14, 2]

I presume that you are not ignorant of the fact that the living Church is the body of Christ (2). The Scripture says, "God made man male and female (3)." The male is Christ, and the female is the Church. Moreover, the Books (4) and the Apostles declare that the Church belongs not to the present, but has existed from the beginning. She was spiritual, just as was our Jesus; but He was manifested in the last days so that He might save us. [3] And the Church, being spiritual, was manifested in the flesh of Christ.

401

400

106

[17, 7]

But when they see how those who have sinned and who have denied Jesus by their words or by their deeds are punished with terrible torture in unquenchable fire, the just, who have done good, and who have endured tortures and have hated the luxuries of life, will give glory to their God (5), saying, "There shall be hope for him that has served God with all his heart."

1034
1032

1. Acts 10:42; 2 Tim. 4:1; 1 Pet. 4:5.
2. Eph. 1:22-23.

3. Gen. 1:27.
4. *The Books*, of course, are the Old Testament Scriptures, while *the Apostles* are the New Testament. The Syriac translation supplies to *the Books* the qualification *of the Prophets*.
5. Apoc. 11:13.

CAIUS, PRESBYTER OF ROME [*fl. ca. A. D.* 198/217]

Little or nothing is known of Caius or Gaius, a presbyter of the Roman Church, beyond that which is recorded by Eusebius: he lived during the pontificate of Pope Zephyrinus, *i.e.*, between 198 A. D. and 217 A. D., and he authored a written disputation with Proclus, a Montanist. Certain of the authentic works of Hippolytus have been betimes falsely attributed to Caius.

DISPUTATION WITH PROCLUS [*ca. A. D.* 198/217]

Of Caius' work, the *Disputation with Proclus,* only a few fragments have been preserved, mostly by Eusebius. The text given by Migne, PG 10, 25-36, is less reliable than that of M. J. Routh, *Reliquiae sacrae,* second edition, 5 volumes, Oxford, 1846 ff., Vol. 2, pp. 123-158. The better source for the Eusebian passages is Schwartz's critical edition of Eusebius in the Berlin Corpus (GCS), which text is reprinted by Kirsopp Lake in his Loeb Classical Library edition of Eusebius.

FRAGMENT IN EUSEBIUS, History of the Church, BK. 2, CH. 25

106a

[2, 25, 5]
It is recorded that Paul was beheaded in Rome itself, and Peter, likewise, was crucified, 431 *during the reign [of Nero]. The account is confirmed by the names of Peter and Paul over the cemeteries there, which remain to the present time. [6] And it is confirmed also by a stalwart man of the Church, Gaius (1) by name, who lived in the time of Zephyrinus, Bishop of Rome. This Gaius, in a written disputation with Proclus, the leader of the sect of Cataphyrygians (2), says this of the places in which the remains of the afore-mentioned Apostles were deposited:* [7] "I can point out the trophies (3) of the Apostles. For if you are willing to go to the Vatican or to the Ostian Way, you will find the trophies of those who founded this Church."

1. The name is variously given as Gaius or Caius, the former being common to Greek, the latter to Latin.
2. The Phrygians or Cataphrygians are the Montanists.
3. Trophies is not an especially brilliant rendering of τὰ τρόπαια, but it is the customary rendering, since we have no corresponding term in English. *Triumphal monuments* answers closely, but not perfectly. The

τρόπαιον was not so much a monument to one's victory as a monument to the defeat of one's enemy. It consisted of the shields, helmets, arms, *etc.,* taken from the enemy and hung on trees or fixed on upright posts or frames. If the enemy allowed the trophy to be put up, it was in itself his confession of defeat. It is obvious that the use of the term τρόπαιον involves, in the present instance, a considerable amount of analogy. Yet, it is equally obvious that there must have been some evidence of cult — some kind of a τρόπαιον — in the places mentioned by Caius. See Hertling and Kirschbaum, *The Roman Catacombs and Their Martyrs,* p. 66 ff.

ST. DIONYSIUS OF CORINTH [*fl. ca. A. D.* 166/174]

The time of the episcopate of St. Dionysius, Bishop of Corinth, can be assigned a specific date only from the fact that he was a contemporary of Pope St. Soter, who ruled the Roman Church from 166 A. D. to 174 A. D.

LETTER TO SOTER OF ROME [*inter A. D.* 166/174]

The Letter of Dionysius of Corinth to Soter of Rome is extant only in a few fragments preserved in Eusebius. M. J. Routh, in the *Reliquiae sacrae,* mentioned above as containing the remains of Caius, has included also the fragments of Dionysius. A more current source, however, is Schwartz's critical edition of Eusebius, in the Berlin Corpus (GCS), reprinted by Kirsopp Lake in the Eusebius of the Loeb Classical Library.

FRAGMENT IN EUSEBIUS, History of the Church, BK. 2, CH. 25

106b

[2, 25, 8]

That both [Peter and Paul] suffered martyrdom at the same time is affirmed as follows, by Dionysius, Bishop of Corinth, when writing to the Romans: "You have also, by your   431 very admonition, brought together the planting that was made by Peter and Paul at Rome and at Corinth; for both of them alike planted in our Corinth and taught us; and both alike, teaching similarly in Italy, suffered martyrdom at the same time."

FRAGMENT IN EUSEBIUS, History of the Church, BK. 4, CH. 23

106c

[4, 23, 9]

There is extant a letter of Dionysius to the Romans, addressed to Soter who was bishop at that time; nor will it be amiss to quote here some passages from it, in which, writing as follows, he comments favorably upon a custom of the Romans, carefully preserved down to the persecution in our own time:

[10] "For from the beginning it has been your custom to do good to all the brethren   434
in various ways, and to send contributions to all the Churches in every city, thereby relieving the poverty of the needy and providing for the brethren in the mines. In this way, through the contributions which have ever been made, you Romans have preserved the ancestral custom of the Romans. This custom your blessed Bishop Soter has not only preserved, but is augmenting, by furnishing an abundance of supplies to the saints and by urging with consoling words, as a loving father his children, the brethren who are journeying (1)."

FRAGMENT IN EUSEBIUS, *History of the Church, BK. 4, CH. 23*

107

[4, 23, 11]

In this same letter, Dionysius also makes mention of the letter of Clement to the Corinthians, indicating that from the beginning it was, according to ancient custom, read in the church. He says, at any rate: "Today we have observed the Lord's holy day, in   434
which we have read your letter. Whenever we do read it, we shall be able to profit   435
thereby, as also we do when we read the earlier letter written to us by Clement."

1. The import of the last phrase is somewhat obscure. Some have taken it to mean that the Roman Church paid the expenses of poor pilgrims visiting there. While this may well have been done, it seems more likely to us that the *brethren who are journeying* is simply another way of referring to all Christians anywhere who may be in need.

EVENING HYMN OF THE GREEKS [2nd / 3rd cent.]

Belonging to the 3rd or perhaps even to the 2nd century, the text of the present work may be found in M. J. Routh, *Reliquiae sacrae*, Vol. 3, p. 515.

108

Joyous light of the holy glory
    Of the immortal Father,
[Who is] heavenly, holy blessed:
    Jesus Christ!

Having come to the setting of the sun,
    Seeing the evening light,
We praise the Father and the Son   230
    And the Holy Spirit of God.

It is right that You be praised
    At all times with holy sounds,
O Son of God, Giver of life: 370
    Therefore the world glorifies You.

QUADRATUS [*fl. ca. A. D.* 125]

Of Quadratus there is no information whatever beyond that which is to be found in Eusebius (*Hist. Eccl.* 4, 3, 1), who says of him: *"When Trajan had reigned for nineteen and one-half years Aelius Hadrian succeeded to the sovereignty. It was to him that Quadratus addressed a treatise, comprising an apology for our religion, because some wicked men were attempting to trouble us. It is still extant and in the hands of many of the brethren; and in fact, we ourselves have a copy. From it can be seen the clear proof of his intellect and of his apostolic orthodoxy."*

Since Hadrian ruled from 117 to 138 A. D., we have a rather narrow span of years for the dating of the work. Yet, it may be dated even more closely. Quadratus was a native of Asia Minor; and possibly he is the same Quadratus mentioned elsewhere by Eusebius as a disciple of the Apostles. Hadrian visited Asia Minor in 123-124 A. D., and again in 129 A. D. No doubt it was on one of these two visits that Quadratus' apology was presented to him.

While the identification of Quadratus, the Apologete of Asia Minor, with Quadratus, the apostolic disciple of Asia Minor, is far from certain, tradition makes of Quadratus the Apologete an Apostolic Father, and we may continue to regard him as such. He must not, however, be identified with another Quadratus, also mentioned by Eusebius, who is known as St. Quadratus, and who was Bishop of Athens in the time of Marcus Aurelius (*A. D.* 161-180).

APOLOGY TO HADRIAN [*A. D.* 123/129]

The fragment given below, as cited by Eusebius (*Hist. Eccl.* 4, 3, 2) is the sole passage that has survived from Quadratus' apology. J. Rendel Harris developed a very complicated theory, according to which portions of the *Apology* were supposedly woven through the *Pseudo-Clementines,* the *Acts of St. Catherine of Sinai,* the *Chronicle* of John Malalas, and the romance, *Barlaam and Josaphat.* The theory has gained no acceptance, in view of the futility of tracing the use of a work which is not extant, and the content of which is mere conjecture.

For the text of the single remaining fragment of the work Migne may be consulted, PG 5, 1265-1266. A more respected source, however, is Funk-Bihlmeyer-Schneemelcher, *Die apostolischen Väter,* Vol. 1, Tübingen 1956, p. 140.

FRAGMENT IN EUSEBIUS, History of the Church, BK. 4, CH. 3

109

[4, 3, 2]

[Quadratus] himself reveals the early date at which he lived, when he relates the following, which is in his own words: "The works of the Savior were ever present, for they   82 were true. Those who were cured and those who were raised from the dead were seen not only while being cured and while being raised. They were ever present, not only while our Savior dwelt among us, but also for a considerable time after He had departed. In fact, some of them have survived to our own time."

ARISTIDES OF ATHENS [*fl. ca. A. D.* 140]

Of Aristides we know nothing beyond the meager information provided by Eusebius, who says of him that he was "a man of faith and devoted to our religion," and in another place implies that he was a philosopher in the city of Athens. Only by dating his work can we provide a date for his life.

APOLOGY [*ca. A. D.* 140]

An Armenian fragment of an apology bearing the title *To Emperor Hadrian Caesar from the Athenian Philosopher Aristides,* and now known definitely to be a part of an Armenian translation of the *Apology* of Aristides, was published by the Mechitarists in 1878, from a 10th-century manuscript. Internal reasons suggest that the work is addressed not to the Emperor familiarly known as Hadrian (Publius Aelius Nerva Traianus Hadrianus), but to his successor, Antoninus Pius, whose fuller name is Titus Aelius Hadrianus Antoninus Pius, and whose reign embraced the years 138 to 161 A. D. The work is generally assigned to the beginning of Antoninus' reign, *ca.* 140 A. D.

In 1889 J. Rendel Harris discovered the complete text of the *Apology* of Aristides in a Syriac translation. Previously the work was known only by its title and by the Armenian fragment mentioned above. With the discovery of the Syriac translation, the startling fact became evident that the Greek text had really been extant all along, having been incorporated into the text of the religious novel falsely attributed to John Damascene: *Barlaam and Josaphat.* Within the latter work, the *Apology* constitutes chapters 26 and 27.

In 1922 and 1924 two large portions of the original Greek text were published from papyri of the British Museum. The *Apology* of Aristides is the oldest extant Christian apology, only a very short fragment of the older apology of Quadratus having been preserved.

For the *Barlaam and Josaphat* text one may consult Migne, PG 96, 1107-1124, or the text in the Loeb Classical Library edition. The Syriac and Greek texts of the apology proper were edited by J. Rendel Harris and J. A. Robinson in the *Texts and Studies* series, Vol. 1, part 1, second edition, Cambridge 1893. The more recently recognized Greek fragments are edited by Grenfell and Hunt in the *Oxyrhynchus Papyri XV,* London 1922, n. 1778, and by H. J. M. Milne, "A New Fragment of the Apology of Aristides," in the *Journal of Theological Studies,* Vol. 25, London 1924, pp. 73-77.

110

[1]

When I saw that the world and all that is in it is moved by a force, I understood that He 132
who moves and maintains it is God; for whatever moves something is stronger than that 179
which is moved, and whatever maintains something is stronger than that which is maintained. 460
I call the One who constructed all things and maintains them *God:* He that is without 156
beginning and eternal, immortal and lacking nothing, and who is above all passions and 178
failings such as anger and forgetfulness and ignorance and the rest. 180

111

[4]

Let us proceed, then, O King, to the elements themselves, so that we may demonstrate 461
concerning them that they are not gods, but corruptible and changeable things, produced 155

out of the non-existent by Him that is truly God, who is incorruptible and unchangeable   152
and invisible, but who sees all things and changes them and alters them as He wills.   158

112

[15]
Christians trace their origin to the Lord Jesus Christ. He that came down from heaven   301
in the Holy Spirit for the salvation of men is confessed to be the Son of the Most High   370
God. He was born of a holy Virgin without seed of man, and took flesh without defile-   230
ment; and He appeared among men so that He might recall them from the error of   781
polytheism. When He had accomplished His wonderful design, by His own free will and   311
for a mighty purpose He tasted of death on the cross. After three days, however, He came
to life again and went up into the heavens.

It is possible for you, O king, to learn to know the report of His coming in the holy
gospel writing, as it is called by us — should you chance to come upon a copy. He had   60
twelve disciples who, after His ascent into the heavens, went out into the provinces of the   404
world (1) teaching about His greatness. In this way one of them came through the places
around about us, announcing the doctrine of truth. Since then, they who continue to
observe the righteousness which was preached by His disciples are called Christians. These
are they who, above every people of the earth, have found the truth; for they
acknowledge God, the Creator and Maker of all things, in the only-begotten Son and in   460
the Holy Spirit.

Other than Him, no god do they worship. They have the commandments of the Lord
Jesus Christ Himself impressed upon their hearts, and they observe them, awaiting the   1011
resurrection of the dead and the life of the world to come. They do not commit adultery   86
nor fornication, nor do they bear false witness, nor covet the goods of other men. They
honor father and mother and love their neighbors; and they render just judgment. What
they would not want done to them, they do not do to another (2). They make appeal
to those who wrong them, and win them to themselves as friends.

They hasten to do good to their enemies. They are gentle and reasonable. They
abstain from every unlawful exchange and from all uncleanness. They despise not the
widow, nor do they distress the orphan. Whoever has, distributes liberally to him that has
not. Should they see a stranger, they take him under roof, and rejoice over him as over a
blood brother. For not after the flesh do they call themselves brethren, but after the
spirit. For the sake of Christ they are ready to lay down their lives. They keep His
commands without wavering, living holy and just lives as the Lord God commanded them;
and they give thanks to Him every hour for all their food and drink and for the rest of
their goods.

1. εἰς τὰς ἐπαρχίας τῆς οἰκουμένης. The ecumene is the civilized world, i. e., the Greek world as opposed to
   that of the barbarians. Yet, it sometimes means even the whole world. It is a question, then, whether to
   translate to the various provinces of the civilized world, or to all the provinces of the whole world. In any
   case, the point is made that the disciples travelled far and wide to spread the gospel.
2. Matt. 7:12; Luke 6:31.

ST. JUSTIN THE MARTYR [*A. D.* 100/110 - *ca. A. D.* 165]

St. Justin the Martyr was born into paganism at Flavia Neapolis, now Nablus, in Palestine, between the years 100 and 110 A. D. As a young man he attached himself successively to the various philosophical schools, being first a Stoic, then a Peripatetic, a Pythagorean, a Platonist, and finally he came to know Christianity. What we know of his life comes to us mostly through biographical details revealed in his own writings. As a Christian philosopher he became an itinerant, eventually arriving in Rome, where he founded a school in which he had Tatian the Syrian for a pupil. The *Martyrium SS. Justini et sociorum* is the authentic account of his martyrdom, according to which he, along with six companions, was beheaded between the years 163 and 167 A. D., most probably in 165 A. D.

Justin was a rather prolific writer, but only two or three of his writings have come down to us, along with a few fragments of other works. The two *Apologies*, sometimes reckoned as but a single work, and the *Dialogue with Trypho the Jew* are extant in a single manuscript *(Paris, No. 450)* of the 14th century. Justin is regarded generally as the most important of the 2nd century apologists. His style is tedious and labored, making him difficult to read; yet, there is a note of intense sincerity in all that he wrote.

FIRST APOLOGY [*inter A. D.* 148-155]

Whether the *First Apology* and the *Second Apology* of Justin constitute two works or one is debatable. Eusebius knew that Justin wrote two apologies; and the single manuscript mentioned above presents what are called the two apologies, the first of sixty-eight chapters, addressed to Antoninus Pius; and the second, of fifteen chapters, addressed to the Roman Senate. Most scholars are today of the opinion that we have only one of the two apologies known to Eusebius, and that our *Second Apology* is in fact an appendix added later by Justin himself to the *First Apology*. If this actually be the relationship between the so-called two apologies, it remains a possibility also that it is really only a single apology with its appendix that Eusebius refers to as two apologies. Whether one apology or two, we will keep to the tradition of referring to them as two. Both parts belong to the years 148 to 161 A. D., the first having been completed by 155 A. D.

The text of both apologies may be found in Migne, PG 6, 327-471; but the standard edition is that of G. Rauschen in the series *Florilegium patristicum*, fasc. 2, 2nd edition, Bonn 1911. Editions by Pfättisch in 1912, Krüger in 1915, and Frasca in 1938 are quite acceptable for scholarly work, but have not dislodged the Rauschen edition from its position as the standard text.

112a

[5]

The truth shall be told. When in ancient times the wicked demons effected their   494
apparitions they defiled women and corrupted boys and presented such fearful sights to men, that those who did not use their reason [λόγος] in judging these occurences were panic-stricken. Not knowing that these were evil demons, they called them gods, and addressed them individually by the name which each demon had given himself. Afterwards, when by true and careful reasoning [λόγος], Socrates attempted to make these things known and to deliver men from the demons, those very demons charged that he introduced unheard of gods, and brought it about through the agency of men who delight in evil that he was put to death as an atheist and impious person. Now they endeavor to do

the very same thing to us. Not only did Socrates condemn these things among the Greeks by reason [λόγος], but even among the barbarians they were condemned by the Word [Λόγος] Himself, who assumed a form and became man, and was called Jesus Christ.   302

113

[6]
So we are called atheists. Well, we do indeed proclaim ourselves atheists in respect to those whom you call gods, but not in regard to the Most True God, the Father of   230
righteousness and temperance and the other virtues, who is without admixture of evil. On the contrary, we reverence and worship Him and the Son who came forth from Him   301
and taught us these things, and the host of other good angels who are about Him and   480
are made quite like Him, and the Prophetic Spirit. We pay homage to them in reason and in truth; and to all who wish to learn, we pass on intact what we have been taught (1).

114

[10]
We have been taught that God, in the beginning, in His goodness and for the sake of   461
men, created all things out of formless matter (2). And if men, by their works, show themselves worthy of His design, they are deemed worthy, so we are told, to make their abode with Him and to reign with Him, being freed of all corruption and passion. Just as in the beginning He created us when we were not, in the same way, we believe, He will regard all those who choose to please Him, because of their choice, as worthy of immortality in communion with Him (3). Our coming into being in the beginning was   680
none of our doing. But now, to follow those things which are pleasing to Him, and to choose them by means of the rational faculties which he has bestowed upon us: to this He persuades us, and leads us to faith.   656

115

[12]
More than all other men, we are your helpers and allies in maintaining peace; for it is our position that it is no more possible for the evil-doer, the avaricious and the treacherous, to hide from God, than it is for the virtuous; and that every man will receive the eternal punishment or reward which his actions deserve. Indeed, if all men recognized   1034
this, no one would choose evil even for a short time, knowing that he would incur the eternal sentence of fire. On the contrary, he would take every means to control himself   1032
and to adorn himself in virtue, so that he might obtain the good gifts of God and escape the punishments.

116

[12]
That all these things (4) should happen was foretold, I say, by our Teacher, Jesus   83
Christ, who is the Son and Apostle (5) of God, the Father and Ruler of all. From Him we have received our name as Christians. We are convinced of the truth of all that He taught us, because whatever He foretold would happen is actually happening. This is the work of God: He tells of a thing before it happens, afterwards showing that it happens   191
as it was foretold.

117

[13]

Is there any intelligent person who will dispute the contention that we are not atheists,   460
when we worship the Creator of everything that exists? We declare, moreover, as we have
been taught, that He has no need of blood offerings and libations and incense. Rather, we
praise Him to the best of our ability by prayer and thanksgiving for all the things which
have been granted us. We have been instructed that the only honor worthy of Him is *not*
to consume by fire those things which He has created for our sustenance, but to employ
them for ourselves and for those in need; and to offer thanks to Him in solemn prayers
and hymns, for our own creation, for the means of achieving health, for the variety of
creation, for the change of seasons, and to beseech Him in prayer that we may exist again
in incorruption through our faith in Him.

Our Teacher of these things, born for this end, is Jesus Christ, who was crucified under
Pontius Pilate, the procurator in Judea in the time of Tiberius Caesar. We will prove that   301
we worship Him reasonably; for we have learned that He is the Son of the True God   230
Himself, that He holds a second place, and the Spirit of Prophecy a third (6). For this
they accuse us of madness, saying that we attribute to a crucified man a place second to   302
the unchangeable and eternal God, the Creator of all things: but they are ignorant of
the mystery which lies therein.

118

[14]

We who formerly delighted in fornication now cleave only to chastity. We who   87
exercised the magic arts now consecrate ourselves to the good and unbegotten God. We   89
who valued above all else the acquisition of wealth and property now direct all that we
have to a common fund, which is shared with every needy person. We who hated and
killed one another, and who, because of differing customs, would not share a fireside
with those of another race, now, after the appearance of Christ, live together with them.
We pray for our enemies, and try to persuade those who unjustly hate us that, if they
live according to the excellent precepts of Christ, they will have a good hope of receiving
the same reward as ourselves, from the God who governs all.

119

[15]

In regard to chastity, He has this to say: "If anyone look with lust at a woman, he
has already before God committed adultery in his heart (7)." . . . And, "Whoever marries   974
a woman who has been divorced from another husband, commits adultery (8)." . . . According to our Teacher, just as they are sinners who contract a second marriage (9), even   979
though it be in accord with human law, so also are they sinners who look with lustful
desire at a woman. He repudiates not only one who actually commits adultery, but even
one who wishes to do so; for not only our actions are manifest to God, but even our   632
thoughts.

120

[18]

We expect to receive our own bodies again, even though they be dead and buried in   1013
the earth. [19] . . . Because you have never seen a dead person rise, you disbelieve. But
just as in the beginning you would not have believed that from a little drop such persons
might be produced, and yet you see them so produced, so now in the same way realize
that it is not impossible for human bodies, after they have been resolved and, like seeds,
dissolved into earth, to rise again in God's appointed time and put on incorruption.

121

[21]

We have been taught that only they may aim at immortality who have lived a holy
and virtuous life near to God. We believe that they who live wickedly and do not repent   1034
will be punished in everlasting fire.   1032

122

[30]

But lest anyone should pose the objection: "What prevents us from supposing that He
whom we call Christ was a man born of men, and that He performed what we call His
mighty works by the art of magic, and in this way appeared to be the Son of God?" — we   82
shall presently offer proof, not believing those who only speak, but being compelled to
belief by those who prophesied before the events. With our own eyes we are witness to
things that have happened and are happening just as they were predicted. And this, we   300
think, will appear to you as the strongest and surest proof (10).   81

122a

[33]

And again, hear how Isaias expressly foretold that He was to be born of a virgin. He   300
stated the following: "Behold, a virgin shall conceive and bear a son; and for his name
they shall say 'God-with-us' (11)." . . . The phrase *Behold, a virgin shall conceive* means,
certainly, that the virgin shall conceive without intercourse. For if she had had intercourse   781
with anyone at all, she would not be a virgin. But the power of God, coming upon the
Virgin, overshadowed her, and caused her, while yet a Virgin, to conceive.

122b

[36]

When you hear the words of the Prophets, spoken as it were personally, do not imagine   20
that they are spoken by the inspired persons themselves. It is the Divine Word who moves   21
them. Sometimes He tells things which are going to happen, as one who foretells the
future. Sometimes He speaks as in the characterization of God the Father and Master of
all; sometimes as in the characterization of Christ; sometimes in the role of the people
replying to the Lord or to His Father.

123

[43]

We have learned from the Prophets and we hold it as true that punishments and
chastisements and good rewards are distributed according to the merit of each man's   770
actions. Were this not the case, and were all things to happen according to the decree of
fate, there would be nothing at all in our power. If fate decrees that this man is to be   775
good, and that one wicked, then neither is the former to be praised nor the latter to be
blamed.

Furthermore, if the human race does not have the power of a freely deliberated choice
in fleeing evil and in choosing good, then men are not accountable for their actions,   636
whatever they may be. That they do, however, by a free choice, either walk upright or
stumble, we shall now prove (12). . . . God did not make man like the other beings, the   505
trees and the four-legged beasts, for example, which cannot do anything by free choice.

Neither would man deserve reward or praise if he did not of himself choose the good;
nor, if he acted wickedly, would he deserve punishment, since he would not be evil by

choice, and could not be other than that which he was born. [44] The Holy Prophetic
Spirit taught us this when He informed us through Moses that God spoke as follows to the   20
first created man: "Behold, before your face, the good and the evil. Choose the good (13)."

124

[52]

The prophets have proclaimed His two comings. One, indeed, which has already taken
place, was that of a dishonored and suffering Man. The second will take place when, in   347
accord with prophecy, He shall come from the heavens in glory with His angelic host;   1012
when He shall raise the bodies of all the men who ever lived. Then He will clothe the   1034
worthy in immortality; but the wicked, clothed in eternal sensibility, He will commit   1032
to the eternal fire, along with the evil demons.   1033

125

[53]

Why should we believe a crucified man, that He is the Firstborn of the unbegotten
God, and that He will pass judgment on the whole human race, if we had not found   392
testimonies published about Him before He came and was made Man, and if we had not
seen these predictions fulfilled?   81

126

[61]

Whoever is convinced and believes that what they are taught and told by us is the   834
truth, and professes to be able to live accordingly, is instructed to pray and to beseech
God in fasting for the remission of their former sins, while we pray and fast with them.
Then they are led by us to a place where there is water; and there they are reborn in   822
the same kind of rebirth in which we ourselves were reborn: in the name of God, the   230
Lord and Father of all, and of our Savior, Jesus Christ, and of the Holy Spirit (14),   826
they receive the washing with water. For Christ said, "Unless you be reborn, you shall   823
not enter into the kingdom of heaven (15)." . . . The reason for doing this, we have   820
learned from the Apostles.

Since we had no awareness of our first birth, but were compelled to be born of the
moist seed through the mutual union of our parents, and were raised in bad habits and
in evil training, and so that we might not remain as children of necessity and ignorance,
but rather of deliberate choice and knowledge, and in order to obtain in the water the   836
remission of past sins, there is invoked over him who wishes to be reborn and who has
repented of his sins, the name of God, the Father and Master of all. . . . This washing
is called illumination (16), because it enlightens the intelligence of those who learn these
things. Furthermore, the one being illuminated is washed also in the name of Jesus
Christ, who was crucified under Pontius Pilate, and in the name of the Holy Spirit, who   20
predicted through the prophets everything concerning Jesus.

127

[63]

These words [of the Prophets], then, have become the proof that Jesus Christ is the   81
Son and Apostle of God, being of old the Word, appearing at one time in the guise of   300
fire, and at another time as an incorporeal image. And now, by the will of God and for   236
the sake of the human race, He has become man, and has born all the torments which   370
the demons instigated the senseless Jews to inflict upon Him. . . . And again, as we have   362
shown, Jesus, while still in the midst of the [Jews], said: "No one knows the Father   302
except the Son nor the Son except the Father, and those to whom the Son has given a
revelation (17)."

Although the Jews were always of the opinion that it was the Father of all who had spoken to Moses, it was in fact the Son of God, who is called both Angel and Apostle, who spoke to him; they are, therefore, justly accused by both the Prophetic Spirit and by Christ Himself of knowing neither the Father nor the Son. They who assert that the Son is the Father are proved to know neither the Father, nor that the Father of all has a Son, who is both the first-born Word of God and is God. Formerly He appeared to Moses and to the other prophets in the form of fire and as an incorporeal image; and now, in the times of your reign, having become man, as we said, by a Virgin and by the will of the Father, for the salvation of those who believe in Him, He allowed Himself to be treated with contempt and to suffer so that by death and resurrection He might conquer death.

781

375

128

[65]
After we have thus washed the one who has believed and has assented, we lead him to where those who are called brethren are gathered, offering prayers in common and heartily for ourselves and for the one who has been illuminated, and for all others everywhere, so that we may be accounted worthy, now that we have learned the truth, to be found keepers of the commandments, so that we may be saved with an eternal salvation. Having concluded the prayers, we greet one another with a kiss. Then there is brought to the president of the brethren bread and a cup of water and of watered wine (18); and taking them, he gives praise and glory to the Father of all, through the name of the Son and of the Holy Spirit; and he himself gives thanks at some length in order that these things may be deemed worthy (19).

860

861

230

When the prayers and the thanksgiving are completed, all the people present call out their assent, saying: "Amen!" *Amen* in the Hebrew language signifies *so be it.* After the president has given thanks, and all the people have shouted their assent, those whom we call deacons give to each one present to partake of the Eucharistic bread and wine and water; and to those who are absent they carry away a portion.

868

871

[66] We call this food *Eucharist;* and no one else is permitted to partake of it, except one who believes our teaching to be true and who has been washed in the washing which is for the remission of sins and for regeneration, and is thereby living as Christ has enjoined. For not as common bread nor common drink do we receive these; but since Jesus Christ our Savior was made incarnate by the word of God and had both flesh and blood for our salvation, so too, as we have been taught, the food which has been made into the Eucharist by the Eucharistic prayer set down by Him, and by the change of which our blood and flesh is nourished (20), is both the flesh and the blood of that incarnated Jesus.

954

874

856

864

851

The Apostles, in the Memoirs which they produced, which are called Gospels, have thus passed on that which was enjoined upon them: that Jesus took bread and, having given thanks, said, "Do this in remembrance of Me; this is My Body (21)." And in like manner, taking the cup, and having given thanks, He said, "This is My Blood (22)." And He imparted this to them only. The evil demons, however, have passed on its imitation in the mysteries of Mithra. For, as you know or are able to learn, bread and a cup of water together with certain incantations are used in the initiation to the mystic rites.

60

852

862

129

[67]
Afterwards we continually remind each other of these things. And those who have possessions come to the aid of all those who are poor; and we are always at one with each other. For everything that has been given to our use, we praise the Creator of all through His Son Jesus Christ and through the Holy Spirit. On the day which is dedicated

to the sun, all those who live in the cities or who dwell in the countryside gather in a
common meeting, and for as long as there is time the Memoirs of the Apostles (23) or
the writings of the prophets are read. Then, when the reader has finished (24), the   61
president verbally gives a warning and appeal for the imitation of these good examples.

Then we all rise together and offer prayers, and, as we said before, when our prayer
is ended, bread is brought forward along with wine and water, and the president likewise   860
gives thanks to the best of his ability (25), and the people call out their assent, saying the   861
Amen. Then there is the distribution to each and the participation in the Eucharistic
elements, which also are sent with the deacons to those who are absent. Those who are
wealthy and who wish to do so, contribute whatever they themselves care to give; and   868
the collection is placed with the president, who aids the orphans and the widows, and
those who through sickness or any other cause are in need, and those who are imprisoned,
and the strangers who are sojourning with us — and in short, he takes care of all who are
in need.

The Day of the Sun is the day on which we all gather in a common meeting, because
it is the first day, the day on which God, changing darkness and matter, created the   461
world; and it is the day on which Jesus Christ our Savior rose from the dead. For He   84
was crucified on the day before that of Kronos (26); and on the day after that of
Kronos, which is the Day of the Sun, He appeared to His Apostles and disciples, and
taught them these things which we have also submitted to you for your consideration.

1. Certain translators have been at considerable pains to re-arrange various phrases of this passage, in the hope
   of obviating the two alleged theological difficulties therein. These supposed difficulties are first, that
   Justin seems to say that he worships angels, and second, by the term *other good angels,* he seems to make
   Christ one of the angels. It will not do, of course, to point out that as sent from God, Christ may be and in
   fact often is termed an Angel; for the problem consists in Justin's apparently making insufficient distinction
   between Christ and the created angels. However, if we bear in mind that Justin is generally admitted to have
   been the possessor of subordinationist tendencies, we can simply admit that his manner of expression is neither
   acceptable nor yet surprising.

   And as to the first difficulty, surely *worship – προσκυνέω –* is a sufficiently vague term that a part of it
   may be given even to created angels. We are satisfied that the above translation is an accurate representation
   of what Justin wrote; and we will do no violence to the natural meaning of his phrases to make them
   harmonize better with what we might think he ought to have written. There are theological difficulties in
   the above passage, no doubt. But we wonder if those who make a great deal of these difficulties do not
   demand of Justin a theological sophistication which a man of his time and background could not rightly be
   expected to have.
2. Cfr. Plato, *Timaeus* 51 A. Justin often uses Platonic terminology, but not necessarily in a precisely Platonic
   sense. In Justin, this passage need not be regarded as a denial of the *creatio ex nihilo* which he seems to
   affirm in other places, as in the *Second Apology* 5.
3. Cfr. Plato, *Phaedo* 83 E.
4. Justin has been referring to the persecution of Christians.
5. Cfr. Heb. 3:1.
6. This is one of the passages frequently cited as an indication of Justin's probably having held subordinationist
   opinions.
7. Matt. 5:28.
8. Matt. 5:32.
9. διγαμίας. Whether Justin condemns only simultaneous bigamy, or also successive bigamy; and, if the
   latter, when even the first spouse is dead, is not clear.
10. In the next chapters following (31 to 53), Justin is occupied in demonstrating the fulfillment in Christ of
    the Scriptural prophecies.
11. Is. 7:14.
12. The argument itself, which we omit, is principally this: that the same man pursues both good and evil,
    frequently wavering and changing his mind. But if he were set upon a path by fate, to waver or change
    were not possible. Besides, if fate decreed that some men are to be evil and others are to be good, then
    fate itself would be the cause of both good and evil, and would be in opposition to itself.
13. Deut. 30:15 and 19.
14. Matt. 28:19.
15. John 3:3.
16. φωτισμός.
17. See Matt. 11:27 and Luke 10:22.

18. ἄρτος καὶ ποτήριον ὕδατος καὶ κράματος. κρᾶμα is already a mixture of water and wine, – a thing for which we have no single term in English, – so the text presents a difficulty. In the presence of already watered wine, what was the water for? Besides, reading the text strictly, the cup followed by the two terms in the genitive case would indicate that both the water and the watered wine were in the same cup. It would appear to be a lapse of Justin's pen. He meant, I suggest, to write "a cup of water and of wine", or "a cup of watered wine", – but inadvertently either combined and repeated or partially separated his ideas, writing "a cup of water and of watered wine." In chapter 67 he refers back to this passage, even prefacing his remark "as we said before" – and there he writes "bread is brought forward along with wine and water."

19. καὶ εὐχαριστίαν ὑπὲρ τοῦ καθηξιῶσθαι τούτων παρ᾽ αὐτοῦ ἐπὶ πολὺ ποιεῖται. Another satisfactory translation might be: "and he gives thanks at some length in order that these things before him may be deemed worthy."

20. The change referred to here is the change which takes place when the food we eat is assimilated and becomes a part of our own body.

21. Luke 22:19; Matt. 26:26; Mark 14:22; 1 Cor. 11:23-24.

22. Luke 22:20; Matt. 26:27-28; Mark 14:24; 1 Cor. 11:25.

23. As Justin himself explains in chapter 66 of this same *First Apology*, the *Memoirs of the Apostles* are the Gospels.

24. εἶτα παυσαμένου τοῦ ἀναγινώσκοντος.

25. ὅση δύναμις αὐτῷ.

26. Kronos is the Greek counterpart of the Roman god Saturn: hence, the Day of Kronos is Saturday. Presumably it will not have escaped the gentle reader's attention that the Day of the Sun is Sunday.

SECOND APOLOGY [*inter A. D.* 148-161]

As previously noted, the so-called *Second Apology* is probably an appendix, by Justin himself, to the first. See the introductory notes to the *First Apology,* p. 50 above.

130

[6]

To the Father of all, who is unbegotten, no name is given; for anyone who has been   174 given a name has received the name from someone older than himself. Father and God and Creator and Lord and Master are not names but appellations derived from His beneficences and works. His Son, who alone is properly called Son, who was both with Him and was begotten by Him before anything was created, when in the beginning the   256 Father created and put everything in order through Him – He is called Christ, from His   284 being anointed and from God's putting everything in order through Him. This name 'Christ' contains an unknown significance, just as also the appellation 'God' is not a name   135 but the notion implanted in the nature of men of a thing which can hardly be explained. 'Jesus', His name as Man and Savior also has a significance; for indeed, He also became Man, as we have said, having been conceived according to the will of God the Father, for the sake of believing men and for the defeat of the demons.   374

131

[13]

After God we worship and love the Word who is from the unbegotten and inexpressible   301 God, since He even became Man for us, so that by becoming a partaker in our passions   370 He might also work their cure.   349

DIALOGUE WITH TRYPHO THE JEW [*ca. A. D.* 155]

St. Justin's *Dialogue with Trypho the Jew* is the oldest extant Christian apology against Judaism. Its text has come down to us through the single Paris manuscript of the 14th century, which, unfortunately, is not complete. The introduction and a large part of chapter 74 are lost. The work is generally assigned to about the year 155 A. D., by which time the *First Apology* had already been written.

Trypho is probably a historical person, and is likely to be identified with a certain Rabbi Tarphon, mentioned in the Mishnah.

Migne's text will be found in PG 6, 471-800. The standard edition, however, is that of G. Archambault, *Justin, Dialogue avec Tryphon* (text and translation), 2 vol., Paris 1909.

132

[5]

[Old man:] " 'If the world is produced (1), necessarily souls too are produced; and 502 perhaps there is a time when they do not exist. For they were produced for the sake of men and other living things, even if you say that they were produced entirely separate, and not with their appropriate bodies.'

[Justin:] " 'That seems to be correct.'

[Old man:] " 'Then they are not immortal?'

[Justin:] " 'No, since it appears to us that the world is produced.'

[Old man:] " 'Yet, I do not say that all souls die; for that would be a god-send for the wicked. But what? The souls of the pious remain in some better place, the unjust and evil 996 in a worse, awaiting the time of judgment. Thus, those indeed who will be judged worthy of God will never die; but others will be punished for so long as God wills them to exist and to be punished. . . . For whatever things exist after God or will at anytime exist, have a corruptible nature, and are such as may be blotted out and no longer exist. God alone 155 is unbegotten and incorruptible, which is why He is God. Everything else after Him is produced and corruptible (2).' "

133

[6]

[Old man:] " 'The soul is either life, or it has life. If, however, it were life, then it 502 would make some other thing to live, but not itself; just as also movement moves something else rather than itself. No one would deny that the soul lives. If it lives, however, it lives not as life itself, but as the partaker of life; and the partaker of anything is other than that in which it partakes. The soul partakes of life, since God wills it to live. It will not even partake, then, whenever He does not wish it to live; for life is not a property of the soul, as it is of God. Just as a man does not live forever, and the body is not forever united to the soul, but whenever this union must be broken the soul leaves the body and the man exists no longer; in the same way, whenever the soul must cease to exist, the spirit of life is removed from it and the soul exists no longer, but it returns 504 again to the place from whence it was taken.' "

133a

[11]

[Justin:] "I have read, Trypho, that there will be a final law, and a covenant the most authoritative of all, which must be observed by all men who seek after the inheritance of God. That law on Horeb is old, and was only for you (3); but this is for all in

general. A law set down after another law abrogates that which was before it, and a   52
covenant made later likewise voids that which was earlier. An eternal and final law, the
Christ, is given to us, a faithful covenant after which there shall be no law, no precept, no
commandment. Have you not read this which Isaias says: 'Hear me, hear me, my people;
and you kings, give ear to me; for a law shall go forth from me, and my judgment shall be   300
a light to the nations. My righteousness approaches swiftly, and my salvation shall go
forth, and the gentiles shall hope in my arm (4).' "

133b

[11]
    [Justin:] "If, therefore, God proclaimed a new covenant which was about to be
established, and this for a light to the gentiles, we see and are persuaded that through
the name of this crucified Jesus Christ men turn to God from their idols and other
wrong-doing, and practice piety and maintain their confession even unto death; and
by the works and by the accompanying miracles it is possible for everyone to understand   13
that this is the new law, and the new covenant, and the expectation of those who among
every nation are awaiting the good things of God. The true spiritual Israel, descendants
of Juda and Jacob and Isaac and Abraham, — that Abraham whom God approved by His
testimony, on account of his faith, although he was in the state of having his foreskin,
and blessed him and called him the father of many nations (5), — are we who have been
led to God through this crucified Christ."   374

134

[23]
    [Justin:] "The Scriptures and the facts themselves oblige us to confess that Abraham   795
received circumcision for a sign and not for justification. Justly, then, was it said
concerning his people, that the soul which shall not have been circumcised on the eighth
day shall be destroyed out of his kindred (6). Furthermore, the inability of female
offspring to receive circumcision in the flesh proves that this circumcision was given as
a sign, and not as a work of justification. For God has given also to females the ability
to observe all the things that are righteous and virtuous."

134a

[23]
    [Justin:] "If circumcision was not necessary before Abraham, nor before Moses the   52
sabbath observance and festivals and sacrifices, then, similarly, they are not necessary
now, when in accordance with the will of God, Jesus Christ the Son of God has been
born without sin, of a Virgin of the offspring of Abraham."   781

134b

[40]
    [Justin:] "The mystery, then, of the lamb which God commanded to be sacrificed   51
as the Passover, was a type of Christ. With its blood, by reason of faith in Him, they
anoint their own homes, — that is, they who believe in Him. . . . The two identical
goats which were ordered to be offered during the feast, one of which was the
scapegoat and the other ror sacrifice, were a proclamation of the two comings of Christ:
of the first coming, in which He was sent out as a scapegoat, when the elders of your
people and the priests laid hands on Him and put Him to death; and of His second
coming, when, in that same place in Jerusalem, you shall recognize Him who was
dishonored by you, and who was a sacrificial victim for all sinners who desire to

repent, fasting the fast which Isaias prescribed, 'bursting asunder the knots of forcible agreements (7),' and to keep the other precepts likewise enumerated by him, which also I have quoted (8), and which those believing in Jesus do observe."

135

[41]
[Justin:] "Also, sirs," I said, "the offering of fine wheat flour which was prescribed   892
to be offered on behalf of those cleansed from leprosy was a type of the Bread of the
Eucharist, the celebration of which our Lord Jesus Christ prescribed in memory of the
passion He suffered on behalf of those men who are cleansed in their souls of every   849
evil. . . . Moreover, as I said before, concerning the sacrifices which you at that time
offered, God speaks through Malachias, one of the twelve (9), as follows: 'I have no   894
pleasure in you, says the Lord; and I will not accept your sacrifices from your hands;
for from the rising of the sun until its setting, my name has been glorified among the
gentiles; and in every place incense is offered to my name, and a clean offering: for
great is my name among the gentiles, says the Lord; but you profane it (10).' It is
of the sacrifices offered to Him in every place by us, the gentiles, that is, of the Bread
of the Eucharist and likewise of the cup of the Eucharist, that He speaks at that time;
and He says that we glorify His name, while you profane it."

135a

[44]
[Justin:] "It is necessary to hasten to learn in what way forgiveness of sins and a   831
hope of the inheritance of the promised good things may be yours. There is no other
way than this: acknowledge this Christ, be washed in the washing announced by
Isaias (11) for the forgiveness of sins; and henceforth live sinlessly."

136

[48]
[Justin:] "Now certainly, Trypho," I said, "it is inescapable that this is the Christ   301
of God, even if I be unable to prove that He pre-existed as the Son of the Creator of   302
all things, being God, and that He was born a man by the Virgin. But since it is   311
completely proven that this is the Christ of God, whoever He be, if I have not demonstrated
that He pre-existed and that He submitted, in accord with the will of the Father, to be
born a man of like passions with us and to have flesh, still, it would be just to say that   349
He is the Christ, even if it were to appear that He was born man of men and it were
proven that He became the Christ by election. Indeed, my friends, there are some of our
race (12)," I said, "who confess that He is the Christ, and yet hold that He is man born
of men. I do not agree with them, nor would I, even if the greater part of those who now
agree with me were to say so; for we have been warned by Christ Himself not to be
persuaded by human doctrines, but by those proclaimed by the blessed prophets and
taught by Himself."

137

[61]
[Justin:] "Friends," I said, "I will give you another testimony, from the Scriptures,   256
that God begot before all creatures a Beginning, who was a certain Rational Power from
Himself, and whom the Holy Spirit calls the Glory of the Lord, or sometimes the Son,
sometimes Wisdom, sometimes an Angel, sometimes God, sometimes Lord and Word. On   261
another occasion He calls Himself Commander-in-Chief (13), when He appeared in the   301

form of a man to Jesus, the son of Nave (14). He can be called by all these names, because He ministers to the will of the Father and was begotten by the Father's will. We see things happen similarly among ourselves: for whenever we utter some word, we beget a word — yet, not by any cutting off, which would diminish the word in us when we utter it. We see a similar occurence when one fire enkindles another. It is not diminished through the enkindling of the other, but remains as it was; and that which was enkindled by it appears to exist by itself, not diminishing that from which it was enkindled." 265

138

[65]

[Justin:] "[That the Scriptures contradict each other] — I will not have the effrontery 25 at any time either to suppose or to say such a thing. If a Scripture which appears to be of such a kind be brought forward, and there be a pretext for regarding it as contradictory, 27 since I am totally convinced that no Scripture is contradictory to another, I shall admit instead that I do not understand what is spoken of, and shall strive to persuade those who assume that the Scriptures are contradictory to be rather of the same opinion as myself."

138a

[80]

And Trypho replied to this, "I remarked to you, sir, that you are anxious to be safe 1016 in everything, and you cling to the Scriptures. But tell me, do you really profess that this place, Jerusalem, will be rebuilt? And do you expect that your people will be gathered together and that they will rejoice with Christ in the company of the patriarchs and prophets, both with those of our race and with those who became proselytes before your Christ came? or have you proceeded to admit this in order to have the appearance of overcoming us in controversy?"

At this I said, "I am not such a wretched person, Trypho, that I would say other than what I think. As I admitted to you before, I and many others are of this opinion, and we believe absolutely that this will happen. But still, I signified to you that there are many Christians of pure and pious faith who do not share this belief. . . . But I and such other 1017 Christians as judge rightly in everything believe that there will be . . . a thousand years in which Jerusalem will be built up, adorned and enlarged, as the prophets Ezechiel and Isaias and the others declare."

140

[95]

[Justin:] "The whole human race can be said to be under a curse. . . . If, then, for 383 the sake of the whole human race, the Father of all wished His Christ to take upon Himself the curse of all, knowing that after crucifixion and death He would raise Him up, why do you Jews so speak of Him, who submitted to these things in accord with the will of the Father, as if He were cursed, instead of weeping for yourselves? For even though His Father effected that He suffer these things on behalf of the human race, still, you did not act out of obedience to the will of God. Neither were you engaged in pious practice when you slew the prophets. And let no one among you say: 'If the Father wished Him to suffer this, so that His wound might become a healing for the human race, neither have we done wrong.' If, however, you admit this, while repenting your sins, and recognize this to be the Christ and keep His commandments, then, as I have said, the remission of sins will be yours."

141

[100]

[Justin:] "Since it is written of Him in the Memoirs of the Apostles that He is the   302
Son of God, and since we call Him Son, we have understood that before all creatures   61
He proceeded from the Father by His will and power — for in the words of the Prophets   300
He is addressed in one way or another as Wisdom and Day and East and Sword and Stone
and Rod and Jacob and Israel — and that He became Man by the Virgin so that the   781
course which was taken by disobedience in the beginning through the agency of the
serpent, might be also the very course by which it would be put down. For Eve, a virgin
and undefiled, conceived the word of the serpent, and bore disobedience and death. But   784
the Virgin Mary received faith and joy when the angel Gabriel announced to her the glad
tidings that the Spirit of the Lord would come upon her and the power of the Most High
would overshadow her, for which reason the Holy One being born of her is the Son of
God. And she replied: 'Be it done unto me according to thy word (15).' "

142

[102]

[Justin:] "Because God knew that it would be good, He created both angels and   486
men free to do what is righteous; and He limited the times up to which He knew it   505
would be good for them to have the exercise of free choice."

143

[103]

[Justin:] "[It is recorded] in the Memoirs which, I say, were composed (16) by   61
[Christ's] Apostles and their followers, that His perspiration fell down like drops of   66
blood (17), while He prayed and said, 'If it be possible, let this cup pass (18).' "   64

144

[110]

[Justin:] "It is evident that no one can terrify us or hold us in servitude, who have   404
believed in Jesus over all the earth. For, though beheaded and crucified and thrown to   88
the beasts and in chains and fire and subjected to all the other tortures, we do not give
up our confession. On the contrary, the more do such things happen, the more do others
in greater numbers become faithful worshippers of God through the name of Jesus. Just
as with the vine, when someone cuts away the fruit-bearing parts it grows up again and
puts forth other branches both flourishing and fruitful — it happens in the same way with
us."

144a

[117]

[Justin:] "There is not one single race of men — whether barbarians or Greeks, or of   404
whatever name they may be called, either wagon-dwellers or those who are called homeless
or herdsmen who dwell in tents — among whom prayers and thanksgivings are not offered
to God the Creator of all things, in the name of the crucified Jesus."

146

[141]

[Justin:] "If they repent, all who desire it will be able to obtain mercy from God.   751
Scripture (19) foretells that they shall be blessed, saying, 'Blessed is he to whom the Lord

imputes no sin (20).' It means one who has repented of his sins, so that he might receive from God the remission of sins, and not, as you and some like you in this deceive yourselves, saying that though they be sinners, since they acknowledge God, the Lord will not impute sin to them."

1. γεννητός.
2. The entire passage above, as also the next below, is represented as part of the conversation between Justin and the old man who set Justin on the path to Christianity; and which conversation is now being reported to Trypho by Justin.
3. *I. e.,* the Jews.
4. Is. 51:4-5.
5. Gen. 17:5.
6. Gen. 17:14 [Septuagint].
7. Is. 58:6 [Septuagint]. Justin apparently understands this to imply "setting aside the covenant to which you were formerly bound."
8. The other precepts enumerated by Isaias are recounted by Justin in Ch. 15 of the dialogue.
9. *I. e.,* one of the twelve lesser prophets, so-called from the shortness of their respective writings.
10. Mal. 1:10-12.
11. Is. 58:11.
12. Some read *of your race,* the better to identify these with the Ebionites, Christians of Jewish origin, who denied the divinity of Christ. Others retain the reading *of our race,* and deny that the passage refers to the Ebionites. Most choose the more obvious course: they retain the reading *of our race,* and still regard the reference as being to the Ebionites, on the grounds that Justin uses the word *race* in the looser sense of any group in some way identifiable as a unit, in the present instance meaning *of our persuasion* or *of our faith.*
13. Jos. 5:15 [Septuagint].
14. Jesus, the son of Nave, is Josue, the son of Nun.
15. Luke 1:38.
16. συντετάχθαι.
17. Luke 22:44.
18. Matt. 25:39.
19. ὁ λόγος.
20. Ps. 31 [32]:2.

THE RESURRECTION

Four fragments, the first of which is of considerable length (more than fifteen pages in Von Otto's edition), of a treatise on *The Resurrection* are preserved in St. John Damascene's *Sacra parallela,* wherein they are ascribed to Justin. The work is of obvious antiquity, having been used by both Irenaeus and Tertullian, neither of whom, however, names the author of the work. The authenticity of the fragments is probable enough, but by no means certain.

The text of the fragments may be found in Migne PG 6, 1571-1592; but the better source for them is volume 3 of J. C. T. von Otto's *Corpus apologetarum christianorum saeculi secundi* (9 volumes, Jena 1847-1872), pp. 210-249, 258; or K. Holl's *Fragmente vornicänischer Kirchenväter aus den Sacra parallela,* in the series *Texte und Untersuchungen* 20, 2, Leipzig 1899, pp. 36-49.

147

[8]
    Indeed, God calls even the body to resurrection, and promises it everlasting life. When   1011
He promises to save the man, He thereby makes His promise to the flesh: for what is man
but a rational living being composed of soul and body? Is the soul by itself a man? No,   500
it is but the *soul of a man.* Can the body be called a man? No, it can but be called the
body of a man. If, then, neither of these is by itself a man, but that which is composed of
the two together is called a man, and God has called man to life and resurrection, He has
called not a part, but the whole, which is the soul and the body.

148

[10]

The resurrection is of the flesh which died; for the spirit does not die. The soul is in the body, which cannot live without a soul. The body, when the soul departs from it, is not. The body is the house of the soul; and the soul, the house of the spirit. These three, in those who have a genuine hope and unquestioning faith in God, will be saved.

504

EXHORTATION TO THE GREEKS [*inter A. D.* 260 / 302]

Although Justin is known to have written a *Discourse Against the Greeks,* the work which has come down to us under his name and with a similar title, the *Cohortatio ad Graecos,* cannot be regarded as other than spurious. The attitude to Greek philosophy exhibited in this work of thirty-eight chapters is not the attitude of Justin. It has been dated variously from 180 to 360 A. D.; but the greater probability is that it belongs to the pre-Constantinian period, and to a period of extended peace: hence, between 260 and 302 A. D.

The Migne text is in PG 6, 241-312; but the standard edition is that of Von Otto's *Corpus apologetarum christianorum saeculi secundi,* Vol. 3, — unless one prefer that of E. J. Goodspeed, *Die ältesten Apologeten,* Göttingen 1914, which, in fact, presents an excellent text of all the second century apologists, Theophilus of Antioch excepted.

149

[8]

Since, therefore, nothing true is able to be learned about religion from your teachers, who by their mutual contradiction have supplied you with sufficient proof of their own ignorance, I regard it as reasonable to turn to our forefathers, who in point of time have very much of a precedence over your teachers, and who have taught us nothing of their own imagining, nor have they disagreed among themselves and tried to overturn each other's positions; but, without arguing and without contradiction, they have taught us the very knowledge which they received from God.

Neither by nature nor by human reasoning is it possible for men to know things so great and so divine; but such knowledge can be had only as a gift, which in this case descended from above upon the holy men, who had no need of the art of words, nor of saying anything in a quarrelsome or contentious manner, but only of presenting themselves in a pure manner to the operation of the Divine Spirit, so that the Divine Plectrum Himself, descending from heaven and using righteous men as an instrument like a harp or lyre, might reveal to us the knowledge of things divine and heavenly.

20

21

22

149a

[13]

Ptolemy, the King of Egypt, when he had constructed a library in Alexandria, and had filled it by collecting books from everywhere, afterwards learned that ancient histories written in Hebrew letters had been carefully preserved. Desiring to know these writings, he sent for seventy wise men from Jerusalem who knew both the Greek and the Hebrew languages, and appointed them to translate the books. . . . He supplied attendants to care for their every need, and also to prevent their communicating with each other, so that it might be possible to know the accuracy of the translation, by their agreement one with another. When he found that the seventy men had given not only the same meaning, but even in the same words, and had failed to agree with each other by not so much as a single word, but had written the same things about the same things, he was struck with amazement, and believed that the translation had been written with divine authority (1).

29

150

[22]

I think it necessary to keep in mind this too, that Plato never calls Him Creator, but rather, the *fashioner* of the gods; and furthermore, according to the opinion of Plato, there is a great difference between the two. Indeed, in need of nothing else, the Creator creates the creature out of His own capacity and authority; but the fashioner does his constructing when he has received from matter the wherewithal for his production.

461

1. This is the Aristean account of the translating of the Septuagint, so-called because it is first recited in the *Letter of Aristeas,* a document which dates from about the end of the third century B. C. Many of the fathers accepted the Aristean account at face value, and thereby regarded the Septuagint as an inspired translation.

TATIAN THE SYRIAN [*fl. ca. A. D.* 165/175]

Very little is known of Tatian's life, and even less of his death. He was by birth a Syrian, born into paganism. Like Justin, he sought the true philosophy and found it in Christianity. His wanderings brought him to Rome, where he was a pupil in Justin's school: but whether he was already a Christian when he came to Rome, or was converted there by Justin, is not known.

Tatian was in all things an extremist. He returned to the East about the year 172 A. D., where he founded a gnostic sect of encratites known as *Aquarii,* because of the fact that their fanatical rejection of the use of wine was so inflexible that they substituted water for wine even in the Eucharistic elements. Others rejected or discouraged second marriages; but Tatian's sect rejected even first marriages, which, quite possibly, is a factor to be reckoned with in accounting for the early disappearance of his followers.

He is best remembered for his having arranged a harmony of the Gospels, called the

Diatessaron. Until the fifth century this was the official form of the Gospels used in the Liturgy of the Syrian Church; and it seems to have had a considerable influence upon the Gospel text of the whole Church. Whether the original language of his *Diatessaron* was Greek or Syriac is still debated. Only fragments of the work have survived in either of these languages; but the entire text can be reconstructed from extant translations in Latin, Arabic, and, quite remarkably, Middle Low Franconian. A commentary on the *Diatessaron,* by Ephraim the Syrian, has survived in its entirety in an Armenian translation.

ADDRESS TO THE GREEKS [*ca. A. D.* 165/175]

Besides the *Diatessaron,* the only other extant work of Tatian is the *Address to the Greeks,* written not in Syriac but in Greek. It is to be dated after the death of Justin, *ca. A. D.* 165; but whether before or after Tatian's founding of the sect of *Aquarii,* shortly after 172 A. D., cannot be said with certainty. We cannot be far wrong in dating the work between the years 165 and 175 A. D.

Tatian knew no moderation in discourse, and his *Address* is filled with vituperation and invective. He decries the immorality of the Greek pagans, especially as evidenced by examples of their sculpture. In so doing, he unwittingly provides antiquarians with a valuable descriptive list of Greek statuary, matched with the names of the artists who created the works.

The text of the *Address* is found in Migne, PG 6, 803-888; but the standard text for scholarly purposes is that of E. Schwartz, *Tatiani Oratio ad Graecos,* in the series *Texte und Untersuchungen* 4, 1, Leipzig 1888.

152

[4]

Our God has no introduction in time. He alone is without beginning, and is Himself the   156
beginning of all things. God is a spirit (1), not attending upon matter, but the Maker of   460
material spirits and of the appearances which are in matter. He is invisible and untouch-   152
able, being Himself the Father of both sensible and invisible things. This we know by the
evidence of what He has created; and we perceive His invisible power by His works (2).   131

153

[5]

God existed in the beginning. But we have been taught that the beginning is the power   252
of the Word. For the Master of the universe, who Himself is the foundation (3) of all,   284
insofar as no creature was yet made, was alone. But inasmuch as He was all power, He   256
was the foundation of things visible and invisible; and with Him was the Word Himself,
who was in Him, and who sustains all things by a rational power.

By His simply willing it, the Word springs forth; and the Word, not proceeding in
vain, becomes the first-begotten work of the Father. We know Him (4) to be the
beginning of the world. He was begotten through communication, and not by a cutting
off; for what is cut off is separated from the original substance; but that which proceeds   257
from something by communication, and which accepts the choice of arrangement, does   253
not diminish that from which it is taken. For just as from one torch many fires are
lighted, and the light of the first torch is not lessened by the igniting of the many torches,
so also the Word, proceeding from the power of the Father, has not rendered the
Progenitor wordless.

154

[5]
    Matter is not without a beginning, like God; nor is it of equal power with God,   468
through being without a beginning. It is begotten, and not produced by any other begotten
being; but it is brought into existence by Him alone who is the Creator of all things.   460

155

[6]
    We believe that there will be a resurrection of bodies after the consummation of all   1011
things, and not as the Stoics affirm, according to certain periodic cycles in which the
same things are eternally produced and destroyed for no useful purpose; but that it will
take place once, at the completion of our times — and forever, according to the studied
arrangement which pertains to men alone — for the purpose of judgment. . . . And if we   1020
appear to you as carpers and babblers, it does not trouble us; for we believe in this
doctrine. Just as I had no being before I was born and did not know who I was and
existed only in the substantial basis (5) of fleshly matter, and after I once was not, was
then born and have obtained through birth the certainty of my own existence: in just
the same way, having been born and then through death existing no longer, and seen no   1013
longer, I shall exist again — just as formerly I was not, but was afterwards born.

156

[7]
    The heavenly Word, who is Spirit begotten by the Father, and Word from the rational   284
potency, made man an image of immortality in imitation of the Father who begot Him.   512
In that way, as incorruption pertains to God, so man, sharing in the portion of God,   480
might have immortality too. Indeed, the Word, before ever men were made, was the   481
Creator of the angels. Each of these species of creatures was created free, not having the   486
nature of good, which pertains only to God, and which is brought to perfection by men
through their freedom of choice. Thus, the wicked man is justly punished, having become   505
depraved of himself; and the just man is worthy of praise for his honest deeds, since it   775
was in his free choice that he did not transgress the will of God.

157

[13]
    The soul is not in itself immortal, you Greeks, but mortal (6). But it is also possible   502
for it not to die. If it does not know the truth, it dies and is set loose along with the
body, and rises again with the body at the consummation of the world, to be punished by   1011
receiving death in deathlessness. Otherwise, however, if it acquires the knowledge of God,
it does not die, although it is loosed for a time.

158

[13]
    In the beginning, indeed, the Spirit was a companion to the soul; but the Spirit   753
abandoned it because the soul was not willing to follow the Spirit. The soul, however,   761
retaining as it were a spark of the Spirit's power, and unable, because of its separation,
to discern the perfect, — during its wandering while seeking God it fashioned many gods,
following the sophistries of the demons. The Spirit of God, however, is not with all.
Rather, He makes His dwelling with those who live justly, and joins in an intimate union
with the soul; and by prophecies He announces hidden things to the rest of the souls (7).

159

[15]

Further, it is necessary for us now to seek what once we had, but have lost: indeed,   753
to unite the soul with the Holy Spirit, and to strive after union with God. . . . The perfect
God is without flesh; but man is flesh. The bond of the flesh is the soul; that which   500
encloses the soul is the flesh. Such is the form of man's constitution: and if it be like a
temple, God desires to dwell in it through the Spirit, His Representative; but if it be
not such a habitation, then man excels the beasts only in that he has articulate speech,
and in other respects his manner of life is like theirs and he is not a likeness of God.   512

160

[21]

We are not playing the fool, you Greeks, nor do we talk nonsense, when we report that   301
God was born in the form of a man.

1. John 4:24.
2. Cfr. Rom. 1:20.
3. ὑπόστασις.
4. *I. e.,* the Word.
5. ὑπόστασις.
6. Although often cited as evidence that Tatian denied the immortality of the soul, it is not at all clear that
   the passage involves such a denial. On closer examination, in fact, it appears that Tatian refers to the loss
   of salvation as a kind of death; and when he says that the unfaithful soul is punished by death in a state
   of being unable to die, he seems to affirm the eternity of punishment.
7. Apparently the term *Spirit* throughout this passage refers to the Holy Spirit, and not the spirit of the
   trichotomy of body, soul and spirit.

ATHENAGORAS OF ATHENS [† *paulo post A. D.* 180]

Nothing at all is known of Athenagoras except what little can be gleaned from his own writings; for in all ancient literature he is mentioned only once, Methodius of Olympus [known also as Methodius of Philippi, Methodius of Tyre, or Methodius of Patara] having taken passing note of him in his treatise *De resurrectione.*
Athenagoras was a Christian philosopher of Athens, if we can trust the manuscript title of his *Supplication for the Christians;* and he was a contemporary of Justin and Tatian. In rhetorical ability he far exceeds Justin, writing a very attractive style of Greek; and whereas Tatian was given to polemical contentiousness, Athenagoras knows better than to antagonize with insults those whom he hopes to influence. Of the time of his birth and how long he lived, we have not an inkling; and of his death, not the manner, but only that it took place soon after 180 A. D.

SUPPLICATION FOR THE CHRISTIANS [*ca. A. D.* 177]

Athenagoras' *Supplication for the Christians* was written between 176 and 180 A. D., probably in 177. It is an appeal for understanding, addressed to the Emperor Marcus Aurelius and to his son, the Emperor Commodus, who had been given the imperial title in 176 A. D. The work refutes the accusations made by pagans against Christians, of atheism, cannibalism, and incest, and ends in a calm entreaty for just judgment. Unlike that of Tatian, Athenagoras' pen provides light without heat.

The Migne text is found in PG 6, 889-972; but it has been superseded by several other editions. Probably that of E. Schwartz, *Athenagorae libellus pro Christianis,* in the series *Texte und Untersuchungen* 4, 2, Leizig 1891, can still be called the standard edition; but a much more recent one is that of P. Ubaldi and M. Pellegrino, *Atenagora,* (text with Italian translation), Turin 1947.

161

[4]
Is it not unreasonable to apply the name of atheist to us, who distinguish God from matter and teach that matter is one thing and God another, and that there is a great difference between them, the Deity being unbegotten and eternal, able to be known by reason and understanding alone, while matter is produced and perishable?   156

162

[7]
As witnesses of the things we have come to know and believe, we have the prophets, who made pronouncements about God and about the things of God, under the influence of the Spirit of Inspiration (1). You too will perhaps admit, surpassing others as you do in perception and in reverence for the real Deity, that it would be irrational to cease believing in the Spirit from God, who moved the mouths of the prophets like musical instruments, and to attend to human opinions.   21   558

163

[9]
In an ecstasy beyond their natural powers of reasoning, and moved by the Divine Spirit, [the prophets] spoke out the things with which they had been possessed, the Spirit making use of them after the manner of a flute-player breathing into a flute.   21

164

[10]

I have sufficiently demonstrated that we are not atheists, since we acknowledge one | 156
God, unbegotten, eternal, invisible, incapable of being acted upon, incomprehensible, | 152
unbounded; who is known only by understanding and reason; who is encompassed by | 173
light and beauty and spirit and indescribable power; by whom all things, through His | 284
Word, have been produced and set in order and are kept in existence. We recognize also | 230
the Son of God. Let no one think it laughable that God should have a Son. For we do | 237
not conceive of either God the Father or the Son as do the poets (2), who, in their
myth-making, represent the gods as no better than men. The Son of God is the Word of
the Father, in thought and in actuality. By Him and through Him all things were
made, the Father and the Son being one. Since the Son is in the Father and the
Father is in the Son by the unity and power of the Spirit, the Mind and Word (3) of
the Father is the Son of God.

And if, in your exceedingly great wisdom, it occurs to you to inquire what is meant
by 'the Son', I will tell you briefly: He is the First-begotten of the Father, not as having | 251
been produced, — for from the beginning God had the Word in Himself, God being
eternal mind and eternally rational, — but as coming forth to be the model and
energizing force of all material things, which were like a nature without attributes and an
inert earth, in which the heavier parts lay mixed up with the lighter.

The Prophetic Spirit also confirms this reasoning, when He says, "For the Lord made
me the beginning of His ways for His works (4)." The Holy Spirit also, who works in | 269
those who speak prophetically, we regard as an effluence of God, flowing out and
returning like a ray of the sun. Who, then, would not be astonished to hear those
called atheists, who speak of God the Father and of God the Son and of the Holy
Spirit, and who proclaim Their power in union and Their distinction in order? Nor is
our theology confined to these; for we recognize also a multitude of angels and ministers | 480
whom God, the Creator and Designer of the world, by means of His Word, set in their
places and gave into their charge the elements and the heavens and the world and what
is in it, and the good order of all.

165

[24]

Just as we assert that there is a God, and a Son who is His Word, and a Holy Spirit, | 230
united in power — the Father, the Son, and the Spirit, the Son being the Mind, Word, and | 261
Wisdom of the Father, and the Spirit an effluence like light from fire: so also do we
recognize that there are other powers which are in relation with matter and use it. . . .
For the origin of the angels was in view of their exercising providence for God over the | 480
things He created and which were put in order by Him.

166

[31]

If we were persuaded that this present life were the only one we should live, then it
might be possible to suspect us of sinning, of being enslaved to flesh and blood or made
dishonest by greed and passion. Since, however, we know that God is present both night | 189
and day to what we think and what we say, and that He, being light to all things, sees | 632
what is in our hearts, we are persuaded that when we are removed from this present life
we shall live another life, better than the present one, and not earthly but heavenly. Then
we shall abide near God and with God, changeless and free from suffering in the soul,
not as flesh, but as a heavenly spirit — or, if we fall with the rest, a worse one and in | 1044
fire; for God has not made us as sheep or beasts of burden, a mere incidental work, that | 1032
we should perish and be annihilated. In view of all this it is not likely that we should
desire to do evil, nor to deliver ourselves over to the great Judge for punishment.

167

[33]
Our concern is not with words, but with example and with the teaching of deeds: 977
either a person should remain as he was born, or be content with one marriage; for a   979
second is but a specious adultery. "For whoever divorces his wife," He says, "and marries
another, commits adultery (5)." Neither is a man allowed to divorce her whose virginity   64
he has ended, nor may he marry again. Anyone who deprives himself of his first wife,
even if she be dead, is a hidden adulterer. In breaking the bond of flesh with flesh, which
union was formed for the intercourse of the race, he is resisting the hand of God, inasmuch
as, in the beginning, God made one man and one woman.

1. Literally, *by an inspired Spirit:* Πνεύματι ἐνθέῳ.
2. It is a reflection of the Greeks' exalted notion of the work of the poet that the term here employed (the
   same term which also is used for the artist and composer), and which is the etymological source of our
   word *poet,* is simply ποιηταί, literally, *makers* or *creators.*
3. Νοῦς καὶ Λόγος.
4. Prov. 8:22.
5. Matt. 19:9.

THE RESURRECTION OF THE DEAD [*ca. A. D.* 177 / 180]

Athenagoras' *The Resurrection of the Dead* is a later work than his *Supplication for the Christians,* and can otherwise be dated only as between the years 177 and 180 A. D. It is a work of decidedly philosophical orientation, and proves the fact of universal resurrection from the reasonableness thereof. Taking the purely philosophical approach, little can be said today for the proof of resurrection that is not already said by Athenagoras.

The Migne text is in PG 6, 973-1024. It is superseded, however, by the editions of Schwartz and Pellegrino, in the same volumes referred to above in regard to Athenagoras' *Supplication for the Christians.*

168

[12]
God did not create man in a purposeless enterprise; for He is wise, and no work   463
performed by wisdom is without purpose. Nor was it through any need of His own, for   465
He is in want of nothing; but to a Being in need of nothing at all, none of His own
productions can contribute anything needful. And again, He did not create man for the
sake of any of the other works which He produced; for nothing which uses reason and
judgment has been created or is created for the use of another creature, whether greater
or less than itself; but such are created for the sake of their own life and existence.
. . . Therefore, if man has been made neither foolishly nor without a purpose − and
none of the works of God are done foolishly, insofar as the purpose of the Creator is
concerned − nor for any need of the Creator Himself, nor for that of any of the other
creations which He has produced, it is quite clear, then, that although the commonest
and foremost opinion is that God created man for Himself and for the sake of the
goodness and wisdom which are the hallmark of all His creation, yet, according to the
reason which most nearly touches upon those who were created, it was for the sake of
their own life that He made them; and their life is not enkindled for a brief time, to be   502
completely snuffed out afterwards.

169

[12]

That, however, which was generated for the sake of its own life and existence — since this cause belongs to it by nature and is recognized only by the fact that the creature exists — can never admit of any cause which would completely annihilate its existence.   502 This cause is seen to be directed to perpetual existence; therefore, the being so produced must be preserved forever, doing and experiencing what accords with its nature, each of its parts contributing what belongs to it. Thus the soul exists and continues unchanged in the nature in which it was made, and performs what is natural to it. . . . And the body is moved to what is proper to it in accord with its nature, and undergoes the changes allotted to it; and among the other changes of age, appearance and size, is the resurrection. 1011 For the resurrection is a species of change, the last of all, and a change for the better in those things which remain at that time.

170

[15]

If every example of human nature is made up jointly of an immortal soul and the body   500 with which it is united at creation; and if God has decreed such an origin, such a life   503 and course of existence, neither for the nature of the soul itself nor for the nature of the body separately, but for men who are composed of the two, so that having passed through life they may arrive at one common end, still composed of the same elements from which they were made and with which they lived, it is absolutely necessary, since one living being is formed of the two, experiencing whatever the soul experiences and whatever the body experiences, doing and performing whatever requires either sensual or rational judgment, that the whole series of these experiences must be referred to one and the same end.

ST. THEOPHILUS OF ANTIOCH [† *ca. A. D.* 185 / 191]

St. Theophilus was the seventh bishop of Antioch, the sixth successor of Peter. Little is known of him beyond the few details which can be gathered from his *To Autolycus.* He was born near the Euphrates, and was converted from paganism to Christianity as an adult, after having made a careful study of the Scriptures. He died between the years 185 and 191 A. D.

TO AUTOLYCUS [*ca. A. D.* 181]

Of Theophilus' writings only one work has survived, an apologetic work in three books, *To Autolycus.* The third book contains a chronology of the world which ends with the death of Marcus Aurelius on March 17, in 180 A. D. It is assumed, then, that the work was written *ca.* 181 A. D.

The Migne text, PG 6, 1023-1168, is superseded by the text of J. C. T. von Otto, *Corpus apologetarum christianorum saeculi secundi,* Vol. 8, Jena 1861, which is still generally regarded as the standard edition, in spite of the 1938 Turin edition of S. Frasca: *Justinus, Apologie: Segue: Theophilus Antiochenus, Gli tre libri ad Autolico. Testo, versione, introduzione.*

171

[1, 4]

He is without beginning, because He is unbegotten. He is unchangeable inasmuch as He is immortal. He is called God [ϑεός] because of His having placed [τεϑεικέναι] everything in the security which He Himself affords, and because of ϑέειν; for ϑέειν means to run, to move, to operate, to nourish, to foresee, to govern, and to make everything come alive (1). He is Lord because He rules over all things; Father, because He is before all   530 things; Designer and Creator, because He is Maker and Creator of all things; Most High,   460 because He is above everything; Almighty, because He Himself rules and encompasses all.   158 . . . And God has made all things out of those which were not into those which are, so   461 that by His works His greatness may be known and understood.   466

172

[1, 6]

Consider, O man, His works: the changes of the seasons at set times, the changes in   131 weather, the well-ordered course of the planets, the well-ordered progress of days and   132 nights and months and years, . . . the providence by which God arranges that nourishment is at hand for all flesh, and the subjection in which He has ordained that all things are subservient to mankind. . . . He alone is God, who made light out of darkness, who brought forth light from among His treasures, who made the storehouses of the south wind (2) and the treasure chambers of the deep and the boundaries of the seas.

173

[1, 7]

When you have put off mortality and have put on incorruption, then you shall be worthy to see God. For God will raise up your flesh immortal with your soul; and   1011 then, having become immortal, you shall see the Immortal, if you will believe in Him   758 now; and then you will realize that you have spoken against Him unjustly. [8] But   771

you do not believe that the dead will be raised. When it happens, then you will
believe, whether you want to or not; but unless you believe now, your faith then will
be reckoned as unbelief.

And why do you not believe? Do you not know that faith is foremost in all matters?   10
For what farmer is able to reap, unless first he have faith, and trust the seed to the   561
earth? Or who is able to journey across the sea, unless first he have faith to trust
himself to the ship and to the pilot? What sick person is able to be cured unless first
he have faith to trust himself to the physician? Who is able to learn either an art or a
science, unless first he devote himself faithfully to the teacher? If, then, the farmer   558
believes in the earth, and the sailor believes in the ship, and the sick man believes in the
physician, will not you yourself wish to believe in God, when you have so many pledges   560
from Him?

174

[1, 12]

Are you unwilling to be anointed (3) with the oil of God? It is on this account that   840
we are called Christians: because we are anointed with the oil of God.   841,842

175

[1, 14]

At the same time I came upon the Sacred Scriptures of the holy prophets, who   15
recited through the Spirit of God the things which have happened in the manner in which   21
they happened, and the present events as they are happening, and the future events in the
very order in which they will be accomplished. I acknowledged, therefore, the proof
afforded by things happening as they have been predicted, and I do not disbelieve, but,   558
obedient to God, I believe.

176

[1, 14]

Give studious attention to the prophetic writings and they will lead you on a clearer   1034
path to escape the eternal punishments and to obtain the eternal good things of God. He   1043
who gave the mouth for speech and formed the ears for hearing and made eyes for
seeing will examine everything and will judge justly, granting recompense to each
according to merit. To those who seek immortality by the patient exercise of good   771
works, He will give everlasting life, joy, peace, rest, and all good things, which neither   759
has eye seen nor ear heard, nor has it entered into the heart of man (4). For the   1045
unbelievers and for the contemptuous, and for those who do not submit to the truth but
assent to iniquity (5), when they have been involved in adulteries and fornications and
homosexualities and avarice and in lawless idolatries, there will be wrath and indignation,
tribulation and anguish (6): and in the end, such men as these will be detained in ever-   1032
lasting fire.

177

[2, 3]

It is the attribute of God — of the Most High and Almighty and of the living God —   154
not only to be everywhere, but also to hear all and to see all; for He can in no way be   189
contained in a place. If He were, the place containing Him would be greater than He is;
for that which contains is greater than that which is contained. God is not contained, but is
Himself the place of everything.

178

[2, 4]

    Plato and those of his school do indeed acknowledge that God is unbegotten, and   468
that He is the Father and Creator of all things; but then they posit that matter as well   460
as God is uncreated, and maintain that matter is coeval with God. But if God is
uncreated and matter is uncreated, then, according to the Platonists God is no longer
the Creator of all things; nor, insofar as their opinion holds, is the monarchy of God
established.

    Furthermore, inasmuch as God is uncreated, He is also unchangeable; so also, if
matter were uncreated, it would be unchangeable and equal to God; for that which is
created is alterable and changeable, while that which is uncreated is unalterable and
unchangeable. And what great thing were it, if God made the world out of existing   461
matter? Even a human artist, when he obtains material from someone, makes of it
whatever he pleases. But the power of God is made evident in this, that He makes out
of what does not exist whatever He pleases; and the giving of life and movement   462
belongs to none other, but to God alone.

179

[2, 10]

    In the first place, [the prophets and the Sibyl] taught us as with one voice that He   461
created everything out of that which did not exist; for nothing is coeval with God. He,   468
however, being His own place (7) and lacking nothing and existing before the ages, willed
to make man, by whom He might be known (8). For the sake of man, therefore, He   466
prepared the world; for that which is created is by the same token in need, while the
uncreated is in need of nothing. God, therefore, having His own Word internally in His
very organs, begot Him, emitting Him along with His own Wisdom, before all things. He   265
had this Word for a Helper in the things which He made, and through Him were all   284
things created. He is called Beginning [ἀρχή], because He rules [ἄρχει] and has dominion
over everything which was fashioned by Him.

    He, then, being Spirit of God and Beginning and Wisdom and Power of the Most High,
descended upon the prophets and through them spoke of the creation of the world and   21
of all the rest; for the prophets did not exist when the world came to be, but there was   237
Wisdom, which was in Him and which was of God, and His Holy Word, who is eternally
present with Him.

180

[2, 15]

    The three days before the luminaries were created are types of the Trinity (9): God,   230
His Word, and His Wisdom.   232

181

[2, 16]

    Moreover, those things which were created from the waters were blessed by God, so   790
that this might also be a sign that men would at a future time receive repentance and   836
remission of sins through water and the bath of regeneration (10) — all who proceed to
the truth and are born again and receive a blessing from God.

182

[2, 22]

You will, therefore, say to me, "You said that God cannot be contained in a place. How now, then, do you say that He walked around in Paradise?" Hear what I say. The God and Father of all, indeed, is not contained, and is not found in a place; for there is no place of His rest. But His Word, through whom He created all things, being His   261
Power and His Wisdom, assuming the person of the Father and Lord of the universe,   236
went to the garden in the person of God, and talked with Adam. The Divine Scripture itself teaches us that Adam said he had heard the voice.

And what else is this voice, but the Word of God, which also is His Son, – not as poets and writers of myths tell of the sons of gods begotten of intercourse, but, as truth recounts, the Word which always exists internally in the heart of God? For before anything was created, He had this Counsellor, being His own Mind and Thought; and   256
when God wished to create what He had decided upon, He begot this uttered Word, the   265
First-born of all creation, not emptying Himself of the Word, but having begotten the Word, and conversing always with His Word.

This is what the Holy Scriptures teach us, as do all the inspired men (11), one of   67
whom, John, says, "In the beginning was the Word, and the Word was with God (12)," showing that at first God was alone, and the Word was in Him. Then he says, "And the Word was God; all things were made through Him, and without Him was made nothing (13)." The Word, then, being God and being generated from God, is sent to any place at the will of the Father of the universe; and when He comes, having been sent by Him and being found in place, He is both heard and seen.   290

183

[2, 25]

For the first man, disobedience resulted in his expulsion from Paradise. It was not   612
as if there were any evil in the tree of knowledge; but from disobedience man drew   611
labor, pain, grief, and, in the end, he fell prostrate in death.

184

[2, 27]

Someone, however, will say to us, "Was man made by nature mortal?" Certainly not.   522
"Was he, then, immortal?" Neither do we say that. But someone will say, "Was he, then, made nothing?" Not so, I reply. By nature, in fact, he was made neither mortal nor immortal. For if God had made him immortal from the beginning, He would have made him God. Again, if He had made him mortal, it would seem as if God were the cause of his death. He made him, then, neither mortal nor immortal, but, as we said above, capable of either. Thus, if he should incline to the ways of immortality, keeping   505
the command of God, he should receive from God the reward of immortality, and become God. If, however, he turn aside to the ways of death, disobeying God, he should become   639
for himself the cause of death. For God made man free and self-determining.

185

[3, 12]

Moreover, in regard to the righteousness which the law enjoined, the Prophets and   20
the Gospels are found to be consistent with each other, because they all spoke as being   50
inspired by the one Spirit of God.

186

[3, 15]

Far be it from Christians that to do such deeds (14) should enter their mind; for   86
temperance dwells with them, self-restraint is practiced, monogamy is observed, chastity   977
is guarded, injustice is exterminated, sin is rooted out, righteousness is exercised, law is
administered, reverence is preserved, God is acknowledged: truth controls, grace guards,
peace protects, the holy word guides, wisdom teaches, life directs, God reigns.   681

1. The first of these two etymologies is found also in Herodotus, *Hist.* 2, 52. The second is put in the mouth
   of Socrates in Plato's *Cratylus* 397 D. Other etymologies proposed in antiquity include ϑεωρεῖν, *to behold,*
   and αἴϑειν, *to burn.* See Bardenhewer, *Geschichte der altkirchlichen Literatur,* Vol. 1, p. 303, n. 1.
2. Job 9:9.
3. χρισϑῆναι. The cleverness of Theophilus' remark, largely lost in English, rests upon the literal meaning of
   Christ: i.e., the Anointed One. It is as if he had said: "Are you unwilling to be Christed with the oil of
   God? It is because we are so Christed that we are called Christians." For oil, Theophilus uses the word
   ἔλαιον, the common olive oil used by wrestlers. One would think that χρῖσμα, the more precious and
   sweet-smelling unguent, would have been a better choice of words.
4. 1 Cor. 2:9.
5. Rom. 2:8.
6. Rom. 2:8-9.
7. αὐτὸς ἑαυτοῦ τόπος ὤν no doubt signifies "being sufficient unto Himself."
8. Here we stand at the brink of the mystery of creation. Man has always asked, why did God create him;
   and the answer which Christianity has always given is, that He might be known. But how could God,
   existing alone and entirely self-sufficient and lacking nothing, desire to be known by another? The
   answer is given, but the mystery remains, cloaked now in an anthropomorphism. The arguments of the
   God-lover of Antioch are no more logical, in the face of the inexplicable, than are those of the
   Platonists against whom he scored a few chapters above. Yet, his answer is correct, and we know it by
   our unalterable faith. We can only say triumphantly that the illogical arguments of the philosophers
   are wrong, but the illogical arguments of the God-lover are correct. Christendom wants to know why God
   created; and it supplies the answer, that He might be known. It is as much as men can know; and we
   may well suspect that even in the light of beatitude the anthropomorphic cloak will not be stripped
   entirely away.
9. Τριάδος: this is the first use of the word τρίας in reference to the Godhead.
10. Titus 3:5.
11. οἱ πνευματοφόροι.
12. John 1:1.
13. John 1:3.
14. Theophilus has been speaking of the excesses of the pagans.

EPITAPH OF ABERCIUS [*ca. A. D.* 180 / 200]

Abercius, the composer of his own epitaph, was Bishop of Hierapolis in Phrygia
Salutaris. The two fragments of the epitaph now in the Lateran Museum in Rome
were discovered near Hierapolis in 1883 by the Scots archeologist, W. Ramsey.
The same archeologist had discovered a year earlier an epitaph of a certain \
Alexander, which was in a style imitative of that of Abercius, and which, fortunately,
bore a date, convertible to 216 A. D. With the aid of the epitaph of Alexander and
a fourth century biography of Abercius, it has been possible to reconstruct the
complete text of the Abercius epitaph, although only about 20% of the text is
contained on the two fragments.

The text has been printed many times, and we will refer the reader only to Adolph
Harnack's *Zur Abercius-Inschrift* in the series *Texte und Untersuchungen* 12, 4b,

Leipzig 1895; and C. M. Kaufmann, *Handbuch der altchristlichen Epigraphik,* Freiburg im Breisgau 1917, pp. 169-178, where a photograph of the fragmentary monument is given.

187

The citizen of a prominent city, I erected this
While I lived, that I might have a resting place for my body.
Abercius is my name, a disciple of the chaste shepherd
Who feeds His sheep on the mountains and in the fields,
Who has great eyes surveying everywhere,
Who taught me the faithful writings of life.
He sent me to Rome to contemplate a kingdom,   434
And to behold a queen in a golden robe and golden sandals.
There I saw a people who had the resplendent seal;
And I saw the plain of Syria and all the cities, even Nisibis   404
Beyond the Euphrates. And everywhere I had associates,
Having Paul as a companion. Everywhere faith led the way   877
and everywhere set food before me, — fish from the fountain   851
Mighty and pure, which the chaste virgin caught, —
And gave this to friends to eat, always
Having good wine, giving mixed wine with bread.   860
Standing by, I, Abercius, ordered this to be inscribed;   871
Truly, I was in my seventy-second year.
May everyone who is in accord with this and who understands
    it pray for Abercius.   1001
Nor, indeed, shall any man place another in my tomb.
And if he do, he shall place in the Roman treasury two
    thousand pieces of gold,
And with my deserving fatherland, Hierapolis, one thousand
    pieces of gold.

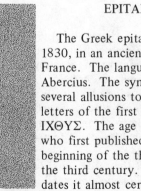

EPITAPH OF PECTORIUS [*inter A. D.* 350-400]

The Greek epitaph of Pectorius was found almost complete in seven fragments in 1830, in an ancient Christian cemetery in the neighborhood of Autun in southern France. The language of the inscription is very similar to the much older epitaph of Abercius. The symbolism of the fish is again quite prominent. In fact, besides the several allusions to Christ as the Fish within the text of the epitaph, the initial letters of the first five verses of the eleven-verse inscription form the acrostic ΙΧΘΥΣ. The age of the epitaph has been much controverted. Cardinal J. P. Pitra, who first published it, concluded with G. B. de Rossi that it belonged to the beginning of the third century. E. le Blant and J. Wilpert assigned it to the end of the third century. The letters of the inscription, however, belong to a style which dates it almost certainly between the years 350 and 400 A. D.

For the text of the Pectorius epitaph, see J. Quasten, *Monumenta eucharistica et liturgica vetustissima,* pars 1, Bonn 1935, pp. 24-26; or better, C. M. Kaufmann, *Handbuch der altchristlichen Epigraphik,* Freiburg im Breisgau 1917, pp. 178-180, where also a photograph of the monument is printed. Both of these sources contain also the Epitaph of Abercius, our preceding selection.

187a

O divine child of the heavenly Fish, earnestly desire
   a holy heart,
Having received among mortals the immortal fountain
Of the wondrous waters. Refresh your soul, beloved,   836
In the eternal waters of munificent wisdom.
Receive the honey-sweet food of the Savior of the saints,
Being hungry (1), eat, having the Fish in your hands.   851
Fatten me with Fish straightway (2), I beseech you,
   Master and Savior.
I pray you, O light of the dying, that mother may rest well.   1001
Aschandius, father, beloved of my soul,
With my sweet mother and brothers
In the peace of the Fish, remember your Pectorius.

1. ΠΙΝΑΩΝ. Some have read πίνων, but we prefer to read πεινάων.
2. ΑΡΑ. Some have read ἆρα, but we prefer to read ἄρα.

ST. HEGESIPPUS [*fl. ca. A. D.* 180]

St. Hegesippus was born in the East, probably a Hellenistic Jew. The time and occasion of his conversion to Christianity is not known. He visited Rome in the time of Pope St. Anicetus (155-156 A. D.). The time of his death is not known, but there are reasons for supposing that he wrote his *Memoirs* about the year 180 A. D.

MEMOIRS [*ca. A. D.* 180]

Hegesippus' *Memoirs,* an account in five books of his journey to various centers of Christianity, a journey made for the express purpose of gathering information on the true doctrine of Christianity, in order to enable him the better to combat gnosticism, is extant only in a few fragments, none of any great length, principally in Eusebius, but also in Stephen Gobarus as given by Photius. There is a single remark concerning him in George Syncellus.

The texts of the few fragments may be found in Migne, PG 5, 1307-1328; and in

A. Hilgenfeld's article "Hegesippus", in the *Zeitschrift für wissenschaftliche Theologie*, Vol. 19, 1876, pp. 177-229. For the Eusebian fragments, of course, it will be best to consult E. Schwartz's critical edition of Eusebius in the Berlin Corpus.

FRAGMENT IN EUSEBIUS, History of the Church, BK. 4, CH. 22.

188

[4, 22, 1]

Hegesippus, indeed, in the five books of Memoirs *which have come down to us, has left a complete record of his own opinion. In these books he shows that he journeyed as far* 405 *as Rome and became acquainted with a great many bishops, and that he heard the same* 420 *doctrine from all. It is interesting to hear what he says after some remarks about the letter of Clement to the Corinthians:*

[2] "And the Church of the Corinthians has continued in the correct doctrine to the time of Primus, who has become Bishop in Corinth, and with whom I conversed at length on my way to Rome, when I spent some days with the Corinthians, during which time we were mutually refreshed in the correct doctrine. [3] When I had come to Rome, I made a succession up to Anicetus (1), whose deacon was Eleutherus. And after Anicetus, 432 Soter succeeded; and after him, Eleutherus. In each succession and in each city there is 440 a continuance of that which is proclaimed by the Law, the Prophets, and the Lord. 51

---

1. The manuscript evidence of the Greek, supported by the Syriac, is διαδοχὴν ἐποιησάμεν μέχρις Ἀνικήτου. It is conjectured that διαδοχὴν should be corrected to διατριβήν, making the passage mean that Hegesippus came to Rome and remained there up to the time of Anicetus. Support for this view is found in Rufinus, who reads *permansi ibi.* It is true that there is a certain obscurity about the text as it stands; but it appears to us that this obscurity is greatly exaggerated by those who propose to change the reading. It is maintained that if Hegesippus had composed a list or succession of the Bishops of Rome from Peter on, Eusebius would have given us all of it. Well, I should think he ought to have done so, if he had it available; but I have no way of knowing the state of the Hegesippus manuscript that was in Eusebius' possession. And in any case, I would hesitate to say anything more definite in a matter of this kind than that I would wish Eusebius might have given us the whole list — and when I meet him in eternity, I shall certainly ask him why he did not.

Besides pointing out the futility of arguing about what Eusebius ought to have done, we must note this also: if the conjectured reading be adopted, and it be read that Hegesippus came to Rome and stayed there up to the time of Anicetus, then we must take into account Eusebius' remark in *Hist. Eccl.* 4, 11, that Hegesippus came to Rome in the time of Anicetus and remained there until the time of Eleutherus. First of all, that Hegesippus remained in Rome until the time of Eleutherus is possible but not very likely. The remark is probably the result of an inadvertence or faulty memory of a source which Eusebius did not re-check at the moment.

But it is one thing to suggest that Eusebius erred in this way, and quite another to involve him in direct contradictions within his own work. And if the suggested emendation of the text in *Hist. Eccl.* 4, 22, be adopted, then we have Eusebius contradicting himself. All in all, I would want a better reason than a bad translation in Rufinus and a poorly turned phrase in Hegesippus for changing the text, when it is confirmed by all the Greek manuscripts, by the Syriac, and when changing it results in making Eusebius clearly contradict himself in the same book.

ST. MELITO OF SARDES [† *inter A. D.* 171 / 190, *ca.* 177]

Biographical details of St. Melito, Bishop of Sardes in Lydia, are virtually non-existent, save for a notice taken of him by St. Polycrates of Ephesus in his famous letter to Pope St. Victor (below, § 190a); and even Polycrates says little enough of him, to wit: he was one of the great lights of Asia, had never married, and was already dead when Polycrates was writing, *ca. A. D.* 190.

About 170 A. D. Melito wrote an *Apology for Christianity,* addressed to Marcus Aurelius. He was, in fact, quite a prolific writer; but, except for a complete *Homily on the Passion,* discovered only thirty years ago, his numerous writings have survived only in a fair number of small fragments. The *Homily on the Passion* is a precious work, well worth study, although we take no occasion here to cite it. It was published by its discoverer, Campell Bonner, in the series *Studies and Documents,* No. 12, London 1940. The fragments, preserved as citations in Eusebius and in Anastasius of Sinai, can be found collected in the Migne edition, PG 5, 1207-1232, or better, J. C. T. von Otto, *Corpus apologetarum christianorum saeculi secundi,* Vol. 9, Jena 1872. For the Syriac fragments, the better source is I. Rucker, *Florilegium Edessenum anonymum,* in the *Sitzungsberichte* of the Berlin Academy, Berlin 1933, pp. 12-16 and 67-73.

FRAGMENT IN ANASTASIUS OF SINAI, The Guide, CH. 13

189

[13]
It is in no way necessary in dealing with persons of intelligence to adduce the actions of Christ after His Baptism as proof that His soul and His body, His human nature, were like ours, real and not phantasmal. The activities of Christ after His Baptism, and especially   310
His miracles, gave indication and assurance to the world of the Deity hidden in His flesh.   82
Being God and likewise perfect man, He gave positive indications of His two natures (1):   301
of His Deity, by the miracles during the three years following after His Baptism; of His   322
humanity, in the thirty years which came before His Baptism, during which, by reason of
His condition according to the flesh, He concealed the signs of His Deity, although He was   256
the true God existing before the ages (2).

FRAGMENT IN EUSEBIUS, History of the Church, BK. 4, CH. 26

190

[4, 26, 14]
When, therefore, I went to the East and came to the place where these things were   41
preached and done, I learned accurately the books of the Old Testament; and I send you the list in order, these being their names: Five books of Moses, Genesis, Exodus, Numbers, Leviticus, Deuteronomy; Jesus Nave; Judges; Ruth; four books of Kingdoms; two of Paralipomenon; Psalms of David; Proverbs of Solomon, and also Wisdom; Ecclesiastes; Song of Songs; Job; of the prophets, Isaias, Jeremias, the twelve in one book, Daniel, Ezechiel, and Esdras. I have made extracts from these, arranging them in six books (3).

---

1. τὰς δύο αὐτοῦ οὐσίας.
2. Probably this Anastasian fragment is from Melito's work entitled *On God Incarnate.*
3. The present fragment is cited by Eusebius as being from the introduction to Melito's work entitled *Extracts,* addressed to a certain Onesimus.

ST. POLYCRATES OF EPHESUS [*ca. A. D.* 125 – *ca. A. D.* 196]

For the extremely meager biographical details which we have of St. Polycrates, Bishop of Ephesus, we are indebted to his own letter to Pope St. Victor. Polycrates was 65 years of age when he wrote the letter, *ca. A. D.* 190 – hence, he was born about the year 125 A. D. Among his kinsmen there were seven other bishops. He died about the year 196 A. D.

LETTER TO VICTOR OF ROME [*ca. A. D.* 190]

The letter of Polycrates of Ephesus to Victor of Rome is one of the prime sources for the history of the Quartodeciman controversy. Polycrates was the leader of those bishops of Asia Minor who opposed Victor's order in regard to arranging the date of Easter so that it would fall always on a Sunday. Polycrates held a synod with his fellow-bishops, and informed Victor by letter of the reasons for which they had determined to continue following the only custom they knew, that of observing the 14th Nisan, no matter the day of the week. Only a sizeable fragment of the letter is extant, preserved by Eusebius (*Hist. Eccl.* 5, 24, 2-8). In Eusebius' account, Victor thereupon excommunicated the dioceses of Asia and all the Quartodecimans, as those who observed the 14th Nisan were called. Eusebius' information in this regard, however, is held in considerable suspicion; and it is generally supposed that Irenaeus and others who pleaded for toleration succeeded in staying Victor's hand before ever his censure was leveled.

The fragment in question may be found in Migne, PG 5, 1357-1362; but it is better, of course, to consult E. Schwartz's critical edition of Eusebius in the Berlin Corpus (GCS).

190a

[5, 24, 1]

But of the bishops of Asia, who confidently affirmed that they must hold to the old　102
custom handed down to them (1), Polycrates was the leader; and he himself, in the　107
writing which he addressed to Victor and to the Roman Church, set forth in the following
words the tradition which had come down to him:

[2] "As for us, then, we observe the precise day, neither adding nor taking away. For even in Asia great lights have gone to sleep, who will rise again on the day of the coming　1011 of the Lord, when He comes in glory from the heavens to seek out all the saints – Philip of the twelve Apostles, who sleeps in Hierapolis, and his two daughters who grew old in virginity, and his other daughter who regulated her life in the Holy Spirit and who rests in Ephesus.

[3] "Moreover, there is also John, who reclined at the bosom of the Lord (2), and who became a priest wearing the high priest's mitre, and a witness and a teacher. [4] He fell asleep at Ephesus. Then there is also Polycarp in Smyrna, both bishop and martyr; and Thraseas, both bishop and martyr, from Eumenia, who fell asleep in Smyrna.

[5] "And what is to be said of Sagaris, bishop and martyr, who fell asleep in Laodicea? or of the blessed Papirius? and of Melito, the eunuch, who regulated his life entirely in the Holy Spirit, and who sleeps at Sardes while awaiting the visitation (3) from heaven in which he will rise up from the dead?

[6] "These all kept the fourteenth day of the Passover, according to the Gospel, deviating in no way, but adhering to the rule of faith. So also do I, Polycrates, the least of all among you, in accord with the tradition of my kindred, some of whom I have followed closely. Seven of my kinsmen were bishops, and I am the eighth; and my

kinsmen always observed the day when the people put away the leaven. [7] Therefore, brethren, I, who am sixty-five years old in the Lord, and who have been acquainted with the brethren throughout the world, and who have read through the entire Holy Scriptures —   435 I am not frightened by things said as threats. Those greater than I have said, 'We must obey God rather than men (4).' "

[8] *He adds to this, concerning the bishops who were present with him when he wrote, and who thought as he did, saying:* "I could also mention the bishops who were present   433 with me, whom you requested me to call together, and whom I have called together. Their names, were I to write them down, are most numerous. These, on seeing that I am the least of men, gave approval to the letter, knowing that I did not bear my gray hairs in vain, but have always regulated my life in Christ Jesus."

[9] *Thereupon Victor, who presided over the Church of Rome, immediately attempted to cut off from the common unity the dioceses of Asia and the Churches which agreed with them, as heterodox; and he inveighed against them by letters declaring all the brethren there to be absolutely excommunicate.* [10] *But this was not pleasing to all the bishops. They besought him rather to consider the things of peace, of unity with neighbor, and of charity. Their letters are extant, in which they sharply rebuke Victor.*

1. The custom, from which they are called Quartodecimans, dictated that Easter must be celebrated on the 14th Nisan, regardless of the day of the week on which that date occurred. Victor's custom, with the rest of the Catholic world, insisted upon certain adjustments to make the Easter celebration coincide only with a Sunday. That both Eusebius and Jerome praise Polycrates highly for his orthodox doctrine and practice is indicative of the fact that the Quartodeciman controversy was in their day a dead issue.
2. John 13:23.
3. ἐπισκοπήν.
4. Acts 5:29.

ST. IRENAEUS [*ca. A. D.* 140 – *ca. A. D.* 202]

St. Irenaeus was the second bishop of Lyons, succeeding the martyred bishop St. Pothinus in the year 177 or 178 A. D., when he himself was perhaps about 37 years old. He was a native of Asia Minor, probably of Smyrna, where in his youth he had been a pupil of St. Polycarp. His passage to Gaul, where we meet him as an esteemed presbyter of the Church of Lyons immediately before the death of his episcopal predecessor, is one of history's mysteries. To exchange figs for frogs is incredible.

True to his name of Peacemaker, as Eusebius remarks, it was Irenaeus who sought to make peace between Victor of Rome and Polycrates of Ephesus, when Victor was threatening excommunication against the latter. After this incident of about the year 190 A. D., Irenaeus disappears from history and is presumed to have died about the year 202 A. D. Not until Gregory of Tours wrote his *History of the Franks* do we find Irenaeus mentioned as a martyr; and such late testimony is necessarily suspect, especially in view of the fact that Eusebius, who has good knowledge of Irenaeus, says nothing of his supposed martyrdom.

DETECTION AND OVERTHROW OF THE GNOSIS FALSELY SO-CALLED *or* AGAINST HERESIES [*inter A. D.* 180 / 199]

Irenaeus is certainly the most important theologian of the second century; and the most prominent of his writings is the *Detection and Overthrow of the Gnosis Falsely So-called* , generally cited simply as the *Adversus haereses*. Until the Chenoboskion finds of 1946, we had very little of the actual gnostic writings, and for what little we knew of the gnostics we were largely dependent upon Irenaeus' great refutation. Nor has his work lost its value through the discovery of some of the original works which were for centuries known only by means of quotations from them in Irenaeus. In short, the *Adversus haereses* remains one of our primary sources for a knowledge of the gnostic sects.

The five books of the *Adversus haereses* were written in Greek between the years 180 and 199 A. D. The Greek text has not survived in its entirety, but can be almost completely reconstructed from its numerous citations in Hippolytus, Eusebius, and Epiphanius, and from papyrus fragments and *catenae* (books of selected passages, generally organized according to subject matter). The complete work is extant in a very old Latin translation. There is some probability that Cyprian of Carthage already knew this Latin translation, and indeed, some authors date it as early as 200 A. D. Further, there is extant the text of a very literal Armenian translation of the fourth and fifth books; and there are extant also some twenty-three fragments of one or more Syriac translations.

Migne reprints the 1710 text of Massuet, in PG 7, 433-1224. The standard text is still that of W. W. Harvey, *Sancti Irenaei episcopi Lugdunensis libros quinque adversus haereses,* 2 volumes, Cambridge 1857. A new edition is badly needed.

191

[1, 10, 1]

For the Church, although dispersed throughout the whole world even to the ends of	404
the earth, has received from the Apostles and from their disciples the faith in one God,	102
Father Almighty, the Creator of heaven and earth and sea and all that is in them (1);	157
and in one Jesus Christ, the Son of God, who became flesh for our salvation; and in the	460
Holy Spirit, who announced through the prophets the dispensations and the comings, and	230
the birth from a Virgin, and the passion, and the resurrection from the dead, and the	302

bodily ascension into heaven of the beloved Christ Jesus our Lord, and his coming (2)   781
from heaven in the glory of the Father to re-establish all things (3); and the raising up   391
again of all flesh of all humanity, in order that to Jesus Christ our Lord and God and   1012
Savior and King, in accord with the approval of the invisible Father, every knee shall   301
bend of those in heaven and on earth and under the earth, and that every tongue shall   392
confess Him (4), and that He may make just judgment of them all; and that He may send
the spiritual forces of wickedness (5), and the angels who transgressed and became   491
apostates, and the impious, unjust, lawless and blasphemous among men, into everlasting   1034
fire; and that He may grant life, immortality, and surround with eternal glory the just   1043
and the holy, and those who have kept His commands and who have persevered in His
love, either from their beginning or from their repentance.

192

[1, 10, 2]
As I said before, the Church, having received this preaching and this faith, although   420
she is disseminated throughout the whole world, yet guarded it, as if she occupied but   102
one house. She likewise believes these things just as if she had but one soul and one   404
and the same heart; and harmoniously she proclaims them and teaches them and hands   405
them down, as if she possessed but one mouth. For, while the languages of the world are   100
diverse, nevertheless, the authority of the tradition is one and the same.

Neither do the Churches among the Germans believe otherwise or have another
tradition, nor do those among the Iberians, nor among the Celts, nor away in the East,
nor in Egypt, nor in Libya, nor those which have been established in the central regions
of the world. But just as the sun, that creature of God, is one and the same throughout
the whole world, so also the preaching of the truth shines everywhere and enlightens all   89
men who desire to come to a knowledge of truth.

Nor will any of the rulers in the Churches, whatever his power of eloquence, teach
otherwise, for no one is above the teacher (6); nor will he who is weak in speaking
detract from the tradition. For the faith is one and the same, and cannot be amplified
by one who is able to say much about it, nor can it be diminished by one who can say
but little.

192a

[1, 12, 2]
Such beings as the Homeric Jove, . . . dear friend, will not seem to you to have a   150
greater power than He who is the God of the universe. For the latter, as soon as He
thinks, actually accomplishes what he has willed; and as soon as He wills, He also
thinks that which He has willed. Therefore, thinking what He wills, and then willing
what He thinks, He is all thought, all will, all mind, all light, all eye, all ear, all fountain   175
of every good.

192b

[1, 13, 5]
When after much effort the brethren had converted her, she persevered for a long time   916
in confession, weeping and lamenting over the defilement which she had suffered from
this magician.

193

[1, 13, 7]

    [The gnostic disciples of Marcus] have deluded many women in our own district of   916
the Rhone, by saying and doing such things. Their consciences branded as with a hot
iron (7), some of these women make a public confession (8); but others are ashamed to
do this, and in silence, as if withdrawing from themselves the hope of the life of God,
they either apostatize entirely or hesitate between the two courses.

194

[1, 22, 1]

    We hold, however, the rule of truth, according to which there is one almighty God, who   157
formed all things through His Word, and fashioned and made all things which exist out   158
of that which did not exist; in which regard the Scripture says: "For by the Word of   284
the Lord were the heavens established, and all their strength by the Spirit of His   461
mouth (9)." And again, "All things were made through Him, and without Him was
made nothing (10)." From *all,* however, there is no exception; and the Father made   460
all things through Him, whether visible or invisible, whether of sense or of intelligence,   232
whether temporal and for a certain dispensation or eternal and through the ages.

195

[1, 27, 2]

    [Marcion], moreover, mutilated the Gospel according to Luke, removing all that is   69
written about the generation of the Lord; and he removed much of the teaching of the   66
Lord's utterances, in which the Lord is recorded as confessing most clearly that His
Father is the Maker of the universe. He also persuaded his followers that he himself
was more truthful than those Apostles who have handed down the Gospel; and he   63
furnished them not with the Gospel but with a small part of the Gospel.   60

196

[2, 1, 1]

    Nor is He moved by anyone; rather, freely and by His Word (11) He made all things.   463
For He alone is God, He alone is Lord, He alone is Creator, He alone is Father, He alone   157
contains all and commands all to exist.

197

[2, 6, 1]

    Although the power of God is invisible, it bestows upon all a profound mental   130
intuition and a perception of His most powerful and omnipotent presence. Whence, even
if no one knows the Father except the Son, nor the Son except the Father, and those
to whom the Son has given a revelation (12), nevertheless all do know this, at least, that
there is one God and Lord of all, because the reason (13) implanted in their minds moves
them and reveals it to them.

198

[2, 9, 1]

    Creation itself reveals Him that created it; and the work made is itself suggestive of   131
Him that made it; and the world manifests Him that arranged it. Every Church through-   100
out the whole world has received this tradition from the Apostles.

199

[2, 10, 4]

Men, indeed, are not able to make something from nothing, but only from existing   461
material. God, however, is greater than men first of all in this: that when nothing existed
beforehand, He called into existence the very material for His creation.

199a

[2, 11, 1]

It is easy to demonstrate from the very words of the Lord that He acknowledges one   61
Father, Creator of the world and Fashioner of man, who was proclaimed by the Law and   460
by the Prophets; and that He knows no other, this being God over all. He teaches also
that the adoption of sons by the Father, which is eternal life and which takes place   157
through Himself, is conferred on all the just.   387

199b

[2, 13, 3]

Far removed is the Father of all from those things which operate among men, the   151
affections and the passions. He is simple, not composed of parts, without structure,
altogether like and equal to Himself alone. He is all mind (14), all spirit, all thought (15),   150
all intelligence, all reason, all ear, all eye, all light, all fountain of every good; and this is   175
the manner in which the religious and the pious are accustomed to speak of God.

200

[2, 13, 8]

[The various heretical gnostics] transfer the generation of the uttered word of men to   256
the eternal Word of God, attributing to Him a beginning of utterance and a coming into
being in a manner like to that of their own word. In what manner, then, would the Word   265
of God — indeed, the great God Himself, since He is the Word — differ from the word of
men, were He to have the same order and process of generation?

201

[2, 22, 4]

He came to save all through Himself, — all, I say, who through Him are reborn in God,   373
— infants, and children, and youths and old men. Therefore He passed through every   834
age, becoming an infant for infants, sanctifying infants; a child for children, sanctifying   835
those who are of that age, and at the same time becoming for them an example of piety,
of righteousness, and of submission; a young man for youths, becoming an example for
youths and sanctifying them for the Lord. So also He became an old man for old men
so that He might be the perfect teacher in all things, — perfect not only in respect to   62
the setting forth of truth, but perfect also in respect to relative age, — sanctifying the
elderly and at the same time becoming an example to them. Then He even experienced
death itself, so that He might be the firstborn from the dead, having the first place in all
things (16), the originator of life (17), before all and preceding all.

202

[2, 26, 3]

But what if someone should ask us whether every individual of all the things which   189
have been made and which are being made is known to God; and whether each one of
these, according to His providence, has received a quantity peculiar to itself? Upon our

affirming this and acknowledging that not one of the things which have been made or are being made or which will be made escapes the knowledge of God, but through His   195
providence each one of them receives and has received its special nature and rank and individuation and quantity, . . . — if anyone, then, upon receiving our testimony and affirmation of this, should proceed to count up the sand and pebbles of the earth, and to think out the causes of the number he supposes he has found, would not his labor be in vain? And would not such a man be justly declared mad and irrational by all who have sense?

203

[2, 28, 2]

If, however, we are not able to find explanations for all those passages of Scripture   25
which are investigated, we ought not on that account seek for another God besides Him   157
who exists. This would indeed be the greatest impiety. Things of that kind we must leave to God, the One who made us, knowing full well that the Scriptures are certainly perfect, since they were spoken by the Word of God and by His Spirit.   20

204

[2, 28, 6]

Inflated unreasonably, however, you boldly claim to know the indescribable mysteries   239
of God, when even the Lord Himself, the Son of God, allowed that the Father alone   351
knows the very hour and day of judgment, when He plainly stated: "Of that day, however, and the hour, no one knows, not even the Son, but the Father only (18)." If, then, the Son was not ashamed to refer the knowledge of that day to the Father, but said what was true, neither ought we be ashamed to reserve to God what are questions of major importance to us; for no one is above the teacher (19).

If, then, someone say to us: "How, indeed, is the Son produced from the Father?" — we answer him, that no one understands that production or generation or calling or revelation or whatever name be given to His generation, which in fact is indescribable. Neither Valentine nor Marcion nor Saturnine nor Basilides (20) nor Angels nor Archangels nor Principalities nor Powers but only the Father who generated and the Son who was born. Since, therefore, His generation is indescribable, those who attempt to set forth the generations and productions cannot be in their right mind, when they undertake to describe the indescribable.

205

[2, 30, 9]

Of His own accord and by His own power He made all things and arranged and   460
perfected them; and His will is the substance of all things (21). He alone, then, is   463
found to be God; He alone is omnipotent, who made all things; He alone is Father,   157
who founded and formed all things, visible and invisible, sensible and insensate,   158
heavenly and earthly, by the Word of His Power (22). And He has fitted and arranged   188
all things by His Wisdom; and while He comprehends all, He can be comprehended by   173
none. He is Himself the Designer, Himself the Builder, Himself the Inventor, Himself the Maker, Himself the Lord of all. . . .

This Father of our Lord Jesus Christ is revealed through His Word, who is His Son —   260
through Him is He revealed and made manifest to all to whom He is revealed. For they know Him, those to whom the Son has given revelation. The Son, however, always co-existing with the Father, of old and from the beginning, always reveals the Father to   256
the Angels and Archangels and Powers and Virtues and to all to whom God wishes to give revelation.

206

[2, 34, 2]

If any persons maintain, in regard to this matter, that souls, which began but recently   502
to exist, cannot endure for very long, but to be immortal they must be unborn (23),
or if they had a beginning by way of generation they must die with the body itself:
let them learn that to be without beginning and without end, to be truly and always the   156
same, and to remain ever without change, belongs to God alone, who is Lord of all.
All things, however, which are from Him, all that have been made and which will be
made, receive each their own beginning of existence; and inasmuch as they are not   468
unbegotten, in this way they are inferior to Him who made them. They perdure, however,
and continue through a length of ages, according to the will of God their Maker; for
indeed, He makes them to be in the beginning, and afterwards gives them continuance.   530

207

[2, 34, 3]

In the same way that the heavens which are above us, the firmament and the sun and   468
the moon and the rest of the stars and all their grandeur, did not always exist, but have
been created and continue for a long time according to the will of God, so also he will   530
not be far wrong who thinks likewise of souls and spirits and each and every created
thing; for everything that has been made had a beginning to its own existence, and will
continue for as long as God wills it to exist and to continue.

208

[3, 1, 1]

We have learned the plan of our salvation from none other than those through whom
the gospel came down to us. Indeed, they first preached the gospel, and afterwards, by
the will of God, they handed it down to us in the Scriptures, to be the foundation and
pillar of our faith. . . . They went forth to the ends of the earth, spreading the good
news of the good things which God has sent to us, and announcing the peace of heaven   60
to men, who indeed are all equally and individually sharers in the gospel of God. Matthew   61
also issued among the Hebrews a written Gospel in their own language, while Peter and   64
Paul were evangelizing in Rome and laying the foundation of the Church. After their   432
departure, Mark, the disciple and interpreter of Peter, also handed down to us in writing   65
what had been preached by Peter. Luke also, the companion of Paul, set down in a book   66
the Gospel preached by him. Afterwards, John, the disciple of the Lord who reclined at   67
His bosom (24), also published a Gospel, while he was residing at Ephesus in Asia.

209

[3, 3, 1]

It is possible, then, for everyone in every Church, who may wish to know the truth,   102
to contemplate the tradition of the Apostles which has been made known throughout the
whole world. And we are in a position to enumerate those who were instituted bishops
by the Apostles, and their successors to our own times: men who neither knew nor   440
taught anything like these heretics rave about. For if the Apostles had known hidden
mysteries which they taught to the elite secretly and apart from the rest, they would
have handed them down especially to those very ones to whom they were committing
the self-same Churches. For surely they wished all those and their successors to be
perfect and without reproach, to whom they handed on their authority.

210

[3, 3, 2]

But since it would be too long to enumerate in such a volume as this the successions   422
of all the Churches, we shall confound all those who, in whatever manner, whether through   102
self-satisfaction or vainglory, or through blindness and wicked opinion, assemble other than
where it is proper, by pointing out here the successions of the bishops of the greatest
and most ancient Church known to all, founded and organized at Rome by the two most   434
glorious Apostles, Peter and Paul, that Church which has the tradition and the faith which   432
comes down to us after having been announced to men by the Apostles. For with this
Church, because of its superior origin, all Churches must agree, that is, all the faithful in
the whole world; and it is in her that the faithful everywhere have maintained the
Apostolic tradition (25).

211

[3, 3, 3]

The blessed Apostles [Peter and Paul], having founded and built up the Church [of   432
Rome], they handed over the office of the episcopate to Linus. Paul makes mention
of this Linus in the Epistle to Timothy (26). To him succeeded Anencletus; and after   42
him, in the third place from the Apostles, Clement was chosen for the episcopate. He had
seen the blessed Apostles and was acquainted with them. It might be said that He still
heard the echoes of the preaching of the Apostles, and had their traditions before his
eyes. And not only he, for there were many still remaining who had been instructed by   102
the Apostles.

In the time of Clement, no small dissension having arisen among the brethren in Corinth,   434
the Church in Rome sent a very strong letter to the Corinthians, exhorting them to peace   435
and renewing their faith. . . . To this Clement, Evaristus succeeded; and Alexander
succeeded Evaristus. Then, sixth after the Apostles, Sixtus was appointed; after him,
Telesphorus, who also was gloriously martyred. Then Hyginus; after him, Pius; and
after him, Anicetus. Soter succeeded Anicetus, and now, in the twelfth place after the
Apostles, the lot of the episcopate has fallen to Eleutherus. In this order, and by the
teaching of the Apostles handed down in the Church, the preaching of the truth has come
down to us.

212

[3, 3, 4]

Polycarp, however, was instructed not only by the Apostles, and conversed with many
who had seen Christ, but was also appointed bishop of the Church in Smyrna, by the   440
Apostles in Asia. I saw him in my early youth; for he tarried a long time, and when   62
quite old he departed this life in a glorious and most noble martyrdom. He always taught
those things which he had learned from the Apostles, and which the Church had handed   102
down, and which are true. To these things all the Churches in Asia bear witness, as do
also the successors of Polycarp even to the present time. . . . Once he was met by Marcion,
who said to him, "Do you recognize me?" and Polycarp replied, "I recognize you as the
firstborn of Satan!"

213

[3, 4, 1]

When, therefore, we have such proofs, it is not necessary to seek among others the   450
truth which is easily obtained from the Church. For the Apostles, like a rich man in a   102
bank, deposited with her most copiously everything which pertains to the truth; and   104

everyone whosoever wishes draws from her the drink of life (27). For she is the entrance
to life, while all the rest are thieves and robbers. That is why it is surely necessary to   420
avoid them, while cherishing with the utmost diligence the things pertaining to the Church,   415
and to lay hold of the tradition of truth. What then? If there should be a dispute over
some kind of question, ought we not have recourse to the most ancient Churches in which   422
the Apostles were familiar, and draw from them what is clear and certain in regard to that
question? What if the Apostles had not in fact left writings to us? Would it not be
necessary to follow the order of tradition, which was handed down to those to whom they
entrusted the Churches?

214

[3, 11, 7]
   There is such certainty surrounding the Gospels that the heretics themselves bear   61
witness to them; and starting from the Gospels, each one of them attempts to establish   69
his own doctrine. The Ebionites, using only the Gospel of Matthew, are confuted by it   64
when they make false suppositions concerning the Lord. Marcion, who mutilates that of   66
Luke, is proved a blasphemer of the only existing God, by those parts which are still
retained. Those who separate Jesus from the Christ, saying that Christ remained unsub-   302
jected to suffering and that it was Jesus who suffered, would be able to correct their   347
errors if they would make use of the Gospel of Mark and read it with a love of truth.   65
Those who follow Valentine, making copious use of the Gospel of John to illustrate   67
their conjugations (28), will by that very Gospel be proved to have said nothing rightly.

215

[3, 11, 8]
   It is not possible that the Gospels can be either greater or fewer in number than they   61
are. Just as there are four regions of the world in which we live, and four universal winds,
and since the Church is disseminated over all the earth, and the pillar and mainstay (29)   404
of the Church is the Gospel, the breath of life, it is fitting that she have four pillars,
breathing immortality on every side and enkindling life in men anew. From
this it is evident that the Word, the Artificer of all, who sits upon the Cherubim and
embraces all things, and who was manifested to man, has given us a four-fold gospel   60
embracing one spirit.

217

[3, 15, 1]
   Neither can anyone (30) contend that Paul was not an Apostle, when he was elected   403
to it, nor can anyone prove Luke guilty of falsehood, when he announces the truth to
us most diligently. Perhaps it was to this end that God set forth through Luke much of   66
the gospel which it is necessary for all to use: that all who follow Luke's later testimony,
in which he treats of the acts and doctrine of the Apostles, having an unadulterated rule
of truth, may be saved. His testimony, therefore, is true, and the doctrine of the
Apostles is open and firm, holding nothing back. They did not teach one body of doctrine
privately and another in public.

217a

[3, 16, 6]
   In all things, however, He is man, the formation of God. Recapitulating man in   310
Himself, the invisible is made visible, the incomprehensible is made comprehensible, and
that which is not subject to suffering is made subject to suffering. The Word, becoming

man, recapitulates all things in Himself, so that just as the Word of God is foremost in
things super-celestial, spiritual, and invisible, so also in things visible and corporeal He   313
might have the primacy; and so that, in taking the primacy to Himself, and in constituting   401
Himself the Head of the Church, He might at the proper time draw all things to Himself.

218

[3, 16, 9]

If the one did indeed suffer while the other remained incapable of suffering; and if
the one, indeed, was born, but the other descended upon Him that was born and afterwards left Him; then it is evident that there were not one but two. . . . Make no
mistake: Jesus Christ the Son of God is one and the same, who by suffering reconciled   302
us to God, who rose from the dead, who is at the right hand of the Father, and perfect   329
in all things. . . . For He Himself truly worked salvation, He Himself is the Word of God,   301
Himself the Only-begotten of the Father, Christ Jesus our Lord.

219

[3, 17, 1]

And again, giving the disciples the power of regenerating in God, He said to them: 752
"Go and teach all nations, and baptize them in the name of the Father, and of the Son,   826
and of the Holy Spirit (31)." This He promised through the Prophets, that in the last
days He would pour out upon His servants and handmaids the ability to prophesy (32).
Therefore He did also descend upon the Son of God made Son of man, becoming   753
accustomed with Him to dwell among the human race, to rest with men, to dwell in the
workmanship of God, working the will of the Father in them, and renewing them from
their old ways into the newness of Christ.

220

[3, 17, 2]

The Lord promised to send us the Paraclete, who would make us ready for God (33).   650
Just as dry wheat without moisture cannot become one dough or one loaf, so also, we
who are many cannot be made one in Christ Jesus, without the water from heaven.
Just as dry earth cannot bring forth fruit unless it receive moisture, so also we, being at
first a dry tree, can never bring forth fruit unto life, without the voluntary rain from
above. Our bodies achieve unity through the washing which leads to incorruption; our   836
souls, however, through the Spirit. Both, then, are necessary, for both lead us on to the
life of God.

221

[3, 18, 6]

If He did not truly suffer, no thanks to Him; and when we shall begin really to suffer,   347
if He Himself did not in reality suffer before us, He will seem to have led us astray when
He exhorted us to be beaten and to turn the other cheek (34). As He misled those [who
maintain that He suffered only in appearance], by seeming to be what He was not, so also
He misleads us, exhorting us to endure what He Himself did not endure. . . . [7] Therefore,   323
as I said before, He united man with God. For if man had not conquered the enemy of   374
man, the foe would not have been rightly vanquished.   314

222

[3, 19, 1]

But not knowing Him, who, from the Virgin, is Emmanuel, they are deprived of   781
His gift, which is life eternal. And not receiving the Word of incorruption, they remain
in mortal flesh and are the debtors of death, not having received the antidote of life.
. . . [2] Nevertheless, what cannot be said of anyone else who ever lived, that He is   301
Himself in His own right God and Lord and Eternal King and Only-begotten and Incarnate
Word, proclaimed as such by all the Prophets and by the Apostles and by the Spirit   81
Himself, may be seen by all who have attained to even a small portion of the truth.
The Scriptures would not have borne witness to these things concerning Him, if, like
everyone else, He were mere man. But that He had in Himself what no other ever had,
that pre-eminent generation by the Most High Father; and that He also experienced that
pre-eminent birth from a Virgin, — the divine Scriptures testify to both in His regard.

223

[3, 21, 10]

The Word Himself, born of Mary who was still a Virgin, rightly received in birth the   779
recapitulation of Adam, thereby recapitulating Adam in Himself (35).   781,376

224

[3, 22, 4]

Consequently, then, Mary the Virgin is found to be obedient, saying: "Behold, O
Lord, your handmaid; be it done to me according to your word (36)." Eve, however,
was disobedient; and when yet a virgin, she did not obey. Just as she, who was then
still a virgin although she had Adam for a husband, — for in Paradise they were both
naked but were not ashamed (37); for, having been created only a short time, they had   521
no understanding of the procreation of children and it was necessary that they first come
to maturity before beginning to multiply, — having become disobedient, was made the   614
cause of death for herself and for the whole human race; so also Mary, betrothed to a
man but nevertheless still a virgin, being obedient, was made the cause of salvation for
herself and for the whole human race. . . . Thus, the knot of Eve's disobedience was   386
loosed by the obedience of Mary. What the virgin Eve had bound in unbelief, the Virgin   784
Mary loosed through faith.   781

224a

[3, 23, 2]

But this man [of whom I have been speaking] is Adam, if the truth be told, the   614
first-formed man. . . . We, however, are all from him; and as we are from him, we have
inherited his title.

225

[3, 23, 5]

Resisting the wanton impulse of the flesh, for he had lost his natural disposition and   612
child-like mind, and had come to a knowledge of evil, [Adam] girded both himself and
his wife with a bridle of continence, fearing God and expecting His coming, and indicating
something such as this: "Inasmuch," he said, "as I have lost by disobedience the mantle   610
of holiness which I had from the Spirit, I do acknowledge that I am worthy of such a   520
covering, which provides no comfort, but stings and irritates the body (38)."

226

[3, 24, 1]

The preaching of the Church truly continues without change and is everywhere the   104
same, and has the testimony of the Prophets and the Apostles and all their disciples.
. . . That in which we have faith is a firm system directed to the salvation of men; and,
since it has been received by the Church, we guard it. Constantly it has its youth
renewed by the Spirit of God, as if it were some precious deposit in an excellent vessel;   105
and it causes the vessel containing it also to be rejuvenated. . . . In the Church, God has
placed apostles, prophets and doctors, and all the other means through which the Spirit   419
works (39); in all of which none have any part who do not conform to the Church.   417
On the contrary, they defraud themselves of life by their wicked opinion and most
wretched behavior. For where the Church is, there is the Spirit of God; and where the
Spirit of God, there the Church and every grace. The Spirit, however, is Truth.

227

[4, 6, 4]

The Lord has taught us that no one is able to know God unless he be taught by God: 134
that is, without God, God cannot be known. However, it is the will of the Father that
God be known. To whomsoever the Son reveals Him, they shall know Him (40).

228

[4, 6, 6]

Through creation itself the Word reveals God as Creator; and through the world,   130
the Lord as Maker of the world; and through His formation of man, the Artificer who   131
formed him; and through the Son, the Father who begot the Son. These things are
presented to all men in the same way; but not all, however, do likewise believe.

228a

[4, 7, 4]

[The Father] is ministered to in all things by His own Offspring, and by the latter's   271
Likeness: that is, by the Son and by the Holy Spirit, by the Word and by the Wisdom,   480
whom all the angels serve and to whom they are subject.   492

229

[4, 11, 2]

God differs from man in this, that God makes, but man is made. Surely that which   153
makes is always the same; but that which is made must receive a beginning, a middle,
addition and increase. God, indeed, creates well; and man is well-created. God
certainly is perfect in everything, being equal and similar to Himself, inasmuch as He is   150
all light, all mind, all substance, and source of all good; and man truly receives advancement and increase towards God.

230

[4, 12, 3]

Inasmuch as in the Law and in the Gospel the first and greatest commandment is to   50
love the Lord God whole-heartedly, and then there is another like it, to love one's
neighbor as oneself (41), it is shown that the Law and the Gospel have one and the same
Author. The precepts of the perfect life, since they are the same in both Testaments,
point out the same God, who certainly has prescribed particular precepts adapted to each,

while for the more prominent and greatest commandments, without which it is not possible to be saved, He recommends the same in both.

231

[4, 14, 1]

    In the beginning, therefore, God formed Adam, not as if needing him, but that He   465
might have someone on whom to bestow His benefits. Not only before Adam, but
before anything was created, the Word glorified His Father, remaining in Him. And
He was Himself glorified by the Father, as He Himself says: "Father, glorify me with
the glory which I had with You, before the world existed (42)." Nor did He need our
service when He ordered us to follow Him; but thus He bestowed salvation upon us.

232

[4, 17, 5]

    Again, giving counsel to His disciples to offer to God the first-fruits from among His   852
creatures, not as if He needed them, but so that they themselves might be neither unfruit-   897
ful nor ungrateful, He took from among creation that which is bread, and gave thanks,
saying, "This is My Body (43)." The cup likewise, which is from among the creation to
which we belong, He confessed to be His Blood.

    He taught the new sacrifice of the new covenant, of which Malachias, one of the twelve   890
prophets, had signified beforehand: " 'You do not do My will,' says the Lord Almighty,   894
'and I will not accept a sacrifice at your hands. For from the rising of the sun to its
setting My name is glorified among the gentiles, and in every place incense is offered to
My name, and a pure sacrifice; for great is My name among the gentiles,' says the Lord
Almighty (44)." By these words He makes it plain that the former people will cease to
make offerings to God; but that in every place sacrifice will be offered to Him, and
indeed, a pure one; for His name is glorified among the gentiles.

233

[4, 18, 2]

    Sacrifice as such has not been reprobated. There were sacrifices then, sacrifices among   892
the people; and there are sacrifices now, sacrifices in the Church. Only the kind has been   890
changed; for now the sacrifice is offered not by slaves but by free men.

234

[4, 18, 4]

    But what consistency is there in those who hold that the bread over which thanks have   851
been given is the Body of their Lord, and the cup His Blood, if they do not acknowledge
that He is the Son of the Creator of the world, that is, His Word, through whom the wood   284
bears fruit, and the fountains gush forth, and the earth gives first the blade, then the ear,
then the full grain on the ear (45)? [5] How can they say that the flesh which has been   879
nourished by the Body of the Lord and by His Blood gives way to corruption and does
not partake of life? Let them either change their opinion, or else stop offering the things
mentioned (46).

    For thanksgiving is consistent with our opinion; and the Eucharist confirms our
opinion (47). For we offer to Him those things which are His, declaring in a fit manner
the gift and the acceptance (48) of flesh and spirit. For as the bread from the earth,   863
receiving the invocation of God, is no longer common bread but the Eucharist,
consisting of two elements, earthly and heavenly, so also our bodies, when they receive
the Eucharist, are no longer corruptible but have the hope of resurrection into eternity (49).

234a

[4, 19, 2]

Truly great are the heavenly treasures. God cannot be measured in the heart; nor   154
can He be comprehended in the mind, He that comprehends the earth in the hollow of   173
His hand. Who knows the measure of His right hand? Who knows but His finger, or
understands His hand — that hand which measures immensity; that hand which by its
own measure takes the measure of the heavens, and which holds in its palm the earth
and its depths; which contains in itself the width and length and depth below and
height above of all creation; which is seen and heard and understood, and which is
invisible?

235

[4, 20, 1]

It was not angels, then, who made us nor who formed us, nor did angels have the
power to make an image of God. It was not some power existing far from the Father
of the universe, nor was it anyone else, other than the Word of the Lord. God had no   284
need of others to make what He had already determined of Himself to make, as if   467
He had not His own hands. For with Him always are the Word and the Wisdom, the   283
Son and the Spirit, through whom and in whom He made all things freely and spon-   230
taneously; and to whom He spoke, saying: "Let us make man in our image and   463
likeness (50)."   233

236

[4, 20, 5]

[The Prophets said], in regard to His greatness and marvelous glory: "No one shall   170
see God and live (51)." The Father is incomprehensible (52); but because of His love
and kindness (53), and because all things are possible with Him, He concedes even this to
those who love Him: that is, to see God, even as the Prophets prophesied (54). For
things that are impossible with men are possible with God (55). Man does not by his
own power see God. But if He wills it, He is seen by men — by whom He wills it, when   172
He wills it, and in the manner in which He wills it. God is powerful in all things. He was
seen through the Spirit of Prophecy, and by His own choice (56) through the Son. He
will also be seen as the Father (57) in the kingdom of heaven. The Spirit prepares man   1041
through the Son of God, the Son leads him to the Father, and the Father gives him
incorruption in eternal life, which comes to everyone by the fact of his seeing God (58).

237

[4, 26, 2]

It is necessary to obey those who are the presbyters in the Church, those who, as we   422
have shown, have succession from the Apostles; those who have received, with the   440
succession of the episcopate, the sure charism of truth according to the good pleasure of   965
the Father. But the rest, who have no part in the primitive succession and assemble   415
wheresoever they will, must be held in suspicion.

238

[4, 27, 2]

The Lord descended into the regions beneath the earth, announcing there the good   390
news (59) of His coming and of the remission of sins conferred upon those who believe   60
in Him.

239

[4, 28, 2]
   As in the New Testament man's faith in God has been increased by the addition of   103
the Son of God, whereby man becomes a partaker of God, so also is there an increase in   313
diligence in our lives, since we are commanded to abstain not only from evil deeds, but
even from the thoughts themselves and from wicked talk and empty language and   632
scurrilous words. So also is the penalty increased of those who do not believe the Word
of God and despise His coming and whose attention is directed to the past; for it is not   1034
merely temporal, but eternal. For to whomsoever the Lord shall say, "Depart from Me,
accursed ones, into the everlasting fire (60)," they will be damned forever; and to
whomsoever He shall say, "Come, blessed of My Father, receive the inheritance of the   1043
kingdom, which has been prepared for you in eternity (61)," they shall receive the
kingdom forever.

240

[4, 33, 2]
   If the Lord were from other than the Father, how could He rightly take bread, which   852
is of the same creation as our own, and confess it to be His Body, and affirm that the   861
mixture in the cup is His Blood?

241

[4, 33, 7]
   [A truly spiritual disciple] shall judge those who make schism and are destitute of the   420
love of God, who look to their own advantage rather than to the unity of the Church, who
for any kind of trifling reason cut apart and divide the great and glorious body of Christ,
and destroy it insofar as they are able — men who talk of peace while making war.
. . . He shall judge also those who are outside the bounds of truth, that is, those who are   415
outside the Church; but he himself shall be judged by no one.

242

[4, 33, 8]
   The true gnosis is the doctrine of the Apostles, and the ancient organization of the   100
Church throughout the whole world, and the manifestation of the body of Christ according   440
to the successions of bishops, by which successions the bishops have handed down the
Church which is found everywhere; and the very complete tradition of the Scriptures,   101
which have come down to us by being guarded against falsification, and which are   104
received without addition or deletion; and reading without falsification, and a legitimate
and diligent exposition according to the Scriptures, without danger and without
blasphemy; and the pre-eminent gift of love, which is more precious than knowledge,   591
more glorious than prophecy, and more honored than all the other charismatic gifts.

243

[4, 33, 9]
   In every place and in every age, the Church, because of the love which she has for   88
God, sends forth to the Father a multitude of martyrs. All the others, however, not only
have nothing of this kind to point to among themselves, but even declare that such
witnessing is not at all necessary.

244

[4, 37, 1]

Those words, however, in which He says: "How often would I have gathered your
children together, but you would not (62)," make clear the ancient law of human   505
liberty; for God made man free from the beginning, so that he possessed his own power   613
just as his own soul, to follow God's will freely, not being compelled by God. For with 700
God there is no coercion; but a good will is present with Him always. He, therefore,   695
gives good counsel to all. In man as well as in angels — for angels are rational — He has 486
placed a power of choice, so that those who obeyed might justly possess the good things   636
which, indeed, God gives, but which they themselves must preserve.

Those who have not obeyed will not be found worthy to possess the good, and will
receive deserved punishment; for God did kindly bestow the good upon them, but they
did not guard it carefully, nor regard it as something precious, but were contemptuous
of His most eminent goodness. . . . God, therefore, has given good, . . .and they who
work with it will receive glory and honor, because they have done good when they were
able to do otherwise. But those who do not do it will receive God's just judgment,
because they did not do good when they were able to do it.

245

[4, 37, 5]

Not merely in works, but even in faith man's freedom of choice under his own control   553
is preserved by the Lord, who says, "Let it be done to you according to your faith (63),"
showing therewith that man has a faith of his own, just as he has judgment especially his
own. And again, "All things are possible to him that believes (64);" and "Go, as you
have believed, so be it done to you (65)." All such expressions demonstrate that man is, 758
as far as faith is concerned, in his own control. For this reason, he that believes in Him
has eternal life; but he that does not believe in the Son does not have eternal life, and
the anger of God will remain upon him (66).

246

[4, 37, 7]

[Paul], an able wrestler, urges us on in the struggle for immortality, so that we may   770
receive a crown, and so that we may regard as a precious crown that which we acquire
by our own struggle, and which does not grow on us spontaneously. And because it comes
to us in a struggle, it is therefore the more precious; and as it is the more precious, let
us love it always the more. Those things which come to us spontaneously are not loved
as much as those which are obtained by anxious care.

247

[4, 39, 2]

If you are obstinately hardened and reject His skillful hand and show yourself
ungrateful to Him for having made you man, you will, by your becoming ungrateful
to God, have lost both life and His skill. To create is proper to the kindness of God;
but to be created is proper to the nature of man. If, then, you will render to Him
what you have, that is, faith in Him and subjection, you will be the recipient of His
skill, and will be a perfect work of God. [3] If, however, you will not believe in Him   695
and will flee His hand, the cause of the imperfection will be in you that did not obey,
but not in Him who called you. He sent, that they might call them in to the marriage
feast; and those who did not obey Him deprived themselves of the royal supper.

The skill of God, therefore, was not lacking, — for He is able to raise up stones as
children of Abraham, — but the man who does not avail himself of that skill is the
cause of his own imperfection. The light does not fail through those who have blinded

themselves; but while it remains the same as it was, the blind are involved in darkness
through their own fault. The light never enslaves anyone by necessity; nor does God
compel anyone unwilling to accept His skill. They, therefore, who have apostatized from   701
the light of the Father, and who have transgressed the law of liberty, have apostatized
through their own fault, since they were created free and with the power of determining
their own opinion.

248

[5, *Preface*]

It will be necessary both for you and for all who read this writing to read it with
full attention to what I have written above, so that you may know the actual substance
of the doctrines against which I am presenting refutations. For it is thus that you will
both refute them properly and will choose refutations already prepared against them;
and by means of the celestial faith, you will reject their opinions as dung. You will,
however, follow the only true and reliable Teacher, the Word of God, Jesus Christ our   301
Lord, who, on account of His great love, became what we are, so that He might bring   372
us to be what He Himself is.

249

[5, 2, 2]

They are vain in every respect, who despise the entire dispensation of God, and deny   502
the salvation of the body and spurn its regeneration, saying that it is not capable of   374
immortality. If the body be not saved, then, in fact, neither did the Lord redeem us with
His Blood; and neither is the cup of the Eucharist the partaking of His Blood nor is   851
the Bread which we break the partaking of His Body (67). . . . As we are His members,
so too are we nourished by means of created things, He Himself granting us the creation,
causing His sun to rise and sending rain as He wishes. He has declared the cup, a part of
creation, to be His own Blood, from which He causes our blood to flow; and the bread,   878
a part of creation, He has established as His own Body, from which He gives increase to
our bodies.   861

[3] When, therefore, the mixed cup and the baked bread receives the Word (68) of God   860
and becomes the Eucharist, the Body of Christ, and from these the substance of our   856
flesh is increased and supported, how can they say that the flesh is not capable of
receiving the gift of God, which is eternal life — flesh which is nourished by the Body   879
and Blood of the Lord, and is in fact a member of Him?

In this regard the blessed Paul says in his Epistle to the Ephesians: "Because we
are members of His Body, from His flesh and His bones (69)." . . . In the same way that   1011
the wood of the vine planted in the ground bears fruit in due season; or as a grain of
wheat, falling on the ground, decomposes and rises up in manifold increase through the
Spirit of God who contains all things; and then, through the Wisdom of God, comes to
the service of men, and receiving the Word (70) of God, becomes the Eucharist, which is
the Body and Blood of Christ; so also our bodies, nourished by it, and deposited in the
earth and decomposing therein, shall rise up in due season, the Word of God favoring them
with resurrection in the glory of God the Father.

250

[5, 3, 2]

God, taking soil from the earth, made man. And surely it is much more difficult and   509
more incredible that from non-existent bones and nerves and veins (71) and the rest of
the human system, He makes him to exist, and in fact raises him up as an animated and
rational living being, than that He restores again that which had been made, for the   1011

reasons already mentioned (72), after it has been dissolved in the earth and has returned to that from which man was made, when in the beginning he had not yet been made. For in the beginning when He willed, He made him who was not; and much more readily will He restore again him who had existed, when He wills that life be given him.

251

[5, 6, 1]

   Those are perfect who have had the Spirit of God continuing in them, and who have   750
preserved their souls and bodies without blame, holding fast to God, that is, to faith in   753
God, while observing justice in regard to their neighbor. [2] Whence also [Paul] says
that this creation is the temple of God: "Do you not know," he says, "that you are a
temple of God, and that the Spirit of God dwells in you? If anyone violate the temple
of God, him will God destroy. For the temple of God, which you are, is holy (73)."
He plainly says, then, that the body is a temple in which the Spirit dwells.

252

[5, 7, 1]

   And again, [Paul] says to the Romans: "But if His Spirit, who raised Jesus from the   1011
dead, dwells in you, He that raised Christ from the dead will make also your mortal
bodies to live (74)." What, then, are mortal bodies? Are they souls? But souls, as
compared to mortal bodies, are incorporeal: for God breathed into the face of man the
breath of life, and man became a living soul (75). The breath of life, however, is   501
incorporeal. And certainly they cannot say that the breath of life is itself mortal. In   502
this regard David says, "And for Him my soul shall live (76)," just as if its substance were
immortal.
   But neither can they say that the spirit is the mortal body. What, then, is there left
to call the mortal body, except that which was shaped, that is, the flesh, of which it is
also said that God will make it to live? It is this which dies and is decomposed, but not   990
the soul nor the spirit. For to die is to lose the vital ability and to become henceforth
without breath and inanimate and incommunicative, and to melt away into those elements
from which it had the beginning of substance. But this happens neither to the soul, for
it is the breath of life, nor to the spirit, for it is simple spirit and not a composite, and
cannot be decomposed, and is itself the life of those who receive it.

253

[5, 10, 1]

   Those men who are not bringing forth fruits of righteousness, being covered as it
were by thorn bushes, if they observe diligence and receive the Word of God as if grafted
on them, they will arrive at the pristine nature of men — that which was made in the   520
image and likeness of God. [2] Just as the wild olive, having been grafted, does not lose   740
the substance of its wood, but changes the quality of its fruit and receives another name,
no longer being called wild olive but fruit-bearing olive (77), so also when a man has been
grafted through faith and receives the Spirit of God, certainly he does not lose the   750
substance of flesh, but changes the quality of the fruit of his works and receives another
name, signifying that which is a change for the better. He is no longer merely flesh and
blood, but is a spiritual man and is called such.

254

[5, 14, 1]

If the flesh were not in a position to be saved, the Word of God would certainly not   360
have become flesh. And if the blood of the righteous were not to be sought after, the
Lord would certainly not have had blood.

255

[5, 16, 3]

Indeed, through the first Adam, we offended God by not observing His command.   614
Through the second Adam, however, we are reconciled, and are made obedient even unto   376
death. For we were debtors to none other except to Him, whose commandment we
transgressed at the beginning.

256

[5, 18, 2]

And thus it is shown that there is one God the Father, who is above all and through   259
all and in all. The Father indeed is above all, and He is the Head of Christ. But the Word 230
is through all, and He is the Head of the Church. The Spirit, however, is in us all, and He 402
is the Living Water (78) which the Lord grants to those who rightly believe in Him and love
Him and who know that there is one Father, who is above all and through all and in us
all (79).

256a

[5, 19, 1]

The Virgin Mary, . . . being obedient to His word, received from an angel the glad   779
tidings that she would bear God (80).

257

[5, 20, 1]

For all these [heretics] are of much later date than are the bishops to whom the   102
Apostles handed over the Churches; and this fact I pointed out most carefully in the   440
third book. It is of necessity, then, that these aforementioned heretics, because they
are blind to the truth, walk in various and devious paths; and on this account the   415
vestiges (81) of their doctrine are scattered about without agreement or connection. The
path of those, however, who belong to the Church, goes around the whole world; for it   404
has the firm tradition of the Apostles, enabling us to see that the faith of all is one and the 420
same.

258

[5, 24, 3]

The devil, however, since he is an apostate angel, is able, as he was in the beginning, to   494
lead astray and to deceive the mind of man for the transgressing of God's commands. And
little by little he can darken the hearts of those who would try to serve him, to the point
that, forgetting the true God, they adore him as if he were God.

259

[5, 31, 2]

For since the Lord went away into the midst of the shadow of death (82) where the   391
souls of the dead were, and afterwards arose in the body, and after the resurrection was   390

taken up, it is clear that the souls also of His disciples, on account of which the Lord
underwent these things, will go away into the place (83) allotted them by God. And   996
there they will delay until the resurrection, waiting to be raised up. After receiving their   1011
bodies, and rising up perfectly, bodily that is, just as the Lord arose, they shall come thus
into the sight of God.

260 ·

[5, 32, 1]

It is necessary to explain in regard to these matters, that it is fitting for the righteous   1016
first to receive the promised inheritance which God promised to the fathers, and then to
reign in it when they rise again to the sight of God in this same state of creation when it
is renewed; and that the judgment should take place afterwards. For it is just that in the
very state of creation in which they labored or were afflicted, having been proved in every
way by suffering, they should receive the fruit of their suffering; and that in the very
state of creation in which they were slain for the love of God, they should be made to
live again; and that in the state of creation in which they endured servitude, they should
reign. For God is rich in all things, and all things are His. It is fitting, therefore, that
creation itself, restored to its pristine state, should serve the righteous without stinting.

261

[5, 33, 3]

The elders who saw John, the disciple of the Lord, remembered that they had heard   62
him say that the Lord taught in regard to those times: "The days will come, in which vines   1016
shall grow, each having ten thousand branches, and on each branch ten thousand twigs;
and in fact, on each twig, ten thousand shoots; and on each and every shoot, ten
thousand clusters; and on each and every cluster, ten thousand grapes; and each and every
grape when pressed shall yield twenty-five measures of wine (84). And when anyone of
the saints takes hold of one of the clusters, another will cry out, 'I am a better cluster,
take me, bless the Lord through me!'" . . . [4] These things, too, Papias, a man of
ancient times who was a hearer of John and a companion of Polycarp, attests in writing
in the fourth of his books (85). He composed five books.

1. Ps. 145 [146]:6. Acts 4:24; 14:15.
2. παρουσίαν.
3. ἀνακεφαλαιώσασθαι τὰ πάντα. Eph. 1:10.
4. Phil. 2:10-11.
5. Eph. 6:12.
6. Matt. 10:24. Luke 6:40. The term employed in the Greek is not δεσπότην but διδάσκαλον; and although
   magistrum means either and is a fair rendering in the old Latin version, those who translate the passage into
   English saying no one is greater than the Master, as one reads in the Ante-Nicene Fathers series, do so only
   at the risk of allowing their theological bias to show. It ought to be clear enough to all that in the present
   context the teacher is the Church itself. Such translators may well plead that master is generally the word
   used in English versions of Scripture; but these versions do not give master an upper-case initial.
7. 1 Tim. 4:2.
8. εἰς φανερὸν ἐξομολογοῦνται.
9. Ps. 32 [33]:6. We have capitalized Word and Spirit, in accord with the thought of Irenaeus.
10. John 1:3.
11. The Greek of this passage is lacking. We are conjecturing that sua sententia et libere in the Latin represents
    something like διὰ τοῦ λόγου αὐτοῦ ἐλευθέρως in the lost Greek.
12. Matt. 11:27; Luke 10:22. Irenaeus cites the passage in the same way that Justin quotes it (§ 127 above).
13. Ratio in the Latin must represent ὁ λόγος in the lost Greek. The concept here is that of Justin's seminal
    word, by which every man possesses a λόγος which is but a seed of the Divine Λόγος. The concept has its
    origins in Plato, but is refined and christianized in Justin.
14. Sensus in the Latin probably represents νοῦς in the lost Greek.
15. Sensuabilitas in the Latin was probably νόησις in the lost Greek.
16. Col. 1:18.
17. The princeps vitae of the Latin version very probably translates ἀρχηγὸς τῆς ζωῆς in the lost Greek, a phrase
    which occurs in Acts 3:15.

18. Mark 13:32.
19. Matt. 10:24. Lk. 6:40.
20. The four men named were proponents of as many gnostic systems; and a special note of the heresy of each is their explanation of the generation of the Son. Up to the present place in the *Adversus haereses* it is precisely their heresies which have been the chief objects of Irenaeus' refutations.
21. *I.e.,* by His will all things are what they are.
22. Heb. 1:3.
23. The sense of the passage demands that we understand *unborn* as meaning *increate* or *without a beginning.* The Latin *innascibiles* readily admits only the meaning *unborn;* but it must certainly represent the term ἀγένητοι in the lost Greek, which term admits equally the meanings *unborn, increate,* and *without a beginning.*
24. John 13:23.
25. Unfortunately the Greek of this very important and much disputed passage is not extant. The ancient Latin version reads: *Ad hanc enim ecclesiam, propter potiorem* [var. *potentiorem*] *principalitatem, necesse est omnem convenire ecclesiam, hoc est, eos qui sunt undique fideles, in qua semper ab his, qui sunt undique conservata est ea quae est ab apostolis traditio.*
26. 2 Tim. 4:21. Which identification, however, is tenuous at best.
27. Apoc. 22:17. Irenaeus would have a better reputation among rhetoricians if he had held as tenaciously to his metaphors as he did to tradition.
28. In Valentinian gnosticism the vast membership in the pleroma is begotten through conjugation of the preceding members, the initial force, the Dyad, apparently being hermophroditic, comprising both Arrhetus, the Unspeakable, and Sige, the Silent. There is a certain sarcasm in Irenaeus' use of the term *conjugation.*
29. 1 Tim. 3:15.
30. The chapter heading indicates what is in any case fairly obvious, that the present passage is directed particularly against the Ebionites.
31. Matt. 28:19.
32. See Joel 2:28.
33. John 16:7.
34. Matt. 5:39.
35. For a short summation of Irenaeus' doctrine of Recapitulation or ἀνακεφαλαίωσις, see J. Quasten, *Patrology,* Vol. 1, pp. 295-296.
36. Luke 1:38.
37. Gen. 2:25.
38. Irenaeus was of the opinion, stated more clearly in a passage immediately preceding the part we have translated, that Adam chose to make himself a garment of fig leaves as a deliberate penance; for the sharp-pointed fig leaves annoyed his flesh, whereas he might have chosen any number of other kinds of leaves more comfortable.
39. i Cor. 12:28.
40. Matt. 11:27. Luke 10:22.
41. Matt. 22:37-39. Deut 6:5 and Lev. 19:18.
42. John 17:5.
43. Matt. 26:26; Mark 14:22; Luke 22:19; 1 Cor. 11:24.
44. Mal. 1:10-11.
45. Mark 4:28.
46. The bread and the cup.
47. ἡμῖν δὲ σύμφωνος τῇ γνώμῃ ἡ εὐχαριστία, καὶ ἡ εὐχαριστία βεβαιοῖ τὴν γνώμην.
48. κοινωνίαν καὶ αἵρεσιν.
49. In translating this passage (§ 234) we have departed from use of Harvey's text, and have followed that of K. Holl, in his *Fragmente vornicänischer Kirchenväter aus den Sacra Parallela,* in Vol. 2, new series, of *Texte und Untersuchungen,* Leipzig 1899. Two of the more important readings peculiar to Holl's edition may be seen in the two footnotes last above.
50. Gen. 1:26.
51. Ex. 33:20.
52. *incapabilis.*
53. *humanitatem.*
54. *prophetabant prophetae.*
55. Luke 18:27.
56. *adoptive.*
57. *paternaliter.*
58. The general meaning of the entire passage is quite clear, in spite of numerous minor obscurities. The Greek of the passage, unfortunately, is not extant. The frequent poor choice of words, several instances of which are evident in the preceding footnotes, are not at all typical of Irenaeus' style, apparent in other

passages where the Greek is extant. The lack of precision and a choice of words sometimes quite ludicrous like *humanitatem,* where the Greek, were it extant, would almost certainly read φιλανθρωπίαν, must be attributed to the Latin translator, whose lack of precision borders on shoddiness.

59. *evangelizantem.*
60. Matt. 25:41.
61. Matt. 25:34.
62. Matt. 23:37.
63. Matt. 9:29.
64. Mark 9:22.
65. Matt. 8:13.
66. John 3:26.
67. 1 Cor. 10:16.
68. A very considerable theological point hinges somewhat upon whether we spell *word* with a capital or a lower case *W.* If the passage be read with a lower case *W,* the *word of God* will refer to the words of institution, and the passage will readily admit of interpretation in accord with the Catholic doctrine of transubstantiation; if with a capital *W,* however, the *Word of God* must be the eternal and personal Word, and the passage will be more in accord with the concept of impanation, which Catholic theology rejects.

    While we ourselves adhere absolutely to the doctrine of transubstantiation, and while affirming that any arguments on the manner of Christ's presence in the Eucharist are of a subtlety not to be expected in so early an author as Irenaeus, we conceive that his actual words and his more likely mentality, in view of this and other passages in which he uses the term ὁ λόγος τοῦ θεοῦ, demand the upper case *W.* Moreover, the verb which we have translated *receives,* ἐπιδέχεται, might as readily be translated *receives in addition* or *admits of.* This is not to say that Irenaeus held impanation. He believed that Christ is really present in the Eucharist, and he was not concerned with how He is present. His language, however, is such that it is more indicative of an impanation mentality than of transubstantiation.

69. Eph. 5:30. The second part of the quotation, *from His flesh and His bones,* is attested by a great many Scripture manuscripts, but not by the more reliable, and is regarded as unauthentic. It is interesting to find it in Irenaeus, or at least in Irenaeus as he has come down to us. The Greek of Irenaeus is extant for the present passage, and the phrase is found both in the Greek and in the early Latin translation.
70. See note 68 above, the same observations applying here. The participle translated *receiving* is προσλαμβανόμενα, and like ἐπιδέχεται, it might also be translated *receiving in addition.* Again, however, to insist upon all its more minute theological implications, however important they be, were to attribute a subtlety to Irenaeus that he, in his circumstances, cannot possibly have had.
71. The words *and veins* are restored to the poorly preserved Greek text from the presumably more accurate Latin.
72. The phrase *for the reasons already mentioned,* like the words *and veins* of the note immediately preceding, are restored to the Greek text from the more accurate Latin.
73. 1 Cor. 3:16-17.
74. Rom. 8:11.
75. Gen. 2:7.
76. Ps. 21 [22]:30.
77. The wild olive tree is the *oleaster,* the cultivated and fruit-bearing tree being the *oliva.*
78. John 7:38-39.
79. Eph. 4:6.
80. *Ut portaret Deum.* The Greek unfortunately is not extant. Probably the sentence structure of the Latin follows closely that of the Greek, in which case the very word θεοτόκος can scarcely have been used. Nevertheless, the concept of θεοτόκος could not be clearer.
81. *vestigia.* The primary meaning of the Latin term is *footprints.* Unfortunately we have no term in English which will do full justice to Irenaeus' very clever metaphor.
82. Ps. 22 [23]:4.
83. The Latin qualifies the place as *invisibilem,* the adjective not being present in the often poorly transmitted Greek text.
84. In all, 2,500,000,000,000,000,000,000,000 measures: two sextillion five hundred quintillion by American reckoning, or two thousand five hundred trillion by British reckoning.
85. In view of the confidence which Irenaeus quite apparently places in the word of Papias, it seems only proper to point out that it was undoubtedly this same affirmation of Millenarianism or Chiliasm in the fourth of Papias' five books of the *Explanation of the Sayings of the Lord* that led Eusebius to term Papias "a man of very little intelligence." Further, be it noted that Eusebius (*Hist. Eccl.* 3, 39, 2 – § 94 above) denies the accuracy of Irenaeus' remark that Papias was a hearer of John.

PRESENTATION OF THE APOSTOLIC PREACHING [*ca. A. D.* 190 / 200]

Irenaeus' *Presentation of the Apostolic Preaching* was known only by its title until the present century, when, in 1904, the complete text of an Armenian version was discovered by Karapet Ter-Mekerttschian. The Armenian version along with a German translation thereof, edited by Ter-Mekerttschian in collaboration with Erwand Ter-Minassiantz was published in 1907 in the series *Texte und Untersuchungen* 31, 1. The Armenian has been republished several times since 1907, and besides the German translation, others have appeared in English, French, Dutch, and Italian. The Armenian, with translations in French and in English, is to be found in the *Patrologia orientalis,* Vol. 12, fasc. 5, Paris 1919.

263

[61]
As to the union, harmony, and peace among the various animals which are by nature   1017
mutually inimical and hostile, the elders (1) say that it will really be so, when Christ comes again to be King over all. In this way there is indicated as if by a parable the gathering together of men of various and different nations in peace and harmony in the name of Christ.   87
. . . And this has already happened: for those who before were quite perverse and who let no evil work undone, now that they have come to know and to believe in Christ and as soon as they have embraced the faith, have changed their manner of living, and they adhere to the severest demands of righteousness.

1. When Irenaeus introduces a chiliastic view, appealing to the authority of the elders (presbyters), it is not rash to suspect that he refers particularly to Papias. In the present instance, while perhaps not precisely rejecting the chiliastic or millenaristic inferences, Irenaeus does suggest that the general peace ascribed by certain of the elders to the millenium is already experienced as a result of membership even in the Church Militant.

FRAGMENTS OF LOST WORKS OF ST. IRENAEUS

Of Irenaeus' works other than the *Adversus haereses* and the *Presentation of the Apostolic Preaching* we possess only titles and fragments. The fragments are collected in the Migne edition, PG 7, 1225-1264, or better, W. W. Harvey, *Sancti Irenaei episcopi Lugdunensis libros quinque adversus haereses,* Vol. 2, Cambridge 1857, pp. 454-511. A new edition is very badly needed. Since all the fragments we cite (numbered as in the Migne edition) are preserved by Eusebius, the best available text will be found to be the Berlin Corpus (GCS) edition of Eusebius.

The student must beware of the so-called Pfaff fragments, published in 1715 from an alleged Turin manuscript, and long since proved to be forgeries.

FRAGMENT 2

From a letter to Florinus, a Roman priest who apostatized and joined the Valentinians. This letter circulated as a treatise under the title *On Sole Sovereignty* or *That God is not the Author of Evil.* The fragment is preserved by Eusebius in his *History of the Church* 5, 20, 4-8.

264

[5, 20, 4]

In the letter to Florinus, of which we have already spoken, Irenaeus mentions again his familiarity with Polycarp, when he says: "These doctrines, Florinus, to put it mildly, are not of sound judgment. These doctrines are not in accord with the Church, and they involve those who accept them in the greatest of impiety. These doctrines not even the heretics outside the Church have ever dared to publish. These doctrines were not handed down to you by the presbyters who came before us and who were the companions of the Apostles.

[5] "When I was still a boy I saw you in Asia Minor with Polycarp, doing splendidly in the royal court and striving to gain his approbation. [6] I remember the events of those days better than the ones of recent years. What a boy learns grows with the mind and becomes a part of him, so that I am able to describe the very place in which the blessed Polycarp sat as he discoursed, his goings and his comings, the manner of his life, his physical appearance, as well as the discourses he delivered to the people, and how he spoke of his familiar conversation with John and with the rest of those who had seen the Lord, and how he would recall their words to mind. All that he had heard from them concerning the Lord or about His miracles and about His teaching, having received it from eyewitnesses of the Word of Life (1), Polycarp related in harmony with the Scriptures.

[7] "These things were told me at that time through the mercy of God; and I listened to them attentively and noted them down, not on paper but in my heart. Continually, by the grace of God, I recall them exactly to mind. I am able to bear witness in the presence of God that if that blessed and apostolic old man had heard any such thing, he would have cried out and stopped his ears; and, as was his custom, he would have said, 'O good God, to what times you have spared me, that I should endure these things!' He would have fled away from the place where, sitting or standing, he had heard such words. [8] This can be plainly seen from his letters which he sent, either to neighboring churches to strengthen them, or to certain of the brethren, to admonish and exhort them."

102
62

63
67

FRAGMENT 3

From a letter to Victor of Rome, in regard to the Quartodeciman controversy over the computation of the date of Easter, preserved by Eusebius in his *History of the Church* 5, 24, 11-18. This is the letter in which Irenaeus besought Pope St. Victor not to excommunicate Polycrates of Ephesus (see above, pp. 82-83.)

265

[In exhorting Victor, Bishop of Rome, not to excommunicate Polycrates for refusing to abandon the Quartodeciman practice, Irenaeus wrote to Victor, saying:] [5, 24, 16]   435
" . . . And when the blessed Polycarp was visiting in Rome in the time of Anicetus, although they disagreed somewhat about certain other things, they immediately made peace with each other, not caring to quarrel in this matter. For neither was Anicetus able to persuade Polycarp not to observe what he had always observed with John, the disciple of our Lord, and the rest of the Apostles; nor was Polycarp able to persuade Anicetus to follow his observance, when Anicetus said that he felt obliged to follow the customs of the presbyters who had preceded him. [17] In this state of affairs they remained in communion with each other, and Anicetus made way for Polycarp to celebrate the Eucharist in his church, by way of doing him honor. They parted from each other in peace, and kept peace in the Church both for those who observed and for those who did not observe."

1. 1 John 1:1.

THE MURATORIAN FRAGMENT [*inter A. D.* 155 / 200]

The *Muratorian Fragment* takes its name from its discoverer, L. A. Muratori, who published it in 1740. It has been variously ascribed to Caius of Rome, Hegesippus, Clement of Alexandria, Melito of Sardes, Polycrates of Ephesus, and perhaps with a greater possibility than attaches to any of the others, to Hippolytus. The safer course, however, is to call it precisely what it is: an anonymous fragment of a date later than *The Shepherd* of Hermas and most probably before the year 200 A. D.

The fragment opens (as also, indeed, it closes) with an incomplete sentence: *quibus tamen interfuit et ita posuit.* Westcott omits the *et;* and Bunsen supplies *ipse non* before *interfuit.* To translate half a sentence is at least near to being a fool's errand; but to alter the text when only half a text stands is somewhat on the other side. But be that as it may: we have in the fragment a fairly orderly treatment of the titles contained in the New Testament; and since the first full remarks treat of the Gospels of Luke and John, presumably the opening line, as it stands, is the conclusion of the author's notice of Mark. It is not unlikely that the remark, of which we have only the conclusion, was something like this: "The second of the Gospels was written by Mark, who was neither a hearer nor a follower of the Lord, but who was a companion of Peter. In his sermons Peter gave no connected account of the words and deeds of the Savior, but preached always from his memory of Him, to suit the needs of his audience; so although Mark was not present with the Lord, Peter preached of Him in his sermons, *at which, however, he was present; and so he wrote."*

The text may be found in L. A. Muratori, *Antiquitates italicae medii aevi,* Vol. 3, Milan 1740, pp. 851-854; or G. Rauschen, *Florilegium patristicum,* fasc. 3, 2nd edition, Bonn 1914, pp. 24-34.

268

. . . . . . at which, however, he was present; and so he wrote. The third book of the   42
Gospel is that according to Luke, the well-known physician, which, after the ascension of   61
Christ, Luke wrote in his own name from what he had learned when Paul associated him   65
with himself as a companion of his journey. Nor did he himself see the Lord in the flesh;   66
but inasmuch as he was thus enabled to proceed, he began his account with the birth of
John. The fourth Gospel is by John, one of the disciples. When his fellow disciples and   67
bishops were urging him, he said, "Fast with me for the three days beginning today, and
whatever will have been revealed to us, let us recount it with each other." On that very   63
night it was revealed to the Apostle Andrew that all the things they had recalled to mind,
John should write them all in his own name. And therefore while various points are
taught in the different books of the Gospels, there is no difference to the faith of believers;
for in all of them all things are spoken under the one guiding Spirit, whether concerning
the nativity, the passion, the resurrection, conversation with His disciples, or His two
advents, the first of which was in the humiliation of rejection and is already past, and
the second in the glory of royal power, which is yet to be. It is no wonder, then, that
John constantly returns to these things even in his Epistles, saying of himself, "What we
have seen with our eyes and have heard with our ears and what our hands have touched,
these things have we written to you (1)." And thus he professes that he is not only the
eye-witness but also the hearer, and moreover, also the writer of all the marvels of the
Lord as they happened (2). The Acts of the Apostles, however, were written by Luke in   403
one book addressed to the most excellent Theophilus; and he makes it clear that these
events took place in his presence, for he omits the passion of Peter, as also the journey
of Paul when he went from the city (3) to Spain. The Epistles of Paul, however, for
those who wish to understand the matter, indicate of themselves from what place (4)

and for what cause they were sent. First of all he wrote to the Corinthians, to check schismatic opinions, then afterwards a second; to the Galatians about circumcision; to the Romans, however, at some length, about the order of Scriptures, and also to show that Christ is foremost in them (5). It is [not] necessary for us to discuss them separately, since the blessed Apostle Paul himself followed the order of his predecessor, John, and wrote to only seven Churches by name. They are, in this order: first, to the Corinthians; second, to the Ephesians; third, to the Philippians; fourth, to the Colossians; fifth, to the Galatians; sixth, to the Thessalonians; seventh, to the Romans. And indeed, although he writes again to the Corinthians and to the Thessalonians for their correction, nevertheless it is shown that there is one Church spread abroad through the whole world; for John,   404 too, in the Apocalypse, though he writes to only seven Churches, yet speaks to all. Besides these, there is one to Philemon, and one to Titus, and two to Timothy, in affection and love, but nevertheless regarded as holy in the Catholic Church, in the ordering of churchly discipline (6). There is also circulated one to the Laodiceans and another to the Alexandrians, forged under the name of Paul, in regard to the heresy of Marcion; and there are several others which cannot be received by the Church, for it is not suitable that gall be mixed with honey. The Epistle of Jude, indeed, and the two ascribed to John, are received by the Catholic Church (7). Both the Wisdom written by the friends of Solomon in his honor, and the Apocalypse of John and that of Peter we receive, which last, however, some of us do not wish to read in church. *The Shepherd*, moreover, was written by Hermas quite recently in our time, in the city of Rome, while his brother, Bishop Pius (8), sat in the chair of the Church of the city of Rome; and, therefore, it too should certainly be read. But it cannot be read publicly to the people in church, for it is neither among the Prophets, whose number is complete to the end of time, nor among the Apostles. Of Arsinous, also called Valentine, and of Miltiades, we receive nothing at all. Those also who wrote the new book of psalms for Marcion, together with Basilides, the founder of the Asian Cataphrygians . . . .

1. 1 John 1:1.
2. *per ordinem.*
3. *ab urbe* = from Rome.
4. *a quo loco.* We would rather have read *to what place.* The Latin of the fragment is extremely poor, but we dare not change so clear and common a phrase.
5. By *Scriptures* is meant the Old Testament. The author's point is that the chief burden of the Old Testament is the foretelling of Christ.
6. *I. e.,* they are regarded as inspired, and are read ceremonially in the Liturgy.
7. *in catholica habentur.* Others change *catholica* to *catholicis,* and translate *are reckoned among the Catholic Epistles.* Changing a word-ending in the fragment is no sin, for the author himself had a most distressing disregard for the conventions of grammar and orthography. However, we distrust the use of the term *Catholic Epistles* so early, especially when the word which *Catholic* qualifies is omitted, implying a very common term. We justify adding *Church* as the word qualified, because *Catholic Church* is a known term even at this early time, and had in fact been used in full just a few lines above. Secondly, to read the phrase as *among the Catholic Epistles* is less consistent with what follows, and forces us, moreover, to wonder that they are mentioned as *among* the Catholic Epistles, when we are not told what the other Catholic Epistles are.
8. Pope St. Pius I [*regn. ca. A. D.* 140 – 154 / 155]

MINUCIUS FELIX [*fl. inter A. D.* 218 / 235]

Biographical details of Minucius Felix are utterly lacking. We can say of him only that he was a Christian, a layman, a Roman, and a rather distinguished member of the legal profession in that city. He is the author of only one work, the dialogue *Octavius,* written between the years 218 and 235 A. D., the only dates which can be assigned even to himself.

OCTAVIUS [*inter A. D.* 218 / 235]

The *Octavius* is preserved in a single Paris manuscript of the 9th century, where it stands as an eighth book of Arnobius' *Against the Pagans.* It is, however, an authentic work of Minucius Felix. A work of very gentle character and of deep insight, it deserves to be much more widely read than it is at present. The date of the work given above is that assigned to it by most authors at the present time; yet, it is by no means certain — a most vexing thing, since a considerable point of historical curiosity hinges upon it. A literary dependence between the *Octavius* and Tertullian's *Apology,* the latter dating from 197 A. D., is obvious. Their arguments are too similar, couched in much the same terms and developed in much the same fashion, to admit of coincidence. Both Minucius and Tertullian wrote in Latin, and whichever of them has temporal priority deserves the title of the first Christian author to write in the Latin language.

The question has been and continues to be much discussed, whether Tertullian depends on Minucius, or Minucius on Tertullian. There is not yet anything like universal agreement on the point, though Tertullian would seem to be in better possession of the title. Should it happen, however, that one find better reason for making Minucius prior to Tertullian, then the date of the *Octavius* must be moved back to before 197 A. D., with a corresponding revision of our notion of when Minucius lived; for the date of Tertullian's similar work, 197 A. D., may be taken as certain.

The Migne text of the *Octavius,* PL 3, 231-360, is superseded by what is still the standard edition, in spite of numerous more recent editions: C. Halm's *M. Minucius Felicis Octavius,* in the series CSEL, Vol. 2, Vienna 1867, pp. 1-71.

269

[18, 4]
    If upon entering some home you saw that everything there was well-tended, neat and   130
decorative, you would believe that some master was in charge of it, and that he was   131
himself much superior to those good things. So too in the home of this world, when you   132
see providence, order, and law in the heavens and on earth, believe that there is a Lord 134
and Author of the universe, more beautiful than the stars themselves and the various parts
of the whole world.

270

[18, 7]
    With a word He commands all the things that exist, arranges them by His wisdom,   170
and perfects them in His power. [8] He cannot be seen, for He is too bright for sight;   173
nor can He be grasped, for He is too pure to touch; nor can He be measured, for He is
too great for the senses. He is infinite and cannot be measured; and how great He is,
is known to Himself alone. Our heart is too narrow to understand Him; and therefore   188
we take His measure worthily by saying that He is immeasurable. [9] I will speak plainly 174
what I think: he that supposes he knows the magnitude of God is diminishing it; he that

does not desire to diminish it does not know it (1). [10] Nor shall you seek the name of God: for God is His name.

Words are needed when it is required to separate a multitude into individuals according to the special characteristics indicated by names. To God, who is alone, the name of God   177
is the whole. If I were to call Him Father, you would think Him made of flesh. If King, you would infer that He is earthly. If Lord, you would understand Him as mortal. Take away these added names and you will behold His splendor. [11] What then of the consent of all men which I have in this matter? I hear the common people. When they   2
raise their hands to heaven they say nothing else but "God!" and "God is great!" and   135
"God is true!" and "If God grant!" Is this the natural speech of the common people, or   130
is it the prayer of a confessing Christian?

271

[31, 5]
We maintain modesty not on the surface but in the mind. We cling freely to the bond   86
of one marriage. In the desire to procreate we know one wife or none. The banquets we   977
attend are not only modest but sober: for we do not indulge in revelry or prolong a feast with strong wine. Rather, we temper our joyousness with gravity. With chaste discourse and even more chaste in body, many of us enjoy rather than boast of the perpetual virginity of a body undefiled. In fact, so far from us is the desire for incest, that some blush even at the thought of a chaste union.

272

[34, 9]
It is more difficult to initiate that which is not, than to repeat that which has been.   1011
[10] Do you think that if something be withdrawn from our feeble eyes, it perishes to God? Every body, whether it withers into dust or is dissolved into moisture or is crumbled into ashes or passes off as a vapor, is removed from our eyes; but a guard is kept over its elements by God. Not subscribing to your belief, we fear no loss in burial, but we practice the old and better custom of burial in the ground.

[11] See, too, how for our consolation all nature suggests the future resurrection. The sun sinks down, but is reborn. The stars go out, but return again. Flowers die, but come to life again. After their decay shrubs put forth leaves again; not unless seeds decay does their strength return. A body in the grave is like the trees in Winter: they hide their sap under a deceptive dryness. [12] Why are you in haste for it to revive and return, while yet the Winter is raw? We must await even the Spring of the body. I am not ignorant of the fact that many, in the consciousness of what they deserve, would rather hope than actually believe that there is nothing for them after death. They would prefer to be annihilated rather than be restored for punishment.

273

[35, 3]
Nor is there either measure or end to these torments. That clever fire burns the limbs   1034
and restores them, wears them away and yet sustains them. Just as fiery thunderbolts   1032
strike bodies but do not consume them; just as the fires of Mount Etna and Mount   1036
Vesuvius and of burning lands everywhere blaze without being wasted; so also that fiery punishment is fed not by consuming those who burn, but is nourished by the unending eating away of their bodies. [4] That they who do not know God are deservedly tortured for their impiety and injustice, none but a godless man can doubt; for the crime of not knowing the Author of all and Lord of all is not less than that of offending Him.

[5] And aside from the fact that ignorance of God is sufficient for punishment, just as

knowledge of Him is an aid to pardon, still, if we Christians be compared to you, although some of us may not be equal to our standards, we shall be found to be much better than you. [6] You forbid adultery, yet you do it. We, however, are known as men only to our wives. You punish crimes when they have been committed. With us, it is a sin even to consider a crime. You fear witnesses. We fear even our own conscience, which we cannot escape. And finally, the jails are full of your people; but there is no Christian there, unless his crime be his religion. Otherwise, he is an apostate.

86

632

1. If anyone thinks that he knows fully the greatness of God, he is guilty of supremely underestimating God. Anyone who fears to run the risk of underestimating God will make no attempt to explain God's greatness, but will simply admit his own lack of knowledge.

TERTULLIAN [*ca. A. D.* 155 / 160 — *ca. A. D.* 240 / 250]

Quintus Septimius Florens Tertullianus was born in Carthage of pagan parents, between the years 155 and 160 A. D. He became a lawyer of considerable repute, and after his conversion, *ca. A. D.* 193, his expert knowledge in the field of law was turned to the defense of Christianity.

Jerome says that Tertullian was a priest. Opinion on this point, however, is still very much divided. J. Quasten remarks that the great respect his writings enjoyed is inexplicable if he were not a cleric. We might counter his argument by stating that great respect for a man's writings may be evidenced in two ways: by appealing to his authority, and by wide use of his works. In Tertullian's case, his writings are quoted considerably by later authors; but oftener than not, in an anonymous manner. This can be accounted for by the genuine excellence of his writings apart from any particular respect for his person. Certainly his writings were widely known and widely read; but again, this is understandable quite apart from his person, when we remember that he was the first to write in Latin, the new vernacular, when Greek was beginning to pass away as a common language in the West. We find nothing in his writings to indicate that he was a priest, or a cleric of any kind; and at the same time, in the manner in which he deals with theological points of particular interest to the laity, he generally reveals the attitude of a layman rather than that of a cleric.

Tertullian's literary activities embrace the years 197 to 220 A. D. Within this span of nearly twenty-five years, his numerous writings fall into three fairly distinct periods: his Catholic period, his so-called semi-Montanist period, and his Montanist period. In the Catholic period, from 197 to 206 A. D., his writings are marked by orthodoxy of opinion. The semi-Montanist period, from 206 A. D. to 212 A. D., it must be understood, represents a period of transition. There is no heresy or schism called semi-Montanism. The term simply indicates that in this period he is wavering. He is virtually a Montanist, without yet having made a definitive break with the Catholic Church. The period is marked by rigorist tendencies and a developing attitude of anticlericalism.

From 213 to 220 A. D. (some extend the period of his writings as far as 223

A. D.) his literary remains indicate that he has passed outright into the camp of the Montanists. His rigorism has become extreme, his anti-clericalism has reached the point of invective, while he takes an exaggerated view of the priestly role of the layman; and he clearly admits the new charismatic prophets and prophetesses of the Montanists.

What of the Tertullianists? Augustine knows such a sect around Carthage at the end of the 4th century. It was he that converted the last of them. Some authors indicate that Tertullian outgrew even Montanism and became the founder of a sect bearing his own name. More likely his name simply attached to the North African Montanists, he being far and away the most prominent person in their circle. But whatever the numerous possibilities, it would seem most unlikely that the name *Tertullianists* was attached to any group in his own lifetime.

After 220 A. D. we hear of him no more, except that certain remarks of Jerome indicate that he lived on for a number of years after 220 and into ripe old age, dying probably as late as 240 and possibly as late as 250 A. D.

The interesting problem of whether it is Minucius Felix or Tertullian who deserves the title of first Christian author to write in Latin is mentioned briefly in the introduction to Minucius' *Octavius* (above, p. 109). As indicated there, while the question is still very much an open one, to most modern authors Tertullian seems to have the better part, the *Octavius* being dependent upon his *Apology*, and not *vice versa*.

APOLOGY [*A. D.* 197]

The *Apology* belongs to Tertullian's Catholic period, having been written in 197 A. D. It is generally regarded as the most important of his writings. In content it is similar to his *Ad nationes*, written earlier in the same year; but it represents a much more careful and polished study. The wide use of the work is demonstrated by its being preserved in no less than thirty-six codices. The Migne text, PL 1, 257-536, is no longer useful. Hoppe's edition in the CSEL, Vol. 69, Vienna 1939, can be used intelligently if one takes the trouble to understand that Hoppe held to the theory that Tertullian himself made two editions of the work, one represented by the text of the *Codex Fuldensis,* the other preserved as the so-called *Vulgata recensio,* which latter he takes for his primary text, reproducing the variants of the *Fuldensis* in the apparatus.

The most recent and best critical edition, which may already be regarded as standard, is that of E. Dekkers in the *Corpus Christianorum,* Vol. 1, Turnhout 1954, pp. 85-171. For his primary readings Dekkers prefers the tradition represented by the *Codex Fuldensis,* mostly relegating the *Vulgata recensio* variants to the apparatus. The opinion that the *Codex Fuldensis* readings represent a more authentic text, while the *Vulgata recensio* is the result of a Carolingian scribe's attempts at normalizing Tertullian's Latin, an opinion once nearly defunct, seems to have revived, and is once more in good repute.

274

[7, 3]
Truth had its beginning along with hatred. As soon as it appeared, there was enmity also.   85
It has as many foes as there are outsiders: among the Jews especially, because of jealousy;   86
among soldiers, for extortion; and nature being what it is, even in our own homes.
[4] Daily we are beset, daily we are betrayed, and how often even in our own meetings

and assemblies we are taken by surprise. [5] Who, as we are accused, ever came upon an
infant whimpering? Who has kept for the judge, just as he found them, the bloody mouths
of Cyclopes and Sirens? Who has ever found some evidence of impurity in his wife? Who
has concealed such crimes when he found them, or was bribed when he arrested these
men? If we always keep hidden, what do we admit when betrayal comes?

[6] Indeed, by whom can such betrayal be made? Surely not by the guilty themselves,
when the obligation of silence is binding upon all mysteries by their very nature. If the   810
Samothracian and Eleusinian make no disclosure, how much more will silence be kept
in regard to such things the betrayal of which will call forth immediate human
punishment, while divine awaits? [7] If, then, they are not their own betrayers, it
follows that it must be outsiders. And whence have outsiders their information, when
religious initations are always hidden from the godless and are wary of witnesses?

274a

[10, 1]
"You do not worship the gods," you say, "and you do not offer sacrifices for the   157
emperors." It is logical that, since we do not offer sacrifices for ourselves, for the same
reason we do not for others — namely, we do not worship the gods. Hence we are
accused of sacrilege and treason. This is the principal charge against us — indeed, it is the
sum total of charges. It is, therefore, worth investigating, whether prejudice and injustice
be not the judge, the one of which does not seek truth, while the other refuses it.

275

[17, 1]
The object of our worship is the One God, who, by the Word of His command, by the   157
Reason of His plan, and by the strength of His Power, has brought forth from nothing   461
for the glory of His majesty this whole construction of elements, bodies and spirits;   466
whence also the Greeks have bestowed upon the world the name ΚΟΣΜΟΣ. [2] He is   130
invisible, and yet He may be seen. He is intangible, and yet His presence is apparent
through His grace. He is immeasurable, and yet He is measured by the human senses.
He is, therefore, as real as He is great. In regard to other things, that which is able to be
seen, to be touched, or to be measured is less than the eyes by which it is seen, than the
hands by which it is touched, and the senses by which it is discovered. But what is truly
infinite is known only to itself.

[3] Thus it is that the measure of God is taken, although He is really immeasurable.
Thus it is that the force of His greatness makes Him known to men, although He is yet
unknown. And this is the crowning guilt of men, that they do not want to know Him   2
of whom they cannot be ignorant. [4] Do you wish to have proof from His many and
mighty works, by which we are supported, by which we are sustained, by which we are
delighted, and even by which we are awe-struck? Would you have it from the witness of
the soul itself? [5] The soul, although it be repressed in the prison of the body, though
it be wrapped around by depraved customs, though it be weakened by lust and passion,
though it be enslaved to false gods, yet, when it revives as from intoxication or from
sleep or from some illness and regains its health, it calls God by that only name which is
proper to the true God.

"Great God! Good God!" and "If God Grant!" are words spoken by all. [6] That
also He is Judge is testified by "God sees," and "I commend to God," and "God will
reward me." O, testimony of the soul, Christian by nature! And finally, as it utters
these words, it looks not to the Capitol, but to heaven. It knows the throne of the
living God: for from Him and from there it came down.

276

[18, 3]

After the present age is ended He will judge His worshippers for a reward of eternal 1043
life, and the godless for a fire equally perpetual and unending. All who have died since 1034
the beginning of time will be raised up again and shaped again and remanded to whichever 1032
destiny they deserve. [4] In times past we laughed at these things. We are from among 1011
you. Men are not born Christians, but become such. 87

276a

[20, 1]

If their antiquity be doubted, if their age does not prove the Scriptures divine, then 50
their majesty does. This is readily understood from a source at hand. That which will 89
so teach is immediately before us: the world, the age, and the sequence of events.
[2] Whatever happens has been foretold. Whatever is seen has been heard about beforehand. . . . [3] While we are experiencing the events, we read of them. While we are
recognizing them, they are proven. I suggest that the fulfillment of prophecy is sufficient 15
witness to the divine origin thereof.

277

[21, 6]

[The sacred writers who warned the Jews] always insisted upon the same point, that 300
in the last cycles of the world God would choose more faithful followers, taking them from
every country and people and place; and upon them He would bestow His grace in
fuller measure because they were receptive of a fuller discipline. [7] Therefore He came 301
to reform and enlighten our receptivity, He whose coming was announced beforehand by
God: Christ, the Son of God. It was announced, therefore, that the Arbiter and Teacher
of this grace and discipline, the Enlightener and Trainer of the human race, would be the
Son of God. His birth, however, was not such that He must blush at the name son or
because of the seed of a father. . . . [9] In fact, the Son of God has no mother in any
sense which would involve impurity. Though to appearances she was married, she did
not enter into a marital union. But first, I shall discuss His substance, so that the manner 781
of His birth may be understood.
[10] We have already said that God fashioned the whole universe by His Word, His 284
Reason and His Power. . . . [11] And to the Word, the Reason and the Power through
which, as we have said (1), God fashioned all things, we do indeed ascribe Spirit as its
proper substance, in which Spirit the Word indwells to give utterance, and Reason is
present in order to arrange, and Power presides for the sake of bringing to completion.
We hold that this which was uttered by God, and which was begotten in that utterance, 265
because of the unity of substance is called God and Son of God; for God too is Spirit. 257
[12] Even when a ray is shot forth from the sun it is a part of the whole; but the sun 152
will be in the ray because it is a ray of the sun, not separated from its substance but
extended therefrom, as light is enkindled from light. The parent material (2) remains
whole and unimpaired even though you derive from it numerous shoots possessed of its
qualities.
[13] So also, that which proceeds from God is God and Son of God, and both are one.
Likewise, as He is Spirit from Spirit, and God from God, He is made a second by count
and in numerical sequence, but not in actual condition; for He comes forth from the
source (3) but does not separate therefrom. [14] Therefore, that Ray of God, as was
ever foretold in the past, descended into a certain Virgin and was formed flesh in her 311
womb, and was born God and man combined. The flesh, formed by the Spirit, is 323
nourished, grows into manhood, speaks, teaches, acts, and is the Christ. 332

278

[22, 4]

The business [of the fallen angels, who are the demons], is to corrupt mankind.   494
Thus, from the very first, spiritual wickedness augured man's destruction. Therefore do
they inflict diseases and other grievous misfortunes upon our bodies; and upon the soul
they do violence to achieve sudden and extraordinary excesses. [5] Their marvelous
subtlety and elusiveness give them access to both parts of man's substance. . . . [8] Every   483
spirit is winged, both angels and demons. Therefore are they everywhere in a moment.   484
The whole world is but one place to them. What and where anything happens they can   489
know and tell with equal facility. Their swiftness is thought of as divine, because their
substance is not understood.

279

[37, 4]

We are but of yesterday, and already we have filled all your world: cities, islands,   85
fortresses, towns, marketplaces, the camp itself, tribes, companies, the palace, the senate,
the forum. We have left you nothing but your temples only! [5] We can match the
numbers of your armies; and from one province we shall come to be many. For what
war would we not be fit and eager, even if of unequal strength, when we are so willing to
be slain, if it were not that according to our discipline, it is better to be killed than to kill?
[6] Unarmed and without rebellion but simply as dissenters we could carry on the contest
against you, by merely separating ourselves from you in ill-will. If such a force as we are
were to desert you for some remote corner of the world, the very loss of so many citizens
of whatever kind would cause your empire to blush for shame, and vengeance would be
had by that very forsaking.

[7] Without doubt you would be frightened at your loneliness, at the silence of things,
and at that certain stupor as of a dead world. You would have to seek for someone whom
you might govern, and you would have left to you more enemies than citizens. [8] As it
is, you have fewer enemies because of the multitude of Christians: almost every citizen in
nearly every city in which Christians are found. But you prefer to call us enemies of the
human race rather than enemies of human error.

280

[38, 4]

Among us there is nothing to be said, nothing to be seen, nothing to be heard, of the   86
madness of the circus, the immodesty of the theater, the brutality of the arena, and of
the vanity of physical culture.

281

[39, 1]

Now I myself will explain the practices of the Christian society. . . . We are a body   405
joined together by religious conviction, unity of discipline, and by hope. [2] We assemble   412
in a meeting and comprise a congregation, so that we might surround God with our prayers,
as if by force of arms. Such violence is pleasing to God. We pray even for the emperors,
for their ministers and those in power, for the condition of the world, that peace may
prevail, and that the end may be stayed. [3] We assemble to recall the divine Scriptures,
if any condition of the present times makes it needful to be forewarned or to reflect. And
in any case, with holy words we nourish our faith, uplift our hope, strengthen our trust,
and confirm the discipline by the inculcating of precepts.

[4] In the same place there are exhortations, corrections and divine censure. Judgment
is passed with the greatest of gravity, as among men who are certain of the presence of

God; and it is the greatest foretaste of the future judgment, when anyone has sinned so
grievously that he is cut off from communication in prayer and assembly and from every
holy transaction. [5] Certain approved elders preside, who have received that honor not for
a price but by the witness of character; for nothing that pertains to God is to be had for a
price. Even if there is some kind of a treasury, it is not made up of huge grants, as if
they were the price of religion. Each one puts in a small amount on the monthly day, or
when he wishes, accordingly as he wishes and is able. No one is compelled, and it is given
freely.

[6] These are, as it were, the deposits of piety. For they are not expended therefrom
on feasts and drinking parties and in thankless houses of gluttony, but for the support and
burial of the poor, for boys and girls without parents and destitute of means, for the aged
quietly confined to their homes, for the shipwrecked; and if there are any in the mines
or in the islands or in the prisons, if it be for the reason that they are worshippers of God,
then they become the foster-sons of their confession. [7] But it is mainly the practice
of such a love which leads some to put a brand upon us. "See," they say, "how they love   86
one another"; for they themselves hate each other. "And how ready they are to die
for one another," they themselves being more inclined to kill each other.

281a

[39, 11]
We who are so united in mind and in soul do not hesitate to share everything that we   977
have. Everything is held in common among us, except our wives. [12] In this matter in
which other men maintain a partnership, our partnership is dissolved.

281b

[39, 14]
You attack our humble meals on the grounds that they are extravagant as well as
infamously criminal. The remark of Diogenes is referred to us: "The people of Megara
give banquets as if they were to die tomorrow; but they build as if they were never to
die!" [15] The straw in another's eye is seen more readily than the tree trunk in one's
own (4). The air is fouled by the belching of so many tribes, courts, and sub-courts.
When the Salii are about to dine, it is necessary to take a loan. The accountants will have
to calculate the tithes of Hercules and the costs of his sacrifical banquets. The most
exquisite of cooks is drafted for the Apaturia, the Dionysia, and the Attic mysteries.
The firemen are called out because of the smoke at a banquet of Serapis. But objection
is made only to the dining-couch of the Christians!

[16] The purpose of our meal is shown by its name: it is called by a word which to
the Greeks means *love* (5). However much it may cost, it is gain to incur expense in
the name of piety, since by this refreshment we comfort the needy. . . . [17] If the
motive of our banquet is honorable, judge from that motive the rest of our order of discipline.
What pertains to the office of religion admits of nothing vile and nothing immodest.
No one reclines without first participating in prayer to God. Enough is eaten to satisfy   120
hunger, and as much is drunk as befits the chaste.

[18] They satisfy themselves, as men who remember that God is to be worshipped
even through the night. They converse, as men who know that God hears. After they
have washed their hands and lamps have been brought in someone is called forth to the
center to sing to God, either from the divine Scriptures or as he is able from his own
composing. This is the proof of how he has drunk. The banquet ends likewise in prayer.
[19] They depart, then, . . . to observe the same care of modesty and chastity as
befits those who have partaken not so much of a meal as of a religious exercise (6).

282

[40, 1]
On the contrary, they deserve the name of faction who conspire in hatred of good and   85
virtuous men, who cry out against innocent blood, offering it as a vain pretext in defense
of their hatred that they consider the Christians to be the cause of every public disaster
and of every misfortune which has befallen the people from the earliest times. [2] If
the Tiber rises to the city walls, if the Nile does not rise to the fields, if the weather
continues without change, if there is an earthquake, if famine, if pestilence, immediately,
"Christians to the lion!" So many for one beast?

283

[44, 3]
It is with your own people that the jail is always bulging, with your own people that   86
the mines are always sighing, with your own people that the beasts are always fattening,
with your own people that the producers of gladiatorial shows always make flocks of
criminals food for beasts. No one there is a Christian, unless he is there for that very
reason. And if he is there for other cause, he is no longer a Christian.

284

[48, 12]
Then will the entire race of men be restored to receive its just deserts according to   1034
what it has merited in this period of good and evil, and thereafter to have these paid out   1043
in an immeasurable and unending eternity. [13] Then there will be neither death again,
nor resurrection again, but we shall be always the same as we are now, without changing.
The worshippers of God shall be always with God, clothed in the proper substance of
eternity. But the godless and those who have not turned wholly to God will be punished   1032
in fire equally unending; and they shall have from the very nature of this fire, divine as
it were, a supply of incorruptibility.
[14] Even the philosophers knew the difference between ordinary and secret fire.
There is a great difference between that which serves man's needs and that which is seen
in the judgment of God, whether it casts thunderbolts from heaven or belches from the
earth through mountain peaks; for it does not consume what it burns, but while it destroys
it also repairs. [15] Mountains remain though they burn always; and one who is struck
by lightning is preserved so that he can no longer be consumed by fire. This shall be a
proof of the eternal fire, and this an example of the endless judgment which feeds itself:
mountains burn and continue to exist. What, then, of the wicked and of the enemies of
God?

285

[50, 12]
Crucify us, torture us, condemn us, destroy us! Your wickedness is the proof of our   86
innocence, for which reason does God suffer us to suffer this. When recently you
condemned a Christian maiden to a panderer rather than to a panther (7), you realized
and confessed openly that with us a stain on our purity is regarded as more dreadful than
any punishment and worse than death. [13] Nor does your cruelty, however exquisite,
accomplish anything: rather, it is an enticement to our religion. The more we are hewn   88
down by you, the more numerous do we become. The blood of martyrs is the seed of
Christians (8)!

---

1. See § 275 above. It will be evident from the present passage why it was necessary that the terms *Word,*
   Reason, and *Power* in passage 275 be given upper case initials.
2. *materia matrix.*
3. *a matrice.*

4. Matt. 7:3. Luke 6:41.
5. ἀγάπη.
6. *disciplinam.*
7. *ad lenonem . . . potius quam ad leonem:* literally, *to a procurer rather than to a lion.* No doubt the *substitutio felix* will be suffered by the reader for the sake of preserving the rhetorical device.
8. *Semen est sanguis Christianorum.*

THE TESTIMONY OF THE SOUL [*inter A. D.* 197 / 200]

Written between 197 and 200 A. D., *The Testimony of the Soul* is an apologetic work of Tertullian's Catholic period. The argument of the work is that we have a natural apprehension of God's existence. Migne's text, PL 1, 607-618, no longer serves scholarly purposes. The edition of A. Reifferscheid and G. Wissowa in the Vienna Corpus (CSEL), Vol. 20, Vienna 1890, pp. 134-143, is excellent; but we prefer the more recent edition of R. Willems in the Corpus Christianorum, Vol. 1, Turnhout 1954, pp. 175-183.

286

[3, 2]

Finally, in every instance of vexation, contempt, and abhorrence, you pronounce the 610
name of Satan. He it is whom we call the angel of wickedness, the author of every error, 494
the corrupter of the whole world, through whom man was deceived in the very beginning
so that he transgressed the command of God. On account of his transgression man was 614
given over to death; and the whole human race, which was infected by his seed, was made
the transmitter of condemnation.

THE SHOWS [*inter A. D.* 198 / 200]

The treatise on *The Shows,* dating from between 198 and 200 A. D., is another work of Tertullian's Catholic period. Migne's text, PL 1, 630-662, is no longer useful. The Reifferscheid-Wissowa edition in volume 20 of the CSEL, Vienna 1890, pp. 1-29, is still quite acceptable, though we ourselves prefer the edition of E. Dekkers in *Corpus Christianorum,* Vol. 1, Turnhout 1954, pp. 227-253.

287

[2, 4]

No one denies, because there is no one who does not know, what nature moreover 130
suggests: that God is the Creator of the universe, the same universe which is such a good 680
thing and is at the same time a free gift to man.

THE DEMURRER AGAINST THE HERETICS [*ca. A. D.* 200]

Also from Tertullian's Catholic period, written about the year 200 A. D., is the *De praescriptione haereticorum,* which we translate *The Demurrer Against the Heretics.* In this work Tertullian draws upon his legal training, applying the law of *praescriptio,* in concept virtually the same as that which lawyers of our own time call a *demurrer,* to the controversies between Catholics and heretics.

It seems to us that the usual English title given the work, *The Prescription Against the Heretics,* is at best confusing. *Prescription,* to any modern lawyer, is the concept of rights deriving through undisturbed use. Thus, one may claim title to land by right of prescription, on the grounds of having had actual and undisturbed though legally unfounded use of the land for a specified and acknowledged period of time. This concept is totally foreign to the legal provision invoked by Tertullian, who was actually trying to prevent application of what we call *prescription.*

In Roman law, *praescriptio* was invoked by a defendant against the plaintiff to bar entry of the suit in the form submitted by the plaintiff. If granted by the court, the *praescriptio* barred the suit *ad limina,* which simply means that the case was dismissed. This is almost the same as the current legal concept of the *demurrer,* which is invoked by a defendant when he pleads that the plaintiff's case, even if it be true as to fact, is insufficient in law, there being an obvious defect in the legal aspects of the plaintiff's pleadings which constitutes reason why his case should be dismissed. If there be any difference between Roman *praescriptio* and English *demurrer,* it is in the fact that presentation of a demurrer generally assumes a willingness to admit the truth of the plaintiff's allegations, while *praescriptio* implies nothing in this regard. In spite of this obvious defect in our use of the term *demurrer,* we believe it a better translation of *praescriptio* than the extremely misleading and quite irrelevant term *prescription.*

Tertullian invokes two *praescriptiones* or *demurrers* in the work (1): *a)* Christ sent the Apostles as preachers of the Gospel, so none others ought to be received; and *b)* what the Apostles preached can be discovered only through Apostolic Churches, so only those in agreement with Apostolic Churches ought to be given a hearing. It is rather a complicated way of presenting a common and simple argument. The demanding of evidence of apostolicity is generally a strong and effective argument, but Tertullian's clothing of it in legal form and his use of *praescriptio* seems only to cloud the issue.

Migne's text, PL 2, 12-74, is no longer serviceable. Emil Kroymann's edition appeared in the Vienna Corpus (CSEL), Vienna 1942, pp. 1-58. Our translation is based on the more recent edition of R. F. Refoulé in the *Corpus Christianorum,* Vol. 1, Turnhout 1954, pp. 187-224.

288

[7, 12]
    After Jesus Christ, there is no need of further search; nor, after the Gospel, is there any   104
further inquiry. [13] Inasmuch as we believe, we desire nothing further to believe. For   60
beyond what we already have, we believe there is nothing further that we ought to believe.

289

[9, 3]
    But at the outset I propose this: that there is something specific and definite   568
established by Christ, which the pagans are by all means obliged to believe, and therefore to
seek so that they may find it and be able to believe (2). [4] However, there can be no
indefinite seeking for that which has been established as specific and definite. It is to   104
be sought until you find it; and when found, it is to be believed. Nor is there anything
further to do, except to keep what you have believed, while believing this also: that
there is nothing else to be believed and, therefore, nothing else to be sought, after you
have found and have believed what has been established by Him, who gives you no other
command except to seek what He has established. [5] If, indeed, any man doubts this,   401
proof will be shown that we are what Christ has established.

290

[13, 1]

There is, however, a rule of faith; and so that we may acknowledge at this point what
it is we defend, it is this precisely that we believe: [2] There is one only God, and none   157
other besides Him; the Creator of the world who brought forth all things out of nothing   461
through His Word, first of all sent forth. [3] This Word is called His Son; and in the   284
name of God He was seen at various times by the patriarchs, and has always been heard   260
in the Prophets; and at last He was brought down from the Spirit and Power of God the   236
Father into the Virgin Mary, and was made flesh in her womb; and having been born   311
from her, came forth as Jesus Christ.   300

[4] Thenceforth He preached a new law and a new promise of the kingdom of heaven;   302
worked miracles; was crucified, rose again on the third day; and having ascended into   80
heaven, sat at the right of the Father; [5] sent the Holy Spirit with vicarious power to   291
lead those who believe; is going to come in glory to take the saints into the enjoyment   392
of eternal life and of the heavenly promises, and to condemn the godless to eternal fire,   1034
after the resurrection of both classes and their restoration in the flesh. [6] This rule,   1043
as will be proved, was taught by Christ, and admits of no questions among us, except   1012
those which heresies bring in and which make men heretics.

291

[19, 3]

Wherever it shall be clear that the truth of the Christian discipline and faith are   100
present, there also will be found the truth of the Scriptures and of their explanation, and   101
of all the Christian traditions.

292

[20, 4]

The Apostles — a title which means 'those who have been sent forth' — immediately   420
chose by lot Matthias as the twelfth, in the place of Judas, on the authority of a prophecy   422
which is in one of the psalms of David (3). They obtained the promised power of the
Holy Spirit for miracles and eloquence, and after first bearing witness to faith in Jesus
Christ in Judea, and having established Churches there, they next went forth into the
world and preached the same doctrine of the same faith to the gentiles. [5] They then
founded Churches in cities one after another, from which other Churches borrow the
sprout of faith and seeds of doctrine, and are daily borrowing them, so that they may
become Churches. [6] And it is in this way that they may regard themselves as apostolic;
for they are the offspring of apostolic Churches.

[7] Any group of things must be classified according to its origin. Therefore although
the Churches are so many and so great, there is but the one primitive Church of the
Apostles, from which all others are derived. [8] Thus, all are primitive, all are apostolic,
because all are one. The communication of peace, the title of brotherhood, and the bond
of hospitality prove her unity: [9] privileges which no other principle governs except the
one tradition of the same sacrament (4).

293

[21, 1]

From this, then, we draw up our demurrer: if the Lord Jesus Christ sent the Apostles   422
to preach, no others ought to be received except those appointed by Christ. [2] For no   102
one knows the Father except the Son, and him to whom the Son gives a revelation (5).
Nor does it seem that the Son has given revelation to any others than the Apostles,   104

whom He sent forth to preach what He had revealed to them. [3] But what they
preached, that is, what Christ had revealed to them — and here again I must enter a
demurrer — can be proved in no other way except through the same Churches which the
Apostles founded, preaching in them themselves *viva voce* as they say, and afterwards
by their Epistles. [4] If these things are so, then it follows that all doctrine which agrees
with the apostolic Churches, those nursuries and original depositories of the faith, must
be regarded as truth, and as undoubtedly constituting what the Churches received from
the Apostles, what the Apostles received from Christ, and what Christ received from
God. [5] And indeed, every doctrine must be prejudged as false, if it smells of anything
contrary to the truth of the Churches and of the Apostles of Christ and God. [6] It
remains, then for us to demonstrate whether this doctrine of ours, of which we gave
the rule above (6), accords with the tradition of the Apostles, in which case all other   420
doctrines proceed from falsehood. [7] We communicate with the apostolic Churches
because there is no diversity of doctrine: this is the witness of truth.

294

[23, 10]
    Moreover, if Peter was reproached [by Paul] because, after having lived with the   451
gentiles, he later separated himself from their company out of respect for persons, the
fault certainly was one of procedure and not of doctrine (7).

295

[28, 1]
    Grant, then, that all have erred; that the Apostle was mistaken in bearing witness; that   100
the Holy Spirit had no such consideration for any one Church as to lead it into truth,   450
although He was sent for that purpose by Christ (8), who had asked the Father to make
Him the Teacher of truth (9); that the Steward of God and Vicar of Christ (10)
neglected His office, and permitted the Churches for a time to understand otherwise
and to believe otherwise than He Himself had preached through the Apostles: now, is   420
it likely that so many and such great Churches should have gone astray into a unity of
faith?

295a

[30, 2]
    [Marcion and Valentine], on account of the ever-restless curiosity with which they   415
also infected the brethren, were more than once expelled; Marcion, indeed, with the two
hundred sesterces which he had brought into the Church. Finally banished to perpetual
excommunication (11), they broadcast the poisons of their doctrines. [3] Afterwards
Marcion professed repentance (12) and agreed to the condition granted him: that he
should be received in peace if he restored to the Church all those others also, whom he
had been training for perdition. Death prevented him from so doing.

296

[32, 1]
    Moreover, if there be any [heresies] bold enough to plant themselves in the midst of   422
the apostolic age, so that they might seem to have been handed down by the Apostles   102
because they were from the time of the Apostles, we can say to them: let them show
the origins of their Churches, let them unroll the order of their bishops, running down in   440
succession from the beginning, so that their first bishop shall have for author and
predecessor some one of the Apostles or of the apostolic men who continued steadfast

with the Apostles. [2] For this is the way in which the apostolic Churches transmit their lists: like the Church of the Smyrnaeans, which records that Polycarp was placed there by John; like the Church of the Romans where Clement was ordained by Peter. [3] In just this same way the other Churches display those whom they have as sprouts from the apostolic seed, having been established in the episcopate (13) by the Apostles.

[4] Let the heretics invent something like it. After their blasphemies, what could be unlawful for them? [5] But even if they should contrive it, they will accomplish nothing; for their doctrine itself, when compared with that of the Apostles, will show by its own diversity and contrariety that it has for its author neither an Apostle nor an apostolic man. The Apostles would not have differed among themselves in teaching, nor would an apostolic man have taught contrary to the Apostles, unless those who were taught by the Apostles then preached otherwise.

[6] Therefore, they will be challenged to meet this test even by those Churches which are of much later date — for they are being established daily — and whose founder is not from among the Apostles nor from among the apostolic men; for those which agree in the same faith are reckoned as apostolic on account of the blood ties in their doctrine. [7] Then let all heresies prove how they regard themselves as apostolic, when they are challenged by our Churches to meet either test (14). [8] But in fact they are not apostolic, nor can they prove themselves to be what they are not. Neither are they received in peace and communion by the Churches which are in any way apostolic, since on account of their diverse belief (15) they are in no way apostolic.

297

[36, 1]
Come now, if you would indulge a better curiosity in the business of your salvation, run through the apostolic Churches in which the very thrones (16) of the Apostles remain still in place; in which their own authentic writings are read, giving sound to the voice and recalling the faces of each. [2] Achaia is near you, so you have Corinth. If you are not far from Macedonia, you have Philippi (17). If you can cross into Asia, you have Ephesus. But if you are near to Italy, you have Rome, whence also our authority derives (18). [3] How happy is that Church, on which Apostles poured out their whole doctrine along with their blood, where Peter endured a passion like that of the Lord, where Paul was crowned in a death like John's (19), where the Apostle John, after being immersed in boiling oil and suffering no hurt, was exiled to an island.

298

[37, 1]
These things being so, in order that we may be judged to have the truth, — we who walk in the rule which the Churches have handed down from the Apostles, the Apostles from Christ, and Christ from God, — admit that the reasonableness of our position is clear, defining as it does that heretics ought not to be allowed to challenge an appeal to the Scriptures, since we, without using Scripture, prove that they have nothing to do with the Scriptures. [2] If they are heretics, they cannot be Christians, because it is not from Christ that they have gotten what they pursue of their own choosing, and from which they incur the name heretic (20).

[3] Not being Christians, they have acquired no right to Christian literature; and it might be justly said to them, "Who are you? When and from where did you come? Since you are not of mine, what are you doing with what is mine? Indeed, Marcion, by what right do you chop in my forest? By whose permission, Valentine, do you divert my streams? By what authority, Apelles, do you move my boundary markers? [4] And the rest of you, why do you sow and graze here at your own pleasure?

This is my property, which I have long possessed, which I possessed before you came, and for which I have a sure title from the very authors whose property it was. [5] I am the heir of the Apostles. As they carefully prepared their will, as they committed it to a trust, and as they sealed it with an oath, so do I hold the inheritance. [6] You, certainly, they always held as disinherited, and they rejected you as strangers and enemies."

299

[40, 1]

But it will be asked, by whom is the sense of those passages interpreted so that they make for heresies? [2] By the devil, of course, whose wiles pervert the truth and who, by the mystic rites of idols, imitates even the essential parts of the divine sacraments (21). [3] He too baptizes some, his own believers and faithful followers; he too promises the remission of sins by a washing. [4] And if memory serves me, Mithra signs his soldiers there on the forehead. He celebrates also a sacrifice of bread, and brings forth an image of the resurrection, and plaits a crown beneath a sword (22). [5] What must we say to his limiting his high priest to a single marriage? He too has his virgins, and he too his celebates.

808

820
842

964

300

[41, 1]

I must not omit a description of heretical conduct, how frivolous, how worldly, how merely human it is, without seriousness, without authority, without discipline, as fits their belief. [2] First of all, it is doubtful who is a catechumen and who a believer; for they have like access, they hear alike, and they pray alike — even heathen, if any happen along. They will throw what is holy to dogs and cast pearls before swine (23) — but not genuine ones, of course. [3] They would have simplicity to consist in the overthrow of discipline, attention to which on our part they call pandering. And they give peace to anyone who comes along (24).

[4] It is of no concern to them how diverse be their views, so long as they conspire to erase the one truth. All are puffed up, all offer knowledge. Before they have finished as catechumens, how thoroughly learned they are! [5] And the heretical women themselves, how shameless are they! They make bold to teach, to debate, to work exorcisms, to undertake cures, and perhaps even to baptise. [6] Their ordinations are casual, capricious, and changeable. Now they put neophytes in office, and again, men who are attached to the world; and at another time, our apostates, so that they can hold them by glory when they cannot by truth. [7] Nowhere is promotion easier than in the camp of the rebels, when merely to be there is service outstanding. [8] So it is that today one man is bishop, tomorrow another; today, a deacon, and tomorrow he is a lector; today, a priest, who is tomorrow a layman. For even on laymen do they enjoin the functions of the priest-hood.

957

956
951

1. Both demurrers are in Ch. 21:the first in verse 1, the second in verses 3-5. See our § 293 below.
2. Matt. 7:7.
3. Ps. 108 [109]:8 — καὶ τὴν ἐπισκοπὴν αὐτοῦ λάβοι ἕτερος. See also Acts 1:20.
4. *Sacramentum* is a military oath of allegiance, and refers here not to the Eucharist, as might first be supposed, but to the faith, which is traditional, and perhaps to the instrument of the tradition of faith, such as a creed. Tertullian's own creed or *sacramentum* is found in Ch. 13 of his *Demurrer,* § 290 above.
5. Matt. 11:27; Luke 10:22.
6. § 290.
7. *utique conversationis fuit vitium, non praedicationis.*
8. John 14:26.
9. John 15:26.
10. *I.e.,* the Holy Spirit.

11. *in perpetuum discidium relegati.*
12. *paenitentiam confessus.*
13. *I.e.,* having been given a bishop.
14. The two tests which Tertullian has just presented are *apostolic origin,* and, where that is impossible because of late origin, *apostolic doctrine.* Apostolic origin is possessed not only by those Churches founded by an actual Apostle, but also by those founded by an apostolic man. An apostolic man, as Tertullian explains, is *one who continued steadfast with the Apostles.* Probably he means the term to include not only such a one as received his doctrine directly from an Apostle, but even some of those who were later in the apostolic age and received their doctrine from hearers of the Apostles. For example, Polycarp, a hearer of John, was certainly an apostolic man by Tertullian's definition; and probably he would include also Irenaeus, who was a hearer of Polycarp, within the ranks of apostolic men.
15. *ob diversitatem sacramenti.* See note 4, p. 123 above.
16. *cathedrae.*
17. Some manuscripts add: *habes thessalonicenses.*
18. *unde nobis quoque auctoritas praesto est.*
19. John the Baptist, who, like Paul, was beheaded.
20. *Heresy* comes to English from the Latin *haeresis,* from the Greek αἵρεσις, the root meaning of which is *choice.*
21. *res sacramentorum divinorum.*
22. In the initiations to the several ranks of Mithraism, there were lustrations of various kinds to signify the washing away of guilty stains. Sexual intercourse was regarded as fouling, and perfect continence was praiseworthy. The Mithraic ritual included a consecration of bread and water, or of bread and a mixture of water and wine. The initiation ceremony was called a *sacramentum,* because of the oath which the neophyte took — *sacramentum* in one of its technical senses being the oath of allegiance taken by conscripts in the army. The signing of the forehead to which Tertullian refers was not an unction, but a branding with a hot iron — again, like that which was done to a soldier before he swore the *sacramentum.* One of the titles of rank within Mithraism was, in fact, that of *miles,* or *soldier.* Franz Cumont *(The Mysteries of Mithraism,* p. 156) notes: "The mystic that aspired to the title of *miles* was presented with a crown on a sword. He thrust it back with his hand and caused it to fall on his shoulder, saying that Mithra was his only crown. Thereafter, he never wore one, neither at banquets nor when it was awarded to him as a military honor, replying to the person who conferred it: 'It belongs to my god,' that is to say, to the invincible god."
23. Matt. 7:6.
24. *Pacem quoque passim cum omnibus miscent.* There is probably a *double-entendre* in the Latin, which we have not quite managed in English.

PRAYER [*inter A. D.* 200 / 206]

Although it already shows signs of considerable rigorism, Tertullian's work on *Prayer,* written between the years 200 and 206 A. D., is regarded as belonging still to his Catholic period. Migne's text, PL 1, 1149-1196, is no longer useful. The Reifferscheid-Wissowa edition in the series CSEL, Vol. 20, Vienna 1890, pp. 180-200, is still excellent, but may be regarded as having yielded its place as standard edition to the much more recent text of G. F. Diercks in the *Corpus Christianorum,* Vol. 1, Turnhout 1954, pp. 257-274; or perhaps, deserving of even better reputation is Diercks' even more recent edition of the same work in the series *Stromata,* fasc. 4, Utrecht and Antwerp 1956, pp. 17-36. The last named serves as the text for our present translation.

300a

[6, 2]

Nevertheless, we had rather understand *give us this day our daily bread* (1) in a spiritual sense. For Christ is our Bread, because Christ is Life, and bread is life. "I am," He said, "the Bread of Life (2);" and shortly before: "The Bread is the Word of the Living God, which comes down from heaven (3)." And then, that His Body is included in the term bread (4): "This is My Body (5)." In asking, therefore, for our daily bread, we petition for continued existence in Christ and indivisibility from His Body.

852

301

[19, 1]

Likewise, in regard to days of fast (6), many do not think they should be present at   873
the sacrificial prayers, because their fast would be broken if they were to receive the Body
of the Lord. [2] Does the Eucharist, then, obviate a work devoted to God, or does it bind
it more to God? [3] Will not your fast be more solemn if, in addition, you have stood at
God's altar? [4] The Body of the Lord having been received and reserved (7), each point   865
is secured: both the participation in the sacrifice and the discharge of duty.

1. Matt. 6:11; Luke 11:3.
2. John 6:35.
3. John 6:31ff.
4. In this 6th chapter of the *De oratione* Tertullian says that in asking for our daily bread we ask really for
   three things: ordinary food for our corporal sustenance, and spiritual food, which latter is really two
   things: not only sustenance for the soul, but even the very Body of Christ in the Eucharist.
5. Matt. 26:26; Mark 14:22; Luke 22:19.
6. *de statione diebus.* The word *fast,* occuring below in the same verse and again in verse 3, represents in
   both instances the word *statio.* In *The Shepherd* of Hermas, *Par. 5, 2,* it is explained that *to keep a
   station* means *to fast.*
7. *accepto corpore Domini et reservato.* The two terms, *accepto* and *reservato,* would seem to indicate
   something more than the mere pleonasm of *taking and receiving* at the altar. It is probably a reference
   to carrying home a particle of the Eucharist for later reception. It appears, then, that Tertullian is
   saying that if anyone is afraid that his strict fast would be broken by receiving the Eucharist, he need
   not for that reason remain away from the Mass. He can attend the Mass, take the Eucharist home with
   him, and consume it when the time of the fast is over. Thus he will observe both obligations: that of
   participating in the sacrifice of the Mass, and that of keeping the fast on the station days, which were
   Wednesday and Friday. Fasting on Wednesday and Friday is commanded already in the *Didache 8, 1*
   (§ 5 above).

PATIENCE [*inter A. D.* 200 / 206]

The treatise on *Patience* belongs to the years between 200 and 206 A. D., and was
used by Cyprian in his *De bono patientiae.* It belongs, of course, to Tertullian's
Catholic period. Migne's text, PL 1, 1249-1274, is no longer useful. Kroymann's,
in CSEL, Vol. 47, Vienna 1906, pp. 1-24, is still quite satisfactory, although we have
preferred to use the more recent edition of J. G. Ph. Borleffs in *Corpus Christianorum,*
Vol. 1, Turnhout 1954, pp. 299-317, in the preparation of the following translation.

301a

[9, 1]

Not even that kind of impatience is to be excused, where, in the loss of loved ones, some
assertion of a right to grief is defended. Consideration of the Apostle's declaration must be
set before us, where he says: "Lest you should grieve at the falling asleep of anyone, like
the pagans who lack hope (1)." [2] And rightly so: for believing in the resurrection of
Christ, we believe also in our own, for whose sake He both died and rose again. Therefore,   1011
since there is certainty as to the resurrection of the dead, grief on account of death is
empty, as empty also is impatience in grief.

[3] Why should you grieve, if you do not believe he has perished? Why should you
bear impatiently the temporary withdrawal of one whom you believe will return? That
which you think is death is only a departure. He that goes before us is not to be mourned,
though of course he may be longed for. But even that longing must be tempered with
patience. Why should you bear immoderately the departure of one whom you will soon
follow?   582

[4] Besides, impatience in such matters bodes ill of our hope, makes a lie of our faith;

and we wound Christ when we do not accept with equanimity the summoning of any by Him, as if they were to be pitied. [5] "I desire," says the Apostle, "to be taken now and to be with the Lord (2)." How better is the desire he expresses! If we grieve impatiently   1041 when others have obtained the desire of Christians, we show ourselves unwilling to obtain it.

1. 1 Thess. 4:13.
2. Phil. 1:23.

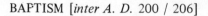

BAPTISM [*inter A. D.* 200 / 206]

Also of his Catholic period is Tertullian's work on *Baptism,* written between the years 200 and 206 A. D. It is sometimes designated the only pre-Nicene treatise on any of the Sacraments; but, while this is technically correct, we ought to bear in mind while terming it such that Tertullian's *Repentance,* dating from *ca.* 203 A. D., is virtually a treatise on both Baptism and Penance; and there are a number of other pre-Nicene works which treat specifically of various aspects of individual Sacraments, such as treatises on re-baptism, on monogamy, *etc.*

Migne's text, PL 1, 1197-1224, is no longer useful. The Reifferscheid-Wissowa text in CSEL, Vol. 20, Vienna 1890, pp. 201-218, has yielded its place as the standard edition to that of J. G. Ph. Borleffs in the *Corpus Christianorum,* Vol. 1, Turnhout 1954, pp. 277-295.

302

[1, 1]
A treatise on our sacrament of water, by which the sins of our earlier blindness are   820
washed away and we are released for eternal life will not be superfluous. . . . [2] Vipers   822
and asps, as is true of serpents in general, are found in dry and waterless places. [3] But   836
we, little fishes, are born in water after the manner of our ΙΧΘΥΣ (1), Jesus Christ; nor
can we be otherwise saved, except by abiding permanently in the water.   831

303

[4, 1]
The Spirit who in the beginning hovered over the waters would continue to linger as   800
an influence upon the waters (2). . . . [4] All waters, therefore, by reason of the original   822
sign at their beginning, are suitable, after God has been invoked, for the sacrament of sanctification. The Spirit immediately comes from heaven upon the waters, and rests upon them, making them holy of Himself; and having been thus sanctified they absorb at the same time the power of sanctifying. [5] Even so, there is a similitude well-adapted   790
to the simple act: that since we are defiled by sins, as if by dirt, we are washed in water.

303a

[5, 5]
An angel intervened and stirred up the pool at Bethsaida (3). They who were complaining of ill-health watched for him; for whoever was first to descend into the waters ceased, after washing, to complain. That figure of a bodily healing was the pre-announcement of a spiritual healing, according to the rule that things carnal always come   51
beforehand as a figure of things spiritual (4). [6] When the grace of God afterwards advanced among men, it came more fully upon the waters and upon the angel: and

they who formerly healed bodily ills now heal the spirit; they who worked temporal salvation now renew the eternal; they who set free only one and only once a year now save whole peoples daily, taking away death by the washing away of sins. The guilt being removed, the penalty, of course, is also removed.

304

[7, 1]

    After coming from the place of washing we are thoroughly anointed with a blessed unction, from the ancient discipline by which in the priesthood they were accustomed   841
to be anointed with a horn of oil, ever since Aaron was anointed by Moses. . . . [2] So   840
also with us, the unction runs on the body but profits us spiritually, in the same way   842
that Baptism is itself a corporal act by which we are plunged (5) in water, while its   824
effect is spiritual, in that we are freed from sins. [8, 1] After this, the hand is imposed   836
for a blessing, invoking and inviting the Holy Spirit.   792

305

[10, 4]

    Even the Lord Himself said that unless He first ascended to the Father, the Spirit would not otherwise descend. Thus, what the Lord was not yet conferring, certainly the servant was not able to supply. Accordingly, we find afterwards in the Acts of the Apostles that those who had the Baptism of John had not received the Holy Spirit;   821
indeed, they had not so much as heard of Him (6).

306

[12, 1]

    Since it is in fact prescribed that no one can attain to salvation without Baptism,   831
especially in view of that declaration of the Lord, who says: "Unless a man shall be born of water, he shall not have life (7)," there immediately arise scrupulous, or rather, audacious doubts on the part of some, as to how, in accord with that precept, salvation may be attained to by the Apostles, who, except for Paul, we do not find baptized in the Lord. [2] . . . I have heard — the Lord is my witness — doubts of that kind (8)!

307

[13, 3]

    The law of washing has been imposed, and the form has been prescribed: "Go," He   230
says, "teach the nations, washing them in the name of the Father and of the Son and of   823
the Holy Spirit (9)."   826

308

[15, 1]

    We have one and only one Baptism in accord with the Gospel of the Lord as well as with the letters of the Apostle, inasmuch as he says: "One God, and one Baptism, and one Church in the heavens (10)." [2] The question, however, of what is to be observed in regard to the heretics may be worthwhile treating. The assertion (11) is made in our   415
regard. Heretics, however, have no fellowship in our discipline. That they are outsiders is testified to by the very fact of their excommunication (12). I ought not recognize in their regard a precept binding upon me; for we and they have not one God nor one, that is, the same, Christ. Therefore, neither is their Baptism one with ours, because it is not the same.

Since they have it not rightly, doubtless they have it not at all; and what they do   803
not have is not to be counted. Thus, they cannot receive, because they do not have it   830
to give. But we have already discussed this point more fully in Greek (13). [3] We,
therefore, enter the font once; once are our sins forgiven, because they ought never be   799
repeated.

309

[16, 1]

We have, indeed, a second font, one with the former: namely, that of blood, of   833
which the Lord says: "I am to be baptized with a baptism (14)," when He had already
been baptized. For He had come through water and blood (15), as John wrote, so that
He might be baptized with water and glorified with blood. [2] He sent out these two
Baptisms from the wound in His pierced side (16), that we might in like manner be
called by water and chosen by blood, and so that they who believed in His blood might
be washed in the water. If they might be washed in water, they must necessarily be so
by blood (17). This is the Baptism which replaces that of the fountain, when it has not
been received, and restores it when it has been lost.

310

[17, 1]

For the conclusion of our brief subject, it but remains to impress upon you the manner
of observance in giving and in receiving Baptism. In giving it, certainly, the primary right   828
is had by the high priest, that is, the bishop; and after him, the presbyters and the
deacons, though not without authority from the bishop, on account of the honor of the
Church, which, when preserved, peace is preserved. [2] Besides these, even a layman has   829
the right; for that which is equally received can be equally given — unless bishops or
presbyters or deacons are already engaged in instructing in the Lord! — because the word
ought not be hidden from anyone. Hence Baptism, too, which is likewise the gift of God,
is able to be administered by all.

But how much more is the discipline of reverence and modesty incumbent upon laymen,
seeing that these powers belong to their superiors, lest they assume to themselves the
specific office of the bishop. Emulation of the episcopate is the mother of schisms.
"All things are lawful," the most holy Apostle has said, "but not all are expedient (18)."
[3] It will suffice, of course, in cases of necessity, that you so act as the circumstances of
place and time and person compel you. When the situation of one in danger is urgent,
then the steadfast courage of the one giving help is permitted as exceptional; for he would
be guilty of the loss of a human being if he were to refrain from bestowing what he could   831
freely give. ...

[5] But if those writings which are wrongly called *Acts of Paul* defend the example of
Thecla as a license for women to teach and baptize, let them know that in Asia the
presbyter who composed that writing, as if he were augmenting Paul's fame from his own,
after having been convicted and having pleaded that he did it out of love for Paul, was
removed from his office. For how could it seem credible that he who did not permit a
woman even to learn in a formal manner, would grant to a female the power of teaching
and baptizing? "Let them be silent," he says, "and at home consult their own husbands (19)!"

310a

[18, 4]

According to circumstance and disposition and even age of the individual person, it   831
may be better to delay Baptism; and especially so in the case of little children. Why,

indeed, is it necessary — if it be not a case of necessity (20) — that the sponsors too be thrust into danger, when they themselves may fail to fulfill their promises by reason of death, or when they may be disappointed by the growth of an evil disposition? [5] Indeed, the Lord says, "Do not forbid them to come to me (21)."

Let them come, then, while they grow up, while they learn, while they are taught to whom to come; let them become Christians when they will have been able to know Christ! Why does the innocent age hasten to the remission of sins? . . . [6] For no less cause should the unmarried also be deferred, in whom there is an aptness to temptation,— in virgins on account of their ripeness as also in the widowed on account of their freedom,— until either they are married or are better strengthened for continence. Anyone who understands the seriousness of Baptism will fear its reception more than its deferral. Sound faith is secure of salvation!

758

1. Though the present work is, of course, written in Latin, the word *fish* is given in Greek. ἰχθύς, or *fish*, is the well-known early Christian acrostic of Ἰησοῦς Χριστὸς Θεοῦ Υἱὸς Σωτήρ — *Jesus Christ, Son of God, Savior.*
2. *super aquas* instinctorum *moraturum.* Others read *s. a.* intinctorum *m.*, making the clause mean *would continue to linger over the waters of the baptized.*
3. John 5:2ff.
4. See 1 Cor. 15:46.
5. *mergimur.*
6. Acts 19:1-5.
7. John 3:5.
8. In reply to the objection Tertullian points out what he regards as several possibilities: how it may be that the other Apostles were in fact baptized; how that the Lord perhaps allowed the Baptism of John to suffice in their cases; how their very faith in Him and complete abandonment to Him might suffice; and he declares withal the very audaciousness of anyone who would presume to judge the Apostles.
9. Matt. 28:19. Tertullian's quoting of the passage reads: *"Ite inquit docete nationes tinguentes eas in nomine patris et filii et spiritus sancti."* Our use of the term *form* in our translation is not a theological anachronism, for Tertullian uses the very term *forma.*
10. Eph. 4:4-6.
11. *I.e.*, that there is but one Baptism.
12. *ademptio communicationis.*
13. Tertullian wrote only a few treatises in Greek, and none of them are extant.
14. Luke 12:50.
15. 1 John 5:6.
16. John 19:34.
17. See Matt. 22:14. Tertullian seems to be making the distinction that we accept a call to Baptism of Water, but are ourselves chosen by God for Baptism of Blood, which is martyrdom.
18. 1 Cor. 6:12; 10:23.
19. 1 Cor. 14:34-35.
20. *si non tam necesse est.*
21. Matt. 19:14; Luke 18:16.

REPENTANCE [*A. D.* 203 / 204]

The treatise on *Repentance* was written in the year 203 or 204 A. D., and belongs to Tertullian's Catholic period. While he insists strongly that post-Baptismal Penance can be received only once, it is probable that he does so from pedagogical and psychological considerations, and not on theological grounds, nor even as a matter of actual practice. He urges that after Baptism, this second repentance ought never be necessary at all; and he fears to lead others into sin by suggesting that Penance may be received more than once. Yet, he hints strongly that when necessary it may be repeated; for, after stressing the point of the singularity of second repentance, he urges that should one fall into sin he must not be ashamed to be set free again; and then he declares *(7, 13, § 314 below)*: "Medicine must be repeated for a repeated sickness." Origen, a late contemporary of Tertullian, can be found giving advice on the selection of a regular confessor (§ *485a below*).

The Migne edition, PL 1, 1227-1248, is no longer serviceable, and has been superseded by several more recent editions. The standard text is that of Borleffs, published most recently in the *Corpus Christianorum,* Vol. 1, Turnhout 1954, pp. 299-340.

311

[2, 11]

A good deed has God for its debtor, just as also an evil one; for a judge is the rewarder   770
in every case.

312

[4, 1]

If there be repentance (1), pardon will on that account be granted for every sin, whether   836
committed in flesh or in spirit, whether in deed or in desire, by the same God who otherwise determines their punishment in the judgment.

313

[6, 4]

How very inconsistent it is, to expect pardon of sins when repentance has been   923
subverted and is not completed. This is the same as holding out the hand for merchandise
without offering the price! Repentance is the price which the Lord has set for the
awarding of pardon. The compensation through repentance is what He proposes for the
buying back of safety from punishment.

314

[7, 10]

[The devil's] poisons are foreseen by God; and although the gate of repentance has   799
already been closed and barred by Baptism, still, He permits it to stand open a little.
In the vestibule He has stationed a second repentance, which He makes available to those   928
who knock — but only once, because it is already the second time, and never more, because   907
further were in vain. [11] Is not even this once enough? You have that which you
did not now deserve; for you have lost what you had received. If the Lord's indulgence
grants you the means by which you might restore what you have lost, be thankful for a
benefit which has been repeated, and which has in fact been amplified. [12] For it is a
greater thing to restore than it is to give, since it is worse to have lost than never to have
received at all.

If anyone becomes a debtor to the second repentance, certainly his spirit should not be
immediately downcast and undermined by despair. [13] By all means, let it be irksome   908
to sin again; but let it not be irksome to repent again. Let it be shameful to be endangered
again; but let no one be ashamed to be freed again. Medicine must be repeated for a
repeated sickness. [14] You will show your gratitude to the Lord if you do not refuse
what He offers you again. You have offended, but you are still able to be reconciled.
You have One to whom you may make satisfaction, and indeed He is willing!

315

[9, 1]

In regard to this second and single repentance, then: — since it is such a serious affair,   904
so much the more laborious is its examination. It is not conducted before the conscience   907

alone, but it is to be carried out by some external act. [2] This act, which is more   916
usually expressed and spoken of by the Greek word, is *exomologesis* (2), by which we   910
confess our sin to the Lord, not indeed as if He did not know it, but because satisfaction   911
is arranged by confession, of confession is repentance born, and by repentance is God   923
appeased.

[3] Thus, confession is a discipline for man's prostration and humiliation, enjoining a
manner, even as regards dress and food, conducive to mercy. [4] It commands one to lie
in sackcloth and ashes, to cover the body with mourning, to cast the spirit down in
sorrow, to exchange the sins which have been committed for a demeanor of sorrow; to
take no other food or drink except what is plain, not, of course, for the sake of the
stomach, but for the sake of the soul; and most of all, to feed prayers on fasting; to
groan, to weep and wail day and night to the Lord your God; to bow before the   925
presbyters, to kneel before God's refuge places (3), and to beseech all the brethren for
the embassy of their own supplication.

[5] Confession is all of this, so that it may excite repentance; so that it may honor
God by fear of danger; so that it may, by its own pronouncement against the sinner,
stand in place of God's indignation; and so that it may by temporal mortification, I will
not say frustrate, but rather expunge the eternal punishments. [6] Therefore, while it
abases a man, it raises him; while it covers him with squalor, the more does it cleanse
him; while it condemns, it absolves. In so far as you do not spare yourself, the more,
believe me, will God spare you!

316

[10, 1]
Most men, however, either flee from this work (4), as being an exposure (5) of   916
themselves, or they put it off from day to day. I presume they are more mindful of
modesty than of salvation, like those who contract a disease in the more shameful parts
of the body and shun making themselves known to physicians; and thus they perish
along with their own bashfulness. . . . [5] Why do you flee from the partners of your
misfortunes as you would from those who would deride? The body is not able to take
pleasure in the trouble of one of its members. It must necessarily grieve as a whole and
join in laboring for a remedy.

[6] With one and two individuals, there is the Church; and the Church, indeed, is
Christ. Therefore, when you cast yourself at the knees of the brethren, you are
dealing with Christ, you are entreating Christ. In the same way, when they shed tears
over you, it is Christ who suffers, Christ who implores the Father. When it is a son
who asks, the request is always more easily granted. [7] How very grand is the reward
of modesty, which the concealing of our sin promises (6)! If in fact we conceal something
from the notice of men, shall we at the same time hide it from God? [8] Are, then,
the good opinion of men and the knowledge of God to be equated? Is it better to be
damned in secret than to be absolved in public (7)? [9] "But it is a miserable thing
thus to come to confession!" Yes, evil leads to misery (8). But where there is repentance
misery ceases, because it is thereby turned to salvation.

317

[12, 1]
If you are inclined to draw back from confession, consider in your heart the hell   908
which confession extinguishes for you, and imagine first the magnitude of the penalty,   1030
so that you will not hesitate about making use of the remedy. [2] What do you think
of that storehouse of eternal fire when certain of its smoke-holes rouse such a pressure   1032
of flames that nearby cities either already are no more, or are daily in expectation of
destruction? [3] The grandest mountains part asunder in the birth of their eternal fire,

and though they part asunder, though they are devoured, yet they never come to an end — which proves to us the perpetuity of the judgment.

[4] Who will not regard these occasional punishments inflicted on the mountains as examples of the impending judgment (9)? Who will not agree that such sparks are but a few missiles and random darts from some unimaginably great center? [5] Therefore, when you know that after the initial support of the Lord's Baptism there is still in confession a second reserve against hell, why do you desert your salvation? Why do you hesitate to approach what you know will heal you?

1. This statement, as will be clear if it be restored to its context, is made particularly in regard to the repentance which should precede Baptism, and the pardon which comes through Baptism. The passage, then, should not be cited in reference to the Sacrament of Penance, as if it were said of confessional powers, nor in reference to the so-called unforgiveable sins, which some — with Tertullian himself, at least in his later life and perhaps even now — excluded from confessional jurisdiction. We point this out because of the frequency with which the passage is found mis-applied.
2. ἐξομολόγεσις = confession.
3. Not *caris* but *aris*. Even in pre-Christian times the pagan altar was a place of refuge for the criminal; and *ara* is found in various idiomatic phrases in which it is best translated as a *place of refuge*. There is manuscript evidence for both readings; but *caris* is to be rejected.
4. *I.e.,* confession.
5. *publicationem.*
6. Obviously Tertullian says this in irony.
7. *palam.*
8. This is undoubtedly the sense of a badly corrupted line: *Malo enim amans si pervenitur.*
9. The great eruption of Mount Vesuvius was in the year 79 A. D. It erupted again, however, in 203 A. D. It is because of the apparent freshness of this latter event in Tertullian's mind that the present work is usually assigned to the year 203 or 204 A. D. Being at heart a gullible sceptic, I accept the date but reject the dubious basis of its establishment.

TO MY WIFE [inter A. D. 200 / 206]

To My Wife belongs to the years between 200 and 206 A. D., therefore, to Tertullian's Catholic period. He wrote in all three treatises on marriage and remarriage: a second, *An Exhortation to Chastity,* in his semi-Montanist period, and a third, *Monogamy,* in his Montanist period.

In this first of the three treatises he urges that his wife not remarry in the event of his death; or that, if she do remarry, her spouse be a Christian.

Migne's text, PL 1, 1274-1304, is no longer an adequate instrument for scholarly purposes. Kroymann's text in CSEL, Vol. 70, Vienna 1942, pp. 96-124, required only a few slight revisions for inclusion in the *Corpus Christianorum,* Vol. 1, Turnhout 1954, pp. 373-394.

318

[2, 5, 2]

"Do not," He says, "cast your pearls to swine, lest they trample them and turn about to destroy you also (1)." Your pearls are in fact the marks of your daily conduct. The more care you take to conceal them, so much the more suspect will you make them, and the more you will expose them to the curiosity of a pagan. [3] Can you hide it when you sign your bed or your body? when with a breath you blow away some impurity (2)? When during the night you rise to pray? And will you not seem to be engaged in some magic rite? Will a husband not know what you secretly taste before taking any food? And if he were to know that it is Bread, would he not believe it to be that bread which it is said to be (3)? [4] And will he, ignorant of the reason for these things, simply endure them?

858
865
872

320

[2, 8, 4]

Shall a faithful Christian woman be ashamed to marry one of the faithful because he
has not much goods, when she would be enriched for the future by a husband who is   972
poor? [5] . . . Should (4) she hesitate and investigate and speculate repeatedly whether
he will be suitable to receive her dowry, when God has entrusted him with His own   980
property? [6] How shall we suffice for the telling of that happiness of that marriage which 890
the Church arranges, which the sacrifice strengthens, on which the blessing sets a seal, which 974
the angels proclaim, and which has the Father's approval?   480

1. Matt. 7:6.
2. A common exorcism, still performed in the rite of Baptism.
3. Possibly this means only that the pagan husband will think that the Eucharist which his wife is reserving
   secretly at home and which she takes before meals is only ordinary bread. More likely, however, it means
   that when he spies her so taking the Eucharist when she thinks she is unobserved, he will believe it to be
   what rumor reports of it: that it is bread dipped in the blood of a murdered infant.
4. Another tradition of dividing the text makes this passage not a part of 2, 8, 5, but the beginning of a
   new chapter, 2, 9, 1.

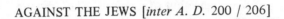

AGAINST THE JEWS [*inter A. D.* 200 / 206]

The treatise *Against the Jews* is usually assigned to Tertullian's Catholic period, and
between the years 200 and 206 A. D. Further, it is generally agreed that chapters 9
through 14 do not constitute an authentic part of the present work, but are an
addition made largely from a re-working of parts of Book 3 of Tertullian's *Adversus
Marcionem,* representing a clumsy attempt of one of Tertullian's friends to complete
the work. Although it is possible to hold for authenticity of the entire work, we will
cite nothing from the questionable chapters.

Migne's text, PL 2, 597-642, is no longer serviceable. Kroymann's text in Vol. 70
of the CSEL, Vienna 1942, pp. 251-331, has had only slight revisions made in it for
inclusion in the *Corpus Christianorum,* Vol. 2, Turnhout 1954, pp. 1339-1396.

320a

[7, 4]

In whom else have all nations believed, if not in the Christ, who has already come? The   85
Parthians and the Medes and the Elamites; and they who inhabit Mesopotamia, Armenia,
and Cappodocia; and they who dwell in Pontus and Asia, in Phrygia and Pamphylia;
sojourners in Egypt and inhabitants of the parts of Africa beyond Cyrene, Romans and
foreign residents; yes, and Jews in Jerusalem, and other peoples: by this time even the
various tribes of Getulians, and the many boundaries of the Moors, and all the confines
of Spain, and the various nations of Gaul; and the places of the Britons, inaccessible to
the Romans, but already subjugated to Christ; and of the Sarmatians and Dacians and
Germans and Scythians, and of the many remote tribes and provinces and islands unknown
to us and which we are scarcely able to enumerate — [5] in all these places the name of
Christ, who has already come, is reigning; and before Him the gates of all cities are
opened, and none are closed to Him before whom iron bars are crumbled and bronze
gates are thrown wide. . . . [9] The name of Christ, however, is extending everywhere.
Everywhere He is believed. He is worshipped by all the nations enumerated above. He
rules everywhere. He is everywhere adored.

AGAINST HERMOGENES [*inter A. D.* 200 / 206]

Another work of Tertullian's Catholic period, and from the years between 200 and 206 A. D., is the treatise *Against Hermogenes.* An artist, Hermogenes was a gnostic of Carthage; and in writing against him Tertullian probably made use of an earlier treatise, now lost, *Against the Heresy of Hermogenes,* by Theophilus of Antioch.

The Migne text, PL 2, 197-238, no longer serves the needs of scholars. Emil Kroymann's text, in the CSEL, Vol. 47, Vienna 1946, pp. 126-176, is reprinted, with some emendations of the apparatus, in the *Corpus Christianorum,* Vol. 1, Turnhout 1954, pp. 397-435. The text used as the basis of our present translated selections is the edition of J. H. Waszink in the series *Stromata,* fasc. 5, Utrecht and Antwerp 1956.

321

[3, 3]

We say that the name of God always existed with Himself and in Himself, but the name   151
of Lord not always. There is a difference in what is to be understood by each of the   156
terms. God, of course, is the name of the substance itself, which is Divinity; Lord, however, is not the name of a substance but of a power. The substance, I maintain, always existed with its own name, which is God. The name Lord came afterwards, when, of course, something was added. [4] Ever since those things began to exist, over which the power of the Lord might act, from that very moment, through the accession of power, He both became Lord and received that name. God is Father, and likewise, God is Judge; but it does not follow that He is always Father and Judge, simply on the grounds that He is always God; for He could not be Father before the Son was, nor Judge before there   292
was sin (1).

322

[4, 3]

Whatever special property God has, it must necessarily be unique, so that it can belong   157
to Him who is One. [4] But what can be unique and singular except that to which nothing can be equated? What can be principal, if not that which is above all, if not that which is before all and from which all things are? [5] It is by being the sole possessor of these qualities that He is God; and by being sole possessor, that He is One. And if another should have them, then there will be as many gods as there are beings who possess the qualities proper to God. It is thus that Hermogenes implies two gods: he introduces   468
matter as equal to God. [6] God, however, must be One, because that which is supreme is God; but nothing can be supreme except that which is unique; but nothing can be unique if something else can be made its equal. Matter, however, will be made equal to God, if it be reckoned as eternal.

323

[8, 1]

Worse than that, by contending that God made all things out of matter, Hermogenes   461
even makes matter superior to God, and subjects God to it. If God used matter in the work of creating the world, matter is thereby found to be the superior, since it provided Him with the material for His work; and thus God were seen to be subject to matter, whose substance He needed. There is no one who does not need him whose property he uses; and there is no one who is not subject to him whose property he needs to make use of. And again, there is no one who, by using the property of another, is not inferior

to him whose property he uses; and there is no one who allows his property to be used by another, who is not thereby superior to him whom he allows to use it.

Therefore, matter itself, no doubt, was not in need of God, but rather lent itself to God, who needed it — rich and abundant and liberal as it was, to One who was, I suppose, too small and weak and too unskilled to make what He wanted out of nothing. [2] What a grand benefit matter conferred upon God, that today He should have something whereby He can be known as God and be called the Almighty — except that He is no longer almighty, if He was not able to do this also: to make all things out of nothing. [3] To be sure, matter would also have conferred something on itself in getting itself acknowledged together with God, as coequal to God and even as His helper — except that Hermogenes is the only man who ever knew this, along with those patriarchs of the heretics, the philosophers. At any rate, up to the present time it has escaped the Prophets and the Apostles, and, I think, Christ too.

158

324

[16, 3]

I do not see how Hermogenes can escape the fact that God, in whatever way He created evil out of matter, either of His own will or of necessity or for some reason, cannot be regarded as the author of evil. Further, if the author of evil is He that actually made it, matter being merely associated with Him by providing Him with its substance, then the reason for which matter was introduced is dismissed (2). For, if matter is assumed so that God will not seem to be the author of evil, nevertheless, God is still, through the instrumentality of matter, shown to be the author of evil. Matter, then, having been excluded because the reason for its having been introduced is dismissed, it remains that God undoubtedly made all things out of nothing. [4] We shall see whether this includes evil things, when it becomes apparent what things are evil, and whether those things really are evil which at present you regard as such.

469

461

325

[17, 1]

This rule [that all things were created out of nothing] is upheld by the fact of God's being unique. He is the unique God for this reason alone, that He is the sole God; and He is the sole God for this reason alone, that nothing existed along with Him. So too, He must be the first, because all else is after Him. All else is after Him because all else is from Him — and from Him because they are created out of nothing. The account of Scripture, then, is correct: "Who has known the mind of the Lord? or who has been His counsellor? or whom has He consulted? or who showed Him the way of wisdom and knowledge? who gave, and recompense will be made to him (3)?"

158
468
461

326

[19, 1]

Thus [the opposition] has seized upon the opportunity provided by certain words, in accord with the usual practice of heretics, of twisting the simplest things. For instance, they would have it that the *beginning* (4) itself, in which God made both heaven and earth, was like something substantial and corporeal, and is able to be understood as matter. [2] We, however, defend for every word its proper meaning; that *principium* means *beginning* (5), and that this word was used quite appropriately in regard to things then taking their inception. Nothing which has becoming is without a beginning; nay, rather, its beginning is the very moment of its starting to become. Thus *principium* or *initium* is a word signifying *inception,* and not the name of a substance.

461

327

[20, 3]

I too, then, claim for myself the support of this passage of Scripture (6), because it   461
mentions both God who made something, and the things which He made; but whence
He made them is not stated. Since in every work there are three principal elements:
the one who makes, and that which is made, and that from which it is made — there
are three names to be mentioned in a correct description of a work: the person of the
maker, the kind of thing made, and the form of material used. If the material is not
mentioned, while both the artifact and the one who made the artifact are mentioned,
it is clear that he made the artifact from nothing; for the source would also have been
mentioned, if he had made his artifact from something.

328

[21, 2]

I say that even if Scripture did not expressly declare that all things were made out   461
of nothing, just as neither does it say that they were made out of matter, there was not
so great a necessity of expressly indicating that all things were made out of nothing, as
there would have been of declaring their having been made out of matter. In the case
of that which is made out of nothing, it is clear that it is made out of nothing, since it
is not shown to have been made out of something; and there is no danger of its being
thought to have been made out of something, when from what it was made is not
stated. . . .

[4] Therefore, if God was able to make all things out of nothing, Scripture can
omit mention of the fact that He did make them out of nothing; but if, of course,
He had made them from matter, it ought by all means have been stated that He made
them out of matter; for the former would certainly be understood, even if it were not
stated; but the latter would be in doubt, unless it were stated.

1. Hermogenes, if Tertullian reports him correctly, had argued that matter was not created but was itself
   eternal. His supporting argument was that the name Lord, like that of God, is eternal; but if He was
   Lord eternally, there had to be something else eternal over which He was Lord. In refuting him,
   Tertullian unfortunately denies that Lord is an eternal title, saying that from eternity God is God, but
   not until creation can He be called Lord. In continuing the argument he seems also to say that the
   Son is not eternal. How his words are to be interpreted may, of course, be debated: but he uses the
   very expression which, 125 years later, will designate the rankest sort of Arianism.
2. Hermogenes, unwilling to make God the author of evil, introduced matter as pre-existing, in order to
   explain the existence of evil. Tertullian counters that if God used pre-existing matter in fashioning
   what is evil, He still must be regarded as the author of evil: so there was no reason to posit pre-existing
   matter in the first place. Tertullian seems not to have met his opponent's objection head-on; and in
   any case, it must be admitted that Tertullian is not entirely above simplifying an opponent's position
   in order to make an easier refutation.
3. Rom. 11:34-35. Is. 40:14.
4. *principium.*
5. *initium.*
6. *I.e.,* Gen. 1:1 — In the beginning God made heaven and earth.

THE VEILING OF VIRGINS [*ca. A. D.* 206 *nisi forte* 213]

The treatise on *The Veiling of Virgins* belongs to the year 206 A. D., to the
beginning of Tertullian's so-called semi-Montanist period, when he began to pass
gradually but perceptibly from orthodoxy to heresy; or, according to some
authors, to about the year 213 A. D., when he was already a Montanist.

Migne's text, PL 2, 888-914, is no longer useful to the scholar. The edition
of Eligius Dekkers is in the *Corpus Christianorum*, Vol. 2, Turnhout 1954, pp.

1209-1226. As the basis for our translations we have used the text of G. F. Diercks in *Stromata,* fasc. 4, Utrecht and Antwerp 1956, pp. 39-60.

328a

[1, 3]
 The rule of faith, indeed, is altogether one, alone unchangeable and irreformable. It   420
is as follows: to believe in òne only almighty God, the Creator of the world; and in His 157
Son, Jesus Christ, born of the Virgin Mary, crucified under Pontius Pilate, raised up 158,460
from the dead on the third day, received into heaven, and now sitting at the right of the 302
Father, waiting to come to judge the living and the dead during the resurrection of the 781,392
flesh. [4] This law of faith remaining the same, the other points of discipline and 1011
practice admit newer correction, since, of course, the grace of God works and perfects 105
up to the end.

328b

[1, 5]
 What, then, is the administrative office of the Paraclete, if not this? — that discipline 20
be directed, that the Scriptures be revealed, that the understanding be reshaped, and that
progress be made to those things which are better.

329

[2, 1]
 Throughout Greece and certain of its barbaric provinces, a majority of the Churches
veil their virgins. And, lest any ascribe the practice to Greek or barbarian social custom (1),
there are places under this sky (2) where the practice is observed. But I have proposed
as a standard those Churches which the Apostles themselves or apostolic men founded, 422
and, I think, among these, those which are earlier than others. And these, then, have 102
equal authority in regard to custom, because they have weightier appeal to antiquity and
to predecessors than do those which are later. [2] What shall we observe? What shall
we cherish? We cannot be contemptuous of a custom which we cannot condemn. No
more can we call it strange, since we find it not among strangers but among those to
whom we do in fact communicate the right to peace and the name of brotherhood.
With them we have one faith, one God, the same Christ, the same hope, the same 820
sacraments of washing (3) — let me say it all at once: we are one Church. 420

330

[6, 1]
 Writing to the Galatians, [the Apostle] says: "God sent His own Son, born of a 781
woman (4)," who certainly is admitted to have been a virgin, even if Ebion deny it. I
acknowledge, too, that the angel Gabriel was sent to a virgin (5). But when he blesses
her, he ranks her not among virgins but among women: "Blessed art thou among
women (6)." The angel also knew that even a virgin may be a woman. . . . [4] Certainly
there is nothing here that may be regarded as having been spoken prophetically, as if by
saying "born of a woman" the Apostle was naming her as one who was about to become
a woman, that is, married; for he was not able to name her as formerly a woman, of whom
Christ was not to be born, that is, one who had known man. But she who was present,
she who was a virgin, was called a woman in consequence of the meaning of this word
applied in the widest sense to a virgin as included in the universal class of women (7).

1. *gentilitati.* Here we have a word in the process of its forming. Normally in ecclesiastical Latin *gentilitas* means paganism. Here, however, the meaning of *social custom* is quite evident. The word has taken a step towards what we mean by *gentility.*
2. *I.e.,* in Carthaginian Africa, Tertullian's native place, to which he had returned in *A. D.* 195, after an extended residence in Rome.
3. *eadem lavacri sacramenta.* The plural number is a little puzzling. We dismiss immediately, however, the notion that he might have meant Baptism and Penance. Surely only Baptism can be so designated. No doubt it is merely a piece of unsound rhetoric, as one might say: "Their Baptism is the same as our Baptism: we have the same *Baptisms.*"
4. Gal. 4:4.
5. Luke 1:26-27.
6. Luke 1:28.
7. Only by a misunderstanding of the passage is this argument sometimes presented as a denial on the part of Tertullian, of Mary's virginity. It is precisely the opposite. Involved and abstruse, it takes a while to sink in — but in all, when properly understood, it is a fairly good argument. Tertullian says in effect: Scripture calls Mary a virgin at the time of the Annunciation. St. Paul, however, refers to her as a woman, in reference to Christ's being born of her. But Paul cannot thereby mean that she was not a virgin at the time of Christ's birth. For if Mary, a virgin at the time of the Annunciation, was not to be still a virgin at the time of Christ's birth, Paul would not have called attention to it, because it would have been in no way remarkable. That a woman who bears a child is a virgin is worth notice; that she is not a virgin requires no notice. Nor could she have formerly known man, for she is called a virgin at the Annunciation. So when Paul calls her a woman, whatever he means, he is not thereby distinguishing woman from virgin. Tertullian concludes that she is called a woman merely as a generic term, and a virgin more specifically. In the present passage, then, so far from denying her virginity, Tertullian is proved to have believed in the virginity of Mary *ante partum,* while saying nothing whatever of virginity *in partu* and *post partum.* Her virginity *in partu* and *post partum* he does in fact deny in another place *(see § 359 below).*

AGAINST MARCION [*inter A. D.* 207-212]

The treatise in five books *Against Marcion* is Tertullian's longest single work. An early edition consisted most probably of book 1 only, which was written about the year 207 A. D. A second edition, consisting perhaps of books 1 to 3, belongs to the years 207 and 208 A. D. Between 208 and 212 A. D. books 4 and 5 were added, and the work took its present form. Although it is of his semi-Montanist period, the treatise is of special value, since it is the principal source for our knowledge of the heresy of Marcion.

The Migne text, PL 2, 246-524, is no longer of much use to the scholar. The text of Emil Kroymann first made its appearance in CSEL, Vol. 47, Vienna 1906, pp. 290-650. The Kroymann edition, with revisions in the critical apparatus, has now appeared again, in the *Corpus Christianorum,* Vol. 1, Turnhout 1954, pp. 441-726.

331

[1, 3, 1]

Christian truth, however, has distinctly declared, "If God be not one, He does not   157
exist"; for we more properly believe that that which is not what it must be does not exist
at all. [2] So that you may know, however, that God must be one, ask what God is,   175
and you will find that such is the case. In so far as a human being is able to formulate
a definition of God, I formulate such a definition as the conscience of every man may   130
acknowledge; God is the Great Supreme Being existing in eternity, unbegotten, uncreated,   156
without beginning, and without end.

332

[1, 10, 1]

Indeed, He was recognized from the very beginning as their Creator by the objects   131

of creation themselves, which were brought forth for just this purpose: that He might be
known as God. ... [3] For the knowledge of God is, from the beginning, an endowment   135
of the soul.

334

[1, 18, 2]
    It is our definition that God must be known first from nature, and afterwards He is   130
authenticated from instruction: by nature, from His works; by instruction, from His   137
revelations.   11

335

[2, 5, 5]
    I find that man was constituted by God with a freedom of both his own will and his   505
own power; for I observe in him the image and likeness of God by nothing so clearly as
by this, the characteristic of his estate. [6] ... That such is his estate has been confirmed
even by the fact of the law which was then imposed upon him by God. [7] For a law
would not be imposed upon one who did not have it in his power to render the obedience
due to law. Nor again, would the penalty of death be attached to transgression, if contempt   636
for the law were impossible to man within the freedom of his will.

337

[3, 19, 3]
    [The cross of Christ] is the wood of which also Jeremias gives you an inkling when,   853
in prophecy, he tells the Jews that they would say: "Come, let us throw wood onto his
bread (1)," meaning the body. [4] For thus did the Lord in His Gospel reveal it also to
you, calling His Body bread, so that from that time onward you might understand that He
gave a figure of His own body to bread (2). The prophet of old pictured His body as
bread; and the Lord Himself has afterwards done that whereby the sign is to be interpreted.

338

[3, 24, 3]
    We confess that a kingdom has been promised to us on earth, but before heaven and   1016
in another state of existence. It will be after the resurrection for a thousand years in
the divinely built city of Jerusalem, let down from heaven (3), which the Apostle also
calls "our mother from above (4)." And, declaring that our πολίτευμα, that is, our
citizenship, is in heaven (5), he states thereby that it is in fact a city in heaven. [4]
This also Ezechiel knew (6), and the Apostle John saw (7); and the word of the new
prophecy, which is part of our faith (8), attests to the foretelling that there would be as
a sign an image of this city exhibited before its manifestation.
    Moreover, this prophecy has been quite recently fulfilled on an expedition to the East.
It is agreed even by pagan witnesses that in Judaea a city was suspended in the sky early
every morning for forty days. As the day advanced every outline of its walls vanished,
or if anyone approached, there was nothing. [5] We say that this city has been provided
by God for receiving the saints after the resurrection and for refreshing them with every
truly spiritual good, to compensate them abundantly for those things which in this world
we have either despised or lost; for it is both just and worthy of God to give joy to His
servants in that very place where they suffered for the sake of His name. This is the
reason for the sub-celestial kingdom.
    [6] After its thousand years are over, during which period the resurrection of the
saints will be completed, who will rise earlier or later according to their merits, there will

be the destruction of the world and the conflagration at the judgment. We shall then be
changed in an instant into the angelic substance, evidently through the outer garment of   1044
incorruption; and we shall be transported into the heavenly kingdom.

339

[4, 2, 1]

I pass on now to a description of the Gospel — not that of Jewry but of the Pontus (9)   61
— which has sometimes been adulterated; and I shall now indicate the order which we   69
shall follow. First of all, we take the position that the evangelical testament (10) has as
its authors Apostles, upon whom the task of promulgating the Gospel was imposed by the   67
Lord Himself. And if there are also apostolic men, they are not on their own, but are   64
with the Apostles. . . . [2] Of the Apostles, then, John and Matthew first introduce the   66
faith to us, and of the apostolic men, Luke and Mark refresh it for us.   65

340

[4, 4, 1]

I say that my [Gospel] is the true one; Marcion says that his is. I affirm that Marcion's   69
is adulterated; Marcion, that mine is. How shall it be settled between these two, except
on the grounds of time — by ascribing authority to that which is found to be more ancient,
and by assuming corruption in the case of that which is convicted of being the more
recent? . . . [5] Since Marcion emends, he confirms both points: that the Gospel in
which he changes what is found is the prior one; and that his is the more recent, which
he has put together from the emendation of ours, making his new one.

341

[4, 5, 1]

In short: if it is evident that that is the truer which is earlier, if that is the earlier   102
which is from the very beginning, if that is from the beginning which was authored by   422
the Apostles, then it will likewise be evident that that has been handed down by the
Apostles, which has been held sacrosanct in the Churches of the Apostles. Let us see   40
what milk the Corinthians drained from Paul; against what standard the Galatians were   42
measured for correction; what the Philippians, Thessalonians, and Ephesians read; what   431
even the nearby Romans sound forth, to whom both Peter and Paul bequeathed the Gospel
and even sealed it with their blood.

[2] We have, too, the Churches fostered by John. And even if Marcion rejects his
Apocalypse, still, the order of their bishops, when reckoned up, will depend upon John   440
as their author. The excellence of other Churches is recognized in like manner. I say,
therefore, that in these Churches — and not only in those founded by Apostles but in
the Churches throughout the world which are united with them in the fellowship of the   66
sacrament (11) — the Gospel of Luke, which we defend with all our strength, has stood   69
from the beginning of its publication. That of Marcion, however, is unknown to most;
and there are none who know it who do not condemn it.

[3] It has, of course, its churches also, but they are its own, as late as they are
spurious. And should you want to know their origin, you will more easily find them
apostate than apostolic, with Marcion, of course, their founder, or someone of Marcion's
swarm. Even wasps make honey-combs, and the Marcionites make churches. The same
authority of the apostolic Churches will defend the other Gospels, which we possess   61
through them and because of their using them. I mean the Gospels of John and Matthew,   67
while that issued by Mark may be affirmed to be Peter's, whose interpreter Mark was.   64
And the digest by Luke men are accustomed to ascribe to Paul (12).   65

342

[4, 34, 4]

I maintain, then, that Christ now made the prohibition of divorce conditional: "If   975
anyone should dismiss his wife for the purpose of marrying another."

"Whoever dismisses his wife," He says, "and marries another, commits adultery; and
whoever marries her who has been dismissed by her husband, is equally an adulterer (13)"
— dismissed, then, for that very reason for which dismissal is not permitted: to marry
another. And he that marries a woman who has been dismissed unlawfully is as much
an adulterer as he that marries one who has not been dismissed. [5] The marriage
which is not rightly dissolved is permanent. To marry again, however, while there is a
permanent marriage, is adultery. Therefore, if he conditionally forbade the dismissing
of a wife, He did not forbid it absolutely; and what He did not forbid absolutely, He
permitted in certain cases, where the reason for prohibition was not present.

And thus His teaching is not contrary to Moses, whose precept — I do not yet say He
confirms it — He partially observes. . . . Indeed, in your sect, what is a husband to do,
if his wife commit adultery? Shall he keep her? But your own Apostle, you know,
would not join the members of Christ to a prostitute (14). [6] The justice of divorce,
therefore, has Christ, too, for its defender. Henceforth Moses must be considered as
confirmed by Christ, Moses having permitted divorce for the same cause that Christ permits
it: if there should be found any unchaste commerce on the part of the woman. For in
the Gospel of Matthew He says: "Whoever dismisses his wife, except for the cause of
adultery, makes her commit adultery (15)." And thus he too is regarded as an adulterer,
who marries a woman who has been dismissed by her husband.

343

[4, 40, 3]

Having taken bread and having distributed it to His disciples, He made it His own Body   853
by saying, "This is My Body (16)" — that is, the 'figure of My Body.' A figure, however,
there could not have been, unless there was in truth a body. Some empty thing, which is   310
a phantasm, were not able to satisfy a figure (17). Or, if He pretended that bread were
His Body, because in truth He lacked a Body, then He must have given bread for us (18).
It would support the vanity of Marcion, had bread been crucified (19)! But why call His
Body bread, and not rather a pumpkin, which Marcion had in place of a brain (20)!
Marcion did not understand how ancient is that figure of the Body of Christ, who said
Himself through Jeremias: "They have devised a device against Me, saying, 'Come, let
us throw wood onto his bread (21)' " — the cross, of course, upon His Body (22).

344

[5, 1, 1]

Nothing is without origin except God only. Inasmuch as origin occupies first place in   564
the condition of all things, so also must it necessarily take precedence in the treatment
of them, so that agreement may be reached in regard to their condition; for you could
not find the means to examine the quality of a thing, unless first you have certainty of
its existence by knowing its origin. And since in the course of my little work I have
been brought to this point, I wish to know from Marcion the origin even of the Apostle
Paul. Something of a new disciple, I am the follower of none other; but at the same
time, I can believe nothing except that nothing ought to be believed rashly — and anything
is indeed rashly believed if it is believed without an examination of its origin.

345

[5, 9, 3]

In regard to that which is called the resurrection of the dead, it is necessary to defend   1011

the proper meaning of the terms *of the dead* and *resurrection*. The word dead signifies   990
merely that something has lost the soul, by which faculty formerly it lived. The body is
that which loses the soul, and by its loss becomes dead. The term *dead,* then, applies to
a body. Moreover, if resurrection is of the dead, and *dead* applies only to a body, the
resurrection will be of a body. [4] Again, the word *resurrection* applies to nothing else   1013
except that which has fallen. *To rise* may be said of that which never in any way fell,
but which was always lying down. But *to rise again* can be said only of that which has
fallen; for by *rising again* that which fell is said to *re-surrect.* The syllable *re* always
implies iteration. We say, therefore, that a body falls to the ground in death, a fact which
is self-evident in accord with the law of God. For it was to the body that it was said:
"Earth you are, and unto earth you shall return (23)." Thus, that which came from the
earth shall return to the earth; and that which returns to the earth falls; and that which   611
falls, rises again.   375

[5] "Because by a man came death, by a man also comes resurrection (24)." Here,
by the word *man,* who consists of a body, as we have often shown already, I understand
that it is a fact that Christ had a body. And if we are all made to live in Christ as we
were made to die in Adam, then, as in the flesh we were made to die in Adam, so also   614
in the flesh are we made to live in Christ. Otherwise, if the coming to life in Christ
were not to take place in that same substance in which we die in Adam, the parallel
were imperfect.

1. Jer. 11:19.
2. *ut et hinc iam eum intellegas corporis sui figuram pani dedisse.* Others read *corpori* and *panis,* for which,
   however, there is unsatisfactory manuscript evidence. Further, no such change is necessary, the passage
   being quite intelligible as it stands. See below, § 343, with its final note.
3. Apoc. 21:2.
4. Gal. 4:26.
5. Phil. 3:20.
6. Ezech. 48:30-35.
7. Apoc. 21:2.
8. *I.e.,* Montanism.
9. Marcion's homeland was in the Pontus.
10. *evangelicum instrumentum.*
11. *de societate sacramenti. I.e.,* in the bond of the faith.
12. The Gospel of Luke, considered to be a digest of Paul's teaching.
13. Luke 16:18.
14. 1 Cor. 6:15. Marcion rejected all of the Old Testament and most of the New. He retained, however, the
    Gospel of Luke, Paul's companion, and most of the Epistles in the Pauline tradition. Hence, Marcion
    making Paul and his own sometimes distorted understanding of Paul his cornerstone, Tertullian sarcastically
    refers to Paul as the Marcionites' *own Apostle.* It should be observed, too, that whatever we think of
    Tertullian's view of how Luke 16:18 is to be understood, his position might appear to have been stronger
    had he cited instead the correlative passage in Matt. 5:32, where the seeming condition "except on
    account of immorality" is expressed. In fact, he does cite Matthew presently as corroborating his view;
    but he had to exclude Matthew at the outset because the whole of Matthew's Gospel was rejected by the
    Marcionite sect.
15. Matt. 5:32.
16. Luke 22:19.
17. *figuram capere non posset.*
18. *I.e.,* on the cross.
19. Tertullian is arguing against Marcion's Docetism, which held that Christ had no real body, but only a
    phantasm, the appearance of a body. Attempting to make that position ridiculous, Tertullian says that
    if Christ had no real body, then, when He said over the bread, "This is My Body," He must have meant
    that His Body was bread. And then it would have been that bread were nailed to the cross for our
    salvation.
20. *cordis loco.*
21. Jer. 11:19.
22. Some have misunderstood this entire passage, as if it were a denial of the Real Presence of Christ in the
    Eucharist, when in fact it is an emphatic affirmation of the same. The problem, of course, is in the
    phrase "figure of My Body," which, however, must not be divorced from the clear statement immediately
    preceding it, and the explanation which follows it. The passage from Jeremias, cited also in 3, 19, 3
    [§ 337 above] makes the use of the term *figura* intelligible. The bread of Jeremias 11:19 is a figure,

a type as it were, of Christ's Body. Whatever one say of the text tradition of the Scripture passage, for Tertullian the wood is the cross, and the bread is Christ. Hence, when He took bread and "made it His own Body, by saying, 'This is My Body,' " He thereby gave substance to the figure in Jeremias, and thereby enabled the prophecy of laying wood on bread to be fulfilled – *i.e.*, by actually making bread the figure of His Body, as it had already been pre-figured in Jeremias.

23. Gen. 3:19.
24. 1 Cor. 15:21.

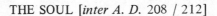

THE SOUL [*inter A. D.* 208 / 212]

Also of Tertullian's semi-Montanist period, dating from between the years 208 and 212 A. D., is the treatise on *The Soul*. Except for the *Adversus Marcionem*, this were the longest of his writings.

The Migne text, PL 2, 646-752, is no longer useful. The series CSEL in Vol. 20, Vienna 1890, offers the text of A. Reifferscheid and G. Wissowa. Even this is now largely replaced by the text established by J. H. Waszink, published originally in a separate edition at Amsterdam in 1947, and now reprinted in *Corpus Christianorum*, Vol. 2, Turnhout 1954, pp. 781-869.

346

[7, 1]

In hell the soul of a certain man is put to grief, is punished in flames, and suffers excruciating thirst; and it implores a drop of moisture from the finger of a happier soul (1). [2] Do you suppose that the end of the blessed poor man and of the miserable rich man is imaginary? And why is the name Eleazar (2) there if this is not an actual occurrence? But even if it is to be regarded as imaginary, it is still a testimony to the truth. For if the soul had no bodily substance (3), the image of a soul could not embrace the image of bodily substance; nor would the Scriptures lie about the limbs of a body, if such did not exist (4).

1032

501

346a

[9, 1]

When we assert that the soul has body of a quality proper to itself, by that fact we at the same time assert the existence of the other accidents of corporality. Either they belong to the soul, since we have shown it to be a body, having qualities peculiar to itself in accord with the special nature of its body; or, if these accidents are not present, that too is in accord with the special nature of the soul's corporality, from which are absent certain qualities which are present in all other bodies. Nevertheless, we shall not be inconsistent if we solemnly profess that whatever are the usual characteristics of corporality, these are found also with the soul, such as location, confinement, and the threefold dimensions by which philosophers measure all bodies, that is, length and breadth and height.

501

348

[21, 5]

A wicked tree will not yield good fruits, unless it be grafted; nor will a good tree yield wicked fruits, unless cultivated thereto (5). Indeed, stones will become children of Abraham, if they be formed in Abraham's faith; and a brood of vipers may bring forth fruits of penitence, if they reject the poison of their malignant nature (6). [6] This can be brought about by the strength of God's grace, more powerful even than nature itself,

650

696

holding as subject to itself even our faculty of free will which is said to be
αὐτεξούσιος (7). But since this faculty is itself both natural and mutable, in whatever
direction it is turned, its nature so inclines it.

349

[22, 2]

We define the soul as born of the breath of God, immortal, corporal, having form,   501
simple in substance, acquiring knowledge by its own operation, showing itself in various   502
ways, free to choose, subject to misfortunes, changeable according to natural inclinations,   613
rational, the mistress, she who divines, descended from a single source (8).

349a

[27, 1]

How, then, is a living being conceived? Is the substance of both body and soul formed
together at the same time, or does one of them precede the other? We do indeed
maintain that both are conceived, formed and perfected at the same time, as also they
are born together; nor is there any moment intervening in their conception, which
would give a prior place to either. [2] Consider the first events in the light of the last.
If death is defined as nothing other than the separation of body and soul, then life, the   990
opposite of death, should be defined as nothing else but the union of body and soul.
If the separation occurs by means of death at one and the same time to both substances,
then the pattern of union must likewise give assurance that, in reference to life, it occurs
simultaneously to both substances. [3] We acknowledge, therefore, that life begins with
conception, because we contend that the soul begins at conception. Life begins when the
soul begins.

350

[41, 3]

God alone is without sin. The only man without sin is Christ; for Christ is also   301
God.   345

351

[55, 3]

To no one is heaven open. I do not mean it is closed, for after all, the earth is still   996
safe. When the world shall pass away, the kingdoms of the heavens shall be unlocked.
[4] But shall our rest be in the ether with the boy-chasers of Plato (9)? or in the air
with Arius? or around the moon with the Endymions of the Stoics? "Certainly not,
but in paradise," you say, "to which place the patriarchs and prophets have already
gone in the retinue of the Lord's resurrection!" How is it, then, that the region of
paradise which was revealed to John in the spirit, and which was seen beneath the
altar (10), displays no souls therein except those of the martyrs? How is it that Perpetua,
that most heroic martyr, on the day of her passion, in a vision of paradise, saw only
martyrs there? . . . [5] . . . The only key to paradise is your blood. You have our
little book *On Paradise* (11), in which we prove that every soul is detained in Hades until
the day of the Lord (12).

352

[58, 1]

Every soul, therefore, is shut up in Hades? Do you admit it? Whether you do or   996

not, it is a fact. And there are already punishments and rewards there; and there you
have a poor man and a rich one (13). . . . [6] The soul does not perform all its operations with the assistance of the flesh; and divine judgment pursues even simple thoughts
and mere desires. "Whoever shall look in lust has already committed adultery in his   632
heart (14)." Therefore and on this account it is most fitting that the soul, without
waiting for the flesh, be punished for what it did without the partnership of the flesh.
And for pious and benevolent thoughts in which it shared not with the flesh, without
the flesh it shall be refreshed. . . . [8] In short, if we understand that prison of which
the Gospel speaks to be Hades, and if we interpret the last farthing (15) to be the light
offense which is to be expiated there before the resurrection, no one will doubt that the   1000
soul undergoes some punishments in Hades, without prejudice to the fullness of the
resurrection, after which recompense will be made through the flesh also.

1. Luke 16:22 ff.
2. He means, of course, Lazarus; and *Lazari* is found already in the *editio princeps* and following editions.
   Eleazari is the reading, however, of the sole manuscript, the 9th-century *Codex Agobardinus*.
3. *corpus.*
4. See also § 346a, § 349, and especially § 355 below; and it will be clear that Tertullian, while he *seems*
   to say that the soul is corporeal, really has only a rather odd understanding of what corporality is.
5. See Luke 6:43.
6. See Matt. 3:7-9.
7. *I.e.,* completely self-determinative.
8. The final somewhat cryptic remark must be understood in the light of 27, 9, where Tertullian writes:
   "Therefore the entire abundance of souls comes from one man." He distinguishes between the seed of
   the body and the seed of the soul, both of which, however, are transmitted at the same time and by the
   same coition, the act of generation reproducing the whole man, soul and body. Thus, as our bodies are
   descended from Adam, so also are our souls. Plainly, this is Traducianism.
9. *cum puerariis Platonis.*
10. Apoc. 6:9.
11. Unfortunately not; for it is one of the seven works of Tertullian which we know only by their titles.
12. In chapter 58 of the present work, § 352 below, Tertullian notes that already in Hades and before the
    resurrection souls are either rewarded or punished. Therefore, it is not proper to cite the present
    passage, as some have done, to show that Tertullian believed reward and punishment was delayed until
    after the general judgment.
13. Luke 16:22 ff.
14. Matt. 5:28.
15. Matt. 5:25-26.

THE FLESH OF CHRIST [*inter A. D.* 208 / 212]

The treatise on *The Flesh of Christ*, written between the years 208 and 212 A. D.,
is of Tertullian's semi-Montanist period. The Migne text, PL 2, 754-792, is no longer
suitable for scholarly purposes, and is entirely superseded by the edition of Emil
Kroymann, first published in CSEL, Volume 70, Vienna 1942, pp. 189-250, now
reprinted with only slight revisions in the apparatus, in *Corpus Christianorum*, Vol.
2, Turnhout 1954, pp. 873-917.

353

[5, 2]
But tell me now, you murderer of truth, was the Lord not really crucified? And having   310
been really crucified, did He not really die? And indeed, having really died, did He not
really rise again? [3] Did Paul falsely determine to know nothing among us except Him
who was crucified (1)? Did he falsely insist that He was buried? falsely teach that He rose
again? Then our faith is also false, and all that we hope for from Christ is but a phantasm.
You wickedest of men, you excuse the murderers of the Lord! For Christ suffered nothing

from them, if He did not really suffer anything. Spare the one hope of the whole world. Would you destroy the indispensable dishonor of the faith? However it may be unworthy of God, it is needful to me. I am saved, if I am not ashamed of my Lord. "Whoever will be ashamed of Me," He says, "of him also will I be ashamed (2)."

[4] I find no other reasons for shame — which might, by my contempt of shame, prove me shameless in a good sense, and foolish in a happy way. The Son of God is crucified: and I am not ashamed that it ought be cause for shame. The Son of God is dead: and it is believable, because it is folly. And having been buried, He rose again: it is certain, because it is impossible. [5] But how will all these things be true of Him, if   311
He Himself was not true; if He did not really have in Himself what might be crucified, what might die, what might be buried and rise again — the flesh, of course, suffused with blood, built up over bones, interwoven with nerves, entwined with veins? His flesh knew how to be born and how to die — human without doubt, as born of man and therefore   313
mortal — this flesh in Christ is man and son of man.

[6] Or why is Christ man and son of man, if in Him there is nothing of man and nothing from man? . . . [7] The origins of both His substances display Him as man and   322
as God: from the one, born, and from the other, not born; from the one, flesh, and from the other, spiritual; from the one, weak, and from the other, exceedingly strong; from the one, dying, and from the other, living. . . . [8] Would you with a lie divide Christ in halves? He was all truth. Believe me, He chose to be born, rather than to make a lie of any part of Himself.

354

[6, 9]

It is plain that those angels [who appeared, along with the Lord, to Abraham] bore   483
a flesh which was not properly their own; for their nature is of a spiritual substance,— and, if in some way corporeal, yet, in a manner peculiar to themselves, — but is able to assume for a time the appearance of human flesh, so that they could be seen and could converse with men. [10] Since, then, we have not been told whence they assumed flesh, it but remains for our understanding not to doubt that it is a property of the angelic power to take upon itself a body from nothing material.

354a

[7, 3]

I do not accept what you introduce apart from Scripture and on your own authority.   10

355

[11, 4]

If [the soul] has something by which it exists, that must be its body. Everything   501
which exists is a body of its own proper kind. Nothing is incorporeal except that which does not exist (3).

356

[14, 1]

"But Christ," they say, "also bore the nature of an angel." For what reason? And   371
why did He take human nature? Might both be for the same reason? Christ bore human nature in order to be man's salvation — to restore, of course, that which had been lost. Man had been lost; it was necessary that man be restored. But there was no such reason why Christ would take upon Himself angelic nature. [2] And even if perdition   491
is the lot of angels in that fire prepared for the devil and his angels (4), no restoration   1033

was ever promised them. Christ received no command from the Father to save the angels. What the Father neither promised nor commanded, Christ was not able to undertake (5).

357

[16, 2]

   We maintain, however, that what has been laid aside in Christ is not the flesh of sin, but the sin of flesh: not the material thing, but its state (6); not the substance, but its flaw (7); and this is in accord with the authority of the Apostle, who says, "He has laid aside sin in the flesh (8)." [3] And although elsewhere he says that Christ was "in the likeness of sinful flesh (9)," he does not mean that He took upon Himself the likeness of flesh, as if it were but an image of a body and not its reality; but he wishes it to be understood that the likeness is to flesh which sinned, because the flesh of Christ, which committed no sin itself, was the same kind as that in which there was sin, though not to be equated (10) with it in regard to vice. [4] From this, then, we affirm that the flesh of Christ is the same as that which in man is prone to sin (11), but in which in Him sin had been laid aside. Christ has flesh without sin, which men can have only with sin.

310
345

358

[16, 5]

   Again, — and let this be said to all those who do not think that our flesh was in Christ (12), because He was not conceived through the seed of man, — let them remember that Adam himself was made of this flesh without the seed of man. As the earth was converted into this flesh without the seed of man, so also was the Word of God able to pass into the material of flesh without the agency of that seed. . . . [17, 2] He that was to inaugurate a new kind of birth must Himself be born in a new way, concerning which Isaias foretold that the Lord would give a sign. And what is that sign? "Behold, a virgin shall conceive in the womb and bear a son (13)." A virgin did afterwards conceive and bear Emmanuel, which name means *God with us.*

   . . . [17, 4] And again, lest I depart from my argumentation on the name of Adam: why is Christ called Adam by the Apostle, if as man He was not of that earthly origin? But even reason defends this conclusion: that God recovered His image and likeness in a procedure similar to that in which He had been robbed of it by the devil. [5] For it was while Eve was still a virgin that the word of the devil crept in to erect an edifice of death.

   Likewise, through a Virgin, the Word of God was introduced to set up a structure of life. Thus, what had been laid waste in ruin by this sex, was by the same sex re-established in salvation. Eve had believed the serpent; Mary believed Gabriel. That which the one destroyed by believing, the other, by believing, set straight.

781

784

359

[23, 2]

   [Mary] was a virgin, in so far as a husband is concerned; and not a virgin, in so far as child-bearing is concerned. . . .[3] Although she was a virgin when she conceived, she became a wife by bearing her child (14). . . . [5] Indeed, she ought to be said to be not a virgin rather than a virgin, because she became a mother at a leap, as it were, before she became a wife.

781
782

1. 1 Cor. 2:2.
2. Matt. 10:33; Mark 8:38; Luke 9:26.
3. Tertullian's frequent statement that the soul is itself corporeal becomes intelligible in the light of the

present statement, which makes corporality a necessary concomitant of existence. He makes it clear that the corporality of the soul is something different from the corporality of the body, frequently noting, as he does here, that the corporality of the soul or of any spiritual substance is *sui generis*.

4. Matt. 25:41.
5. Through the rest of the chapter Tertullian continues to argue against the unnamed heretics who say that Christ assumed angelic nature. After a great many *aiunt's,* or the equivalent thereof, he finally mentions that the Ebionites say that Christ was mere man, but had an angel in Him. It may be, afterall, that it was only the Ebionites whom Tertullian had in mind, with his indefinite "they say."
6. *naturam.*
7. *culpam.*
8. Rom. 8:3. Tertullian writes: *"Evacuavit peccatum in carne."*
9. If the immediately preceding remark is in fact an imperfect citation of Rom. 8:3, then the present situation is not *alibi*, as Tertullian says, but in the same place.
10. We read, with Kroymann's most recent edition: *non vitio adaequanda*. Others read *non vitio Adae. Quando* . . . . The latter would explicitly exempt Christ from original sin. It is not the fact that we doubt, but only the reading.
11. *cuius natura est in homine peccatrix.*
12. *I.e.,* that Christ's flesh was the same kind as ours.
13. Is. 7:14; Matt. 1:23.
14. *in parte suo.* Tertullian strenuously defends the virginity of Mary *ante partum.* He denies virginity *in partu,* believing that the birth of Christ came about in the natural manner, thus opening the womb. While this is merely a question of physical virginity, he seems also to have denied virginity *post partum,* holding that the *brethren of Jesus* were in fact later children of Mary and Joseph. In any case, if he is something less than precise in regard to the latter point, he does seem to say such in a manner stronger than mere implication; and he was so understood by those close to his own time. Helvidius appealed to Tertullian as to an authority for that same opinion; and it was in reference to this opinion that Jerome said: "As to Tertullian I have nothing else to say except that he was not a man of the Church."

THE RESURRECTION OF THE DEAD [*inter A. D.* 208 / 212]

The treatise on *The Resurrection of the Dead* is quite intimately connected with the treatise on *The Flesh of Christ,* and was written very soon after the latter, belonging also to the semi-Montanist period, to the years between 208 and 212 A. D.

The Migne text, PL 2, 795-886, cannot be depended upon for scholarly investigations. The text established by Emil Kroymann is in CSEL, Vol. 47, Vienna 1906, pp. 25-125; but it is now in turn replaced by the text of J. G. Ph. Borleffs, in *Corpus Christianorum,* Vol. 2, Turnhout 1954, pp. 921-1012.

359a

[1, 1]

The resurrection of the dead is the assurance of Christians. Through it we are believers (1). 558 Truth compels us to believe it, the truth which God makes known.

360

[5, 6]

"And God made man (2)," it says. [7] The procedure is, without doubt, vastly   509 different; and that, of course, because of the condition of the things made. For the creatures which were made were inferior to him for whom they were made; — if, indeed, they were made for man, to whom they were soon rendered subject by God. Rightly, then, as servants, they came forth into the world at a bidding and at a command and solely by a vocal ordinance. Man, on the contrary, as their master, was fashioned by God Himself.

361

[6, 2]
    Indeed, a great affair was in progress when that clay was being fashioned [into man]. 509
It is honored, then, as often as it feels the hand of God, when it is touched, when it is
pulled, when it is drawn out, when it is moulded. [3] Think of God being wholly
employed and devoted to it, whose lines He was determining by His hand, His eye, His
labor, His judgment, His wisdom, His providence, and above all else, His affection. In
whatever way the clay was pressed out, He was thinking of Christ, the Man who was one
day to be: because the Word, too, was to be both clay and flesh, as the world was then.
[4] Thus it was that the Father did say beforehand to the Son: "Let us make man in 233
our image and likeness. And God made man," — that is, the creature which He 512
fashioned, — "to the image of God," — of Christ, of course, — "He made him (3)."

362

[8, 2]
    No soul whatever is able to obtain salvation, unless it has believed while it was in the
flesh. Indeed, the flesh is the hinge of salvation. In that regard, when the soul is 808
deputed to something by God, it is the flesh which makes it able to carry out the 820
commission which God has given it. [3] The flesh, then, is washed, so that the soul 836
may be made clean. The flesh is anointed, so that the soul may be dedicated to holiness. 840
The flesh is signed, so that the soul too may be fortified. The flesh is shaded by the 846
imposition of hands, so that the soul too may be illuminated by the Spirit. The flesh 792
feeds on the Body and Blood of Christ, so that the soul too may fatten on God. They 851
cannot, then, be separated in their reward, when they are united in their works. 877

363

[11, 5]
    Certainly you have among your philosophers men who maintain that this world is
without a beginning and was not created. But a majority, almost all even of the heresies,
allow it a beginning and a maker, and ascribe its creation to our God. [6] Firmly
believe, therefore, that He made it wholly out of nothing; and by believing that He has 461
such powers, you will have found the knowledge of God. But some persons, too weak
to believe this at first, would rather have it, as the philosophers say, that the universe
was made by Him from some matter already pre-existing (4). . . . [9] If God produced
all things out of nothing, He will also be able to draw forth from nothing the flesh which
has fallen into nothing; or, if He shaped other things out of matter, He will also be
able to call forth the flesh from something else, from wherever it has been swallowed up. 1011
[10] And surely He that created is competent to re-create, since it is a much greater
thing to produce than it is to re-produce, and to give a beginning than to maintain in
existence. You may be sure, therefore, that to restore the flesh is easier than to initiate
it.

364

[14, 10]
    We say, first of all, that it must be believed that the judgment of God is full and 1011
perfect, in such a way that it is final and therefore perpetual; and that it is just, since 1020
it is not less severe with some than with others; and that, full and perfect, it is worthy
of God, since it is in keeping with His patience. It follows, then, that the fullness and
perfection of the judgment consists in nothing else than in its representing of the interests

of the whole man. [11] Since the whole man is comprised in the union of both substances (5), he must appear in both; for it is necessary that he who passed through life in his entirety be judged in his entirety. Therefore, as he lived, so shall he be judged, because he must be judged concerning the way in which he lived. Life is the reason for judgment, and it must be investigated in as many substances as those in which it functioned.

365

[63, 1]

Therefore, the flesh shall rise again: certainly of every man, certainly the same flesh, and certainly in its entirety. Wherever it is, it is in safe keeping with God through that most faithful Agent between God and man, Jesus Christ (6), who shall reconcile both God to man and man to God, the spirit to the flesh and the flesh to the spirit.

    1012
    1013

1. *Illam credentes sumus.* The import of the line is that *the resurrection is the key-stone of our faith.* To translate Tertullian in a literal fashion and still retain intelligibility is often well-nigh impossible.
2. Gen. 1:27.
3. Gen. 1:26-27.
4. *de materia . . . subiacenti.*
5. *I.e.,* body and soul.
6. 1 Tim. 2:5.

AN EXHORTATION TO CHASTITY [inter A. D. 208 / 212]

    Also of the years between 208 and 212 A. D., and of his semi-Montanist period, is Tertullian's treatise *An Exhortation to Chastity.* It is addressed to a friend, recently widowed, urging him not to marry again: for although God tolerates second marriages, they are really a kind of fornication. Whereas in *To My Wife* Tertullian praised Christian marriage, now he can only praise virginity and continence, while regarding even first marriages as degrading. He quotes the Montanist prophetess Prisca in the present work; but he has not as yet made a full break with the Church.

    The Migne text, PL 2, 913-930, is no longer of scholarly usefulness, having been superseded by the text of Emil Kroymann, in CSEL, Vol. 70, Vienna 1942, pp. 125-152, reproduced with only minor emendations in *Corpus Christianorum,* Vol. 2, Turnhout 1954, pp. 1015-1035.

366

[7, 2]

    Vain shall we be if we consider that what is not lawful for priests is lawful for the laity. [3] Are not we of the laity also priests? For it is written, "A kingdom also, and priests to God and His Father has He made us (1)." The authority of the Church and the dignity which pertains to those sanctified by God in the assembly of order (2) has established a difference between those in orders and the laity (3). Where there is no assembly of ecclesiastical order, you both sacrifice and baptize, and you are a priest to yourself alone. Indeed, where there are three, there is the Church, even be they laymen. [4] . . . Therefore, if you have in yourself, when necessary, the right of a priest, it behooves you to keep also the discipline of a priest, even when it is not necessary for you to exercise the right of a priest. As a digamist, would you baptize? As a digamist, would you sacrifice? [5] How much more serious a crime is it for a digamist layman to act the part of a priest, when the priest himself who became a digamist is deprived of his priestly function.

    "But," you say, "allowance must be made for necessity." No necessity is excused, if it could have been avoided. Therefore, do not be found in digamy, and you will not expose

    951

    829
    866

    979

    964

yourself to the necessity of performing those ministrations which are forbidden to a
digamist. [6] God wills us all to be so disposed that we might properly administer His
sacraments at any time. So true is this, that unless the laity also observe the rules which
pertain to those who are chosen as priests, how will there be any priests, since they are
chosen from among laymen? We must contend, therefore, that the obligation of
abstaining from a second marriage rests first on the layman, since none other but a layman
who has been married only once can become a priest.

1. Apoc. 1:6.
2. *et honor per ordinis consessus sanctificatos deo.* The *consessus ordinis* or *assembly of order* is apparently a
   technical term for the clergy, the clerical estate, men in orders, Holy Orders.
3. *inter ordinem et plebem.*

THE CROWN [*A. D.* 211]

Another treatise of Tertullian's semi-Montanist period is *The Crown,* written in
211 A. D. It concerns the problems of a Christian in military service.
    The Migne text, PL 2, 73-102, is not suitable any more for scholarly purposes,
having been superseded by Emil Kroymann's text, in CSEL Vol. 70, Vienna 1942,
pp. 153-188, reprinted with some emendations in the apparatus, in the *Corpus
Christianorum,* Vol. 2, Turnhout 1954, pp. 1039-1065.

367

[3, 2]
    To put it briefly, let me turn to Baptism. When we are about to enter the water — no,   822
just a little before, — in the church and under the hand of the bishop (1) we solemnly
profess that we renounce the devil and his pomps and his angels (2). [3] Thereupon we are   825
immersed three times, complying somewhat more amply with what the Lord enjoined
in the Gospel. Then, when we are taken out, we taste first of all a mixture of milk and
honey; and from that day for a whole week we abstain from the daily bath. The
Sacrament of the Eucharist, which the Lord commanded to be taken at meal times and by
all, we take even before daybreak in congregations, but from the hand of none others   897
except the presidents (3).   898
    We offer sacrifices for the dead on their birthday anniversaries (4). [4] We regard it   1001
as unlawful to fast or to worship on our knees on the Lord's Day. We rejoice in the same
privilege from the Paschal Day until Pentecost (5). We take anxious care lest something   851
of our Cup or Bread should fall upon the ground. At every forward step and movement,   859
when coming in and going out, when putting on our clothes, when putting on our shoes,
when bathing, when at table, when lighting the lamps, when reclining, when sitting, in all
the ordinary occupations of our daily lives, we furrow our forehead with the sign.   125

1. *sub antistitis manu.*
2. *contestamur nos renuntiare diabolo et pompae et angelis eius.* The precise terms will be interesting since they
   are so very like those still in use.
3. *nec de aliorum manu quam praesidentium sumimus.*
4. *pro nataliciis annua. I.e.,* on the anniversary of their death, their birthday into eternal life.
5. See § 651z below, where we find that in 325 A. D. the First Ecumenical Council of Nicaea, for the sake of
   uniformity of liturgical practice, in its 20th canon forbade the custom of those "who are bending their
   knees on Sunday and on the days of Pentecost."

IDOLATRY [*A. D.* 211 *aut* 212]

The treatise on *Idolatry* was written in 211 or 212 A. D., and thus it belongs still to Tertullian's semi-Montanist period. Migne's text, PL 1, 663-696, is no longer useful. The Reifferscheid-Wissowa text of the CSEL Vol. 20, Vienna 1890, pp. 30-58, is reprinted with emendations of the apparatus, in *Corpus Christianorum,* Vol. 2, Turnhout 1954, pp. 1101-1124.

368

[7, 1]

Zeal for the faith will pray at length and in tears over this: that a Christian comes from   875
idols to the church; that he comes from the workshop of the adversary to the house of
God; that he lifts up to God the Father hands which are the mother of idols; that he
worships God with those same hands which otherwise are employed in worship against God.
Shall he touch the Body of the Lord with those same hands which give bodies to demons?
[2] Nor does that suffice. If it be not enough that those hands receive from others What
they contaminate, they even give to others What they have contaminated. [3] The makers
of idols are chosen for ecclesiastical orders! How wicked! The Jews laid hands on Christ
once, but these men mangle His Body daily. Oh, hands to be cut off! Let it now be seen
whether or not it was said only figuratively, "If your hand causes you to offend, cut if
off (1)." What hands deserve more to be cut off than those which cause offense to the
Body of the Lord?

1. Matt. 18:8.

ANTIDOTE AGAINST THE SCORPION [*A. D.* 211 *aut* 212]

Tertullian's *Antidote Against the Scorpion* is a defense of martyrdom against the opinion of certain gnostics who held that God did not demand such ultimate heroism. It belongs to his semi-Montanist period, and was written in 211 or 212 A.D.

Migne's text, PL 1, 121-154, is entirely superseded by that of August Reifferscheid and George Wissowa in CSEL Vol. 20, Vienna 1890, pp. 144-179, reprinted with emendations in the critical apparatus, in the *Corpus Christianorum,* Vol. 2, Turnhout 1954, pp. 1069-1097.

368a

[15, 3]

And if a heretic wants a faith backed by public record, let the archives of the empire
speak, as would the stones of Jerusalem. We read the lives of the Caesars. In Rome Nero
was the first to stain with blood the rising faith. Peter was girded about by another (1),   431
when he was made fast to the cross. Paul obtained a birth suited to Roman citizenship,
when in that city he was given re-birth by an ennobling martyrdom. [4] When and
wherever I read these things, I learn to suffer. Nor is it of any concern to me whichever
I follow as teachers of martyrdom, whether the declarations of the Apostles, or their
deaths — except that in their deaths I recall their declarations also.

1. John 21:18.

TO SCAPULA [*A. D.* 212]

The treatise *To Scapula,* dating from late in the year 212 A. D. at the end of Tertullian's semi-Montanist period, is addressed to that Proconsul of Africa who had re-instituted bloody persecutory measures against the Christians. Tertullian warns him against, or, to be more accurate, threatens him with the wrath of God.

The Migne text, PL 1, 697-706, no longer serves scholarly purposes. The edition of T. Bindley, *Tertulliani De Praescriptione haereticorum, Ad martyres, Ad Scapulam,* Oxford 1893, has yielded its place of standard edition to the text established by E. Dekkers in *Corpus Christianorum,* Vol. 2, Turnhout 1954, pp. 1127-1132.

369

[2, 10]

It ought to be clear enough to you that we do indeed act under a discipline of divine   85
patience, since, although we are such a multitude of men, almost the greater part of any   87
city, we conduct ourselves quietly and modestly. Perhaps we are better known as individuals than as a group, nor are we recognized in any other way than by the reformation of our former vices.

FLIGHT IN TIME OF PERSECUTION [*A. D.* 213]

Whereas in the treatises *To My Wife* and on *Patience* Tertullian had allowed that in time of persecution we are permitted to flee from place to place in order to escape torture, and had in fact stated that it is better to flee than to be arrested and run the risk of denying, his usual rigorism has now increased and has taken over even in the present area. He now holds, in the treatise on *Flight in Time of Persecution,* that to so flee is contrary to the will of God.

Tertullian gives ample evidence in the work that he is now a Montanist outright, taking occasion several times to denounce those who do not receive the Paraclete, *i.e.,* those who do not accept the new revelations of the Paraclete, made through the Montanist prophets and prophetesses. The work belongs to the year 213 A. D.

The Migne text, PL 2, 103-120, is no longer useful. J. J. Thierry revised the text he first published at Hilversum, 1941, for inclusion in the *Corpus Christianorum,* Vol. 2, Turnhout 1954, pp. 1135-1155, which latter may now be regarded as the standard edition.

370

[12, 2]

But that you should redeem with money a man whom Christ has redeemed with His   374
own blood, how unworthy it is to God and His providence! On your behalf He did not spare His own Son (1) from being cursed for us; for cursed is he that hangs on the tree (2); . . . and He was delivered up to death, even to death on the cross (3). All this, that He might purchase us from our sins. . . . [3] And the Lord indeed redeemed him from the angels who rule the world, from powers, from eternal judgment, from everlasting death. But you bargain for him with an informer or a soldier or some petty thief of a ruler, under the fold of the tunic as they say, as if he were stolen goods, though Christ bought him in the face of the whole world, yes, and gave him his freedom.

1. Rom 8:32.
2. Deut. 21:23; Gal. 3:13.
3. Phil. 2:8.

AGAINST PRAXEAS [*post A. D.* 213]

The treatise *Against Praxeas,* written after 213 A. D., or perhaps even in that very year, is a work of Tertullian's Montanist period. He accuses Praxeas of various Trinitarian heresies, and denounces him quite bitterly as being responsible for the condemnation in Rome of the new prophets and prophetesses of Montanism.

The Migne text, PL 2, 154-196, is no longer of much use to scholars. The text of Emil Kroymann appeared in the series CSEL, Vol. 47, Vienna 1906, pp. 227-289; and the text of Ernest Evans was published by the SPCK, London 1948. The two are collated and reworked with numerous emendations of apparatus, the resultant appearing as the Kroymann-Evans text in *Corpus Christianorum,* Vol. 2, Turnhout 1954, pp. 1159-1205. The last serves as the basis for the present translations.

371

[2, 1]

We do indeed believe that there is only one God; but we believe that under this   237
dispensation, or, as we say, οἰκονομία, there is also a Son of this one only God, His Word   262
[*Sermo*], who proceeded from Him, and through whom all things were made and without   284
whom nothing was made (1). We believe that He was sent by the Father into a Virgin   781
and was born of her, God and man, Son of Man and Son of God, and was called by the   302
name Jesus Christ. We believe that He suffered and that, in accord with the Scriptures,   311
He died and was buried; and that He was raised again by the Father to resume His place   347
in heaven, sitting at the right of the Father; and that He will come to judge the living   391
and the dead. We believe that He sent down from the Father, in accord with His own   392
promise, the Holy Spirit, the Paraclete, the Sanctifier of the faith of those who believe in   285
the Father and in the Son and in the Holy Spirit.   230

[2] That this rule of faith has been current since the beginning of the Gospel, before   100
even the earlier heretics, – much more, then, before Praxeas, who is but of yesterday, – will be apparent both from the lateness itself of all heresies, and from the utter novelty of this Praxeas of Yesterday. In this we have a presumptive principle against all heresies: whatever is first is true, whatever is late is spurious.

[3] But while keeping to this demurrer always, there must, nevertheless, be place for   105
reviewing, for the sake of the instruction and protection of various persons. Otherwise it might seem that each perverse opinion is not examined but simply pre-judged and condemned. This is especially so in the case of the present heresy, which considers itself to have the pure truth when it supposes that one cannot believe in the one only God in   293
any other way than by saying that Father, Son, and Spirit are the very selfsame Person.
[4] As if One were not All even in this way, that All are One – through unity of substance, of course!

And at the same time the mystery (2) of the οἰκονομία is safeguarded, for the Unity is   238
distributed in a Trinity (3). Placed in order, the Three are Father, Son, and Spirit. They are Three, however, not in condition, but in degree (4); not in substance, but in form (5); not in power, but in kind (6); of one substance, however, and one condition, and one power, because He is one God of whom these degrees and forms and kinds are taken into account in the name of the Father, and of the Son, and of the Holy Spirit.

372

[4, 1]

I believe that the Spirit proceeds not otherwise than from the Father through the   272
Son (7).

373

[7, 1]

   Then, therefore (8), even the Word [*Sermo*] Himself takes His own aspect and attire (9),   252
His own sound and voice, when God says: "Let there be light (10)." This is the perfect   262
nativity of the Word, while He is proceeding from God. Formed by Him first for the sake   265
of what was to be thought out in the name of Wisdom, — the Lord formed me as the   261
beginning of His ways (11), — then He was begotten to carry all into effect: — when He
prepared the heavens, I was present there (12).
   Thus, the Father makes Him equal to Himself; and the Son, by proceeding from Him,
was made the first-begotten, since He was begotten before all things; and the only-
begotten, because He alone was begotten of God, in a manner peculiar to Himself, from
the womb of His own heart, to which even the Father Himself gives witness: "My heart
has poured forth My finest Word (13)."

374

[7, 8]

   Who will deny that God is body, although God is spirit (14)? For spirit has a body of   152
a quality peculiar to itself, in its own form. [9] But if even invisible things, whatever they
are, are like God both as regards His body and His form, on which account they are visible
to God alone, how much more, then, shall He not be without substance, who is sent   252
forth from God's substance! Therefore, whatever was the substance of the Word, I call   258
That a Person, and I defend for Him the name of Son; and since I acknowledge Him as   259
Son, I assert that He is second after the Father (15).

375

[8, 5]

   I would not hesitate to call the Son a stem from the root and a river from the fountain
and a ray from the sun; because every source is a parent, and everything that issues from
the source is an offspring. Much more is this true of the Word [*Sermo*] of God, who even
receives the name Son as His proper designation. The stem is not separated from the root
nor the river from the fountain, nor the ray from the sun. Neither, then, is the Word
separated from God.
   [6] Following, therefore, the form of these examples, I profess that I do call God and His
Word, — the Father and His Son, — two. For the root and the stem are two things, but
conjoined; the fountain and the river are two kinds, but indivisible; the sun and the ray   258
are two forms, but coherent ones. [7] Anything which proceeds from another must
necessarily be a second to that from which it proceeds; but it is not on that account
separated from it. Where there is a second, however, there are two; and where there is
a third, there are three. The Spirit, then, is third from God and the Son (16), just as the   273
third from the root is the fruit from the stem, and third from the fountain is the stream
from the river, and third from the sun is the apex of the ray.

376

[9, 1]

   Keep always in mind the rule of faith which I profess and by which I bear witness   230
that the Father and the Son and the Spirit are inseparable from each other, and then you
will understand what is meant by it. Observe, now, that I say the Father is other, and the   238
Son is other, and the Spirit is other. This statement is wrongly understood by every
uneducated or perversely disposed individual, as if it meant diversity and implied by that
diversity a separation of Father, Son, and Holy Spirit.
   I say this, however, out of necessity, — since they contend that the Father and the Son

and the Spirit are the selfsame Person, thus extolling the monarchy at the expense of the   293
οἰκονομία (17), – that the Son is other than the Father not by diversity but by
distribution. He is not other by division but by distinction; for the Father is not the
same as the Son, since they differ one from another by a kind of measure (18). [2]   257
The Father is the whole substance, while the Son, indeed, is a derivation and portion   259
of the whole (19) as He Himself professes: "Because the Father is greater than I (20)."   258
In the psalm His minority is sung as being a little less than the angels (21). Thus the   290
Father is other than the Son, because He is greater than the Son; because He that
begets is other than Him that is begotten; because He that sends is other than Him
that is sent; because He that makes something is other than Him through whom He
makes it.

[3] Happily the Lord Himself used this expression in regard to the Person of the
Paraclete, signifying not division but disposition: "I will ask the Father," He says, "and
He will send you another Advocate, the Spirit of truth (22)." Thus He showed that the
Son is other than the Father. He showed in the Paraclete a third degree, just as we believe   237
that the Son is a second degree, by reason of the order observed in the οἰκονομία.

377

[13, 5]

We who by the grace of God examine the times and the motives of the Scriptures, and   230
who are disciples not of men but especially of the Paraclete (23), – we do indeed define
that there are two, Father and Son, and with the Holy Spirit even a third, in accord with
the principle of the οἰκονομία, which distinguishes as to number, lest, as your perversity   302
would infer, the Father Himself be believed to have been born and to have suffered –
which, in fact, it is not lawful to believe, since it has not been handed down. [6] That
there are two Gods and two Lords, however, is a statement which we will never allow
to issue from our mouth – not as if the Father and the Son were not God, nor the Spirit   301
God, and each of them God; but formerly two were spoken of as Gods and two as   266
Lords (24), so that when Christ would come, He might both be acknowledged as God and   232
be called Lord, because He is the Son of Him who is both God and Lord.

378

[25, 1]

The Father and the Son are distinguished by what is proper to each. He promises to
send the Paraclete also, for whom He will ask the Father, after He has ascended to the
Father; and He calls the Paraclete 'another' (25). How it is that He is 'another' we have
already explained (26). Further, He says, "He will receive of what is mine (27)," just as
He Himself had received from the Father. Thus the connection of the Father in the Son,   270
and of the Son in the Paraclete, produces three who, though coherent, are distinct one   238
from another. These three are one (28), and yet not one: for "I and the Father are   235
one (29)" was said in regard to their unity of substance, but not in regard to a singularity
of number.

379

[27, 6]

This, then, must be the point of our inquiry: How the Word [Sermo] became flesh, whether   262
as if by being transfigured in the flesh, or by actually being clothed in the flesh. Certainly   321
it was by actually being clothed in flesh; for it is still necessary to believe that God is   322
immutable and unchanging, inasmuch as He is eternal. [7] Transfiguration, however, is
the very destruction of what formerly was; for anything that is transfigured into something

else ceases to be what it was and begins to be what it was not. God, however, neither ceases to be, nor can He become other than He is. The Word, indeed, is God; and the Word of the Lord endures forever (30), by continuing of course, in His own proper form. Since He cannot be transfigured, it follows that His becoming flesh must be understood in just this sense, that He really comes to be in the flesh, and is made visible, is seen, and is touched by means of that flesh, and that all else in this matter must be understood in the same way.

[8] For if the Word had become flesh by a transfiguration and change of substance, then Jesus would have one substance produced out of two, flesh and spirit, a mixture such as electrum, of gold and silver; and He would be neither gold nor silver, – that is, neither spirit nor flesh, – but the one would be changed by the other, and a third produced. [9] And then, when He was made flesh, Jesus were no longer God, for the Word had ceased to be. ... [10] In fact, however, we find Him expressly set forth as God and man, as this same psalm suggests: "Because God was born man therein, and He built it up by the will of the Father (31)." ... [11] We see a twofold state, not   324
confused but conjoined in one person, Jesus, God and man.

Of Christ, I defer what I have to say. The property of each substance is so preserved,   332
that the spirit performed its own actions in Him, such as miracles and feats and signs, while the flesh carried on the affections proper to it, such as being hungry when He was tempted by the devil, being thirsty when He was with the Samaritan woman, weeping   348
for Lazarus, being troubled at death, and at last, actually dying. [12] But had some   349
third substance been formed from the confusion of the two, such as electrum, there would be no such distinct proofs apparent of either substance. By a transference of functions, the spirit might have performed corporal deeds, and the flesh might have done spiritual deeds; or there might have been neither corporal nor spiritual evidences, but some third kind as a result of that confusion.

1. John 1:3.
2. *sacramentum.*
3. This is the first usage of the Latin word *Trinitas* in respect to the Godhead. The corresponding Greek term, τρίας, had already been used by Theophilus of Antioch (§ 180 above).
4. *non statu sed gradu.*
5. *nec substantia sed forma.*
6. *nec potestate sed specie.* Whether or not Tertullian is entirely free of Subordinationism can be debated; but he certainly gives us no cause to think him in any way a Modalist. In fact, it is Modalism that he is here arguing against. Nevertheless, in putting the passage into English, it is difficult to find any translation of *specie* that will be entirely free of modalist overtones. We are conscious of the fact that, after giving the matter much thought and finally settling for *kind,* we have not done him a perfect service.
7. *a Patre per Filium.*
8. *Tunc igitur.* Given the context of the present passage, the temporal connotations of these words cannot be escaped. Tertullian is slipping again into a pre-Arian Arianism (see above, § 321, n. 1).
9. *speciem et ornatum.*
10. Gen. 1:3.
11. Prov. 8:22.
12. Prov. 8:27.
13. Ps. 44 [45]:2.
14. John 4:24. See § 355 above.
15. If this is Subordinationism, it is not clearly so.
16. *Tertius est Spiritus a Deo et Filio.*
17. Tertullian uses οἰκονομία as synonymous with *dispensatio* (see above, § 371), by which he means the relationship actually existing between the persons of the Trinity.
18. *modulo alius ab alio.*
19. *derivatio totius et portio.*
20. John 14:28.
21. Ps. 8:6.
22. John 14:16.
23. This is one of the clear indications that Tertullian is now fully in the camp of the Montanists, who claim special revelation and continued charisms.
24. By the term *formerly* he means in the Old Testament. Earlier in this same chapter Tertullian cited numerous such Scripture passages as *The Lord said to my Lord* (Ps. 109 [110]:1), *the Lord rained ... brimstone and*

fire from the Lord (Gen. 19:24), and also *the Word was with God and the Word was God* (John 1:1), as proof that there are two, each of whom is called Lord and God.

25. John 14:16.
26. See above, § 376.
27. John 16:14.
28. 1 John 5:7.
29. John 10:30.
30. Is. 40:8.
31. Ps. 86 [87]:5. That he calls it the same psalm is merely a reference to the fact that he had already quoted the same verse in 27, 5.

MONOGAMY [*post A. D.* 213]

The treatise on *Mongamy* was written after 213 A. D. and belongs to Tertullian's Montanist period. The Migne text, PL 2, 930-954, is now entirely superseded by the text of E. Dekkers in *Corpus Christianorum,* Vol. 2, Turnhout 1954, pp. 1229-1253.

380

[8, 2]

It was a Virgin who gave birth to Christ; and she would marry once only, after she brought Him forth. The reason for this was that both titles to sanctity might be exhibited in Christ's parentage, born as He was of a Mother who was both a Virgin and a wife to one husband.

781
783

381

[8, 4]

Peter alone [among the Apostles] do I find married, and through mention of his mother-in-law. I presume he was a monogamist; for the Church, built upon him, would for the future appoint to every degree of orders none but monogamists. As for the rest, since I do not find them married, I must presume they were either eunuchs or continent (1).

964
430

382

[10, 1]

A woman, after the death of her husband, is bound not less firmly but even more so, not to marry another husband. . . . [4] Indeed, she prays for his soul and asks that he may, while waiting, find rest; and that he may share in the first resurrection (2). And each year, on the anniversary of his death, she offers the sacrifice.

979
1001

890

1. St. Polycrates of Ephesus knew that the Apostle Philip had three daughters (see above § 190a).
2. See *Against Marcion* 3, 24, 6, in § 338 above.

MODESTY [*ca. A. D.* 220]

The treatise on *Modesty,* written about the year 220 A. D., belongs to Tertullian's Montanist period. The Migne text, PL 2, 980-1030, is long since outmoded by the Reifferscheid-Wissowa edition in CSEL Vol. 20, Vienna 1890, pp. 219-273; and this has in turn been replaced by the text of E. Dekkers in *Corpus Christianorum,* Vol. 2, Turnhout 1954, pp. 1281-1330.

383

[1, 6]

I hear that there has even been an edict, and indeed, a peremptory one. A pontiff —   902
sovereign, of course — that is, a bishop of bishops (1) — has declared: "I remit the sins
both of adultery and of fornication, for such as have done penance." [7] Oh, edict to
which it is not possible to subscribe a "well-done!"

384

[4, 4]

With us even clandestine unions, that is, unions which have not been professed before-   980
hand in the presence of the Church, run the risk of being judged as adultery and fornication; 972
nor can they escape the charge of such crime by being afterwards woven together under a
covering of matrimony.

385

[5, 14]

There stands the idolater, there the murderer, and between them an adulterer. They   901
sit as one in the performing of the duties of penance. They tremble in sackcloth and   902
ashes; they weep with the same lament; they go about with the same prayers; they   904
make supplication on the same knees; they invoke the same mother. [15] What will
you do, gentlest and most humane discipline? Either you must be this same to all of
them — for blessed are the peace-makers (2) — or, if not to any, then you must come
over to us (3). Can you condemn once and for all the idolater and the murderer, while
withdrawing the adulterer from their midst? the adulterer, who is successor to the idolater,
predecessor to the murderer, and companion to both? That is respect of persons, while
abandoning the more pitiable penitents!

386

[18, 18]

But if the clemency of God extends to those who are still ignorant and unbelieving,
then certainly repentance will be an invitation to receive clemency. It must be remembered,   911
however, in regard to that kind of penance which is done after having received the faith,   906
that for lesser sins (4) it will be able to obtain pardon from the bishop; but for the   901
greater and irremissible sins (5), from God only.

386a

[20, 2]

There is extant a work of Barnabas addressed to the Hebrews (6), a man so sufficiently   907
strengthened by God, that Paul put him next to himself in the observance of abstinence:
"Or is it I alone and Barnabas who have not the right to do this (7)?" And, of course,
this letter of Barnabas is more generally received by the Churches than is the apocryphal
Shepherd of adulterers (8).

[3] Warning the disciples to omit all that is elementary and to strive for perfection,
and not to lay again a foundation of repentence on works of the dead (9), he says:
"For it is impossible for those who were once enlightened, who have both tasted the
heavenly gift and become partakers of the Holy Spirit, and who have tasted the sweet
Word of God, when they shall have fallen away, — their time already fleeting, — to be
recalled again in repentance, crucifying again for themselves the Son of God, and making
of Him a mockery. [4] For the earth that drinks in the rain that often falls upon it, and

produces vegetation that is of use to those by whom it is cultivated, receives a blessing from God; but that which brings forth thorns is worthless and is near to being cursed, and its end is in being burned (10)."

387

[21, 7]

"But," you say, "the Church has the power of forgiving sins." This I acknowledge.   900
And I account it even more than you do, since I have the Paraclete Himself, who says through the new prophets: "The Church is able to forgive sins; but I will not do it, lest they might commit others too (11)." [8] What if a pseudo-prophetic spirit has made that declaration? But the part of a subverter were more to recommend himself by clemency, and to lead others into sin; or, if he has been eager to simulate the Spirit of Truth, then indeed the Spirit of Truth is able to indulgently pardon fornicators, but wills not to do it, in order to prevent more wide-spread evil (12).

[9] I now inquire into your opinion, to see whence you usurp this right for the Church. Do you presume, because the Lord said to Peter, "On this rock I will build my Church, I have given you the keys of the kingdom of heaven (13)," or "whatever you shall have bound or loosed on earth will be bound or loosed in heaven (14)," that the power of   430
binding and loosing has thereby been handed on to you, that is, to every Church akin to Peter? [10] What kind of man are you, subverting and changing what was the manifest intent of the Lord when He conferred this personally upon Peter? On *you,* He says, I will build my Church; and I will give to *you* the keys, not to the Church; and whatever *you* shall have bound or *you* shall have loosed, not what *they* shall have bound or *they* shall have loosed.

387a

[22, 1]

But you even pour out this power [of forgiving sins] upon your martyrs. As soon as   935
anyone by common agreement has put on the bonds — soft ones, in the new and nominal imprisonments — immediately adulterers beset him, immediately fornicators gain access to him; instantly prayers echo around him, instantly pools of tears of all the polluted surround him; nor are any more anxious to buy their way into prison than those who have lost the Church. [2] Men and women are violated in the darkness made familiar to them by their habitual indulgence of lust; and they seek peace at the hands of those who are risking their own. Others flee to the mines and return from there as communicants, when already another martyrdom is necessary because of the new sins committed after martyrdom.

[3] "But who on earth and in the flesh is without fault?" . . . Imagine now a martyr already under the sword and with head poised, . . . imagine him already at the stake and with the fire made ready — in the very certainty, I mean, of possessing martyrdom: who allows a man to forgive those sins which have been reserved to God, by whom they have been condemned with no excuse possible, which, so far as I know, not even Apostles, themselves martyrs, have judged as remissible? [4] In brief, Paul had already been condemned to fight with the beasts at Ephesus when he decreed the ruin of the incestuous man. Let it suffice for a martyr to have atoned for his own sins which he will have accomplished at a great price.

Who has redeemed another by his own death, except the Son of God alone? For even in His very passion, He freed the thief. For this purpose He came, that, being Himself entirely free of sin and holy in every respect, He might die for sinners. [5] You, then, who imitate Him in forgiving sins, if you have done no sin yourself, suffer freely for me. But if you, too, are a sinner, how will the oil of your little torch be able to suffice for yourself and for me?

1. Two identifications have been made of the *pontifex scilicet maximus quod est episcopus episcoporum* as author of the so-called edict mentioned in the present very famous passage: Callistus of Rome and Agrippinus of Carthage. That it was Callistus who issued the 'peremptory edict' is supported by H. Koch, A. von Harnack, P. Battifol, E. Goeller, J. Hoh, D. van den Eynde, E. Caspar, B. J. Kidd, W. Koehler, J. Haller, K. Mueller, and H. Stoeckius. That it was Agrippinus is maintained by G. Bardy, K. Preysing, A. Ehrhard, P. Galtier and B. Poschmann. With so many able names on either side it is scarcely necessary to note that the question is in no way settled. It does seem to the present writer that Agrippinus has the part of greater likelihood. Summary treatment of the question can be found in J. Quasten, *Patrology*, Vol. 2, pp. 204-207, 234-235, and 312-313.

2. Matt. 5:9.

3. An invitation to the whole Church to join with Tertullian and the Montanists! In chapter 2 of *De pudicitia,* Tertullian refers to the fact that there are certain sins which may obtain *veniam* or forgiveness, calling them *remissible.* Idolatry and adultery, however, along with murder, he accounts as irremissible. In chapter 3 he calls these irremissible sins *mortalia,* while making it clear that by irremissible he means that they cannot be forgiven through ecclesiastical penances, but by God only. See also § 386 below.

4. *levioribus delictis.*

5. *maioribus et inremissibilibus.*

6. It is not the anonymous and so-called *Epistle of Barnabas* that Tertullian refers to as a work of Barnabas, but our own canonical *Epistle to the Hebrews.* Barnabas' authorship of the latter is not especially probable; but Paul's authorship of it is virtually impossible.

7. 1 Cor. 9:6.

8. Tertullian employs such sarcasm on *The Shepherd* of Hermas because that work announced a further opportunity for repentance, and because its author's attitude toward second marriage after the death of a spouse was considerably more relaxed than his own.

9. Heb. 6:1.

10. Heb. 6:4-8.

11. If the change of persons within the quotation seems strange and suggestive of varying interpretations, it must be read in the light of verse 16 of this same chapter, in which Tertullian declares: "The Church itself is properly and principally that very Spirit, in whom is the Trinity of one Divinity, Father and Son and Holy Spirit."

12. His reasoning is, in effect: "If this statement is really made by a pseudo-prophetic spirit, in imitation of the Paraclete — why, then it is clear that since it imitates the Paraclete, it must truly represent what the Paraclete might in fact reveal." Such specious reasoning is not entirely absent from Tertullian's earlier writings, but in his last works it becomes more frequent and more transparent.

13. Matt. 16:18-19.

14. Matt. 16:19.

ST. HIPPOLYTUS OF ROME [†A. D. 235]

St. Hippolytus is the first anti-pope, and the only one of the two or three dozen anti-popes of various times to whom the Church accords the title of *sanctus* and the honors of the altar. Beyond a few key facts, and many of these doubtful in some degree, not a great deal is known of him. Though we first meet him in Rome, and his entire career is connected with that city, there is every reason to believe that he was not a Roman by birth, and that his origins are other than Latin. It may, in fact, be taken as certain that he was from the East, and as a near certainty that he had Alexandrian connections; for he exhibits a thorough knowledge of Greek philosophy and his theological attitudes betray a dependence upon Alexandrian thought.

Hippolytus came into conflict with Pope St. Callistus, taking an extremely rigorous view in the question of the reconciliation and re-admission of sinners when Callistus was taking an attitude that may have shown an unaccustomed lenience. Elected Bishop of Rome by a small group of devoted followers, Hippolytus became first anti-pope in the time of Callistus (217-222), and his schism continued through the the reigns of Pope St. Urban I and Pope St. Pontianus, until 235 A. D. In the latter year both Pontianus and Hippolytus were exiled by the Emperor Maximin Thrax to Sardinia. Pontianus resigned his see in September of 235 A. D., in order to enable the Roman Church to elect his successor; possibly Hippolytus did the same. In any case, he and Pontianus seem to have been reconciled to each other in Sardinia, where both died very soon as martyrs. The schism at an end, already in 235 A. D. the united community elected Pope St. Anterus (235-236) whose successor, Pope St. Fabian (236-250), brought the bodies of both martyrs from Sardinia to Rome.

Hippolytus' literary activity was quite prodigious, almost as extensive as Origen's; and like Origen, only a small part of his writings have survived intact. A statue, probably of the third century and probably marking his burial place, was discovered in 1551 A. D., and is presently in the Lateran Museum. It depicts Hippolytus seated in a chair; and on the chair is graven his Paschal Table and a list of the titles of his works.

Hippolytus' position of anti-pope, strangely enough, was literally forgotten at an early date, and Pope St. Damasus I (366-384) honored his tomb with an inscription that calls him a follower of Novatian, but recalls also that he was a martyr who, before his death, admonished his followers to be reconciled to the Church. A tradition grew up, current as early as St. Jerome, that Hippolytus had been bishop of Porto Romanus, one of the suburban Roman sees.

THE ANTICHRIST [*ca. A. D.* 200]

Of Hippolytus' dogmatic treatises only one is preserved in its entirety: *An Explanation from the Scriptures of the Christ and of the Antichrist,* better known simply as *The Antichrist.* It is judged to have been written about the year 200 A. D., and Hippolytus refers to it as a work of his own in his *Commentary on Daniel,* written *ca. A D.* 204. There are extant three manuscripts of the Greek text, and also extant are versions in Georgian and in Old Slavonic, along with fragments of an Armenian version.

The Migne text, PG 10, 725-788, is entirely superseded by the critical edition of H. Achelis in the Berlin Corpus (GCS), Vol. 1 part 2, Leipzig 1897, pp. 1-47.

388

[2]

    All of these prophets were under the influence of the Holy Spirit and were fittingly   21
honored by the Word Himself. Like musical instruments, they had the Word ever in   270
themselves, as if He were a plectrum; and when moved by Him, they announced what
God willed. Not by their own power did the prophets speak (1) — let there be no
mistake about that — nor did they make their announcements according to their own
pleasure.

389

[3]

    [The Word of God] casts away none of His servants, none does He despise as unworthy
of His divine mysteries. . . . He is compassionate to all, and desires to save all. He desires   200
to reinstate all as sons of God, and to call all the saints into one perfect man. For there is
one Son of God, through whom we too, being regenerated through the Holy Spirit, desire   285
to become all as one perfect and heavenly man.

    [4] Although He was without flesh, the Son of God took on flesh from the Holy Virgin,   311
like a bridegroom putting on a robe, which He wove for Himself in the sufferings of the   781
cross, so that by uniting our mortal body to His own power, and mixing the corruptible   370
with the incorruptible and the weak with the strong, He might save man who was perishing.   347
The beam of the loom, therefore, is the suffering of the Lord which he endured on the
cross; the warp on it is the power of the Holy Spirit; the woof is the holy flesh, woven
by the Spirit; the thread is the grace which, through the love of Christ, binds and unites
the two in one; the combs are the Word; the workers are the patriarchs and prophets, who
weave the beautiful and perfect tunic of Christ, reaching to His feet; and the Word, passing
through them like the combs, by their means finishes weaving whatever the Father wills.

1. The idea expressed is similar to that of 2 Peter 1:21; but it is in no way linguistically dependent upon the
   Scripture passage.

COMMENTARY ON DANIEL [*ca. A. D.* 204]

    Of Hippolytus' exegetical writings the best preserved is his *Commentary on Daniel.*
Dating from about the year 204 A. D., it is the oldest extant exegetical treatise of
Christian origin. The entire text of an Old Slavonic version is extant, along with
large parts of the original Greek. The Scripture text which Hippolytus comments is
that of Theodotian; and he includes also the deuterocanonical sections. For
Hippolytus, Susanna is the Church, the Bride of Christ, persecuted by two peoples,
the Jews and the pagans. In Bk. 4, Ch. 23, it is stated that Christ was born on
Wednesday, December 25th, in the 42nd year of the reign of Augustus (who ruled
from 30 B.C. to 14 A.D.). This, were it authentic, would be the earliest reference
to Christ's birth as being on December 25th; however, the passage is generally
regarded as an interpolation.

    The Migne text, PG 10, 641-700, is entirely superseded by the critical edition of
G. N. Bonwetsch in the Berlin Corpus (GCS), Vol. 1 part 1, Leipzig 1897, pp. 1-340.

390

[1, 16]

    "And she said to her maids, 'Bring me oil (1).' " Indeed, faith and love prepare oil and   840
cleansing unguents for those who are washed. But what were these unguents if not the

commands of the Holy Word? And what the oil, if not the power of the Holy Spirit? It is with these, after the washing (2), that believers are anointed as with a sweet-smelling oil. All these things were prefigured through the blessed Susanna for our sakes, so that we of the present time who believe in God, might not regard as strange the things which now are done in the Church, and that we might believe that all of them have been set   300
forth in figures by the patriarchs.

390a

[4, 6]

Neither does Scripture falsify anything, nor does the Holy Spirit deceive His servants,   25
the prophets, through whom He is pleased to announce to men the will of God.   20

1. Dan. 13:17 (or, in the Septuagint, Sus. 1:17). In the passage quoted, it is Susanna who is speaking.
2. *I.e.*, Baptism.

AGAINST THE HERESY OF A CERTAIN NOETUS [*inter A. D.* 200/210]

Hippolytus' so-called homily *Against the Heresy of a Certain Noetus,* dating from between the years 200 and 210 A. D., is not a homily at all, but a large fragment of an anti-heretical work. We know that Hippolytus' lost *Syntagma* or *Against All Heresies* treated of thirty-two heretics from Dositheus to Noetus; and it is commonly held that the present so-called homily is actually a fragment of the *Syntagma.* There are yet authors, however, who admit the work as being an authentic writing of Hippolytus, but believe, because of its considerable length, that it is part of an independent treatise devoted entirely to Noetus.

The text of Migne, PG 10, 803-830, is superseded by the edition of P. Nautin, *Hippolyte: Contre les hérésies, fragment, étude et édition critique,* Paris 1949.

391

[10]

God, existing alone and having nothing coeval with Himself, willed to create the world.   468
. . . Besides Himself there was no one; but though He was alone, He was mighty. For He   463
was not without reason (1), not without wisdom (2), not without power, and not without   256
counsel. All things were in Him, and He was All. When He willed and in the manner in
which He willed and in the times determined by Himself, He made known His Word,   284
through whom He created all things. When He wills, He does. When He thinks, He carries
out. When He speaks, He manifests. When He forms anything, He contrives it in wisdom.
All things that are made, He fashions through reason and wisdom: creating them by reason,
and arranging them by wisdom. He made them, therefore, as He willed; for He was God.   252

But He begot the Word as the Author and Counsellor and Fashioner of those things
which have been made. And since He had this Word within Himself, invisible to the created
world, He made Him visible. First of all giving vocal utterance, and then begetting Light
from Light, He sent Him forth, His own Mind, as Lord of creation. Before, He was visible
only to Himself, and invisible to the created world; but now He makes Him visible so that
by His being made manifest the world might see Him and be able to be saved.

392

[11]

Thus, there appeared another besides Himself (3). When I say 'another', however, I do   257
not mean that there are two Gods. Rather, it is as if there were light from light, or

water from a fountain, or a ray from the sun. For there is but one power, which is from the All; and the Father is the All, from whom comes the Power, the Word. This, indeed, is the Mind, which came forth into the world and was made manifest as the Son of God.

393

[15]
The blessed Paul says: "For what was impossible to the law, in that it was weak, — God, sending His own Son in the likeness of sinful flesh, has condemned sin in the flesh, in order that the justification of the law might be manifested among us, who walk not according to the flesh but according to the spirit (4)." What Son of His own, then, 302
did God send down through the flesh, if not the Word, whom He addressed as Son because He was about to be born as such? And in being called Son, He takes the 256
common name of tender affection among men. For when He was without flesh and as yet by Himself, the Word was not yet perfect Son, although He was already perfect 324
Word, the Only-begotten.

Nor was the flesh able to subsist (5) by itself apart from the Word, because it had its subsistence (6) in the Word. In this way, then, one perfect Son of God has been manifested. [16] And these, indeed, are testimonies to the incarnation; and there are many others. But let us look again to the subject of immediate concern, which is, brethren, that the Father's Power, that is, the Word, came down from heaven, and not the Father Himself.

394

[17]
Let us believe, then, dear brethren, according to the tradition of the Apostles, that 102
God the Word came down from heaven into the holy Virgin Mary, in order that, taking 781
flesh from her and taking also a soul, I mean a rational soul, and thus becoming all that 310
man is except in regard to sin, He might save the fallen and confer immortality on such 312
men as believe in His name. In all this, then, the word of truth is demonstrated to us: 345
namely, that the Father is one, and His Word, through whom He created all things, is 376
present with Him. 284

In later times, as we said before, the Father sent forth this Word for the salvation of 290
men. The Law and the Prophets announced this Word as one who was destined to come 300
into the world. And in just the way in which it was announced of Him, did He come and manifest Himself, made a new man of the Virgin and the Holy Spirit. As the Word, He had from the Father what is heavenly, just as from the old Adam he had what is 313
earthly, having become incarnate through the Virgin. He came forth into the world and, in the body, showed Himself to be God, although it was as perfect man that He came 321
forth. For He was made man, not in appearance nor in seeming, but in truth.

1. ἄλογος.
2. ἄσοφος.
3. There is no omission of text between § 391 and § 392.
4. Rom. 8:3-4.
5. ὑποστῆναι.
6. τὴν σύστασιν.

THE APOSTOLIC TRADITION [ca. A. D. 215]

With the exception of the *Didache*, Hippolytus' work on *The Apostolic Tradition*, dating from about the year 215 A. D., is the earliest and most important of the various Church Orders, providing as it does a considerable body of extremely valuable information on the Liturgy and upon the hierarchical organization of the Church.

In 1910 E. Schwarz made the claim that an Ethiopic work known since the 17th century as *The Egyptian Church Order* represented substantially *The Apostolic Tradition* of Hippolytus, which until then had been known only as the title of one of his supposedly lost works. Schwarz's theory was proven to the satisfaction of most modern scholars by R. Hugh Connolly in 1916, with the publication of his book *The So-called Egyptian Church Order and Derived Documents*.

The original Greek text of *The Apostolic Tradition* remains lost except for a few fragments which can be gleaned from such later Greek documents as *The Apostolic Constitutions*. However, there are translations extant in Sahidic and Bohairic Coptic, in Ethiopic, as mentioned above, in Arabic, and in Latin. These versions are mostly very much interpolated and reworked, except for the Latin, which is a quite literal 4th century translation. Unfortunately only a portion of the Latin version is extant, and that in a 5th century palimpsest of Verona. From the extant Latin, however, and by comparing it with the other versions, it is possible to reconstruct almost the entire Greek text in its original form.

It is interesting to trace the interdependence of the versions. The Latin is the oldest extant; but the extant Sahidic is almost as old, dating from about the year 500 A. D. The Bohairic was made from a rather poorly transmitted copy of this Sahidic. The extant Arabic was made from a different and non-extant Sahidic version. The Ethiopic translation was made from a lost Arabic, not connected with the extant Arabic; and the lost Arabic upon which the Ethiopic depends is believed to have been made from another lost Sahidic version.

Our translations below are made mostly from the Latin or Greek texts, supplying only where necessary from the oriental versions; and with the lateness of the latter in mind we have taken care to give nothing that cannot be substantiated as authentic with Hippolytus.

Perhaps the best editions, besides that of Connolly mentioned above, are E. Hauler, *Didascaliae apostolorum fragmenta Veronensia latina,* Leipzig 1900 (*editio princeps* of the Latin version); G. Horner, *The Statutes of the Apostles or Canones Ecclesiastici,* London 1904 (Ethiopic, Arabic, Bohairic); F. X. Funk, *Didascalia et Constitutiones apostolorum,* Vol. 2, Paderborn 1905, pp. 97-119; Burton Scott Easton, *The Apostolic Tradition of Hippolytus,* Cambridge 1924; G. Dix, *The Treatise on the Apostolic Tradition of St. Hippolytus of Rome,* London, 1937.

394a

[2]

Let the bishop be ordained after he has been chosen by all the people. When someone pleasing to all has been named, let the people assemble on the Lord's Day with the presbyters and with such bishops as may be present. All giving assent, the bishops shall   958
impose hands on him, and the presbytery shall stand by in silence. Indeed, all shall   960
remain silent, praying in their hearts for the descent of the Spirit.   961

Then one of the bishops present shall, at the request of all, impose his hand on the one who is being ordained bishop, and shall pray thus, saying: [3] "God and Father of our   959
Lord Jesus Christ, Father of mercies and God of all comfort (1), who dwell on high and attend to the lowly (2), who know all things before they come to pass: you that have given boundaries to your Church through your Word of grace, predestining from the beginning the just offspring of Abraham, making them princes and priests so as not to leave your sanctuary without a ministry, from the beginning of the world you have been well-pleased to be glorified in those (3) you have chosen. Pour forth now that power   965
which comes from you, from your Royal Spirit (4), which you gave to your Beloved Son

Jesus Christ and which He bestowed upon His holy Apostles, who established in every place the Church of your sanctification for the glory and unceasing praise of your name. You that know the hearts of all (5), grant to this your servant, whom you have chosen for the episcopate, to feed your holy flock (6) and to serve without blame as your high priest, ministering night and day to propitiate unceasingly before your face; and to offer to you the gifts of your holy Church; and by the Spirit of the high-priesthood to have the authority to forgive sins (7), in accord with your command; to assign lots (8), in accord with the authority which you gave to the Apostles; and to please you in meekness and purity of heart, offering to you an odor of sweetness (9): through your Son, Jesus Christ our Lord, through whom be glory, might, and honor to you, to the Father and the Son with the Holy Spirit, both now and through the ages of ages. Amen."

925

[4] And when he has been made bishop let all salute him with the kiss of peace, because of his having been made worthy. The deacons shall then bring the offering to him; and he, imposing his hand on it, along with all the presbytery, shall give thanks, saying: "The Lord be with you." And all shall respond, "And with your spirit." "Hearts aloft!" "We keep them with the Lord." "Let us give thanks to the Lord." "It is right and just." And then he shall continue immediately:

"We give you thanks, O God, through your beloved Son Jesus Christ, whom in these last days you have sent to us as Savior and Redeemer and as the angel of your will; He that is your inseparable Word, through whom you made all things, and who is well-pleasing to you; whom you sent from heaven into the womb of a Virgin, and who, dwelling within her, was made flesh and was manifested as your Son, born of the Holy Spirit and of the Virgin; who, fulfilling your will and winning for Himself a holy people, extended His hands when it was time for Him to suffer, so that by His suffering He might set free those who believed in you; who also, when He was betrayed to His voluntary suffering, in order that He might destroy death and break the bonds of the devil and trample hell underfoot and enlighten the just and set a boundary (10) and show forth His resurrection, took bread and gave thanks to you, saying: 'Take, eat: this is My Body, which is broken for you.' Likewise with the cup too, saying: 'This is My Blood, which is poured out for you. Whenever you do this, you do it in my memory (11).'

"Remembering, therefore, His death and resurrection, we offer to you the bread and the cup, giving thanks to you, because of your having accounted us as worthy to stand before you and minister to you. And we pray that you might send your Holy Spirit upon the offering of the holy Church. Gather as one in the fullness of the Holy Spirit your saints who participate; and confirm their faith in truth so that we may praise and glorify you through your Son Jesus Christ, through whom be glory and honor to you, to the Father and the Son with the Holy Spirit, in your holy Church, both now and through the ages of ages. Amen."

230

394b

[8]

When a presbyter is to be ordained, the bishop shall impose his hand upon his head, while the presbyters touch the one to be ordained; and the bishop shall speak after the fashion of those things said above, where we prescribed what was to be said in the ordination of a bishop (12), praying and saying:

960
959

"God and Father of our Lord Jesus Christ, look upon this your servant and grant him the Spirit of grace and the counsel of a presbyter, so that he may support and govern your people with a pure heart, as also you looked upon your chosen people and commanded Moses to choose presbyters, whom you filled with your Spirit, which you gave to your servant. And now, O Lord, grant that there may be ever preserved among us the Spirit of your grace, and make us worthy that, in faith, we may give praise to you and minister to you in simplicity of heart: through your Son Jesus Christ, through whom be glory

and honor to you, to the Father and the Son with the Holy Spirit, in your holy Church,   230
both now and through the ages of ages. Amen."

394c

[9]
When a deacon is to be ordained he is chosen after the fashion of those things said   960
above (13), the bishop alone in like manner imposing his hands upon him as we have   952
prescribed. In the ordaining of a deacon, this is the reason why the bishop alone is to   953
impose his hands upon him: he is not ordained to the priesthood, but to serve the bishop   954
and to fulfill the bishop's command. He has no part in the council of the clergy, but is   959
to attend to his own duties and is to acquaint the bishop with such matters as are
needful. He does not receive that Spirit which the presbytery possesses and in which the
presbyters share. He receives only what is entrusted to him under the authority of the
bishop.

For this reason, then, the bishop alone shall ordain a deacon. On a presbyter, however,
let the presbyters impose their hands because of the common and like Spirit of the clergy.
Even so, the presbyter has only the power to receive, and has not the power to give. That
is why a presbyter does not ordain the clergy; for at the ordaining of a presbyter, he but
seals while the bishop ordains.

Over a deacon, then, let the bishop speak thus:

"O God, who have created all things and have set them in order through your Word;
Father of our Lord Jesus Christ, whom you sent to minister to your will and to make clear
to us your desires, grant the Holy Spirit of grace and care and diligence to this your
servant, whom you have chosen to serve the Church and to offer in your holy places the
gifts which are offered to you by your chosen high priests, so that he may serve with a
pure heart and without blame, and that, ever giving praise to you, he may be accounted by
your good will as worthy of this high office: through your Son Jesus Christ, through
whom be glory and honor to you, to the Father and the Son with the Holy Spirit, in your   230
holy Church, both now and through the ages of ages. Amen (14)."

394d

[10]
If a confessor has been in chains for the name of the Lord, hands are not imposed   958
on him for the diaconate or presbyterate; for he has the honor of the presbyterate by
the fact of his confession. But if he is to be ordained a bishop, hands are to be imposed
upon him. If, however, he is a confessor who was not summoned before the authorities
and was not punished in chains and was not imprisoned, but was offered private and
passing indignity for the name of the Lord, even though he confessed, hands are to be
imposed upon him for every office of which he is worthy.

394e

[10]
The bishop shall give thanks as we have prescribed (15). Certainly it is not necessary   898
for him to recite the exact words which we have set down, by learning to say them from
memory in his giving thanks to God. Rather, let each one pray according to his ability.
Indeed, if he is able to pray in an accomplished manner and with a lofty style of prayer,
it is well. But even if he has only a moderate ability in praying and in giving praise, let
no one forbid it, so long as his prayer is of sound faith.

394f

[11]

When a widow is to be appointed, she is not to be ordained, but is designated by being   957
named such. . . . A widow is appointed by words alone, and is then associated with the
other widows. Hands are not imposed upon her, because she does not offer the oblation
and she does not conduct the Liturgy (16). Ordination is for the clergy because of the
Liturgy; but a widow is appointed for prayer, and prayer is the duty of all.

394g

[12]

A lector is appointed by the bishop's giving him the book; for he is not ordained.   956

394h

[14]

Hands are not imposed upon a subdeacon; but he shall be designated by name as one   955
who may serve the deacon.

394i

[21]

At dawn a prayer shall be offered over the water. Where there is no scarcity of water   822
the stream shall flow through the baptismal font or pour into it from above; but if water
is scarce, whether as a constant condition or on occasion, then use whatever water is
available.

Let them remove their clothing. Baptise first the children; and if they can speak for   835
themselves, let them do so. Otherwise, let their parents or other relatives speak for them.
Next, baptize the men, and last of all the women. The latter must first let down their
hair and put aside any gold or silver ornaments they may be wearing. Let no one take
any foreign object into the water with him.

When it is time for the Baptism the bishop shall give thanks over the oil, which he   811
puts into a vessel. This is called the *oil of thanksgiving*. Then he shall take other oil
and exorcise it. This is called the *oil of exorcism*. A deacon shall hold the oil of
exorcism and shall stand to the left of a presbyter. Another deacon shall hold the oil
of thanksgiving, and shall stand to the right of the presbyter. The presbyter then takes
hold of each of those to be baptized and commands him to renounce, saying:

"I renounce you, Satan, and all your servants and all your works."

When he has renounced all these the presbyter shall anoint him with the oil of
exorcism, saying:

"Let all spirits flee far away from you."

After all these things have been done, let him be given over to the bishop or presbyter   828
who will baptize. Let them stand naked in the water, a deacon going down with them   824
likewise (17). When the one being baptized goes down into the water, the one baptizing
him shall put his hand on him and speak thus:

"Do you believe in God, the Father Almighty?"   826

And he that is being baptized shall say:

"I believe."

Then, having his hand imposed upon the head of the one to be baptized, he shall baptize
him once. And then he shall say:

"Do you believe in Christ Jesus, the Son of God, who was born of the Holy Spirit, of
the Virgin Mary, and was crucified under Pontius Pilate and died and was buried, and
rose up again on the third day, alive from the dead, and ascended into heaven, and sat at
the right of the Father, about to come to judge the living and the dead?"

And when he says: "I believe," he is baptized again.

And again he shall say:

"Do you believe in the Holy Spirit and the holy Church and the resurrection of the flesh?"

The one being baptized then says: "I believe." And so he is baptized a third time (18).   825

And afterwards, when he has come out, he is anointed with the consecrated oil (19); and the presbyter says:

"I anoint you with the holy oil in the name of Jesus Christ."

And so each one then drys himself; and immediately they put on their clothes. Then they come into the church.

[22] The bishop, imposing his hand on them, shall make an invocation, saying: 843

"O Lord God, who made them worthy of the remission of sins through the Holy Spirit's   836
washing unto rebirth, send into them your grace so that they may serve you according to your will: for there is glory to you, to the Father and the Son with the Holy Spirit, in the holy Church, both now and through the ages of ages. Amen."

Then, pouring the consecrated oil into his hand and imposing it on the head of the   841
baptized, he shall say:

"I anoint you with holy oil in the Lord, the Father Almighty and Christ Jesus and the Holy Spirit."

And signing them on the forehead he shall kiss them and say: 842

"The Lord be with you."

And he that has been signed shall say:

"And with your spirit."

Thus shall he do with each. And immediately afterwards they shall pray at one with all the people; and not until all these things have been completed shall they pray with the faithful. And when they have finished praying, they shall give the kiss of peace.

[23] And then the deacons immediately bring the oblation to the bishop; and he   860
eucharists the bread into the antitype of the Body of Christ; and the cup of mixed wine,   851
for an antitype of the Blood, which was shed for all who believe in Him (20); and milk   853
and honey mixed together for the fulfillment of the promise made to the fathers, which spoke of a land flowing with milk and honey, that is, the very flesh of Christ which He gave and by which they who believe are nourished like little children, since He makes   877
sweet the bitter things of the heart by the gentleness of His word; and water also, for an   823
offering as signifying the washing, so that the inner part of the man, which is of the soul (21), may receive the same as the body.

Indeed, the bishop shall explain the reason for all these things to those who partake. Breaking the Bread into individual particles which he then distributes, he shall say:

"Heavenly Bread in Christ Jesus!"

And he that receives shall answer:

"Amen!"

And the presbyters, or, if they are not enough, the deacons too, shall hold the cups   868
and shall stand by in reverence and modesty: first, he that holds the water; second, the   871
milk; third, the Wine. They who receive shall taste three times of each, while he that gives the cup says:

"In God the Father Almighty."

And the one receiving says:

"Amen."

"And in the Lord Jesus Christ."

[And he shall say:

"Amen (22)."]

"And in the Holy Spirit and in the holy Church."

And he shall say:

"Amen."

So it shall be done to each one. And when these things are completed let each hasten to do good works and to please God and to live justly, devoting himself to the Church, practicing what he has learned, and advancing in the service of God.

Now we have delivered to you in brief the things concerning holy Baptism and the holy oblation. You have already been instructed about the resurrection of the flesh and all else that is taught in the Scriptures. But if there is anything more they ought to be told, let the bishop impart it to them in private, after their Baptism, and let no unbelievers   810
know it until they have been baptized. This is the white stone of which John said: "There is upon it a new name written, which no one knows except him that receives the stone (23)."

1. 2 Cor. 1:3.
2. Ps. 112 [113]:5-6.
3. The Greek and the Latin readings almost certainly mean *in those persons,* but they do admit the interpretation of the generally less reliable Ethiopic, *in those places.* The former is much more likely the intent of the prayer.
4. Ps. 50 [51]:14.
5. Acts 1:24.
6. Acts 20:28; 1 Pet. 5:2.
7. John 20:22-23.
8. *dare sortes* or δίδόναι κλήρους — *i.e.,* to establish others in the clerical estate through ordination.
9. Eph. 5:2.
10. *terminum figat.*
11. *quando hoc facitis, meam commemorationem facitis.*
12. See § 394a, above. This is to be taken also, however, in the light of § 394e, below.
13. See § 394b, above.
14. The last half of the prayer is preserved through the Ethiopic and in the *Testament of Our Lord;* and these sources substitute a doxology familiar to their time and place. We have re-introduced the doxology found in other parts of the Latin version of the work.
15. *I.e.,* in the ordination ceremonies described in §§ 394 a, b, and c, above. By the time the Ethiopic and Arabic versions were made, extemporaneous prayer had been supplanted entirely by set forms. Those versions attempt to correct the passage by omitting the negative from the next line: *Certainly it is (not) necessary. . . .*
16. Here and in the next line, *Liturgy* is the reading of the Sahidic. The Ethiopic and the Arabic have *she has not a sacred ministry* in the first instance, and *because of their ministry* in the second.
17. The passage seems to mean that the one baptizing, the one being baptized, and the deacon assisting, are all standing naked in the water; and this may in fact be the case. Or, the term *them* may be intended to refer to the candidates for baptism as a group, though taken singly; and then the *likewise* may simply mean that the deacon also goes into the water, while implying nothing of his attire or lack thereof. Probably the one baptizing stood at the edge of the font, while the deacon entered the water with the candidate; and probably it was only the candidate who was naked. These people were accustomed to attend the Roman baths and would find no impropriety in the usage.
18. The *Canons of Hippolytus,* a fifth century revision of the present work, and of Egyptian origin, adds that at each of the three 'baptisms', the one baptizing should say: *I baptize you in the name of the Father and of the Son and of the Holy Spirit, the Trinity in unity.* Neither the Latin nor the oriental versions of *The Apostolic Tradition* prescribes such a form. Note however that what is required in the baptismal form is a distinct expression of God, One and Three: and such expression is contained within the ceremony which Hippolytus so closely describes: "Do you believe in God, the Father Almighty, . . . in Christ Jesus, the Son of God, . . . in the Holy Spirit? I believe!"
19. *I.e.,* the oil of thanksgiving.
20. The Greek of this passage is not extant, and in translating the Latin we have omitted its obvious interpolations. The Latin reads: *Et tunc iam offeratur oblatio a diaconibus episcopo et gratias agat panem quidem in exemplum, quod dicit Graecus antitypum, corporis Christi; calicem vino mixtum propter antitypum, quod dicit Graecus similitudinem, sanguinis, quod effusum est pro omnibus, qui crediderunt in eum.* This may be rendered in more literal fashion: *And then immediately the oblation is offered to the bishop by the deacons; and he thanks-gives the bread forsooth into the exemplar — as the Greek says, the antitype — of the Body of Christ; the cup of mixed wine for the antitype — as the Greek calls the likeness — of the Blood, which was poured out for all who shall have believed in Him.* The passage presents no theological difficulty if one bear in mind that in respect to the Eucharist, bread is the type, whereas the body of Christ Himself is the antitype.
21. *quod est animale.*
22. The words in brackets are a conjectural restoration, the text of this interchange reading: *Et gustent, quo percipient, de singulis ter dicente eo, qui dat: In Deo patre omnipotenti. Dicat autem, qui accipit: Amen. Et domino Iesu Christo et spiritu sancto et sancta ecclesia. Et dicat: Amen. Ita singulis fiat.*
23. Apoc. 2:17.

AGAINST THE GREEKS [ante A. D. 225]

The treatise *Against the Greeks,* which Hippolytus wrote before the year 225 A. D., is lost except for a rather lengthy fragment preserved in St. John Damascene's *Sacra parallela.* The text in Migne, PG 10, 795-802, is superseded by that of K. Holl, *Fragmente vornicänischer Kirchenväter aus den Sacra parallela,* in *Texte und Untersuchungen,* Vol. 20, Fasc. 2, Leipzig 1899, pp. 137-143.

395

[2]

It dare not be said of God that in one thing He is able and in another unable. We believe, therefore, that the body too is resurrected. For even if it becomes corrupt, it is   1013
not utterly destroyed. The earth receives its remains and preserves them; and they become like seed, wrapped up in the richer part of the earth, to spring up and bloom. That which is sown, is sown as bare grain; and at the command of the creating God it buds and is raised up in glorious array — but not unless it first dies and is dissolved and is mingled with the earth.

Not in vain, then, do we believe in the resurrection of the body. Moreover, while it is dissolved at its proper time because of the transgression which took place in the beginning,   611
and is committed to the earth as to a furnace, to be reshaped again, not in its present   1044
corruption, but pure and no longer corruptible, so also to every body its own soul will be returned; and the soul, being clothed with it again, will not be grieved but will rejoice with it, the pure abiding in the pure. Just as the soul now abides with the body in this world in righteousness, and finds the body in no way uncoöperative, so to, in all joy it   1012
will receive the body again.

The unrighteous, however will receive their bodies unchanged, neither freed from suffering and disease, nor glorified, but in those ills in which they died; and whatever they were before they were raised to life and reunited, and however they lived in faithlessness, according to that shall they be faithfully judged.

396

[3]

Standing before [Christ's] judgment, all of them, men, angels, and demons, crying out   1020
in one voice, shall say: "Just is your judgment (1)!" And the justice of that cry will be   771
apparent in the recompense made to each. To those who have done well, everlasting   1043
enjoyment shall be given; while to the lovers of evil shall be given eternal punishment.   1034
The unquenchable and unending fire awaits these latter, and a certain fiery worm which   1032
does not die and which does not waste the body (2), but continually bursts forth from the body with unceasing pain. No sleep will give them rest; no night will soothe them; no   1036
death will deliver them from punishment; no appeal of interceding friends will profit them. For neither are the righteous any longer seen by them, nor are they themselves worthy of remembrance.

1. Ps. 118 [119]:137. Apoc. 16:7.
2. See Judith 16:21 [16:17, in the Septuagint]; Is. 66:24; Mark 9:42-45.

PHILOSOPHOUMENA *or* REFUTATION OF ALL HERESIES [*post A. D.* 222]

Liturgists will believe that *The Apostolic Tradition* is the most important of Hippolytus's writings; while theologians are equally convinced that such honor belongs to his *Philosophoumena* or *Refutation of all Heresies.* The *Philosophoumena* was written after the year 222 A. D.; and of the ten books which comprised the work, only eight are extant, books 2 and 3 remaining lost. The work was known in antiquity as *The Labyrinth,* and was variously attributed to Tertullian, Novatian and to Caius of Rome. Book I was re-discovered in 1701, handed down as a work of Origen; and books 4 through 10 came to light in 1842. In 1851 the eight books were published as a work of Origen; and not until 1859 was the work finally restored to the corpus of Hippolytus.

The Migne text, PG 16/3, 3017-3454 (*apud* Origen) is entirely superseded by the edition of P. Wendland in the Berlin Corpus (GCS), Vol. 26, Leipzig 1916, pp. 1-293.

396a

[9, 12]

[Callistus] even permitted women, if they were unmarried and burning up at an unsuitable time of life, or if they did not wish to lose their own dignity by a lawful marriage, to take a man of their choosing as bedfellow, whether slave or free, and to regard such a one as a husband, though not lawfully married (1). For this reason women who were reputed to be   970 believers began to take drugs to render themselves sterile, and to bind themselves tightly   969 so as to expel what was being conceived, since they would not, on account of relatives and excessive wealth, want to have a child by a slave or by any insignificant person. See, then, into what great impiety that lawless one has proceeded, by teaching adultery and murder at the same time!

397

[10, 32]

The one God, the first and only, both Creator and Lord of all things, had nothing   157 coeval with Himself, neither infinite chaos, nor immeasurable water, nor solid earth,   460 nor dense air, nor hot fire, nor gentle breeze, nor the azure roof of the great heavens. No,   468 he was one, to Himself alone; and when He so willed, He created those things which   463 before had no existence other than in his willing to make them and inasmuch as he had   189 knowledge of what would be: for he has also foreknowledge. He first created, however, the diverse elements of the things which would come into existence, fire and air, water and earth, from which various elements he then made his own creation.

398

[10, 33]

Therefore this sole and universal God, by reflecting, first brought forth the Word — not   265 a word as in speech, but as a mental word, the Reason for everything. Him only did He produce from what existed: for the Father Himself was Being, from which He produced Him. The Word was the cause of those things which came into existence, carrying out in   284 Himself the will of Him by whom He was begotten, and without being unaware of the mind of the Father; for, at the same time that He came forth from Him by whom He was begotten, he became the latter's firstborn Voice (2), and He has in Himself the ideas which were conceived beforehand in the Father.

And thus, when the Father commanded the world to be, the Word put His commands one by one into effect, thereby pleasing God. . . . For whatever He willed, God made. He created these things through the Word; nor was it possible for them to be produced in a manner other that that in which they were produced. He signified that He created accordingly as He willed, when He gave a name to creation. He shaped the ruler of all these things, and fashioned him of all composite substances. He did not intend to make Him God and fail; nor an angel, — make no mistake, — but a man. If he had willed to make you God, He could have done so. You have the example of the Word. He willed man, and He made you man. But if you wish to become also God, obey Him that made you and do not now resist, so that when you are found faithful in what is a small matter, you may be enabled to be entrusted also with what is a great matter (3).

Only His Word is from Himself, and is therefore also God, becoming the substance of   257
God (4). The world was made from nothing. Therefore it is not God; and it admits   461
of being dissolved whenever the Creator so wishes. And God, who created it, did not
and never does make what is evil. He makes what is beautiful and good, because He that   469
makes it is good. . . . In the latter days the Father sent forth this Word; for He desired   290
no longer to speak through a prophet nor to be conjectured about, through being announced   302
in an obscure manner.   300

On the contrary, He intended the Word to be seen with our own eyes, so that the world, when it saw Him, might revere the One who was issuing commands not in the person of prophets and who was terrifying the soul not by an angel, but who was Himself present — He that had spoken.

We know that this Word took on flesh from a Virgin, thereby putting on the old man   311
in a new way; that He passed through every period of life, so that He might Himself be a   781
law for every age, that, by being present among us, He might exhibit His own manhood   373
as a model for all men; and that He might prove by the example of Himself that God made nothing evil, and that man is self-determining, having the ability to will or not to will, and being capable of both. We know that this Man was made from that of which we   613
are made; for had He not our same existence, in vain would He command us to imitate   313
the Teacher. And if that Man happened to be of a different substance, how could He demand similar behavior of me, who am born weak? How would this be good and just?

399

[10, 34]

For Christ is the God over all, who has arranged to wash away sin from mankind,   301
rendering the old man new. God called man His image from the beginning, showing His   374
love for you by a figure. If you obey His solemn injunctions and become a good imitator   376
of Him who is good, you will become like Him and will be honored by Him. For God is
no niggard; and He has made you a god for His own glory.

1. Stripped of vituperative rhetoric, the charge which Hippolytus is making is simply that Callistus had permitted free women to marry slaves, in spite of civil legislation to the contrary.
2. The distinction that Hippolytus is making between the Reason and the Voice is the well-known distinction, subordinationist in conception, of the internal Word (λόγος ἐνδιάθετος) and the uttered Word (λόγος προφορικός).
3. 2 Pet. 1:4.
4. οὐσία ὑπάρχων θεοῦ, which phrase might also be translated somewhat in this fashion: *the substance of the Word arising from that of God.*

AGAINST THE HERESY OF ARTEMON [*ca. A. D.* 230]

Hippolytus' treatise *Against the Heresy of Artemon* dates from about the year 230 A. D. No mention was made of Artemon in the *Philosophoumena,* called by some in antiquity *The Labyrinth.* Perhaps the present work was written as a kind of supplement to the *Philosophoumena;* and Theodoret of Cyr refers to it as *The Little Labyrinth.* We noted before that *The Labyrinth* was attributed by some in ancient times to Caius of Rome; and Photius knew a codex with a marginal note attributing even *The Little Labyrinth* to Caius.

All that is extant of the work is some very short fragments preserved by Eusebius in Bk. 5, Ch. 28 of his *History of the Church.* The best source for the text of the fragments, then, will be Schwartz's edition of Eusebius, in the Berlin Corpus (GCS), Vol. 9, part 1, Leipzig 1903.

FRAGMENT IN EUSEBIUS, History of the Church, BK. 5, CH. 28

400

[5, 28, 15]

[The followers of Artemon] have not feared to lay hands upon the Sacred Scriptures, saying that they have corrected them. . . . [18] Nor is it likely that they themselves are ignorant of how very bold their offense is. For either they do not believe that the Sacred Scriptures were spoken by the Holy Spirit, in which case they are unbelievers; or, if they regard themselves as being wiser than the Holy Spirit, what else are they but demoniacs?

ST. CLEMENT OF ALEXANDRIA [*ca. A. D.* 150 — 211/216]

Titus Flavius Clemens, St. Clement of Alexandria, was born of pagan parents, probably at Athens, about the year 150 A. D. After becoming a Christian he journeyed to Italy, Syria, and Palestine, seeking Christian teachers for his own instruction. Finally he met the celebrated Pantaenus in Alexandria, and was so attracted to the master that he settled there and became, in order, Pantaenus' pupil, associate, assistant, and finally succeeded him as director of the school of catechumens, attaining the latter position about the year 200 A. D. Two or three years later he was forced by the persecution under Septimius Severus to flee from Egypt. He died in Cappadocia between the years 211 and 216 A. D., without ever having seen Egypt again.

EXHORTATION TO THE GREEKS [*ante A. D.* 200]

The *Protreptikos* or *Exhortation to the Greeks* is the first of Clement's three great works, and it dates from before the year 200 A. D. It is closely related to earlier Christian apologies; but still, Clement has found a new approach. He no longer finds it necessary to rescue Christianity from the onslaughts of slander and calumny; rather, he is deeply concerned with the educative function of the Logos, the Divine Word, throughout the history of mankind. This being his concern, the work bears some claim to being a theology of history.

The Migne text, PG 8, 49-246, is no longer serviceable, in view of Otto Stählin's critical edition in the series GCS, Vol. 12, Leipzig 1936, pp. 3-86.

401

[1, 7, 1]

The Word, then, the Christ, is the cause both of our ancient beginning — for He was in God — and of our well-being. And now this same Word has appeared as man. He alone is both God and man, and the source of all our good things. It is by Him that we are taught to live well and then are sent along to life eternal. . . . [3] He is the New Song, the manifestation which has now been made among us, of the Word which existed in the beginning and before the beginning. The Savior, who existed before, has only lately appeared. He that has appeared is in Him that is; for the Word that was with God (1), the Word by whom all things were made, has appeared as our Teacher; and He, who bestowed life upon us in the beginning, when, as our Creator, He formed us, now that He has appeared as our Teacher, has taught us to live well so that, afterwards, as God, He might furnish us abundantly with eternal life.

301
302
284
373
256

402

[4, 63, 2]

Human art, moreover, fashions houses and ships and cities and pictures; but how should I tell what God makes? Behold, the whole world — that is His work; and the heavens and the sun and angels and men, the works of His fingers (2). [3] How great, indeed, is the power of God! His mere willing it is the creation of the world; and God alone created it, because He is God in fact. By a mere exercise of His will He creates, and His simple volition is followed by its coming to be.

460

158

403

[6, 68, 2]

For into all men in general, and indeed, most particularly into those who are engaged   135
in intellectual pursuits, a certain divine emanation has been instilled, [3] by reason of
which they confess, if somewhat reluctantly, that God is one, indestructible and unbegotten,
and that somewhere above in the heavenly regions, in His proper and familiar vantage point,
He truly and eternally exists.

404

[9, 82, 1]

I could adduce for you a myriad of Scriptures, of which not one serif shall pass   20
away (3) without being fulfilled; for the Mouth of the Lord, the Holy Spirit, has spoken
these things.

405

[10, 110, 1]

The Divine Power, moreover, radiating with an unsurpassable speed and with a readily   89
obtainable benevolence, has filled the whole earth with the seed of salvation. No, it was   404
not without divine care that the Lord accomplished such a great work in so short a time.
Despised as to appearance but in reality adored, the Expiator, the Savior, the Soother,
the Divine Word, He that is quite evidently true God, He that is put on a level with the   301
the Lord of the universe because He was His Son, − and the Word was in God (4), −   232
[2] He that was not entirely disbelieved in when first He was heralded, nor altogether   310
unknown when He took up the person of man and reshaped Himself in the flesh − He
enacted the drama of human salvation. [3] For He was a genuine champion and a
fellow-champion with the creature. Brought down most speedily to all men, and having
risen from the will of the Father more quickly than the sun, with perfect ease He made
God shine upon us.   80
Whence He was and who He Himself was, was demonstrated by what He taught and did.   387
He showed Himself as the Herald of a truce, our Mediator and Savior, the Word, the Font   388
of Life and Peace poured out over the face of the earth; and through Him, so to speak, the
universe has already become an ocean of good things. [11, 111, 1] . . . The first man,
when He was in Paradise, played in childlike abandon, because he was a child of God; but
when he gave himself over to pleasure . . . he was seduced by lust, and in disobedience the
child became a man. Because he did not obey his Father, he was ashamed before God.   374
. . . [2] The Lord then wished to release him from his bonds. Having put on flesh − this
is a divine mystery − He vanquished the serpent and enslaved the tyrant death; and most   376
wonderful of all, man, who had been deceived by pleasure and bound by corruption, had
his hands unbound and was set free. [3] O mystic wonder! The Lord was laid low, and
man rose up! He that fell from Paradise receives even better as the reward for obedience:
heaven itself.

405a

[11, 113, 3]

Just as night would be over everything in spite of the other stars, if the sun did not   370
exist, so also, had we not known the Word and been illuminated by Him, we would have
been no different from fowls that are being fed, fattened in darkness and nourished for
death.

1. John 1:1.
2. Ps. 8:4.
3. Matt. 5:18; Luke 16:17.
4. John 1:1.

THE INSTRUCTOR OF CHILDREN [*ante A. D.* 202]

The *Paidagogos* or *The Instructor of Children* was written after the *Protreptikos*, to which it is a kind of sequel, and before the year 202 A. D. It continues the development of the idea of the educative function of the Logos, who is presented as the instructor or tutor of converts in the conduct of their lives. The second and third books of the *Paidagogos* turn to the problems of the homely affairs of Christians in a pagan society. It is an extremely informative work, in which Clement appears as a kind of 3rd-century Emily Post.

The Migne text, PG 8, 247-684, is entirely superseded by Otto Stählin's edition in the GCS, Vol. 12, Leipzig 1936, pp. 87-340.

406

[1, 5, 23, 1]

Again, there is Isaac . . . who is a type of the Lord. He was a child, just as the Son; for he was the son of Abraham, as Christ is the Son of God. He was a sacrificial victim,   381 as was the Lord. Yet, he was not immolated as the Lord was. Isaac did, however, at least carry the wood for a sacrifice, as the Lord carried the cross. [2] And he laughed mystically, prophesying that the Lord would fill us with joy, who are redeemed from corruption by the Blood of the Lord. But he did not suffer. Not only did Isaac suddenly yield the first place in suffering to the Word, but there is even a hint of the   301 divinity of the Lord, in Isaac's not being slain.

407

[1, 6, 26, 1]

When we are baptized, we are enlightened. Being enlightened, we are adopted as   836 sons. Adopted as sons, we are made perfect. Made perfect, we are become immortal.   755 "I say," he declares, "you are gods and sons all of the Most High (1)." [2] This work   751 is variously called grace, illumination, perfection, and washing (2). It is a washing by which we are cleansed of sins; a gift of grace by which the punishments due our sins are remitted; an illumination by which we behold that holy light of salvation — that is, by which we see God clearly; and we call that perfection which leaves nothing lacking. [3] Indeed, if a man know God, what more does he need? Certainly it were out of place to call that which is not complete a true gift of God's grace. Because God is perfect, the gifts He bestows are perfect.

408

[1, 6, 41, 3]

When the loving and benevolent Father had rained down the Word, that Word then   877 became the spiritual nourishment of those who have good sense. [42, 1] O mystic   230 wonder! The Father of all is indeed one, one also is the universal Word, and the Holy Spirit is one and the same everywhere; and one only is the Virgin Mother. I love to   416 call her the Church. This Mother alone was without milk, because she alone did not   781 become a wife. She is at once both Virgin and Mother: as a Virgin, undefiled; as a Mother, full of love.

Calling her children about her, she nourishes them with holy milk, that is, with the Infant Word. . . . [3] The Word is everything to a child: both Father and Mother, both Instructor and Nurse. "Eat My Flesh," He says, "and drink My Blood (3)." The Lord   850 supplies us with these intimate nutriments. He delivers over His Flesh, and pours out His Blood; and nothing is lacking for the growth of His children. O incredible mystery!

409

[1, 8, 62, 3]

Nothing exists except that which God causes to be. There is nothing, therefore,   460
which is hated by God; [4] nor is there anything hated by the Word. Both are one,   257
both are God; for he says: "In the beginning the Word was in God, and the Word was   258
God (4)."

409a

[1, 12, 98, 3]

We have in the conduct of the Lord an unmistakable model of incorruptibility, and   373
are following in the footsteps of God.

409b

[1, 12, 99, 1]

Indeed, we are educated not for war but for peace. In war there is need for much   373
equipment, and provisions (5) are required in abundance. Peace and love, however, are
plain and simple sisters, and need neither arms nor abundant supplies. Their nourishment
is the Word; and the Word is He by whose leadership we are enlightened and instructed,
and from whom we learn frugality and humility, and all that pertains to the love of truth,
the love of man, and the love of beauty and goodness.

To say it in but a word: through the Word we become like God by a close union in
virtue. . . . [2] And as for these who have been reared under this influence — their manner
of walking and reclining at table, their eating and sleeping, their marital relations and
manner of life, and the rest of their upbringing, acquires a greater dignity. For such a
training as is imparted by the Word is not overly severe, but well-tempered.

410

[2, 2, 19, 4]

The Blood of the Lord, indeed, is twofold. There is His corporeal Blood, by which we   857
are redeemed from corruption; and His spiritual Blood, that with which we are anointed.   851
That is to say, to drink the Blood of Jesus is to share in His immortality (6). The strength
of the Word is the Spirit, just as the blood is the strength of the body. [20, 1] Similarly,
as wine is blended with water, so is the Spirit with man (7). The one, the Watered Wine,   861
nourishes in faith, while the other, the Spirit, leads us on to immortality. The union of
both, however, — of the drink and of the Word, — is called the Eucharist, a praiseworthy   877
and excellent gift. Those who partake of it in faith are sanctified in body and in soul.
By the will of the Father, the divine mixture, man, is mystically united to the Spirit and
to the Word.

410a

[2, 3, 36, 3]

Divine Scripture, addressing itself to those who love themselves and to the boastful,   50
somewhere says most excellently: "Where are the princes of the nations, and those who
rule over the beasts which are upon the earth; they that take their diversion among the
birds of the air; they that hoard up silver, and the gold in which men trust — and there
is no end to their acquiring it; they that work in silver and in gold and are solicitous?
There is no searching of their works; they have vanished and have gone down into
Hades (8)."

411

[3, 1, 1, 1]

The greatest of all lessons, so it would seem, is to know oneself. For whoever   133
knows himself will know God; and knowing God, he will become like God, not by
wearing gold ornaments and robes which reach to the feet, but by doing good and by
requiring as few things as possible.

412

[3, 1, 1, 5]

But that man in whom reason (λόγος) dwells is not shifty, not pretentious, but has   754
the form dictated by reason (λόγος) and is like God. He is beautiful, and does not
feign beauty. That which is true is beautiful; for it, too, is God. Such a man becomes
God because God wills it. [2, 1] Rightly, indeed, did Heraclitus say: "Men are gods,
and gods are men; for the same reason (λόγος) is in both (9)." That this is a mystery
is clear: God is in a man, and a man is God, the Mediator fulfilling the will of the
Father. The Mediator is the Word (Λόγος) who is common to both, being the Son of
God and the Savior of men.

413

[3, 12, 97, 2]

A multitude of other pieces of advice to particular persons is written in the holy   406
books (10): some for presbyters, some for bishops and deacons; and others for   952
widows (11), of whom we shall have opportunity to speak elsewhere.   957

1. Ps. 81 [82]:6.
2. χάρισμα καὶ φώτισμα καὶ τέλειον καὶ λουτρόν. A knowledge that such are the various names given to
   Baptism will be of assistance in arriving at a better understanding of numerous Scripture passages, where
   these or related terms are used, notably: Rom. 5:2; 5:15; 7:25; Eph. 5:26; Titus 3:5; Heb. 6:4;
   7:11; 10:32; and James 1:17.
3. John 6:55.
4. John 1:1.
5. Read τροφή, instead of τρυφή.
6. ἀφθαρσίας, rightly understood, may often be translated *immortality* rather than *incorruption*. Neither body
   nor soul individually constitutes a man; and the Greek Fathers often term the separation of body and soul
   corruption. Hence, corruption is often synonymous with death; and in view of the resurrection and reunion
   of body and soul, salvation is termed incorruption, which may be better understood as immortality.
   Moreover, while some few earlier writers may have been uncertain as to the resurrection of the unjustified,
   by the time of Clement the term incorruption has already a special and technical meaning, referring to the
   resurrection and reunion of body and soul in the case of the just; and it carries with it the unexpressed but
   superimposed notion of salvation, but without denying in any way a resurrection to damnation for the
   unjustified.
7. This, with what follows, may be taken as an indication of a rather keen theological insight in Clement, a
   rather forceful expression of the fact that in receiving the Eucharist with worthy dispositions, we receive not
   only the Body and Blood of Christ, but receive also an increase of the indwelling Holy Spirit.
8. Baruch 3:16-19. While our chief interest in this passage is in Clement's use of the term Divine Scripture, —
   ἡ θεία · · · γραφή, — we include his full citation, since it is from a seldom-quoted and deuterocanonical
   book.
9. Heraclitus, fragment 62, in H. Diels, *Die Fragmente der Vorsokratiker*, Berlin 1903.
10. ταῖς βίβλοις ταῖς ἁγίαις can as easily be translated *the Holy Bible*.
11. αἱ μὲν πρεσβυτέροις, αἱ δὲ ἐπισκόποις καὶ διακόνοις, ἄλλαι χήραις . . . The term *widow* may here be
    taken, as quite often it may, as synonymous with *deaconess*.

STROMATEIS *or* MISCELLANIES [*post A. D.* 202]

In the second of his three great works, the *Paidagogos,* Clement remarked that the Word first exhorts, then trains, and finally teaches us. Since the *Protreptikos* was a work of exhortation and the *Paidagogos* a work of training, some have concluded that Clement intended to write a trilogy, of which the final installment would be a work of teaching. It seems to me that this view, though it is virtually universally accepted, reads a great deal into his remark; nor am I entirely certain that exhortation, training, and teaching is necessarily a tricotomy.

But be that as it may, while it is almost universally held that Clement intended to produce such a trilogy, it is also quite generally agreed that the *Stromateis,* though it is the third of Clement's three great works, does not constitute the third part of the supposed trilogy. If he ever intended a trilogy, it is clear that he abandoned such a project after writing the *Paidagogos.* It was at the end of the introduction to the *Paidagogos* that Clement made the remark referred to above; and it seems to me that while the *Protreptikos* may be regarded as having covered his ideas of the Word in His hortatory function, the *Paidagogos* may be regarded as having covered both the training and teaching functions of the Word. In Clement's mind, after all, the difference between a trainer and a teacher is in the age of the one under discipline: children are trained, while teaching is for adults. The *Paidagogos* actually deals, of course, with the latter, but under the figure of the former, we being the children of a divine Father.

The term *Stromateis* is an interesting one. It is suggestive of *table-cloths, bed-clothes, horse-blankets, throw rugs,* and means, more precisely, *patch-work quilts.* It is from the last-named concept that the Greeks apply it as a title to books of the sort that we call *Miscellanies.* It is, then, as the title indicates, a kind of mix-mash — one thinks of Abraham of St. Clare's *Heilsames Gemisch-Gemasch* — or catch-all of various topics, treated in eight books.

The text of Migne, PG 8, 685-1392, and 9, 9-602, is entirely superseded by the critical edition of Otto Stählin in the GCS, Vol. 15, Leipzig 1906, reprinted in 1939 and again in 1960; and Vol. 17, Leipzig 1909, pp. 3-102. Vol. 15 contains books 1 through 6; Vol. 17, books 7 and 8.

416

[2, 2, 5, 2]
"And what is hidden and open, I know. For wisdom, the craftsman of all things, has taught me (1)." [3] You have, in brief, the professed aim of our philosophy (2). The learning of these things, along with the pursuit of right conduct, leads through Wisdom, the Craftsman of all things, to the Ruler of all, who is difficult to grasp and apprehend, ever receding and withdrawing from him that pursues.

130
174

417

[2, 2, 8, 4]
But faith, which the Greeks disparage and regard as useless and barbarous, is a voluntary preconception, the assent of piety (3); "the substance of things hoped for, the evidence of those things which are not seen (4)," according to the divine Apostle (5). "For by it most especially did the men of old have testimony borne to them; and without faith it is impossible to be pleasing to God (6)." [9, 1] Others, however have defined faith as an intellectual assent to a thing unseen, since certainly the proof of a thing unknown is manifest assent. . . . [6] He, then, that believes in the Divine Scriptures with firm judgment, receives, in the voice of God, who gave the Scriptures,

557
553
567
568
552

559
558

an unquestionable proof. Nor by proof does faith become more firm. Blessed, therefore,   560
are those who have not seen and yet have believed (7).

418

[2, 4, 14, 3]

For knowledge is a state of mind that results from demonstration; but faith is a   560
gift which leads on from what is undemonstrable to what is universal and simple, to   554
what is neither concomitant to matter, nor matter itself, nor subject to matter.   555
. . . [15, 5] Aristotle, however, says that faith is that decision, which follows upon
knowledge, as to whether this or that be true (8). Faith, then, is superior to knowledge,   563
and is its criterion.

419

[2, 6, 31, 1]

Such a change as this, by which someone comes from unbelief to belief, and, while   555
hoping and fearing, yet believes, is of divine origin. Indeed, faith appears to us to be   582
the first inclination toward salvation; after which hope and repentance and even fear,   591
advancing in company with moderation and patience, lead us on to love and to
knowledge (9).

420

[2, 23, 145, 3]

That Scripture counsels marriage, however, and never allows any release from the   974
union, is expressly contained in the law: "You shall not divorce a wife, except for
reason of immorality (10)." And it regards as adultery the marriage of a spouse, while
the one from whom a separation was made is still alive. . . . [146, 2] "Whoever takes
a divorced woman as wife commits adultery (11)," it says; for "if anyone divorce his
wife, he debauches her (12);" that is, he compels her to commit adultery. [3] And not
only does he that divorces her become the cause of this, but also he that takes the
woman and gives her the opportunity of sinning; for if he did not take her, she would
return to her husband.

420a

[3, 10, 68, 1]

Who are the two or three who begin by gathering together in the name of Christ,   972
and in whose midst is the Lord (13)? Are not the three man, wife, and child, since a wife
is joined to a man by God?

420b

[3, 12, 84, 2]

If, however, marriage, though commanded by the Law, were yet sinful — really, I do   972
not see how anyone could say that he knows God and yet say that sin has been
commanded by God. If the Law is sacred, then marriage is a holy estate.

421a

[5, 1, 5, 4]

We confront them with an argument unanswerable: It is God who speaks and comes   50

to our aid in writing, in regard to each one of the points which I am discussing.
[6, 1] Who, then, is so impious as to disbelieve in God, and to demand proofs from God
as from men?

423

[5, 11, 71, 3]

    If, then, abstracting from all that pertains to bodies and to such as we call corporeal,   178
we cast ourselves into the greatness of Christ, and then advance into His immensity by   175
holiness, we may reach somehow to the conception of the Almighty, knowing not what   153
He is, but what He is not. [4] Neither form nor motion, however, nor standing, nor
sitting, nor place, nor right, nor left are to be conceived of as belonging to the Father
of the universe, although these things are written of Him. What each of these means
will be shown in its proper place. [5] The First Cause, therefore, is not located in a
place, but is above place and time and name and conception. On this account did Moses
also say, "Show yourself to me (14)," indicating most clearly that God cannot be
taught to men nor expressed in words, but can be known only by an ability which He
Himself gives.

424

[5, 12, 81, 6]

    Nor is it possible to predicate any parts of [God]. For what is one is indivisible, and   151
thereby infinite — not in regard to its being clearly inconceivable, but in regard to its   154
being without dimensions and not having limits, for which reason it is without form and   175
name. [82, 1] And if we somehow name Him, we do not do so properly, when we
supply such names as the One, or the Good, or Mind, or That Which Is, or Father, or
God, or Creator, or Lord. We so speak not as supplying His name; but in our need we
use beautiful names so that the mind may have these as a support against erring in other
respects.

    [2] For each one by itself does not express God, but all together they are indicative of
the power of the Omnipotent. Predicates are expressed either from what belongs to things   158
themselves, or from their relationship to each other; but nothing of this is applicable in
reference to God. [3] Neither is He apprehended by the science of demonstration; for
it depends upon primary and better known principles, while there is nothing antecedent
to the Unbegotten.

425

[5, 13, 87, 1]

    That which in other ages was not known has now been clearly shown and has now   135
been revealed to the sons of men (15). [2] Indeed, there was always a natural
manifestation of the one almighty God, among all right thinking men; and the majority,
who had not entirely divested themselves of shame in the presence of the truth,
apprehended the eternal beneficence through divine providence. . . . [5, 14, 133, 7] The
Father and Creator of all things, therefore, is apprehended by all by means of an innate
power and without instruction, in a manner suitable to all. . . [8] Nor is it possible for
any race to live anywhere, whether they be tillers of the soil or nomads, nor even be they
city-dwellers, without being imbued with faith in a Higher Being.

426

[6, 9, 71, 1]

    The one who has deeper wisdom (16) is such that he is subject only to the affections which exist for the maintenance of the body, such as hunger, thirst, and the like. [2] In regard to the Savior, however, it were ridiculous to suppose that the body demanded, as a body, the necessary aids for its maintenance. For He ate, not for the sake of the body, which had its continuance from a holy power, but lest those in His company might happen to think otherwise of Him, just as afterwards some did certainly suppose that He had appeared as a mere phantasm. He was in general dispassionate; and no movement of feeling penetrated Him, whether pleasure or pain (17).

347
310
349

427

[6, 13, 107, 2]
Even here in the Church the gradations of bishops, presbyters, and deacons happen to be imitations, in my opinion, of the angelic glory and of that arrangement which, the Scriptures say, awaits those who have followed in the footsteps of the Apostles, and who have lived in perfect righteousness according to the Gospel.

406
952
488
60

428

[6, 14, 108, 4]
When we hear, "Your faith has saved you (18)," we do not understand [the Lord] to say simply that they will be saved who have believed in whatever manner, even if works have not followed. [5] To begin with, it was to the Jews alone that He spoke this phrase, who had lived in accord with the law and blamelessly, and who had lacked only faith in the Lord.

758
760

429

[6, 17, 156, 5]
God knows all things, not only those that are, but those also that shall be, and how each shall be. Foreseeing their individual movements,
He surveys all things, and hears all things (19),
[6] seeing inside the naked soul; and He possesses from eternity the conception of each thing individually. . . . [7] In one glance He views all things together and each thing by itself.

189

430

[6, 17, 157, 4]
The thoughts of virtuous men are produced by divine inspiration. The soul is disposed in the way it is, and the will of God is conveyed to human souls, by special divine ministers who assist in such service. For regiments of angels are distributed over nations and cities; and perhaps some even are assigned to particular individuals.

683
684
493

433

[7, 10, 57, 3]
Faith, then, is a comprehensive knowledge, so to speak, of the essentials; but knowledge is the strong and firm proof of what is accepted through faith, and which is built upon faith by the Lord's teaching, and which leads to infallibility and understanding and to sudden comprehension. [4] And it seems to me that the first saving change is from paganism to faith, as I said before; and the second is that from faith to knowledge. This latter develops into love, and afterwards presents the one loving to Him that is loved, and the one knowing to Him that is known. [5] And such a one, perhaps, has already attained the condition of being like to an angel (20).

563
565

595
590
757

433a

[7, 12, 70, 4]

And one is not really shown to be a man in the choice of a single life; but he   968
surpasses men, who, without pleasure or pain, has disciplined himself by marriage, by
the begetting of children, and by care for the household; who, in his solicitude for the
household, has been inseparable from God's love; and who has withstood every temptation
arising through children and wife or through domestics and possessions. [5] He, however,
who is without a family (21), for the most part escapes temptation. Caring, then, for
himself alone, he is surpassed by one who is inferior to him in what pertains to his own   984
salvation, but is superior to him in the conduct of life (22).

434

[7, 12, 78, 7]

Righteous conduct also is twofold: that which is done for love, and that which is   912
done through fear. [79, 1] For indeed, it is said, "The fear of the Lord is pure, remaining   914
forever and ever (23)." Those who, because of fear, turn to faith and righteousness, remain
forever. Fear does, in fact, motivate to abstaining from evil; but love, building up to free
action, exhorts to the doing of good.

435

[7, 17, 107, 3]

From what has been said, then, it seems clear to me that the true Church, that which   416
is really ancient, is one; and in it are enrolled those who, in accord with a design (24),   400
are just. . . . [5] We say, therefore, that in substance, in concept, in origin and in eminence,   414
the ancient and Catholic Church is alone, gathering as it does into the unity of the one   421
faith which results from the familiar covenants, — or rather, from the one covenant in   420
different times, by the will of the one God and through the one Lord, — those already   202
chosen, those predestined by God who knew before the foundation of the world that
they would be just.

1. Wis. 7:21.
2. Here *philosophy* means *religion*. The usage is clear, since Clement is opposing Christianity, which he calls
"the barbarian philosophy which we follow," to the Greek philosophical systems, in which latter, Clement
indicates (in Bk. 1, Ch. 4 and Ch. 5), the Greeks of the pre-Christian era were justified and found
righteousness. Soon the word φιλοσοφία will mean purely and simply a life of Christian asceticism; and
with the growth of monasticism, it will mean the monastic life, in which sense it is used quite frequently
in the 4th century.
3. The terms προλήψις = *preconception,* and συγκατάθεσις = *assent,* are borrowed from Stoic philosophy, in
which the preconception is an instinctive or implanted notion, and the assent is of the mind to such a
conception.
4. Heb. 11:1.
5. Clement attributes *Hebrews* to St. Paul.
6. Heb. 11:2 and 6.
7. John 20:29.
8. Ἀριστοτέλης δὲ τὸ ἐπόμενον τῇ ἐπιστήμῃ κρίμα, ὡς ἀληθὲς τόδε τι, πίστιν εἶναί φησι. The line is not,
however, in Aristotle. The statement appears to mean, and the Latin translation in Migne so takes it,
*[Aristoteles autem, id, quod consequitur scientiam, judicium, quo verum esse hoc aut illud judicamus,
dicit esse fidem]*, that a judgment, based on knowledge, as to the truth or falsity of something, is faith.
It is hard to believe that Clement could so define faith, or that he could approve such a definition even
if he thought it to be Aristotle's.

Besides, the proposition is entirely illogical in view of Clement's subsequent comment, that faith is
therefore superior to knowledge and the criterion of knowledge. The Greek construction does barely
admit of another interpretation (entirely excluded in the Latin translation!); and while we have faithfully preserved the ambiguity of the Greek in our translation above, it is certain that it must be
understood along with Clement's comment, somewhat in this fashion: *Aristotle says that the judgment
brought to bear upon some item of supposed knowledge, as to whether such be true or false, is faith;*

faith, therefore, is the criterion of knowledge. This will not, of course, satisfy a theologian; and it is not very profound; but at least it does not defy logic.

9. There follows a quotation from the so-called *Letter of Barnabas,* which Clement expressly attributes to the Apostle Barnabas.

10. Matt. 5:32; 19:9.

11. *Ibid.,* also Lk. 16:18.

12. Mark 10:11. Clement, however, reads: ἐὰν γάρ τις ἀπολύσῃ γυναῖκα, μοιχᾶται αὐτήν, which changes the sense considerably. While the actual words used seem to indicate that Clement has in mind Mark 10:11, the content of the remark is closer to Matt. 5:32.

13. Matt. 18:20.

14. Ex. 33:13.

15. Eph. 3:5.

16. ὁ γνωστικός, literally, *the gnostic.* Clement uses the term in reference to those who practice the true faith, and without the odious overtones which the term generally has. Clement's gnostic, then, is the true gnostic, as distinguished from the gnostic falsely so-called. Unfortunately for our language, it is the latter who finally came into sole possession of the name.

17. This is not to be taken as a denial of the Lord's having had a sensible body; for Clement continues the paragraph, using much the same language and terminology in regard to the Apostles, and in fact in regard to all true gnostics, who do indeed experience pleasure and pain, but do not suffer themselves to be moved immoderately by these or by any of the other sensations to which the body is naturally subject. The word *penetrated* is a quite literal translation of παρεισδύεται, but it ought to be understood more in the meaning of *subjugated.* Again, our clause: *He was in general quite dispassionate,* is a quite literal rendering of: αὐτὸς δὲ ἁπαξαπλῶς ἀπαθὴς ἦν. Those who translate it: *But He was entirely impassible,* really say much more than the Greek says; and they give a handle to a heresy which cannot be found in Clement.

18. Matt. 9:22; Mark 5:34; Luke 8:48.

19. Homer, *Iliad* Γ 277.

20. Luke 20:36.

21. τῷ δὲ ἀοίκῳ. More literally, *he, however, who is homeless.*

22. An excellent passage, deserving of much meditation. Some, however, have concluded from the above remarks that Clement regarded the married state as superior to virginity. It should be clear from the concluding sentence that he did not. Yet, Clement does give wonderful testimony to the simple fact that, although virginity ordered toward salvation is a higher state than marriage, even when the latter is, as it should be, ordered toward salvation, still, one who bears up well under the superior trials and temptations of the married state may yet surpass one who leads the more or less carefree life of a celibate.

23. Ps. 18 [19]:10.

24. One might ordinarily translate κατὰ πρόθεσιν as *purposely* or *of set purpose.* In view of what follows, however, it would appear that Clement is stressing the fact that these just or righteous men are what they are because God has so providentially ordained it. They are just, then, in keeping with God's plan, *i.e., in accord with a design.* Taking the passage in its entirety it is clear that Clement extends membership in the Church to all those who have been predestined to salvation – even those who lived in the centuries before redemption was accomplished by Christ. It is not clear, however, that he restricts membership in the Church to *only* the predestined. If Clement errs, his error is not so evident as that in the condemned propositions of Hus and Quesnel, which implied that membership in the Church belongs to all and only the predestined.

WHO IS THE RICH MAN THAT IS SAVED? [*inter A. D.* 190/210]

Clement's *Who is the Rich Man that is Saved,* written between the years 190 and 210 A. D., is a literary homily on Mark 10:17-31. Apparently Clement had wealthy people among his charges; for he takes the consoling view that when the Lord said: 'Go, sell whatsoever you have and give it to the poor,' He did not really mean anything quite that drastic.

The Migne text, PG 9, 603-652, is superseded by the critical edition of Otto Stählin, GCS, Vol. 17, Leipzig 1909, pp. 157-191.

[21, 1]

A man by himself, working and toiling at freedom from passion, achieves nothing. But   657
if he plainly shows his great desire and complete sincerity in this, he will attain it by the

addition of the power of God. [2] Indeed, God conspires with willing souls. But if they   690
abandon their eagerness, the spirit which is bestowed by God is also restrained. To save   700
the unwilling is to exercise compulsion; but to save the willing belongs to Him who bestows
grace.
    [3] Nor does the kingdom of heaven belong to the sleeping and the lazy; rather, the
violent take it by force (1). . . . [4] On hearing these words (2), the blessed Peter, the
chosen, the pre-eminent, the first among the disciples, for whom alone with Himself the   430
Savior paid the tribute (3), quickly grasped and understood their meaning. [5] And what
does he say? "Behold, we have left all and have followed you (4)!"

436a

[23, 2]
    On the other hand, hear the Savior: ". . . [4] I am He that feeds you. I give Myself   877
as Bread, of which he that has tasted experiences death no more; and I supply daily the   879
Drink of immortality. [5] I am the Teacher of lessons concerning the highest heavens.   873
On behalf of you I contended with death, and I paid the death which you owed for your 871,374
former sins and for your unbelief towards God."   383

437

[33, 2]
    You, however, shall not judge who is worthy and who unworthy. For it is possible   1034
that you might err in your opinion. When in doubt and ignorance it is better to do good   1032
to the unworthy for the sake of the worthy, than to guard against the less good and
thereby fail to fall in with the sincere. [3] For by being too cautious, and by aiming
to test who you will or will not find worthy to be received, it is possible for you to
neglect some that are dear to God; and for this the penalty is punishment in eternal
fire.

438

[42, 2]
    After the death of the tyrant, the [Apostle John] came back again to Ephesus   440
from the Island of Patmos; and, upon being invited, he went even to the neighboring   406
cities of the pagans, here to appoint bishops, there to set in order whole Churches, and   951
there to ordain to the clerical estate such as were designated by the Spirit.

1. Matt. 11:12.
2. Our Savior had said that it was easier for a camel to pass through the eye of a needle than for a rich man to
   enter heaven. His disciples met His statement with the question, "Who, then, can be saved?" Clement is now
   referring to our Savior's reply to that question, with which words the present chapter opens: "With men this
   is impossible, but with God all things are possible."
3. See Matt. 17:27.
4. Matt. 19:27; Mk. 10:28.

HYPOTYPOSEIS or SKETCHES [inter A. D. 190/210]

    Photius was still able to read a complete text of Clement's *Hypotyposeis* or *Sketches*,
written between the years 190 and 210 A. D.; but Photius, blessed man, read many
good things that no one since has seen. The work was in eight books, but has
survived only in a few short Greek excerpts, preserved mostly by Eusebius,
Pseudo-Oikomenios, and John Moschus. A longer fragment in Latin translation stems

from Cassiodorus. Photius passed very severe judgment on the work, citing its many rank heresies; and withal, he expressed his doubt of its authenticity. Since we have only a few fragments, and since there is no reason to doubt their authenticity, no judgment can safely be rendered on Photius' remarks.

The text in Migne, PG 9, 729-750, is no longer much cited, since the edition of Otto Stählin in GCS, Vol. 17, Leipzig 1909, pp. 195-215.

FRAGMENT IN EUSEBIUS, History of the Church, BK. 6, CH. 14

439-440

[6, 14, 1]

To put it briefly, [Clement] has given in the Sketches *abridged accounts of all the* **42** *canonical Scripture, and he does not omit the disputed books* (1) — *I mean Jude and the rest of the Catholic Epistles, and Barnabas and the so-called Apocalypse of Peter.* [2] *The Epistle to the Hebrews, moreover, he attributes to Paul, and says that it was written to the Hebrews in the Hebrew language, and that Luke translated it carefully and gave it out to the Greeks. Hence, the same style of expression is found in this epistle and in the Acts.* . . . [5] *Again, in the same books, Clement gives the tradition of the earliest presbyters in regard to the order of the Gospels, referring to it in this manner:* **61**

"The Gospels containing the genealogies," *he says,* "were written first. [6] The **64** circumstances which occasioned that of Mark were these: When Peter preached the Word **66** publicly at Rome, and declared the Gospel by the Spirit, many who were present requested **65** that Mark, who had been for a long time his follower and who remembered his sayings, **431** should write down what had been proclaimed. Having composed the Gospel, he gave it to those who had requested it. [7] When Peter learned of this, he did not positively forbid it, but neither did he encourage it. John, last of all, seeing that the plain facts (2) had **67** been clearly set forth in the Gospels, and being urged by his acquaintances, composed a spiritual Gospel under the divine inspiration of the Spirit." *So much for Clement.*

FRAGMENT OF COMMENTARY ON THE FIRST EPISTLE OF JOHN, PROBABLY ALSO FROM THE Sketches, AND SURVIVING IN THE LATIN OF CASSIODORUS: Adumbrationes Clementis Alexandrini in epistulas canonicas.

442

[On 1 John 1:1]

When [John] says: "What was from the beginning (3)," he touches upon the generation **251** without beginning of the Son, who is coeval with the Father. "Was," therefore, is indicative **256** of an eternity without a beginning, just as the Word Himself, that is, the Son, being one with the Father in regard to equality of substance, is eternal and uncreated. That the Word always existed is signified by the saying: "In the beginning was the Word (4)."

1. τὰς ἀντιλεγομένας.
2. τὰ σωματικά, literally, *the bodily things: i.e.,* the somatic as opposed to the pneumatic. The Gospel of John is here termed τὸ εὐαγγέλιον πνευματικόν.
3. 1 John 1:1. — "I write of what was from the beginning."
4. John 1:1.

ORIGEN [*ca. A. D.* 185 — 253/254]

There are more biographical details available for Origen than for any of the earlier theologians, mostly because the sixth book of Eusebius' *History of the Church* is devoted almost entirely to him. He was born about the year 185 A. D. at Alexandria, the child of Christian parents. When his father, St. Leonidas, was martyred in the persecution of Septimius Severus, in the year 202 A. D., Origen's mother prevented him from accompanying his father to martyrdom by the simple expedient of hiding his clothes. It is generally stated that he castrated himself, probably soon after the death of his father; but the statements which lead to this conclusion are open to other interpretation and the facts are far from certain.

It was under the direction of Origen, successor to Clement, that the school of Alexandria reachest its greatest prominence. About 212 A. D. he journeyed to Rome, where he made the acquaintance of Hippolytus. He left Alexandria again about the year 215 A. D., when the Emperor Caracalla was looting the city and persecuting its teachers. Going to Caesarea in Palestine, he preached to the congregation there on Scripture, though he was a layman, at the request of Theoctistus, Bishop of Caesarea, and Alexander, Bishop of Jerusalem. Demetrius, Bishop of Alexandria, raised strong objections to Origen's having been permitted to preach, and demanded his return to Alexandria.

Fifteen years later Origen again passed through Caesarea, on a journey to Greece; and in order to obviate any further objections to a layman's being allowed to preach, Alexander and Theoctistus ordained him to the priesthood. Demetrius was now quite thoroughly enraged at such a flagrant breach of the canons, which, apparently, already demanded that a man be ordained only by the bishop of the diocese of his residence. He called two synods at Alexandria in 230 and 231 A. D., which deposed, degraded, and excommunicated Origen, who then moved to Caesarea in Palestine, where he founded a school patterned after that at Alexandria. During the Decian persecution he was tortured and imprisoned, most likely in Caesarea; and as a result of his sufferings he died at Tyre at the age of sixty-nine, in 253 or 254 A. D.

The disputes known as the Origenist controversies, in respect to the orthodoxy of his doctrine, arose never during his life, but three times after his death: *ca. A. D.* 300, *ca. A. D.* 400, and *ca. A. D.* 550. He was a great scholar and a great theologian, and strove always to be Catholic in his faith. Yet, he came finally to be regarded as a heretic, which accounts largely for the fact that so many of his writings have perished entirely, while much that is extant has suffered terribly at the hands of expurgators, interpolators, and translators.

Much, of course, has been written on Origen; but there remains today a great need for a fresh and thorough re-investigation of his doctrine. It must be pointed out, however, that it is very dubious that such a re-investigation could reach conclusions of any satisfactory degree of certainty. As hinted above, his literary productivity was tremendous. Eusebius compiled a list of his writings, but even the list has perished. Jerome knew the list and said that Origen's writings totalled some two thousand books. Epiphanius gives the figure as six thousand. We possess only a very small fraction of his actual literary output, probably not much more than the hundredth part of what he wrote, and even this is generally in a poor state of preservation.

So, while re-investigation of Origen is much needed, the one who will undertake the task must be prepared for a great deal of conjecture; and while some remarkable discoveries may be made along the way, the total picture will probably remain, in general, an unsatisfactory one in point of certainty of conclusions. One thing we can say of him, and this will not change: that he deserves well the title of greatest scholar of Christian antiquity.

THE FUNDAMENTAL DOCTRINES [*inter A. D.* 220-230]

Origen was the first to attempt a manual of dogmatic theology, the Περὶ ἀρχῶν, generally referred to as *De principiis,* which we may translate *The Fundamental Doctrines.* The work consists of four books, and was written between the years 220 and 230 A. D. Of the original Greek, only a few fragments have survived. Entirely extant, however, is the very free Latin translation by Rufinus, who almost certainly attempted something in the way of expurgating or correcting passages suspect of heresy Jerome's translation, a more literal one, but probably not less biased, as it was designed to show Origen's heresies at their worst, has perished entirely.

It is generally stated that Origen's heresies are nowhere clearer than in his work on *The Fundamental Doctrines.* Nevertheless, it should be noted that he is generally very careful to distinguish between Catholic doctrine and his own speculations, which latter he presents as no more than possibilities which would have to stand the test of acceptance or rejection in the teaching Church. The work undoubtedly suffers from an overly active Platonic influence, and from allegorical interpretation of Scripture; yet, it stands firmly and immovably and without pretence as neither more nor less than a theological monument of absolutely epic proportions.

The Migne text, PG 11, 115-414, is no longer of much scholarly usefulness, and is entirely superseded by the critical edition of P. Koetschau in the Berlin Corpus (GCS), Vol. 22, Leipzig 1913.

N. B. The seven passages below which we have numbered from 443 to 447a inclusive represent a continuous section, nothing of the text having been omitted between these passages.

443

[1, *Preface,* 2]

Although there are many who believe that they themselves hold to the teachings of Christ, there are yet some among them who think differently from their predecessors. The teaching of the Church has indeed been handed down through an order of succession from the Apostles, and remains in the Churches even to the present time. That alone is to be believed as the truth which is in no way at variance with ecclesiastical and apostolic tradition.

101
102

444

[1, *Preface,* 3]

It ought to be known, however, that the holy Apostles, in preaching the faith of Christ, treated with the utmost clarity of certain matters which they believed to be of absolute necessity to all believers, even to those who seemed somewhat dull in regard to the investigation of divine knowledge. Naturally, they left the grounds of their assertions to be investigated by those who would deserve the excellent gifts of the Spirit, and to those who would receive in a pre-eminent degree through the same Holy Spirit the gifts of language, of wisdom, and of knowledge. In other matters, indeed, they stated that certain things are so; but as to the how and the wherefore of their being so, they were silent. They did this, indeed, so that such of their successors as were more studious and who would be lovers of wisdom might have a subject of exercise on which to display the fruit of their talents — those persons, I mean, who should prepare themselves to be fit and worthy for the reception of wisdom.

105

445

[1, *Preface*, 4]

The specific points which are clearly handed down through the apostolic preaching   102
are these: First, that there is one God who created and arranged all things, and who,   157
when nothing existed, called all things into existence; . . . and that in the final period   460
this God, just as He had promised beforehand through the Prophets, sent the Lord Jesus   461
Christ. . . . Secondly, that Jesus Christ Himself, who came, was born of the Father   300
before all creatures; and after He had ministered to the Father in the creation of all   301
things, — for through Him were all things made (1), — in the final period he emptied
Himself and was made man. Although He was God, He took flesh; and having been
made man, He remained what He was, God. He took a body like our body, differing   347
only in this, that it was born of a Virgin and the Holy Spirit.   310

Moreover, this Jesus Christ was truly born and truly suffered; and He endured this
ordinary death, not in mere appearance, but did truly die; for He truly rose again from
the dead, and after His resurrection He conversed with His disciples, and was taken up.
Third, they handed it down that the Holy Spirit is associated in honor and dignity   230
with the Father and the Son.

In His case, however, it is not clearly distinguished whether or not He was born (2),
or even whether He is or is not to be regarded as a Son of God; for these are points
of careful inquiry into sacred Scripture, and for prudent investigation. And it is most
clearly taught in the Churches that this Spirit inspired each one of the holy men, whether
Prophets or Apostles; and that there was not one Spirit in the men of old, and another   50
in those who were inspired after the coming of Christ.

446

[1, *Preface*, 5]

After these points, it is taught also that the soul, having a substance and life proper   996
to itself, shall, after its departure from this world, be rewarded according to its merits.
It is destined to obtain either an inheritance of eternal life and blessedness, if its deeds
shall have procured this for it, or to be delivered up to eternal fire and punishments, if   1034
the guilt of its crimes shall have brought it down to this. And it is also taught that there
will be a time for the resurrection of the dead, when this body which is now sown in
corruption will rise in incorruption, and that which is sown in dishonor will rise in   1011
glory (3).   1013

This also is clearly defined in ecclesiastical teaching, that every rational soul has free
will and choice; also, that it has a struggle against the devil and his angels and opposing   505
powers, in which they strive to burden it with sins, while we, if we live rightly and   494
properly, should endeavor to shake ourselves free of any such disgrace. Whence it follows
also that we do not understand ourselves as being subject to necessity, so as to be entirely
compelled, even against our will, to do either evil or good. For while we make our own
decisions, some powers may perhaps impel us to sin, and others help us to salvation.   492

We are not, however, forced by necessity to act either rightly or wrongly, as is main-   700
tained by those who say that the course and movement of the stars is the cause of human
actions, and not only of those events which take place apart from the freedom of choice,
but of those also which are placed within our power.

But in regard to the soul, whether it is derived from the seed like a shoot (4), so that   508
its source (5) or substance may be found implanted in the very seminal bodies, or whether
it has some other beginning; and this other beginning, whether it be by birth or not; or,
indeed, whether bestowed upon the body from without or not: this is not distinguished
with sufficient clarity in the teaching of the Church.

446a

[1, *Preface*, 6]

In regard to the devil and his angels and opposing powers, the ecclesiastical teaching   491
maintains that these beings do indeed exist; but what they are or how they exist is not
explained with sufficient clarity. This opinion, however, is held by most: that the devil
was an angel; and having apostatized, he persuaded as many angels as possible to fall
away with himself; and these, even to the present time, are called his angels.

447

[1, *Preface*, 7]

There is, moreover, this also in ecclesiastical teaching: that the world was created and   468
took its beginning at a certain time, and is to be destroyed because of its own wickedness.
But what existed before this world, or what will exist after the world, has not become   1016
certain knowledge among the many; for no clear statement in this matter is to be found
in ecclesiastical teaching.

447a

[1, *Preface*, 8]

Moreover, it is of ecclesiastical teaching that the Scriptures were written through the   20
Spirit of God, and that they have not only that meaning which is quite apparent, but   30
also another which escapes most. For the words which are written are the forms of
certain mysteries (6), and the images of divine things. In this matter the opinion of the
whole Church is one: that the whole Law is indeed spiritual; the spiritual meaning which
the Law conveys, however, is not known to all, but only to those on whom the grace of
the Holy Spirit is bestowed in the word of wisdom and knowledge.

448

[1, *Preface*, 10]

This also is in the ecclesiastical teaching: that there are certain angels of God and   480
good powers who minister to Him in accomplishing the salvation of men; but when they   492
were created, or what they are, or how they exist, is not distinguished with sufficient   481
clarity. In regard to the sun, however, and the moon and the stars, as to whether they are
living beings or are without life, there is no clear tradition.

449

[1, 1, 3]

Even though many saints participate in the Holy Spirit, He cannot on that account   750
be understood to be a body, which, being divided into corporeal parts, is partaken of by
each one of the saints. Clearly, He is a Sanctifying Power, in which all are said to participate   753
who have deserved to be sanctified by His grace.   285

450

[1, 1, 5]

We hold that in truth God is indeed incomprehensible and immeasurable. For whatever   173
that may be which we are able to perceive or understand of God, we must of necessity   180
believe that He is far and away better than what we can see of Him.

451

[1, 1, 6]

Since our mind is in itself unable to behold God Himself as He is, it knows the Father   170
of the universe from the beauty of His works and from the elegance of His creatures.
God, therefore, is not to be thought of as being either a body or as existing in a body,   152
but as a simple intellectual Being (7), admitting within Himself no addition of any kind.   151
Thus, He cannot be believed to have within Himself something greater and something lesser.
Rather, He is in every part μονάς (8) and, so to speak, ἑνάς (9). He is the mind and source
from which every intellectual being or mind takes its beginning.

452

[1, 1, 8]

John says in the Gospel, "No one has at any time seen God (10)," clearly declaring   170
to all who are able to understand, that there is no nature to which God is visible: not   152
as if He were indeed visible by nature, and merely escaped or baffled the view of a
frailer creature, but because He is by nature impossible to be seen. And if you should
ask of me what I think even of the Only-begotten Himself, whether I could say that the
nature of God, which is naturally invisible, is not visible even to Him, let not such a
question seem to you to be at once either impious or absurd: for we will give you a   230
logical answer.

For it is just as unsuitable to say that the Son is able to see the Father, as it is
unbecoming to suppose that the Holy Spirit is able to see the Son. It is one thing to   171
see, another to know. To see and to be seen belongs to bodies. To know and to be
known belongs to an intellectual being (11). That, therefore, which is proper to bodies,
is not to be attributed to either the Father or to the Son; but that which pertains to
deity is common to the Father and the Son.

Finally, even He Himself did not say in the Gospel that no one has seen the Father
except the Son, nor anyone the Son except the Father. But He did say, "No one knows
the Son except the Father, nor does anyone know the Father except the Son (12)." By
this it is clearly indicated that whatever among corporal natures is called seeing and being
seen, is termed, between the Father and the Son, knowing and being known — by means
of the power of knowledge, and not by the frail sense of sight. Inasmuch, then, as
neither seeing nor being seen can be properly predicated of an incorporeal and invisible
being, neither is the Father, in the Gospel, said to be seen by the Son, nor the Son by
the Father; rather, They are said to be known.

453

[1, 2, 1]

In the first place, it behooves us to know that in Christ the nature of His deity is   322
one thing, because He is the Only-begotten Son of the Father; and quite another is the
human nature which He put on in these most recent times for the purpose of the
dispensation (13).

454

[1, 2, 10]

Just as no one can be called a father unless there be a son, and no one can be a   468
master unless there be a possession or a servant, so also God could not in fact be called
almighty, if there were not those over whom He might exercise His powers; and
therefore, that God may be shown to be almighty, it is necessary that all things continue
to exist. If anyone would have it that some ages or interstices, or whatever he wishes
to call them, passed away while those things which were afterwards created did not exist,

he would doubtless show thereby that in those ages or interstices God was not almighty, and was afterwards made almighty, from that time when He began to have those over whom He might exercise His powers. In this way He will appear to have received a certain increase, and to have risen from a lower to a higher condition; for it cannot be doubted that it is better for Him to be almighty than not to be so (14).

455

[1, 3, 1]

Although no one, certainly, is able to speak worthily of God the Father, it is   175
nevertheless possible for some knowledge of Him to be obtained by means of visible   179
creatures and from those things which the human mind naturally senses; and it is possible, 130
moreover, for such knowledge to be confirmed by the sacred Scriptures.   10

456

[1, 6, 1]

These subjects, indeed, are treated by us with great anxiety and caution, more in the   1014
manner of discussions and investigations than in that of fixed and definite positions. For we have indicated in the preceding pages those questions which are bounded by clear dogma, which I think I did to the best of my ability when speaking of the Trinity. In these matters, however, our exercise is to be conducted, insofar as we are able, more in the style of a disputation than of an actual defining.

The end of the world, then, and the consummation, will take place when everyone will be subjected to the punishments deserved for his sins; a time which God alone knows, when He will bestow upon each what he deserves. We think, indeed, that the goodness of God, through His Christ, may recall every creature to one end, even His enemies being conquered and subdued.

457

[1, 6, 3]

But whether any of those orders of beings who act under the government of the devil   1014
and who obey his wicked commands will be able sometime in future ages to be converted to goodness because of the presence in them of the faculty of free will; or whether persistent and inveterate wickedness may be changed from habit into nature — but even you who are reading this may judge, whether neither in these temporal ages which are seen, nor in those which are eternal and are not seen, one portion is to differ from another in every respect, even in the final unity and fitness of things.

458

[2, 1, 3]

For how do we live and move and have our being (15), if His power does not surround   530
and hold together the universe? And how is heaven the throne of God, and the earth His footstool, as the Savior Himself declares, except by His power, which fills the whole universe, both heaven and earth, which also the Lord says (16)?

459

[2, 1, 4]

This matter, then, which is so great and has such quantity that it suffices for all the   460
bodies in the world which God willed to exist, and which is the servant and slave of the

Creator in all things, for whatever forms and species He wills, and which receives in itself whatever qualities He wishes to impose upon it — I cannot understand how so many and such great men have thought that this matter is uncreated and not made by God Himself, who is the Creator of all things; nor how they can say that its nature and power are the result of mere chance.

Moreover, I am astonished at how they can find fault with those who deny either God's creative power or His providential administration of the world, and at how they can accuse of impiety those who think that so great a work as the world can exist without a Creator or Overseer, when they themselves do also incur a similar charge of impiety in saying that matter itself is uncreated and co-eternal with the uncreated God.

460

[2, 6, 3]

Nor, on the other hand, was it opposed to the nature of the soul [of Christ], as a rational substance, to receive God, into whom, as we said above, as into the Word and the Wisdom and the Truth, it had already passed (17). Deservedly, therefore, is it also called, along with the flesh which it assumed, the Son of God, the Power of God, the Christ, and the Wisdom of God — either because it was wholly in the Son of God, or because it received the Son of God wholly into itself.

312
323
334

261

And again, the Son of God, through whom all things were created, is named Jesus Christ and Son of Man. For the Son of God is also said to have died, in view of that nature, indeed, which could admit of death. And He is called Son of Man, who is proclaimed as being about to come in the glory of God the Father, in company with the holy angels. And for this reason, throughout Scripture, not only is the divine nature spoken of in human terms, but the human nature is adorned with appellations of divine dignity.

461

[2, 6, 5]

If our having shown above that Christ possessed a rational soul should cause anyone a difficulty, since we have frequently shown throughout all our discussions that the soul is by nature capable both of good and of evil, the difficulty in this matter will be explained in the following manner: It is not possible to doubt that the nature of His soul was indeed the same as that of all others; for otherwise, were it not truly a soul, it could not be called a soul. But truly, since the faculty of choosing good and evil is within the reach of all, this soul which belonged to Christ so chose to love justice, that in proportion to the immensity of its love it did cling to justice unchangeably and inseparably. In this way firmness of purpose, and immensity of affection, and an inextinguishable fire of love, destroyed every inclination for change and alteration, so that what had depended upon choice was, by the effect of long usage, converted into nature.

312
346

It must be believed, therefore, that there was in Christ a human and rational soul, without thinking of it as having had any inclination or possibility of sinning. [6] . . . That soul which has been placed perpetually in the Word, perpetually in Wisdom, perpetually in God, is God in all that it does, in all that it feels, in all that it understands; and being incessantly heated, like iron in a fire, it possessed immutability from its union with the Word of God, and can be called neither convertible nor mutable. It must be supposed that some warmth from the Word of God passed over to each of the saints; and it must be believed that in this soul rested substantially the divine fire itself, from which some warmth may have passed to others.

462

[2, 9, 6]

We have frequently shown above by those declarations of Sacred Scripture, in which　465
we have our strength, that God, the Creator of all things, is good and just and almighty.
He, when in the beginning He created those things which He wished to create, that is,
rational beings, had no other cause for creating them except on account of Himself,
that is, His own goodness.

463

[2, 10, 3]

Now let us see what is meant by the threatening with eternal fire. [4] We find in the　1015
prophet Isaias that the fire with which each one is punished is described as his own; for
he says: "Walk in the light of your fire and in the flame which you have kindled for
yourselves (18)." It seems to be indicated by these words that every sinner kindles for
himself the flame of his own fire and is not plunged into some fire which was kindled
beforehand by someone else or which already existed before him. The food and fuel of
this fire are our sins, which are called wood and hay and stubble by the Apostle Paul (19).

And I think that . . . when the soul has gathered together within itself a multitude of
evil deeds and an abundance of sins, at the appropriate time the whole collection of evils
boils up for punishment and is set on fire for penalty. When the mind itself, or conscience,
by divine power receives into the memory all those things which, when it was sinning, it
impressed upon itself as certain signs and forms, it will see exposed before its eyes a kind
of history of each of its own enormities, the deeds which it foully and shamefully performed
and even impiously committed.

Then also will the conscience itself be harrassed and pierced by its own goads, becoming
witness and accuser against itself. . . . From this, then, it is understood that certain
tortures are produced around the substance of the soul by the harmful influences of the
sins themselves. . . . [5] . . . It is my judgment, however, that it is possible to understand
that there is also another species of punishment. . . . Thus, when the soul shall have been
found to be outside the order and structure or harmony in which, for the sake of its
well-being and useful behavior, it was created by God, and does not harmonize with itself
in the structure of its rational movements, it must be supposed that it will bear the
agonizing penalty of its own dissension, and will feel the punishment of its own inconstancy
and disorderliness. And when this dissolution and tearing asunder of the soul shall have
been accomplished by means of the application of fire, no doubt it will afterwards be　1014
solidified into a firmer structure and into a restoration of itself.

464

[2, 10, 6]

There are many other things hidden from us and known to Him alone who is the　1015
Physician of our souls. For if, because of those diseases which we contract by eating and
drinking, we must occasionally, for the health of the body, make use of a harsh and
biting curative; and if, sometimes indeed, the nature of the disease demanding it, we
must undergo the rigor of the knife and the severity of amputation, and if the disease is
such that it goes beyond even those remedies, and the virulence must at last be cauterized
with fire; how much more understandable it is that God, our Physician, desiring to
alleviate the diseases of our souls, which they contracted from a variety of sins and crimes,
should likewise employ such punitive cures, and should, moreover, employ even the
punishment of fire with those who have so lost their health of soul! . . . That even the
punishment, however, which is said to be inflicted by means of fire, is understood to be

applied remedially (20), is taught by Isaias, who does indeed speak thus in regard to   1014
Israel:
    "The Lord will wash away the filth of the sons and daughters of Sion, and will purify
the blood from the midst of them by the spirit of judgment and by the spirit of
burning (21)." And of the Chaldeans he speaks thus: "You have coals of fire. Sit
upon them, and they will be a help to you (22)." In other passages, he says: "The Lord
will sanctify in a burning fire (23)." And in the Prophet Malachias, it is said: "Sitting,
the Lord will blow, and will purify, and will pour out the purified sons of Juda (24)."

465

[3, 1, 18]
    The human will is not enough for the obtaining of the end; nor is the running of   690
those who are, as it were, athletes, enough for the receiving of the prize of God's high
calling in Christ Jesus (25). For these things are accomplished by God's assistance.
. . . We could not in piety assert that the production of full crops is the work of the
farmer or of him who watered; it is, rather, the work of God (26). Thus, our own
perfection is accomplished neither by our doing nothing, nor yet is it completed by us;
but God does the greater part of it.

466

[3, 3, 5]
    This too, I think, should be investigated in a suitable manner: what are the reasons   507
why a human soul is sometimes moved by good spirits, and at other times, by evil?   210
. . . It seems to me that this cannot be answered otherwise, if we are to show that divine
providence is without any guilty injustice, than by holding that there were certain prior
causes acting upon souls, in consequence of which, before they were born into bodies,
they contracted some kind of guilt in their feelings or movements, on account of which
they have been judged by divine providence as deserving of suffering. For indeed, a soul
always has free will, certainly when it is in this body — nay, even when it is outside the
body.

467

[3, 4, 1]
    In this matter [of temptations besetting men], I think we must inquire in a suitable   503
manner, whether there be in us, that is, in men, who are composed of soul and body and
vital spirit, some other element having its own power to incite, and provoking a movement
toward what is evil.
    The question is wont to be approached by some in this way: whether, for example,
there must be said to be two souls in us, one of which is more divine and heavenly, the
other inferior; or whether, indeed, by the very fact that we inhere in bodies, — which
bodies according to their own proper nature are dead and utterly devoid of life, since it
is from us, that is, from our souls, that the bodily material is vivified, while the bodily
material itself is contrary and inimical to the spirit, — we are drawn and enticed to these
evils which are agreeable to the body; or whether, thirdly, as certain of the Greeks
believed, although our soul is one in substance, it nevertheless consists of plural elements,
one part of it being called rational and another part irrational, while that which is called
irrational is again divided into two dispositions, the concupiscible and the irascible (27).
    These three opinions about the soul which we have just set forth, we have found to be
held by some. That one of them, however, which we mentioned as being the view of
certain Greek philosophers, — that the soul is tripartite, — does not seem to me to be

greatly confirmed by the authority of the divine Scriptures. As to the other two which remain, there can be found a considerable number of passages in the divine writings which seem capable of being applied to them.

467a

[3, 6, 5]

The last enemy, moreover, who is called death, is said to be destroyed for this   1014
reason: so that when death no longer exists there may be nothing left of a sorrowful kind, nor anything of an adverse sort — when there is no longer an enemy. The destruction of the last enemy is to be understood not as if his substance, which was formed by God, is to perish, but because his purpose and inimical will, which proceed not from God but from himself, are to perish. He will, therefore, be destroyed not in such a way that he will no longer exist, but in that he will no longer be an enemy and death. For nothing is impossible to the Almighty, nor is there anything which cannot be healed by its Creator. Indeed, He made all things for this purpose: that they might exist; and those things which He made so that they might exist are not able to not exist (28).

468

[3, 6, 6]

It is to be believed, then, [that into this state of glory which belongs to a spiritual   1014
body], all this bodily substance of ours will be brought, when all things are so restored as to be one and when God will be all in all. This, however, is not to be understood as coming about suddenly, but gradually and by parts, through the passage of infinite and unmeasured ages, during which the process of change and correction will take place perceptibly and individually, some running ahead of others, hastening to the summit by a swifter course, some others following close behind, while others still, indeed, are a long way off. Thus, through the innumerable multitude in the ranks of those progressing from a state of enmity and being reconciled to God, finally the last enemy will be reached, he that is called death, so that even he will be destroyed and will no longer be an enemy.

When, therefore, all rational souls have been restored to a condition of this kind, then   1044
even the nature of this body of ours will be advanced to the glory of a spiritual body.   1013
. . . In regard to the nature of the body, we must know that this body which we now use in degradation and corruption and infirmity is not a different body from that which we shall use in incorruption and in power and in glory. This same body, having cast off the infirmities in which it now is, will be made spiritual and will be transformed into glory, so that the very thing which was a vessel of dishonor, being cleansed, will become a vessel   1043
of honor and an abode of blessedness.

We must believe also that by the will of the Creator it will remain always and unchangeably in this condition, as is confirmed by the declaration of the Apostle Paul, when he says: "We have a house not made with hands, eternal in the heavens (29)."

468a

[4, 1, 6]

While we have been sketching the proof of the divinity of Jesus, we have made use of   301
the prophetic statements concerning Him, and have at the same time demonstrated that   81
the writings which prophesied about Him are divinely inspired.   300,20

469

[4, 2, 4 (al. 4, 1, 11)]

Each man, then, ought to have the meaning of the Sacred Scriptures inscribed in a   30

three-fold manner upon his own soul. Thus, the simple man may be edified as if by the
flesh of the Scriptures — for so we name the obvious sense. He that has ascended somewhat
may be edified as if by the soul of the Scriptures. The perfect man, again, . . . may be
edified by the spiritual Law, which casts a shadow of the good things to come. For just
as man consists of body, soul, and spirit, so also does Scripture, which is the gift of God's
bounty for the salvation of men (30).

470

[4, 4, 1 (al. 4, 1, 28)]

For we do not hold that which the heretics imagine: that some part of the substance   256
of God was converted into the Son, or that the Son was procreated by the Father from   251
non-existent substances, that is, from a substance outside Himself, so that there were a
time when He did not exist. No, rejecting every suggestion of corporality, we hold that
the Word and Wisdom was begotten out of the invisible and incorporeal God, without   265
anything corporal being acted upon, in the manner of an act of the will proceeding from   255
the mind. . . . The expression which we employ, however, — that there never was a time
when He did not exist, — is to be taken with a certain allowance.   230

For these very words *when* and *never* are terms of temporal significance, while whatever
is said of the Father, Son, and Holy Spirit, is to be understood as transcending all time,
all ages, and all eternity. For it is the Trinity alone which exceeds every sense in which
not only *temporal* but even *eternal* may be understood. It is all other things, indeed,
which are outside the Trinity, which are to be measured by times and ages.

1. John 1:3.
2. The original Greek, as previously announced, is not extant. Rufinus reads *natus an innatus;* and it is his
   Latin that we are rendering. Jerome, however, is undoubtedly referring to this same passage, when, in his
   letter to Avitus (94, *al.* 59), he severely censures Origen for not knowing whether the Holy Spirit is *factus
   an infectus, i.e.,* created or increate. One or the other authors has commented that Rufinus' reading of
   natus an innatus reflects a probable Greek of γεννητὸς ἢ ἀγέννητος, while Jerome's *factus an infectus*
   would indicate that he read γενητὸς ἢ ἀγένητος.

   The distinction is not a valid one, since it depends too much upon a supposed difference in the meaning of
   the Greek terms, γεννητὸς from γεννάω and γενητὸς from γενέσθαι, and totally neglects the simple fact
   that whatever etymological distinctions may be possible with the terms γενητὸς and γεννητὸς, in practice
   they are virtually synonymous. Whichever Greek term be used, its precise meaning, whether *born, made
   produced, originated, etc.* must be gotten from the context. Either term could be rendered as Rufinus
   renders it; and either as Jerome renders it. Jerome, however, in building a case against Origen's orthodoxy,
   was interested in painting him as black as possible. On the other hand, the distinction Origen is making
   is hardly between generation and spiration, so Jerome is still right: for in fact, whichever Latin terms be
   used, Origen is still confessing that he does not know whether or not the Holy Spirit is *natus vel factus.*
3. 1 Cor. 15:42-43.
4. *traduce,* from *tradux:* hence the term *traducianism,* which is applied to the opinion which Origen briefly
   describes as an alternative possibility. Traducianism was condemned by Pope St. Anastasius II in a letter
   to the bishops of Gaul, *Bonum atque iucundum,* of August 23, 498. Authenticity of this letter, however,
   is not entirely above question.
5. *ratio.*
6. *sacramentorum.*
7. *natura.* The same again, in the final line of the present passage.
8. *I.e.,* the Alone.
9. *I.e.,* the One.
10. John 1:18.
11. *natura.* And again in the final sentence of the present passage.
12. Matt. 11:27.
13. *pro dispensatione, i.e.,* in accord with the divine plan of salvation.
14. This passage is sometimes advanced as an argument against Origen's having held a creation of the world in
    time, and for his having held an eternal world or an eternal succession of worlds. The passage is at best
    somewhat obscure, and certainly must be read in conjunction with his positive and unequivocal statement
    given in the preface to this very book, selection § 447 above.
15. Acts 17:28.
16. Origen is referring to Jer. 23:24, which he had quoted a few lines above: " 'Do I not fill heaven and
    earth?' says the Lord."

17. The thought seems confused. How much the passage may have suffered in Rufinus' translating it into Latin from the no longer extant Greek, it is impossible to say.
18. Is. 50:11.
19. 1 Cor. 3:12.
20. *pro adjutorio.*
21. Is. 4:4.
22. Is. 47:14-15 [Septuagint].
23. See Is. 10:17 in the Septuagint, and 66:16.
24. See Mal. 3:3.
25. Phil. 3:14.
26. See 1 Cor. 3:7.
27. *in duos rursum dividatur affectus cupiditatis et iracundiae.*
28. The *last enemy, who is called death,* is understood to refer to the devil. The present passage is a part of the evidence indicative of Origen's having believed speculatively that even the devil was to find a final salvation.
29. 2 Cor. 5:1.
30. Origen, as might be expected of a man of his time with a background in Greek philosophy, makes not a two-fold but a three-fold division of man, composing him of body, soul, and spirit, in ascending order of nobility (see § 467 above). To this three-fold composition of man he conforms his three senses of Scripture: *the somatic,* called also the literal, the material, the historico-grammatical, the corporal, and the physical sense; *the psychic,* called also the moral sense; and *the pneumatic,* called also the spiritual, and the allegorical-mystical sense.

COMMENTARIES ON GENESIS [*ante. A. D. 232*]

Origen's *Commentaries on Genesis* date from before the year 232 A. D. Originally a work in thirteen books, it is almost entirely lost, the few extant passages having been preserved in Eusebius' *Praeparatio evangelica* and in the *Philocalia,* an anthology of Origen compiled jointly by Basil the Great and Gregory of Nazianz.

The Migne text is in PG 12, 47-146. A more recent edition still wanting, the edition usually cited is that of C. H. E. Lommatzsch, *Origenis opera omnia,* 25 volumes, Berlin 1831-1848, volume 8.

471

[3, 6]

When God undertook in the beginning to create the world, — for nothing that comes to   189
be is without a cause, — each of the things that would ever exist was presented to His mind. He saw what else would result when such a thing were produced; and if such a result were accomplished, what else would accompany; and what else would be the   194
result even of this when it would come about. And so on to the conclusion of the sequence   190
of events, He knew what would be, without being altogether the cause of the coming to   193
be of each of the things which He knew would happen (1).   638

1. For another but unrelated fragment from the third book of Origen's *Commentaries on Genesis,* see below, § 652a.

HOMILIES ON LUKE [*paulo post A. D. 233*]

The *Homilies on Luke* date from soon after 233 A. D. How many homilies Origen wrote on the Gospel of St. Luke we do not know; but there are thirty-nine extant in the translation of St. Jerome. Of the original Greek only a few fragments of the thirty-fifth homily are extant. The Migne text, PG 13, 1801-1910, is superseded by the critical edition of Max Rauer in the series GCS, Vol. 35, Leipzig 1941.

474

[*Hom.* 1]

The Church has four Gospels; but the heretics have many, including one represented as   61
According to the Egyptians, and another *According to the Twelve Apostles.* Even Basilides   68
made bold to write a gospel, and titled it with his own name. . . . I know a certain gospel   69
called *According to Thomas,* and one *According to Mathias.* We have read many others
too, rather than seem to be ignorant of them, because of those who think they know
something when they are acquainted with such things. But among all of these we approve
none others except those, the four only Gospels, which are received by the Church.

475

[*Hom.* 12]

To every man there are two attending angels, the one of justice and the other of   493
wickedness. If there be good thoughts in our heart, and if righteousness be welling up in   494
our soul, it can scarcely be doubted that an angel of the Lord is speaking to us. If,
however, the thoughts of our heart be turned to evil, an angel of the devil is speaking to
us.

477

[*Hom.* 17]

If we have sinned we ought to say: "My sins I have made known to you and my   916
wickedness I have not hidden. I said, 'I will accuse myself to the Lord, of my injustice (1).' "
If we will do this and will reveal our sins not only to God but also to those who are able
to remedy our wounds and sins, then our sins will be blotted out by Him who says,
"Behold, I have blotted out your iniquities like a cloud, and your sins as the mist (2)."

477a

[*Hom.* 17]

Now, indeed, second and third and fourth marriages, — I will be silent about even   979
more, — are entered upon; and we are not ignorant that such unions cast us out from
the kingdom of God. Not fornication only, but even marriages make us unfit for
ecclesiastical honors; for neither a bishop, nor a presbyter, nor a deacon, nor a widow
is able to be twice married. Perhaps the digamist shall be ejected even from the assembly   951
of the pristine and immaculate in a Church which has neither stain nor blemish: not that   957
he will be sent into eternal fire, but that he may have no part in the kingdom of God.

1. Ps. 31 [32]:5.
2. Is. 44:22.

COMMENTARIES ON JOHN [*A. D.* 226 - 232 *et postea*]

Origen's *Commentaries on John* comprised originally at least thirty-two books.
Only eight books are extant, and these in the original Greek. The first four of the
thirty-two or more books were written most probably at Alexandria between the
years 226 and 229 A. D.; the fifth, perhaps in 230-231 A.D.; part of the sixth in

232 A. D.; and the rest of the books after 232 A. D. The Migne text, PG 14, 21-830, is superseded by the critical edition of E. Preuschen in the Berlin Corpus (GCS), Vol. 10, Leipzig 1903, pp. 1-574.

479

[2, 6 (*al.*, 2, 10, 75)]

We believe, however, that there are three Persons, the Father and the Son and the Holy Spirit; and we believe none to be unbegotten except the Father. We admit, as more pious and true, that all things were produced through the Word, and that the Holy Spirit is the most excellent and the first in order of all that was produced by the Father through Christ. 230 250 284 272

479a

[5, 3 (*apud Eusebium, Hist. eccl.* 6, 25)]

Peter, upon whom is built the Church of Christ, against which the gates of hell shall not prevail (1), left only one Epistle of acknowledged genuinity. Let us concede also a second, which, however, is doubtful. 430 42

480

[10, 4 (*al.*, 10, 5, 19)]

I do not condemn [the Evangelists] if, to serve their mystical view, they have in some way re-arranged actual historical events in an order other than that in which they occurred, so as to tell of what happened in one place as if it had happened in another, or of what happened at a certain time, as if it had happened at another time, and to introduce into what was said in a certain way some variations of their own. For they proposed to speak the truth both pneumatically and somatically (2), in so far as possible; and where this was not possible, to prefer the pneumatic to the somatic. They often preserved the pneumatic truth in what some might call a somatic falsehood. 30 25

481

[19, 6 (*al.*, 19, 23, 152)]

Whoever dies in his sins, even if he profess to believe in Christ, does not truly believe in Him; and even if that which exists without works be called faith, such faith is dead in itself, as we read in the Epistle bearing the name of James (3). 758 760

482

[28, 14 (*al.*, 28, 18, 157)]

Jesus, who died, is a man. [(158)] Even in His own regard, He said: "But now you seek to kill me, a man who has spoken the truth (4)." [(159)] But while it is certainly a man who died, the Truth, Wisdom, Peace and Justice, of whom it is written, "The Word was God (5)," was not a man; and the God who is the Word, and the Truth, and Wisdom and Justice, is not dead. For the Image of the invisible God, the First-born of all creation (6), is incapable of death. [(160)] This man, the most pure of all living beings, bore our sins and weaknesses (7) and died for the sake of the people; for neither did He know sin Himself, — but He was able to remove and to destroy and to blot out every sin of the whole world, all taken upon Himself, who did not sin, — nor was deceit found in His mouth (8). 322 334 383 345

1. Matt. 16:18.
2. See above, § 469, n. 30.

3. James 2:17.
4. John 8:40.
5. John 1:1.
6. Col. 1:15.
7. Is. 53:4. Matt. 8:17.
8. Is. 53:9. 1 Pet. 2:22.

COMMENTARIES ON THE PSALMS [*ante A. D.* 244]

Of Origen's *Commentaries on the Psalms* there were some forty-six books on forty-one psalms, written before the year 244 A. D. No one of the forty-six books is entirely extant, but an enormous number of fragments have been gleaned from various *catenae,* from the *Philocalia,* from the letters of Jerome, from Eusebius, and from numerous other authors. The text printed by Migne is in PG 12, 1053-1320 and 1409-1686. Since Migne but reprints the 18th-century edition of C. de la Rue, the more recent edition is actually that of C. H. E. Lommatzsch, *Origenis opera omnia,* 25 volumes, Berlin 1831-1848, volume 11. For want of a newer and more critical edition, Lommatzsch is still regarded as the standard text.

483

[*To* Ps. 1, no. 4: *Lommatzsch 11, 375: PG 12, 1081A*]
With complete and utter precision the Holy Spirit supplied the very [words of   20
Scripture] through His subordinate authors (1), so that you might ever bear in mind the   23
weighty circumstance of their writing (2), according to which the wisdom of God pervades every divinely inspired writing, reaching out to each single letter. Perhaps it was on account of this that the Savior said: "Not one iota nor even a serif thereof shall be lost from the law until all is accomplished (3)."

484

[*To* Ps. 1: *apud Eusebium, Hist. eccl.* 6, 25]
The twenty-two books according to the Hebrews are these: . . . Genesis, . . . Exodus,   41
. . . Leviticus, . . . Numbers, . . . Deuteronomy, . . . Josue, ... Judges and Ruth, reckoned by them as one, . . . First and Second Kingdoms, which among the Hebrews constitute but one book under the title Samuel, . . . Third and Fourth Kingdoms, reckoned as one, . . First and Second Paralipomenon, reckoned as one, . . . First and Second Esdras, reckoned as one, . . . the Book of Psalms, . . . the Proverbs of Solomon, . . . Ecclesiastes, . . . Song of Songs, . . . Isaias, . . . Jeremias, with Lamentations and the Letter, reckoned as one, . . . Daniel, . . . Ezechiel, . . . Job, . . . Esther, . . . and, outside of these, there is Maccabees (4).

485

[*To* Ps. 4: *Lommatzsch 11, 450: PG 12, 1161*]
I might say that just as an agricultural good, the production of fruits, is brought about   690
through a blending of the farmer's free will in accord with his technical skill, along with that which is not under his free will but issues forth from providence, such as temperate climate and sufficient rainfall, so also is the good of a rational creature a blend of his own free will and of divine power coming to the aid of that man who chooses the most virtuous way. In order that a man may be good and virtuous, therefore, there is the   671
necessity not only of his own free will, along with the divine help which is not within his choosing, but there is the necessity also that he who has become good and virtuous persevere in virtue.

1. διὰ τῶν ὑπηρετῶν τοῦ λόγου, literally, *through the subordinates of the word.*
2. μήποτε καὶ ὑμᾶς διαφεύγῃ ἡ ἀναλογία.
3. Matt. 5:18.
4. Note that Origen begins by stating that there are twenty-two books in the Hebrew canon; and in the enumeration given, there are only twenty-one mentioned, prior to Maccabees. In the text as we have it in Eusebius, it would almost appear that Maccabees is being mentioned as the 22nd book of the Hebrew canon. The phrase ἔξω δὲ τούτων is eloquent, however; and while some have compounded the difficulty by translating it *besides these,* it really means *outside of these.* In fact, it would be quite legitimate to translate this phrase: *excluded from these, however, ...* That Origen accepted Maccabees as an inspired book is, of course, quite beside the point when he is enumerating the Hebrew canon. And incredible indeed is the glaring omission of the Twelve Minor Prophets. He must have included them, and probably between Song of Songs and Isaias. We must look to the twelve minor prophets, and not to Maccabees, in order to bring the enumeration to twenty-two.

Moreover, it is likely that the problem of text transmission is in Eusebius' Greek text; for in Rufinus's Latin version of Eusebius, the Twelve Minor Prophets does in fact stand directly after Song of Songs, just where we would expect to find it. Furthermore, in the prologue to his *Tractatus super psalmos* (§ 882, below), Hilary of Poitiers likewise gives a division of the Hebrew canon into twenty-two books; and while he refers vaguely to tradition as his source, his division is in part so much like Eusebius' account of Origen's words, that we may well wonder whether it may not in fact be a better witness to Origen's catalog than is Eusebius, or, at any rate, than the present state of Eusebius. Down to the fifteenth book, Song of Songs, the enumeration is the same. Hilary then continues: *the Twelve Prophets constitute the sixteenth; then Isaias, and Jeremias along with the Lamentation and the Letter, and Daniel, and Ezechiel, and Job, and Esther bring the number of books to twenty-two.*

HOMILIES ON THE PSALMS [*inter A. D.* 240 - 242]

Jerome knew that Origen wrote 120 homilies on 63 of the psalms. Only nine of so great a number are extant, and even these are preserved only in the Latin translation of Rufinus: five on Ps. 36 [37], two on Ps. 37 [38], and two on Ps. 38 [39]. The nine that are thus extant are to be dated between the years 240 and 242 A. D. Besides these there is extant also, preserved by Eusebius (*Hist. eccl.* 6, 38), a fragment of one of Origen's three homilies on Ps. 82 [83].

The Migne text of the homilies is in PG 12, 1319-1410. Lommatzsch, however, as noted above in regard to the *Commentaries on the Psalms,* is still, for lack of something better, the standard edition. Lommatzsch's text is in his volume 11, along with the commentaries.

485a

[*On* Ps. 37 (38): *Hom.* 2, 6]

For I confess my wickedness (1). We have often spoken a denunciation of our wicked-   916
ness: that is, we have often made a confession of sin. Look, then, to what Divine
Scripture teaches us: that sin is not to lie hidden within us. Perhaps there are some who
have an undigested mass of food shut up within them, or an abundance either of a humor
or phlegm remaining in the stomach where it weighs upon them heavily and to their
discomfort. If they vomit it out, they experience relief. It is the same way with those who
have sinned. If, indeed, they conceal their sin and keep it within them, they will suffer an
internal urging, and may come close to being suffocated by the phlegm or humor of sin.
If, however, a man in such a circumstance becomes his own accuser, as soon as he accuses
himself and confesses, he vomits out his fault and puts in order what was the whole cause
of his illness.

Only be careful and circumspect in regard to whom you would confess your sins. Test   908
first the physician to whom you would expose the cause of your illness. See whether
he knows to seem weak with one who is weak, to weep with one who weeps, and
whether he is acquainted with the art of consoling and comforting. Finally, when he

has shown himself to be a physician both learned and merciful, do whatever he might
tell you, and follow whatever counsel he may give. If after much deliberation he has   918
understood the nature of your illness and judges that to be cured it must be exposed   919
in the assembly of the whole church, follow the advice of that expert physician, and   920
thereby others may perhaps be able to be edified, while you yourself are the more easily   905
healed.

1. Ps. 37 [38]:19.

HOMILIES ON JEREMIAS [*post A. D.* 244]

    Origen's *Homilies on Jeremias* date from after the year 244 A. D., in which year he
had completed his course of *Homilies on the Psalms.* How many the collection
originally comprised is not known. Twenty are extant in the original Greek; and in
Jerome's translation into Latin there are fourteen extant, twelve of which match
homilies extant in the Greek, while two are in addition to the twenty in Greek.
    The Migne text, PG 13, 255-606, is entirely superseded by the edition of E.
Klostermann in the Berlin Corpus (GCS) Vol. 6, Leipzig 1901, pp. 1-232.

486

[*Hom.* 8, 1]
Everyone in the world falls prostrate under sin. And it is the Lord who sets up those   614
who are cast down and who sustains all who are falling (1). In Adam all die, and thus
the world falls prostrate and requires to be set up again, so that in Christ all may be
made to live (2).

1. Ps. 144 [145]:14.
2. 1 Cor. 15:22.

HOMILIES ON EXODUS [*post A. D.* 244]

    Of an unknown number of *Homilies on Exodus,* written after 244 A. D., thirteen
are extant in the Latin translation of Rufinus. Of Origen's original Greek, only a
few fragments of the eighth homily are recoverable. The Migne text, PG 12,
297-396, is entirely superseded by the edition of W. A. Baehrens in the Berlin
Corpus (GCS), Vol. 29, Leipzig 1920.

489

[*Hom.* 5,4]
Look at the great foundation of the Church, that most solid of rocks, upon whom   430
Christ built the Church! And what does the Lord say to him? "O you of little faith,"
He says, "why did you doubt (1)!"

490

[*Hom.* 13, 3]
I wish to admonish you with examples from your religion. You are accustomed to
take part in the divine mysteries, so you know how, when you have received the Body of   851
the Lord, you reverently exercise every care lest a particle of it fall, and lest anything of   859

the consecrated gift perish. You account yourselves guilty, and rightly do you so believe, if any of it be lost through negligence. But if you observe such caution in keeping His Body, and properly so, how is it that you think neglecting the word of God a lesser crime than neglecting His Body?

1. Matt. 14:31.

HOMILIES ON NUMBERS [*post A. D.* 244]

Origen wrote twenty-eight *Homilies on Numbers,* after the year 244 A. D. Only a small fragment of the thirteenth is extant in Greek; but all twenty-eight have survived in the Latin of Rufinus. The Migne text, PG 12, 585-806, is entirely superseded by the edition of W. A. Baehrens in the Berlin Corpus (GCS), Vol. 30, Leipzig 1921.

491

[*Hom.* 7, 2]

Formerly there was Baptism, in an obscure way, in the cloud and in the sea; now however, in full view, there is regeneration in water and in the Holy Spirit. Formerly, in an obscure way, there was manna for food; now, however, in full view, there is the true food, the Flesh of the Word of God, as He Himself says: "My Flesh is truly food, and My Blood is truly drink (1)."

820
836
850

492

[*Hom.* 24, 1]

For the feast of the Passover a lamb was designated for the sacrifice by which the people should be purified. For other feasts sacrifice was made of a male calf; and for still others, of a goat or a ram, of a female goat or a female calf. But these things, about the beasts mentioned, you well know. Of these animals, however, which served for the purification of the people, there is one which is said to be our Lord and Savior. John was greater than all the prophets (2), and he so understood it, when he indicated this of Him by saying: "Behold the Lamb of God! Behold Him who takes away the sins of the world (3)!" . . . So long as there are sins, it is necessarily required that there be also sacrificial victims for sins.

374
380

But suppose, for example, that there had been no sin. If there had been no sin, there would have been no necessity for the Son of God to become a lamb; nor would it have been necessary for Him to take flesh and to be slain. He would have remained that which He was from the beginning, the Word and God. . . . In all these sacrificial victims there was one lamb who was able to take away sin from the whole world. Therefore have other victims ceased to be, because this victim was such that, although one alone, He sufficed for the salvation of the whole world. Others remitted sins by their prayers; but He alone by His power.

360

385

1. John 6:56.
2. *I.e.,* John the Baptist. See Luke 7:26-28.
3. John 1:29.

HOMILIES ON LEVITICUS [*post A. D.* 244]

Origen's *Homilies on Leviticus* were written after the year 244 A. D. How many were originally in the collection is not known; but sixteen are extant in the Latin translation of Rufinus, while almost all of the eighth and a fragment of the fifteenth are extant in the original Greek. The Migne text, PG 12, 405-574, is entirely superseded by the edition of W. A. Baehrens in the Berlin Corpus (GCS), Vol. 29, Leipzig 1920.

493

[*Hom.* 2, 4]

But perhaps some members of the Church may be saying, "Why, it was better, it seems, with the ancients than it is with us. They had various forms of sacrificial offerings by which the forgiveness of their sins was obtained. But with us there is one only forgiveness of sins, that which is given in the beginning through the grace of Baptism. After that, there is no mercy for the sinner, nor is any forgiveness granted."

It is fitting, certainly, that discipline be more strict for a Christian, one for whom Christ died. Sheep and goats and cattle and birds were slain for those of former times. With such things were they sprinkled. For you, however, the Son of God was slain: and it pleases you to sin again? You have heard how many sacrifices for sin there were in the Law; and, therefore, lest those accounts not so much raise up your souls for virtue as cast them down in despair, hear now how many are the kinds of forgiveness of sins in the Gospels.　836

First, there is that by which we are baptized unto the forgiveness of sins. A second　833
forgiveness is found in the suffering of martyrdom. A third is that which is given because　929
of almsgiving. For the Savior says: "Nevertheless, give alms; and behold, all things are clean to you (1)." And there is for us a fourth remission of sins, obtained by our also forgiving our brothers their sins. For so says our Lord and Savior Himself: that if in your heart you forgive your brothers their sins, your Father will also forgive you your sins. But if in your heart you do not forgive your brothers, neither will your Father forgive your sins (2). And thus He taught us to say in prayer, "Forgive us our debts, as we also forgive our debtors (3)."

And there is a fifth remission of sins, when someone converts a sinner from the error of his ways. For thus says Divine Scripture, that whoever causes a sinner to turn back from the error of his ways will save his soul from death and will cover a multitude　912
of sins (4). There is also a sixth remission of sins, through an abundance of charity, as even the Lord Himself says: "Amen, I say to you, many sins are forgiven her, because she has loved much (5)." And the Apostle says: "For charity covers a multitude of sins (6)."

In addition to these there is also a seventh, albeit hard and laborious: the remission of sins through penance, when the sinner washes his pillow in tears, when his tears are day　916
and night his nourishment, and when he does not shrink from declaring his sin to a priest　919
of the Lord and from seeking medicine, after the manner of him who says, "I said, 'To　920
the Lord I will accuse myself of my iniquity', and you forgave the disloyalty of my heart (7)." In this way there is fulfilled that too, which the Apostle James says: "If,　940
then, there is anyone sick, let him call the presbyters of the Church, and let them impose hands upon him, anointing him with oil in the name of the Lord; and the prayer of faith will save the sick man, and if he be in sins, they shall be forgiven him (8)."

494

[*Hom.* 3, 4]

Hear the rule which the Law enjoins: "If someone of the aforementioned shall have　918
sinned," it says, "he shall confess the sin which he sinned (9)." There is something

wonderful hidden in this, whereby confession of sins is commanded. For they are to be confessed, whatever kind they be; and all that we do must be brought forward in public. Whatever we have done in secret, whatever sin we have committed by word alone or even in our secret thoughts — all must be made public, all must be brought forward. It will indeed be brought forward by him who is both the accuser of sin and the instigator thereof. For that one who now incites us to sin is the very one who will accuse us when we have sinned.

If, therefore, we anticipate him in life, and become the accusers of ourselves, we will escape the malice of the devil, our enemy and accuser. . . . You see, then, that confession of sin merits the remission of sin. For if we precede the devil in making our accusation, he will not be able to accuse us. If we become our own accusers, it profits us unto salvation. But if we wait until the devil has accused us, that accusation will deliver us to punishment.

495

[*Hom.* 8, 2]

"And the Lord," it says, "spoke to Moses, saying, 'Speak to the children of Israel;   781
and you shall say to them, "A woman, if she shall have received seed, and if she shall
bear a male child, shall be unclean for seven days (10)." ' " The expression *if she shall
have received seed,* which is placed before the words *if she shall bear a male child,*
would seem to be superfluous. But I wonder whether perhaps the whole statement
has been made in this manner, lest Mary, who, according to the Prophets, would bear a
male child without having received seed, should otherwise be thought to be unclean
by reason of the birth of the Savior. Yet, even without the interjection of the words
if she shall have received seed, Mary were still able to be understood to be not unclean.
For she was not simply a *woman,* but a virgin. Women, indeed, bear the burdens of the
Law. Virgins, however, have immunity therefrom.

496

[*Hom.* 8, 3]

Every soul that is born into flesh is soiled by the filth of wickedness and sin. . . . And   614
if it should seem necessary to do so, there may be added to the aforementioned considerations (11) the fact that in the Church, Baptism is given for the remission of sins; and
according to the usage of the Church, Baptism is given even to infants. And indeed if   831
there were nothing in infants which required a remission of sins and nothing in them   835
pertinent to forgiveness, the grace of Baptism would seem superfluous.

497

[*Hom.* 15, 2]

In regard to grave crimes a place for repentance is conceded only once. Those, however,   633
which are common, and into which we frequently fall, always admit repentance, and are   907
forgiven without cease.   905,908

1. Luke 11:41.
2. Matt. 6:14-15.
3. Matt. 6:12.
4. James 5:20. The term *his soul,* it is clear in the extant Latin of the present text and in the Greek of Scripture, refers to the soul of the sinner. It is generally understood, however, that reference is made indirectly to the salvation of the one who converts the sinner, and whose charity will gain him the remission of his own sins.
5. Luke 7:47.
6. 1 Pet. 4:8.

7. Ps. 31 [32]:5.
8. James 5:14-15.
9. See Lev. 5:5, and the preceding, especially in the Septuagint.
10. Lev. 12:2.
11. Origen had cited numerous Scripture passages indicative of the fact that no one, regardless of his station, is without sin. He cited in particular a line evidently from the Septuagint version of Job 14:4-5, although his manner of quoting it differs slightly even from the Septuagint. Origen quotes: "No one is clean of filth, not even if his life is but a single day."

COMMENTARIES ON ROMANS [*post A. D.* 244]

The fifteen books of Origen's *Commentaries on Romans* were written before his *Commentaries on Matthew*, but still, most probably, after the year 244 A. D. Rufinus' free redaction in ten books is entirely extant; but of the original Greek only a few fragments are recoverable: in various *catenae;* in the *Philocalia* of Basil the Great and Gregory of Nazianz; from other writings of Basil; from a papyrus found at Toura near Cairo in 1941; and from a biblical manuscript, Codex 184 B 64, discovered by E. von der Goltz in one of the Mount Athos monasteries.

A new edition is very badly needed, and at present we have no source for the texts any better than Migne, PG 14, 837-1292. For von der Goltz's Mount Athos text, see O. Bauernfeind, *Der Römerbrieftext des Origenes nach dem Codex 184 B 64 des Athosklosters Lawra,* in *Texte und Untersuchungen,* Vol. 44, part 3, Leipzig 1923.

498

[3, 8]
Inasmuch as [Christ] gave Himself for the redemption of the whole human race, [Paul]   380
said, as we have seen above, that He redeemed those who were bound in the captivity   . 374
of their sins (1), when, separate from God (2), He tasted death for all.   386

500

[5, 8]
Perhaps you may inquire even into this: why, when the Lord Himself told His disciples that they should baptize all peoples in the name of the Father and of the Son and of the Holy Spirit (3), does this Apostle employ the name of Christ alone in Baptism, saying,   827
"We who have been baptized in Christ (4);" for indeed, legitimate Baptism is had only in   826
the name of the Trinity (5).

501

[5, 9]
The Church received from the Apostles the tradition of giving Baptism even to infants.   835
For the Apostles, to whom were committed the secrets of divine mysteries, knew that   831
there is in everyone the innate stains of sin, which must be washed away through water   614
and the Spirit.   836

1. See Rom. 3:24 and 1 Tim. 2:6.
2. Heb. 2:9. Origen's Greek is not extant; but Rufinus translated it *sine Deo.* The accepted reading of Scripture is χάριτι θεοῦ, but there are numerous manuscripts of the Epistle to the Hebrews which have instead the variant reading χωρὶς θεοῦ; and this must have been the reading familiar to Origen.
3. Matt. 28:19.
4. Rom. 3:6.
5. Origen then explains that Paul here speaks of being baptized into Christ's death. In Baptism we share in His death, that we may share also in His resurrection. And, says Origen, where Paul speaks of Baptism in

terms of Christ's death, he cannot properly name also the Father and the Holy Spirit; for it was the Word only who was made flesh, and only where there is flesh can we treat of death in a proper sense.

COMMENTARIES ON MATTHEW [*post A. D.* 244]

Origen wrote twenty-five books of *Commentaries on Matthew,* after the year 244 A. D. Except for a few minor fragments, only eight books, ten to seventeen in the numbering of the original, dealing with Matt. 13:26 – 22:33, are extent in Greek. There is also extant an anonymous Latin translation, covering the section dealing with Matt. 16:13 – 27:65.

The Migne text, PG 13, 829-1800, is superseded by the critical editions of E. Klostermann, in the Berlin Corpus (GCS): Vol. 38, Leipzig 1933, pp. 1-299 (the Latin translation mentioned above); Vol. 40, Leipzig 1935, pp. 1-703 (the Greek text of the eight extant books); Vol. 41, Leipzig 1941 (the few other fragments known, and the indices).

FRAGMENT FROM BK. 1: IN EUSEBIUS, History of the Church, BK. 6, CH. 25

503

[6, 25, 3]

In the first of his books on the Gospel according to Matthew, in which he defends the canon of the Church, Origen bears witness that he knows only four Gospels. He writes as follows: [4] "As to the four Gospels, which alone are indisputable in the Church of God under heaven, I learned from tradition that the first to have been written was that of Matthew, who was formerly a tax-collector, but later an Apostle of Jesus Christ. It was prepared for those who were converted from Judaism to the faith, and was written in Hebrew letters. [5] The second was that of Mark, who composed it under Peter's guidance. . . . [6] The third, the Gospel which was praised by Paul, was that of Luke, written for gentile converts. Last of all, there is that of John."

61
42
64

65
66
67

504

[11, 14]

That which is sanctified through the word of God and prayer (1) does not of its very nature sanctify him who avails himself of it. If this were the case, it would sanctify even him that eats unworthily of the Bread of the Lord, and no one would become infirm or weak on account of this food, nor would they fall asleep. Paul indicated something of this kind in the saying, "This is why many among you are infirm and weak, and why many sleep (2)." In regard to this Bread of the Lord, therefore, there is advantage to him who avails himself of it, when, with undefiled mind and pure conscience, he partakes of the Bread. Therefore, neither by not eating, that is, by not eating of the Bread which has been sanctified by the word of God and prayer, do we suffer the loss of any good thing; nor by eating do we gain the advantage of any good thing.

855
807

875

The cause of our suffering a loss is wickedness and sins; and the cause of our gaining advantage is righteousness and right actions. Such, then, is the meaning of that which is said by Paul, "Neither shall we suffer any loss if we do not eat, nor if we do eat shall we gain any advantage (3)." And indeed, if everything that enters into the mouth goes into the stomach and is cast out into the privy (4), even the food which has been sanctified through the word of God and prayer, being material, goes into the stomach and is cast out into the privy. But in accord with the prayer that comes upon it, and according to the proportion of the faith (5), it becomes a benefit, and is the source of clear vision

864

in the mind, which looks to what is beneficial. It is not the material of the bread but the word which is said over it which is of advantage to the one who eats it not unworthily of the Lord.

These things, indeed, are said of the typical and symbolic body; but much more 853 might be said about the Word Himself, who became flesh and true food, of which he that eats shall surely live forever, no wicked person being able to eat it. For if it were possible for one who continues in wickedness to eat of him who became flesh, the Word and the Living Bread, it would not have been written that everyone who eats of this Bread shall live forever (6).

505

[14, 16]

Certainly it is God who joins two in one, so that when He marries a woman to a man, 972 there are no longer two. And since it is God who joins them, there is in this joining a grace for those who are joined by God. Paul knew this, and he said that just as holy celibacy was a grace, so also was marriage according to the Word of God a grace. He says, "I would that all men were like myself; but each has his own grace from God, one in this way, another in that (7)."

506

[14, 23]

Some of the laws were written not in view of excellence, but by way of accommodation 974 to the weakness of those to whom such laws were given. Something of this is indicated in the saying, "Moses permitted you to divorce your wives, because of the hardness of your hearts (8)." That, however, which is more excellent, and which is superior to a law written because of hardness of heart, is indicated in this: "But from the beginning it was not thus (9)." Even in the New Testament there are some legal injunctions of a kind similar to "Moses permitted you to divorce your wives, because of the hardness of your hearts." For example, because of our hardness of heart and in view of our weakness, it is written: "But lest there be fornication, let each man have his own wife and each woman her own husband (10);" and this: "Let a husband render to a wife her due, and likewise also a wife to her husband (11)."

To these sayings there is subjoined: "But I say this by way of concession, not by way of commandment (12)." And this also, "A wife is bound for so long a time as her 979 husband lives; but if her husband is put to rest, she is free to marry whom she will, only be it in the Lord (13)," was said by Paul in view of our hardness of heart and weakness, to those who do not wish to desire earnestly the greater graces and to become more blessed.

And now, contrary to what was written, some even of the rulers of the Church have 976 permitted a woman to marry while her husband was yet living, thus doing contrary to what was written, where it says: "A wife is bound for so long as her husband lives," and "the wife of a man yet living shall be called an adulteress if she live with another man (14)." Indeed, this is not altogether without reason; for it is probable that this concession, though it be contrary to what was from the beginning ordained by law and written, was permitted in order to avoid worse things.

507

[14, 24]

Even the man who withholds himself from his wife, oftentimes makes her an adulteress, 974 when he does not satisfy her desires, even though he withholds himself under the appear- 975

ance of greater gravity and self-control. And perhaps this man who, so far as it rests   968
with him, makes her an adulteress by not satisfying her desires, is more culpable than one
who has divorced his wife for reasons other than fornication — for poisoning or murder
or any of the most grievous sins. But just as a woman is an adulteress, even though she
seem to be married to a man, while a former husband yet lives, so also the man who
seems to marry her who has been divorced does not marry her, but, according to the
declaration of our Savior, he commits adultery with her.

507a

[14, 25]

[The disciples said to Christ:] "If such be the case of a man with his wife, it is not   712
profitable to marry (15)!" At this the Savior said to them, teaching us that absolute
chastity is a gift given by God — not obtained by ascetical practice alone, but given by
God with prayer: "Not all can accept this teaching; only those to whom it has been
given (16)." . . . If we believe the Scriptures, why then do we lay hold of this saying,
"only those to whom it is given," and no longer attend to this: "Ask, and it shall be
given to you (17)!" . . . God, therefore, will give the good gift, perfect purity in
celibacy and chastity, to those who ask him with the whole soul, and with faith, and in
prayers without ceasing.

508

[16, 8]

[Christ] came and visited with the race of men so that He might serve us by going   373
along ahead to show us the way of salvation, and so that He might give His life as a   370
ransom for the many who would believe in Him. If we might suppose that all were to   386
believe in Him, then He had given His life as a ransom for all. To whom did He pay out
His life as a ransom for the many? Certainly not to God. Was it then to the evil one?   384
Yes, for it was he who ruled over us, until the life of Jesus was given to the deceiver
himself as a ransom for us.

1. 1 Tim. 4:5.
2. 1 Cor. 11:30.
3. 1 Cor. 8:8. *N. B.:* Paul was speaking of food offered to idols, not of the Eucharist.
4. Matt. 15:17.
5. κατὰ τὴν ἀναλογίαν τῆς πίστεως.
6. Matt. 15:18-19. Selection § 504 in its entirety is fraught with apparent difficulties, which, however,
   largely disappear with careful study and consideration. That Origen should have been able to treat
   the Eucharist from the theological position of the *ex opere operato* certainly is not to be expected. His
   reference to the Eucharist as the *typical and symbolic body* should cause no eye to jaundice. He seems
   clear enough elsewhere on the real presence (among others, § 490 above). Neither so orthodox a
   theologian as Bellarmine, who employs the same terms, nor the very definition of Trent, which calls
   the Eucharist a symbol of the one body of which Christ is the head and we the members, can be
   suspected of anything theologically dubious in regard to the Eucharist. Much of the above passage
   becomes somewhat more understandable if we suppose that Origen, in attempting to arrive at some
   understanding of the Eucharist, takes a view which is perhaps theologically more akin to impanation
   than to transubstantiation. In fine, Origen seems almost to be reaching out toward such a theological
   distinction as that of the *Sacramentum tantum* and the *Res et Sacramentum*. That such distinctions
   are yet beyond his grasp should cause no wonderment. Excellent theological considerations in regard
   to the present passage will be found in the footnotes of the Migne edition, Vol. 13, col. 948-952.
7. 1 Cor. 7:7.
8. Matt. 19:8.
9. *Ibid.*
10. 1 Cor. 7:2.
11. 1 Cor. 7:3.
12. 1 Cor. 7:6.
13. 1 Cor. 7:39.

14. Rom. 7:3.
15. Matt. 19:10.
16. Matt. 19:11.
17. Matt. 7:7.

AGAINST CELSUS [*ca. A. D.* 248]

Origen's most important apologetic treatise is his *Against Celsus,* in eight books, written about the year 248 A. D. It is a refutation of *The True Discourse,* a work written about 178 A. D. by Celsus, the pagan philosopher. Celsus' work is not extant as such, but can be almost entirely reconstructed from Origen's refutation of it. The treatise *Against Celsus* is a valuable source for the history of religion; and Eusebius was so taken by the power of Origen's refutation that he declared it an adequate answer even to all future heresies.

The Migne text, PG 11, 641-1632, is entirely superseded by the critical edition of P. Koetschau in the Berlin Corpus (GCS), Vols. 2 and 3, Leipzig 1899.

515

[1, 23]

How much more effective it is — and how better than all those invented explanations (1)!   131
— that when we are convinced by what we see in the excellent orderliness of the world, we
then worship its Maker as the one Author of one effect, which, since it is entirely in   157
harmony with itself, cannot, therefore, have been the work of many makers.

516a

[1, 26]

Certain ones among the Christians, from a desire of excelling in chastity, and in order to   984
worship God in greater purity, refrain even from such physical pleasures as are in accord
with the law.

519

[2, 15]

If [the Evangelists] had not been lovers of truth, but, as Celsus says, inventors of   63
fictions, they would not have written of Peter as having made a denial, nor of the disciples
of Jesus as having been scandalized. For indeed, even if these things happened, who could
have offered proof of their having happened as they did?

520

[2, 16]

We do not regard His suffering as having been in mere appearance; therefore, neither   80
was His resurrection a sham, but real. For if one who was truly dead arises, he truly   347
arises; but one who only appeared to be dead could not in truth arise.

530

[6, 10]

The characteristic of divinity is the announcement of future events, predicted not by   15
human power, and which show in their outcome that it was the Divine Spirit who made
the prediction.

536

[8, 12]

Therefore do we worship the Father of Truth, and the Son who is Truth, who exist   258
as two persons (2), while they are one in unity of mind, in harmony, and in identity of
will. Thus, whoever sees the Son, who is the brightness of God's glory and the image of   264
His substance, will see God in Him; for He is the image of God.

1. The *invented explanations* referred to are the Greek myths.
2. ὄντα δύο τῇ ὑποστάσει πράγματα. A really literal translation is difficult. *Being two individuals as to hypostasis* or *being in substance two individuals* are close, but present to a modern reader certain theological difficulties which would not have occurred to a reader of the Greek in Origen's time. We are satisfied that *who exist as two persons* is a better capturing of the thought.

HOMILIES ON JOSUE [*inter A. D.* 249-251]

Origen's twenty-six *Homilies on Josue* were written between 249 and 251 A. D. All twenty-six are extant in the apparently faithful translation of Rufinus, and a rather extensive fragment of the twentieth is extant also in the original Greek. The Migne text, PG 12, 825-948, is entirely superseded by the edition of W. A. Baehrens, in GCS, Vol. 30, Leipzig, 1921.

537

[*Hom.* 3, 5]

If someone of that people wishes to be saved, let him come into this house, so that   417
he may be able to obtain his salvation (1). . . . Let no one, then, be persuaded otherwise,
nor let anyone deceive himself: outside this house, that is, outside the Church, no one is
saved. For if anyone go outside, he shall be guilty of his own death (2).

538

[*Hom.* 7, 1]

Matthew first made a noise on the sacerdotal trumpet in his own Gospel. Mark also,   42
and Luke and John played upon their own sacerdotal trumpets. Peter blew loudly even   61
on two trumpets in his Epistles; and James also, and Jude. And still it was added to,   64
John blowing a trumpet by means of his Epistles; and Luke, by describing the acts of the   65
Apostles. Last of all, however, there comes the one who said, "I think, however, that   66
God has shown us as Apostles last of all (3)." In his fourteen Epistles he blasts on the   67
trumpets, and throws down from their foundations the walls of Jericho, along with all the   403
engines of idolatry and the teachings of the philosophers.

1. Origen has been expounding upon the salvation that was in the house of Rahab the Harlot, as recounted in the second chapter of Josue; and he indicated that the scarlet cord, hung out of the window of the harlot's house as a sign that those therein should be spared, was in fact scarlet and no other color, so that it might the better serve as a symbol of the saving Blood of Christ. Rahab, the *sapiens meretrix*, knew that no one was to be saved except in the Blood of Christ. Origen now proceeds to make of Rahab's house a figure of the Church, outside of which there is no salvation.
2. See Josue 2:19.
3. 1 Cor. 4:9.

COMMENTARIES ON HEBREWS [*ante A. D.* 254]

The original number of Origen's *Commentaries on Hebrews* is not known, nor can any date be assigned to the writing of the work, except by the date of his death:

254 A. D. at the latest. Only four short fragments are extant, all in the first book of Pamphilus' *Apology for Origen,* of which, indeed, only the first book is extant, and that in the Latin translation of Rufinus.

The texts may be found in Migne, PG 14, 1307-1308; and in Vol. 24, pp. 297-300, of C. H. E. Lommatzsch's *Origenis opera omnia,* 25 volumes, Berlin 1831-1848.

540

[Frag. in Heb.: Lommatzsch 24, 300: PG 14, 1308 C-D]

So also Wisdom, since He proceeds from God, is generated from the very substance of   261
God. Under the figure of a bodily effluence, nevertheless, He is also called a kind of pure   252
and clean effluence of the glory of the Almighty (1). Both of these similes show with
great clarity that there is a community of substance between the Son and the Father. For
an effluence seems to be ὁμοούσιος, that is, of one substance with that body from which it   257
is either an effluence or an exhalation.

1. Wis. 7:25.

ST. CORNELIUS I, POPE [*regn. A. D.* 251-253]

The pontificate of Pope St. Cornelius I, though it was very short, embracing only the years 251 to 253 A. D., is of importance for the history of penitential discipline, and for his dealings with the Novatian schism.

LETTERS

We know that Cornelius wrote seven letters to Cyprian, Bishop of Carthage, with whom he was on excellent terms of friendship; three to Fabius, Bishop of Antioch; one to Dionysius, Bishop of Alexandria; and an encyclical letter to all the Churches. Of these writings, only two letters to Cyprian have survived, and but a fairly lengthy fragment of one of his letters to Fabius. The two to Cyprian were preserved by their inclusion in the Cyprianic corpus of letters, where, of course, they are found in Latin, though the originals must have been in Greek. The fragment of a letter to Fabius is preserved by having been cited by Eusebius (*Hist. eccl.* 6, 43), and thus, of course, is preserved in Greek. All the rest of Cornelius' letters have perished entirely.

The texts of the two letters and the fragment of a third may be found in Migne, PL 3, 712-725 and 733-759. However, for the text of the two letters to Cyprian, preserved as Nos. 49 [*al.* 46] and 50 [*al.* 48] in the corpus of Cyprian's letters, it will be better to consult W. Hartel's Vienna Corpus (CSEL) edition of Cyprian, Vol. 3, part 2, Vienna 1871; while for the extensive fragment of his letter to Fabius it will be better to consult Eusebius' *History of the Church,* 6, 43, in the edition of E. Schwartz in the Berlin Corpus (GCS), Vol. 9, part 2, Leipzig 1908.

LETTER OF CORNELIUS OF ROME TO CYPRIAN OF CARTHAGE. A. D. 252.

546

[*Apud Cyp. Epist.* 49 [*al.* 46] , 2]

    [*Certain men, having fallen into a schism and now seeking reconciliation, besought Cornelius, saying:*] " . . . We are not ignorant of the fact that there is one God, and one Christ the 230 Lord whom we confess, and one Holy Spirit; and that there must be one bishop in the 410 Catholic Church."

LETTER OF CORNELIUS OF ROME TO FABIUS OF ANTIOCH. A. D. 251.

546a

[*Apud Euseb. Hist. eccl.* 6, 43, 11]

    This guardian of the gospel (1), then, did not know that there must be one bishop in 410 the Catholic Church. Yet he was not unaware — how could he be? — that in it there 953 are forty-six presbyters; seven deacons; seven subdeacons; forty-two acolytes; fifty-two 952,954 exorcists, lectors, and porters together; and over fifteen hundred widows and persons in 955 need, all of whom are supported by the grace and kindness of the Master. 956,957

547

[6, 43, 14]

    As [Novatian] seemed about to die, he received Baptism in the bed where he lay, by 824 pouring — if, indeed, such a man can be said to have received it at all. [15] And when he recovered from his illness he did not receive the other things which, in accord with the law of the Church, it is necessary to have; nor was he sealed by the bishop (2). And 845 since this was not done, how could he have the Holy Spirit? 840

1. The reference is to Novatian, and is made in sarcasm; for Novatian was at the head of a rigorist faction.
2. *I. e.*, he was not confirmed.

ST. CYPRIAN OF CARTHAGE [† A. D. 258]

    Caecilius Cyprianus Thascius, St. Cyprian, Bishop of Carthage, often called the African Pope, was born at Carthage of wealthy pagan parents, between the years 200 and 210 A. D. He was converted to Christianity about the year 246 A. D., and was raised to the priesthood soon afterwards. In 248 or 249 A. D. he was made Bishop of Carthage. When the Decian persecution broke out in 250 A. D. he found a safe refuge in the hills outside the city, from where, in comparative safety, he directed his flock by letters to his clergy.

    No doubt Cyprian's action in taking a safe refuge was a prudent course of conduct, and he proved later that he was ready for martyrdom; but his present conduct made him an easy target for the barbs of his enemies, especially when he found it necessary to reprove the faction who wanted an immediate and easy reconciliation of the lapsed. One of this faction, a priest named Novatus, showed his bad faith, when, breaking with Cyprian allegedly because Cyprian was not easy enough with the lapsed, he went to Rome and joined the schism of Novatian, who was an extreme rigorist in respect to the reconciliation of the lapsed, generally denying reconciliation entirely.

    Although Cyprian was on excellent terms with Pope St. Cornelius I (*regn. A. D.* 251-253), he fell out sharply with Cornelius' successor, Pope St. Stephen I (*regn. A. D.* 254-256), on the question of the re-baptizing of converted heretics. It was

the immemorial custom of the African Church to regard Baptism conferred by
heretics as invalid, and in spite of Stephen's severe warnings, Cyprian never yielded.
His attitude was simply that every bishop is responsible for his own actions,
answerable to God alone. The dispute was just at the dangerous stage when an
edict of the Emperor Valerian, renewing the persecutory measures against the
Christians, prevented it from ending in disaster. Stephen was martyred in 256
A. D., and Cyprian, exiled to Curubis in August of 257 A. D., was beheaded near
Carthage on September 14, 258 A. D. He was the first African bishop to die a
martyr's death.

TO DONATUS [*A. D.* 246/247]

The earliest of Cyprian's treatises is that entitled *To Donatus,* written in 246 or 247
A. D. To his friend Donatus (not to be confused with the Donatus from whom the
Donatist schism takes its name), he writes a touching description of the movements of
divine grace which led to his own conversion.

In early collections the treatise was included in the corpus of Cyprian's letters. In
the Migne edition, PL 4, 191-223, it appears as letter no. 1. Migne's text, however, is
now entirely superseded by that of W. Hartel, who restores the work to its rightful
place as an independent monologue, in CSEL, Vol. 3, part 1, Vienna 1868, pp. 3-16.

548

[4]

And I myself was bound fast, held by so many errors of my past life, from which I did   657
not believe that I could extricate myself. I was disposed, therefore, to yield to my clinging
vices; and, despairing of better ways, I indulged my sins as if they were actually part and
parcel of myself. But afterwards, when the stain of my past life had been washed away   836
by means of the water of re-birth, a light from above poured itself upon my chastened
and now pure heart; afterwards through the Spirit which is breathed from heaven, a   752
second birth made of me a new man. And then in a marvelous manner, doubts immed-   683
iately clarified themselves, the closed opened, the darkness became illuminated, what   684
before had seemed difficult offered a way of accomplishment, and what had been thought
impossible was able to be done. Thus it had to be acknowledged that what was of the
earth and was born of the flesh and had lived submissive to sins, had now begun to be
of God, inasmuch as the Holy Spirit was animating it.

THE LAPSED [*A. D.* 251]

Cyprian's treatise on *The Lapsed* was written in 251 A. D., when he had returned
to Carthage from the refuge he had taken during the persecution of Decius. The work
is a warning against too great a leniency in the reconciling of those who had lapsed in
various ways during the persecution. The treatise was read at the Council of Carthage
in the Spring of 251 A. D., and became the basis for a uniform procedure throughout
the Church of North Africa.

The Migne text, PL 4, 465-494, is entirely superseded by the critical edition of W.
Hartel in CSEL, Vol. 3, part 1, Vienna 1868, pp. 235-264.

551

[15]

The Apostle likewise bears witness and says. "You cannot drink the cup of the Lord and the cup of devils. You cannot be a communicant of the table of the Lord and of the table of devils (1)." And again he threatens the stubborn and perverse and denounces them, saying: "Whoever eats the Bread or drinks the Cup of the Lord unworthily, will be guilty of the Body and Blood of the Lord (2)." [16] But they spurn and despise all   916 these warnings; and before their sins are expiated, before they have made a confession of their crime, before their conscience has been purged in the ceremony and at the hand of   925 the priest (3), before the offense against an angry and threatening Lord has been appeased, they do violence to His Body and Blood; and with their hands and mouth they sin against   875 the Lord more than when they denied Him.

552

[17]

The Lord alone is able to have mercy. He alone, who bore our sins, who grieved for   383 us, and whom God delivered up for our sins, is able to grant pardon for the sins which have been committed against Him. . . . Certainly we believe that the merits of the   936 martyrs and the works of the just will be of great avail with the Judge — but that will be when the day of judgment comes, when, after the end of this age and of the world,   392 His people shall stand before the tribunal of Christ.

552a

[25]

Hear what took place in my presence and with myself as witness. It happened that   875 some parents were fleeing; and acting imprudently because of their fear, they left an infant daughter in the care of a nurse. The nurse turned the abandoned child over to the magistrates. In the presence of the idol where the people were gathering, and because she was not, on account of her age, able to eat meat, they gave her bread mixed with wine, which was itself left over after the sacrifice offered by those who are perishing. Afterwards the mother recovered her daughter. But the girl was no more able to speak and point out the crime that had been committed than she had before been able to understand and prevent it.

It came about through ignorance, therefore, that the mother brought the child into our presence when we were offering the Sacrifice. The girl mingled with the saints (4);   890 and then, growing impatient of our prayers and petitions, was at one moment shaken with weeping and at another began to be tossed about by the violent excitement of her mind. As if by the compulsion of a torturer, the soul of that child of still tender years confessed the awareness of the deed by such signs as it could.

When the solemnities were completed, however, and the deacon began to offer the   868 chalice to those present, and when her turn came among the rest of those receiving, the   871 little girl, with an instinct of the divine majesty, turned her face away, compressed her mouth with resisting lips, and refused the cup. The deacon persisted, however; and although she was resisting, he poured some into her mouth from the Sacrament in the cup. The result was that she began to choke and to vomit. The Eucharist was not able to remain in that violated body and mouth. The drink sanctified in the Blood of the Lord (5) burst forth from her polluted stomach. So great is the power of the Lord, and so great His majesty (6)!

553

[28]
Finally, of how much greater faith and more salutary fear are they who, though
bound by no crime of sacrifice or certificate, but since they did take thought of doing   918
such a thing, confess even this to the priests of God in a straightforward manner and in   920
sorrow, making an open declaration of conscience. Thus they remove the weight from
their souls and seek the saving remedy for their wounds however small and slight they
be; for they know that it is written: "God is not mocked (7)."
God cannot be mocked or outwitted; nor can He be deceived by any clever cunning.
Indeed, he but sins the more if, thinking that God is like man, he believes that he can
escape the punishment of his crime by not openly admitting his crime. . . . [29] I   925
beseech you, brethren, let everyone who has sinned confess his sin while he is still in
this world, while his confession is still admissible, while satisfaction and remission made
through the priests are pleasing before the Lord.

1. 1 Cor. 10:21.
2. 1 Cor. 11:27.
3. *sacrificio et manu sacerdotis.*
4. *cum sanctis:* the term being applied to the Christian congregation.
5. *sanctificatus in Domini sanguine potus.*
6. It will no doubt be observed by more skeptical souls that what Cyprian offers as evidence of miraculous
   intervention is more easily explained by the infantile stubbornness of a cranky child who ought to have
   been at home with a reliable baby-sitter instead of being permitted to disturb responsible Christians at
   their prayers. We will not argue on the miracle, since it is not to the point. We include the above passage
   not as miraculous evidence, but because of its wealth of homely detail significant to the Liturgy of Carthage:
   most notably, the deacon as minister of the cup, and infant communion.

   It may well be observed additionally, however, that Cyprian is at great pains to instill in his people a healthy
   fear of God, while emphasizing the sacredness of the Eucharist and the enormity of sacrilege. The examples
   he uses may in fact be a better reflection of the mentality of his people than of himself. And in any case,
   he in no way implies any personal guilt on the part of the infant. So perhaps the good pope of Carthage
   was not such a great booby afterall.
7. Gal. 6:7.

THE UNITY OF THE CATHOLIC CHURCH [*A. D.* 251/256]

The treatise on *The Unity of the Catholic Church* belongs primarily to the year 251
A. D., but a second edition of the work, revised by Cyprian himself, belongs to the
years 255 and / or 256 A. D. It is the most important of Cyprian's treatises, and had
the most lasting effect.
Chapter four of the work is extant in two recensions, the one with so-called
additions having generally been regarded as an interpolated version until in 1902 Dom
Chapman established the fact that both are from the pen of Cyprian himself. In
Chapman's view the edition having the word *primacy* and other expressions interpret-
able as referring to Roman primacy was a re-working of the original, made by Cyprian
himself, rather than a maliciously interpolated version. His theory is now very
generally accepted, with one important difference, however, that the version with
the so-called primacy additions is to be regarded as Cyprian's original, while the
version without those phrases is regarded as Cyprian's own re-casting of the work.
Cyprian's revised version, his second edition, is actually the longer; but it has omitted
those phrases of the original version which were extremely favorable to the Roman
claims of primacy.
According to this latter view, Cyprian's choice of words in the original form of the
work would have been read in Rome as a recognition of the universal authority over the
whole Church, which Rome claimed. Cyprian, indeed, recognized that the Bishop of

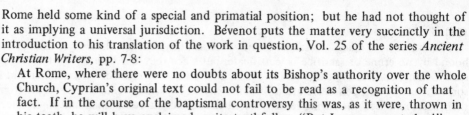

Rome held some kind of a special and primatial position; but he had not thought of it as implying a universal jurisdiction. Bévenot puts the matter very succinctly in the introduction to his translation of the work in question, Vol. 25 of the series *Ancient Christian Writers*, pp. 7-8:

> At Rome, where there were no doubts about its Bishop's authority over the whole Church, Cyprian's original text could not fail to be read as a recognition of that fact. If in the course of the baptismal controversy this was, as it were, thrown in his teeth, he will have exclaimed, quite truthfully: "But I never meant *that!*" — and so he "toned it down" in his revised version. He did not, then, repudiate what he had formerly held. He had never held that the Pope possessed universal jurisdiction. But he had never denied it either; in truth he had never asked himself the question where the final authority in the Church might be. . . . If the foregoing reconstruction is correct, we have in Cyprian's *De ecclesiae catholicae unitate* a good example of what a dogma can look like while still in an early stage of development. The reality (in this case, the Primacy of Rome) is there all the time: it may be recognized by some; by others it may even be denied, and that though much of what they say or do unconsciously implies it. . . . Cyprian is a standing example of what we mean when we speak of the Papal Primacy being "implicit" in the early Church.

The Migne edition, PL 4, 495-520, presents in its chapter four a conflation of the two recensions, and is in general virtually worthless as an instrument for scholarly research. The standard edition is still that of W. Hartel in the Vienna Corpus (CSEL), Vol. 3, part 1, Vienna 1868, pp. 207-233. It must be born in mind, however, that Hartel predates Chapman, and still regarded the edition with references to the primacy as an interpolated text.

555-556

[4]

The Lord says to Peter: "I say to you," He says, "that you are Peter, and upon this   430
rock I will build my Church, and the gates of hell will not overcome it. And to you I   420
will give the keys of the kingdom of heaven: and whatever things you bind on earth shall   401
be bound also in heaven, and whatever you loose on earth, they shall be loosed also in
heaven (1)."

[Cyprian's first edition]	*[Cyprian's second edition]*
And again He says to him after His resurrection: "Feed my sheep (2)." On him He builds the Church, and to him He gives the command to feed the sheep; and although He assigns a like power to all the Apostles, yet He founded a single chair, and He established by His own authority a source and an intrinsic reason for that unity. Indeed, the others were that also which Peter was; but a primacy is given to Peter, whereby it is made clear that there is but one Church and one chair. So too, all are shepherds, and the flock is shown to be one, fed by all the Apostles in single-minded accord. If someone does not hold fast to this	It is on one man that He builds the Church; and although He assigns a like power to all the Apostles after His resurrection, when He says, "As the Father has sent me, so also do I send you; receive the Holy Spirit: if you forgive any man his sins, they shall be forgiven; and if you retain any man's sins, they shall be retained (3)," — nevertheless, in order that unity might be clearly shown, He established by His own authority a source for that unity, which takes its beginning from one man alone. Indeed, the other Apostles were that also which Peter was, being endowed with an equal portion of dignity and power; but the origin is grounded in unity, so that it may be made clear that

unity of Peter, can he imagine that he still holds the faith? If he desert the chair of Peter upon whom the Church was built, can he still be confident that he is in the Church?

there is but one Church of Christ. Indeed, this oneness of the Church is indicated in the Song of Songs, when the Holy Spirit, speaking in the Lord's name, says: "One is my dove, my perfect one, to her mother the only one, the chosen of her that bore her (4)." If someone does not hold fast to this unity of the Church, can he imagine that he still holds the faith? If he resists and withstands the Church, can he still be confident that he is in the Church, when the blessed Apostle Paul teaches this very thing and displays the sacred sign of unity when he says: "One body and one spirit, one hope of your calling, one Lord, one faith, one Baptism, one God (5)"? [5] Most especially must we   420
bishops, who exercise authority in the Church, hold firmly and insist upon this unity, whereby we may demonstrate also that the episcopate itself is one and undivided. Let no one mislead the brotherhood with a lie, let no one corrupt the faith by a faithless perversion of the truth. The episcopate is one, of   421
which each bishop holds his part within the undivided structure. The Church also is one, however widely she has spread among the multitude through her fruitful increase. . . . The Church is bathed in the light of the Lord, and pours her rays over the whole world; but it is one light that is spread everywhere, and the unity of   85
her structure is undivided.

[5] The episcopate is one, of which each bishop holds his part within the undivided structure (6). The Church also is one, however widely she has spread among the multitude through her fruitful increase. . . . The Church is bathed in the light of the Lord, and pours her rays over the whole world; but it is one light that is spread everywhere, and the unity of her structure is undivided (7).

557

[6]
   The Bride of Christ (8) cannot be defiled. She is inviolate and chaste. She knows but   417
one home, and with a chaste modesty she guards the sanctity of one bedchamber. It is
she that keeps us for God, she that seals for the kingdom the sons whom she bore.
Whoever is separated from the Church and is joined to an adulteress is separated from
the promises of the Church; nor will he that forsakes the Church of Christ attain to the
rewards of Christ. He is an alien, a worldling, and an enemy. He cannot have God for
his Father who does not have the Church for his Mother. If anyone outside the ark of
Noah was able to escape, then perhaps someone outside the pale of the Church may
escape. . . . The Lord says, "The Father and I are one (9);" and again, it is written of   230
the Father, Son, and Holy Spirit, "And the three are one (10)."   235
   Does anyone believe that in the Church this unity which proceeds from the divine
stability and which is welded together after the heavenly patterns (11), can be divided,
and can be separated by the parting asunder of opposing wills? Whoever holds not fast
to this unity holds not to the law of God; neither does he keep faith with the Father
and the Son, nor does he have life and salvation.

[7] This sacrament of unity (12), this bond of an inseparably cohering harmony, is indicated in the Gospel when the tunic of the Lord Jesus Christ is in no way divided nor cut apart.

1. Matt. 16:18-19.
2. John 21:17.
3. John 20:21-23.
4. Cant. 6:8.
5. Eph. 4:4-6.
6. *Episcopatus unus est, cuius a singulis in solidum pars tenetur.*
7. *nec unitas corporis separatur.*
8. *I. e.,* the Church.
9. John 10:30.
10. 1 John 5:7.
11. *sacramentis caelestis cohaerentem.*
12. *hoc unitatis sacramentum.*

THE LORD'S PRAYER [*A. D.* 251/252]

Cyprian's treatise on *The Lord's Prayer* belongs to the year 251 or 252 A. D. It has some dependence upon Tertullian's treatise on the same subject; but this dependence is not very extensive, and Cyprian's treatise possesses a deep insight which Tertullian's did not have. The Migne text, PL 4, 519-544, is entirely superseded by the edition of W. Hartel in CSEL, Vol. 3, part 1, Vienna 1868, pp. 265-294.

557a

[12]

After this we say: "Hallowed be thy name (1)," not that we want God to be made   120
holy by our prayers, but because we seek from the Lord that His name may be made holy in us. Indeed, by whom could God be made holy, when it is He that sanctifies? But because He Himself said, "Be holy, as I too am holy (2)," we ask and seek that very thing, so that we who have been made holy in Baptism may persevere in what we have begun to be. For this we do pray daily. We have a daily need of being made holy, so that we who sin daily may be cleansed again of our sins by continual sanctification.
. . . The Apostle says that we have been made holy in the name of the Lord Jesus Christ and in the Spirit of our God (3).

We pray that this sanctification may abide in us, . . . and we make this petition in our constant prayers, we ask it day and night, so that the sanctification and vivification which   672
is received from the grace of God may, by His protection, be preserved.

558

[14]

We continue and say: "Thy will be done on earth as it is in heaven (4)," not as if   696
praying that God may do as He wills, but that we may be able to do what God wills;   650
for who could withstand God and prevent His doing what He wills! But since the devil withstands us, and would prevent our thoughts and deeds from being devoted in all things to obedience to God, we pray and petition that God's will be done in us. And in order that it might be done in us we have need of God's will, that is, of His help and protection, since no one is strong by his own powers, but is safe only by the kindliness and mercy of God.

559

[18]
    As the prayer continues, we ask and say, "Give us this day our daily bread (5)."   879
. . . And we ask that this bread be given us daily, so that we who are in Christ and   873
daily receive the Eucharist as the food of salvation, may not, by falling into some more
grievous sin and then in abstaining from communicating, be withheld from the heavenly
Bread, and be separated from Christ's Body. . . . He Himself warns us, saying, "Unless
you eat the flesh of the Son of Man and drink His blood, you shall not have life in   850
you (6)." Therefore do we ask that our Bread, which is Christ, be given to us daily, so
that we who abide and live in Christ may not withdraw from His sanctification and from
His Body.

1. Matt. 6:9.
2. 1 Peter 1:16. See Lev. 20:7.
3. 1 Cor. 6:11.
4. Matt. 6:10.
5. Matt. 6:11.
6. John 6:54.

TO DEMETRIAN [A. D. 252]

    Cyprian's treatise *To Demetrian* was written in the year 252 A. D., as a refutation
of the charges made by a certain Demetrian, to the effect that it was the impiety of
the Christians which brought the scourges of war, pestilence, famine and drought upon
mankind. The Migne text, PL 4, 544-564, is superseded by that of W. Hartel, CSEL,
Vol. 3, part 1, Vienna 1868, pp. 349-370.

560

[24]
    An ever-burning Gehenna and the punishment of being devoured by living flames will   1032
consume the condemned; nor will there be any way in which the torments can ever   1034
have respite or be at an end. Souls along with their bodies will be preserved for suffering   1036
in infinite agonies. . . . The grief at punishment will then be without the fruit of   991
repentance; weeping will be useless, and prayer ineffectual. Too late will they believe
in eternal punishment, who would not believe in eternal life.

561

[25]
    When once you have departed this life, there is no longer any place for repentance, no   991
way of making satisfaction. Here life is either lost or kept. Here, by the worship of   928
God and by the fruit of faith, provision is made for eternal salvation. Let no one be kept   901
back either by his sins or by his years from coming to obtain salvation. To him who still
remains in this world there is no repentance that is too late.   908

THE DEATH-RATE [A. D. 252/253]

    Cyprian's treatise on *The Death-Rate* belongs to the years 252 or 253 A. D. It was
occasioned by the plague which took so many lives, and which followed immediately
upon the Decian persecution. It is a treatment of the attitude which the Christian

must have in facing death. The Migne text, PL 4, 583-602, is no longer serviceable,
in view of W. Hartel's critical edition in the Vienna Corpus (CSEL), Vol. 3, part 1,
Vienna 1868, pp. 295-314.

562

[6]

If a staid and praiseworthy man should promise you something you would have faith   10
in his promise, and you would not believe that you would be cheated or deceived by one   558
whom you knew to be steadfast in his words and deeds. God is speaking to you, and do
you waver faithlessly with your unbelieving mind? God promises that when you leave
this world you shall have immortality in life eternal, and do you doubt? This is to know
God· not at all. This is to offend Christ, the Teacher of belief, by the sin of disbelief.
For one established in the Church, this is not to have faith in the house of faith.

WORKS AND ALMSGIVING [*A. D.* 253]

Cyprian's treatise on *Works and Almsgiving* dates from the year 253 A. D. It urges
liberal works of charity at a time when so many were impoverished and in reduced
circumstances because of the recent devastating plague. The Migne text, PL 4,
601-652, is entirely superseded for scholarly purposes by the edition of W. Hartel, in
CSEL, Vol. 3, part 1, Vienna 1868, pp. 371-394.

563

[1]

Many and great, most beloved brethren, are the divine blessings by which the abundant
and copious clemency of God the Father and of Christ has both worked and is always
working for our salvation. The Father sent the Son to preserve us and to give us life, so
that He might be able to restore us; and indeed, the Son wished to be sent and to become   376
the Son of Man, so that He might make us the sons of God. He humbled Himself in order
to raise up a people who before were cast down. He was wounded in order to cure our
wounds. He served as a slave in order to draw away to liberty those who were in bondage.
He underwent death in order to hold forth immortality to mortals. These are many and
great gifts of divine mercy.

But still more, what is that providence and how great is that clemency, which provides   530
for us a plan of salvation by which more abundant care is taken for preserving a man
after He has been redeemed. For when the Lord had come and healed those wounds
which Adam bore, and had cured the old venoms of the serpent, to him that He had
cured He gave a law and forbade him to sin again, lest even worse should befall him in
his sinning. We were restricted and shut up in a narrow place by the command of
remaining innocent. Nor would the infirmity and weakness of human frailty be able to
find any aid, had not divine goodness entered again upon the scene to point out the works
of justice and mercy, thereby opening a way of safe-guarding salvation; for whatever   929
stains we subsequently contract we may wash away by almsgiving.

564

[14]

You, then, who are rich and wealthy, buy for yourself from Christ gold purified in   929
fire; for with your filth as if burned away in the fire, you can be like pure gold, if you
are cleansed by almsgiving and by works of justice. Buy yourself a white garment so that,

although you had been naked like Adam, and were formerly frightful and deformed, you may be clothed in the white garment of Christ. And you who are a matron rich and wealthy, anoint not your eyes with the antimony of the devil, but with the collyrium 771
of Christ (1), so that you may at last come to see God, when you have merited before 760
God both by your works and by your manner of living (2).

1. Antimony was used on the eyes as a cosmetic. Collyrium was a liquid eye-salve. Probably there is something in the nature of a pun intended with the latter term, since the very similar word, *collybus*, means foreign exchange, the exchange of the coins of one realm for those of another.
2. See Apoc. 3:18.

THE ADVANTAGE OF PATIENCE [*A. D.* 256]

Cyprian's sermon on *The Advantage of Patience*, written in the year 256 A. D., bears a rather heavy literary dependence upon Tertullian's *De patientia*, in its general treatment and even in the illustrations used. Nevertheless, there is a considerable difference in the spirit of the two works, Cyprian rejecting a mere stoic indifference, while stressing the peculiarly Christian aspects of patience.

The Migne text, PL 4, 622-638, is entirely superseded by that of W. Hartel, CSEL, Vol. 3, part 1, Vienna 1868, pp. 395-415.

565

[6]
[Christ's] every act, even from His first coming, is marked by an accompanying patience. From the first moment when He descended from the sublimity of heaven to earthly things, the Son of God did not disdain to put on the flesh of man; nor, although not Himself a sinner, to bear the sins of others. He put aside His immortality for a time, and allowed 383
Himself to become mortal, so that, although innocent, He might be slain for the salvation of the guilty.

566

[17]
Since with that first transgression of a command strength of body along with 522
immortality departed and infirmity along with death came in; and since strength cannot 611
be regained until immortality is also regained, it is necessary for us while in this state of bodily weakness and infirmity to keep struggling and contending. Nor can this struggle and contest be sustained except by the virtue of patience.

567

[19]
The devil bore impatiently the fact that man was made in the image of God; and 491
that is why he was the first to perish and the first to bring others to perdition. Adam, 520
contrary to the heavenly command, was impatient in regard to the deadly food, and 610
fell into death; nor did he preserve, under the guardianship of patience, the grace 611
received from God.

LETTERS

The Cyprianic corpus of letters contains eighty-one items: sixty-five letters written by Cyprian, and sixteen addressed to him. They constitute an extremely valuable source for the history of his fascinating times; in fact, their importance can scarcely be stressed enough. Suffice it to say that without these letters our knowledge of certain events in the history of the Church in the third century — notably the problems of the lapsed, of Novatianism in part, and the quarrel over the Baptism of heretics — would suffer a great lacuna.

The Migne text, PL 4, 191-438, is entirely superseded by that of W. Hartel, CSEL, Vol. 3, part 2, Vienna 1871. In the numbering of the letters for our selections below, we give first the number of the letter as in Hartel's edition, which follows exactly the numbering of the letters in the Oxford edition of 1682. Where this number is followed by a second number in parentheses, the latter is the numbering as found in the Migne edition, which is, as far as the numbering and text is concerned, a reprint of Stephen Baluzius' edition of 1726. Baluzius had adopted only in part the order followed by Pamelius' edition of 1568. Where we give only one number for the letter, and parentheses are absent, it will be found that the letter is given the same number both in Hartel and in Migne.

LETTER OF CYPRIAN AND COLLEAGUES TO POMPONIUS, BISHOP OF DIONYSIANA. [A. D. ?]

568

[4 (62), 1]
Cyprian, Cecil, Victor, Sedatus, Tertullus, with the presbyters who were present here with them, to their brother Pomponius, greeting! We have read your letter, dearest brother, which you sent by our brother Paconius, asking and desiring that we write back to you what we think ought to be done in regard to those virgins who, although they had once determined to continue firmly in their state of life, were afterwards discovered to have remained side by side in the same bed with men, one of whom you say is a deacon; and yet these same virgins who have confessed that they slept with men insist that they are virgins still. . . .

982
902
904

[3] Let no one think that she can defend herself with the excuse that whether or not she be a virgin may be examined and proved; for both the hands and the eyes of midwives are often deceived. Even if she be examined and be found to be a virgin intact in that part in which a woman can be examined, still she may have sinned in another part of the body which can be corrupted but in which such an examination cannot be made.

Certainly the very lying together, the mutual embrace, the small talk and the kissing, and the disgraceful and foul sleep of the two lying together — how great a dishonor and crime does it confess! If a husband, coming upon his wife, should see her lying with another man, is he not filled with indignation and does he not fall into a rage? and in his jealous grief will he not perhaps take sword in hand? What then of Christ, our Lord and Judge, when He finds His virgin, who is dedicated to Him, lying with another man? How indignant and angry He is, and what penalties He does threaten against such lewd relations! . . .

[4] You have, therefore, acted advisedly and with vigor, dearest brother, in excommunicating (1) the deacon who dallied often with a virgin, and the others, too, who were accustomed to sleep with virgins. But if they shall have separated themselves from each other, then let the virgins be carefully examined by midwives; and, if they shall have been found to be virgins, let them, when they have been received to communion, be admitted to the Church, with this warning, however: that if afterwards they should go back to the same men, or if they should dwell in the same house or under the same

roof with them, they will be cast out with a more grave censure; nor will such persons be easily received back into the Church.

If, however, someone among them shall have been found to be corrupted, let her do full penance, because she that has committed this crime is an adulteress not against a husband but against Christ. Therefore, at a time considered a just interval after she has made a confession of sin, let her return to the Church. But if they continue in their obstinacy and will not separate themselves from each other, let them know that because of such shameless obstinacy we can never admit them to the Church, lest by their sins they might begin to set an example for the ruination of others. Do not let them imagine that the way of life and of salvation is still open to them, if they have refused to obey the bishops and the priests.

LETTER WITHOUT HEADING, FROM THE CLERGY OF ROME TO THE CLERGY OF CARTHAGE. A. D. 250.

568a

[8 (2), 1]

We have learned from Crementius, the subdeacon who came to us from you, that the blessed Pope Cyprian has withdrawn, for the reason specified, "which, indeed, he might rightly do, especially since he is a distinguished person, and in view of the impending conflict . . . (2)."

436

LETTER OF CYPRIAN IN REPLY TO CERTAIN MARTYRS AND CONFESSORS. A. D. 250.

568b

[15 (10), 1]

Although you sent me a letter in which you ask that consideration be given your desire that, after the persecution is over and we begin to gather together again and to meet together with the clergy, peace be then extended to the lapsed, those [aforementioned presbyters] have dared, — contrary to the law of the gospel, contrary even to your respectful petition, before penance has been done, before a confession of the most grave and extremest sin has been made, before a hand has been imposed in penance by the bishop and the clergy, — to offer on their behalf and to give them the Eucharist; that is, to profane the holy Body of the Lord, in spite of what is written: "Whoever shall eat the Bread or drink the Cup of the Lord unworthily, will be guilty of the Body and the Blood of the Lord (3)."

904
906
792

LETTER OF CYPRIAN TO HIS CLERGY. A. D. 250.

569

[16 (9), 2]

Although for lesser sins it is required that sinners do penance for a just time, after which, according to the rule of discipline, they may come to confession and, through the imposition of hands by the bishop and clergy, may receive the right of communication (4), now, in an unpropitious time and while the persecution continues, when peace is not yet restored to the Church itself, they are being admitted to communication, and the offering is made in their name; and, not yet having made a confession of

904
906

sin, not yet having had hands imposed upon them by the bishop and clergy, the   916
Eucharist is given to them, in spite of what is written: "Whoever shall eat the Bread   792
or drink the Cup of the Lord unworthily, will be guilty of the Body and the Blood of   875
the Lord (5)."

LETTER OF CYPRIAN TO HIS CLERGY. A. D. 250.

570

[18 (12), 1]

Inasmuch as I find that there is not yet an opportunity of coming to you, and the
Summer has already begun — a season disturbed by continual and grave illnesses — I
think that we must deal with our brethren. Therefore, those who have received certifi-   935
cates from the martyrs and are able to be assisted by their privileged position before
God, if they should be seized by some misfortune or dangerous illness at a time when
my return is not expected, then, before whatever presbyter is present, or if a presbyter   909
is not found and death begins to be imminent, even before a deacon they are permitted   916
to make their confession of sin, so that a hand may be imposed upon them in penance   927
and they may come to the Lord with the peace which the martyrs, as indicated in letters   906
sent to us, desired to be given them.

LETTER OF CYPRIAN TO HIS CLERGY. A. D. 250.

570a

[29 (24)]

Know, therefore, that I have made Saturus a lector (6), and Optatus the confessor a   956
subdeacon — men whom I had already, by common advice, after examining whether
they were fit in all those things which must be found in those who are being prepared
for the clerical estate, appointed next to the clergy, when one or the other time (7) I
gave to Saturus the reading on the Paschal day; or the time when, while in company
with the teaching presbyters I was carefully testing the readers, I appointed Optatus,
from among the lectors, to be a teacher of the catechumens (8). I have, then, done
nothing new in your absence. That which was begun long ago at the common advice
of all of us, however, has been carried further because of the urgent necessity. I hope,
dearest brethren, that you are well and that you are always mindful of me. Greet the
brotherhood. Farewell.

LETTER OF THE CLERGY OF ROME [SEDE VACANTE] TO CYPRIAN OF CARTHAGE. A. D. 250.

570b

[30 (31), 1]

The presbyters and deacons abiding in Rome, to Pope Cyprian: greetings . . . [8] We   436
hope, most blessed and most glorious Pope, that you are well and that you are always
mindful of us in the Lord (9).

LETTER WITHOUT HEADING, OF CYPRIAN TO THE
LAPSED. A. D. 250.

571

[33 (27), 1]
Our Lord, whose commands we ought to fear and observe, says in the Gospel, by way   401
of assigning the episcopal dignity and settling the plan of His Church: "I say to you that   430
you are Peter, and upon this rock I will build my Church, and the gates of hell will not
overcome it. And to you I will give the keys of the kingdom of heaven: and whatever
things you bind on earth will be bound also in heaven, and whatever you loose on earth,
they will be loosed also in heaven (10)."   406

From that time the ordination of bishops and the plan of the Church flows on through
the changes of times and successions; for the Church is founded upon the bishops, and
every act of the Church is controlled by these same rulers. Since this has indeed been
established by divine law, I marvel at the rash boldness of certain persons who have
desired to write to me as if they were writing their letters in the name of the Church,
"since the Church is established upon the bishop and upon the clergy and upon all who
stand firm in the faith (11)."

Far be it from the mercy of the Lord and His invincible power to permit the ranks of
the lapsed to be called the Church, for it is written: "He is not the God of the dead,
but of the living (12)." Certainly we hope that all may be brought back to life; and
by our petitions and our groans we pray that they may be restored to their former state.
But if some of the lapsed wish themselves to be the Church, and if the Church is among
them and in them, what remains for us except to ask them to deign to admit us to the
Church! It behooves them, therefore, to be submissive and quiet and modest, who,
mindful of their sin, ought to make satisfaction to God instead of writing letters in the
name of the Church when they know well that it is the Church to whom they write.

LETTER OF CYPRIAN TO HIS CLERGY AND TO
ALL HIS PEOPLE. A. D. 250.

572

[39 (34), 3]
Lawrence and Ignatius, though they fought betimes in worldly camps, were true   121
and spiritual soldiers of God; and while they laid the devil on his back with their
confession of Christ, they merited the palms and crowns of the Lord by their illustrious
passion. We always offer sacrifices for them, as you will recall, as often as we celebrate
the passions of the martyrs by commemorating their anniversary day.

LETTER OF CYPRIAN TO ALL HIS PEOPLE. A. D. 251.

573

[43 (40), 5]
They who have not peace themselves now offer peace to others. They who have
withdrawn from the Church promise to lead back and to recall the lapsed to the Church.   416
There is one God and one Christ, and one Church, and one Chair founded on Peter by   410
the word of the Lord. It is not possible to set up another altar or for there to be another   435
priesthood besides that one altar and that one priesthood. Whoever has gathered elsewhere
is scattering.

*LETTER OF CYPRIAN TO ANTONIANUS, A BISHOP
IN NUMIDIA. A. D. 251/252.*

574a

[55 (52), 1]

You wrote also, that I should forward to Cornelius (13), our colleague, a copy of your
letter, so that he might put aside any anxiety and know immediately that you are in
communion with him, that is, with the Catholic Church.   423

575

[55 (52), 8]

Cornelius was made bishop by the decision of God and of His Christ, by the testimony   441
of almost all the clergy, by the applause (14) of the people then present, by the college
of venerable priests and good men, at a time when no one had been made before him —
when the place of Fabian, which is the place of Peter, the dignity of the sacerdotal   434
chair, was vacant. Since it has been occupied both at the will of God and with the   432
ratified consent of all of us, whoever wishes now to become bishop must do so outside.
For he cannot have ecclesiastical rank who does not hold to the unity of the Church.   421

576

[55 (52), 17]

It seemed fitting, dearest brother, after examining each case separately, to admit after
a time those who had received certificates; and those who sacrificed should be received   909
at death, because among the dead there is no confession of sin, nor is it possible to force   991
anyone to repentance if the fruit of repentance be taken away. If the battle come
suddenly, he will be found ready for it, having been strengthened by us. And indeed, if
illness press hard upon him before the battle, he will depart with the comfort of peace
and of being in communion.

576a

[55 (52), 20]

Do not suppose, dearest brother, that for the future either the courage of the brethren
will be lessened, or that martyrdom will fail, because repentance is made easier for the
lapsed and because a hope of peace is offered to the penitent. Indeed, the strength of
the faithful will remain unshaken and the integrity of those who fear and love God with
their whole heart will continue firm and strong. We allow a time of penance even to
adulterers, and peace is given them. Even so, virginity does not on that account fail in   902
the Church, nor does the noble resolve of continence weaken because of the sins of   984
others. The Church flourishes, crowned as it is with so many virgins; and chastity and
modesty retain their noble attraction. The vigor of continence, then, is not broken down
by making penance and pardon easier for the adulterer.

576b

[55 (52), 21]

And indeed, among our predecessors, some of the bishops here in our province did   902
not think that peace should be extended to adulterers; and in the matter of adultery
they completely shut off any opportunity for penance. They did not, however, with-   442
draw from the college of their fellow-bishops (15); nor did they break the unity of the   420
Catholic Church by their continuing the severity of their censure, as were the case if,

because peace was given by some to adulterers, he that did not give it should be
separated from the Church. While the bond of concord remains and the indivisible
sacrament of the Catholic Church continues, each bishop disposes and directs his own   410
work as one who must give an account of his administration to the Lord.

577

[55 (52), 27]
   We think that no one should be held back from the fruit of satisfaction and from   901
the hope of peace, since we know by our faith in the Divine Scriptures, of which God   20
Himself is the author and initiator, both that sinners are brought back to repentance,
and that pardon and forgiveness are not denied the penitent.

578

[55 (52), 29]
   And if, inasmuch as the Lord is merciful and kind, we find that none of those im-   901
ploring and entreating His mercy should be prohibited from doing penance, then peace   925
is able to be extended through His priests. The groans of those who mourn must be   904
taken into account, and the fruit of repentance must not be denied to the sorrowful.
And since among the dead there is no confession, nor in that place can a confession of   991
sin be made (16), those who have repented from the bottom of their heart and have
besought it, must after a time be received into the Church, to be preserved therein for
the Lord.

LETTER OF CYPRIAN TO THE PEOPLE OF THIBAR. A. D. 253.

579

[58 (56), 10]
   Oh, what a day that will be, and how great when it comes, dearest brethren! when   1020
the Lord begins to survey His people and to recognize by examining with divine knowledge the merits of each individual! to cast into hell evildoers, and to condemn our   1030
persecutors to the eternal fire and punishing flame! and indeed, to present to us the   1034
reward of faith and devotion! What will be that glory, and how great the joy of being
admitted to the sight of God! to be so honored as to receive the joy of eternal light   1041
and salvation in the presence of Christ the Lord, your God! to greet Abraham, and   1045
Isaac, and Jacob, and all the patriarchs, apostles, prophets, and martyrs! to rejoice
with the just and with the friends of God in the kingdom of heaven, in the delight of   1043
the immortality that will be given! to receive there what eye has not seen nor ear
heard, what has not entered into the heart of man (17)!
   The Apostle predicts that we will receive even greater things than we perform or
suffer here, when he says: "The sufferings of the present time are not worth comparing
with the brightness about to come upon us and which will be unveiled in us (18)."
When that unveiling has come and when the brightness of God shines about us,
honored by the condescension of the Lord, we shall be as blessed and joyful as they
will remain guilty and miserable — those deserters of God and rebels against God, who
have done the will of the devil, so that it is necessary for them to be tortured along   1033
with him in the unquenchable fire.

LETTER OF CYPRIAN TO CORNELIUS OF ROME. A. D. 252.

580

[59 (55), 14]

With a false bishop appointed for themselves by heretics, they dare even to set sail   434
and carry letters from schismatics and blasphemers to the chair of Peter and to the   451
principal Church, in which sacerdotal unity has its source; nor did they take thought
that these are Romans, whose faith was praised by the preaching Apostle, and among
whom it is not possible for perfidy to have entrance.

LETTER OF CYPRIAN TO A CERTAIN CECIL. [A. D. ?]

581

[63, 4]

Also in the priest Melchisedech we see the Sacrament of the Sacrifice of the Lord   893
prefigured, in accord with that to which the Divine Scriptures testify, where it says:
"And Melchisedech, the King of Salem, brought out bread and wine, for he was a priest
of the Most High God; and he blessed Abraham (19)." That Melchisedech is in fact a
type of Christ is declared in the psalms by the Holy Spirit, saying to the Son, as it were
from the Father: "Before the daystar I begot You. You are a Priest forever, according
to the order of Melchisedech (20)."

The order certainly is that which comes from his sacrifice and which comes down from
it: because Melchisedech was a priest of the Most High God; because he offered bread;   860
and because he blessed Abraham. And who is more a priest of the Most High God than   382
our Lord Jesus Christ, who, when He offered sacrifice to God the Father, offered the
very same which Melchisedech had offered, namely bread and wine, which is in fact His
Body and Blood!

582

[63, 9]

We find that the cup which the Lord offered was mixed; and that what was wine, He   860
called Blood. From this it is apparent that the Blood of Christ is not offered if there is
no wine in the cup; nor is the Sacrifice of the Lord celebrated with a legitimate consecration (21) unless our offering and sacrifice corresponds to the passion. . . . [11] I   891
wonder, indeed, whence this practice has come, that, contrary to evangelic and apostolic
tradition, in certain places water alone, which cannot signify (22) the Blood of Christ, is
offered in the cup of the Lord.

583

[63, 13]

Because Christ bore us all, in that He bore our sins, we see that by the water, people   861
are signified, while in the wine, indeed, the Blood of Christ is shown. And when the
water is mixed with the wine in the cup, the people are made one with Christ, and the
multitude of believers is coupled and joined to Him in whom it believes.

584

[63,14]

If Christ Jesus, our Lord and God, is Himself the High Priest of God the Father;   890

and if He offered Himself as a sacrifice to the Father; and if He commanded that this
be done in commemoration of Himself — then certainly the priest, who imitates that   867
which Christ did, truly functions in place of Christ.

LETTER OF CYPRIAN AND OF HIS COLLEAGUES IN COUNCIL TO THE NUMBER OF SIXTY-SIX: TO FIDUS. A. D. 251/252.

584a

[64 (59), 1]

We have read your letter, dearest brother, in which you indicated in regard to Victor,   900
formerly a presbyter, that our colleague Therapius (23) had rashly granted peace to him
after an insufficient time and in headlong haste, before he had done full penance and
before he had made satisfaction to the Lord God, against whom he had sinned. This   923
matter disturbed us considerably, because it was a departure from the authority of our
decree, in that peace was granted him before the full and lawful time of satisfaction,
without the request nor even the awareness of the people, and with no pressing illness
nor any compelling necessity. . . . Still, we did not think that peace, once granted in
whatever way by a priest of God, should be taken away; and for this reason we have
allowed Victor to avail himself of the communion granted him.

585

[64 (59), 2]

As to what pertains to the case of infants: you said that they ought not to be baptized   834
within the second or third day after their birth, and that the old law of circumcision must   835
be taken into consideration, and that you did not think that one should be baptized and
sanctified within the eighth day after his birth. In our council it seemed to us far otherwise. No one agreed to the course which you thought should be taken. Rather, we all
judged that the mercy and grace of God ought to be denied to no man born.

586

[64 (59), 5]

If, in the case of the worst sinners and of those who formerly sinned much against   831
God, when afterwards they believe, the remission of their sins is granted and no one is
held back from Baptism and grace, how much more, then, should an infant not be held
back, who, having but recently been born, has done no sin, except that, born of the
flesh according to Adam, he has contracted the contagion of that old death from his   614
first being born. For this very reason does he approach more easily to receive the remis-   615
sion of sins: because the sins forgiven him are not his own but those of another.

LETTER OF CYPRIAN TO FLORENTIUS PUPIANUS. A. D. 254.

587

[66 (69), 8]

You have written also that on my account the Church now has a portion of itself in a   420
state of dispersion. In truth, the whole people of the Church are collected together and
made one and joined to each other in an indivisible harmony. They alone have remained
outside who, were they within, would have to be ejected. . . . And the Lord too, in the

Gospel, when the disciples abandoned Him while He was speaking, turned to the twelve and said, "And do you too wish to go away?" Peter answered Him, saying, "Lord, to whom shall we go? You have the word of eternal life: and we believe and know that you are the Son of the Living God (24)."

There speaks Peter, upon whom the Church would be built, teaching in the name of the Church and showing that even if a stubborn and proud multitude withdraws because it does not wish to obey, yet the Church does not withdraw from Christ. The people joined to the priest and the flock clinging to their shepherd are the Church.

430
423

You ought to know, then, that the bishop is in the Church and the Church in the bishop; and if someone is not with the bishop, he is not in the Church. They vainly flatter themselves who creep up, not having peace with the priests of God, believing that they are secretly in communion with certain individuals. For the Church, which is One and Catholic, is not split nor divided, but is indeed united and joined by the cement of priests who adhere one to another.

415

418
421

LETTER OF CYPRIAN IN COUNCIL WITH THIRTY-SIX OTHER BISHOPS, TO CERTAIN CLERGY AND LAITY OF SPAIN. A. D. 256.

588

[67 (68), 3]

The people, in obedience to the precepts of the Lord and in the fear of God, ought to separate themselves from a sinful prelate, nor ought they associate themselves with the sacrifices of a sacrilegious priest, especially inasmuch as they have the power both of electing worthy priests and of refusing the unworthy. [4] This very thing, too, we note, stems from divine authority — that a priest be chosen in the presence of the people and under the eyes of all, and that he be approved as worthy and suitable by public judgment and testimony. . . . [5] That point of divine tradition and apostolic observance is to be kept diligently and held fast, which is indeed observed among us and throughout almost all the provinces, that for the proper celebrating of ordinations all the neighboring bishops of the same province should assemble with that people for whom a prelate is being ordained; and the bishop should be chosen in the presence of the people, who are thoroughly familiar with the life of each one, and who have looked into the doings of each one in respect to his habitual conduct. And we see that this was done by you in the ordination of our colleague Sabinus, so that the episcopate was conferred upon him and hands were imposed upon him in place of Basilides, with the applause of the whole brotherhood and in conformity with the judgment of the bishops.

441

958

LETTER OF CYPRIAN TO STEPHEN OF ROME. A. D. 254.

588a

[68 (67), 1]

Our colleague Faustinus, dearest brother, abiding at Lyons, has written me time and again (25) about matters which I know have certainly been reported to you both by him and also by the rest of our fellow-bishops established in that same province: that Marcian, abiding at Arles, has joined himself to Novatian and has separated himself from the truth (26) of the Catholic Church, and from the unanimity of our corporate priesthood (27). . . . [2] On this account you ought to write a very full letter to our fellow-bishops who are established in Gaul, not to allow Marcian, who is stubborn and proud and inimical to divine mercy and to the salvation of the brotherhood, any longer to

420

insult our college by seeming not yet to be excommunicated by us. . . . [3] Let letters   442
be directed by you into the province and to the people living at Arles by which letters,
when Marcian has been excommunicated, another may be substituted in his place; and
the flock of Christ which is presently held in contempt as having been scattered and
wounded by that proud man will thereby be reassembled. . . . It is for this reason,
dearest brother, that the sacerdotal body is abundant, joined together by the bond of
mutual harmony and by the chain of unity: so that if anyone of our college attempts
to fashion heresy and to wound and lay waste the flock of Christ, the others may inter-
vene and, as useful and merciful shepherds, gather the Lord's sheep into the flock.

LETTER OF CYPRIAN TO A CERTAIN MAGNUS. A. D. 255.

589

[69 (76), 3]
    The Church is one; and it is not possible to be both within and without what is one.   416
If the Church is around Novatian, it was not around Cornelius. And indeed, if it was   415
around Cornelius, who succeeded Bishop Fabian by a legitimate ordination and whom
the Lord glorified with martyrdom even beyond the honor of the priesthood, then Novatian
is not in the Church, nor can he be reckoned as a bishop, since, in contempt of evangelic
and apostolic tradition, he succeeded to no one but sprang up of himself. He that was   422
not ordained in the Church can neither have nor hold the Church in any way.

589a

[69 (76), 5]
    Even the very Sacrifices of the Lord (28) bespeak a Christian unanimity bound to   854
itself by a firm and inseparable charity. When the Lord calls bread made from the union   420
of many granules His Body, He points out our people, whom He was betokening as made
one; and when He calls wine, which is pressed from many grapes and clusters and reduced
to a whole, His Blood, again He signifies our flock, joined together by the blending of a
multitude into one.

590

[69 (76), 12]
    You have asked also, dearest son, what I thought about those who obtain the grace of   824
God while they are weakened by illness — whether or not they are to be reckoned as
legitimate Christians who have not been bathed with the saving water, but have had it
poured over them. On this point, my modesty and reservation prejudges no one. Let
each one consider what he thinks best; and what he thinks best, let him do. In so far
as my poor ability conceives it, I think that the divine benefits can in no way be weakened or mutilated; nor can anything less take place in that case, where that which is
drawn from the divine gifts is accepted with full and entire faith both on the part of
the giver and of the receiver. . . . In the saving sacraments, when necessity compels   790
and when God bestows His pardon, divine benefits are bestowed fully upon believers;
nor ought anyone be disturbed because the sick are poured upon or sprinkled when they
receive the Lord's grace.

LETTER OF CYPRIAN IN COUNCIL WITH THIRTY OTHER BISHOPS OF PROCONSULAR AFRICA TO JANUARIUS AND SEVENTEEN OTHER BISHOPS OF NUMIDIA. A. D. 254/255.

591

[70, 1]

When we were together in council, dearest brothers, we read the letter which you   830
wrote us concerning those who among the heretics and schismatics seem to be baptized,
as to whether they ought to be baptized upon coming to the Catholic Church, which is one.
. . . We express our judgment not as something new; rather, we join with you in mutual
consent to a statute long observed by our predecessors and by ourselves: — namely,
judging and holding it as certain that no one beyond the pale is able to be baptized
outside the Church, since there is one Baptism appointed in Holy Church. . . . How should
one who baptizes grant to another the remission of sins, when he is himself outside the   415
Church and cannot put aside his own sins?

592

[70, 2]

It is necessary for him that has been baptized also to be anointed, so that by his   840
having received chrism, that is, the anointing, he can be the anointed of God and have   842
in himself the grace of Christ. But in turn, it is by the Eucharist that the oil with which   845
the baptized are anointed is sanctified on the altar. He that has neither altar nor church,   803
however, is not able to sanctify that creature, oil. Thus there can be no spiritual anointing among the heretics, since it is evident that oil cannot be sanctified nor can the Eucharist   962
be celebrated among them at all.

LETTER OF CYPRIAN TO QUINTUS, A BISHOP IN MAURETANIA. A. D. 254/255.

592a

[71, 1]

I surely do not know by what presumption certain of our colleagues are led to think   830
that those who have been made wet by heretics ought not to be baptized when they come
to us, on the grounds that, as they say, there is but one Baptism. Indeed there is but
one: because the Church is one, and there can be no Baptism outside the Church.
. . . We hold that those who so approach are not re-baptized among us, but are baptized.   799
. . . [2] They say that in this matter they are following ancient custom, since among the
ancients there were already heretics and the first beginnings of schisms, and there were
those even then who withdrew from the Church after first having been baptized therein;
and that when they returned to the Church and did penance it was not necessary to
baptize them.

We still observe this today: that it is sufficient to impose hands in penance upon those
who have manifestly been baptized and then have gone over from us to the heretics, if
afterwards they recognize their sin and put aside their error and return to the truth and
to their parent. . . . But if he that comes from the heretics was not first baptized in the
Church, but comes entirely as a profane stranger, he must be baptized in order to become
a sheep; for in Holy Church is the one water which makes sheep. . . .[3] One must not
object, however, on the grounds of custom; rather, one must overcome by reasoned
argumentation. For Peter, whom the Lord chose first and upon whom He built His   430
Church, when Paul later disagreed with him about circumcision, did not claim anything   433

for himself insolently nor assume anything arrogantly, so as to say that he held the   435
primacy and that he ought rather to be obeyed by novices and those more recently
arrived.

LETTER OF CYPRIAN TO JUBAIANUS, A BISHOP
IN MAURETANIA. A. D. 254/256.

593

[73, 1]

    You wrote to me, dearest brother, desiring that the thought of my mind be signified   830
to you, in regard to what I might think in the matter of the baptism of heretics, who are
placed beyond the pale and who are established outside the Church, but yet claim for   415
themselves a thing which is neither theirs by right nor which is within their power. This
baptism we cannot reckon as valid or legitimate, since it is evident that it is unlawful
among them. . . . And then too, when we had assembled together, bishops from the
Province of Africa as well as from Numidia, to the number of seventy-one, we again
confirmed this matter with our judgment, deciding that there is but one Baptism, that it
is to be had in the Catholic Church, and that those coming to us from adulterous and
profane water with the necessity of being washed and sanctified by the truth of the
saving water are, therefore, not re-baptized but are baptized by us.   799

594

[73, 7]

    We know that only in the Church, where prelates have been established by the gospel   828
law and by the ordinance of the Lord, is it permitted to baptize and to give the remission   836
of sins. Beyond the pale, however, nothing can be bound or be loosed, where there is no   803
one who is able either to bind or to loose.

595

[73, 9]

    Some, however, say in regard to those who were baptized in Samaria, that when the
Apostles Peter and John came there only hands were imposed on them so that they
might receive the Holy Spirit, and that they were not, however, re-baptized. But we see,
dearest brother, that this situation in no way pertains to the present case. For those in
Samaria who had believed, had believed in the true faith; and it was by the deacon
Philip, whom those same Apostles had sent there, that they had been baptized inside, in
the Church, which is one, and in which alone it is permitted to give the grace of
Baptism and to absolve sins.

    For the reason, then, that they had already received legitimate and ecclesiastical
Baptism, it was not necessary to baptize them again. Rather, that only which was lacking
was done by Peter and John; and thus, prayer having been made over them, and hands   840
having been imposed upon them, the Holy Spirit was invoked and was poured out upon
them. This is even now the practice among us, so that those who are baptized in the   843
Church are then brought to the prelates of the Church; and through our prayer and the   792
imposition of hands, they receive the Holy Spirit and are perfected with the seal of the
Lord.

596

[73, 12]

If someone could be baptized by heretics, he could certainly receive also the remis-   803
sion of sins. If he were to receive the remission of sins, he would be sanctified. If he
were sanctified, he would be made a temple of God. If he were made a temple of God
— now I ask you: of what God? Of the Creator? But that is not possible, because he
does not believe in Him. Of Christ? One who denies that Christ is God cannot become   301
His temple. Of the Holy Spirit? Since the Three are One, how were it possible for the   230
Holy Spirit to be reconciled to him that is an enemy of either the Son or of the Father?   237

597

[73, 18]

After the Resurrection, when the Lord sent the Apostles to the nations, He commanded
them to baptize the gentiles in the name of the Father and of the Son and of the Holy   826
Spirit. How then do some say that though a gentile be baptized beyond the pale and   415
outside the Church, yes, even against the Church, never mind how or of whom, so long
as it be done in the name of Jesus Christ, the remission of sins can follow — when Christ   827
Himself commands the nations to be baptized in the full and united Trinity?

597a

[73, 21]

If the Baptism of public witness and of blood cannot profit a heretic unto salvation,   833
because there is no salvation outside the Church, how much the more worthless is it for   417
him, in secret places and in the caves of robbers, dipped in the contagion of adulterous
water, not merely not to have put off his former sins, but even to have added new and   836
greater ones!

598

[73, 22]

[Catechumens who suffer martyrdom before they have received Baptism with water]   833
are not deprived of the Sacrament of Baptism. Rather, they are baptized with the most
glorious and greatest Baptism of blood, concerning which the Lord said that He had
another Baptism with which He Himself was to be baptized (29).

1. *abstinendo.*
2. The clause we have put within quotation remarks is generally interpreted as having been part of the excuse
   which the clergy of Carthage made for Cyprian's conduct, in the letter which they sent to Rome with the
   subdeacon Crementius. It is now quoted back to them, perhaps somewhat sarcastically, by the clergy of
   Rome.
3. 1 Cor. 11:27.
4. *ius communicationis accipiant.* This seems to be a much broader concept than that of being admitted to
   the Communal Sacrament. It is, we submit, the concept of being in communion as opposed to being in a
   state of excommunication.
5. 1 Cor. 11:27.
6. In a letter of the year 252 A. D., (No. 59 [55], Cyprian to Cornelius), Saturus, probably the same person,
   is called an acolyte.
7. *semel atque iterum.* Sometimes this phrase means *twice*, and sometimes it means *repeatedly*. We must
   remember to ask Cyprian whether he meant it in the strict or in the vague sense.
8. *audientium.*
9. In his letter No. 55 [52], 5 *(Ad Antonianum)*, Cyprian mentions that this present letter in the name of
   the clergy of Rome was composed in fact by Novatian. The Roman See was vacant at this time; and
   Novatian, of course, had not yet launched himself into schism.
10. Matt. 16:18-19.
11. It is clear that Cyprian is quoting back to the lapsed the excuse which they had used in their letter to
    him, in the part in which they were attempting to justify their writing to him.

12. Matt. 22:32.
13. Pope St. Cornelius, *regn. A. D.* 251-253.
14. *suffragio.*
15. *Non tamen a coepiscoporum suorum collegio recesserunt . . . .*
16. It is interesting that in this line both of the common terms for confession of sins are used: *Et quia apud inferos confessio non est nec exomologesis illic fieri potest.*
17. 1 Cor. 2:9.
18. Rom. 8:18.
19. Gen. 14:18-19.
20. Ps. 109 [110]:3-4.
21. *legitima sanctificatione.*
22. *exprimere.*
23. Therapius, Bishop of Bulla Minor.
24. John 6:68-70.
25. *semel atque iterum.* See note 7, in this same series, above.
26. A variant reading has *unitate* in place of *veritate.* A correct understanding of hermeneutic principles requires the retaining of *truth,* it being the less likely and therefore the more probable term. Which is to say, one expects the reading *unity;* and a scribe might easily substitute it for *truth,* but hardly *vice versa.*
27. There are numerous variants in the present phrase; but the thought in all is much as we render it.
28. *dominica sacrificia:* the plural of the term which Cyprian several times employs to signify the Eucharistic Sacrifice. The above line, then, might be translated: "The Mass itself bespeaks a Christian unanimity . . . "
29. Luke 12:50.

ACTS OF THE SEVENTH COUNCIL OF CARTHAGE, CYPRIAN PRESIDING [*A. D.* 256]

The Seventh Council of Carthage, of which Cyprian was president, met with eighty-seven bishops present, in the year 256 A. D. The subject of their meeting was the now hotly controverted question of the baptism of heretics. They refused to acquiesce to the demands of Pope St. Stephen, even in the face of his threats of excommunication. Emissaries were sent to Rome from the council, but Stephen refused to give them audience.

The *Acts* of the council may be found in Mansi, Vol. 1, 951-965, and in Migne, PL 4, 1051-1078. Neither edition any longer serves scholarly purposes, the standard edition being the critical text established by W. Hartel, in the Vienna Corpus (CSEL), Vol. 3, part 1, Vienna 1868.

599a

[*Proem*]

When, at the kalends of September, a great many bishops from the Province of Africa, from Numidia, and from Mauretania, had met together as one in Carthage, along with the presbyters and deacons, and when even a considerable number of the people were present, . . . Cyprian said: You have heard, dearly beloved colleagues, what Jubaianus, our fellow-bishop, has written to me, taking counsel of my poor ability, in the matter of the unlawful and profane baptism of heretics, and what I have written back to him. . . . It but remains that each of us should, in regard to this same matter, bring forward his opinion, judging no one, nor depriving anyone of the right of communion if he should think differently.

406

For neither does anyone of us set himself up as a bishop (1), nor by tyranny and terror does anyone compel his colleagues to the necessity of obedience, since every bishop has his own free will to the unrestrained exercise of his liberty and power, so that neither can he be judged by another, nor is he himself able to judge another. Rather, let us all await the judgment of our Lord Jesus Christ, the one and only one who has both the power of setting us over the governing of His Church, and of judging our conduct in that capacity.

410
435

392

599b

[4]

Novatus of Thamogad (2) said: Although we know that all Scripture bears witness concerning the saving Baptism, still we must express our faith that when heretics and schismatics, who appear falsely to have been baptized, come to the Church, they must be baptized in the everlasting fountain. And therefore, in accord with the testimony of the Scriptures and in accord with the decree of our colleagues, men of most holy memory, all schismatics and heretics who are converted to the Church are to be baptized. Moreover, those who appear to have been ordained are to be received among the laity.

830

442

803

600

[87]

Cyprian of Carthage said: The letter which was written to our colleague Jubaianus expresses quite at length my opinion that according to evangelic and apostolic testimony, heretics, who are called anti-christs and adversaries of Christ, when they come to the Church, must be baptized with the one Baptism of the Church, so that friends may be made of adversaries, and Christians of antichrists.

830

1. A variant reading of certain manuscripts makes the phrase read *as a bishop of bishops*. Probably it is not the technically correct reading, but it is clearly the sense of the passage: no bishop sets himself up as a bishop with authority over other bishops. The term *episcopus episcoporum*, as in the variant, is known as a title of grandeur occasionally accorded to various persons of authority as early as the 4th century; and according to Lucifer of Calaris, it was given by the Arians to Constantius. Except for the manuscript variant in question, we have not seen it in the third century. It was not at this time a special title assigned to the Bishop of Rome; and the attitude expressed in regard to the jurisdictional autonomy of individual bishops is Cyprian's constant attitude, not much stronger in expression here than in certain passages of his letters as early as the year 250 A. D. Yet, in the context of the present question of opposition between Rome and Carthage, it is impossible to believe that in committing himself to the words of the present address, Cyprian did not have Stephen in mind.

2. Novatus, Bishop of Thamogad in Numidia, is not to be confused with the Roman schismatic and anti-Pope Novatus, generally called Novatianus or Novatian; nor yet with the Carthaginian Novatus, a priest who went to Rome to support the Novatian schism.

TREATISE ON RE-BAPTISM [*A. D.* 256/258]

The anonymous *Treatise on Re-Baptism,* preserved in the corpus of Cyprian's writings, is really an anti-Cyprianic treatise, written most probably by an African Bishop between the time of the Council of Carthage of the year 256 A. D. and Cyprian's death in 258 A. D.

The author of the treatise makes an unfortunate distinction between Baptism of water and Baptism of the Spirit, the latter conferred by the imposition of the Bishop's hand. He does not, quite obviously, and could not at this early period, recognize in the latter the separate Sacrament of Confirmation; and he makes his distinction to the detriment of the former, Baptism of water, which he regards as a less necessary adjunct of integral Baptism.

The distinction which he makes is the result of his attempt to fortify the position of those opposed to the re-baptizing of converts from heresy and schism, while being in the unfortunate circumstance of having neither a theology sufficiently developed nor a theological acumen of his own to enable him to do so properly. He found a clever way out of the difficulty: Baptism of water is not to be repeated upon those coming into the Church. It is really only a form anyway, the real Baptism being the Baptism of the Spirit, conferred only by the bishop, through the imposition of hands.

Perhaps the author of the treatise has failed to make a proper distinction in his own mind between the various kinds of impositions of hands, and is thereby confusing the baptismal imposition or Confirmation with the penitential imposition of hands for reconciliation. Moreover, it seems to have escaped the author's attention that in first denying that Baptism is to be repeated and then distinguishing between Baptism of water and Baptism of the Spirit, the latter constituting what is in his mind the more important and necessary Baptism, and then declaring that the latter is to be repeated, his solution is really only a begging of the question along with a rather hideous exposition of his own deficiencies in the area of sacramental theology.

The Migne text, PL 3, 1183-1204, is entirely superseded by that of W. Hartel in the Vienna Corpus (CSEL), Vol. 3, part 3, Vienna 1871, pp. 69-92.

601

[10]

Since our salvation is grounded upon Baptism of the Spirit, which for the most part is   831
had jointly with Baptism of water, whenever Baptism is conferred by us let it be given in its entirety and with solemnity, with all that is prescribed; and let it be conferred without any separation of anything from it. Or, if through necessity, it be conferred by a lesser cleric (1), let us postpone the conclusion (2), so that it may either be supplied by us (3)   828
or be reserved to the Lord for His supplying of it. If, however, it was conferred by those who are strangers to us, let this transaction be corrected as is possible and permissible. Because there is no Holy Spirit outside the Church, it is impossible for there to be any sound faith not only among heretics, but indeed, even among those who are established in schism.

1. *a minore clero.* This is not the technical term *minor cleric, i.e.* a cleric in minor orders, but refers here to any clergyman below the grade of episcopate.
2. *eventum expectemus: i.e.,* that part of the rite constituting confirmation, which the author calls Baptism of the Spirit, is not to be given by a *clerus minor.*
3. *I. e.,* by a bishop, the word being taken as a plural of solidarity.

ST. STEPHEN I, POPE [*regn. A. D.* 254-257]

No writings are known of Pope St. Stephen I, except for two letters, both dating from the year 255 A. D. One is to Cyprian of Carthage, in regard to the controversy over the Baptism of heretics; and another, to the Bishops of Asia Minor, threatening to excommunicate those who re-baptize converts from heresy. Only a very short fragment of each has been preserved: of the first, by inclusion in a letter of Cyprian to Pompey, Bishop of Sabrat, letter No. 74 in the Cyprianic corpus; of the second, by inclusion in the letter of Firmilian, Bishop of Caesarea in Cappadocia, to Cyprian of Carthage, letter No. 75 in the Cyprianic corpus. The best source for the fragments, then, which may otherwise be found in Migne, PL 3, 1128-1129 and 1169-1170, is W. Hartel's edition of Cyprian, CSEL, Vol. 3, part 2, Vienna 1869.

FRAGMENT OF A LETTER OF STEPHEN OF ROME TO CYPRIAN OF CARTHAGE. A. D. 255.

601a

[*Apud Cyp. Epist.* 74, 1]

Among other things either arrogant or not pertinent to the question or self-contradictory,	433
which he wrote clumsily and without foresight, [Stephen] added even that he would say:	435
"If, therefore, someone comes to you from any heresy whatsoever, let nothing be renewed	803
except that which has been handed down (1), namely, that the hand be imposed on him	830

in penance; for the heretics themselves, quite properly, do not baptize those who come to them from each other, but simply admit them to communion."

FRAGMENT OF A LETTER OF STEPHEN OF ROME TO THE BISHOPS OF ASIA MINOR. A. D. 255.

601b

[*Apud Cyp. Epist.* 75, 18]

"But the name of Christ," *[Stephen] says,* "accomplishes much toward the faith and	433
sanctification of Baptism, so that whoever has been baptized anywhere in the name of	790
Christ, immediately receives the grace of Christ." *Still, his argument can be countered*	435
briefly, and he can be told that if Baptism in the name of Christ given beyond the pale	
is valid for the cleansing of a man, then the imposition of hands in the name of the	792
same Christ ought to be valid there for the receiving of the Holy Spirit (2).	

1. This is the justly famous *nihil innovetur nisi quod traditum est*. We cannot pass it by, however, without some comment. The word *innovare* is of very infrequent usage. It means, first of all, *to renew,* and can also mean *to change* or *to innovate.* How the phrase in question is to be translated has been somewhat debated, but has not, I think, at any time been sufficiently treated. It seems obvious, in its context, that for Stephen, *innovare* meant *to renew;* and if this meaning be assigned, the problems of translation disappear.

   Nevertheless, it is quite certain that Cyprian understood it in the sense of *to change* or *to innovate.* We can see, then, why he says Stephen wrote in a clumsy manner: for taken strictly and with the meaning *to innovate,* the phrase would then mean: *let nothing be changed except that which is traditional.* Obviously Stephen could not have meant that, and Cyprian never supposed he did. Even Cyprian took the grammatical connection of *nisi* quite loosely, as others have ever since, and understood that Stephen was saying: *Let nothing be innovated, but keep always to what is traditional.* Cyprian so understood it, and then waxes eloquent and at considerable length, in high indignation, because Stephen has called him an innovator. No doubt Stephen would have liked to call him much more, but what he really said was much less. Cyprian misunderstood the phrase. Had he understood it as Stephen meant it, taking *innovare* in the sense of *to renew,* he would still have disagreed, but perhaps without so much emotion.

We must also point out that when the phrase is rightly understood and put back into its context, it is easily perceived that the manner in which the phrase is so often quoted in modern times, *let nothing be innovated but keep always to what is traditional,* is nothing short of misquotation. What Stephen actually said is, in effect, "In this problem of receiving already baptized converts from heresy, let nothing of that baptismal ceremony be renewed, and renew only what it is traditional to renew: that is, impose hands on them in the penitential rite of reconciliation, for a renewal of their faith after their having been heretics or schismatics."

Since we are compiling a volume of sources and not writing a patristic treatise we cannot now pursue the question further, except only to point out that this matter of the imposing of hands was further misunderstood, as is evidenced by the anonymous *Liber de Rebaptismate* (p. 242 above) as well as by a number of letters related generally to the baptismal quarrel, so that although Stephen explicitly said *impose hands in penance,* some, thinking primarily of imposition of hands as a conferral of the Holy Spirit, and failing to distinguish between different kinds of manual impositions, understood that Confirmation, then joined to the baptismal rite, was to be renewed, though not, of course, the Baptism itself.

2. But Stephen (§ 601a above) did not say "the imposition of hands . . . for the receiving of the Holy Spirit," but rather, "let nothing be renewed except . . . that the hand is to be imposed on him in penance." Thus Stephen not only does not advise iteration of Confirmation, but expressly forbids it by forbidding that anything of the baptismal rite be renewed, while at the same time he orders the penitential imposition of hands for reconciliation. We have here an example of what was referred to in the last paragraph of the footnote immediately preceding: Although Stephen clearly stated that baptized converts from heresy were not to have their Baptism renewed, but that hands should be imposed on them *in penance,* Firmilian's mental processes closed upon *imposition of hands;* and he has in mind not the imposition which was part of the penitential rite, but that which was part of the rite of Confirmation, which for men of his time, of course, was an adjunct to the rite of Baptism.

FIRMILIAN OF CAESAREA [† *ca. A. D.* 268]

Firmilian, Bishop of Caesarea in Cappadocia, was a contemporary of St. Gregory the Thaumaturge and, like the latter, an ardent admirer of Origen; but he is remembered mostly for the moral support that he gave to Cyprian when the Bishop of Carthage was quarreling with Pope Stephen over the question of the Baptism of heretics. He died in the year 268 A. D. or shortly thereafter.

LETTER TO CYPRIAN [*A. D.* 255/256]

Of whatever Firmilian may have written, the only work extant, and that only in Latin translation, is his letter to Cyprian of Carthage, preserved as letter No. 75 in the Cyprianic corpus — the very letter which preserves one of the two extant fragments of letters of Pope St. Stephen I, and which we have already cited (§ 601b above). It is clear from certain expressions in the letter that the original was in Greek; and the Latin vocabulary of the translation is so typically Cyprianic that it seems certain that the extant Latin is Cyprian's own translation. For example, the use of *maiores natu* where *presbyteri* might be expected clearly betrays a Greek origin; and again, the peculiar use of the word *foris,* which we translate *beyond the pale,* when *outside the Church* is meant, is indicative of Cyprian's hand in the translating.

For the text of the letter, one may consult Migne, PL 3, 1154-1178; but the better source is W. Hartel's edition in the collected letters of Cyprian: CSEL, Vol. 3, part 2, Vienna 1871, pp. 810-827.

601c

[75, 7]

And other heretics as well, if they have parted themselves from the Church, can have nothing to do with power and grace, since all power and grace is settled in the Church, where preside presbyters (1) who possess the power both of baptizing and of imposing hands, and of ordaining.

415
803
828
843,960

601d

[75, 8]

Inasmuch as Stephen and those who agree with him contend that the remission of sins and the second birth can take place in the baptism given by heretics, even while they admit that the Holy Spirit is not present among the heretics, let them take thought and understand that there can be no spiritual birth without the Spirit. . . . [9] It is absurd also that they do not think it necessary to inquire as to who it was that baptized someone, on the grounds that he that was baptized is able to receive the grace through the invocation of the trinity of names of the Father and of the Son and of the Holy Spirit.

830

826

602

[75, 16]

But what is his error, and how great his blindness, who says that the remission of sins can be given in the synagogues of the heretics (2), and who does not remain on the foundation of the one Church which was founded upon the rock by Christ, can be learned from this, which Christ said to Peter alone: "Whatever things you shall bind on earth shall be bound also in heaven; and whatever you loose on earth, they shall be loosed in heaven (3);" and by this, again in the gospel, when Christ breathed upon the Apostles alone, saying to them: "Receive the Holy Spirit: if you forgive any man his sins, they shall be forgiven; and if you retain any man's sins, they shall be retained (4)." Therefore, the power of forgiving sins was given to the Apostles and to the Churches which these men, sent by Christ, established; and to the bishops who succeeded them by being ordained in their place (5).

435
803
415

900
440

602a

[75, 17]

In this respect I am justly indignant at this so open and evident stupidity of Stephen: that although he glories so much in the place of his bishopric, and contends that he holds the succession of Peter, on whom the foundations of the Church have been laid, he should introduce many other rocks and establish the new building of numerous Churches, since he defends with his authority that Baptism is found in them! There is no doubt that they who are baptized make up the number of the Church. He, however, that approves their Baptism, affirms from the fact of their having been baptized that the Church is also there (6). He that betrays and deserts unity does not realize that the truth of the Christian rock is being obscured by him and, in a certain way, destroyed.

432
433
435
830
415

1. The actual term used here, *maiores natu*, is a most extraordinary one. We do not know it as a technical term, and it really means *persons of greater age*. Thus, it translates the root meaning of the Greek term πρεσβύτεροι, which term it must certainly represent in the no longer extant Greek original of the letter. *N. B.:* It is clear that in the present instance, *presbyters* means *bishops*.
2. This is a thing which Pope St. Stephen did not say, but which Firmilian attributes to him, as an inescapable consequence of allowing that heretics can validly baptize.
3. Matt. 16:19.
4. John 20:22-23.
5. *qui iis ordinatione vicaria successerunt.* If, in the preceding part of the sentence, Firmilian seems to grant the power of the keys to a local Church, we must bear in mind that his concept of a local Church is not precisely ours. We think of a congregation; but Firmilian supported the Cyprianic theology, in which the bishop is the Church. (See § 571, above).
6. Firmilian seems to have grasped the problem, and he sees that it is a dilemma. And if we must frown that Firmilian's language in regard to Stephen is so intemperate, still, we must admit that he has had the courage to face the dilemma squarely – and we too must admit the existence of the problem: who is a member of the Church? We know that the Church is not a Church of the saved only; and we know that none outside the Church can be saved; but still the problem remains: who is a member of the Church? After more than 1700 years, and after the Second Vatican Council, the problem is still there – or, perhaps it went away for a while in the time of Boniface VIII, and has only now returned in our post-Conciliar era.

NOVATIAN [Anti-pope *A. D.* 251-258]

We first meet Novatian, the more probably correct form of whose name is Novatus, about the year 250 A. D., when he was a priest of great prominence among the clergy of Rome. The two letters addressed by the Roman clergy to Cyprian during the long vacancy prior to the election of Pope St. Cornelius I, letters 30 [31] and 31 [36] in the Cyprianic corpus, were written by Novatian in the name of his confreres; for Cyprian, in his own letter 55 [52] refers to the first of these and states that it was written by Novatian; and the content and style of the second prove that it too is Novatian's work.

No doubt Novatian hoped to be made Bishop of Rome. At any rate, when Cornelius was elected in March of the year 251 A. D., and showed some attitudes of leniency in regard to the lapsed, Novatian suddenly reversed his own lenient views and became a rigorist. According to Eusebius (*Hist. eccl.* 6, 43, 9), he found three guileless bishops in a remote part of Italy, whom he plied with wine until they were no longer in their right senses, and then succeeded in having them consecrate him bishop. From that time until his death in 258 A. D., he is reckoned as an anti-pope. The sect of Novatianists which he founded spread with some success to Spain and to Syria. In the latter place it lasted for several centuries.

The Novatianist schism is characterized not by doctrinal differences but by insistence upon rigorist practices. They forbade entirely second marriages, and refused absolutely any reconciliation to those who lapsed from the faith.

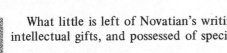

What little is left of Novatian's writings prove him to have been a man of great intellectual gifts, and possessed of special literary talents.

THE TRINITY [*ca. A. D.* 235]

Novatian's treatise on *The Trinity* was written well in advance of his creating a schism, and may be assigned to about the year 235 A. D., if we bear in mind that this is only a very rough approximation. It is the first great Latin contribution to theology to stem from Rome itself. In his development of Trinitarian theology, as evidenced in the present treatise, he was at least a hundred years ahead of his contemporaries. At the same time, however, he did not succeed in shaking off the Subordinationism which he inherited from Justin, Theophilus, Irenaeus, Hippolytus and Tertullian. In fact, in some respects, his Subordinationism is even more deep-seated than theirs; and in his fear of ditheism he makes of the Logos a kind of temporary manifestation of the Father, into whom finally He will return again.

The text of the treatise owes its preservation to the fact of its having been included in certain manuscripts of Tertullian's works. Unfortunately the pertinent manuscripts have perished in more recent times, and the treatise is still extant only because of its early printed editions: Paris, 1545; Basle, 1550; and Antwerp, 1579. Migne's text, PL 3, 885-952, is no longer much used, the standard edition being that of W. Y. Fausset in the series *Cambridge Patristic Texts*, under the title *Novatiani Romanae urbis presbyteri De Trinitate liber*, Cambridge 1909.

603

[2]

Whatever you would state in regard to [God], you would really only be shedding some   173
light upon some condition or power of His, and not upon Himself. What could you   175
fittingly either say or think of Him who is greater than all words and thoughts? But there is one way in which we can attain to a mental grasp of what God is. And how can we do this? How shall we grasp, how shall we understand? We must think of Him as being that which cannot be understood either in quality or in quantity, and of which we cannot possibly conceive.

604

[10]

Neither, then, do we acknowledge as our Christ the Christ of the heretics, who, as it   310
is said, was but an appearance and not a reality; for He had done nothing real among all the actions He performed, if He was Himself a phantasm and not a reality. Nor do we acknowledge one who had nothing of our flesh in Himself, since He received nothing of   313
Mary; nor one who did not come to us, since He appeared as a vision and not in our substance; nor one who put on flesh which was either ethereal or starry, as other heretics would have it. We could perceive no salvation for us in Him, if we could not recognize in Him even the solidity of our flesh.

605

[11]

We do not treat of the substance of [Christ's] body in such a way as to say that He   322
was only and solely a man; rather, we hold that by the association of the divinity of the Word in that very corporality, He was, in accord with the Scriptures, also God.

607

[29]

It is [the Holy Spirit] that effects with water a second birth. He is a kind of seed   800
of divine generation and the consecrator of heavenly birth, the pledge of a promised   752
inheritance (1), and, as it were, a kind of surety bond of eternal salvation. It is He that 753
can make of us a temple of God (2), and can complete us as His house; He that can   756
accost the divine ears for us with unutterable groaning (3), fulfilling the duties of
advocate and performing the functions of defense; He, that is an inhabitant given to
our bodies, and a worker of holiness.

608

[31]

God the Father, founder and creator of all things, who alone knows no beginning,   460
who is invisible, immeasurable, immortal, and eternal, is one God. Neither His greatness   250
nor His majesty nor His power can possibly be — I should not say exceeded, for they   154
cannot even be equalled. From Him, when He willed it, the Word was born, His Son.   156
. . . And the latter, since He was born of the Father, is always in the Father. And I do   157
indeed say *always*, not to prove Him unborn, but born. He that exists before all time   252
must be said to have been in the Father always; for He that exists before all time   255
cannot be spoken of in relation to time. And always must He be in the Father, other-   256
wise the Father were not always the Father. And yet the Father even precedes Him,   259
because it is necessary for the Father to be prior, in order to be the Father.

It is necessary for Him who knows no origin to be antecedant to Him who has an
origin. . . . He, then, when the Father willed it, proceeded from the Father. And He
that was in the Father because He was from the Father, was afterwards with the Father
because He proceeded from the Father — that divine substance, I mean, whose name is   257
Word, and through whom all things were made, and without whom was made nothing.   260
For all things are after Him, because they are made through Him; and properly He is   284
before all things but after the Father, since all things were made through Him, while
He proceeded from Him of whose will all things were made: assuredly, He is God
proceeding from God, causing, as Son, a second Person after the Father, but not taking   230
away from the Father the fact that God is one.

1. Eph. 1:14.
2. 1 Cor. 3:17.
3. Rom. 8:26.

ST. DIONYSIUS, POPE [*regn. A. D.* 260-268]

Pope St. Dionysius is known to have written three letters: one of consolation to the
Church of Caesarea in Cappadocia; and two others, to St. Dionysius the Great, Bishop
of Alexandria. The letter to Caesarea and the second of the two letters to Dionysius
the Great have perished entirely.

Dionysius of Alexandria, in attempting to combat Modalism, had insisted so strongly
on the distinction of Persons of Father and Son that his enemies found occasion to

denounce him to Rome as a subordinationist. Dionysius of Rome then dispatched his two letters to Dionysius of Alexandria, the first defending Trinitarian doctrine against Modalism and Subordinationism; and the second, demanding of Dionysius of Alexandria an explanation of his tenets.

Both letters to Dionysius belong to the year 262 A. D. As stated above, the second of these two letters has perished entirely. All that is extant of the letters of Dionysius of Rome is a fairly lengthy passage from the first letter to his namesake of Alexandria, preserved as a citation in chapter 26 of Athanasius' letter on *The Decrees of the Council of Nicaea.*

The text of the fragment may be found in the proper place in Athanasius, whose writings, however, are badly in need of a new critical edition; or in Migne, PL 5, 109-116; or better, in M. J. Routh, *Reliquiae sacrae,* 5 volumes, 2nd edition, Oxford, 1846 ff.: Vol. 3, pp. 369-403.

LETTER OF DIONYSIUS OF ROME TO DIONYSIUS OF ALEXANDRIA. A. D. 262.

608a

[1]

Next, then, I may properly turn to those who divide and cut apart and destroy the   157
Monarchy, the most sacred proclamation of the Church of God, making of it, as it were, three powers, distinct substances, and three godheads. I have heard that some of your catechists and teachers of the divine word take the lead in this tenet. They are, so to speak, diametrically opposed to the opinion of Sabellius. For he, in his blasphemy, says   293
that the Son is the Father, and vice versa. But they proclaim that there are in some way three Gods, when they divide the Sacred Unity into three substances foreign to each other and completely separate.

It is necessary, however, that the Divine Word be united with the God of the Universe; and the Holy Spirit must abide and dwell in God. Therefore the Divine Trinity must be   230
gathered up and brought together in One, a Summit, as it were — I mean, the omnipotent God of the Universe. . . . [2] Nor are they less to be blamed who hold that the Son is a work, and think that the Lord was made, as if He were one of those things which were   292
truly made. The divine statements bear witness to a generation suitable and becoming to Him, but not to any fashioning or making.

It is a blasphemy, then, and not a common one but the worst, to say that the Lord is in any way a handiwork. For if He came to be Son, then once He was not; but if, as He says Himself, He be in the Father, and if, which you know the Divine Scripture says, Christ be Word and Wisdom and Power, and these attributes be powers of God, then He always existed. But if the Son came into being, there was a time when these attributes did not exist; and, consequently, there was a time when God was without them — which is utterly absurd. . . . [3] Neither, then, may we divide into three godheads the wonderful and divine Unity; nor may we disparage the dignity and exceeding majesty of the Lord by calling Him a work. Rather, we must believe in God, the Father almighty; and in Christ Jesus, His Son; and in the Holy Spirit; and that the Word is united to the God of the Universe. "For," says He, "the Father and I are one (1);" and "I am in the Father, and the Father in me (2)." Thus both the Divine Trinity and the sacred proclamation of the Monarchy will be preserved.

1. John 10:30.
2. John 14:10.

ST. DIONYSIUS THE GREAT OF ALEXANDRIA [*fl. A. D.* 248-265]

Dionysius, the son of wealthy pagan parents, was one of Origen's most remarkable pupils. In 231 A. D. he succeeded Heraclas as head of the catechetical school in Alexandria; and in 248 A. D., he succeeded him again, as Bishop of Alexandria, remaining such until his death in 265 A. D.

Of Dionysius' very extensive writings, only two letters survive in their entirety. Of all his other various works, only fragments remain, preserved mostly by Eusebius, both in his *History of the Church* and in his *Preparation for the Gospel;* and by Athanasius, who wrote a treatise on *The Opinion of Dionysius,* wherein, as might be expected, he quotes him extensively.

REFUTATION AND DEFENSE [*A. D.* 262]

In treating of Pope St. Dionysius (pp. 248-249, above), we had occasion to mention certain accusations of subordinationism made against Dionysius of Alexandria, and letters written to him from Rome in 262 A. D. requiring an explanation of his faith.

Dionysius the Great's reply was a treatise in four books, entitled *Refutation and Defense,* in which he vindicates his orthodoxy. Only a few fragments of the work are extant, in books 7 and 9 of Eusebius' *Preparation for the Gospel,* and in various chapters of Athanasius' *The Opinion of Dionysius.*

The standard source, as for all the remains of Dionysius, is C. L. Feltoe's *The Letters and Other Remains of Dionysius of Alexandria,* in the series *Cambridge Patristic Texts,* Cambridge 1904.

609

[From Bk. 1: *Apud Athan. De sent. Dion.* 15]

There never was a time when God was not the Father. . . . [The Son], being the   256
brightness of Light eternal, is certainly Himself eternal; for as the Light exists always, it is clear that the Brightness likewise exists always. It is by the fact of its shining that the existence of light is perceived, and there cannot be light which does not illuminate. . . . Since, therefore, the Father is eternal, the Son, being Light of Light, is eternal. If there is a parent, there is also a child. But if there were not a child, how and of whom could there be a parent? But both do exist, and they do exist eternally.

610

[From Bk. 1: *Apud Athan. De sent. Dion.* 23]

A word is an effluence from intelligence, and to speak as men do, the intelligence that   265
issues forth by means of the tongue is derived from the heart and passes through the mouth; and it is different from the word which exists in the heart. For after sending the other forth, the latter remains as it was. But the other, which was sent forth, flies off and is carried about in every direction. And thus each is in the other, and each is distinct from the other. They are one, and each is distinct from the other. They are one, and at the same time they are two. Likewise, the Father and the Son were said (1) to be one, and in each other.

---

1. The use of the past tense will be understandable if we but recall the occasion of the four books of *Refutation and Defense:* Dionysius the Great had been called upon by Dionysius of Rome to explain certain remarks of his preaching, which had been reported to Rome as heretical. The import of the final sentence in the present passage, then, is: "It was in *this* frame of reference that I said the Father and the Son are one, and in each other."

ST. GREGORY THE MIRACLE-WORKER [*ca. A. D.* 213 − *A. D.* 270/275]

St. Gregory the Miracle-Worker, or, if you will, the Wonder-Worker or Thaumaturge, was born of wealthy pagan parents at Neocaesarea in the Pontus, about the year 213 A. D. He was called Theodore, and took the name Gregory when he was baptized.

Together with his brother Athenodore, Gregory went to Caesarea in Palestine in 233 A. D. to live with his sister, whose husband was imperial governor of Palestine. Remaining there for five years, he attended Origen's lectures, and was converted to the faith. A few years later he was consecrated the first bishop of his own native city, Neocaesarea. He died there sometime between the years 270 and 275 A. D. The legends which grew up around him account for his title of Thaumaturge; and the great Cappadocian Fathers of the 4th century, Basil and the two Gregory's, venerated him as the founder of the Church in Cappadocia.

Gregory's writings are not particularly extensive, but a fair corpus of Gregorian materials has survived. A new and more critical edition is urgently needed.

THE CREED [*inter A. D.* 260/270]

Sometime in the years between 260 and 270 A. D. Gregory had occasion to compose a short creed, restricting it to an exposition of the Trinity. The text of it in the original Greek was incorporated into the biography of the Thaumaturge written by St. Gregory of Nyssa; and it is to be found also in a large number of manuscripts apart from the biography. Extant also is a Syriac translation; and two independent translations in Latin, one of them by Rufinus.

The text in Greek is given by Migne, PG 10, 983-988; but a much better source, where the Greek, Syriac, and both Latin versions are to be found, is C. P. Caspari, *Alte und neue Quellen zur Geschichte des Taufsymbols und der Glaubensregel*, Christiania 1879, pp. 1-34.

611

One God, the Father of the living Word, of subsistent Wisdom and Power, and of the Eternal image. Perfect Begetter of the Perfect, Father of the only-begotten Son. One Lord, Only of Only, God of God, Image and Likeness of the Godhead, Efficient Word, Wisdom comprehending the constitution of the universe, and Power shaping all creation. Genuine Son of of genuine Father, Invisible of Invisible, and Incorruptible of Incorruptible, and Immortal of Immortal, and Eternal of Eternal.   230 256 264 272

And one Holy Spirit, having substance from God, and who is manifested − to men, that is (1) − through the Son; Image of the Son, Perfect of the Perfect; Life, the Cause of living; Holy Fountain; Sanctity, the Dispenser of Sanctification; in whom is manifested God the Father who is above all and in all, and God the Son who is through all. Perfect Trinity, in glory and eternity and sovereignty neither divided nor estranged.   268 271 277 285 237

Wherefore there is nothing either created or subservient in the Trinity, nor anything caused to be brought about, as if formerly it did not exist and was afterwards introduced. Wherefore neither was the Son ever lacking to the Father, nor the Spirit to the Son; but without variation and without change, the same Trinity forever.

1. This phrase is suspected of being a gloss.

CANONICAL LETTER [*inter A. D.* 254/258]

The *Canonical Letter* is so-called because of its inclusion in the corpus of canonical epistles of the Eastern Church. It appears to have been addressed to a now unknown bishop who had consulted Gregory about various doubts and difficulties occasioned by the incursions of the Boradi and Goths into the Pontus and Bithynia.

The authenticity of the 11th canon, cited below, is disputed, chiefly on the grounds of its being an unnecessary addition somewhat in the manner of an explanation of the authentic canons 7, 8 and 9 of the same letter; and partly also on grounds of the manuscript evidence. That it seems out of place is undeniable; but since we have not the letter which called forth the present letter of Gregory in reply, such argumentation is vain. I am rather of the impression that the passage is very much in the clipped style of Gregory. The question requires further investigation. But whatever the authority of the present passage, this 11th canon does seem to fairly represent the practice less precisely described in canons 7, 8 and 9, of undisputed authenticity.

The text of the *Canonical Letter* may be found in Migne, PG 10, 1018-1048; or better, in Routh's *Reliquiae sacrae,* 2nd edition, Vol. 3, pp. 251-283.

611a

[Canon 11]

Weeping is done outside the gate of the oratory; and the sinner standing there ought to 904 implore the faithful as they enter, to pray for him. Hearing is in the narthex inside the gate, where the sinner ought to stand while the catechumens are there, and afterwards he should depart. "For let him hear the Scriptures and the teaching," it says, "and then be cast out and not be reckoned as worthy of prayer (1)." Submission allows one to stand within the gate of the temple; but he must go out with the catechumens. Assembly allows one to be associated with the faithful, without the necessity of going out with the catechumens. Last of all is participation in the consecrated elements (2).

1. *I.e.,* not unfit to be prayed for, but unworthy to be present and to join in the prayer. The line is given in the manner of a quotation. The rather indefinite φησὶ may perhaps refer to an older canon.
2. The canon is generally referred to as enumerating four classes of penitents. The scholion of Theodore Balsamon, however, specifically notes that it enumerates five such classes. Obviously Balsamon has reckoned even the last, admission to the reception of the Eucharist, as a stage in the penitential discipline rather than as the cessation thereof. The terms employed for the five ways are as follows:
ἡ πρόσκλαυσις = weeping; ἡ ἀκρόασις = hearing; ἡ ὑπόπτωσις = submission; ἡ σύστασις = assembly; and ἡ μέθεξις = participation.

THE COUNCIL OF ELVIRA [*ca. A. D.* 300]

The city of Elvira or Illiberris was at or near the site of the present city of Granada in Spain. Nineteen bishops, including the celebrated Ossius of Cordova, were present, along with twenty-six priests and deacons.

The council was of a reform nature. A large part of its eighty-one canons reflect earlier legislation of African origin. Numerous dates have been assigned as that of the council, the extremes being 250 A. D., proposed by the Oratorian J. Morin in 1651; and 700 A. D., proposed by the Centuriators of Magdeburg, Flacius Illyricus. Neither of these dates can be taken seriously today. The other dates which have been proposed at various times present no grand discrepancy among themselves: 300, 306, 306/313, 313, 314/325 A. D. Opinion today is divided over two possibilities only: ca. 300 A. D. and 306 A. D. The question has been closely studied by V. C. de Clercq *(Ossius of Cordova,* Washington 1954, pp. 87-103); and he concludes with great probability to a date between 295 and 303 A. D., *i.e., ca.* 300 A. D.

The text of the canons may be found in Mansi, Vol. 2, Col. 5-19. A better source, however, where commentary is given along with the texts, and the latter in a more trustworthy edition, is Hefele-Leclercq, *Histoire des Conciles,* I, 1, Paris 1907, pp. 221-264.

CANONS [*ca. A. D.* 300]

611b

[Canon 8]

Likewise, women who have left their husbands for no prior cause and have joined themselves with others, may not even at death receive communion (1).   974

611c

[Canon 9]

Likewise, a woman of the faith who has left an adulterous husband of the faith, and marries another: her so marrying is prohibited. If she has so married, she may not any more receive communion, — unless he that she has left has since departed from this world, — except if perchance the necessity of illness urge that it be given.   975

611d

[Canon 10]

If she whom a catechumen has left shall have married a husband, she is able to be admitted to the fountain of Baptism. This shall also be observed in the instance where it is the woman who is a catechumen. But if a woman of the faithful is taken in marriage by a man who left an innocent wife, and if she knew that he had a wife whom he had left without cause, it is determined that communion is not to be given to her even at death.   976

974

611e

[Canon 12]

A mother, or a parent, or anyone at all of the faithful, if she has plied the trade of a panderer, so that she sold the body of another, — or rather, her own! — it is determined that such as these are not to receive communion even at death.   900

611f

[Canon 13]

Virgins, who have dedicated themselves to God, if they have lapsed from their covenant (2) of virginity and have been enslaved to the same libidinous pleasure: if they do not understand what they have perpetrated (3), it is determined that communion is not to be given to them even at death. But if they are once for all persuaded (4), or if their having been tainted was a lapse caused by the weakness of the flesh, let such women as these do penance all the rest of their lives, keeping themselves away from carnal intercourse, because they would rather be regarded as lapsed (5): it is determined that they may receive communion at death.

900

611g

[Canon 15]

Christian virgins are never, on the pretext of an abundance of daughters, to be given in marriage to pagans, lest a girl just coming into the bloom of youth be destroyed in an adulterous union.

980

611h

[Canon 16]

Heretics, if they do not wish to come over to the Catholic Church, are not to be given Catholic girls in marriage. It is determined that they are to be given neither to Jews nor to heretics, because there can be no companionship between faithful and infidel. If parents disregard this prohibition, it is decided that they are to be excommunicate for five years (6).

980

611i

[Canon 17]

If it should happen that anyone marry his daughters to priests of the idols, it is determined that he is not to be given communion even at death.

980
900

611j

[Canon 18 (al. 19)]

Bishops, presbyters, and deacons may not leave their own places for the sake of commerce, nor are they to be travelling about the provinces, frequenting the markets for their own profit. Certainly for the procuring of their own necessities they can send a boy or a freedman or a hireling or a friend or whomever: but if they wish to engage in business, let them do so within the province.

952

611k

[Canon 19 (al. 18)]

If bishops, presbyters, and deacons, though they be engaged in the ministry, are disclosed as adulterers, it is determined, both in view of the scandal and in view of their wicked crime, that they may not receive communion even at death.

952
902

611l

[Canon 20]

If it is discovered that any of the clergy accepts interest on the loan of money (7),

it is determined that he is to be degraded and that fasting is to be imposed upon him. If   904
it is proved that someone, even a layman (8), has accepted interest; and, already reformed,
he promises that he will cease and will not exact interest any more, it is determined that
he be shown mercy. But if he persists in his wickedness, he is to be ejected from the
Church.

611m

[Canon 21]

    If someone living in a city does not come to Church for three Sundays, fasting is to be   904
imposed on him for a short time, until he is seen to have reformed.

611n

[Canon 22]

    If someone leaves the Catholic Church and goes over to a heresy, and then returns again,
it is determined that penance is not to be denied to such a one, since he has acknowledged   911
his sin. Let him do penance, then, for ten years, and after ten years he may come forward
to communion. If, indeed, there were children who were led astray, since they have not
sinned of their own fault, they may be received without delay.   637

611o

[Canon 24]

    It is determined that all those who were baptized abroad, since the course of their life   899
is utterly unknown, are not to be promoted to the clerical estate in provinces where they
are strangers (9).

611p

[Canon 27]

    A bishop, or any other cleric, may have with him only a sister or a virgin daughter   899
dedicated to God. It is determined that he may by no means have a stranger.

611q

[Canon 30]

    Those who have fornicated (10) in their youth may not be ordained subdeacons, because   902
they might afterwards through subterfuge be promoted to a higher order. If they have
already been ordained at some former time, they are to be removed.

611r

[Canon 31]

    It is determined that youths who have fornicated after having been baptized may, when   907
they have done legitimate penance and when they have been married, be admitted to
communion.

611s

[Canon 32]

    It is determined that if someone, by a grave lapse, falls into the ruin of death (11),   633
he may not do penance in the presence of a presbyter, but rather, in the presence of a   906

bishop. However, if constrained by illness, it is necessary, a presbyter may give him communion, — or even a deacon, if the priest (12) command him.   926

611t

[Canon 33]

It is determined that bishops, presbyters, and deacons, or all clerics stationed in the   964
ministry, are to restrain themselves completely and are to keep themselves away from their wives and are not to beget children. Anyone who does beget children is to be expelled from the honor of the clerical estate (13).

611u

[Canon 38]

During a voyage at sea in a foreign place, or when there is no church in the neighbor-   829
hood, one of the faithful who has kept his Baptism unimpaired (14) and who is not   979
twice-married (15) is able to baptize a catechumen, when there is necessity occasioned by illness, provided that, if such a one survives, he bring him to the bishop, so that it may be completed through the imposition of his hand.

611v

[Canon 39]

Pagans, if they have asked when ill to have the hand imposed upon them: — if it be a   792
question of some of those among them whose lives are honorable, it is determined that the hand may be imposed upon them, and they may become Christians.

611w

[Canon 44]

A woman who was formerly a prostitute, and afterwards has married a husband, if   637
she then comes to a state of belief, it is determined to receive her without delay (16).

611x

[Canon 45]

If a man was formerly a catechumen and for a long time has not come to Church, if   637
someone of the clergy know him as a Christian, or if witnesses from among the faithful speak out for him, it is determined that Baptism is not to be denied him, because he is seen to have put aside the old man.

611y

[Canon 48]

It is determined that the custom is to be abrogated by which those who are being baptized drop coins in the shell (17), lest the priest seem to be distributing for a price what he has received gratis. Nor are their feet to be washed by the priests or clerics (18).   809

611z

[Canon 50]

If, indeed, someone of the clergy or faithful has taken a meal with Jews, it is determined   899
that as a corrective punishment he is to abstain from communion (19).

611aa

[Canon 51]

   He that is converted to the faith from any heresy is never to be promoted to the   951
clerical estate; and if such were ordained in times past, undoubtedly they are to be
deposed.

611bb

[Canon 63]

   If a woman, in the absence of her husband, has conceived in adultery, and has killed   902
that which came of her deed, it is determined that she is not to be given communion
even at death: because she has made twins of her wickedness (20).

611cc

[Canon 68]

   A catechumen, if she has strangled what she conceived in adultery, it is determined that   902
she may be baptized at death.   637

611dd

[Canon 71]

   To defilers of boys communion is not to be given even at death.   902

611ee

[Canon 77]

   If a deacon, ruling a people without a bishop or presbyter, has baptized some of them,
the bishop must bring them to the perfection of it through his blessing. But if they   843
depart from this world beforehand: − by reason of the faith in which he believed, he is   845
able to be justified (21).

1. *nec in finem accipiant communionem.* One might be inclined to interpret this in the sense of *usque ad finem:* − they are not to receive communion until they are dying − especially in view of the fact that Elvira's Latin is anything but Ciceronian. However, it is clear from other canons of this same council that this frequent phrase means precisely what it appears to mean: they are not to receive communion even at death. The best proof of this is Cn. 13, wherein it is decreed that a certain category of sinner may receive communion at death: *eas in finem communionem accipere debere.* If it were allowed that *nec in finem* in Elvira's language means *not until death,* then the provision of Cn. 13 would have to mean that communion could be given only until the sinner was dying, which is clearly nonsense.
2. *pactum.*
3. *non intelligentes quid admiserint.* I.e., not perceiving the gravity of their crime, and, therefore, being unwilling to do penance. The reading *non intelligentes quod amiserint − not understanding what they have lost −* merely approaches the same idea from a different path.
4. *I.e.,* persuaded of the gravity of their fault, so that they are disposed to do penance.
5. *eo quod lapsae potius videantur. Lapsae* is a technical term. A *lapsus* is a particular kind of sinner, one who had lapsed from the faith under the pressure of the persecutions. The import of the canon, then, is this: that a virgin who falls from her vow, if she does not afterwards repent herself, may not even at death receive communion. But if she will repent herself, and is willing to spend the rest of her life in penance, content to be regarded as no better than the *lapsi,* she may expect to be granted the reception of communion when dying.
6. It is clear that *abstineri* does not mean that they are to fast for five years, but they are to abstain from receiving Communion, that is, they are to be excommunicate. The term is known in this sense fifty years earlier, to Cyprian of Carthage, who uses it in his letter no. 4 [62], 4, § 568 above. That it is a technical term, that it means not simply to abstain, but to abstain from receiving Communion, which is to be excommunicate when such abstinence is enforced, is clear also from Canon 79 of the present Council: *Si quis fidelis aleam, id est tabulam, luserit nummis, placuit eum abstineri; et si emendatus cessaverit, post annum communioni reconciliari. − If someone of the faithful has played with dice, that is, at the gaming-board, for money, it is determined that he is to be excommunicate; and if, having reformed, he*

has ceased, after a year he is able to be reconciled to Communion.

7. *usuras accipere.*
8. The inclusion of the laity under the prohibition of taking interest on loans of money is of very dubious authenticity. The 17th canon of the First Council of Nicaea will forbid it only to the clergy. Except for the dubious remark of the present canon, no such condemnation in regard to the laity can be found earlier than the 5th century, when Pope St. Leo I (*Epist.* 4, 3) will declare the practice reprehensible not only for clerics but even for the laity.
9. *in alienis provinciis:* literally, *in foreign provinces.*
10. *fuerint moechati.* This is the same term as that which in C. 19 [18] we translated as *adulterers.* The Latin term is more generic than the English, embracing as it does both fornication and adultery.
11. *ruinam mortis,* that is, grave or mortal sin.
12. Though the present canon uses both the term *presbyter* and *sacerdos,* they appear here to be entirely synonymous. *N. B.* Another version of the present canon determines that to such a sinner as is described therein, neither presbyter nor deacon may give communion, except at the command of the bishop.
13. This is the celebrated canon of Elvira imposing celibacy. The above translation is something less than literal, for the reason that the canon is so badly construed grammatically and rhetorically that a literal translation becomes hopelessly confused, and actually states precisely the opposite of what is the manifest intention of the Fathers of Elvira. The text of the canon reads: *Placuit in totum prohibere episcopis, presbyteris et diaconibus vel omnibus clericis positis in ministerio abstinere se a coniugibus suis et non generare filios: quicumque vero fecerit, ab honore clericatus exterminetur.*
14. *qui lavacrum suum integrum habet:* that is, one who has maintained his baptismal innocence.
15. This is one of the indications that the canons of Elvira actually reflect much earlier legislation, particularly of Africa. Ninety years before Elvira, Tertullian had argued that a layman ought not be twice-married, because he must hold himself ready, in necessity, to baptize. (See above, § 366). The letter of the Council of Carthage of the year 256 A. D. to the clergy and laity of Spain, is indicative of a close relationship between the Spanish and African Churches, and it is apparently a relationship in which Spain is in someway dependent upon Africa, at least in the view of Cyprian, the "African Pope." (See above, § 588). The 2nd Canon of the First Council of Constantinople (381 A. D.) gives recognition to "the custom observed since the times of the Fathers," by which Churches among the barbarians remain juridically subject to the bishop of the place from which missionaries had first come among them. But Cyprian could hardly have laid claim to Spain on this score, since it was already commonly believed that St. Paul had gone to Spain.
16. As a catechumen, of course: she is to be treated no better nor yet any worse than any other pagan seeking to become a Christian. The point of the canon is simply that no special time of penance is to be imposed upon her because of what she was when she was a pagan. There may possibly be in this some recognition of the fact that ignorance can be a mitigating factor in regard to guilt; but certainly it must be taken primarily as a recognition of the remissive effects of the Baptism which will make her a Christian.
17. *I. e.,* the baptismal shell, from which the water was poured.
18. Another reading has *sed* in place of *vel:* nor are their feet to be washed by the priests, *but* by the clerics.
19. *placuit eum a communione abstinere, ut debeat emendari:* literally, *it is determined he is to abstain from communion, so that he may be reformed.* Some of Elvira's Latin constructions are at least odd, and it is impossible to day how *ut* should have the notion of *until;* but no more can it be denied that the idea is here: he is to be denied communion *until* he shows signs of having reformed; *i.e.,* he is to be excommunicated temporarily, as a corrective punishment.
20. We can no more deny that the pun is a cruel one, than we can deny that it is present in the Latin: *eo quod geminaverit scelus.*
21. The awkward change from plural to singular is quite ungrammatical: but so the Latin has it.

ST. PETER OF ALEXANDRIA [† *ca. A. D.* 311]

It is generally assumed that Peter, although he was an anti-Origenist, was head of the catechetical school in Alexandria prior to his being made bishop of that see about the year 300 A. D. After being bishop of Alexandria for about eleven years he died a martyr's death.

Except for a very short letter to the clergy of Alexandria in reference to Meletius of Lycopolis, who had usurped the see of Alexandria when Peter withdrew from the city during the persecution, and who had thereby instigated the so-called Meletian schism, which persisted for several centuries, his writings are extant only in fragments.

PENANCE *or the* CANONICAL LETTER [*A. D.* 306]

Of Peter's tract on *Penance,* written in the year 306 A. D., only fragments are extant, preserved as fourteen canons, embodied in the law collection of the Eastern Church. The fourteen canons are usually referred to, with something less than historical accuracy, as a *Canonical Letter.* A fifteenth canon found in many of the Greek manuscripts is from the same author's treatise on *The Paschal Feast.* For the text of these canons, one may consult Migne, PG 18, 467-508, or better, Cardinal Pitra's *Iuris ecclesiastici Graecorum historia et monumenta,* Vol. 1, Rome 1864, pp. 551-561.

611gg

[Canon 9]
Peter, the first chosen of the Apostles, having been apprehended often and thrown   431
into prison and treated with ignominy, at last was crucified in Rome. And the reknowned Paul, oftentimes having been delivered up and put in peril of death, having endured many evils, and boasting of his numerous persecutions and afflictions, was even himself put to the sword and beheaded in the same city.

THE SOUL [*ante A. D.* 311]

Peter's treatise on *The Soul* cannot be dated except as before the year 311 A. D., the probable year of his death. Only three fragments of the work are preserved, two of them in the treatise *Against the Monophysites,* by Leontius of Byzantium. Leontius cites the passages as being from Book 1 of Peter's work against the Origenist doctrine of the pre-existence of the soul; so we may presume that the work is of at least two books. The title given the work, *The Soul,* is a mere conjecture, a title given the work by common agreement. A third fragment, apparently from the same work, is extant in Syriac. For the texts of the Greek fragments, see J. B. Card. Pitra, *Analecta sacra,* Vol. 4, pp. 193 and 429.

611hh

[Frag. 1]
God said, "Let us make man according to our image and according to our likeness (1)."   507
It is clear from this that man was not formed by the conjunction of the body with some pre-existing type. For if the earth, at a command, brought forth the other animals

endowed with life, how much more certain it is that the dust which God took from the
earth received vital energy from the will and operation of God.   509

1. Gen. 1:26.

ST. METHODIUS OF PHILIPPI [† *ca. A. D.* 311]

Methodius, Bishop of Philippi, was an ardent opponent of Origenism, and a key
figure in the first period of the Origenist controversies, around the year 300 A. D.
Eusebius says nothing of him; consequently, but little is known of him. He is to be
identified with Methodius of Olympus, Methodius of Tyre, and Methodius of Patara;
and he died as a martyr, about the year 311 A. D., probably at Chalcis in Euboea.
Very little remains of his rather extensive writings.

THE BANQUET OF THE TEN VIRGINS *or* ON CHASTITY [*ante A. D.* 300]

Methodius' treatise entitled *The Banquet of the Ten Virgins,* known also as *On
Chastity,* is to be dated before the year 300 A. D., for in it he seems to be still
rather enamored of Origen, whereas after the year 300 he was one of Origen's most
ardent opponents. It is the only one of Methodius' works of which the complete
text has survived in the original Greek. Migne's text, PG 18, 27-220, is entirely
superseded by the critical edition of G. N. Bonwetsch in the Berlin Corpus (GCS),
Vol. 27, Leipzig 1917, pp. 1-141.

611ii

[3, 5]

When Adam, so to speak, had been formed out of clay, and when he was still soft and
moist, not yet hard and incorruptible like a tile, sin ruined him by flowing and dropping
down upon him like water. God therefore moistened him anew and shaped the same clay   311
afresh into an honorable vessel. Having first hardened and solidified it in the virginal
womb, and having united and mingled it with the Word, He brought it forth into life, no   344
longer soft and broken.

612

[3, 6]

Man too was created without corruption. . . . But when it came about that he   611
transgressed the commandment, he suffered a terrible and destructive fall and was reduced   520
to a state of death. The Lord says that it was on this account that He Himself came down
from heaven to the world (1), taking leave of the ranks and armies of the angels. . . . It   488

was to this end that the Word put on humanity: that He might overcome the serpent,
and that He might Himself put down the condemnation which had first come into being   376
when man was ruined. For it was fitting that the evil one should be conquered not by
another, but by that one whom he had deceived, and whom he was boasting that he held
in subjection. In no other way could sin and condemnation be destroyed, except by that   363
same man's being created anew, — he of whom it was said: "Earth you are, and unto
earth you shall return (2)," — and by his undoing the sentence which, because of him,
had been pronounced upon all. Thus, just as in Adam all did formerly die, so again in   614
Christ, who put on Adam, all are made to live (3).

613

[8, 8]
 The illuminated (4) take on the features and the image and the manliness of Christ.   836
The likeness of the form of the Word is stamped upon them; and it is produced in them   754
through sure knowledge and faith. Thus, Christ is born spiritually in each one. It is for
this reason that the Church swells and travails in birth until Christ is formed in us (5), as
if it were that each of the saints, by partaking of Christ, were born a Christ. It is in this
sense that it is said somewhere in Scripture, "Touch not my christs, and work no wickedness on my prophets (6):" those who are baptized in Christ become, as it were, other
Christs, through a communication of the Spirit.

1. εἰς τὸν βίον.
2. Gen. 3:19.
3. 1 Cor. 15:22.
4. οἱ φωτιζόμενοι: *i. e.,* those who have been baptized. See § 407 above.
5. See Gal. 4:19.
6. Ps. 104 [105]:15. *My christs* ought, of course, be rendered in English *my anointed ones.*

ARNOBIUS OF SICCA [† *ca. A. D.* 327]

 Arnobius of Sicca, known also as Arnobius the Elder, was born a pagan and was
for many years a vigorous opponent of Christianity. Finally warned in his dreams,
he was converted to the faith. As a teacher of rhetoric at Sicca in Africa, he numbered Lactantius among his pupils.

AGAINST THE PAGANS [*ca. A. D.* 305]

 According to Jerome's account the bishop of Arnobius' locale was quite skeptical
of the veracity of the latter's conversion; and when Arnobius sought Baptism, the
bishop demanded proof of sincerity. It was in order to offer such proof that

Arnobius wrote, in seven books which apparently constitute his sole literary endeavor, the treatise *Against the Pagans*. Presented as a defense of Christianity against the numerous false charges of its adversaries, and written about the year 305 A. D., the work has little to recommend it. It was written hastily by a man who had very little understanding of Christianity; yet, it does have a certain value of its own: it is a precious source of information on the pagan cults of Arnobius' time.

The Migne text, PL 5, 718-1288, is superseded by the critical edition of A. Reifferscheid in the Vienna Corpus (CSEL), Vol. 4, Vienna 1875.

617

[1, 42]

"You worship one born a man." Even were that true, still, as has been pointed out   301
in passages above, on account of so many and such liberal gifts which have been
bestowed on us by Him, He ought to be called and addressed as God. But since it is
indeed a certitude and beyond the shadow of any earnest doubt that He is God, do you
think that we are about to deny that He is worshipped by us in the highest degree, and
that we call Him the Protector of our body? "Well, then," some raging, angry and
excited man will say, "is that Christ your God?" "God indeed," we shall answer, "and
God of the hidden powers (1)."

618

[1, 43]

Are you able to point out to us or to show us among all those magicians who ever   82
existed through the ages, anyone who did anything similar, even in the thousandth part, to
what Christ did?

619

[1, 54]

But you do not believe these things (2)? Yet, those who beheld them as they took   82
place, and who saw them done before their very eyes, the best witnesses and the surest   63
authorities, both believed them themselves and handed them down to us, their descendants,
with no scanty measure of confirmation, for our belief. "And who might these be?"
perhaps you will ask. Tribes, peoples, nations — indeed, that incredulous human race,
which, if the matter is obvious and, as the saying goes, as plain as the day itself, would
never grant the assent of its belief to events of such a kind. But shall we say that the
men of that time were fools, liars, sluggards and brutes to such a degree that they pretended to have seen what they never saw? that they published with false testimony or
affirmed with childish assertions things which never happened at all? and that when they
could have lived in harmony with you and could have established pleasant relationships,
they went out of their way to incur hatred and to be held in contempt?

621

[2, 5]

What do you say, you ignorant ones, you that are most deserving of tears and pity?
Are you not very much afraid that these things which are so despised by you and which
provide you with material for jesting might afterall be true? And do you not consider at
least within yourselves and among your secret thoughts, the possibility that because in
obstinacy and perversity you refuse this day to believe, time may later confute you and
ceaseless remorse punish you? Do not even these considerations give you faith to
believe? — the fact that in such a brief period of time the holy influences (3) of this great   85

name have spread through every land? that already there is no nation of so barbarous a
behavior and so ignorant of civility, that it has not, under the influence of His love,   87
softened its harshness, and which has not, upon adopting tranquility, passed over into
peaceful dispositions? that men endowed with such great talents — orators, grammarians,
rhetoricians, lawyers, physicians, and even those who pry into the secrets of philosophy
— eagerly seek these teachings, despising those in which, only a little earlier, they had
confidence?

622

[2, 64]
    "But if Christ came as the Preserver of the human race," you say, "why does He not,   724
with equal kindness, free all without exception?" Well, does He not free all alike, when   695
He calls all alike? or does He repel and thrust anyone away from the supreme benevolence,
when He gives to all alike the power of coming to Him — to men of rank, to common folk,
to slaves, to women and boys? "The fountain of life," He says, "is open to all; nor is
anyone turned away or denied the right to drink."
    If you are so fastidious as to spurn the kindness of the offered gift — nay, if you are of
such superior wisdom that you term what Christ offers ridiculous and absurd, why should
He keep on inviting you, when it is but His part to expose the fruit of His bounty to your
own free choice? Plato says that God is not the cause of any man's choosing his lot in
life (4); nor can anyone's will be rightly imputed to another, since the freedom of will is   505
placed within the power of the very one who wills.

623

[3, 19]
    Whatever you would say of God, whatever thought you might conceive about Him in the   177
silence of your mind, it misses the mark and is corrupted in expression; nor can it have the
note of proper signification, since it is expressed in our terms, which are adapted to human
transactions. There is only one thing about the nature of God which man can most   174
certainly understand: you must know and realize that nothing about Him can be brought
out with mortal speech.

1. Possibly the angels are indicated in the phrase *interiorum potentiarum Deus;* or perhaps the forces of nature:
   or does he refer in a kind of general way to all the divine attributes?
2. The miracles of Christ.
3. *sacramenta.*
4. Probably Arnobius has in mind Plato's *Republic* 10, 15 [617 E] : *No divinity shall cast lots for you, but you
   shall choose your own deity. Let him to whom falls the first lot first select a life to which he shall cleave of
   necessity. But virtue has no master over her, and each shall have more or less of her as he honors her or does
   her despite. The blame is his who chooses: God is blameless.* (Paul Shorey translation). St. Justin the
   Martyr is also familiar with the passage (*First Apology* 44, 8).

LACTANTIUS [*ca. A. D.* 250 — *post A. D.* 317]

Lucius Caelius Firmianus Lactantius was an African by birth, a rhetorician by profession, and a Christian by conversion. Born about the year 250 A. D., towards the end of the century he was summoned by Diocletian to his new eastern capital, Nicomedia in Bithynia, to teach rhetoric. Being a Latin rhetorician, however, he had very few pupils in a Greek city; so with nothing worthwhile to do, he decided to write books. By 303 A. D., he had become a Christian, and as such he was obliged by the imperial decree of that year to resign his position as a teacher. In 305 or 306 A. D. he left Bithynia; and we hear of him next about the year 317 A. D., when he was already quite old and living in poverty, summoned by Constantine to come up to Treves as private tutor to his son Crispus. The date of Lactantius' death is not known; but he cannot have survived for very long after 317 A. D.

THE DIVINE INSTITUTIONS [*inter A. D.* 304-310]

The most important of Lactantius' several writings is *The Divine Institutions,* in seven books, written during the years 304-310 A. D. The work has the double purpose of refuting paganism and of setting forth true doctrine. It has its shortcomings and its limitations; but still, it represents the first attempt to produce in Latin a summary exposition of Christian doctrine.

The text offered by Migne, PL 6, 111-822, is entirely superseded by the critical edition of S. Brandt, in CSEL, Vol. 19, Vienna 1890, pp. 1-672, with corrigenda of Brandt and Laubmann, Vol. 27, part 2, Vienna 1897, pp. 30-32.

624

[1, 2, 5]

There is no one so uncivilized nor of such barbarous manners that he does not, when   131
he raises his eyes to heaven, even if he know not by what god's providence all this which
he beholds is governed, understand something from the very magnitude of things, their
motion, arrangement, constancy, usefulness, beauty, and proportion, and that this could
not possibly be if it were not established in wonderful order, having been fashioned on
some greater design.

625

[1, 3, 7]

The gods, if there be any, will be less powerful, each having just so much in himself.
The nature of power, however, is such that it is able to be perfect in him in whom it
resides wholly, rather than in him in whom there is but a small part of the whole. God,
if He is perfect, as indeed He must be, cannot be otherwise than One, so that the totality   157
may be in Him. [8] The powers and abilities of the gods, then, must necessarily be
weaker, because there is lacking in each just as much as is found in the others. Therefore,
the more there are, so much the less will they be.

626

[1, 4, 1]

The prophets, who were many, preach one God. They declare the One; and indeed,   15
filled with the Spirit of God, they predicted, as if with a single and harmonious voice,

things that were to be. [2] Nevertheless, those who are ignorant of the truth do not
think the prophets ought to be believed; for they say that those voices were not divine
but human. They make an announcement about the one God, so of course they must be
either madmen or liars! [3] Yet, we see that their prophecies have been fulfilled or are
daily being fulfilled; and their divination, agreeing as it does in one opinion, teaches
that they were not mad. For who would be able, were his mind disturbed, not so much
to foretell future events, but even to speak coherently?

627

[2, 7 (al. 8), 1]
    It is necessary, therefore, especially in that matter on which hinges the whole plan of   559
life, for each one to have confidence in himself, and to rely on his own judgment and   564
individual capacity for investigating and weighing the truth, rather than to be deceived
by believing the errors of others, as if he were utterly lacking in reason. [2] God gives
to every man a proportionate share of wisdom (1), so that men may be able both to seek
out things unheard, and to weigh things heard. Neither because some went before us in
time do they thereby outstrip us in wisdom; for if it is given to all equally, it cannot be
appropriated by those who precede us. [3] Like the light and brightness of the sun, it
cannot be dissipated; for, just as the sun is a light to the eyes, wisdom is a light to the
human heart. [4] Well then, since to be wise, that is, to seek the truth, is natural to
everyone, they deprive themselves of wisdom who approve the findings of their ancestors
without making any judgment; and like sheep, they are led by others.

628

[2, 8 (al. 9), 8]
    Let no one inquire of what materials God made those so great and wonderful works;   461
for He made all things out of nothing. . . . [26] Without wood, a carpenter will build
nothing, because the wood itself he is not able to make. Not to be able, however, is a
quality of weak humanity. [27] But God Himself makes His own material, because He   158
is able. To be able is a quality of God; and, were He not able, neither would He be
God. [28] Man makes things out of what already exists, because he is weak as a
consequence of being mortal; and because of his weakness, he is of limited and moderate
power. God, however, makes things from what does not exist, because He is strong on   156
account of His eternity; and because of His strength, His power is immeasurable, having
neither end nor limitation, like the life itself of the Maker.

629

[3, 27, 1]
    What then? Do [the philosophers] make similar precepts? Indeed they do, very many;   11
and frequently they approach the truth. But those precepts have no weight, because they   559
are human. They lack the greater authority, that which is divine. Therefore, no one
believes them; for the listener thinks that he is himself as much of a man as is he that
makes the precept.

631

[4, 4, 1]
    From these things it is clear that wisdom and religion are closely interconnected.   1
Wisdom looks toward children and it exacts love. Religion looks toward slaves and it
exacts fear. Just as children ought to love and honor their father, so too slaves ought
to worship and venerate their master. [2] Since God, however, who is one, sustains the

twofold character of both father and master, we ought to love Him, because we are His children, and fear Him, because we are His slaves. It is not possible, therefore, either for religion to be separated from wisdom, or for wisdom to be severed from religion; for it is the same God who, on the part of wisdom, ought to be known, and who, on the part of religion, ought to be honored. [3] But wisdom precedes, and religion follows, because to know God is first, and to worship Him is consequent.

632

[4, 8, 6]

The Holy Writings teach, and in these there is surety, that the Son of God is the Word of God, and that the other angels are the breathings (2) of God. A word is breath sent forth with a vocable signifying something. [7] But since a breath and a word are brought forth from different parts, inasmuch as a breath proceeds from the nostrils and a word from the mouth, the difference between this Son of God and the angels is great. Those breaths went forth silent from God, because they were created not to hand on the doctrine of God, but for service. [8] But the Son, though He be also Himself a breath, proceeds as a word, with voice and sound, from the mouth of God, for this reason: that He might use His voice for the people, that is, that He might become the teacher of the doctrine of God, laying the heavenly secret before men. [9] Rightly, then, is He called the Speech *[Sermo]* or Word *[Verbum]* of God.

301
302
265

373
260
262

632a

[4, 9, 1]

[In regard to the Son of God:] The Greeks express it better with the term λόγος than we do by *verbum* or *sermo;* for λόγος signifies both *sermo* and *ratio,* that He is both the *vox* and the *sapientia* of God (3).

260
262

633

[4, 12, 1]

Therefore, the Holy Spirit of God came down from heaven, and chose the holy Virgin into whose womb He would enclose Himself. Filled with the presence of the Holy Spirit, she conceived; and without any contact with man, her virginal womb was suddenly fruitful.

781

634

[4, 13, 1]

The Most High God and Parent of all, therefore, when He wished to transfer His religious worship, sent from heaven the Teacher of Righteousness (4), so that in Him or through Him, He might give a new Law to new worshippers; not through a man, as He had done before, — but still, He willed that, like a man, He should be born, so that He might be like the Father on High in every way. [2] For God the Father Himself, the Origin and Principle of all things, since He is without parents, is very correctly called ἀπάτωρ (5) and ἀμήτωρ (6) by Trismegistus (7); for by no one was He procreated. It was necessary, then, for the Son too, to be born twice, so that He might also be both ἀπάτωρ and ἀμήτωρ. [3] For in the first and spiritual birth, He was ἀμήτωρ, because He was generated by God the Father alone, without the office of a mother. [4] In the second and carnal birth, He was ἀπάτωρ, inasmuch as He was procreated in the virginal womb, without the office of a father, so that, bearing a middle substance between God and man, He might, as it were, take this weak and fragile nature of ours by the hand and lead it on to immortality. [5] He was made (8) both Son of God in the spirit and Son

373

250

301

781
321
375

of man in the flesh: that is, both God and man.

635

[4, 28, 2]

It is on this condition that we are made to exist: that we pay the debt of service   1
justly owed to the God who makes us to exist, and that we recognize and follow only
Him. [3] We are fastened and bound [*religati*] to God by this bond of piety. It is from
this that *religion* takes its name, and not, as Cicero (9) interpreted it, from re-electing
[*religendo*].

636

[4, 29, 3]

When we speak of God the Father and of God the Son, we do not speak of them as   258
diverse, nor do we separate them from each other; for without the Son the Father
cannot be; nor separated from the Father, can the Son be. Indeed, without the Son,
the Father cannot be so named, nor can the Son be generated without the Father.
[4] Since, therefore, the Father makes the Son, and the Son makes the Father (10),
both have one mind, one spirit, one substance. The former is like a bubbling fountain,   259
while the latter is like a stream flowing therefrom; the former like the sun, the latter
like a ray extending from the sun. . . . [13] Therefore, since the mind and the will of
the one are in the other, or rather, since there is but one in both, it is right that both
are called one God; for whatever is in the Father flows over to the Son, and whatever is
in the Son descends from the Father.

637

[4, 30, 1]

But since many heresies have come about, and because the people of God have been
cut apart at the instigation of demons, the truth must be briefly marked out by us, and
must be placed within its own proper domicile. Thus, if anyone wishes to draw the water
of life, he will not be turned aside to broken cisterns which hold no supply, but he will
know the abundant fountains of God; and when he has been watered there, he will lay
hold of perpetual light. . . . [10] But all of those ensnared in demoniacal deceits, which
they ought to have foreseen and to have guarded against, have through their imprudence
lost the name and worship of God. Whether they be called Phrygians (11), or Novatians,
or Valentinians, or Marcionites, or Anthropians, or whatever else, having lost the name of
Christ, they have ceased to be Christians, and have put on human and foreign names.

[11] It is, therefore, the Catholic Church alone which retains true worship. This is   417
the fountain of truth; this, the domicile of faith; this, the temple of God. Whoever does
not enter there or whoever does not go out from here, he is a stranger to the hope of life
and salvation. . . . [13] Because, however, all the various groups of heretics are confident
that they are the Christians, and think that theirs is the Catholic Church, let it be known:
that is the true Church, in which there is confession and penance, and which takes a   900
salubrious care of the sins and wounds to which the weak flesh is subject.   908

638

[5, 3, 17]

It is no wonder that you, who are far removed from the Wisdom of God, understand
nothing of the things you have read; for not even the Jews, who were well-read in the
Prophets from the beginning, and to whom the mystery (12) of God was consigned,   300
knew what they were reading. [18] Learn, then, if you have any sense at all, that it is

not because He worked miracles that we believe in Christ and that He is God, but   14
because we have seen that in Him were fulfilled all the things which were announced to us   8
beforehand by the predictions of the prophets.

640

[5, 13, 11]

When the rabble sees men lacerated by various kinds of tortures, and that they keep   88
their patience unconquered in the face of their wearied executioners, they must think, as
is in fact the case, that neither the agreement of so many nor the perseverance of the dying
can be without meaning, and that mere patience without the help of God could not
overcome such tortures. [12] Robbers and strong-bodied men cannot be made to endure
lacerations of this kind. They cry out and groan. They are overcome with grief, because
they lack inspired patience. But our people — I will be silent about men — our boys and
frail women silently vanquish their torturers, and even fire cannot extract a groan from
them. . . . [14] Behold! the weaker sex and those of tender age suffer burning and
laceration of the whole body, not of necessity, but voluntarily, because they trust in
God.

641

[6, 5, 10]

From this, therefore, it is clear that the knowledge of good and evil is one thing, but   540
virtue is another; for knowledge can exist without virtue. . . . [11] Virtue is not the
knowing of good and evil. Rather, virtue is the doing of good and not-doing of evil.
Knowledge, however, is in fact joined to virtue in such wise that knowledge precedes
virtue and virtue follows knowledge. Cognition is of no value unless it is followed by
action.

642

[6, 23, 33]

Lest anyone think that he can circumvent the divine commands, these points are   974
added in order to remove all occasion of chicanery or deceit: he is an adulterer, who   975
married a woman divorced from her husband, or who divorced a wife on account of
any crime except adultery, so that he might marry another; for God did not wish the
body (13) to be broken and torn apart.

643

[7, 6, 1]

Now let us seal the whole argument with a brief summarization. The world was made   466
for this reason, that we might be born. We, in turn, are born, that we might know God,
the Maker of the world and of us. We know, in turn, that we may worship. And again,
we worship so that we may receive immortality as the reward of our labors — for the
worship of God entails great labors indeed. And, in turn, we are recompensed with the
reward of immortality so that, having been made like the angels, we may serve the Most   480
High Father and Lord forever, and may be an everlasting kingdom unto God. [2] This
is the sum of things; this is the secret of God; this, the mystery of the world.

643a

[7, 7, 2]

It is easy, however, to show that almost all truth has been divided among the phil-   559 osophers and sects. Nor do we, therefore, subvert philosophy as the Academicians are wont to do. . . . Rather, we show that no sect was so far off course, nor any of the philosophers so inane, that they did not perceive something of the truth. . . . [4] If, however, there were someone who would collect the truth dispersed among individual philosophers and scattered among the sects, and reassemble it in one body, most assuredly he would not disagree with us. But no one can do this, unless he have experience and knowledge of the truth; and to know the truth belongs only to him who has been taught by God.

645

[7, 9, 4]

God is not to be grasped by us, whether by sight or by any other feeble sense: rather,   171
He is observed with the eyes of the mind, when we see His illustrious and marvelous   130
works. [5] As to those who have denied altogether the existence of God, I would say that they were not only not philosophers, but not even men. Like dumb animals, they seemed to be composed of a body only, discerning nothing by the soul, and referring everything to the bodily senses. They thought that nothing existed except that which they beheld with their eyes.

646

[7, 21, 1]

First of all, therefore, we hold that the power of God is so great that He can grasp even incorporeal beings and manage them as He will. For the angels, too, fear God, because   483
they are able to be punished by Him in a certain indescribable manner; and the demons are   1033
in dread, because they are tortured and punished by Him. [2] What wonder, then, if souls, even though they be immortal, are subject to being acted upon by God? For, since they have nothing solid and tangible in them, they cannot be acted upon by solid and corporeal things. Since they live only as spirits, they are tangible to God alone, whose power and substance is spiritual.

[3] The Holy Writings (14) teach us, however, that the impious are to be given punishments. Because they committed sins in their bodies, they will again be clothed with flesh, so that in their bodies they can make expiation. Yet, it will not be that flesh which God put upon man. It will be similar to the earthly flesh, but indestructible and lasting forever, so that it will be able to hold together under torture and under eternal fire, the   1034
nature of which is different from the common fire we use for the necessities of life, and   1032
which is extinguished unless it is nourished by fuel of some material kind.

[4] That divine fire, however, lives forever of its own accord and keeps strong without any nutriment. Neither does it have any smoke mixed in it. It is pure and liquid, and fluid like water. Neither is it driven upward by some force, as our fire is, which, because of the taint of the earthly body by which it is held, is compelled to leap forth along with the intermingled smoke and to fly up into the sky with a tremulous movement. [5] The same divine fire, then, by one and the same force and power, will both consume the wicked and re-create them; and as much as it takes away from their bodies, that much also will it replace, while it will be for itself its own supply of eternal food. This fact the poets carried over to the vulture of Tityus (15). Thus, without any wasting of bodies, which constantly regain their substance, it will only burn and inflict with a sense of pain.

[6] But also when God will judge the just, it is likewise in fire that He will try them.   1000
At that time, they whose sins are uppermost, either because of their gravity or their number, will be drawn together by the fire and will be burned. Those, however, who have been imbued with full justice and maturity of virtue, will not feel that fire; for they have something of God in them which will repel and turn back the strength of the flame. [7] So great is the strength of innocence, that the fire shrinks from it harmlessly.

It has received from God this power, that it burns the impious but is subservient to the just.

Neither, however, should anyone imagine that souls are to be judged immediately after death. All are detained in one common place of confinement, until that time comes when the Great Judge will make an investigation of their deserts. [8] Then those whose justice is proved will receive the reward of immortality. Those, however, whose sins and crimes are revealed, will not rise again, but will be buried in the same darkness with the impious, destined for sure punishment.

995

996

1012

647

[7, 24, 1]

The Son of the Most High and Mighty God will come, therefore, to judge the living and the dead. ... [2] Truly, when He shall have destroyed injustice and shall have rendered the great judgment, and shall have restored to life all the just who ever were, even from the beginning, He will remain among men for a thousand years, and He will rule them in a most righteous reign. ... [3] Those who will then be alive in the flesh will not die, but during that same thousand years they will generate an infinite multitude, and their offspring will be holy and dear to God. [4] Those, however, who will be raised from the dead will preside as judges over the living.

392

1016

The pagans (16), indeed, will not be entirely blotted out; rather, in the victory of God, some will be left so that the just may triumph over them and subject them to perpetual servitude. [5] During this same time the prince of demons, who is the contriver of all evil, will be bound in chains, and he will be imprisoned for the thousand years of heavenly rule when justice will reign on earth, so that he can do no harm to the people of God. ... [7] In short, the world itself will rejoice and all things in nature will be glad, being rescued and set free from the domination of evil and wickedness and crime and error. [8] During this time beasts will not feed on blood, nor birds on prey; but all will be peaceful and tranquil (17). ... [7, 26, 5] When, however, the thousand years are over, the world will be renewed by God, and the heavens will be folded together, and the earth will be changed. And God will transform men into the likeness of angels, and they will be as white as snow; and they will remain always in the presence of the Almighty, and will sacrifice to their Lord and serve Him forever. [6] At that same time there will be that second and public resurrection of all, in which the unrighteous will be raised up for everlasting tortures.

1012

1. *Dedit omnibus pro virili portione sapientiam.* The term *pro virili portione* is a technical term in law, found in the terminology of wills. It means a proportionate or equal share. Here, apparently, it means not necessarily an equal portion, but a sufficient amount: a share equal to the task.
2. *spiritus.*
3. λόγος can mean either the *external* or the *internal word, i.e.,* the *spoken word* or the *conceived word.* It has also, then, the abstract meaning of *reason,* the power of mind which finds expression through words. *Verbum* and *sermo* are generally synonymous, translatable simply as *word. Sermo,* however, means also *speech,* both the abstract sense of the faculty thereof, and in the concrete sense of that which is produced through the exercise of that faculty. Moreover, it is applicable to that product taken either singly or in the aggregate, so that *sermo* is not merely the synonymn of *verbum* in the sense of a *single word,* but may also be a *statement* — a meaning by no means foreign to *verbum,* but which attaches to it perhaps less frequently — or even a lengthy *treatise* — the latter being not a normal use of *verbum* at all, though it does very rarely occur even in this meaning. *Ratio* has such an extraordinary number of meanings that it is often a uselessly vague term, though in the present instance it is clear that it is the *ratio* which translates λόγος: hence, the *internal word* or its process. *Vox* means either the sounding *voice,* or the *sound* which the voice produces. Accordingly, it is translated *voice, word, vocable,* the last noun being rare enough in English that perhaps we must point out that a *vocable* is a spoken word regarded as a sound, apart from its meaning. *Sapientia* is *wisdom,* and in the present instance it is that which hinges upon *ratio* or *reason.* The meanings we have given are, of course, by no means exhaustive, and only a moment's thought will no doubt produce more. And if I do not err, every one of the terms noted above — *internal word, external word, spoken word, conceived word, word, speech, statement, treatise, sound, voice, vocable, reason, wisdom, verbum, sermo, vox, ratio, sapientia* — every one, I say, can be translated by the term λόγος.

4. It is perhaps worth nothing that the term *doctor[em] iustitiae* is identical to the much-discussed term *moré hassedeq* of the Dead Sea scrolls. The term occurs also in Joel 2:23, where, however, the Septuagint corrupts it to τὰ βρώματα εἰς δικαιοσύνην – *foods unto righteousness.*
5. *I.e.,* the Unfathered.
6. *I.e.,* the Unmothered.
7. An enormous number of astrological and alchemical works, authored during a period of perhaps as much as seventeen hundred years, from ancient until early modern times, are attributed to Hermes Trismegistus and to Mercurius Trismegistus.
8. The term used is indeed *factus est;* but it is in no way a denial or contradiction of what is soon to be formalized in the Nicene Creed, *genitum, non factum.* The term here lays no stress upon being made, but is used for lack of a handier way of expressing the fact of his existing, while hinting too at the relationship between Father and Son. See in 4, 29, 4 (§ 636) how Lactantius says that the Father makes the Son, and the Son makes the Father, when clearly the point of his remark is that the Father is a Father because He has a Son, and the Son is a Son because He has a Father. It would be perfectly legitimate in the present instance to translate *factus est* simply as *is,* instead of the more literal *was made.*
9. *De natura deorum* 2, 28.
10. See § 634, n. 8, above.
11. *I.e.,* the Montanists, also called Cataphrygians.
12. *sacramentum.*
13. *I.e.,* the union of marriage, which makes one flesh of two.
14. *Sanctae litterae* is Lactantius' normal term for the Holy Scriptures. See also above, § 632.
15. Tityus was punished by a vulture which constantly nibbled on his liver, which in turn constantly renewed itself, so that the vulture was never without liver and Tityus never without pain. He is known to Homer, Virgil, Tibullus, Ovid, Lucretius, Horace, and myself.
16. *gentes.*
17. Between 7, 24, 8 and 7, 26, 5, we must omit an interesting but too lengthy portion of the account, containing numerous further details of the millenium, which is to begin when the world is 6000 years old, and which, though various historians disagree on details, most do agree, will be in not more than about 200 years hence. (Since Lactantius was writing about the year 310 A. D., we may conclude that he expected the millenium to commence about the year 500 A. D.) Just before the end of the thousand years, the prince of demons will be turned loose upon the world, to incite wars. The wrath of God will fall upon the nations (*i.e.,* the pagans), destroying them to a man. The sun will stand still for three days, melting the life out of those impious and warlike people. During those three days, the just will be hidden away within the bowels of the earth. When this last judgment is completed, the just will stand forth again, but the wicked will have utterly perished. For seven years the forests will grow, and no tree will be cut. The armaments of the pagans will be burned, apparently sufficing for firewood, in place of the forests which are not to be touched. There will be no more wars, but only peace and eternal rest. The account continues, then, as above, at 7, 26, 5.

THE DEATHS OF THE PERSECUTORS [*inter A. D.* 316/320]

The attribution of the treatise on *The Deaths of the Persecutors* to Lactantius is still questioned by some. At present the best argument for its authenticity is that Jerome calls Lactantius its author; and there is nothing in the work to forbid Lactantius' authorship. I strongly suspect that a better argument for its authenticity is one which has not yet been sufficiently developed, and will be found eventually in a study of the style and vocabulary of the work. Lactantius' Latin is very peculiarly his own; and even a cursory reading of *The Deaths of the Persecutors* leaves one with the impression that it was written by the author of *The Divine Institutions:* Lactantius.

The work records the death of Maximin Daia († 313 A. D.) and the death of Diocletian († *ca.* 316 A. D.). And since it regards Licinius as a protector of the faith, it must have been written before 320 A. D., when he too became a persecutor. We cannot prove Lactantius alive after 317 A. D., which is not to say that he was not still alive in 320 A. D., but in any case, an earlier rather than a later date within the period 316-320 A. D. is preferable. That it was in fact written in 317 A. D. is not improbable. And whatever the authenticity of the work, that it is genuine to the period in which it apparently belongs is not disputed.

The Deaths of the Persecutors has survived in a single manuscript of the 11th century. The Migne text, PL 7, 189-276 is probably satisfactory enough; but it is not regarded as a safe edition since the publication of the critical text of S. Brandt in CSEL, Vol. 27, part 2, Vienna 1897, pp. 171 ff.

647a

[2, 5]

When Nero was already reigning (1) Peter came to Rome, where, in virtue of the per- 431 formance of certain miracles which he worked by that power of God which had been given to him, he converted many to righteousness and established a firm and steadfast temple to God. [6] When this fact was reported to Nero, he noticed that not only at Rome but everywhere great multitudes were daily abandoning the worship of idols, and, condemning their old ways, were going over to the new religion. Being that he was a detestable and pernicious tyrant, he sprang to the task of tearing down the heavenly temple and of destroying righteousness. It was he that first persecuted the servants of God. Peter, he fixed to a cross; and Paul, he slew.

1. *A. D.* 54-68.

FIRST COUNCIL OF ARLES [*A. D.* 314]

The Council of Arles, in the city of Provence still bearing that name, was convened in the year 314 A. D. by the Emperor Constantine, chiefly because of the importunities of the Donatists, who were dissatisfied with the decision of the Council of Rome of the previous year. The council still pronounced against the Donatists, upholding the validity of Caecilian's episcopal consecration. A rather large representation of bishops were present, it being virtually a general council of the West; but St. Augustine certainly exaggerates when he refers to it as "a plenary council of the whole Church." Marinus, Bishop of Arles, presided; and Pope Sylvester, who had just succeeded Melchiades in the See of Rome, sent legates to represent himself.

Twenty-two disciplinary decrees were passed, many of which are virtually the same as certain of the canons of the Council of Elvira of *ca.* 300 A. D. The canons of Arles were conducted to Rome in cover of the short letter which precedes canon 1 in the *Collectio* of Mansi: *Marinus and the assembly of bishops who were gathered in the city of Arles, to their most holy lord and brother, Sylvester: What we have decreed in common counsel we signify to Your Charity, so that for the future all may know what must be observed.*

For the text of the acts of Arles one may consult Mansi, Vol. 2, 471-476; or Hefele-Leclercq, *Histoire des Conciles,* I, 1, Paris 1907, pp. 280-294. The latter source has both text and commentary.

CANONS [*A. D.* 314]

647b

[Canon 2]
   Concerning those who have been ordained to the ministry in whatever places: they are   899
to remain in those same places.

647c

[Canon 8]
   Concerning the Africans, because they follow their own peculiar law and re-baptize: It
is determined that if someone come to the Church from heresy, let them ask him his creed;
and if they see that he has been baptized in the Father and the Son and the Holy Spirit,   830
only is the hand to be imposed upon him, so that he may receive the Holy Spirit (1).   826
But if, upon being interrogated, he does not respond with this Trinity, he is to be   906
baptized.

647d

[Canon 11]
   Concerning girls of the faith, who are married to pagans: it is determined that they   980
are to be separated from communion for a while.

647e

[Canon 15]
   Concerning deacons, whom we have known to offer in many places: it is determined   866
that this must never happen (2).

647f

[Canon 21]
   Concerning presbyters and deacons, who are wont to leave their own place in which   899
they were ordained, and transfer themselves to another place; it is determined that they
are to serve those places to which they are attached. But if, having left those places,
they wish to transfer themselves to another place, they are to be deposed.

1. See above, §§ 601 and 601a-d, with their pertinent notes. Stephen said that nothing was to be renewed
    except the imposition of hands *in penance*. Was it ever his intention that the Confirmational imposition
    of hands should be renewed? Whatever the case, and even if the latter practice was begun in honest
    misunderstanding, it gained the ascendancy; and it remains today the practice of the Church to require
    valid orders on the part of the minister of valid Confirmation.
2. *De diaconibus quos cognovimus multis locis offerre, placuit minime fieri debere.* The meaning of this
    canon is not beyond dispute, and rather than place anything of an interpretation upon it, we have made a
    complete sacrifice of rhetorical style for the sake of a literal translation. The question remains: what does
    it mean? It has been held that this canon forbids deacons to distribute communion in churches to which
    they have not been assigned. I see several objections to this proposed interpretation: *a)* it places a very
    strange meaning upon *offerre; b)* it is repetitious of canons 2 and 21 of this same council; *c)* it does not
    require such a great emphasis, almost horror, as is expressed in its terse prohibition: *placuit minime fieri
    debere.*

    It seems to us the likely and almost certain interpretation of the canon is this: some deacons, perhaps
    by reason of the unsettled conditions of the last years of the persecutions, in the absence of a priest or
    bishop, were arrogating to themselves the functions of a priest and were attempting to offer the holy
    sacrifice of the Mass. Properly horrified at such sacrilege, the Fathers of Arles condemned it roundly and
    implied that such unspeakable infractions ought never to have happened, while forbidding that such should
    ever happen again. In support of this interpretation is the simple fact that it is what the words of the
    canon, in their most natural sense, seem to mean; and in fact, in canon 19 of this same council, the verb
    offerre clearly means *to offer Mass.*

With this interpretation in mind, then, canon 15 might be rendered into better English: *Concerning deacons, who, we are aware, have in many places offered Mass: it is determined that such a thing must never be.*

COUNCIL OF NEOCAESAREA [*inter A. D.* 314/325]

The Council of Neocaesarea, a city of Pontine Asia Minor, was held sometime between the Councils of Ancyra and Nicaea, *i.e.*, between 314 A. D. and 325 A. D. An earlier date is preferable to a later one, and it is entirely possible that it was held in the same year as Ancyra. Nineteen bishops were present, ten of whom had been present also at Ancyra. It is likely that Vitalis of Antioch was president at Neocaesarea. The council published fifteen disciplinary canons, the Greek text of which is still extant.

For the acts, see Mansi, Vol. 2, 539-548; or Hefele-Leclercq, *Histoire des Conciles* I, 1, Paris 1907, pp. 327-334.

CANONS [*inter A. D.* 314/325]

647g

[Canon 1]

If a presbyter has married a wife, let him be removed from the ranks. But if he has fornicated or has committed adultery, let him be thrust out completely and let him subject himself to penance (1).   964

647h

[Canon 2]

If a woman marries two brothers (2), let her be thrust out until death. But at death, if she promises to dissolve the marriage if she should recover, let her, as a merciful kindness, have repentance (3). But if, though about to die, the woman or her husband clings to such a marriage, repentance will be very difficult for the survivor.   980

647i

[Canon 11]

A presbyter is not to be ordained before he is thirty years of age, even if he be a man especially worthy; rather, he must wait. For the Lord Jesus Christ was baptized (4) in His thirtieth year, and then He began to teach.   899

1. To be removed from the ranks or lists means that he is to be deposed, reduced to the lay state. To be thrust out completely means, of course, to be excommunicated, in which condition he will find himself among the penitents, laboring for re-admission even to the lay state.
2. The canon does not, of course, envision simultaneous bigamy, which were unthinkable. It speaks of a digamous woman, and not because she is a digamist, but because her second marriage is with her brother-in-law, in the first degree of affinity.
3. *I.e.*, she may, as a humane touch, if she is repentant and promises to dissolve the forbidden union, be given Communion on her death-bed.
4. ἐφωτίσθη.

ARIUS THE ARCHHERETIC [*ca. A. D.* 270 – *A. D.* 336]

Arius, the archheretic, seems to have been a native of Libya, born there perhaps about the year 270 A. D. During the episcopate of Peter of Alexandria (300-311 A. D.) he joined himself to the partisans of Meletius of Lycopolis for a short time. After separating from the schismatics, he succeeded, about the year 307 A. D., in having himself ordained a deacon. After having been excommunicated for criticising the measures taken against the Meletians, he managed to have himself re-instated, and was ordained to the priesthood in 311 A. D. by Achillas (311-312 A. D.), Peter's successor. Alexander (312-328 A. D.), the successor of Achillas, placed him in charge of the church of Baucalis. Whether Baucalis is the name of a place or of the church itself, or of a person for whom the church was named, is uncertain.

Whether or not Arius ever met or heard Lucian of Antioch is questionable. But he did borrow somewhat from Lucian's teaching, which had strong subordinationist overtones; and he claimed Lucian for his master. By 318 A. D. Arius was in serious doctrinal conflict with Alexander; but not until 323 A. D. did his heretical teachings break like a storm upon the Church of Alexandria.

It is not our place to give a summation of the history of Arianism. Enough to say that Arius taught that the Word had been created out of nothing, and that there was a time when He did not exist. Indeed, he was willing to affirm that the Word is not a creature like the other creatures; and even that He is God — but not true God. In the face of his positive teachings, however, these hedging statements are mere persiflage. The doctrine that the Father and the Son are not of the same essence is a disastrous one, and leads directly to the radical Arian position of the Eunomians of fifty years later: the Father and the Son are in every respect unlike.

There is no reason to doubt the essential facts of the early accounts of Arius' death: In spite of his numerous condemnations, by subterfuge he convinced Constantine in a personal interview in 336 A. D. of his orthodoxy. At the emperor's command, and in accord with decisions already reached at councils in Tyre and Jerusalem in 335 A. D., Arius was to be re-admitted on the next day to communion. But having waited so long upon Constantine, in returning from the palace he was caught short in the streets of Constantinople; and while relieving himself in a secluded place behind the forum, his bowels burst out of him and he died on the spot.

The literary remains of Arius are very slight. A letter to Eusebius of Nicomedia, from about the year 318 A. D., is preserved by Epiphanius and by Theodoret; and there are two Latin versions of the same. A credal letter to Alexander, dating from about the year 320 A. D., is preserved by Athanasius and Epiphanius, and, in a Latin version, by Hilary. A letter to Constantine, dating from the year 327 A. D., by which Arius hoped to prove to the emperor his orthodoxy, is preserved by Socrates and by Sozomen. A considerable number of fragments, mostly short and all or nearly all belonging to his work entitled *Thalia,* which means *The Banquet,* can be gleaned from Athanasius, Marcellus of Ancyra, and Anastasius of Sinai. The letters mentioned above and all or most of the fragments can be found in Migne, which, however, is no longer a satisfactory source for them.

The Athanasian fragments and the passages cited by Theodoret and Epiphanius may be gotten from the critical editions of those authors in the Berlin Corpus (GCS); but here we must bear in mind that the purpose of the editors of these critical editions is not to establish the text of Arius, but the text of the author with whom they are dealing, and who cites Arius. The best and most convenient source for all the scant literary remains of Arius is Gustave Bardy's *Recherches sur Saint Lucien d'Antioche et son école,* Paris 1936, pp. 217-295. Since it is Bardy's intention to establish the text of Arius, while the Berlin Corpus editors, quite properly in view of the nature of their works, attempt to establish the text of the authors who report Arius, it is Bardy's text which is presently regarded as the standard edition for the fragments of Arius, and which is the basis of our present translations.

THE BANQUET [ca. A. D. 320]

Arius' work *The Banquet,* written at Nicomedia about the year 320 A. D., is extant only in a fair number of fragments, preserved as quotations in several works of Athanasius, and some few other authors. As noted above, the best and most convenient source for the fragments is Bardy.

There is reason to believe that *The Banquet* was partly in prose and partly in verse. Probably it contained some of the songs which Arius wrote to popularize his teachings; and Athanasius speaks of the dissolute meter of the work and of its effeminate melodies.

648

Fragment III: *Apud* Athanasius, *Discourses Against the Arians* 1, 5, and *Encyclical Letter to the Bishops of Egypt and Libya* 12; in Bardy, p. 261.

God was not always a Father; indeed, there was a time when God was alone, and He   292
was not yet a Father. Afterwards, however, He became a Father. The Son was not always; for inasmuch as all things were made out of what did not exist, the Son of God, too, was made out of what did not exist; and as all that are made do exist as creatures and works, He too is a creature and a work; and since formerly all things did not exist, but were afterwards made, so also there was a time when the Word of God did not Himself exist; and before He was begotten, He was not; rather, He has a beginning of existence.

648a

Fragment IV: *Apud* Athanasius, *Discourses Against the Arians* 1, 5, and *Encyclical Letter to the Bishops of Egypt and Libya* 12; in Bardy, pp. 262-263.

For God was alone, and the Word was not with Him. Afterwards, when He wanted to   292
fashion us, then He made Him. And from the time He was produced, He called Him Word and Son and Wisdom, so that through Him He might fashion us. And as all things, which formerly did not exist, were made to exist by the will of God, so also He, who formerly did not exist, was produced by the will of God. For the Word is not the proper and natural offspring of the Father, but even He was produced by grace. For God, who existed, made the Son, who had not existed, by His will, by which will also He made all things, and fashioned them and created them, and caused them to come into existence.

648b

Fragment XII: *Apud* Athanasius, *Discourses Against the Arians* 1, 6, and *Encyclical Letter to the Bishops of Egypt and Libya* 12; in Bardy, pp. 268-269.

For moreover, indeed, the Son does not only not know the Father precisely, for He   292
is lacking in comprehension; but the Son does not even perceive His own essence.

650

Fragment II: *Apud* Athanasius, *The Councils of Rimini and Seleucia* 15; in Bardy, pp. 256-257.

God Himself, therefore, in His nature, is inexpressible to all. He alone has no one His   292
equal, nor like to Him, nor of equal glory. We call Him unbegotten, because of Him whose nature is that He is begotten. We praise Him as having no beginning, because of Him who has a beginning; and revere Him as eternal, because of Him who was born in time (1). He

that is without beginning established the Son as the beginning of things created; and by adopting Him, He advanced Him to be His own Son. According to His own proper subsistence He has nothing that is proper to God. For He is neither equal nor is He consubstantial (2) to Him. . . . There is, therefore, a Trinity, but not of like glories. Their substances (3) are not mingled with each other; and one is more glorious than the other in the immensity of their glories. The Father, according to substance (4), is alien to the Son, because He exists without beginning. Understand that the Monad was; but the Dyad was not, until it came into existence. . . . Wisdom came into existence as Wisdom, at the will of the wise God. . . . One equal to the Son, the Superior is able to beget; but more excellent, or superior, or greater, He cannot.

650a

The *Hodegos* Fragment: *Apud* Anastasius of Sinai, *The Guide* 21, in Migne, PG 89, 284 A; and in Bardy, p. 288.

Admirably does John say, "In the beginning was the Word (5)," that is, the spoken   292
Word (6) of God. For he does not say, "In the beginning was the Son," but the
uttered Word (7) of God.

1. There is an omission by haplographical error in the Migne text. The lines should read:
   τοῦτον ἄναρχον ἀνυμνοῦμεν   διὰ τὸν ἀρχὴν ἔχοντα,
   αἴδιον δὲ αὐτὸν σέβομεν   διὰ τὸν ἐν χρόνῳ γεγαότα.
2. ὁμοούσιος.
3. αἱ ὑποστάσεις.
4. κατ᾽ οὐσίαν.
5. John 1:1.
6. τὸ ῥῆμα.
7. ὁ λόγος ὁ προφορικός.

LETTER OF ARIUS TO ALEXANDER OF ALEXANDRIA [*ca. A. D.* 320]

The letter of Arius, with a number of co-signatories, to Alexander, Bishop of Alexandria, dates from about the year 320 A. D. The tone of the letter, on the surface, is one of cold respect — an attitude which but thinly disguises its writer's genuine contempt. Not even in protesting his orthodoxy does he succeed in veiling his heresy; and he ends by bidding a final farewell to his bishop.

The text of the letter is preserved by Epiphanius in his work entitled *A Medicine Chest against Heresies* 69, 7-8, in Migne, PG 42, 213-216; or better, in Holl's critical edition in GCS, Vol. 37, Leipzig 1933, pp. 157-159; by Athanasius in his *The Councils of Rimini and Seleucia* 16, in Migne, PG 26, 708-712; or better, in Opitz's critical edition in GCS, Vol. 3, part 1, Leipzig 1935, pp. 12-13; and by Hilary, in Latin translation, in *The Trinity* 4, 12-13, and again, 6, 5-6, in Migne, PL 10, 104-107 and 160-161. The best source, however, is Gustave Bardy, *Recherches sur Saint Lucien d'Antioche et son école*, Paris 1936, pp. 235-238.

651

To our Blessed Pope and Bishop, Alexander, the presbyters and deacons send greetings   436
in the Lord. Our faith from our forefathers, which also we have learned from you, Blessed   292
Pope, is this: We acknowledge one God, alone unbegotten, alone eternal, alone without beginning, alone true, alone possessing immortality, alone wise, alone good, alone sovereign, judge of all, governor, dispenser, immutable and unchangeable, just and good, this God of the Law and of the Prophets and of the New Testament; who begot an only-begotten Son

before times' ages, through whom also He made the ages and all things; and who begot Him, not in appearance but in truth, by His own will making Him subsist, immutable and unchangeable, a perfect creature of God, but not as one of the creatures; offspring, but not as one of the offsprings; not as Valentine taught, that the offspring of the Father was an issue; nor as the Manichaean explained, that the offspring was partially of the same substance of the Father (1); nor as Sabellius, who, defining the Monad, speaks of a Son-Father; nor as Hieracas, a lantern from a lantern, or a lamp in two parts; nor that He who existed before was afterwards begotten or created over again into a Son; even as you yourself, Blessed Pope, have often condemned in the midst of the church and in council session those who introduce these opinions; but, as we said, created at the will of God before times and before ages, and gaining life and existence from the Father, and whose glories were also called into existence along with Him by the Father. For in giving to Him the inheritance of all things, the Father did not deprive Himself of those things which He had as unoriginated in Himself; for He is the source of all. Thus there are three hypostases (2). And indeed, God, the cause of the coming about of all things, is most singularly without beginning. But the Son, begotten by the Father apart from time, and who was created and founded before the ages, did not exist before He was generated; but begotten apart from time before all else, alone was made to subsist by the Father. For He is not eternal, or co-eternal, or co-unoriginate with the Father (3); nor does He have being together with the Father, as they would have it who introduce two unoriginated principles, and speak of certain things as being in relation to certain others (4); but God is indeed before all things, being the Monad and beginning of all. Therefore He is also before the Son, as we have learned even by your own preaching in the midst of the church. In so far, then, as He has from God His being, His glories and life, and all that is given Him, in this sense is God His origin. For He begins from Him, inasmuch as He is His God and is before Him. But if the saying "from Him (5)" and "from the womb (6)" and "I came forth from the Father and have come (7)" be understood by some as meaning part of His same substance (8) and as an issue, then, according to them, the Father is compounded and divisible and mutable and corporal, and so far as they are concerned, the incorporeal God bears the consequences of corporality. We wish, Blessed Pope, to bid you farewell in the Lord (9).

1. μέρος ὁμοούσιον τοῦ πατρὸς τὸ γέννημα.
2. Epiphanius and Hilary add: *Father, Son, and Holy Spirit.* This, however, is certainly not Arius' thought when he speaks of a Trinity. Arius' Trinity is made up of a Monad and a Dyad. The Monad is the Father, while the Dyad is composed of His two most glorious creatures, the Son, who is less than the Father, and the Holy Spirit, who is less then the Son.
3. The omission of τῷ πατρί in Bardy is apparently an inadvertence, since it is found in all three primary sources: Epiphanius, Athanasius, and Hilary.
4. οὐδὲ ἅμα τῷ πατρὶ τὸ εἶναι ἔχει, ὡς τινες λέγουσι τὰ πρός τι, δύο ἀγεννήτους ἀρχὰς εἰσηγούμενοι.
5. Rom. 11:36.
6. Ps. 109 [110]:3.
7. John 16:28.
8. ὡς μέρος αὐτοῦ ὁμοουσίου.
9. The signatories to the letter, as given by Epiphanius alone, are: *Arius, Aeithales, Achillas, Carpones, Sarmatas, and another Arius, Presbyters; Deacons: Euzoius, Lucius, Julius, Menas, Helladius, and Gaius; Bishops: Secundus of Pentapolis, Theonas of Libya; and Pistus, whom the Arians appointed in Alexandria.* The final clause, in explanation of who Pistus was, obviously cannot have formed part of the original text of the letter. Secundus of Pentapolis is to be identified with him that historians more frequently refer to as Secundus of Ptolemais; and Theonas of Libya is more familiarly known as Theonas of Marmarica.

LETTER OF ARIUS TO EUSEBIUS OF NICOMEDIA [*ca. A. D.* 318]

The letter of Arius to Eusebius of Nicomedia dates from the year 318 A. D., or shortly thereafter. Eusebius, Bishop of Nicomedia, was even then closely allied with Arius, and remained throughout his life an ardent proponent of the Arian doctrines. It is, then, a friendly letter; and like every troubled priest, Arius complains that he is persecuted by his bishop.

The text of the letter is preserved by Theodoret, *History of the Church* 1, 5, which is found in Migne, PG 82, 909-912; or better, the critical edition of Parmentier and Scheidweiler in the Berlin Corpus (GCS), Vol. 19, second edition, 1954, pp. 25-27; also by Epiphanius in his *A Medicine Chest against Heresies* 69, 6, in Migne, PG 42, 209-212; or better, in the critical edition of Holl, in GCS, Vol. 37, Leipzig 1933, pp. 156-157. Again, the best and most convenient source is Bardy's *Recherches sur Saint Lucien d'Antioche et son école,* Paris 1936, pp. 226-228.

651a

The bishop (1) largely destroys us and persecutes us, and does his worst against us, and has even turned us out of the city as godless men, because we do not agree to what he publicly preaches: "Eternal God, eternal Son; like Father, like Son; unoriginated (2), the Son co-exists with God; He is eternally born, He is unoriginate-born (3); neither by mental conception nor by the slightest temporal interval does God precede the Son; eternal God, eternal Son; the Son is of God Himself." . . . But what is it that we say and believe and did teach and do teach? That the Son is not unoriginated (4), neither in   292
any way partially unoriginated (5), nor from any essential substratum (6). Rather, that
by will and counsel He subsisted before time and before ages, fully God, only-begotten,   301
unchangeable; and before He was begotten – that is, created – or separated or
established, He did not exist. For He was not unoriginated. We are persecuted because
we said that the Son had a beginning, but God is without beginning. We are persecuted
because we said that He is from what did not exist. We have so spoken, however,
because neither is He partially God (7), nor is He from any essential substratum. For
this we are persecuted. You know the rest.

1. Alexander of Alexandria.
2. ἀγεννήτως. More literally, *the Son co-exists unbegottenly with God.* It seems best to use *unoriginated* here rather than *unbegotten,* as also in several other places in the present selection, since Arius himself a few lines further on uses the term *created* as a synonymn for *begotten,* when he says: καὶ πρὶν γεννηθῇ ἤτοι κτισθῇ . . . . Since Nicene theology uses *begotten* expressly to distinguish from *created,* we hope to have avoided some confusion here by saying *unoriginated* rather than *unbegotten.* Let it be noted also that Alexander, in calling the Son unbegotten, uses what is now unorthodox terminology, but understands it in orthodox fashion. Arius, in calling the Son begotten, uses what is now orthodox terminology, but understands it in a heretical way.
3. ἀγεννητογενής. It is an error to translate this word *begotten by the unbegotten.* Arius is ridiculing what he takes to be contradictions in Alexander's terminology.
4. ὅτι ὁ υἱὸς οὐκ ἔστιν ἀγέννητος.
5. οὐδὲ μέρος ἀγεννήτου κατ᾿ οὐδένα τρόπον.
6. οὔτε ἐξ ὑποκειμένου τινος.
7. καθότι οὐδὲ μέρος θεοῦ ἐστιν.

FIRST COUNCIL OF NICAEA [*A. D.* 325]

The first ecumenical council of the Church and the first council of Nicaea was convened in that city, now called Isnik, in Bithynia, in the year 325 A. D., by the order of Constantine, his purpose being to put an end to the quarrels and dissensions which had arisen over the doctrine of the heresiarch Arius. The number of bishops in attendance at Nicaea is variously given in early sources, but the number 318 is perhaps that most often given, and it is the figure now generally accepted. It is, in any case, a safe approximation.

The vast majority of the Fathers of the Council were from the oriental region of the Church, the West being represented only by Ossius of Cordova, Caecilian of Carthage, Marcus of Calabria, Nicasius of Dijon, and Domnus of Strido in Pannonia. Pope Sylvester was not himself present, but was represented by two priests of Rome, Vitus and Vincent, or, according to some sources, Victor and Vincent.

Who it was that gave the opening address at the Council is the subject of considerable disagreement. But it is hardly more than a point of historical curiosity, in any case. It seems fairly certain, however, that it was Ossius of Cordova who was president of the Council; and it is his signature which is found first in the lists of the signatories. Immediately after the signature of Ossius are the signatures of the legates of Pope Sylvester, the Roman priests, Victor or Vitus, and Vincent.

The precise day on which the Council opened is uncertain. There is reason to believe that there were some informal preliminary sessions as early as the middle of May, while the Fathers were awaiting the arrival of the emperor. Upon Constantine's appearance, the Council opened solemnly on June 19th or 20th. The final session was on August 25th. In these two or three months, the great Council had condemned Arianism, promulgated for all time that Jesus Christ is God and consubstantial *(homoousios)* with the Father, dealt with the problem of the date of Easter, prepared a letter to the Egyptian bishops by way of settling the Meletian Schism, pronounced a number of canons, and had formulated the Creed of Nicaea, which remains today in one way or another the touchstone of the faith.

The exact number of the canons promulgated by Nicaea has been in the past very much disputed. The Greek and Latin collections of conciliar decrees, collections made in the fourth and fifth centuries, attribute only twenty canons to Nicaea, and it is this number and those canons which are now universally accepted as being of Nicene authority. We do know, however, that subject matter for at least one other canon was discussed, and finally rejected: the question of imposing clerical celibacy. When some of the Fathers of the Council wanted to have a canon drawn up which would forbid a married clergy the old one-eyed Paphnutius of the Upper Thebaid, who was much respected for the personal austerities of his long life and for the sufferings he had undergone in the recent persecutions, presented his argument against requiring something so difficult. He was himself, of course, a celibate, and was in any case far beyond any suspicions of personal interest. His arguments prevailed, and the Council did not require celibacy of the clergy.

Fortunately for the Western Church, the attitude of the earlier local Council of Elvira, reflected also in other local councils only a little later than Elvira, soon prevailed anyway in the West. And celibacy remains today, as it has been throughout the many centuries, a great source of strength to the Church throughout the West.

Unfortunately, of the Acts of the Council of Nicaea, only three pieces remain: the Creed, the twenty canons, and the synodal decree. For the text of these, along with a great amount of collateral material by way of history, early commentary, more recent commentary, lists of signatories, etc., see Mansi, Vol. 2, 635-1082. The text of the Creed and the canons, along with much valuable history and commentary, will be found in Hefele-Leclercq, *Histoire des Conciles,* I, 1, Paris, 1907, pp. 335-362.

THE CREED OF NICAEA [A. D. 325]

If there be any who expect to find here the so-called Nicene Creed recited in the Liturgy, they will be disappointed. The substance is here, of course; but the liturgical creed, though generally referred to loosely as the Nicene Creed, is actually the revision of the Nicene Creed still often referred to as the Nicene-Constantinopolitan Creed, under the misapprehension that it originated as a re-statement of the Creed of Nicaea made at Constantinople in 381 A. D. This so-called Nicene-Constantinopolitan Creed was certainly in existence as early as 374 A. D., and was first referred to as a Creed of Constantinople at the Council of Chalcedon in 451 A. D. (see below, pp. 398-399).

St. Basil attributed the writing of the Creed of Nicaea to Hermogenes, later Bishop of Caesarea in Cappadocia, but at Nicaea still a deacon. Hermogenes was in fact secretary to the Council, and no doubt he did *write* the Creed; but it is impossible to suppose that he composed it, although that is certainly what Basil meant. St. Hilary says that it was Athanasius, also a deacon at the Council, who composed the Creed. Besides the fact that it is well-nigh impossible to believe that the Fathers would have accepted a creed from a deacon, or that any but a deacon of most recent times would have been so brash as to offer one, Athanasius himself contradicts Hilary and denies that honor to himself when he states that the Creed of Nicaea was composed by Ossius of Cordova.

This statement of the authorship has every likelihood, and certainly Athanasius was in a position to have firsthand knowledge of its composition, whereas Basil and Hilary were not. In so far as we may attribute the writing of the Creed of Nicaea to any one man, then, we may say that it was Ossius of Cordova who composed it. We must keep in mind, however, that the Creed cannot in any strict sense be called the work of one man: it is a joint effort of the Fathers of the Council. In their hands it was debated, pulled apart and re-worked, until it was the masterpiece that has stood the test of time.

A convenient source for the Greek text of the Creed will be Hefele-Leclercq, *Histoire des Conciles* I, 1, Paris 1907, pp. 443-444, where the critical text of A. Hahn is reprinted, along with some notes on the variants.

651f

We believe in one God, the Father Almighty, Maker of all things visible and invisible.   157
And in one Lord Jesus Christ, the Son of God; the only-begotten, begotten of the   158
Father, that is, of the substance of the Father; God of God, Light of Light, true God   460,252
of true God; begotten, not made; of the same substance as the Father; through   257,284
whom (1) all things were made, both those in heaven and those on earth; who for us   370
men and for our salvation came down, took flesh, and was made man, suffered, and   302
rose up on the third day, ascended into heaven, and will come to judge the living and   347
the dead. And in the Holy Spirit. But those who say there was a time when He was   391
not, and that He was made out of what did not exist, or who say that He is of another   392
hypostasis or substance, or that the Son of God is created or subject to change or   256
alteration, the Catholic Church anathematizes.

1. Note that the antecedent of *whom* is not *Father,* but *Lord Jesus Christ.* The Father is the Creator, but it is the Son who does the Father's work of creation. The Father creates through the agency of the Son, through whom all things were made. These, of course, are attributions: for all the external activities of the Trinity are the works not of particular Persons but of the Godhead.

CANONS OF THE COUNCIL OF NICAEA [*A. D.* 325]

The ancient historian Theodoret mentions that the Council of Nicaea decreed twenty canons of ecclesiastical discipline. Twenty years later Gelasius of Cyzicus makes much the same remark, and quotes the full text of the canons in the same order in which they are commonly accepted today. Rufinus, the historian and translator, renders the same twenty canons into Latin. However, he divided the sixth and eighth canons each into two, so that he numbers the twenty as twenty-two. Over the years a great many other canons, largely extracted from later councils, were cited as being Canons of Nicaea, and the collection grew. However, as we have already noted, it is more or less universally agreed among historians today that there were twenty canons decreed at Nicaea; and they are the twenty of which Gelasius quotes the texts.

The Greek text of the twenty canons with a Latin translation by Gentian Hervé is to be found in Mansi, Vol. 2, 667-678; the Latin version of Dionysius Exiguus, also twenty canons, in the same place, 677-684; the Latin version of Isidore Mercator, also twenty canons, 683-692; the Latin version of Rufinus, twenty canons in twenty-two, 701-704; the Latin version of a fourteenth century Arabic paraphrase of the same twenty canons, 709-720; a Latin version of an Arabic collection of eighty (!) canons of Nicaea, 952-982; the Latin version of an Arabic collection of eighty-four (!) canons of Nicaea, followed by fifteen additional decrees of Nicaea in regard to monks and hermits, nineteen additional decrees on various ecclesiastical matters, and still another twenty-five additional decrees, all translated from Arabic into Latin by Abraham Ecchellensis, 981-1054. The Prisca, a Latin version so-called by Dionysius Exiguus because of its supposed antiquity, can be found in Mansi, Vol. 6 1125-1131. A very ancient Latin version differing both from Dionysius and from the Prisca was discovered by Scipio Maffei in the eighteenth century, in a manuscript at Verona. This too may be found in Mansi, Vol. 6, 1195-1201.

A convenient source for the standard Greek text, in type fonts much more legible than the ligatured Greek of Mansi, is Hefele-Leclercq, *Histoire des Conciles*, I, 1, Paris 1907, 528-620, where they are accompanied by excellent historical commentary.

651g

[Canon 1]

If anyone has been castrated by surgeons operating on him during an illness, or by barbarians, he is to remain in the clerical estate; but if someone enjoying good health has castrated himself, this matter is to be investigated, and his belonging to the clerical estate is to be at an end, and in the future such persons must never be brought forward (1). But since it is clear that this applies to those who do such a thing intentionally and who dare to castrate themselves, it follows, then, in regard to those who have been made eunuchs by barbarians or by their masters, that the canon (2) admits such men as these, be they found worthy, into the clerical estate.

899
951
966

651h

[Canon 2]

Since many things, either through necessity or because of pressures brought to bear by men, have taken place contrary to the ecclesiastical canon (3), in that men but recently come over to the faith from a pagan life and instructed for only a short time are led immediately to the spiritual washing and at the same time as their Baptism advance (4) to the episcopate or presbyterate, it seemed to be proper that in the future such things should not be done, since for catechetical instruction and for further

899
966

probation after Baptism, time is necessary. The Apostle speaks wisely when he says, "Not a neophyte, lest being puffed up with pride he fall into the judgment and snare of the devil (5)." For the future, if some natural (6) sin be discovered in a person, and it be proven by two or three witnesses, let his belonging to the clerical estate be at an end. Whoever acts contrary to this and dares to be disobedient to the great council runs a risk in regard to the clerical estate (7).

651i

[Canon 3]
    The great council absolutely forbids a bishop, presbyter, deacon and any other cleric   899 to have a woman (8) living with him, except it be his mother, or sister, or aunt, or any person only on whom suspicion cannot fall.

651j

[Canon 4]
    A bishop ought certainly be chosen by all the others of the province (9). But if this   899 is too difficult, because of urgent necessity, or because of the length of the journey, then   961 at least three shall assemble in the same place, and the votes of those absent having been communicated in writing, let the consecration (10) take place. The confirmation of the proceedings, however, belongs in each province to the metropolitan.

651k

[Canon 5]
    In regard to those who have been excommunicated (11), whether they be of the clerical   899 or of the lay estate, the sentence of the bishops of each province is to remain in force, in accord with the canon which says very plainly: Those who have been excommunicated by some are not to be re-admitted by others (12). However, it should be investigated, lest it might have happened that they were excommunicated (13) through meanness or contentiousness or some such disposition on the part of the bishop.
    Moreover, so that this fitting investigation may take place, it seemed proper that there should be each year in each province two synods a year, so that through this assembling in common of all the bishops of the province, such investigation may be undertaken; and thus it will be clear to everyone that those whose disobedience to the bishop is established are justly excommunicated, until it shall please the assembly of the bishops to mercifully modify the judgment. The synods are to be held, one before the forty days of lent (14), so that with the casting out of every meanness a pure gift may be offered to God; and the second at about the season of autumn.

651l

[Canon 6]
    Let the ancient custom which is followed in Egypt and Libya and the Pentapolis   899 remain in force, by which the Bishop of Alexandria has the supervision of all those places, since this is also the custom of the Bishop of Rome (15). Similarly, in regard to Antioch and the other provinces, let the inherited rights of the Churches be preserved. Certainly it is quite clear that if someone has been made bishop without the consent of the metropolitan, the great council defines that such a one is not a bishop. If, however, the vote was participated in by all, and was made in discernment and in accord with the canons, but it is yet opposed by reason of the contentiousness displayed by two or three, let the vote of the majority prevail.

651m

[Canon 7]

Since custom and ancient tradition demonstrate that the Bishop of Aelia (16) is to be honored, let him have a position of honor (17) without prejudice to the dignity of the metropolis (18).

899

651n

[Canon 8]

In regard to those who call themselves Cathari (19), when they are converted to the Catholic and Apostolic Church, the holy and great council decrees that hands being imposed on them they are thus to remain in the clerical estate (20). But before all else, it is necessary that they acknowledge in writing that they will conform to and follow the teachings of the Catholic and Apostolic Church: that is, they will be in communion with persons twice-married; and with those who fell away in the persecution, for whom a season has been set and a definite time determined (21). Thus, in all things they are to follow the teachings of the Catholic Church.

In all places, then, whether in villages or in cities, where it is found that they are the only ones ordained, those who are found in the clerical estate are to remain in their position. But if there is a bishop or presbyter of the Catholic Church there, where some are converted, it is clear that the bishop of the Church (22) is to have the dignity of bishop, and he that was named bishop by the so-called Cathari is to have the honor of being a presbyter, if the bishop deems it best not to permit him to share in the honor of the title (23). If this is not satisfactory to him, then he is to assign him a place as a rural bishop or presbyter (24), by which it may be seen that he is in every way a member of the clerical estate, while the presence of two bishops in the same city is thereby avoided.

799
962
906

979

651o

[Canon 9]

If some presbyters have been promoted without an examination, or if examined about their sins they confessed them, and although they confessed them some men were moved, contrary to the canon, to impose hands on such as these, the canon does not approve them: for the Catholic Church demands that they be free of anything reprehensible.

899
966

651p

[Canon 10]

Those of the lapsed (25) who have been ordained either through the ignorance or in spite of the knowledge of those who ordained them are no exception to the ecclesiastical canon, and when they are known they are to be deposed.

966

651q

[Canon 11]

In regard to those who transgressed without compulsion or without confiscation of their property or without danger or something of the sort, which happened during the usurpation of Licinius (26), it is decided by the council, even though they are unworthy of mercy, to treat them, nevertheless, with kindness. Those, then, who are truly repentant, shall, as already baptized (27), spend three years among the hearers, and seven years among the kneelers, and for two years they shall participate with the people in prayers, but without taking part in the offering (28).

904

651r

[Canon 12]

Those who were called by grace and at first demonstrated their zeal and threw aside   904
their military belts, but afterwards returned like dogs to their own vomit, so much so
that some have even given money and presents in order to be re-admitted to military
service, are to be ten years with the kneelers, after having spent a period of three years
with the hearers. In all of these (29) there is to be an examination of their disposition,
and of the character of their repentance. Those who by fear and tears and patience and
good works prove that their conversion is real and not simulated, when they have completed
the prescribed time among the hearers, may fittingly participate in the prayers (30),
after which it is at the discretion of the bishop to treat them with an even greater
kindness. Those, however, who behave indifferently, and who regard the manner of their
attending church a sufficient demonstration of their conversion, must fulfill their time
completely.

651s

[Canon 13]

In regard to those (31) who are dying, the ancient and canonical law is even now to   909
be observed, so that if someone is dying, let him not be deprived of the last and most   904
necessary Viaticum (32). But if, after his life has been despaired of and he is again in
communion, it happens that he recovers and is again among the living, he is to be only
among those who participate in the prayers. Generally in the case of anyone who is
dying of some disease, when he asks to participate in the Eucharist, let the bishop give
it to him after due investigation.

651t

[Canon 14]

In regard even to catechumens who have lapsed, the holy and great council decided   904
that for three years they are to be among the hearers only, after which they may pray
with the catechumens.

651u

[Canon 15]

Because of the existence of great disorder and contentions, it was decided to abolish   899
everywhere the custom which has, contrary to the canon, prevailed in some localities,
so that neither a bishop nor a presbyter nor a deacon is to move from city to city.
But if anyone, after this decision of the holy and great council, should attempt some
such thing, or should engage himself in such an affair, his contrivance is absolutely
without authority, and he is to return to the Church for which he was ordained
bishop or presbyter (33).

651v

[Canon 16]

Those who neither have the fear of God before their eyes, nor consider the   899
ecclesiastical canon, but recklessly retire from their Church, whether they be presbyters
or deacons or any others enrolled in the register (34): they are in no wise acceptable
for advancement to another Church, but by all means the necessity of their returning
to their own dioceses (35) must be urged upon them. If they continue as they are,
excommunication is to be their lot. But if it should even happen that someone
attempts to snatch away the subject of another, not having obtained the consent of

the proper bishop from whom he that is enrolled in the register has escaped, and if he ordains him in his own Church, the ordination shall be invalid.

651w

[Canon 17]

Since many who are enrolled in the register (36), pursuing a course of avariciousness and love of filthy lucre, have forgotten the divine maxim which says: "He has not given his money at interest (37)," and having put out their money for usury, they demand a percentage in interest (38), the holy and great council has decided that if anyone after the publication of this decree receives interest for the service of a loan, or engages in the business of usury in any way, or demands half again as much, or devises any other scheme for filthy lucre, he is to be deposed from the clerical estate, and his name stricken from the register.

899

651x

[Canon 18]

It has come to the attention of the holy and great council that in some localities and cities deacons give the Eucharist to presbyters, although neither the canon nor the custom permits those who do not offer sacrifice to give the Body of Christ to those who do offer the sacrifice. This, too, has become known: that some deacons are now receiving the Eucharist even before the bishops. All this is to be discontinued, and the deacons are to keep within their own proper bounds, knowing that they are the servants of the bishop and that they are less than presbyters. They are to receive the Eucharist, in accord with their rank, after the presbyters, either a bishop or a presbyter giving it to them. And neither are the deacons permitted to sit among the presbyters; for this is contrary to rule and order. If anyone, after these directives, still does not tender his obedience, he is to be deposed from the diaconate (39).

898

651y

[Canon 19]

In regard to the Paulianists (40), when they wish to return to the Catholic Church, the rule is to be observed that they are without exception to be re-baptized. If any of them in times past were numbered in the clerical estate (41), they may, if they appear to be blameless and without fault, be ordained by the bishop of the Catholic Church after they have been re-baptized. But if, upon examination, they be found unfit, they must be deposed. Similarly, in regard to the deaconesses, as with all who are enrolled in the register (42), the same procedure is to be observed. We have made mention of the deaconesses, who have been enrolled in this position, although, not having been in any way ordained, they are certainly to be numbered among the laity.

826

963

957

651z

[Canon 20]

Since there are some who are bending their knee on Sunday and on the days of Pentecost (43), the holy council has decided, so that there will be uniformity of practice in all things in every diocese, that prayers are to be directed to God from a standing position.

898

---

1. *I.e.,* for ordination. The passive of the verb προάγω is so often met in such a context as this, and without further qualification, that compilers of dictionaries would be quite justified in assigning to it a secondary meaning: *to be ordained.*

2. It used to be said that the reference to *the canon* was a reference to the so-called *Apostolic Canons*, Nos. 20-22 [*al.* 21-23]. Since F. X. Funk and others have shown conclusively that the *Apostolic Canons* are much later than Nicaea, it is now sometimes said that this term in the present instance makes reference to a pre-Nicene canon which has not come down to us. However, it seems perfectly clear to me that since the second part of the present canon is by way of interpreting the first part, the reference here to *the canon* is simply a reference to itself. The import of the second part of the canon is this: *But since our canon specifies those who do violence to themselves, then it is clear that in accord with* the canon, *these others may be admitted to the ranks of the clergy.* We have, moreover, a vague apprehension that this second sentence of the canon reads very much like a gloss.

3. Here, quite obviously, the reference cannot be a reflexive one upon the present canon itself; nor can it, as some authors said until recently, refer to Canon 79 [*al.* 80] of the *Apostolic Canons,* which we now know to be a work of the early fifth century. It may be that it refers to some specific pre-Nicene canon now lost, or more likely, it is a reference in a vague way to what is already more or less understood to be ecclesiastical law. The term κανών, which we regularly render *canon,* certainly admits to being translated by a number of less precise terms, such as *rule, norm, standard, etc.*

4. Here we have the verb προσάγω in the active infinitive. Much the same may be noted here as was said of προάγω in the passive, in § 651g, n. 1, above.

5. 1 Tim. 3:6.

6. The word used is ψυχικόν, and strangely enough it must be taken as virtually synonymous with σωματικόν, carrying with it, as it does, a sense of opposition to πνευματικόν. The phrase simply means *a sin of the flesh.*

7. Both those ordaining and those ordained contrary to the canon, both those maintained and those being maintained in the ranks of the clergy contrary to the canon, run the risk of being deposed from the clerical estate.

8. συνείσακτον = *mulierem subintroductam.*

9. ἐν τῇ ἐπαρχίᾳ. The word still means the civil province. When ecclesiastical provinces begin to have boundaries differing from the civil, the word will be borrowed for ecclesiastical usage.

10. χειροτονίαν.

11. τῶν ἀκοινωνήτων.

12. Here it is clear that the term *canon* refers not merely to some general apprehension of law, rule, or custom, but some very definite item of legislation. Of the pre-Nicene councils whose decrees have come down to us, both the 53rd canon of Elvira and the 16th of Arles state that an excommunicated person can be received back again only in the same place or by the same bishop by whom he was excommunicated. Elvira relates it to the person of the bishop, Arles to the place of jurisdiction; but clearly the meaning is the same in both: bishops are not to disregard or override the excommunications levelled by their peers.

13. ἀποσυνάγωγοι: literally, *those who are put out of the synagogue.*

14. πρὸ τῆς τεσσαρακοστῆς: literally, *before the period of forty days.*

15. The point of the first part of the canon is that the Bishop of Alexandria's jurisdiction over certain other bishops is confirmed. The concept of a patriarchate is, in fact, in the process of forming. The Bishop of Alexandria has jurisdiction not only of a civil province, as have the metropolitans mentioned in canon 4 of this same council (§ 651j); but his jurisdiction extends over all the Churches of all the provinces of the civil diocese of Egypt, along with the various provinces of Libya and the Pentapolis, or Cyrenaica. This much is clear. The problem is in the line referring to the Bishop of Rome. The Bishop of Alexandria is to retain his prerogatives, *since this is also the custom of the Bishop of Rome.* Is it also the custom of the Bishop of Rome to have jurisdiction over the bishops of adjacent territories, providing a justification for others to do likewise? Or is it the custom of the Bishop of Rome to recognize the prerogatives of the Bishop of Alexandria, giving the council precedent for doing likewise?

16. Aelia is Jerusalem.

17. τὴν ἀκολουθίαν τῆς τιμῆς.

18. In this case the metropolis is Caesarea in Palestine. The situation is a strange one. A suffragan bishop, he of Jerusalem, is to have a position of honor above that of his metropolitan, the Bishop of Caesarea; but yet he is subject to the jurisdiction of the latter. This somewhat anomalous situation was now and again the cause of some friction until 451 A. D., when Jerusalem was made a patriarchate.

19. The Cathari are the Novatianists.

20. So much hinges upon the clause ὥστε χειροθετουμένους αὐτοὺς μένειν οὕτως ἐν τῷ κλήρῳ, that we have chosen to sacrifice rhetoric for the sake of a very literal translation. There are three opinions as to how this clause is to be understood: *a)* The great medieval Greek canonists Balsamon and Zonaras, followed in more recent times by Van Espen and Beveridge, understood that the imposition of hands referred to was their former ordination, while yet they were Novatianists; and in this view, the canon is recognizing the validity of their orders. *b)* Gratian understood precisely the opposite, that it means hands are to be imposed in a re-ordination of such clerical converts, and upon this re-ordination they are to remain among the clergy. *c)* More commonly held is the view that the imposition of hands is not to be understood as referring to ordination at all, but to the reconciliatory imposition of hands. Thus their orders are recognized, and they have only to submit to the penitential rite of reconciliation, and they may take their place among the Catholic clergy.

Not much can be made of the fact that the participle χειροθετουμένους is in the present passive. English would prefer a past participle passive in the interpretation of the first view, and a present participle passive for either the second or the third view. No such distinction is necessary in the Greek idiom. Nor can much be based on arguing the meaning of the adverb οὕτως, which can have the sense either of *in this way* or *therefore*, and will accommodate itself to any of the three views. The meaning of the passage is simply ambiguous.

21. *I.e.*, for whom a period of penance has been set, and for whom a time of reconciliation is determined.
22. *I.e.*, the Catholic bishop.
23. He is to have the honor of bearing the episcopal title. Apparently, if the Catholic bishop judges in the particular circumstances that it will cause no difficulties, he may allow the converted Novatianist bishop to remain in the city with the title of bishop, but without jurisdiction. The alternatives, as expressed in the canon, are that the converted bishop be reduced to the rank of simple priest in the city, or he may go out to the country as a rural bishop or priest. Acesius, the Novatianist Bishop of Constantinople, was present at the Council of Nicaea. He was a man generally quite highly regarded by the Catholic bishops, and his presence in the council probably accounts for the very conciliatory attitude of the canon. However, Acesius himself remained adamantly against second marriages and against any reconciliation of the lapsed, and the sect of Novatianists was still in existence a hundred years later.
24. ἢ χωρεπισκόπου ἢ πρεσβυτέρου.
25. τῶν παραπεπτωκότων = *lapsorum*. This is the technical term for those who apostatized in time of persecution. It was already the practice of Cyprian of Carthage to admit the *lapsi* to penance and reconciliation, while forbidding them for all time to be accepted into the ranks of the clergy, even the minor ranks.
26. Licinius, after meeting with Constantine in Milan in 312 A. D., at which meeting it was decided between the two emperors to renew and enhance the peace which had resulted from the Galerian edict of Toleration of 311 A. D., did actually follow after Constantine in granting toleration and even certain privileges to the Christian religion. It is now so well-known as to be almost a cliché, that Constantine's Edict of Milan fails historical accuracy on three points: it is an instrument not of Constantine, but of Licinius; it is not an edict but a rescript; and it is not of Milan but of Nicomedia. Be that as it may, Licinius afterwards instituted repressive measures against Christians around the end of 319 A. D. He fell before Constantine and his armies in what has every appearance of a religious war to save Christianity, in 324 A. D.
27. οἱ πιστοί.
28. The canon knows three classes of penitents: the *hearers*, who were permitted only in the vestibule of the church and were dismissed with the catechumens; the *kneelers*, who took their place in the nave of the church, and who also were dismissed with the catechumens, but who, while in the nave of the church, knelt or prostrated themselves while the faithful stood; and, though the term itself does not appear in the canon, the *standers*, who stood with the faithful, remained for the entire Mass, but could not receive Communion.
29. ἐφ᾽ ἅπασι δὲ τούτοις. Since the construction is of ἐπὶ + dative, the meaning may be either temporal *(through all these years)* or personal *(in all these persons*, or *in all such cases)*. However, this is purely a linguistic problem, as the effect is much the same in any case, especially since it is clear from what follows that their examination is to be a continual watching through the time of their penance, and not some particular examination at the conclusion of their years of penance.
30. The present canon deals with those who renounced their army careers when Licinius re-instituted certain persecutory measures against the Christians, and then fearing for themselves, obtained their re-admission to the army at the expense of their faith. If they show special signs of contrition during their three years as hearers, they may by-pass their ten years as kneelers and become standers immediately. For explanation of these terms, see note 28 to the previous canon. The present canon, like the last, knows three classes of penitents. Gregory the Miracle-Worker, in his *Canonical Letter*, knows four classes, his *weepers* preceding the present three (see § 611a above).
31. Obviously the canon is speaking of those who have not yet completed a canonical period of penance, during which they were not to be admitted to the reception of the Eucharist, and are now found to be dying. Perhaps this canon was called forth — and reference is made to more ancient practice — by reason of the fact that the comparatively recent Council of Elvira (*ca. A. D.* 300) had designated nineteen cases in which the Eucharist was to be denied even *in extremis*.
32. τοῦ ἐφοδίου. The original and first meaning of τὸ ἐφόδιον is *provisions for a journey*. It is the precise equivalent of the Latin, now English, *viaticum*.
33. A similar canon was decreed at Elvira. However, as we have pointed out before, the vague reference to *the canon*, as in the present instance, need not be taken as a reference to any specific previous legislation; and it is not likely that the Fathers of Nicaea would place so great a weight of authority upon Elvira as they seem, by the wording of the present canon, to find in whatever are their precedents for their canon. Probably it is a reference only to what was previously and for a long time regarded as legitimate practice within the Church.

34. *I.e.*, who are clerics. The phrase ἐν τῷ κανόνι ἐξεταζόμενοι is a somewhat circumlocutory synonym for οἱ ἐν τῷ κλήρῳ. The same phrase occurs further on in this same canon, and twice also in canon 17 of this same council.

35. τὰς παροικίας.

36. One who is enrolled in the register is a cleric. See note 34 to canon 16, above.

37. Ps. 14 [15]:5.

38. ἑκατοστὰς ἀπαιτοῦσιν. This may also be translated: *They demand an interest rate of one per cent per month,* this being the more specific meaning of ἑκατοστάς. I take it, however, that the canon is not interested in condemning a particular rate, but is using the term more generically as referring to any rate of interest at all.

39. In itself the canon seems clear enough; but it presents certain problems in envisioning just how the abuses it condemns could possibly have existed. There is a physical difficulty about the existence of such abuses. With but one bishop in a city, and the priests present accustomed to concelebrate with him, how *could* a deacon give the Eucharist to the priests? Or, if some priests were present who were not concelebrating, how, in any case, could anyone receive before the bishop, the principal concelebrant?

By way of solution to these problems, it is suggested that first of all the canon takes up the problem of the deacon as minister of the cup: that such a one might have been administering the chalice to the priests themselves who were concelebrating with the bishop is at least conceivable. Next, the canon speaks of *some* deacons or *certain* deacons, who were receiving before *the bishops.* Here it may be supposed that it is not the celebrating bishop who is spoken of, but a visiting bishop or bishops who might be present without celebrating. The specification of *certain* deacons is probably significant, and may refer to a deacon of a special class, one who served the local ordinary in a more particular capacity, such as later came to be known as an *archdeacon.* Such a one, enjoying an easier intimacy with his bishop, might well have begun to arrogate certain prerogatives to himself, such as receiving the Eucharist before the non-celebrating visiting bishop who might be present, or before non-celebrating priests, all of whom ought to receive the Eucharist in order of their clerical rank, immediately after the concelebrants of the Mass and before anyone else.

40. The Paulianists were followers of the anti-Trinitarian heresy of Paul of Samosata, who was deposed from the See of Antioch by a council of the year 269 A. D.

41. *I.e.*, one who had taken orders in the Paulianist sect.

42. *I.e.*, the register of the clergy. See above, canon 16, n. 34. The latter part of the present canon, dealing as it does with the deaconesses, has been the subject of much discussion and argumentation. It seems clear to me, however, that the canon is simply pointing out that the deaconesses, too, are to be re-baptized, and if they be found fit, may continue in the capacity of deaconesses. But why should the canon make mention of the deaconesses, when the same applies to anyone converted from the Paulianist sect, *i.e.*, that they must be re-baptized? The last sentence explains the reason for this special mention of the deaconesses. Apparently there is, within the ranks of the deaconesses, something of the same arrogant spirit which called forth the preceding canon 18, against an arrogant spirit among the deacons. As if to reprove those deaconesses who take too much upon themselves, the canon points out that although their names are enrolled in the register of the clergy, this is by a sort of convenient but not entirely consistent practice. They are not deaconesses by virtue of any rite of ordination, and therefore are not actually clerics at all, though they be enrolled in the register of the clergy, but belong really to the lay estate.

43. See § 367 above, where Tertullian mentions already in the year 211 A. D. that this same practice is forbidden. From Tertullian's manner of phrasing the matter, it seems clear that the otherwise obscure phrase of the above canon, *on the days of Pentecost,* should be interpreted as meaning *from Easter until Pentecost.*

EUSEBIUS PAMPHILUS OF CAESAREA IN PALESTINE [*ca. A. D.* 263 – *A. D.* 340]

Eusebius, the Father of Ecclesiastical History, was born at Caesarea in Palestine about the year 263 A. D. Beginning with the time of Origen's sojourn there, Caesarea had gradually developed into a very respectable center of learning, the presbyter Pamphilus continuing the scholarly traditions of Origen. It was under the master Pamphilus that Eusebius studied; and it was out of respect and veneration for his teacher that he took his name and called himself Eusebius Pamphilus or Eusebius Pamphili, implying Eusebius, *son of* Pamphilus.

In 313 A. D. Eusebius was made Bishop of his native Caesarea, and soon found himself caught up in the Arian controversy. To what extent, if at all, Eusebius was ever an actual Arian, is a very questionable matter. He was a great scholar, but not much of a theologian. He was seeking a middle course, in order to reconcile the Arian and orthodox parties. As a consequence, he occupied something of a semi-Arian position throughout the rest of his life. He was pronounced excommunicate at a Council of Antioch in 325 A. D., because he would not sign a formula directed against Arius; and in the Council of Nicaea in the same year, he continued his peace-making activities, advocating out of due time that which later came to be called Homoianism — the vague acceptance of the likeness of Father and Son to each other, without reference to their *ousia, i.e.,* their substance or essence.

However, under the at least friendly constraint exercised by Constantine, he signed the Nicene Creed, probably without any firm internal convictions. Soon afterwards he was rather openly defending his name-sake, Eusebius, Bishop of Nicomedia; and he had a part in the Council of Tyre in 335 A. D., at which St. Athanasius was pronounced excommunicate and sent into exile. He had always the ear of Constantine, and has been called a prototype of all weak-kneed court bishops. Well — perhaps; but on the whole, it appears to us that Church historians have in times past judged their father very severely. A whole new study of Eusebius' relationship to the Arian problems is badly needed.

THE CHRONICLE [*ca. A. D.* 303]

Among Eusebius' earliest works, written about the year 303 A. D., is *The Chronicle.* Eusebius himself gives the work the title Χρονικοὶ κανόνες καὶ ἐπιτομὴ παντοδαπῆς ἱστορίας Ἑλλήνων τε καὶ βαρβάρων — *Chronicle Rolls and Epitome of the Complete History of the Greeks as well as of the Barbarians.* The title impresses one as being that of a rather generous undertaking.

The original Greek has perished except for a few fragments. The entire work has survived in a sixth century Armenian translation; and the second part of the work, that in which the history of the world is set down in chronological tables, is extant in a Latin version prepared by St. Jerome in 380 A. D. Both the Armenian version, however, and Jerome's Latin, are based not upon the original, but upon a version which continued Eusebius' original down to the year 325 A. D. And Jerome himself made many insertions in the work, and continued it down to the year 378 A. D.

Our selections are from Jerome's Eusebius, the *Hieronymian Chronicle,* the text of which can be found in Migne, PG 19, 101-598, which, however, so far as any scholarly purposes are concerned, has been completely superseded by the critical edition of Rudolf Helm in the Berlin Corpus (GCS), Vol. 47, Berlin 1956. This latter, the basis of our few translated selections, is a new edition, combining the materials of GCS Vols. 24 and 34, published in 1913 and 1926 respectively.

The work no longer has much importance of its own; but since it was so widely used in the Middle Ages, it is yet of considerable value when studying the relationship of later historians to their sources.

651aa

[*Ad An. Dom.* 42]

Second year of the two hundred and fifth olympiad: the Apostle Peter, after he has   431
established the Church in Antioch, is sent to Rome, where he remains as bishop of that   432
city, preaching the gospel for twenty-five years.

651bb

[*Ad An. Dom.* 43]

Third year of the two hundred and fifth olympiad: the Evangelist Mark, interpreter of   65
Peter, announces Christ in Egypt and Alexandria.

651cc

[*Ad An. Dom.* 68]

Fourth year of the two hundred and eleventh olympiad: Nero is the first, in addition   431
to all his other crimes, to make a persecution against the Christians, in which Peter and
Paul died gloriously at Rome.

HISTORY OF THE CHURCH [*inter A. D.* 300-325]

Eusebius' great work, that which has made his name a household word for more than sixteen hundred years, is his *History of the Church,* written between the years 300 and 325 A. D.

The entire work is extant in the original Greek, in several manuscripts. Moreover, there is extant a very faithful Syriac translation made in the fourth century; and also completely extant is the Armenian version, based on the Syriac. Besides these, Rufinus' Latin translation, which continued the work down to 395 A. D., is extant. It is not a faithful translation of the Greek; and unfortunately, it was through Rufinus' version that the work of Eusebius was so popular in the West in the middle ages. Some few fragments of a Coptic version have been published by W. E. Crum.

According to E. Schwartz, editor of the critical edition in the Berlin Corpus, four editions of Eusebius' text are distinguishable: the first edition, books 1 through 8, appearing in 312 A. D.; the second edition, adding book 9, in 315 A. D.; the third, adding book 10, in 317 A. D.; and the fourth, revising passages concerning Licinius and giving an account of his downfall, in 325 A. D. More recently, H. J. Lawlor has suggested an earlier date for the first edition; and the opinion is in fact gaining ground that the first seven books were written before the outbreak of persecution under Diocletian, *i.e.*, before the year 303 A. D.

The Migne text, PG 20, 45-906, is worthless, except for the usual special purposes. The standard edition is that of E. Schwartz in the Berlin Corpus, Vol. 9, parts 1-3, Leipzig 1903, 1908, and 1909 respectively. Parts 1 and 2 are the text, while part 3 contains the introductions and indices. Kirsopp Lake's translation in the *Loeb Classical Library* is accompanied by a Greek text which is a reprint of Schwartz's text.

651dd

[2, 14, 6]

In the same reign of Claudius (1), the all-good and gracious providence which watches   431
over all things guided Peter, the great and mighty one among the Apostles, who, because
of his virtue, was the spokesman for all the others, to Rome.

652

[2, 15, 1]

But such a great light of religion shone on the minds of those who heard Peter, that   65
they were not satisfied to hear only once, nor with the unwritten teaching of the divine
proclamation; but with every possible plea they besought Mark, whose Gospel is extant,
since he was Peter's follower, to leave behind also a written statement of the teaching
which had been given to them orally. Nor did they leave off before they had persuaded
the man; and in this way they became the cause of the Scripture called the Gospel
According to Mark. [2] But knowing, through a revelation made to him by the Spirit,
what had been done, it is said that the Apostle was pleased with the zeal of the man, and
ratified the Scripture in the Churches. [3] Clement gives this account in the sixth book
of the *Sketches* (2); and the Bishop of Hierapolis, Papias by name, confirms him.

[4] It is said also that Peter's first Epistle, in which he makes mention of Mark, was   42
composed in Rome itself; and that he himself indicates this, referring to the city
figuratively as Babylon, in these words: "She that is the elect in Babylon greets you,
as does also my son, Mark (3)." [16, 1] They say that this Mark was the first to be
sent to preach in Egypt the Gospel which, indeed, he had written, and that he was the
first to establish churches in Alexandria itself.

[2, 25, 5-7]

See Caius of Rome, § 106a, *above.*

[2, 25, 8]

See St. Dionysius of Corinth, § 106b, *above.*

652a

[3, 1, 1]

Such, indeed was the state of affairs among the Jews. The holy Apostles and   404
disciples of the Savior, however, were scattered throughout the whole world. Thomas,
as tradition holds, received Parthia by lot; Andrew, Scythia; John, Asia, busying
himself among the people there until he died at Ephesus. [2] Peter, however, seems
to have preached to the Jews in the diaspora in the Pontus and in Galatia, Bithynia,
Cappadocia, and in Asia; and at last, having come to Rome, he was crucified head
downwards, the manner in which he himself had thought it fitting to suffer. Is it
needful to say anything of Paul, who fulfilled the gospel of Christ from Jerusalem to
Illyricum, and afterwards in the time of Nero was martyred in Rome? These facts
are word for word as stated by Origen in the third book of his *Commentaries on
Genesis* (4).

652b

[3, 2]

After the martyrdom of Paul and Peter, Linus was the first appointed to the   431

episcopacy of the Church at Rome. Paul, writing from Rome to Timothy, mentions 42
him in the salutation at the end of the Epistle (5).

653

[3, 3, 1]

 There is but one Epistle of Peter agreed upon, that called his first; and the ancient 42
presbyters used it as unquestioned in their own writings. We have determined, indeed,
that the alleged second is not canonical; but nevertheless, since it has appeared useful
to many, it is studied with the other Scriptures. [2] On the other hand, as for the Acts
attributed to him, and the Gospel bearing his name, and the Preaching said to be his,
and the so-called Apocalypse, we know nothing at all of their having been handed down
among Catholics, for no ecclesiastical author among the ancients nor of our own time has
made use of their testimonies. ... [4] So much, then, for the works attributed to
Peter, of which I recognize only one Epistle as genuine and agreed upon by the ancient
presbyters. [5] The fourteen of Paul are obvious and certain; but wait, it is not right to
ignore that some have disputed the Epistle to the Hebrews, saying that it was rejected by
the Church at Rome as not being by Paul.

654

[3, 7, 6]

 If anyone compare the words of our Savior to the rest of the historian's accounts of 83
that whole war, how would he not be amazed and admit the truly divine and supernaturally
wonderful character of both the foreknowledge and the foretelling of our Savior (6)?

654a

[3, 13]

 When Vespasian had ruled for ten years, his son Titus succeeded him as emperor (7). 423
In the second year of the latter's reign, Linus, bishop of the Church at Rome, having
held his office for twelve years, handed it on to Anencletus. After Titus had ruled for
two years and as many months, his brother Domitian succeeded him (8). ... [3, 15]
In the twelfth year of the same reign, Clement succeeded Anencletus, who had been
bishop of the Church at Rome for twelve years.

656

[3, 25, 1]

 At the present point it seems reasonable to recapitulate the writings of the New 42
Testament which have been mentioned. The holy quaternion of the Gospels should be
put in the first place; and following them, that writing called the Acts of the Apostles.
[2] After this must be reckoned the Epistles of Paul. Following these, there is the
Epistle of John, called the first; and likewise to be acknowledged is the Epistle of
Peter. Placed after these, if it seem desirable, is the Apocalypse of John, the arguments
concerning which we will examine at the proper time. These, then, are the recognized
books.

 [3] Among the disputed books, which are nevertheless known to most, there are
extant the Epistles said to be of James, and of Jude, and the second of Peter; and the
second and third attributed to John, whether they happen to be by the Evangelist, or by
someone else having that same name. [4] Among the spurious writings must be
reckoned the Acts of Paul, the writing called *The Shepherd,* the Apocalypse of Peter,
and in addition to these, the Epistle attributed to Barnabas, and the so-called *Teachings*

of the Apostles (9); and too, as I said, the Apocalypse of John, if it so be judged.
For, as I said, some reject it, while others include it among the recognized books.

[3, 39, 1-6]
  See St. Papias, § 94, *above.*

658

[3, 39, 11]
  The same author [Papias] presents other accounts as if they had come to him from
unwritten tradition, and some strange parables and teachings of the Savior, and some
other more mythical accounts. [12] Among them, indeed, he says that there will be a   1016
period of about a thousand years after the resurrection of the dead, when the kingdom
of Christ will be set up in material form on this earth. I suppose that such ideas came   1017
to him through a perverse reading of the apostolic accounts, he not realizing that they
had spoken mystically and in figures. [13] For he appears to have been a man of very
little intelligence, if one may so speak on the evidence of his words. But he is responsible
for the fact that so many ecclesiastical writers after him, relying on the antiquity of the
man, held the same opinion: for instance, Irenaeus, and whoever else may have held the
same views.

[3, 39, 14-16]
  See St. Papias, § 95, *above.*

[4, 3, 2]
  See Quadratus, § 109, *above.*

[4, 22, 1-3]
  See St. Hegesippus, § 188, *above.*

[4, 23, 9-10]
  See St. Dionysius of Corinth, § 106c, *above.*

[4, 23, 11]
  See St. Dionysius of Corinth, § 107, *above.*

[4, 26, 14]
  See St. Melito of Sardes, § 190, *above.*

[5, 20, 4-8]
  See St. Irenaeus, § 264, *above.*

[5, 24, 1-10]
  See St. Polycrates of Ephesus, § 190a, *above.*

[5, 24, 16-17]
See St. Irenaeus, § 265, *above.*

[5, 28, 15-18]
See St. Hippolytus, § 400, *above.*

[6, 14, 1-7]
See St. Clement of Alexandria, § 439-440, *above.*

[6, 25, 1-2]
See Origen, § 484, *above.*

[6, 25, 3-6]
See Origen, § 503, *above.*

[6, 43, 11]
See Pope St. Cornelius I, § 546a, *above.*

[6, 43, 14-15]
See Pope St. Cornelius I, § 547, *above.*

1. A. D. 41-54.
2. In Bk. 6, Ch. 14, Eusebius quotes Clement's account from the *Hypotyposeis* or *Sketches,* where a very different impression is given. See above, § 439-440.
3. 1 Pet. 5:13.
4. It is clear that Eusebius professes to be citing Origen exactly, and the above passage is certainly to be regarded as containing a fragment of Origen's very incompletely preserved *Commentaries on Genesis.* We cite it here under Eusebius, however, rather than under Origen, because of the Valesian doubt, still unresolved, as to precisely where the citation from Origen begins: whether with Thomas, or whether with Peter.
5. 2 Tim. 4:21. Irenaeus makes the same identification of Linus (see above, § 211).
6. The historian referred to in this passage is Josephus. Eusebius has recounted from Josephus certain of the horrors which accompanied the destruction of Jerusalem, and has recalled the Savior's having wept over the city, and His prophetic utterances in regard to Jerusalem's destiny. The point he makes is that Josephus' historical account verifies the fulfillment of our Savior's prophetic utterances.
7. On June 24, *A. D.* 79.
8. On Dec. 13, *A. D.* 81: hence, not two years and two months, but two years and five and one-half months.
9. The *Didache.*

PREPARATION FOR THE GOSPEL [*inter A. D.* 314/320]

The *Preparation for the Gospel,* all fifteen books of which are extant in the original Greek, was written after 314 A. D. and before 320 A. D. The object of the work is to refute pagan polytheism, and to show the superiority of Judaism, which served to prepare for the gospel, the good news of man's salvation.

The Migne text, PG 21, 21-1408, is inadequate, and was already much outmoded even before the publication of Karl Mras' critical edition in the Berlin Corpus (GCS), Vol. 43, part 1, Berlin 1954, and part 2, Berlin 1956.

661a

[1, 4]

Persians, when they have become pupils of the Savior, no longer marry their own   87
mothers. Neither do the Scythians, since the word of Christ has penetrated their lands,
any longer feed on human flesh. Other tribes of barbarians no longer have unlawful
relations with their daughters and sisters; nor do men fall madly in love with men and
indulge those pleasures which are contrary to nature.

662

[2, 6]

By nature and by reflections which are spontaneous, or rather, divinely inspired,   130
anything beautiful and useful which exists is taken as indicating the name and substance 131
of God. For all men make a presumption based on common conclusions, and introduce   135
a Creator of the universe, every rational and intelligent man doing this by his natural
reflections. They do not, then, reach this conclusion by a supposition following upon a
reasoning process.

663

[6, 11]

And if it must needs be said that foreknowledge of events is not the cause of the   190
occurence of those events — for a foreknown sinner, when he sins, does not thereby   193
hold God within his power — why, what is even more wonderful, we do in fact say that
the event about to take place is the cause of the existence of the foreknowledge
concerning it. For not because it is known does it take place; but because it is about
to take place, it is known. A distinction must be made. Indeed, we will not concede
to the interpretation which some make: that something absolutely must come about
because what is foreknown must necessarily be about to take place. For we do not say   192
that because it was foreknown that Judas would become a traitor, it was therefore of
utter necessity that Judas become a traitor.

PROOF OF THE GOSPEL [*inter A. D.* 316/322]

The *Proof of the Gospel* is something in the way of a sequel to the *Preparation for
the Gospel*. The latter showed the superiority of Judaism over paganism; and the
present work answers the Jewish objection that Christianity has accepted from Judaism
its promises and blessings, while rejecting the obligation of the Law. Eusebius replies
to the charge in twenty books, of which only the first ten, along with a large fragment
of the fifteenth, are extant. The work may be dated between the years 316 and 322 A.

The Migne text, PG 22, 13-794, is no longer useful, being entirely superseded by
the critical edition of I. A. Heikel in the Berlin Corpus (GCS), Vol. 23, Leipzig, 1913.

664

[1, 10]

When the fulfillment arrived just as the prophets had in fact predicted, the early form of
worship ceased and was forthwith put aside in favor of the true and more sublime worship.
Here, indeed, was the Christ of God, of whom it had been prophesied from the earliest
beginnings of time that He was about to come to men, and that He would be slaughtered   380
like a sacrificial animal in behalf of the whole race of men. . . . The great and valued   383
ransom of Greeks as well as of Jews; the cleansing of the whole world; that which is   386

given for the life of all men; the pure victim for every defilement and sin; the Lamb of
God; the innocent sheep which is the beloved of God; the little lamb of prophecy,
through whose divine and mystical teaching all of us, who are from among the gentiles,
have found the remission of former sins, and through whom even such of the Jews as had
hoped in Him are freed from the curse of Moses — when, I say, all this is found to be in   300
accord with the testimony of the Prophets, and when we have a daily celebrating of the
memory of His Body and of His Blood, regarded as worthy of worship and as a sacrifice
more sublime than those of antiquity, then certainly we no longer think that it could be
in accord with the dictates of religion to fall back into those first and weak foreshadowings,
which are symbols and images but which do not embrace the same truth.

665

[3, 5]
   Dare you suppose that [the Apostles] did not see at a glance the end of their Teacher,   84
and what sort of a death necessarily was awaiting Him? Why, then, after His most
ignominious end, did they persist in theologizing (1) Him when He was among the
dead, and in courting the same kind of suffering? And who is there that ever, for any
kind of doctrine, freely and with full awareness chose such a punishment?

666

[3, 5]
   But if [the miracles of Christ] were lies invented according to a mutual agreement   63
among [His disciples], what a wonder it is that such a number were able to keep to their
agreement about their fabrication, even in the face of death, and that no coward among
them ever retired from the association and made a premature repudiation of the things
agreed upon; nor did they ever announce anything in contradiction to the others,
bringing to light what had been put together among themselves.

667

[4, 1]
   For when God willed it, seeing that He is the only good of good (2) and the source
and beginning of everything, many participants in His treasures were produced. It was
just then that every rational creature was about to be sent forth; some as incorporeal,
intelligent and divine powers,— Angels, indeed, and Archangels,— immaterial and entirely   480
pure spirits; and besides these, there were the souls of men supplied with a nature that   483
is independent and of free will in respect to the choosing of what is noble or its opposite.   505

668

[4, 3]
   The content of the theology set before us is indeed beyond all comparison, nothing   239
like this ever having been advanced when dealing with corporeal matters. By the sharpest
kind of intellectual perception it represents the Son as having been begotten, not in the
manner of one who at any time did not exist and afterwards at some time came to be,   252
but as one who existed before the ages of time, both pre-existing and existing eternally
with the Father as the Son; and not as truly unbegotten, having been begotten of the   256
unbegotten Father, but truly as the only-begotten, as Word and God of God. Neither
was He projected from the substance of the Father by a dividing, nor by a cutting off,
nor by a separating. Rather, it teaches us what is beyond our power of reason and
expression, that from eternity, or what is better to say, before all ages, He was invested
with being at the will and power of the inexpressible and incomprehensible God.   173

669

[4, 12]

The divine plan (3) in His regard was such that if anyone seek the reason for Christ's dying, he will find that there was not one reason but many. First, indeed, as the Word teaches: so that He might have dominion over the living and the dead. Second, so that, by being sacrificed for us and by becoming a cursed thing on our behalf, He might wipe away our sins. Third, so that He might be offered to the God of all on behalf of the whole world, as if He were an animal for a sacrifice to God, and a great sacrifice. Fourth, so that He might Himself, with secret words, bring about the destruction of the demoniacal workings which lead so many astray. The fifth is this: so that, holding out to His acquaintances and disciples the hope of a life with God after death, – and this not by words nor by mere vocables and speech, but by deeds, setting also before their eyes the proclamation which had been made in words, – He might bring on to completion those already more willing and those of greater courage; and so that with His rejection He might proclaim a religious polity to all, to Greeks and barbarians alike.

374
380

373

386

671

[5, 3]

Inasmuch as [Melchisedech], a priest of the pagans, never was known to offer flesh in his sacrifices, but only wine and bread; and inasmuch as he blessed Abraham, he is surely by this token our first Lord and Savior — He from whom all the priests sent out to all peoples offer a spiritual sacrifice in accord with ecclesiastical regulations, representing by wine and bread the mysteries of His Body and of His saving Blood. Melchisedech had by divine inspiration a prior knowledge of these mysteries, and of things employed as figures of things to come.

893

866
898
860

673

[10, 1]

[Christ] took upon Himself the toils of the suffering members, and He made our ills His own, and in accord with the laws of the love of mankind, He endured exceeding pain and toiled beyond measure for all of us. Not this only did the Lamb of God do, but He also endured chastisement and punishment on our behalf, which He did not Himself deserve. It was, rather, on account of our many errors that He made Himself the source of the remission of our sins, even undergoing death for us.

380

383

1. θεολογοῦντες. The verb can mean either to speak of God and of things divine, or to deify or prove divine. Its present use no doubt conveys both these meanings simultaneously.
2. I.e., the only source of what is good, in view of the fact that goodness begets goodness. Another translation, though it misses a part of this flavor, might be *the greatest good*.
3. οἰκονομία.

ECCLESIASTICAL THEOLOGY [*A. D.* 337/338]

Eusebius' *Ecclesiastical Theology* is a work in three books, written in the year 337 or 338 A. D. The work constitutes a more detailed refutation of Marcellus of Ancyra than was his *Against Marcellus*, two books, published in 336 A. D. It is probably true that Marcellus had Sabellian tendencies; but the Trinitarian doctrine which Eusebius presents as the true doctrine of the Church is nothing more than rank Subordinationism. In spite of its heresies, the work has survived in its entirety, as has also the *Against Marcellus*.

The text in Migne, PG 24, 825-1046, is entirely superseded by that of E. Klostermann, in GCS, Vol. 14, Leipzig 1906, pp. 59-182.

674

[2, 14]

It must necessarily be agreed that there is some One who is divine, ineffable, good, simple, not composed, uniform, transcending all things (1), Very God, Very Word, Very Light, Very Life, Very Beauty, Very Good, and in fact whatever someone might conceive of that is better than these; or rather, above every thought and beyond every conception 180
and explanation; and that this One's only-begotten Son is like an image of the Father, 264
born of Him, and is in fact completely and utterly like to Him who begot Him; and that 252
He is God, and Mind, and Word, and Wisdom, and Life, and Light, and the image of Him 261
who is Very Beauty and Very Good. He is not in fact the Father, but the only-begotten Son of the Father; nor is he in fact the Unbegotten and the Unbegun, but having been born of Him, there is ascribed to Him a begetter and a beginning (2).

1. τὸ ἐπέκεινα τῶν ὅλων: literally, *the far side of all things.*
2. If the passage seems orthodox enough until this last remark, that we must ascribe to the Son a beginning, we must bear in mind that Eusebius does carry with him certain Arian conceptions. Even the rest of the passage, which on a cursory reading may appear orthodox, will not stand inspection. It is in fact a statement of Arian theology; and never is Eusebius more of an Arian than in the present instance. True, his statement that the Son is completely and utterly like the Father is a verbal denial of Anomoianism, the radical Eunomian Arianism; and his theology here exposed is that of the moderate Arian party.

Yet, the whole of the passage is devoted to showing how the Son differs essentially from the Father; and it must, like all Arianism, lead any logical man to Anomoianism. Eusebius has called the Father *Very* God, while he calls the Son God. He is one of those who was, according to Athanasius (*De synodis* 17), willing to confess that Christ is God, but not true God. The *Acts* of the Second Council of Nicaea (*A. D.* 787) quote a letter of Eusebius to Alexander of Alexandria, otherwise lost; and among the few passages quoted is one stating that Eusebius said in this letter: *The Son Himself, indeed, is certainly God; but He is not true God.* (See Mansi, Vol. 13, col. 318B and 701D.) In the letter to Alexander, written before the First Council of Nicaea, Eusebius' term for *Very God* or *True God* was ἀληθινὸς θεός. In the present passage his term is αὐτόθεος.

ALEXANDER OF ALEXANDRIA [† A. D. 328]

Alexander, Bishop of Alexandria from 312 to 328 A D., was one of the key figures at the Council of Nicaea in 325 A. D. His pontificate was troubled by the continuing Meletian schism, one of the matters discussed at Nicaea; and worse, it was during his pontificate that the Arian heresy arose, the principal item on the Nicene agenda.

LETTERS

Epiphanius knew a collection of seventy letters of Alexander. Probably it contained, as is usual with such collections, letters received by him as well as letters sent by him. Today only four such are known, two written by him and two received by him. The letter of Arius to Alexander has already been treated of, p. 277 above; and the letter of Eusebius Pamphilus to Alexander was quoted in footnote No. 2 to § 674, immediate above. The two letters written by Alexander are both encyclical letters. The earlier of the two was written about the year 319 A. D., addressed to his fellow-bishops everywhere, and gives serious warning against Eusebius of Nicomedia. The entire letter is preserved by Socrates (*Hist. eccl.* 1, 6) and by Gelasius of Cyzicus (*Hist. concil. Nic.* 2, 3). His other encyclical letter, the only item of his meagre literary remains with which we shall now concern ourselves, is addressed, according to Theodoret (*Hist. eccl.* 1, 4), to Alexander of Byzantium (Constantinople). Opitz has suggested that it is more likely that Alexander of Thessalonica is meant; but in any case, it was destined for all the non-Egyptian bishops. It was written in 324 A. D., immediately after the condemnation of Arius in the Council of Alexandria; and its purpose is to warn bishops against the machinations of Arius.

The text can be found in Migne, PG 18, 547-572; but since the letter comes to us through having been quoted in full by Theodoret (*Hist. eccl.* 1,4), it were better to consult the critical edition of Theodoret by Parmentier and Scheidweiler in the Berlin Corpus (GCS), Vol. 19, second edition, Berlin 1954. But perhaps the best edition is still that in H. G. Opitz' *Athanasius' Werke*, Vol. 3, part 1, *Urkunden zur Geschichte des arianischen Streites 318-328*, Berlin and Leipzig, 1934, pp. 19-29.

ENCYCLICAL LETTER OF ALEXANDER OF ALEXANDRIA TO ANOTHER BISHOP ALEXANDER AND TO ALL NON-EGYPTIAN BISHOPS. A. D. 324.

675

[4]

Moreover, that the Son of God was not produced out of what did not exist, and that   251
there never was a time when He did not exist, is taught expressly by John the Evangelist, who writes this of Him: "The only-begotten Son, who is in the bosom of the Father (1)." The divine teacher, because he intended to show that the Father and the Son are two and inseparable from each other, does in fact specify that He is in the bosom of the Father. Moreover, that the Word of God is not to be included among those things which were produced out of what did not exist, is stated by the same John: "Through Him were all things made (2)."

676

[7]

    Since, therefore, the hypothesis "from what did not exist" is clearly most impious,   256
it is necessary for the Father to be Father eternally. He is the Father because of the
eternal presence of the Son, on whose account He is styled Father. And the Son being
eternally present with Him, the Father is eternally perfect, experiencing no lack of any
good thing. Not in time, nor after any interval, nor out of what did not exist, did He
beget the only-begotten Son.

679

[12]

    Therefore His proper dignity as unbegotten must be reserved to the Father, no one   250
being called the cause of His existence. To the Son must be accorded the honor which
befits HIm, ascribing to Him a generation from the Father without beginning. And, as we   256
have already said, we are to render worship to Him, only piously and religiously saying
of Him the *was* and the *eternal* and the *before ages;* not, however, rejecting His divinity,   259
but ascribing to Him in all things an exact likeness in the image and in the character of
the Father. To the Father alone, however, do we ascribe the peculiar circumstance of
being the Unbegotten; for the Savior Himself has said, "My Father is greater than I (3)."

680

[12]

    In addition to this pious belief in regard to the Father and the Son, we confess, as   266
the divine writings teach us, one Holy Spirit, who moved (4) both the holy men of the Old   50
Testament and the divine teachers of that styled the New. And in one only Catholic   416
Church, that which is Apostolic. . . . After this, we acknowledge the resurrection of the   421
dead, of which Jesus Christ our Lord became the firstling; who bore a body not in   422
appearance but in truth, derived from Mary the Mother of God (5); who for the   1011
remission of sins came in the fullness of time to dwell among the race of men, was   310
crucified and died, but did not, for all of that, suffer any diminution of His Godhead.   780
He rose from the dead, was taken up into heaven, and sits to the right of the Majesty   374
on high.   391

1. John 1:18.
2. John 1:3.
3. John 14:28.
4. Reading κινῆσαν in place of καινίσαν.
5. The *Theotokos:* ἐκ τῆς θεοτόκου Μαρίας.

APHRAATES THE PERSIAN SAGE [*ca. A. D. 280 – post A. D.* 345]

Of Aphraates, the oldest of the Fathers of the Syrian Church, there is virtually a total lack of biographical information. He was born about the year 280 A. D., and died after 345 A. D. He is invariably known as *the Persian sage;* he was an ascetic; and probably he was a bishop, but his see is not known.

TREATISES [*inter A. D.* 336-345]

Of the writings of Aphraates, twenty-three *Taḥwâytâ* or *Treatises,* often wrongly called *Homilies,* are extant in the original Syriac. The first ten were written in 336-337 A. D., the next twelve in 343-344 A. D., and the last, the twenty-third, in the year 345 A. D.

The standard edition is that of J. Parisot in *Patrologia Syriaca,* Vol. 1, Paris 1895, col. 5-1050, and Vol. 2, Paris 1907, col. 1-150.

681

[1, 19]

This, then, is faith: that a man believe in God, the Lord of all, who made the heavens and the earth and the seas and all that is in them; and He made Adam in His image; and He gave the Law to Moses; and He sent forth His Spirit upon the prophets; and afterwards, He sent His Christ into the world. Also, that a man believe in the resurrection of the dead; and moreover, that he believe in the Sacrament of Baptism. This is the belief of the Church of God.

	460
	230
	1011
	820

682

[6, 12]

And Christ received the Spirit not by measure, but His Father loved Him and delivered all into His hands, and set Him over all His treasure. For John said: "Not by measure did the Father give the Spirit to His Son; but He loved Him and delivered all into His hands (1)."

341

683

[6, 14]

Therefore, dearly beloved, we too have received of the Spirit of Christ; and Christ dwells in us, accordingly as it is written that the Spirit said through the mouth of the prophet as follows: "I will dwell among them, and will walk about among them (2)." Let us, therefore, prepare our temples for the Spirit of Christ; and let us not grieve Him, so that He will not depart from us. Remember the word of the Apostle, when he warns us, "Grieve not the Holy Spirit, in whom you have been signed unto the day of redemption (3)." For from Baptism we receive the Spirit of Christ. At that same moment in which the priests invoke the Spirit, heaven opens, and He descends and rests upon the waters; and those who are baptized are clothed in Him. For the Spirit is absent from all those who are born of the flesh, until they come to the water of re-birth; and then they receive the Holy Spirit.

Indeed, in the first birth they are born possessed of an animal spirit, which is created within man, nor afterwards does it ever die, for it is written: "Adam became a living soul (4)." But in the second birth, that through Baptism, they receive the Holy Spirit from a particle of the Godhead (5); nor is He afterwards subject to death. For when

753
270

761

836
800
614

506
502
990

men die, the animal spirit is buried with the body, and it is deprived of sensation; but
the heavenly Spirit which they received returns, in accord with His nature, to Christ.
. . . From that man, however, who received the Spirit from the water and then grieved
Him, — He departs from him until the man dies; and then in accord with His nature
He returns to Christ and accuses the man of having grieved Him.

684

[7, 1]

    Of all those who have been born and who have put on flesh, there is one only who   345
is innocent: namely, our Lord Jesus Christ, who in fact testifies to such in His own
regard. For He says, "I have overcome the world (6)." The prophet too testifies of
Him: "He did no sin, nor was wickedness found in His mouth (7)." And the blessed
Apostle says, "He that knew no sin was made to be sin, on our behalf (8)." And how
was He made to be sin? Only in that He took up sin, which He had never done, and
fastened it to the cross (9). Again the Apostle says, "Many run in the race, but one
receives the crown (10)."

    Moreover, among the sons of Adam there is none besides Him who might enter the   614
race without being wounded or swallowed up. For sin has ruled from the time Adam
transgressed the command. By one among the many was it swallowed up; many did
it wound, and many did it kill; but none among the many killed it until our Savior came,   374
who took it on Himself and fixed it to His cross. Yet, though it is fastened to the cross,
its goad remains to the end and will sting many; and then the goad will be broken.

685

[7, 3]

    For anyone who has been wounded in a battle ought not be reluctant to put himself   916
in the care of a wise physician, because he was overcome and lost the battle. And when
he has been healed, he will not be rejected by the king, but will again be counted and
reckoned in his army. So also he that has been struck by Satan ought not be ashamed
to bewail his folly, and to give it up, and to seek a remedy in repentance. . . . If,
however, anyone is ashamed, he will not be able to be cured, since he does not wish to
make his ills known to the physician, who receives two denarii (11), so that with them
all who have been wounded may be made whole.

    [4] You physicians, then, who are the disciples of our illustrious Physician, you ought
not deny a curative to those in need of healing. And if anyone uncovers his wound   908
before you, give him the remedy of repentance. And he that is ashamed to make
known his weakness, encourage him so that he will not hide it from you. And when   920
he has revealed it to you, do not make it public, lest because of it the innocent might   921
be reckoned as guilty by our enemies and by those who hate us.

686

[8, 3]

    Therefore be instructed by this, you fool, that each and every one of the seeds is   1013
clothed in its own body. Never do you sow wheat and reap barley, and never did you
plant a vine and have it produce figs; but everything grows in accord with its own
nature. So also the body which was laid in the ground is the same which will rise again.
And in regard to the corrupting and wasting of the body, you ought to be instructed by
the figure of the seed; for the seed, when it falls to the ground, decays and is corrupted,
and from its own decaying it grows and blooms and bears fruit.

687

[8, 6]

In regard, then, to this resurrection of the dead, my beloved, I will instruct you as 1011
well as I can. For from the beginning God created Adam. From the dust He shaped 509
Him and raised him up. And if, when Adam did not exist, He made him from nothing, 461
how much easier will it now be for Him to raise him up; for he has been sown like a
seed in the earth.

689

[12, 6]

For our Savior ate the passover with His disciples on that night celebrated on the 852
fourteenth (12). And the sign of the Passover He fulfilled in truth with His disciples.
For after Judas had departed from them, He took bread and blessed it, and gave it to
His disciples, and said to them: "This is My Body; take, eat of this, all of you." So
too He pronounced a blessing upon the wine, and said to them: "This is My Blood,
the new covenant (13), which for many is poured out, to the remission of sins. In
like manner do this in memory of Me, whenever you gather together (14)."

But the Lord was not yet arrested. After having spoken thus, the Lord rose up from
the place where He had made the Passover and had given His Body as food and His
Blood as drink, and He went with His disciples to the place where He was to be arrested.
But He ate of His own Body and drank of His own Blood, while He was pondering on
the dead. With His own hands the Lord presented His own Body to be eaten, and
before He was crucified He gave His blood as drink; and He was taken at night on the
fourteenth, and was judged until the sixth hour; and at the sixth hour they condemned
Him and raised Him on the cross.

690

[12, 10]

For Israel was baptized in the midst of the sea on that Passover night, on the day 820
of salvation; and our Savior washed the feet of His disciples on the Passover night — 809
which is the Sacrament of Baptism (15). And you knew already, my beloved, that
until this night when the Savior instituted true Baptism (16) and when He conferred
it upon His disciples, the Baptism with which the priests were baptizing was that
Baptism of which John said: "Do penance for your sins (17)."

And on that night of His passion and death He showed them the Sacrament of
Baptism, just as the Apostle has stated: "You have been buried with Him in Baptism
unto death, and you have risen up with Him in the power of God (18)." Know then, 821
my beloved, that the Baptism of John was of no value for the forgiveness of sins, but
for repentance.

691

[14, 11]

And our Savior, the great King, made the rebellious world to be at peace with His 374
Father, though we were all sinners. He took away the sin of all of us and He became 383
the messenger of reconciliation between God and His creature. Though we are all sinners 387
and rebels, He sought for us our reconciliation with Him.

692

[17, 2]

But still, it is for us a certainty that our Lord Jesus is God, the Son of God; and the 301

King, the Son of the King; Light from Light; Creator, and Counsellor, and Guide, and
the Way, and the Savior, and the Shepherd, and the Gatherer, and the Gate, and the
Pearl, and the Lamp. He is called by many names. But we shall leave aside all of them
and prove that He who came from God is God and the Son of God.

693

[20, 12]

And Abraham said to the rich man, "There is a great abyss separating us from you;   991
they cannot come from you to us, nor from us to you (19)." This shows that after
death and resurrection there will be no repentance. Neither can the wicked repent and   1042
enter the kingdom, nor can the righteous any longer sin and go to perdition. This is the   1043
great abyss.

693a

[21,13]

And Jesus handed over the keys to Simon, and ascended and returned to Him who had   430
sent Him.

694

[22, 15]

And the Life-giver, the destroyer of death, shall come; and He shall take away his   1012
power over the just and over the wicked. And the dead shall rise with a mighty voice,
and death shall be emptied out and despoiled of his every captive. And for the judgment   1020
shall all the children of Adam be gathered together, and each and every one shall go to
the place assigned to him. The resurrection of the righteous leads them among the living;
and the rising up of the wicked delivers them to death.

696

[22, 19]

Again, heed the Apostle, who says, "Each and every one shall receive his reward   1046
in accord with his work (20)." Who labored little shall receive his reward according to
his remissness; and who ran well will be rewarded according to how he ran. . . . And
again the Apostle says, "Star exceeds star in brightness; so also the resurrection of the
dead (21)." Know then, that even when the sons of men shall enter into life, still,
reward shall exceed reward, and glory shall exceed glory, and recompense shall be greater
than recompense.

697

[22, 22]

And again, in regard to punishment, I say that not all men are equal. He that sinned   1035
much is much tormented. He that offended not so much is less tormented. Some shall
go into outer darkness, where there is weeping and gnashing of teeth (22). And others
shall be cast into the fire, in accord with their deserts; for it is not written that they
shall gnash their teeth, nor is that place accounted as dark. And some shall be cast into
another place, a place where their worm shall not die and their fire shall not be quenched;
and they shall be a wonder to all flesh (23). Others shall have the door closed in their
faces, and to them the judge will say, "I do not know you (24)."

698

[23, 3]

Indeed, because the first human being gave ear and listened to the serpent, he received the sentence of malediction, by which he became food for the serpent; and the curse passed on to all his progeny. . . . But a gate has been opened for seeking peace, whereby   614 the mist has lifted from the reason of the multitude; and light has dawned in the mind; and from the glistening olive, fruits are put forth, in which there is a sign of the   841 sacrament of life (25), by which Christians are perfected, as well as priests and kings   840 and prophets. It illuminates the darkness, anoints the sick, and leads back penitents   940 in its secret sacrament.

699

[23, 48]

For great is the gift which He that is good has given to us. While not forcing us,   740 and in spite of our sins, He wants us to be justified; and while He is in no way aided by our good works, He heals us that we may be pleasing in His sight. When we do not   759 wish to ask of Him, He is angry with us. He calls out to all of us constantly: "Ask   713 and receive; and when you seek, you shall find (26)."

701

[23, 61]

That God is one, and that we are to confess, worship, praise, exalt, honor, sanctify,   387 and glorify His majesty, we do indeed acknowledge through Jesus, His Son, our Savior, who chose us and drew us near to Him; and through whom we acknowledge Him and become His adorers and a people and a church and an assembly that is holy. Glory and honor be to the Father and to His Son, and to His living and holy Spirit, from the   230 mouths of all who praise Him, whether above or below. Forever in eternity, so be it and so be it.

1. John 3:34-35.
2. Lev. 26:12.
3. Eph. 4:30.
4. Gen. 2:7; 1 Cor. 15:45. Some will prefer to translate the quotation: "Man became a living soul."
5. مب كرُّا والحدهُّاُ:
6. John 16:33.
7. Is. 53:9. See also Mal. 2:6.
8. 2 Cor. 5:21.
9. Col. 2:14.
10. 1 Cor. 9:24.
11. In the two denarii there may possibly be a reference to the parable of the good Samaritan (see Luke, 10:35); but whether or not such is the reference, the passage is obscure. Does he mean only that it costs but little to be made whole, or was some kind of a stipend receivable from a penitent? While 16th century Alsatian seems to have technical terms for a fee paid to the confessor, the *Beichtpfennig* or the *Beichtgeld*, (see Johannes Pauli, *Schimpf und Ernst,* Strassburg 1522, No. 298 and No. 302), we know of no evidence whatever for such a thing in antiquity. To allow that such were the custom of the 4th century Persian Church would require much better evidence than the present obscure remark.
12. The 14th day of Nisan.
13. W. Wright has suggested that the reading *the new covenant* can be amended to the more familiar *of the new covenant* by prefixing ? to زَكَمَ . J. Parisot points out, however, that the reading as it stands is supported by the Arabic version of Tatian's reading of Matthew, by the Armenian version of the present treatise of Aphraates, and even by a liturgical text in a certain Paris manuscript (*Cod. syr. Paris.*71, fol. 133 b). See also Ephraim, *Homilies (for Holy Week)* 4, 6, § 708 below.
14. Matt. 26:26-28; Mark. 14:22-24; Luke 22:18-20; 1 Cor. 11:23-25.
15. We should perhaps note in passing that both statements are incorrect: neither does the Feast of the Passover commemorate Israel's passage through the Red Sea, nor did the washing of the disciples feet constitute sacramental Baptism.
16. هُصب تبوت فُنؤَمَ مَحمدةُ،نكَما وَعُزُا — literally, *then the Savior gave the Baptism of truth.*

17. Matt. 3:2.
18. Rom. 6:4-5; Col. 2:12.
19. Luke 16:26.
20. 1 Cor. 3:8.
21. 1 Cor. 15:41-42.
22. Matt. 8:12.
23. Is. 66:24.
24. Matt. 25:12.
25. The reference is to the olive oil, used in the various sacramental anointings.
26. Matt. 7:7; Luke 11:9.

THE COUNCIL OF SARDICA [A. D. 342/343]

Sardica or Serdica is the name given in antiquity to the city now known as Sofia, the capital of Bulgaria. The more traditional date given for the Council of Sardica, 347 A. D., stems from erroneous statements of the early Greek historians, Socrates and Sozomen. Mansi attempted without much success to establish the date as 344 A. D. It is now generally accepted that 342 A. D. is a possible date, while 343 A. D. is a near certainty.

About ninety bishops from the West, including Illyricum, were present at the Council, and about eighty from the East, representing in all some forty-eight provinces. It appears that Ossius of Cordova presided at the Council. The Eusebian party, when they found that Athanasius and others whom they had previously condemned were to be seated at the Council, hurriedly held a council of their own, and then withdrew utterly from Sardica by night, on the pretext that they must hasten away in order to present their personal congratulations to the Emperor on his victory over the Persians.

The Council had been summoned in order to put an end to the disputes between East and West which had arisen over Athanasius and certain of his colleagues. Its actual effect, however, was only to further embitter the already strained relations. The boundary between the Eastern and Western Empires was the Pass of Succa, serving also as the boundary between Thrace and Illyricum, and joining Sardica and Philippopolis, i.e., Sofia and Plovdiv. This boundary now became also the boundary between two communions.

CANONS [A. D. 342/343]

The canons of Sardica are twenty in number in the Greek text, but twenty-one in the Latin. The content of both series is basically the same, however, the discrepancy in numbering arising from a different ordering and division of the canons. Whether Greek or Latin is the original language of the canons is a point of some dispute. It is not at all unlikely that the Council provided an official text of the canons in both languages.

Our translations will be of the Greek text. Mansi, in Vol. 3, 5-38, provides a Greek text along with the Latin versions of Dionysius and Isidore. The Prisca will be found in Mansi, Vol. 6, 1140-1152. In Hefele-Leclercq, *Histoire des Conciles* I, 2, Paris 1907, pp. 760-804, the Greek text is given, along with the Latin version of Dionysius.

702a

[Canon 3]

Bishop Ossius said: It is necessary also to impose this decree, that bishops are not to go over from their own province to another province in which there are bishops already established, except perhaps, lest it might seem that we are closing the door on charity, they be invited there by their own brothers. And this must likewise be seen to: if in any province one of the bishops has some cause against his brother and fellow-bishop, neither of them is to call in as arbiters the bishops of another province (1). 899

But if any bishop loses the judgment in some case, and still believes that he has not a bad but a good case, in order that the case may be judged anew, if it pleases Your Charities, let us honor the memory of the Apostle Peter, by having those who gave the judgment write to Julius, Bishop of Rome, so that, if it seem proper, he may himself send arbiters, and judgment may be made again by the bishops of a neighboring province. But if the case cannot be shown to be such as to warrant being heard again, let the judgment once given not be set aside, but let the judgment remain as it was given. 432 435

702b

[Canon 4]

Bishop Gaudentius (2) said: If it pleases you, it is necessary to make an addition to this decree which the fullness of Your Unalloyed Charity has proposed, so that if some bishop be deposed by the judgment of the bishops sitting in the neighborhood (3), and if he declare that he will seek further redress, another should not be appointed to his see until the bishop of Rome can be acquainted with the case and render a judgment. 435

702c

[Canon 5]

Bishop Ossius said: It is proper that if some bishop has been accused, and the bishops of his own region have gathered together and have removed him from his rank, and he then took refuge in an appeal to the most blessed bishop of the Church of the Romans; and if the latter wishes to hear him, and if he thinks it just to re-open the examination of the case, then he should deem it proper to write to the bishops who are closest to that bishop in the province, that they are to examine the details carefully and meticulously, and render judgment in the matter according to what they believe to be true. 435

But if anyone demands that his case be heard again, and by his own entreaty he wishes the bishop of the Romans to send priests as his personal legates to judge the case, it is in the power of the bishop (4) to do whatever seems right to him; and if he decides that he ought to send them, and that they are to have the authority of him that sent them when they render judgment along with the bishops, this too must be allowed. But if he considers that the judgment of the case and the decision rendered upon the bishop is already sufficient, he will do whatever seems best to him in his most prudent counsel. The bishops responded: the matters so stated are approved.

1. The point of this part of the canon is that judgment is to be rendered first by the bishops of the province in which the difficulty arises. The next part of the canon provides for appeal to Rome, if the first judgment is not accepted.

2. Gaudentius, Bishop of Naissus, in Illyricum.
3. We have rendered the phrase quite literally, and it will readily be seen that it is not clear whether it means the bishops of his own province, or the bishops of a neighboring province. It seems more likely to us, taking the canon in conjunction with canon 3 to which this present canon is proposed as addition or clarification, that the bishops of the neighborhood are the bishops of the same province as he that is on trial. The import of the canon, then, is simply this: that if he appeals to Rome, as is provided for in canon 3, his see is not to be regarded as vacant until Rome has rendered judgment through its arbiters.

Others, however, regard the phrase as referring to bishops of the neighboring province, who, in accord with canon 3, have sat with arbiters from Rome and have rendered judgment again against the bishop, deposing him from his see. If this view be taken, then the present canon provides for a second appeal to Rome, with the bishop of Rome himself to render judgment. This does not seem to us to be a likely interpretation.
4. *I.e.,* the Bishop of Rome.

ST. EPHRAIM [*ca. A. D.* 306 - *A. D.* 373]

St. Ephraim, called the *lyre of the Holy Spirit,* is the great classic author of the Syrian Church. He was born at Nisibis about the year 306 A. D., probably of Christian parents, and was a pupil of James, Bishop of Nisibis. He was ordained to the diaconate before the year 338 A. D., and remained all his life a deacon.

The very considerable remains of Ephraim, nearly all of which is in poetic forms of one kind or another, is an almost untouched storehouse of treasures. He himself wrote only in Syriac, but many of his works were translated very early into Greek and Armenian, and to a lesser extent in other oriental languages.

Until quite recently the principal and standard editions of Ephraim were as follows: J. S. and S. E. Assemani, *S. P. N. Ephraem Syri opera omnia quae extant, graece, syriace, latine,* 6 Vols., Rome 1732-1746; G. Bickell, *S. Ephraem Syri carmina nisibena,* Leipzig 1866; and T. J. Lamy, *S. Ephraem Syri hymni et sermones,* 4 Vols., Mechlin 1882-1902. These, with a few other works, were the best available; yet, they were quite incomplete and not at all adequate for the demands of modern scholarship. However, the critical edition of Ephraim's works in the *Corpus Scriptorum Christianorum Orientalium* (CSCO), begun in the early fifties, has made magnificent strides in the last few years, and is approaching completion. Already 26 volumes have been published in the Syriac series, 13 volumes of the Syriac texts with 13 matching volumes of translations (one in Latin, the work of R. M. Tonneau, and the other twelve in German, the work of Edmund Beck).

Besides the 26 volumes in the Syriac series, two volumes have appeared in the Armenian series: CSCO 137 / Arm. 1, *Saint Éphrem: Commentaire de l'Évangile Concordant: Version Arménienne,* edited by Louis Leloir, Louvain 1953; and CSCO 145 / Arm. 2, the same, translated into Latin by Louis Leloir, 1954. In addition to the above, there is in the Georgian series a life of Saint Ephraim: CSCO 171 / Georgian 7, *Vies Géorgiennes de S. Syméon Stylite l'ancien et de S. Éphrem,* edited by Gérard Garitte, Louvain 1957, pp. 78-117; and CSCO 172 / Georg. 8, the same in Garitte's Latin translation, Louvain 1957, pp. 54-81.

Further, in the *subsidia* series of the CSCO, there are four volumes of valuable mongraphs pertinent to the study of Ephraim: CSCO 180 / Sub. 12, *L'Évangile d'Éphrem d'après les oeuvres éditées,* by Louis Leloir, Louvain 1958; CSCO 220 / Sub. 18, *Doctrines et Méthodes de S. Ephrem d'après son Commentaire de l'Évangile Concordant,* Louis Leloir, Louvain 1961; CSCO 227 / Sub. 19, *Le Temoignage d'Éphrem sur le Diatessaron,* Louis Leloir, Louvain 1962; and CSCO 266 / Sub. 26, *History of the School of Nisibis,* Arthur Vööbus, Louvain 1965.

N. B. Since writing the above notice of St. Ephraim two further volumes have appeared in the Armenian series of the CSCO, the text and translation of his *Exposition of the Gospel,* Թարգմանութիւն Աւետարանի *(Tarkmanoutiun Avedarani):* George A. Egan, *Saint Ephrem: An Exposition of the Gospel,* (Armenian text), CSCO Vol. 291 / Arm. 5, Louvain 1968; and the English translation, also by Egan, CSCO Vol. 292 / Arm. 6, Louvain 1968.

HYMNS OF THE EPIPHANY

Ephraim's *Madrāsē d-denhā* or *Hymns of the Epiphany* are thirteen in number in Edmund Beck's critical edition, *Des heiligen Ephraem des Syrers Hymnen de Nativitate (Epiphania),* CSCO 186 / Syr. 82, Louvain 1959, pp. 144-191. They are not presently datable. Beck regards the present hymn, No. 10, as unauthentic (CSCO 187 / Syr. 83, p. x); but we will, nevertheless, quote stanzas 1 and 14, because they are so frequently referred to by theological authors.

703

[10, 1]
Adam sinned and earned all sorrows,   612
And the world, following his lead, all guilt.   614
And it took no thought of how it might be restored,
But only of how its fall might be made more pleasant for it.
[Resp.] Glory to Him that came and restored it!   376

704

[10, 14]
He that is Good takes care in two respects: 700
He wills not to repress our freedom,
Nor yet does He allow that we abuse it.
For had He repressed it He had taken away its strength,
And had He abandoned it He had deprived it of His help.

HOMILIES

For most of Ephraim's Mēmrē, a term which answers closely to *Homilies,* except that the Mēmrā is a poetic form, we are still dependent upon the edition of Lamy. The present selections are from a group of eight such *Homilies,* found in Lamy, Vol. 1, pp. 399-566, under the heading *Sermones in hebdomadam sanctam, diem resurrectionis et dominicam novam.* Their texts stem from manuscripts of the 14th and 17th centuries.

706

[4, 1]

Simon, My follower, I have made you the foundation of the holy Church. I betimes   43C
called you Peter (1), because you will support all its buildings. You are the inspector of
those who will build on earth a Church for Me. If they should wish to build what is
false, you, the foundation, will condemn them. You are the head of the fountain from
which My teaching flows, you are the chief of My disciples. Through you I will give
drink to all peoples. Yours is that life-giving sweetness which I dispense. I have chosen
you to be, as it were, the first-born in My institution, and so that, as the heir, you may
be executor of my treasures. I have given you the keys of my kingdom. Behold, I have
given you authority over all my treasures!

707

[4, 4]

Our Lord Jesus took in His hands what in the beginning was only bread; and He   852
blessed it, and signed it, and made it holy in the name of the Father and in the name   860
of the Spirit; and He broke it and in His gracious kindness He distributed it to all His
disciples one by one. He called the bread His living Body, and did Himself fill it with
Himself and the Spirit.

And extending His hand, He gave them the Bread which His right hand had made
holy: "Take, all of you eat of this, which My word has made holy. Do not now regard
as bread that which I have given you; but take, eat this Bread, and do not scatter the   851
crumbs; for what I have called My Body, that it is indeed. One particle from its crumbs   859
is able to sanctify thousands and thousands, and is sufficient to afford life to those who
eat of it. Take, eat, entertaining no doubt of faith, because this is My Body, and whoever
eats it in belief eats in it Fire and Spirit. But if any doubter eat of it, for him it will   855
be only bread. And whoever eats in belief the Bread made holy in My name, if he be   877
pure, he will be preserved in his purity; and if he be a sinner, he will be forgiven." But   929
if anyone despise it or reject it or treat it with ignominy, it may be taken as a certainty
that he treats with ignominy the Son, who called it and actually made it to be His Body.

708

[4, 6]

After the disciples had eaten the new and holy Bread, and when they understood by
faith that they had eaten of Christ's body, Christ went on to explain and to give them   849
the whole Sacrament. He took and mixed a cup of wine. Then He blessed it, and signed
it, and made it holy, declaring that it was His own Blood, which was about to be poured
out. . . . Christ commanded them to drink, and He explained to them that the cup which   851
they were drinking was His own Blood: "This is truly My Blood, which is shed for all
of you. Take, all of you, drink of this, because it is a new covenant in My Blood. As
you have seen Me do, do you also in My memory. Whenever you are gathered together
in My name in Churches everywhere, do what I have done, in memory of Me. Eat
My Body, and drink My Blood, a covenant new and old."

1. ܟܐܦܐ , *Kēfā, i.e.* Rock or Peter.

SONGS OF PRAISE

Beck's critical edition of Ephraim's *Hymns of the Nativity,* CSCO 186 / Syr. 82,
Des heiligen Ephraem des Syrers Hymnen de Nativitate (Epiphania), Louvain 1959,

includes in an appendix, pp. 191-227, six hymns under the heading *Carmina Sōgyâtâ*. The term *sōgītâ* may be taken as an *ode* or a *song of praise*. The first of these six *sōgyâtâ* is the same hymn which appears as the eighteenth of the *Hymns on Blessed Mary* in Lamy's edition, Vol. 2, p. 605. Beck regards this hymn as unauthentic, because in stanza 2 *virginitas in partu* is mentioned, and in stanza 20 Mary is called *Mother of God* (CSCO 187 / Syr. 83, pp. x-xi). We will, nevertheless, translate certain stanzas from Beck's text, because they are so frequently referred to by theological writers.

710a

[1, 1]
Awake, my harp, your songs
   in praise of the Virgin Mary!
Lift up your voice and sing
   the wonderful history
Of the Virgin, the daughter of David,
   who gave birth to the Life of the World.

779

[1, 2]
Who loves you is amazed;
   and who would understand is silent and confused,
Because he cannot probe the Mother
   who gave birth in her virginity.
If it is too great to be clarified with words
   the disputants ought not on that account cross swords with your Son.

782

711

[1, 12]
In the womb of Mary the Infant was formed,
   who from eternity is equal to the Father.
He imparted to us His greatness,
   and took on our infirmity.
He became mortal like us and joined his life to ours,
   so that we might die no more.

311

375

[1, 20]
This Virgin became a Mother
   while preserving her virginity;
And though still a Virgin
   she carried a Child in her womb;
And the handmaid and work of His Wisdom
   became the Mother of God.

781

779

HYMNS ON VIRGINITY

The grouping which Lamy in his edition refers to as *Hymns on the Church and on Virginity,* Vol. 2, pp. 773-810, includes four hymns under the heading *On Oil and the*

Olive. These same four, under the same sub-heading, *On Oil and the Olive,* appear as Nos. 4 through 7 of the *Hymns on Virginity, Madrãs̄e d-'al btūlūtâ,* in Edmund Beck's new critical edition: *Des heiligen Ephraem des Syrers Hymnen de Virginitate,* CSCO 223 / Syr. 94, Louvain 1962. The selection we offer below is from the hymn which Lamy calls No. 4 *On Oil and the Olive,* and which Beck calls No. 7 *On Virginity.* Our translation is based on the text of Beck.

712

[7, 6]
That oil is a friend
  of the Holy Spirit, and His servant.
Like a disciple, it accompanies Him,
  that with which the priests and the anointed are sealed.
By means of the oil, the Holy Spirit impresses
  His seal upon the sheep;   798
Like a signet pressed in wax,
  He impresses His seal.
So also the invisible seal of the Spirit
  is impressed on our bodies with the oil
With which we are anointed in Baptism,
  whereby we bear His seal.

THE NISIBENE HYMNS

The Nisibene Hymns or *Madrãs̄e da-Nṣībâyē,* so-called after Ephraim's native city of Nisibis, were seventy-seven in number, of which all except Nos. 8 and 22-24 are extant in the original Syriac. They are among the few works of Ephraim which can presently be dated. Nos. 1 through 21 were written between the years 350 and 363 A. D.; Nos. 25 to 30 about the year 370 A. D.; Nos. 31 to 34, about the year 364; and Nos. 35 through 77, between the years 363 and 373 A. D.

The standard edition is that of Edmund Beck, *Des heiligen Ephraem des Syrers Carmina Nisibena,* CSCO 218 / Syr. 92, Louvain 1961 (hymns 1 - 34); and CSCO 240 / Syr. 102, Louvain 1963 (hymns 35 - 77). Beck's German translations of the same are in CSCO 219 / Syr. 93, Louvain 1961, and CSCO 241 / Syr. 103, Louvain 1963.

719

[27, 8]
You alone and your Mother
  are more beautiful than any others;
For there is no blemish in you,
  nor any stains upon your Mother.   786
Who of my children
  can compare in beauty to these?

721

[73, 1]
Behold, my beloved, beneath the earth
  are the corpses, the bodies of the entombed;

But in heaven are the alms-givers.   996
   Earth and heaven
Bear the remains of men,
   and both would cry out
Were the just to be treated unjustly.

Response: Praise to the Son who, with a blast of His trumpet,   1011
         will open the graves and the dead will rise.

COMMENTARIES ON SACRED SCRIPTURE

Of Ephraim's various commentaries on Scripture, only the *Commentary on Genesis* and *Commentary on Exodus* (Vol. 152 / Syr. 71 with translation in Vol. 153 / Syr. 72) and the Armenian version of his *Commentary on the Diatessaron* (Vol. 137 / Arm. 1, with translation in Vol. 145 / Arm. 2) have thus far appeared in the critical editions of the CSCO. A new edition is badly needed of the numerous fragmentary commentaries. Our source for the text of the following fragment, commenting on Joel 2:24, is Vol. 2, p. 252, of the Assemani edition.

ON JOEL 2:24

725

"And your floors shall be filled with wheat, and the presses shall overflow equally with   849
wine and oil." . . . This has been fulfilled mystically by Christ, who gave to the people   840
whom He had redeemed, that is, to His Church, wheat and wine and oil in a mystic
manner. For the wheat is the mystery of His sacred Body; and the wine His saving Blood;
and again, the oil is the sweet unguent with which those who are baptized are signed, being
clothed in the armaments of the Holy Spirit.

HYMNS AGAINST HERESIES

The *Hymns against Heresies* or *Madrā̆šē d-luqbal yulpā̂nē* comprise a group of hymns which older editions referred to as *Polemic Madrashes.* The standard edition of the text is now Edmund Beck's *Des heiligen Ephraem des Syrers Hymnen contra Haereses,* CSCO 169 / Syr. 76, with his German translation in CSCO 170 / Syr. 77, Louvain 1957.

729

[53, 12]
To Moses He revealed His name:
   WHO AM, He called Himself,   140
Which is the name of His essence.
   And never did He name
Any other with this name,
   as He did with His other names,
With which many were named;

therefore, by this one exclusive name
He let it be known that He alone
   is Being: which can be said of no other.

THE COUNCIL OF LAODICEA [*inter A. D.* 343/381]

The Council of Laodicea in Pacatian Phrygia has left sixty canons, largely of a disciplinary nature; but, unfortunately, no authentic list of the signatories of the Council has been preserved, a fact which makes virtually impossible any reasonable degree of precision in the dating of the council.

In the various ancient collections of canons, the canons of Laodicea occupy various relative positions among the canons of the other fourth century councils. Baronius and Binius held that Laodicea was a pre-Nicene council of about the year 314 A. D. Tillemont, Ceillier, and Hefele place it between Sardica and First Constantinople, that is, between 343 and 381 A. D. Pagius would have it in 363 A. D., and Boudinhon, after 381 A. D. Obviously we cannot in this place engage in any lengthy discussion of the problem of the date of the Council, and will only point out that all pre-Nicene dates are equally impossible, if the wording of that part of Canon 7 condemning the Photinians be accepted. Those who insist on a pre-Nicene date are not unaware of this problem, however, and obviate the difficulty of the Photinians being a somewhat post-Nicene phenomenon by declaring that either the word is not pertinent to the authentic text, or else some unknown group of Photinians is meant, some group other than that post-Nicene sect to which the name is generally applied.

As to the other extreme date, Theodoret of Cyr, about the year 450 A. D., was already able to appeal to the authority of Laodicea. Historians today see no reason for giving the Council a post-Constantinopolitan date at all, and it is more or less universally accepted that the Council is most certainly of the fourth century, almost certainly post-Nicene, and very probably post-Sardican. The Council of Laodicea, then, very probably belongs within the period 343 to 381 A. D.; and there seems to be a general apprehension that within this period, an earlier date is preferable to a later one.

CANONS [*inter A. D.* 343/381]

The canons of the Council of Laodicea in Phrygia are preserved in Greek, and in two of the usual Latin versions: Dionysius and Isidore. Formerly it was believed that the leaves of the Prisca which ought to have contained the Canons of Laodicea had perished; but now it is more generally accepted that the Canons of Laodice never were in the Greek manuscript of which the Prisca is a version Further, it is believed that the Greek text extant is not the original text, but one which has been somewhat paraphrased. The reader will notice even in our English translations, which are fairly literal, that the so-called canons seem rather to be a statement of what the canon was, rather than the actual wording of a decree or law.

For the text of the canons, Greek and Latin as referred to above, see Mansi, Vol. 2, 563-594. A more convenient source for the Greek, easier on the eye than Mansi's ligatured Greek, is Hefele-Leclercq, *Histoire des Conciles* I, 2, Paris 1907, pp. 995-1026, where also there are valuable commentaries.

745a

[Canon 1]

That we have determined, in accord with the ecclesiastical canon, that those who freely and lawfully enter upon second marriages, not contracting marriage secretly, — after the passage of a short time, and devoting themselves to prayers and to fastings, communion may be given to them in clemency. 979

745b

[Canon 5]

That ordinations are not to be conducted in the presence of hearers (1). 904

745c

[Canon 7]

That those who are converted from heresies, that is, from the Novatians, or, indeed, from the Photinians, or Quartodecimans, be they catechumens or among those whom they call faithful, are not to be received until they have anathematized every heresy, and especially that in which they were involved. And thereafter, those who among them were called faithful, when they have memorized the formula of faith and have been anointed with the holy chrism, may participate in the Holy Mystery (2). 906

745d

[Canon 8]

That those who are converted from the heresy called that of the Phrygians (3), even if they be among those whom they account as clergy or even among those called their great ones (4), — after they have been very carefully instructed, they are to be baptized by the bishops and presbyters of the Church. 826

745e

[Canon 10]

That those who are of the Church are not to join their children indiscriminately in marriage with heretics. 980

745f

[Canon 11]

That the so-called presbyteresses or presidentesses (5) are not to be ordained in the Church (6). 957

745g

[Canon 12]

That bishops are to be appointed to ecclesiastical leadership by the judgment of the 441 metropolitans and their surrounding bishops, after they have been examined at length as to their knowledge of the faith and quite frankly as to their deportment.

745h

[Canon 13]

That the election of those about to be ordained to the priesthood (7) is not to be referred to the people.

951

745i

[Canon 15]

That none others are to be permitted to sing in Church except the cantors inscribed on the register, who go up to the ambo and chant from the parchments.

956

745j

[Canon 21]

That subdeacons (8) are not to have a place in the diaconicum (9), nor are they to touch the sacred vessels.

955

745k

[Canon 22]

That a subdeacon is not to wear a stole (10), nor abandon the doors.

898

745l

[Canon 23]

That a lector or cantor is not to wear a stole (11), even when reading or chanting.

898

745m

[Canon 24]

That sacred persons (12) from presbyters (13) to deacons (14), and one after another through the ecclesiastical rank, from subdeacons (15) to lectors (16) or cantors (17) or exorcists (18) or porters (19) or those of the rank of ascetics (20) are not to enter a tavern.

952
955
956
899

745n

[Canon 41]

That a sacred person or cleric is not to travel without canonical letters.

899

745o

[Canon 42]

That a sacred person or cleric is not to travel except at the command of the bishop.

899

745p

[Canon 44]

That women are not to come near the altar.

899

745q

[Canon 48]

That those who have been illuminated (21) are, after Baptism, to be anointed with   842
celestial chrism, and thus become partakers in the kingdom of Christ.   846

745r

[Canon 58]

That the Sacrifice is not to be offered in homes by bishops or by presbyters.   898

745s

[Canon 59]

That psalms of private origin are not to be read in the church, nor uncanonical books,   40
but only the canonical books of the Old and New Testaments.

745t

[Canon 60]

These are the books of the Old Testament which ought to be read: 1. Genesis of the   41
World; 2. Exodus from Egypt; 3. Leviticus; 4. Numbers; 5. Deuteronomy; 6. Jesus of
Nave; 7. Judges, Ruth; 8. Esther; 9. First and Second of Kingdoms; 10. Third and
Fourth of Kingdoms; 11. First and Second of Paralipomenon; 12. First and Second
Esdras; 13. Book of One Hundred and Fifty Psalms; 14. Proverbs of Solomon; 15.
Ecclesiastes; 16. Song of Songs; 17. Job; 18. Twelve Prophets; 19. Isaias; 20. Jeremias
and Baruch, Lamentations and Letters (22); 21. Ezechiel; 22. Daniel.

These are the books of the New Testament: the four Gospels, according to Matthew,   42
according to Mark, according to Luke, and according to John. The Acts of the Apostles.
The seven Catholic Epistles, as follows: one of James, two of Peter, three of John, one of
Jude. The fourteen Epistles of Paul: one to the Romans, two to the Corinthians, one to
the Galatians, one to the Ephesians, one to the Philippians, one to the Colossians, two to
the Thessalonians, one to the Hebrews, two to Timothy, one to Titus, one to Philemon (23).

1. The *hearers* constituted one of the classes of penitents. See Canons 11 and 12 of Nicaea (§ 651q and
   § 651r above); and the *Canonical Letter* of St. Gregory the Miracle-Worker, § 611a above.
2. *I.e.,* they may be admitted to the reception of the Eucharist.
3. *I.e.,* the Cataphrygians or Montanists. Their baptismal formula was not Trinitarian: hence, their Baptism
   was invalid.
4. Hefele-Leclercq agrees with Zonaras and Balsamon that this obscure phrase refers to their more important
   clergy, higher clergy, or teachers.
5. τὰς λεγομένας πρεσβύτιδας, ἤτοι προκαθημένας.
6. Hefele-Leclercq, whom we follow, reads ἐν τῇ Ἐκκλησίᾳ. Mansi, however, ἐν ἐκκλησίᾳ: and Dionysius
   Exiguus, *in ecclesiis.* The problem is fairly obvious: does the canon forbid their ordination as an
   institution in the structured Church? or does it forbid their ordination inside a church edifice, but permit
   their ordination outside a church building? Isidore Mercator's Latin is probably farther from the authentic
   text than any, in his wording; yet, by his circumlocutions he arrives at an unambiguous statement which is
   undoubtedly the sense of the canon: "Women who among the Greeks are called *presbyteresses,* but by us
   are named *older widows, women once-married,* and *women on the register,* are not to be stationed in a
   church as if they were ordained." The *priestesses* here spoken of, then, are in fact *deaconesses.* See also
   Epiphanius, *Adv. haer. panarium* 79, 3-4.
7. The term ἱερατεῖον is to be taken as embracing both priesthood and episcopate.
8. ὑπηρέτας.
9. Much as we would like to comment intelligently upon this canon, we are at a distinct disadvantage in not
   knowing what a *diaconicum* was. The term is a noun, τὸ διακονικόν, (or possibly ὁ διακονικός, since we
   have it only in the dative), made of the adjective meaning *serviceable* or *menial;* and it is suggested that it
   refers to the sacristy and the duties of a deacon about the sacristy. But did a deacon have any duties
   about the sacristy? In any case, the canon is generally interpreted as containing a broad prohibition of a
   subdeacon's usurping the role of a deacon. I am not myself much enamored of the idea that the *diaconicum*

was the sacristy, or a place set aside in or near the sacristy for the deacons; and I see no reason at all why τὸ διακονικὸν should not mean simply *the role of a deacon*. The rhetoric of the present canons is already so dreadful that the tautology of *a place in the role* can scarcely be regarded as damaging.

10. ὡράριον φερεῖν.
11. The term is the same as in the previous canon: ὡράριον φερεῖν.
12. ἰερατικούς.
13. πρεσβυτέρων. In several other canons of this same council it is clear that the term *presbyter* means a priest, as distinct from a bishop: *e.g.*, Canon 57, wherein presbyters are forbidden to undertake anything without the knowledge of the bishop. In the present instance, however, the term would seem to embrace both bishops and priests, unless perhaps the Fathers of Laodicea felt that any bishop would be so far removed from attendance upon a tavern that it were insulting even to mention him as included in the prohibition.
14. διακόνων.
15. ὑπηρετῶν.
16. ἀναγνωστῶν.
17. ψαλτῶν.
18. ἐφορκιστῶν.
19. θυρωρῶν.
20. τοῦ τάγματος τῶν ἀσκητῶν.
21. τοὺς φωτιζομένους. *Illumination* is one of the classical terms for Baptism. It is interesting, however, that this same short canon uses also the term τὸ βάπτισμα. Canon 45 of this same council, decreeing *that there is to be no admission to Baptism after the second week of the forty days of Lent*, employs the noun τὸ φώτισμα.
22. Thus in the manuscripts; but Zonaras corrects it to *the Letter*.
23. The sixtieth canon is present in the Greek text and in Isidore, but is missing from Dionysius Exiguus. The scriptural canon which it announces is complete as we have it today, except for the omission of the deuterocanonical books of Tobias, Judith, Wisdom, Jesus Sirach, and First and Second Machabees; and, from the New Testament, the Apocalypse. The omission of the deuterocanonical books from a Syrian scriptural canon of the fourth century is perhaps not so surprising as is the inclusion of one of those books, Baruch. It must be remembered, however, that quite probably Baruch was at one time admitted even to the Jewish canon, and was only later excluded; and it was in fact generally received as canonical even by those Christians who consistently excluded the other deuterocanonical books. Neither is the omission of the Apocalypse from the New Testament canon cause for any surprise. It is not to be found in the Syriac Scriptures, and was excluded by St. Cyril of Jerusalem and even by St. John Chrysostom; and it was generally held at least in suspicion in the East, although in the West it was almost universally received from the earliest times.

ST. ATHANASIUS [*ca. A. D. 295 - A. D. 373*]

St. Athanasius was born near Alexandria about the year 295 A. D. Ordained a deacon in 319 A. D., he accompanied his bishop, Alexander, to the Council of Nicaea in 325 A. D., serving as his secretary. In 328 A. D. he succeeded Alexander in the See of Alexandria. His career as principal champion of Nicene doctrine against the onslaughts of the Arians was a stormy one. Exiled from his see five times, he finally regained his place again in 366 A. D., and his last years, until his death in 373 A. D., were spent in comparative peace.

A critical edition of Athansius' writings, to comprise three volumes, has been in progress since 1934. The general title of the work is *Athanasius' Werke herausgegeben im Auftrage der Kirchenväter-Kommission der Preussischen Akademie der Wissenschaften.* Only two parts have thus far appeared, both the work of H. G. Opitz: Vol. 2, part 1, pp. 1-280, *Die Apologien*, Berlin and Leipzig 1935; and Vol. 3, part 1, pp. 1-76, *Urkunden zur Geschichte des arianischen Streites 318-328,* Berlin and Leipzig 1934. There are also a few of his works in early translations in the various oriental languages in the *Corpus Scriptorum Christianorum Orientalium* (CSCO). Except for these several items, it may be said that in general the Migne edition, however inadequate it may be, remains at present the standard edition.

TREATISE AGAINST THE PAGANS [*ca. A. D. 318*]

Athanasius' *Treatise against the Pagans* and his *Treatise on the Incarnation of the Word (Oratio de incarnatione Verbi)* are, according to Jerome, but two parts of a single work, written about the year 318 A. D., which Jerome refers to as *Adversum gentes duo libri.*

The first part of the work, the *Oratio contra gentes,* is a refutation of pagan beliefs. The Migne text, PG 25, 3-97, remains the standard edition.

746

[34, 3]

[The soul] is fashioned according to the image of God, and according to His likeness is it made; as also the Divine Scripture indicates when it says, as if from the mouth of God: "Let us make man according to our likeness (1)." Therefore, when [the soul] puts aside all the filth of sin which covers it, and retains only what is pure according to that image, then quite properly, when it has been so brightened, it beholds as in a mirror the Word, the Image of the Father; and through Him it reasons to the Father, whose image the Savior is. [4] Or, if the soul's own teaching is insufficient because of the external things which cloud the mind and prevent its seeing what is superior, it is still possible for it to attain to a knowledge of God from the things that are seen; for creation, as if in written characters and by means of its order and harmony, declares in a loud voice its own Master and Creator.

512

264

131

747

[35, 1]

For God, being good and loving to mankind, and caring for the souls which He made, since He is by nature invisible and incomprehensible, and since His existence transcends that of every created being, on which account the human race, made out of nothing while He is not made at all, was unlikely to reach a knowledge of Him, — for this reason God,

170

173

by His own Word, gave to creation such order as is found therein, so that while He is by nature invisible, men might yet be able to know Him through His works.   131

1. Gen. 1:26.

TREATISE ON THE INCARNATION OF THE WORD [ca. A. D. 318]

As noted above, the *Oratio de incarnatione Verbi* is, according to Jerome, the second part of a single work, of which the first part is the *Oratio contra gentes*. Both parts belong to about the year 318 A. D.

The purpose of this second part is to show that the Incarnation is the sole remedy for man's fallen nature, and his single hope of restoration.

The Migne text, PG 25, 95-198, remains the standard edition.

748

[2, 3]
But others, among whom there is Plato, so reknowned among the Greeks, contend that   460
God has made all things out of previously existing and uncreated matter; — as if God could   461
have made nothing unless the matter already existed, just as in the case of a carpenter, who must needs have wood already at hand if he is to be able to work at all! . . . [3, 1] Thus, then, do they vainly speculate. But the divine teaching and the faith according to Christ   463
brands their vain reasoning as godless. It knows that creation was not spontaneous, because it is not improvident; nor was it from pre-existing matter, because God is not weak. On the contrary, through His Word, God made all things to exist out of what   284
did not exist and out of what had no previous existence, as He said through Moses: "In the beginning God made the heavens and the earth (1)."

749

[4, 4]
But men, negligent and refusing to look to God, devised and contrived evil for themselves — as was stated in the former treatise (2) — and received the condemnation   611
of death with which they had been threatened. From that time on they no longer remained as they had been made, but were corrupted in accord with their own devices; and death held sway over them as a king. For transgression of the commandment turned   522
them back to their natural state, so that just as they had come into existence out of nothingness, likewise they might rightly expect the corruption of their existence in the course of time.

750

[5, 1]
God not only made us out of nothing, but He also gave us freely, by the grace of the   461
Word, a life divinely oriented. But men rejected the things of eternity and, on the   611
prompting of the devil, turned to the things of corruption. They became the cause of   522
their own corruption in death; for, as I said before, they were by nature corruptible, but were destined, by the grace of the communion of the Word, to have escaped the consequences of nature, had they remained good. [2] Because of the Word and His dwelling among them, even the corruption natural to them would not have affected them.

751

[9, 1]

The Word perceived that the corruption of men could be undone in no other way   363
whatever, but only by death. Neither could such a one as the Word suffer death, being   375
immortal and Son of the Father. For this reason, then, He takes to Himself flesh
capable of dying, so that this flesh, by partaking of the Word who is superior to all,
might be worthy to suffer death in place of all, and might, because of the Word dwelling
in it, remain incorruptible, so that from then on corruption might be stayed from
everyone, by the grace of the resurrection. Then, by offering to death the body which
He Himself had taken, as a sacrifice and offering free of every stain, He forthwith removed   380
death from all His fellowmen, by that sentencing of a substitute. [2] Since He, the Word
of God, is over all, by offering His own temple and bodily·component for the life of all,   383
He surely satisfied the debt by His death. And thus, too, the incorruptible Son of God,
being joined with all by the similarity of flesh, He surely clothed all in incorruptibility   386
through the promise of resurrection.

751a

[47, 2]

And while in times past demons, occupying springs or rivers or trees or stones, cheated   494
men by deceptive appearances and imposed upon the credulous by their juggleries, now,
after the divine coming of the Word, an end is put to their deceptions. For by the sign   125
of the cross, a man but using it, their wiles are put to flight.

752

[54, 3]

He became man so that we might be made God; and He manifested Himself in the   375
flesh, so that we might grasp the idea of the unseen Father; and He endured the insolence
of men, so that we might receive the inheritance of immortality.

1. Gen. 1:1.
2. See *Treatise against the Pagans* 3, 5.

ENCYCLICAL LETTER TO ALL BISHOPS EVERYWHERE [*A. D.* 339]

The *Encyclical Letter to All Bishops Everywhere* is Athanasius' earliest extant
polemical writing, belonging to about the middle of the year 339 A. D. It is a call
for all bishops, his fellow-ministers, to regard his cause as their own, and to assist
him in rescuing his churches from Gregory, the usurping Arian bishop.

The Migne text, PG 25, 221-240, has happily been superseded by the critical
edition of H. G. Opitz in his *Athanasius' Werke* 2, 1, Berlin and Leipzig 1935, pp.
169-177.

752a

[5]

And now this wonderful Gregory accuses before the governor those who pray in
their own homes; and he takes every opportunity to insult their ministers. His conduct is   831
of such violence, then, that many run the risk of not being baptized, and many have no
one to visit them in sickness and distress, a circumstance which they regret even more
bitterly than their illness. For while the ministers of the Church are under persecution,

the people condemn the impiety of the Arian heretics, and choose rather to be sick and 906
to run the risk, than to permit a hand of the Arians to come upon their head. 909

APOLOGY AGAINST THE ARIANS [ca. A. D. 347]

The *Apology against the Arians* is a work of Athanasius, of about the year 347 A. D. It is largely a collection of documents which Athanasius published in his own defense.

The passage which we translate below is from a letter quoted in full in chapter 76 of the present *Apology*. The letter was addressed to certain civil authorities in Egypt, over the signatures of the priests and deacons of the Mareotis, and was written in defense of Athanasius against certain false charges which had been made against him. Though the *Apology* itself was written in 347 A. D., the letter in question bears a date convertible to Sept. 8, 335 A. D.

The Migne text, PG 25, 247-410, is now entirely superseded by that of Opitz, *Athanasius' Werke*, 2, 1, Berlin and Leipzig 1935, pp. 87-168.

753

[76]
When Theognis, Maris, Macedonius, Theodorus, Ursacius, and Valens, as if sent by all 951
the bishops who were assembled at Tyre (1), came into our diocese, alleging that they had
been given a mandate to investigate certain ecclesiastical matters, among which they also
spoke of the breaking of a cup of the Lord, they had been falsely informed by Ischyras,
whom they brought with them, who calls himself a presbyter but who is not a presbyter. 960
For he was ordained by the presbyter Colluthus who pretended to the episcopate and who
was afterwards ordered by the common synod of Ossius and the other bishops joined with
him to be but a presbyter, as he formerly was. And as a consequence, all those who had
been ordained by Colluthus reverted to the same estate in which they formerly were, and
thus Ischyras himself, it would seem, is a layman.

1. Council of Tyre, *A. D.* 335.

LETTER CONCERNING THE DECREES OF THE COUNCIL OF NICAEA [A. D. 350/351]

The *Letter Concerning the Decrees of the Council of Nicaea* is a genuine Athanasian work of the year 350 or 351 A. D. It is a defense of Nicene terminology, which was under attack as being non-Scriptural.

The Migne text, PG 25, 415-476, is superseded by Opitz's edition in *Athanasius' Werke* 2, 1, Berlin and Leipzig 1935, pp. 1-45.

754

[11]
And then, too, God creates, while creating is also attributed to men; and God, indeed, is 177
Being, while men too are said to be, having received even this gift from God. And yet, does 141
God create as men do? Or is His being like that of man? No indeed. Rather, we take
these terms in one way in regard to God, and understand them in a different way for men.
Indeed, God creates by calling into existence that which did not exist, requiring nothing 461
in order to do it; but men work with some existing material, first praying and obtaining
the ability of making, from that God who fashioned all things through His own proper

Word. And again, men, who have no capacity for self-existence, are in fact circumscribed
in place, and exist at the pleasure of the Word of God (1).   154

God, however, exists of Himself, transcends all things, and is circumscribed by none.
He is within all things according to His own goodness and power, but outside of all
according to His own proper nature. Just as the way in which men create is not the
same as the way in which God creates, so also man's generation is in one way, while the   265
Son is from the Father in another way. For the offspring of men are as a portion of
their fathers, since the very nature of bodies is to be not a simple thing, but unsettled
and composed of parts. In begetting, men pour out something of themselves; and again,
in taking food, they regain something in themselves. And it is on this account that men
in their time become the fathers of many children.

God, however, being without parts, is Father of the Son without division and without   151
being acted upon. For neither is there an effluence from that which is incorporeal, nor
is there anything flowing into Him from without, as in the case of men. Being simple in
nature, He is Father of one only Son. On this account is that Son the only-begotten, and
alone is He in the bosom of the Father; and alone is He acknowledged by the Father as
being from Him, when He says, "This is My beloved Son, in whom I am well pleased (2)."

And He is the Word of the Father, from which fact also it is possible to perceive that
the Father is neither acted upon nor divided. Not even among men is a word begotten
passively or by a process of divisions; and much less then, could this be the case with
the Word of God.

755

[20]

The generation of the Son from the Father is otherwise than that which accords with   257
the nature of men; and He is not only like, but is in fact inseparable from the substance
of the Father. He and the Father are indeed one, as He did say Himself (3); and the Word
is ever in the Father and the Father in the Word, as is the way of radiance in relation to
light. The term itself indicates this; and the Council, so understanding the matter, did
well, therefore, when it wrote *homoousios,* so that it might defeat the perverseness of the
heretics, while proclaiming that the Word is other than created things.

756

[22]

If some persons regard God as being a compound, as is the case of accident with   151
substance, or as having some external envelopment and as being encompassed, or as having
anything about Him which completes His substance, as if when we say *God* or name Him
Father we were not signifying His invisible and incomprehensible substance, but something   173
about it, — then let them complain of the Council's having written that the Son is from
the substance of God.

Let them reflect, however, that in so considering, they utter two blasphemies: for not
only do they treat of God as something corporeal, but they even say falsely that the Lord
is not Son of the Father Himself, but of what is about Him. . . . If the Word is not said   251
to be from God in the sense of a son, genuine and natural, from a father, but only as   257
are the creatures inasmuch as they are created and as all things are said to be from God,
then neither is He from the substance of the Father, nor again is the Son Himself a Son
according to substance, but rather in consequence of grace, just as we are called sons
according to grace. But if He alone is from God as a genuine Son, as in fact He is, then
may the Son rightly be said to be from the substance of God.

[23] And again, such is the meaning of the example drawn from light and radiance.   263
For the holy men have not said that the Word is related to God in the manner of fire
enkindled from the heat of the sun, and which is afterwards readily extinguished; for

this were an external work and a creature of its maker. Rather, they all evangelize Him as Radiance, signifying thereby that He is properly and indivisibly from the substance of the Father, and that He is one with the Father.

757

[27]

 And in regard to the Word's external co-existence with the Father, and that He is   231 not of other substance or essence (4) than that which is proper to the Father, as they declared in the Council, you may hear again from the industrious Origen: " . . . Let him understand well who dares to say, 'There was a time when the Son was not,' that he is indeed saying, 'There was a time when Wisdom was not, and when Word was not, and when Life was not.' " . . . You see, we are proving that this same opinion has been handed down from father to father.

 But you, you modern Jews and disciples of Caiphas, how many fathers can you cite for your phrases? Indeed, you can quote not even one who was intelligent and wise. All abhor you, except the devil alone; for he alone is your father in such an apostasy. In the beginning he sowed you with the seeds of this impiety, and now he persuades you to slander the Ecumenical Council, because it committed to writing not your doctrines, but those which from the beginning were handed down by those who were eye-witnesses and ministers of the Word. For the faith which the Council confessed in writing is the faith of the Catholic Church. In order to establish this, the blessed fathers wrote as they did, while condemning the Arian heresy.

1. καὶ συνεστῶτες ἐν τῷ τοῦ Θεοῦ Λόγῳ.
2. Matt. 3:17.
3. John 10:30.
4. καὶ μὴ ἑτέρας οὐσίας ἢ ὑποστάσεως. The *or* here is not disjunctive but explicative. Athanasius almost invariably uses the term *hypostasis* as meaning *essence* rather than *person:* hence, for him, it is a synonym for *ousia (substance)*.

LETTER ON THE OPINION OF DIONYSIUS [*A. D.* 350/351?]

 The *Letter on the Opinion of Dionysius* is a work of quite uncertain date. It generally appears in the manuscripts as an appendix to the *Letter Concerning the Decrees of the Council of Nicaea;* and it is only as a convenience and not out of any real conviction that it is frequently assigned the same date as the latter work, *i.e.* 350 or 351 A. D. It might even be said that these are the least likely dates of all. As an appendix, it might have been written before the work to which it is joined, or it might have been written some years afterwards, and only subsequently joined to it; but were it written at the same time as the work itself, its content would more likely have been incorporated within the work.

 Certain Arians were claiming Dionysius, a former Bishop of Alexandria (248-265 A. D.) as a support for their views. Athanasius' present work is a defense of the orthodoxy of Dionysius, the purpose of which is the blocking of the Arian appeal to his authority.

 The Migne text, PG 25, 479-522, is now superseded by Opitz's edition, *Athanasius' Werke* 2, 1, Berlin and Leipzig 1935, pp. 46-47.

759

[9]

 In the beginning, indeed, was the Word (1); but at the consummation of the ages   311

the Virgin conceived in the womb, and the Lord was made man. And He that is indicated   323
by both statements is indeed but one; for the Word was made flesh (2). But the things   332
that are said about His divinity and about His Incarnation must be interpreted properly
and with consideration for the particular context. In writing of the human attributes of   334
the Word, one must know also what concerns His divinity; and he that expounds about
His divinity must not be ignorant of what pertains to His coming in the flesh. Discerning
each with the skill of an approved money-changer, however, he will keep to the straight
path of piety. When, therefore, he speaks of His weeping, he knows that the Lord, having
become man, exhibited His humanity by His weeping, while as God He raised Lazarus;
and he knows that the Lord hungered and thirsted physically, while divinely He fed five
thousand with five loaves; and he knows that while a human body lay in the tomb, it was
raised up as the body of God by the Word Himself.

1. John 1:1.
2. John 1:14.

THE MONKS' HISTORY OF ARIAN IMPIETY [*A. D.* 358]

Athanasius had taken refuge in a monastery in 358 A. D., and the monks asked
him to write for them a history of the Arians. Only a quite substantial fragment of
this work, his *The Monks' History of Arian Impiety,* has been preserved. The extant
part covers the years 335 to 357 A. D.
 The Migne text, PG 25, 691-796, is superseded by Opitz's edition, *Athanasius'*
Werke 2, 1, Berlin and Leipzig 1935, pp. 183-230.

759a

[52]
 If a decision was made by the bishops, what concern had the emperor with it? Or if it   411
was but a threat of the emperor, what need then was there of the designated bishops?
When in the world was such a thing ever before heard of? When did a decision of the
Church receive its authority from the emperor? Or rather, when was his decree even
recognized? There have been many councils in times past, and many decrees made by
the Church; but never did the fathers seek the consent of the emperor for them, nor
did the emperor busy himself in the affairs of the Church.
 The Apostle Paul had friends among those who belonged to the household of Caesar,
and in writing to the Philippians he sent greetings from them: but never did he take
them as associates in his judgments. But now we witness a novel spectacle, which is a
discovery of the Arian heresy: heretics have assembled together with the Emperor
Constantius, so that he, by alleging the authority of the bishops, may exercise his power
against whomsoever he will, and while he persecutes may yet avoid the name of persecutor.

DISCOURSES AGAINST THE ARIANS [*inter A. D.* 358-362]

The three *Discourses against the Arians,* written between 358 and 362 A. D.,
constitute Athanasius' principal dogmatic work. In some manuscripts, and in the
Maurist edition which constitutes also the Migne text, there are four discourses.
The fourth is spurious, a later addition, actually a work against the Marcellians, and
not the work of Athanasius. We will translate selections only from the authentic
work, the first three books.
 The Migne text, PG 26, 11-468 [526], remains at present the standard edition.

760

[1, 14]

When these points have been demonstrated, then they speak even more impudently: 256
"If there never was a time when the Son was not, and if He is eternal and co-exists with
the Father, then you are saying that He is not a Son at all, but the Father's brother." O
dull and contentious men! Indeed, if we said only that He co-existed eternally, and had
not called Him Son, their pretended difficulty would have some plausibility. But if while
saying that He is eternal, we confess Him as Son of Father, how were it possible for Him   252
that is begotten to be called a brother of Him that begets? . . . For the Father and the
Son were not generated from some pre-existing source, so that they might be accounted
as brothers.

Rather, the Father is the source and begetter of the Son; and the Father is father, not
being born of anyone; and the Son is son, not brother. And if He is called the eternal
offspring of the Father, He is rightly so called. For the substance of the Father was
never imperfect, as it were if what is proper to it were to be added afterwards. Neither
was the Son begotten as man from man, and thereby of later existence than His Father.
He is offspring of God; and as the proper Son of a God who is eternal, He exists
eternally. It is proper for men to beget in time, because of the imperfection of their
nature; but the offspring of God is eternal, because God's nature is ever perfect.

760a

[1, 23]

Why is it, upon hearing that God has a Son, they reflect upon themselves and deny   176
it; but if they hear that He creates and makes, they devise no objections based upon   177
the condition of men? Even in the matter of creation they ought to interpose human
notions and supply God with materials, so that they could also deny that God is the
Creator, and finally wallow with the Manicheans. But if the very notion of a God
transcends such thoughts, and upon merely hearing of Him one believes and knows
that He exists, not as we are but as God is; and that He creates not as men create but
as a God creates: then surely He begets not as men beget but as a God begets — for it
is not God who imitates men.

761

[1, 29]

"But look," they say, "God is always a Maker, and the power of creating does not   468
grow upon Him afterwards. Does it follow, then, that since it is He that is the Creator of
all, His works are also eternal? And is it wrong to say even of them, that they were not
before they came to be?"

These Arians are senseless. . . . However, so as not to leave even a weak argument
unnoticed, they must be told that although God always had the power to create, yet
the things made had not the power of being eternal. For they are out of nothing, and
before they came to be, they were not. And things which did not exist before they   461
came to be — how could these have the power to co-exist with the ever-existing God?
. . . But the Son, being not a creature but proper to the substance of the Father, always   251
is. For since the Father always is, what is proper to His substance must always be: and   256
this is His Word and Wisdom. That creatures should not be in existence does not detract
from the Creator, for He has the power of shaping them when He will. But for the
offspring not to eternally co-exist with the Father is a disparagement of His substance.   284
His works, then, as He willed, were shaped through His Word: but the Son is eternally   257
the proper offspring of the Father's substance.

762

[1, 42]

The Word was not impaired in receiving a body, as if He had been seeking to receive   342
something beneficial to Himself; but rather, He gave divinity to that which He put on,
and moreover, with it He graced the human race. . . . For inasmuch as the powers in
heaven, the Angels and Archangels, were ever worshipping Him, and do even now worship
the Lord in the person of Jesus, the fact that the Son of God is still worshipped when He
became man is for us a grace and an extraordinary exaltation; for now the heavenly
powers will not be astonished at seeing all of us, who have with Him a common nature,   313
introduced into their realms. And this had not been the case if He that existed in the
form of God had not taken on Himself the form of a servant, thereby humbling Himself
and making His body submissive even to death.

763

[1, 51]

Adam, the first man, altered his course, and through sin death came into the world.   614
. . . When Adam transgressed, sin reached out to all men.

764

[2, 21]

If, as you hold, [the Son] is made from what did not exist, how then is He in turn   251
able to bring into being things which had no being? But if He, a creature, can fashion   462
another creature, then indeed, the same power to fashion others must be conceded to
every creature. And if thus you would have it, then what need is there of the Word,
since inferior created beings may be brought into existence by superior created beings?
Or, in any case, everything that comes into existence could have heard God's commands
in the beginning, "Become," and "Be made," and could thus have been fashioned. Yet,
this is not written, nor could it so be. For none of the creatures is an efficient cause (1),   284
and all are made by the Word. Nor could the Word have wrought all things if He were
Himself numbered among the creatures. Neither are the angels able to create, since they
too are creatures, in spite of what may be said by Valentine and Marcion and Basilides,
and you who but echo those men.

764a

[2, 27]

But they would allege: "Behold, it was through Moses that He led the people out of   462
Egypt, and through Him He gave them the Law; and Moses, nevertheless, was but a man;
therefore it is possible for like to be brought into existence through like."

When they say such a thing as that, they ought to veil their faces the better to hide
their shame. Moses was not sent to be a creator, nor to call into existence things which
were not, nor to fashion men like himself, but only to be the minister of words to the
people and to Pharao, the King. This is quite a different matter; for to minister is the
work of servants, of created beings; while to fashion and to create belongs to God alone,
to His own Word and Wisdom. When it comes to the matter of creation, therefore, we
shall find none but God's Word; for all things were made in Wisdom (2), and without the   284
Word nothing was made (3).

764b

[2, 29]

Neither did the Word become a creator by being taught how to create. Rather, being   264
the Image and Wisdom of the Father, He does the things of the Father. Nor did the   261
Father create the Son for the purpose of making the things created; for behold, although
the Son does exist, even yet the Father is seen working, as the Lord Himself says, "My
Father works even to the present time, and I too work (4)."

765

[2, 56]

"In the beginning was the Word." Even if no works had been created, it still were
true: the Word of God was, and the Word was God (5). But His becoming man would   360
not have taken place, if the need of men had not become a cause. The Son, then, is not
a creature; for if He were a creature, He would not have said, "He begets Me (6)."   251
Creatures are from without, and are works of the one who creates them. The Begotten
however, is not from without and is not a work, but is from the Father and is proper   252
to His essence. Others, then, are creatures; but the Word of God is His only-begotten Son.   257

766

[2, 59]

God's love of man is such that to those for whom first He is the Creator, He afterwards,   755
according to grace, becomes a Father also. The latter He does when men, who are His
creatures, receive into their hearts, as the Apostle says, the Spirit of His Son, crying,
"Abba, Father (7)." It is these who, by their having received the Word, have gained
from Him the power to become the children of God; for, being creatures by nature,
they could not otherwise become sons than by receiving the Spirit of the natural and   387
true Son. To bring this about, therefore, the Word became flesh (8) — so that He might
make man capable of divinity.

767

[2, 68]

"Still," they will say, "even if the Savior be a creature, God were able merely to speak   361
and thereby undo the curse." And their hearer will hasten to join in, saying, "Without   363
His coming among us at all, God were able merely to speak and thereby undo the curse."   257
It is necessary, however, that we look to what was better for mankind, and not consider
merely what was possible for God to do. Before the building of Noah's ark, He might
have destroyed the men who were then transgressors; but He did it after the ark. Even
without Moses, He might have but spoken and have led the people out of Egypt; but it
was fitting to do it through Moses. Even without the judges God might have saved the
people; but it was profitable for the people that for a time judges be raised up among
them.

The Savior, likewise, might have come among us from the beginning; or, when he did
come, might not have been delivered over to Pilate. Nevertheless, He came at the fullness
of time (9), and to those who were searching for Him, He said, "I am He (10)." Whatever
He does is profitable for men, and were not fitting in any other way; and whatever is
profitable and fitting, for this He makes provision (11). . . . If, as was in His power, God
had but spoken, and thus had loosed the curse, the power of Him that spoke would have
been demonstrated; but man would have become such as Adam was before the fall, having
received grace from without, and not having it united to the body — for such was His
condition when he was placed in Paradise.

Or perhaps he had become even worse, now that he had learned to transgress. This being his condition, were he again seduced by the serpent, there were then fresh need for God to issue a command and loose the curse. Thus would the need become interminable; and men, being enslaved to sin, would remain under guilt not less than before: ever sinning, ever in need of pardon, and never being freed; and being themselves flesh, ever subject to the Law because of the infirmity of the flesh. [2, 69] Again, if the Son were a creature, man would have remained always mortal and would never have been joined to God; for a creature, while itself seeking one to so join it, could not have joined other creatures to God. Neither could a portion of creation, while itself in need of salvation, become creation's salvation. 375 376

Lest such be the turn of events, He sends His own Son, and His Son takes on created flesh and becomes Son of Man: so that, while all were under sentence of death, He, being other than all, might on behalf of all offer His own body to death, and henceforth it were as if the letter of that sentence had been carried out, as if all had died through Him — for all died in Christ (12); and all through Him might henceforth be free from sin and from the curse which came through sin, and might truly abide for ever, risen from the dead and clothed in immortality and incorruption. 383 386

767a

[2, 70]

The fact is, then, that the Word is not from things created, but is rather Himself their Creator. For this reason did He assume a body created and human: so that, having renewed it as its Creator, He might deify it in Himself, and thus might introduce all of us in that likeness into the kingdom of heaven. A man would not have been deified if joined to a creature, nor if the Son were not true God (13); neither would a man have been brought into the Father's presence if He had not been the Father's natural and true Word who had put on the body. Since we could have had nothing in common with what is foreign, we would not have been delivered from sin and from the curse if that which the Word put on had not been natural human flesh; so also, the man would not have been deified if the Word which became flesh had not been by nature from the Father and true and proper to Him. 284 257

The union, therefore, was of just such a kind, so that He might unite what is man by nature, to Him who is in the nature of the Godhead, thereby assuring the accomplishment of salvation and His deification. Let those, therefore, who deny that the Son is by nature from the Father and proper to His essence, deny also that He took true human flesh from the Ever-Virgin Mary. In neither case would it have been profitable to us men: if the Word were not by nature true Son of God, or if the flesh which He assumed were not true flesh (14). 310 783

768

[3, 3]

[The Lord said:] "I am in the Father, and the Father in Me (15)." The Son is in the Father, insofar as it is given us to understand, because the whole being of the Son is proper to the Father's essence, as radiance is from light, and as a stream is from a fountain. Therefore, whoever sees the Son sees what is proper to the Father; and knows thereby that the Son's being, since it is from the Father, is in the Father. The Father, moreover, is in the Son, since the Son is what is proper to the Father, as in radiance the sun, or in a word the thought, or in a stream the fountain. Whoever thus contemplates the Son, contemplates what is proper to the Father's essence, and knows that the Father is in the Son. Since the Image (16) and the Godhead of the Father is the being of the Son, it follows that the Son is in the Father, and the Father in the Son. On this account, having already said, "The Father and I are one (17)," He adds quite reasonably, "I am in the Father, and the Father is in Me (18)." He shows thereby the identity of the Godhead and the unity of essence. 257 263 264

[3, 4] They are one, not as one thing now divided into two, but really constituting only 237
one; nor as one thing twice named, so that the same becomes at one time the Father and at
another His own Son. This latter is what Sabellius held, and He was judged a heretic. On 293
the contrary, they are two, because the Father is Father and is not His own Son; and the
Son is Son, and is not His own Father. Their nature is one, because the Offspring is not
unlike (19) its Parent, and is in fact his Image (20); and all that is the Father's is the Son's.

The Son, then, is not another God, for He was not gotten from without. Otherwise, if
Godhead could be conceived of as foreign to that of the Father, there would be a multiplicity.
As it is, if the Son be other, as an Offspring, still He is the Same as God. He and the Father
are one in propriety and peculiarity of nature, and in the identity of one Godhead, as has
been said.

769

[3, 6]

Nor is this Shape (21) of the Godhead [which is the Son] merely partial, but the fullness 257
of the Father's Godhead is the Being of the Son, and the Son is whole God. Although He
was equal to God, He did not estimate being equal to God a thing to be eagerly retained (22);
and again, since the Godhead and the Image (23) belonging to the Son is that of none other 264
than the Father, this is what He says: "I am in the Father (24)." Thus, "God was reconciling
the world to Himself in Christ (25);" for the propriety of the Father's essence is the Son, in
whom creation was being reconciled.

Thus, what things the Son does, are works of the Father; for the Son is the Image of the 387
Father's Godhead, which does those works. He, then, that looks on the Son, sees the 283
Father; for in the Father's Godhead the Son both is and is contemplated; and the Paternal
Image which is in the Son shows forth in Him the Father; and thus, the Father is in the
Son.

770

[3, 24]

This is what John writes when He says, "In this we know that we abide in Him and He in 753
us: because He has given us of His Spirit (26)." It is, then, through the grace given us of 754
the Spirit, that we come to be in Him, and He in us; and since this Spirit is the Spirit of
God, through His coming to be in us and our having the Spirit, we are reasonably considered
as coming to be in God; and thus, God is in us. But we do not, afterall, come to be in the
Father in the way in which the Son is in the Father. That He may be in the Father the Son
does not merely partake of the Spirit; neither does He receive the Spirit, but rather the
Spirit is what He imparts to all. Neither does the Spirit unite the Word to the Father; but
rather, the Spirit receives from the Word. The Son, then, is in the Father as His proper Word
and Radiance. 260

We, however, apart from the Spirit, are strange and distant from God. Thus, our being 263
in the Father is not of ourselves, but is in the Spirit who is in us and who abides in us, and
whose presence in us we preserve by our confession of the faith (27). ... [3, 25] ... It is
then, the Spirit to whom it pertains to be in God, and not we of ourselves; and, since we 755
are sons and gods because of the Word in us, so also, because of the Spirit's being in us, —
the Spirit who is in the Word which is in the Father, — we shall be in the Son and in the
Father, and we shall be accounted as having become one in Son and in Father.

Therefore, when someone falls from the Spirit through any wickedness — that grace 761
indeed remains irrevocably with those who are willing to repent after such a fall. Otherwise,
the one who has fallen is no longer in God, because that Holy Spirit and Advocate (28) who
is in God has deserted him.

771

[3, 31]

Afterwards He became man; and, as the Apostle says, the Godhead dwelt bodily in the   332
flesh (29), which is as if he had said: "Being God, He had His own body; and using this   348
as an instrument, He became man for the sake of us. That is why the properties of the
flesh are said to be His: since He was in the body, He is said to experience hunger, thirst,
suffering, weariness, and the like, suchever as pertain to the flesh. Those works, however,
which are proper to the Word Himself, such as raising the dead, restoring sight to the blind,
and curing the woman who had an issue of blood, – these He did through His own body.   333
The Word, then, bore the infirmities of the flesh as proper to Himself (30); for the flesh   334
was His. The flesh ministered to the works of the Godhead, because the Godhead was in
it. The body was God's. . . . He carries our infirmities, and He Himself bears our sins, so
that it might be made evident that He has become man for the sake of us, and that the body   370
in which He bore our sins is His own body. He received no hurt Himself, however, by
bearing our sins in His body on the tree, as Peter puts it (31); and yet, we men were set
free of our own infirmities, and were filled with the righteousness of the Word.

772

[3, 34]

In order the better to understand the infirmities ascribed to Him because of the flesh,   347
and that the nature of the Word is such that He is not subject to being acted upon from   348
without (32), listen carefully to the blessed Peter, who will be a trustworthy witness to
what concerns the Savior. Thus does he write in his Epistle, saying: "Christ, therefore,
having suffered for us, in the flesh (33)."

Doubtless, then, when He is said to hunger, to thirst, to toil, to be unaware, to sleep,
to weep, to inquire, to flee, to be born, to refuse the cup, and all else that belongs to the
flesh, it might in each case be rightly said, "Christ, therefore, hungering and thirsting 'for
us, in the flesh';" and, "saying He did not know, and suffering blows, and toiling 'for us,
in the flesh';" and again, "being exalted, and being born, and growing 'in the flesh';" and
"being afraid and hiding 'in the flesh';" and, "saying, 'If it be possible, let this cup pass from
Me (34),' and being wounded and violently apprehended 'for us, in the flesh';" and in
short, all such things "for us, in the flesh."

This, then, is why the Apostle himself said, "Christ, therefore, having suffered," not in
His Godhead, but "for us, in the flesh": so that this passivity might be acknowledged
as belonging not properly and by nature to the Word Himself, but properly and by nature
to the flesh itself. Let no one, then, be scandalized because of these evidences of humanity;
rather, let him know that while by nature the Word Himself is not subject to being acted
upon (35), yet, since He has put on flesh, these things are ascribed to Him, because they
are proper to the flesh and the body itself is proper to the Savior.

773

[3, 41]

Although the Word did indeed become flesh, it is to the flesh that passivities (36) are   347
proper; and although the flesh bears divinity in the Word, it is to the Word that grace and   332
power belong. He performed the Father's works, then, through the flesh; but nonetheless
was the passivity of the flesh exhibited in Him. Thus, He inquired and then raised Lazarus;
He chided His Mother, saying: "My hour is not yet come (37);" and forthwith He turned
the water into wine. Indeed, He was true God in the flesh, and He was true flesh in the   323
Word. Out of His works, therefore, He made known both His own Father, and Himself,
the Son of God. By the passivities of the flesh He demonstrated that He bore a true body,
and that it was proper to Him.

774

[3, 42]

Let us examine what He said: "But of that day and the hour no one knows, neither the   351
angels, nor the Son (38)," . . . After saying, "nor the Son," He relates to the disciples the
things which will precede that day, and says that this and that shall be, and then the end.
Now, He that speaks of what will precede that day also has full knowledge of that day which
will follow upon the events foretold. And if He had not known the hour, He would not have
signified the events preceding it, not knowing when that hour would be. . . . [3, 43] . . . He
says in the Gospel, concerning Himself in His human character, "Father, the hour is come,
glorify your Son (39)."

Certainly, then, it is plain that as the Word He knows also the hour and the end of all things,
although as man He is ignorant of it; for ignorance is proper to man, and especially in these
matters. This, moreover, pertains to the Savior's love of man; for, inasmuch as He was made
man, He is not ashamed, because of the ignorant flesh, to say, "I do not know," — so that He
may demonstrate that, although as God He knows, according to the flesh He is ignorant.
This, then, is why He did not say, "nor does the Son of God know": lest the Godhead appear
to be ignorant; but simply, "nor the Son": so that the ignorance may be of the Son as born
of man.

775

[3, 61]

If, then, as we have already shown, the Son is other than all things; and rather, through   253
Him the works came to be: — then, let not *by will* be said of Him, or He will have come to
be, in the same way in which those things exist which came to be through Him. Paul, for
example, not being such beforehand, came afterwards to be an Apostle *by the will* of
God (40). . . . Things which once were not, but happened afterwards from causes
external to themselves, — these the Creator wills to make; but His own Word begotten
of His nature He does not deliberately will (41). . . . [3, 62] . . . Ashamed to call Him a
work or a creature, or to say that before His generation the Word of God was not, they yet   254
assert in another way that He is a creature. They bring forward the question of *willing*,
and say, "Unless He has *by will* come to be, then it was by necessity and against His will
that God has a Son." Who is it, then, who imposes necessity upon Him, O most wicked men,
who twist everything to support your heresy? What is contrary to *will*, they see; but what
is greater and transcends it, they do not grasp. Indeed, what is beside purpose is contrary
to *will*, but what is in accord with nature transcends and supersedes *willing*.

1. ποιητικὸν αἴτιον, *i.e.,* a producing cause, the cause of further *creatio ex nihilo.*
2. Ps. 103 [104]:24.
3. John 1:3.
4. John 5:17.
5. John 1:1.
6. Prov. 8:25 [Septuagint].
7. Gal. 4:6.
8. John 1:14.
9. Gal. 4:4.
10. John 18:5.
11. πρόνοιαν ποιεῖται, *i.e.,* He works providentially.
12. See 2 Cor. 5:14.
13. Athanasius recalls to mind, without making direct reference to it, the Arian subterfuge: "the Son is God,
but not true God."
14. The Son, then, is homoousios or consubstantial with the Father; and we are homoousios or consubstantial
with Christ.
15. John 14:10.
16. τοῦ εἴδους.
17. John 10:30.
18. John 14:10.

19. ἀνόμοιον is the very word which Athanasius uses. It is a quick jab, but a forehanded one, and does not miss its mark, the radical Arians, called Eunomians and Anomoians, whose formula was κατὰ πάντα ἀνόμοιος – *the Father and the Son are unlike in all things.*
20. ἡ εἰκών.
21. ἡ μορφή.
22. Phil. 2:6.
23. τὸ εἶδος. The same term is used twice more below.
24. John 14:10.
25. 2 Cor. 5:19.
26. 1 John 4:13.
27. τῇ ὁμολογίᾳ.
28. ἅγιον καὶ παράκλητον Πνεῦμα.
29. See Col 2:9.
30. *I.e.,* of course, the Word-made-flesh, the God-man. If it began to appear a few lines above in the present selection that Apollinaris or even Nestorius might justifiably claim the authority of Athanasius, it is now clear and becomes increasingly clearer that Athanasius does not regard the union effected in the God-man as a mere clothing with flesh, but sees in the God-man in fact a single person with two natures.
31. 1 Pet. 2:24.
32. Ἵνα δὲ καὶ τὸ ἀπαθὲς τῆς τοῦ Λόγου φύσεως, καὶ τὰς διὰ τὴν σάρκα λεγομένας ἀσθενείας αὐτοῦ γινώσκειν τις ἀκριβέστερον ἔχῃ, ... Considerable circumlocution is employed in our translation, necessitated by the lack of any suitable English equivalent to the Greek term τὸ ἀπαθές. The usual translation *impassibility* means little or nothing to modern readers.
33. 1 Pet. 4:1.
34. Matt. 26:39.
35. *I.e.,* the Word Himself is *impassible.* See note 32, above.
36. τὰ πάθη.
37. John 2:4.
38. Mark 13:32.
39. John 17:1.
40. 1 Cor. 1:1.
41. προβουλεύεται as opposed to βουλεύεται in the antithetic clause.

FOUR LETTERS TO SERAPION OF THMUIS [*A. D.* 359-360]

The four letters of Athanasius to Bishop Serapion of Thmuis, written at the end of 359 and early in 360 A. D., actually form a unified work, having been written in quick succession, addressed all to the same person, and more especially since they deal all with the same subject: Catholic doctrine on the Holy Spirit in refutation of the Pneumatomachian doctrine.

In point of fact, letters two and three of the so-called four originally constituted but one letter together. Moreover, the first seven of the twenty-three chapters of letter four do not actually belong to letter four, and may have been extracted from another letter to Serapion, or they may perhaps be from a treatise belonging to an earlier period of Athanasius' career.

Besides the present quasi-treatise made up of three or four letters, there are still extant two other letters of Athanasius to Serapion: a rather short one of the year 339 A. D., which found its way into the collection of Athanasian Festal Letters; and another of the period 356-358 A. D., giving an account of the death of Arius.

The standard edition is still that of the Maurists, the text given by Migne, PG 26, 522-676.

777

[1, 1]

Dearly beloved and truly most longed for of men, you have written to me in sorrow   292 about certain persons who, although they have departed from the Arians because of the blasphemy of the latter against the Son of God, do nevertheless disparage the Holy Spirit.

These persons say that He is not only a creature, but even that He is one of the
ministering spirits, and that He differs from the angels only in degree (1). Indeed, this
is but a feigned quarrel with the Arians, while it remains a frank contradiction of the
pious faith; for just as those who deny the Son thereby deny also the Father, in like
manner those who disparage the Holy Spirit thereby disparage also the Son.

778

[1, 16]

    The Father has always been Father, and the Son has always been Son. Just as the   237
Father is never about to be the Son, so also the Son is never about to become the
Father. Just as the Father never ceases being the Father alone, so also the Son never
ceases being the Son alone. Consequently it is utterly insane to think or to speak of a
brother of the Son, or to attribute to the Father the name of grandfather. Never in the
Scriptures is the Spirit called Son, lest He might be reckoned as a brother. Nor is He   275
called son of the Son, lest the Father might be termed a grandfather. The Son, however,
is called Son of the Father, while the Spirit is called Spirit of the Father; and thus the
Godhead of the Holy Trinity is one, as also the faith therein.

779

[1, 20]

    Inasmuch as there is in the Holy Trinity oneness of essence and equality in rank, who,   237
then, would dare to separate either the Son from the Father, or the Spirit from either
the Son or the Father? Or who would be so rash as to say that the Trinity is dissimilar   282
and of a diverse nature within Itself? Or that the Son is of other substance than the   266
Father? Or that the Spirit is foreign to the Son? Again, if anyone should inquire,
demanding, "But how is this? How, when the Son is in us, is it said that the Father
is in us? Or how, since there is afterall a Trinity, is that Trinity in One to be explained?   283
Or how, there being one in us, is it said that the Trinity is in us?"   239

    Well now, let such a questioner first isolate refulgence from the light, or wisdom
from the wise; or let him at least explain it. But if he is not able to do even this, then
how much closer to insanity is the temerity of one who would make an inquiry about
God! Indeed, as the saying has it, the Godhead is not brought into proof with words,
but into faith and reverence in the company of prudent reasoning. . . . Just as the Son
is the only-begotten, so also the Spirit, given and sent by the Son, is one and not many;
nor is He one comprised of many, but He alone is the Spirit; for, since the Son, the
living Word, is one, so also must His sanctifying, enlightening and life-giving Gift be one,
perfect and complete — the Gift who is said to proceed (2) from the Father, because He
shines forth from and is sent from and is given by the Word, who is confessedly from the
Father.

780

[1, 24]

    We are all said to be partakers of God through the Holy Spirit. "Do you not know,"   753
it says, "that you are a temple of God, and the Spirit of God dwells in you? If   754
anyone ruins the temple of God, him will God ruin; for it is holy, this temple of God,
which is just what you are (3)." If the Holy Spirit were a creature, there could be no
communion of God with us through Him. On the contrary, we would be joined to a   267
creature, and we would be foreign to the divine nature, as having nothing in common
with it. . . . But if by participation in the Spirit we are made partakers in the divine
nature (4), it is insanity for anyone to say that the Spirit has a created nature and not

the nature of God. Indeed, this it is whereby those in whom He is, are made divine; and if He makes men divine, it cannot be doubted that His is the nature of God.

781

[1, 26]

If, therefore, the Spirit fills all, and is present in the Word in the midst of all, while   484
the angels are reckoned as inferior in this regard, and are only to be found where they are
sent, then there can be no doubt, as you say, that the Spirit is neither from among
created things nor, indeed, is He an angel; rather, He is superior to the angelic nature.

782

[1, 28]

But what is also to the point, let us note that the very tradition, teaching, and faith   231
of the Catholic Church from the beginning, which the Lord gave, was preached by the
Apostles, and was preserved by the Fathers. On this was the Church founded; and if
anyone departs from this, he neither is nor any longer ought to be called a Christian:
there is a Trinity, holy and perfect, acknowledged as God, in Father, Son, and Holy
Spirit, having nothing foreign or external mixed with It, not composed of a fashioner
and an originated, but entirely creative and fashioning; It is consistent in Itself,
indivisible in nature, and Its activity is one. The Father does all things through the Word   283
in the Holy Spirit; and thus the unity of the Holy Trinity is preserved; and thus there   238
is preached in the Church one God, "who is over all, and through all, and in all (5)."
He is *over all* as Father, as beginning, as source; and *through all,* through the Word; and
in all, in the Holy Spirit.

It is a Trinity not merely in name or in a figurative manner of speaking; rather, It is a
Trinity in truth and in actual existence. Just as the Father is He that is, so also His Word
is one that is, and is God over all. And neither is the Holy Spirit non-existent, but
actually exists and has true being. Less than these the Catholic Church does not hold, lest
she sink to the level of the Jews of the present time, imitators of Caiphas (6), or to the
level of Sabellius. Nor does she add to their number by speculation, lest she be carried   293
into the polytheism of the Greeks.

And because this is the faith of the Church, let them somehow understand that the
Lord sent out the Apostles and commanded them to make this the foundation of the
Church, when He said: "Go out and instruct every people, baptizing them in the name of
the Father and of the Son and of the Holy Spirit (7)."

783

[3, 1]

The peculiar relationship of the Son to the Father, such as we know it — we will find   257
that the Spirit has this, to the Son. And since the Son says, "everything whatsoever that   268
the Father has is mine (8)," we will discover all these things also in the Spirit, through
the Son. And just as the Son was announced by the Father, who said, "This is My
beloved Son, in whom I am well-pleased (9)," so also is the Spirit of the Son; for, as the   270
Apostle says, "He has sent the Spirit *of His Son* into our hearts, crying, 'Abba!
Father (10)!' " . . . Hence, if the Son, because of His peculiar relationship to the Father,
and because of His being the Offspring of the Father's own substance, is not a creature,
but is of the same substance of the Father (11), then neither is the Holy Spirit a creature.
To say otherwise were impious, because of His peculiar relationship to the Son, and
because out of Him He is given to all, and what He has is of the Son.

784

[3, 6]

The Spirit, then, being established in us, the Son and the Father come; and they   283
make their dwelling in us (12). For the Trinity is indivisible, and its Godhead is one;
and there is one God over all and through all and in all (13). This is the faith of the
Catholic Church; for on the Trinity the Lord founded it and rooted it, when He said
to His disciples, "Go out and instruct every people, baptizing them in the name of the
Father and of the Son and of the Holy Spirit (14)." But if the Spirit were a creature,   234
He would not have joined Himself with the Father, lest the Trinity be dissimilar (15)
within Itself, lest It have united in Itself anything strange or foreign. Indeed, what could   268
be lacking in God, that He should assume any foreign substance, and be glorified with it?
Inconceivable (16)!

784a

[3, 6]

Whoever believes in the Father knows the Son is in the Father, and the Spirit not   266
outside the Son; and in this way he believes also in the Son and in the Holy Spirit.   268
Since the Godhead of the Trinity is one, It is known out of the one Father. This is
the stamp of the Catholic faith (17). [3, 7] But those who defame the Spirit and call
Him creature, if they do not repent of the things they have said, or if they are
disdainful of the things about to be said — they ought to be ashamed (18). If they
allow that there is a Trinity, and that they have faith in the Trinity, then let them say
whether the Trinity always was, or whether there was a time when the Trinity was not.
Indeed, if the Trinity is eternal, the Spirit is not a creature, because He co-exists
eternally with the Word and in Him.

As for the creatures, there was a time when they were not. But if He is a creature,   270
and the creatures are brought forth out of what did not exist, then plainly there was a
time when there was not a Trinity but a duality. And what more impious thing might
anyone say? The [Tropicists] (19) say that the Trinity has come together out of
change and progress; that there was a Dyad, which awaited the production of a creature
which would come together with Father and Son and become the Trinity.

It is inconceivable how such an idea could ever come into the mind of a Christian!
For just as the Son, being eternal, is not a creature, so also the Trinity is eternal, and
there is no creature in It; and therefore the Spirit is not a creature. As It ever was,
so It is even now. And as now It is, so always It was. It is a Trinity, and in It are
Father and Son and Holy Spirit. And there is one God, Father over all and through all
and in all, who is blessed unto the ages. Amen.

1. καὶ βαθμῷ μόνον αὐτὸ διαφέρειν τῶν ἀγγέλων.
2. ἐκπορεύεσθαι.
3. 1 Cor. 2:16-17.
4. 2 Pet. 1:4.
5. Eph. 4:6.
6. See Matt. 26:57-65.
7. Matt. 28:19.
8. John 16:15.
9. Matt. 3:17.
10. Gal. 4:6.
11. ὁμοούσιος τοῦ Πατρός.
12. John 14:23.
13. Eph. 4:6.
14. Matt. 28:19.
15. The Arian term ἀνόμοιος, by which the radical Arians denied even any similarity between Father and Son,
   is here negated by Athanasius even in respect to the relationship between Father and Holy Spirit.
16. For those whose intellectual curiosity is ensnared by the term — the Greek reads: Μὴ γένοιτο.
17. The Benedictine editors conclude Chapter 6 with *It is known out of the one Father*, making *This is the*

stamp of the Catholic faith the beginning of Chapter 7. We have corrected the division in a way which seems more natural.

18. *They ought to be ashamed* renders the Greek καταδυέτωσαν. The literal meaning of the Greek is *Let them go down,* but it often means also *Let them hide themselves,* or *Let them hide themselves for shame.* The thought keeps coming back to us, however, that there may be here an ellipsis. Perhaps Athanasius' native delicacy prevented him from completing the classical phrase which, in its customary Homeric style, would have read: καταδυέτωσαν εἰς 'Αἴδαο δόμους.

19. Athanasius has taken to calling the heretics against whom he is writing *Tropicists;* but they are, afterall, still the Pneumatomachians, and not another group of heretics. He uses the word in derision, calling them Tropicists from their habit of explaining any passages of Scripture adverse to their position in a *tropical* or *metaphorical* sense.

LETTER CONCERNING THE COUNCILS OF RIMINI AND SELEUCIA [*A. D.* 361/362]

It was formerly a well-accepted theory that this entire lengthy report, with the exception of chapters 30, 31, and 55, was written immediately after the Council of Seleucia closed, that is, within the few days or weeks after October 1, 359. In this theory, chapter 55 is a postscript added by Athanasius himself, shortly after the body of the work had been completed; for chapter 55 consists of a letter of Emperor Constantius to the Bishops assembled at Rimini, together with their reply to it; and chapters 30 and 31, which suppose the death of Constantius, were added in a later recension by Athanasius, after the death of Constantius in 361 A. D.

H. G. Opitz, however, in the introduction to his critical edition, rejects this hypothesis of later insertions, and holds that the entire work was composed after the death of Constantius, but probably before February 21, 362, at which date Athanasius returned from exile: therefore, late in 361 or early in 362 A. D.

The Migne text, PG 26, 681-794, is now entirely superseded by the critical edition of Opitz, referred to above, *Athanasius' Werke* 2, 1, Berlin and Leipzig 1935, pp. 231-278.

785

[5]

[The Fathers of the Ecumenical Council of Nicaea], without prefixing consulate,   452
month, and day, wrote concerning Easter: "The following has been decided." And it
was at that time decided that all should comply. But concerning matters of faith, they
did not write: "It has been decided," but "Thus the Catholic Church believes." And   102
thereupon they confessed how they believed. This they did in order to show that their   104
judgment was not of more recent origin, but was in fact of Apostolic times; and that
what they wrote was no discovery of their own, but is simply that which was taught
by the Apostles (1).

786

[35]

When, however, we hear "I am who is (2)," and "In the beginning God made   140
heaven and earth (3)," and, "Hear, O Israel, the Lord your God is one Lord (4),"
and "So says the Lord almighty (5)," we understand nothing else but the simple,   151
blessed, and incomprehensible essence (6) of Him that is; for though we are unable to   173
grasp what He is, yet, hearing *Father,* and *God,* and *Almighty,* we understand that   175
nothing else is meant but the very essence of Him that is.

787

[51]
    And again, if, as we said before, the Son is what He is, not by participation (7),   257
but, while all originated things have by participation the grace of God, He is the Father's   261
Wisdom and Word, of which all things partake; it necessarily follows, then, that He, being   260
the deifying and enlightening power of the Father, by which all things are deified and
made alive, is not of substance foreign to the Father, but is of the same substance (8).
For by partaking of Him, we partake of the Father, because the Word is proper to the
essence of the Father. Therefore, if He Himself were also of participation, and not of   264
His essence, the Divinity and Image of the Father, He would Himself have been deified   754
and could not deify others (9).

1. Athanasius is comparing the conduct of the Fathers of Nicaea to that of the Fathers of Seleucia, much to
   the embarassment of the latter, who had produced the infamous dated creed. In chapter 3 of the present
   work, Athanasius says of the Seleucian party of Ursacius of Singidunum: "Writing what it pleased them to
   believe, they prefix to it the consulate, the month, and the day of the current year; and thereby demonstrate
   to all sensible people that their faith is not from of old, but from the present time, having its beginnings in
   the reign of Constantius."
2. Ex. 3:14.
3. Gen. 1:1.
4. Deut. 6:4.
5. See Gen. 17:1-4.
6. *οὐσία, i.e.,* substance or essence.
7. *οὐκ ἐκ μετουσίας.*
8. *ὁμοούσιος.*
9. *Others* is clearly implied, and stands in the Maurists' Latin column, although the word itself is not found in
   the Greek text.

ON THE INCARNATION OF THE WORD OF GOD AND AGAINST THE ARIANS [*ca. A. D.* 365]

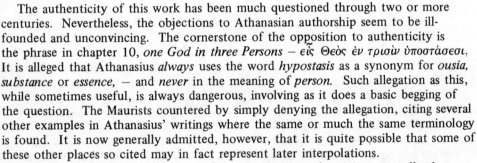

    The authenticity of this work has been much questioned through two or more
centuries. Nevertheless, the objections to Athanasian authorship seem to be ill-
founded and unconvincing. The cornerstone of the opposition to authenticity is
the phrase in chapter 10, *one God in three Persons* – εἷς Θεὸς ἐν τρισὶν ὑποστάσεσι.
It is alleged that Athanasius *always* uses the word *hypostasis* as a synonym for *ousia,
substance* or *essence,* – and *never* in the meaning of *person.* Such allegation as this,
while sometimes useful, is always dangerous, involving as it does a basic begging of
the question. The Maurists countered by simply denying the allegation, citing several
other examples in Athanasius' writings where the same or much the same terminology
is found. It is now generally admitted, however, that it is quite possible that some of
these other places so cited may in fact represent later interpolations.
    In demonstrating the inadequacy of the attacks on authenticity, generally three
points are made:
    a) The phrase in chapter 10, wherein *hypostasis* is used in the sense of *person,*
might itself be a later interpolation, while the work itself remains authentic.
    b) At the Council of Alexandria in the year 362 A. D. Athansius agreed that
hypostasis can be used in the meaning of *person.* Consequently, in a work of *ca.
A. D.* 365, he might easily use such terminology as that of chapter 10, even if it be
true that he had never used it before.
    c) There is ancient testimony to Athanasian authorship of the work; for it is cited
under the name of Athanasius by Theodoret of Cyr († *ca. A. D.* 466), in his
dialogue *Eranistes or Polymorphus* 2 and 3, (PG 83, 180 and 293).
    We will be safe in joining with such authorities as Bardenhewer and Quasten in
holding that the work may be regarded as probably authentic, since no substantial
case has been made against its authenticity.

The Maurist edition, the text of which is reprinted by Migne, PG 26, 983-1028, is still the standard.

788

[8]

Accordingly, the Son of God became Son of Man, so that the sons of man, that is, of   755
Adam, might become sons of God. The Word begotten of the Father from on high,   340
inexpressibly, inexplicably, incomprehensibly and eternally, is He that is born in time   302
here below, of the Virgin Mary, the Mother of God (1), — so that those who are in the   780
first place born here below might have a second birth from on high, that is, of God. He,   781
then, has on earth only a Mother, while we have in heaven only a Father. And for this
reason He calls Himself Son of Man: so that we men might call God our Father in
heaven. "Our Father," He says, "who art in heaven (2)."   313

Therefore, just as we servants of God are made sons of God, so too the Master of
servants is made the mortal son of his own servant, that is, of Adam, so that the sons of   754
Adam, who are mortal, might become the sons of God, in accord with the saying, "He
gave them the power to become the children of God (3)." So too the Son of God
tasted death because of the fleshliness of His father, so that the sons of man might
partake of the life of God, through God, their Father according to the Spirit. He,
therefore, is by nature Son of God; we, however, by grace.

789

[10]

When the Seraphim glorify God, saying thrice, "Holy, holy, holy Lord Sabaoth (4),"   232
they are glorifying Father, Son, and Holy Spirit (5). And likewise, just as we are baptized   234
in the name of the Father and of the Son, so also in the name of the Holy Spirit (6);
and we are made sons of God, not of gods. For it is Father, Son, and Holy Spirit who
is Lord of hosts. For the Godhead is one, and there is one God in three Persons (7).   238

790

[21]

And when [Christ] says, "Father, if it be possible, let this chalice pass from Me; yet,   330
not My will be done, but Yours (8);" and "the spirit is ready, but the flesh is weak (9),"   331
He gives evidence therein of two wills, the one human, which is of the flesh, and the
other divine, which is of God. That which is human, because of the weakness of the
flesh, shrinks from suffering. That, however, which is divine, is ready. Then too, Peter,
hearing about the passion, says, "Cheer up, Lord (10);" but the Lord, chiding him, says,
"Get behind Me, Satan; you are a scandal to Me, because you are mindful not of the
things of God but of the things of men (11)." This too, then, is to be understood in the
same way: for, having been made in the likeness of men, as a man He shrinks from
suffering; but being God and, in accord with the divine substance, really being not subject
to suffering, He readily accepts suffering and death.

1. ἐκ παρθένου θεοτόκου Μαρίας.
2. Matt. 6:9.
3. John 1:12.
4. Is. 6:3. In regard to the term *Sabaoth*, see note 123 to § 849 below.
5. It may be well to call attention to the fact that no matter what one may think of the implied interpretation of Scripture, the statement itself, quite obviously, is true.
6. Matt. 28:19.
7. Μία γὰρ ἡ θεότης καὶ εἷς Θεὸς ἐν τρισὶν ὑποστάσεσι.
8. Matt. 26:39.

9. Matt. 26:41; Mark 14:38.
10. Mark 16:22.
11. Mark 16:23.

FESTAL LETTERS

St. Athanasius continued what had been the laudable practice engaged in already a century earlier by his predecessor six times removed, St. Dionysius of Alexandria, of addressing an Easter pastoral letter each year to all his suffragans. Of the Greek originals, only fragments are preserved; the number of fragments is considerable, however, and a good many have been discovered since the publication of the collected fragments by Migne, PG 26, 1431-1444. Unfortunately, the newer fragments have not yet been assembled in a single source. The Coptic fragments of seventeen of these Easter — or perhaps Lenten were more accurate — pastorals have been edited by L. Th. Lefort, *S. Athanase: Lettres Festales et Pastorales en Copte,* CSCO 150 / Cop. 19, Louvain 1955, with translation in French in CSCO 151 / Cop. 20, Louvain 1955.

Greek was not generally understood in Upper Egypt, and there was a practical necessity for a Coptic version of the letters. It may be taken as a certainty that the Coptic version of at least some of the letters enjoyed an official status, and was the product of whatever passed for Athanasius' Archiepiscopal Chancery. Thirteen of the letters are extant in Syriac, published by Cureton in 1848 and reprinted by Cardinal Mai in the *Nova bibliotheca patrum* 6, Rome 1853.

Along with the Syriac Mai printed an unreliable Latin translation, made by a Maronite from an Italian version. Migne reprinted this poor Latin version in PG 26, 1351-1432. A few other fragments are available in Syriac; and eight fragments are preserved through an Armenian version of a treatise by the Patriarch Timothy the Cat († *A. D.* 477).

THE THIRTY-NINTH FESTAL LETTER [*A. D.* 367]

Of all Athanasius' Easter or Lenten pastorals, the thirty-ninth, of the year 367 A. D., is perhaps the most interesting; for it contains a listing of the canon of both the Old and the New Testaments. In the Old Testament Athanasius excludes from the canon the deuterocanonical books, admitting their use, however, as devotional reading. In the New Testament he lists precisely the twenty-seven books of our present canon, and states for the first time that these and only these are to be admitted as canonical. Athanasius' New Testament canon corresponds exactly to that which was finally promulgated as official by the Council of Trent.

Of this thirty-ninth Festal Letter, the Greek is extant in a fragment containing the important section on the Scriptural Canon (Migne, PG 26, 1435-1440); and there are five sizeable and somewhat overlapping fragments extant in Coptic, containing also the part pertaining to the canon, for which see Lefort, CSCO 150 / Cop. 19, pp. 15-22 and 58-62. Our translations below are made from the Greek of Migne in comparison with the Coptic of Lefort.

791

The Old Testament, then, consists of all together twenty-two books in number, — which   41
also, I have heard, is traditionally the number of written characters used by the Hebrews, —
the order of which, and the name of each, being as follows: first, there is Genesis; then

Exodus; then Leviticus; and after this is Numbers; and then Deuteronomy; and following these is Jesus son of Nave; and Judges; and after this is Ruth; and again, following after these are four books of Kingdoms, of which the first and second are counted as one, and the third and fourth likewise as one; and after these there is a first and second of Paralipomenon, likewise counted as one; then Esdras (1), a first and second in one; and after this is a book of Psalms; and then one of Proverbs; then Ecclesiastes; and Song of Songs; and besides these, there is Job; and then the Prophets, the twelve counted as one book; then Isaias; Jeremias, and along with it, Baruch, Lamentations, and the Letter; and after these, Ezechiel; and Daniel. It is of these so far enumerated that the Old Testament consists (2).

Again, it is not tiresome to speak of the New (3). There are the four Gospels: according to Matthew; according to Mark; according to Luke; and according to John; and then, after these, the Acts of the Apostles; and the seven Epistles of the Apostles, called Catholic, which are: one of James, two of Peter; then three of John; and after these, one of Jude; in addition to these there are the fourteen Epistles of the Apostle Paul, written in this order: first, to the Romans; then two to the Corinthians; and after these, to the Galatians; and then to the Ephesians; then to the Philippians; and then to the Colossians; and two to the Thessalonians; and the one to the Hebrews (4); and then two to Timothy; and one to Titus; and the last, the one to Philemon; and then there is the Apocalypse of John.

42

These are the fountains of salvation at which they who thirst may be satisfied with the words they contain. Only in these is the teaching of piety proclaimed (5). Let no man add to these, nor take away from them. It was in respect to these that the Lord shamed the Sadducees when He said, "You err, because you do not know the Scriptures (6)." And He spoke in reproof of the Jews, saying, "Search the Scriptures, for it is they that bear witness to Me (7)."

For the sake of greater clarity I must necessarily add this remark also: there are other books besides the aforementioned, which, however, are not canonical. Yet, they have been designated by the Fathers to be read by those who join us and who wish to be instructed in the word of piety: the Wisdom of Solomon; and the Wisdom of Sirach (8); and Esther; and Judith; and Tobias; and the Teaching attributed to the Apostles (9); and the Shepherd (10). Those which I mentioned earlier, beloved, are included in the canon, while these latter are but recommended for reading. No mention whatever need be made of the Apocrypha (11), which are the inventions of heretics who write them as they choose, decorating them with a freely bestowed antiquity, so that they may offer them as ancient writings, and thus have occasion, through the use of them, to cheat guileless people.

1. **ⲘⲚ̄Ⲛ̄ⲤⲰⲤ ⲈⲤⲀⲢⲀ** is omitted from the Coptic and must be supplied from the εἶτα Ἐσδρας of the Greek text. Since the description of the work as two books counted as one is present in the Coptic, it is quite clear that the omission of **ⲘⲚ̄Ⲛ̄ⲤⲰⲤ ⲈⲤⲀⲢⲀ** is a mere scribal misadventure.
2. Note that six works, now accepted as canonical, are missing. It will shortly be seen that Athanasius classes Wisdom, Sirach, Tobias, Judith and Esther as pious and worthy books, but uncanonical. Of Machabees he makes no mention at all, which helps to explain its omission from the Ethiopic version of Scripture.
3. The more precise Coptic adds the word **ⲆⲒⲀⲐⲎⲕⲎ** .
4. The Coptic has Hebrews between Corinthians and Galatians. Otherwise, the order is the same.
5. A few lines below we will see that Athanasius mentions certain other books as uncanonical (some of which belong now to the canon as deuterocanonical books), but which are recommended by the Fathers for the private reading of converts, who wish to be instructed in the word of piety. We may, then, very easily assume that εὐαγγελίζεται, which we render *proclaimed,* has the technical meaning of being *read in the Liturgy.*
6. Matt. 22:29. The Coptic edition of the letter completes the quotation: " . . . **ⲞⲨⲦⲈ ⲦϬⲞⲘ Ⲙ̄ⲠⲚⲞⲨⲦⲈ** . . . nor the power of God."
7. John 5:39.
8. While presumably the Coptic enjoys not quite the same authenticity as the Greek text, again it has a greater accuracy in point of fact, when it writes: **ⲦⲤⲞⲪⲒⲀ Ⲙ̄ⲠϢⲎⲢⲈ Ⲛ̄ⲤⲒⲢⲀⳉ** – the Wisdom *of the son* of Sirach.

9. The Greek phrase is καὶ διδαχὴ καλουμένη τῶν Ἀποστόλων, which certainly pin-points the work as being that which we know familiarly as the *Didache*. The Coptic version adds, after the phrase "the Teaching attributed to the Apostles," a parenthetical remark, apparently to distinguish our familiar *Didache* from some other now unknown *Didache:* "I do not mean the one which purports to correct Deuteronomy."
10. *The Shepherd* of Hermas, now classed among the apocryphal Apocalypses.
11. *I.e.,* the Pseudepigrapha.

SYNODAL LETTER TO THE BISHOPS OF AFRICA [*inter A. D.* 368/372]

The present work is preserved in the corpus of Athanasius' writings, but is in fact, as its Greek title indicates, the product of a synod of ninety bishops of Egypt and Libya, Athanasius among them. And again as the Greek title indicates, it is a letter against the Arians, addressed to the bishops of non-Egyptian Africa. More specifically, the term Africa here embraces Carthage with Proconsular Africa, Numidia, the Mauretanias, the provinces of Tripolitania and Byzacenum, and possibly also Sardinia and the Balearic islands.

The Maurist edition reprinted by Migne (PG 26, 1028-1048) remains the standard text, for want of a new critical edition. A considerable portion of the work, however, is quoted by Theodoret in his *Ecclesiastical History*, thus Parmentier's edition of Theodoret in the Series GCS, Vol. 19, is useful in respect to the present work. A Syriac version in a British Museum codex has not yet been published; and there is also an old Latin translation in a Berlin codex. For more precise bibliographical information, see Quasten, *Patrology*, Vol. 3, 1960, p. 56.

792

[2]
But the word of the Lord which came through the Ecumenical Council at Nicaea remains forever (1).   452

792a

[6]
The bishops [at Nicaea] wrote as they did, not as men inventing phrases of them-   230
selves, but as having the witness of the Fathers. Indeed, nearly one hundred and thirty   231
years ago former bishops of Great Rome (2) and of our city wrote and censured those
who were saying that the Son was a creature and not of the same substance (3) as the
Father (4). And Eusebius (5), who was bishop of Caesarea and who was at first a
supporter of the Arian heresy, knew this; but afterwards, having subscribed in this
very council at Nicaea, he wrote to his own people, declaring his assent as follows:
"We know that even of old certain eloquent and distinguished bishops used the term
homoousios in respect to the Godhead of the Father and the Son."   257

1. See 1 Pet. 1:25.
2. *Great* Rome, to distinguish the seat of Christendom from Constantinople, the *New* Rome.
3. ὁμοούσιον.
4. The present synodal letter cannot be dated earlier than 368 A. D. nor later than 372. It belongs, most likely, to the year 369 or 370 A. D. The correspondence to which Athanasius (for we take it that he is, afterall, the principal author of the present letter) is referring is certainly that of Dionysius of Rome with Dionysius of Alexandria (see above, p. 504 ff.), which, however, must be dated *ca. A. D.* 262/263, not yet 110 years before Athanasius' present remarks.
5. Note that it is Eusebius Pamphilus, the Historian, that Athanasius refers to, and not the radical Arian, Eusebius of Nicomedia and Constantinople; for it was Eusebius Pamphilus who was Bishop of Caesarea. The precise position of Eusebius Pamphilus in respect to Arianism has always been somewhat enigmatic.

LETTER TO EPICTETUS OF CORINTH [*A. D.* 370/371]

Epictetus, Bishop of Corinth, had written to Athanasius, requesting his views in regard to certain Trinitarian and primarily Christological questions which were being agitated in Corinth by groups of docetist-minded Arians and Apollinarists. The present letter, later adopted by the Council of Chalcedon (451 A. D.) as constituting an excellent expression of its own views, is Athanasius' reply to Epictetus. It is to be dated in 370 or 371 A. D.

Besides the original Greek, the letter is extant also in two Latin versions, two Armenian versions, and a Syriac version. The last, however, has been corrupted by the introduction of Apollinarist views.

The edition of Migne, PG 26, 1049-1070, remains at present the standard.

794

[6]

The incorporeal Word appropriated as His own the properties of the body. Certainly when the body was struck by the attendant, He spoke as one who was suffering: "Why do you strike Me (1)?" And though the Word is by nature intangible, nevertheless He said, "I gave My back to whips and My cheek to blows; and I did not avert My face from the shame of being spat upon (2)." For what the human body of the Word suffered, the Word, being linked with that body, ascribed to Himself, in order that we might be enabled to partake of the Godhead of the Word. And it was a paradox, that the same one who was suffering was not suffering. He was suffering, inasmuch as His own body suffered, and He was in this suffering body; but He was not suffering, because the Word, being by nature God, is not subject to suffering. And indeed, He, the Incorporeal, was in a body which was subject to suffering.

The body, then, had in itself the Word, who was not subject to suffering, thereby causing the infirmities of this body to disappear. But this He did, and so it came about, that by His taking what is ours and offering it in sacrifice, it might be done away with; and further, that by His cloaking us in what is His, He might make the Apostle say: "This corruptible body must put on incorruptibility, and this mortal body must put on immortality (3)."

[7] This did not come about figuratively (4), as some have supposed. Inconceivable! Rather, the Savior having in truth become man, the salvation of the whole man was accomplished. For if the Word was in the body figuratively, as some would have it, — and by saying figurative they mean in mere appearance, — then it is found that, in accord with the most impious Manichean doctrine, both the salvation of men and their resurrection are spoken of as being in appearance. Nevertheless, our salvation is not a phantasm, nor does it pertain to the body only; but truly, the salvation of the whole man, soul and body alike, has been accomplished in the Word Himself. That, then, which came forth from Mary, was, according to the Divine Scriptures, human by nature; and the body of the Lord was a true one — a true one, since it was the same as ours. For Mary was our sister, inasmuch as we are all from Adam.

310
347

332

380

314

313

1. John 18:23.
2. Is. 50:6.
3. 1 Cor. 15:53.
4. θέσει.

LETTER TO ADELPHIUS, BISHOP AND CONFESSOR, AGAINST THE ARIANS [*A. D.* 370/371]

Adelphius had been Bishop of Onuphis, but was now in exile in the Thebaid, a victim

of the Arian party. This, no doubt, is the reason for his being styled *confessor* in the title of the letter. The present letter is in response to one of Adelphius to Athanasius, in which Adelphius had reported the Arian charge of creature worship against the adherents of Nicene Christology. In his reply Athanasius traces the error back to the Valentinians, Marcionites, and Manicheans; and in paragraph three he makes the special point that Orthodox Christians do not worship the human nature of Christ as such, but the Incarnate Word, God become Man.

Besides the Greek text, the work is extant also in Syriac and Armenian versions, the latter not yet published. The Maurist edition reprinted by Migne, PG 26, 1071-1084, remains at present the standard edition of the Greek text.

795

[3]

We do not worship a creature. Inconceivable! For such an error belongs to heathens   342
and Arians. Rather, we worship the Lord of creation, the Incarnate Word of God. For   334
if the flesh, too, is in itself a part of the created world, still, it had become God's body.
Nor, indeed, the body being such, do we divide it from the Word and adore it by itself;
neither, when we wish to worship the Word, do we separate Him from the flesh. Rather,
as we said before, knowing that the Word was made flesh (1), we recognize Him as God
even after He has come in the flesh. Who, then, is so lacking in sense that he would say
to the Lord: "Leave the body, so that I may worship You?"

1. John 1:14.

SERMON TO THE NEWLY BAPTIZED [*ante A. D.* 373]

Athanasius' *Sermon to the Newly Baptized*, which can only be dated as before the year 373, the year of Athanasius' death, is known only from a short passage quoted by St. Eutyches, Patriarch of Constantinople († 582 A. D.), in his *Sermo de paschate et de sacrosancta Eucharistia*. The passage stands at the conclusion of Eutyches' sermon (PG 86, 2401). There is no other evidence for a work of this title by Athanasius, and apparently this is the sole surviving fragment. It is impossible to speculate on the authenticity of the fragment, much less on the date of Athanasius' sermon. On the other hand, there is no reason to suspect it of being spurious. If the language seems a bit unlike that of Athanasius in his usual style — a difficult judgment to make of so short a passage — it may be only that Eutyches has paraphrased him somewhat.

The fragment was first extracted from Eutyches and placed among the collected fragments of Athanasius by Cardinal Mai, *Nova bibliotheca patrum* 2, p. 583, where it stands as fragment No. 7. Mai's edition is reprinted by Migne, PG 26, 1325.

802

The great Athanasius, in his sermon to the newly baptized, says this: You shall see
the Levites bringing loaves and a cup of wine, and placing them on the table. So long   860
as the prayers of supplication and entreaties have not been made, there is only bread
and wine. But after the great and wonderful prayers have been completed, then the   864
bread is become the Body, and the wine the Blood, of our Lord Jesus Christ. *And*   856
again: Let us approach the celebration of the mysteries. This bread and this wine, so
long as the prayers and supplications have not taken place, remain simply what they

are. But after the great prayers and holy supplications have been sent forth, the Word comes down into the bread and wine — and thus is His Body confected.

ST. JULIUS I, POPE [regn. A. D. 337-352]

Pope St. Julius' letter, of which the opening words are Ἀνέγνων τὰ γράμματα *(Acknowledging your letter),* is preserved in its entirety in Athanasius' *Apology against the Arians,* Ch. 20-35. The letter was written by Julius in 341 A. D., pre-dating Athanasius' work by only six years. It is a defense of Athanasius, written at the request of a Roman synod, and was sent to the bishops of the Eusebian party at Antioch. It stands not only as a defense of Athanasius, but as a reproach to the Eusebian bishops for their attitude of disrespect to the Council of Nicaea and to the Roman See. One of the great historical documents for the history of the primacy, the best source for its text is Opitz's critical edition of Athanasius: *Athanasius' Werke* 2, 1, Berlin and Leipzig 1935, pp. 87-168.

806a

[*Of Julius,* 22: *of Athanasius,* 35]

For if it is entirely as you say, that some offense was committed by those persons, judgment ought to have been made, not as it was, but according to the ecclesiastical canon. It behooved all of you to write to us, so that the justice of it might be seen as emanating from all (1). For they were bishops who suffered; and they were not ordinary Churches which suffered, but were those which the Apostles themselves had governed. And above all, why was nothing written to us about the Church of the Alexandrians? Are you ignorant that the custom has been to write first to us, and then for a just decision to be passed from this place?   433   435

If, then, any such suspicion rested upon the bishop there (2), notice of it ought to have been written to the Church here. But now, after they have done as they pleased, they want to obtain our concurrence, although we never condemned him (3). Not thus are the constitutions of Paul, not thus the traditions of the Fathers. This is another form of procedure, and a novel practice. I beseech you, bear with me willingly: what I write about this is for the common good. For what we have received from the blessed Apostle Peter, these things I signify to you.

1. The Latin version has *ut ita ab omnibus quod iustum esset decerneretur — so that it might be seen by all that it was just.* However, that is not what the Greek means: ἵνα οὕτως παρὰ πάντων ὁρισθῇ τὸ δίκαιον — *so that the justice of it might be seen as emanating from all.* The use of παρὰ with the genitive πάντων conveys not the meaning that the justice of it must be seen *by all,* but that it must be seen *as coming from all.*
2. *I.e.,* at Alexandria, the bishop being Athanasius.
3. *I.e.,* Athanasius.

ST. CYRIL OF JERUSALEM [*ca. A. D.* 315 - *A. D.* 386]

The place and date of birth of St. Cyril, Bishop of Jerusalem, are unknown — but Jerusalem and *ca.* 315 A. D. are the usual conjectures. He was made Bishop of Jerusalem in 348 A. D., consecrated by the proper bishop, Acacius, metropolitan of Caesarea; but unfortunately, Acacius was an Arian, and suspicions began to settle upon Cyril, as if he had made doctrinal concessions in order to obtain his appoint- ment. Yet, he soon came into conflict with Acacius and the Arians, as a defender of Nicene doctrine.

Cyril generally preferred the term *homoiousios* to *homoousios;* but he was one of those who understood the term in an orthodox sense. Not orthodox enough for the orthodox and not Arian enough for the Arians, it is no wonder that his career was a stormy one, and that he was expelled three times from his see. At least he enjoyed peace in his declining years, regaining his see in 378 A. D., after the death of the Emperor Valens; and he continued on in Jerusalem unmolested until his death in 386 A. D.

CATECHETICAL LECTURES [*ca. A. D.* 350]

Except for a letter to Constantius, a homily on John 5:5, and four short fragments of other homilies, the only genuine writing of Cyril which has survived the ages is the *Catechetical Lectures.* The *Lectures* are twenty-four in number, the first being a kind of introductory discourse, and the rest being numbered from one to twenty-three. Of these, the first 18 are pre-baptismal discourses delivered to the *illuminandi* during Lent; and the last five, delivered to the neophtes during Easter week, are on the liturgical ceremonies of the three Sacraments which they had received during the Easter Vigil. The lectures may have been delivered as early as 347 or 348, when Cyril was yet a simple priest; but much more probably they were delivered in 350 A. D., by which time he had succeeded Maximus in the See of Jerusalem.

It is perhaps worthwhile noting that the lectures were delivered orally, and were taken down in short-hand. The form in which they have come down to us, then, is that of a transcript made by someone in the audience, and not that of Cyril's own manuscript.

The authenticity of the introductory discourse, the *Procatechesis,* and of the first eighteen of the numbered lectures, is more or less universally acknowledged. Not so, however, with the last five lectures, the *Mystagogic Catecheses.* On the authenticity of these last five there is sharp dispute, some holding yet for Cyril's authorship, while others attribute them to Cyril's successor, John of Jerusalem (*A. D.* 386-417). Proponents of John's authorship hold that the liturgical development reflected in these last five lectures is such that they must not be dated before the decade 390- 400. To make such a distinction of liturgical practice over such a short period as 40 to 50 years strikes us as being a bit thin. Proponents both of Cyril and of John are able to advance fairly strong arguments, however, in support of their positions; and perhaps Quasten's offhand suggestion deserves deeper consideration: that Cyril is the original author even of the last five lectures, but that they were revised by John. For a brief summation of the question of authenticity, any treatment of which is beyond the scope of the present work, see Quasten, *Patrology,* Vol. 3, pp. 364-366.

The text given by Migne, PG 33, 331-1128, is a reprint of the Maurist edition of 1720. The standard edition is still that of W. K. Reischel and J. Rupp, *S. Cyrilli*

Hierosolymorum archiepiscopi opera quae supersunt omnia, 2 Vol., Munich, 1848-1860.

807

[*Ad lectorum monitum* (1)]:

These catechetical lectures for those about to be illuminated (2) you may loan to   810
those who are coming forward to Baptism, and to believers who have already received
the Washing (3), so that they may have them for their reading; but do not give them
at all (4) either to the catechumens (5) or to any others who are not Christians. For
this you will answer to the Lord. And if you make a copy, write this in the beginning,
as if the Lord were watching (6).

808

[1,3]

Just as those who are conscripting soldiers examine the age and physical condition of
those being drafted, so also the Lord in enlisting souls examines their dispositions. If
anyone harbors hypocrisy even in secret, He rejects that man as unfit for true service.   711
But whoever is found worthy, to him He readily gives His grace. Holy things He does
not give to dogs (7); but where He perceives a good conscience, there He gives the
wondrous and salvific seal, at which demons tremble and which angels recognize. Thus
are the former put to flight, while the latter gather about it, as something pertaining   798
to themselves.

They, then, who receive this spiritual and saving seal require also the dispositions
pertaining to it. Just as a writing-pen or a dart has need of one to employ it, so also
does grace have need of believing hearts. [1, 4] . . . It is God's part to confer grace,   656
but yours to accept and guard it. Do not, therefore, spurn grace, because it is freely
given; but having received it, guard it religiously.

809

[1, 5]

Cleanse your vessel (8) that you may receive grace more abundantly; for although   796
the remission of sins is given to all equally, the communion of the Holy Spirit is bestowed
in proportion to the faith of each (9). If you have labored little, you will receive little;
but if your labor has been great, great will be your reward. You are running for yourself;
see to your own interests.

810

[2, 19]

The Lord is loving toward men, swift to pardon but slow to punish. Let no man, then,
despair of his own salvation. Peter, the first and foremost of the Apostles, denied the Lord   430
three times before a little servant girl; but he repented and wept bitterly. Weeping is
demonstrative of repentance from the depth of the heart, which is why he not only
received the forgiveness of his denial, but also kept his apostolic dignity without forfeit.

810a

[3, 4]

Since man is of a twofold nature, composed of body and soul, the purification also   822
is twofold: the corporeal for the corporeal and the incorporeal for the incorporeal. The   823

water cleanses the body, and the Spirit seals the soul. Thus, having our heart sprinkled
by the Spirit and our body washed with pure water (10), we may draw near to God.
When you go down into the water, then, regard not simply the water, but look for
salvation through the power of the Holy Spirit. For without both you cannot attain to
perfection. It is not I who say this, but the Lord Jesus Christ, who has the power in this
matter.

And He says, "Unless a man be born again" — and He adds the words "of water and
of the Spirit, — he cannot enter into the kingdom of God (11)." He that is baptized
with water, but is not found worthy of the Spirit, does not receive the grace in
perfection. Nor, if a man be virtuous in his deeds, but does not receive the seal by   831
means of the water, shall he enter into the kingdom of heaven. A bold saying, but not
mine; for it is Jesus who has declared it.

810b

[3, 6]

[John the Baptist] was sanctified by the Holy Spirit while yet he was carried in his   285
mother's womb . . . . John alone, while carried in the womb, leaped for joy (12); and
though he saw not with the eyes of the flesh, he recognized the Master by the Spirit.

811

[3, 10]

If any man does not receive Baptism, he does not have salvation. The only exception   831
is the martyrs, who, even without water, will receive the kingdom. . . . For the Savior   833
calls martyrdom a Baptism, saying: "Can you drink the cup which I drink, and be
baptized with the Baptism with which I am to be baptized (13)?" Indeed, the martyrs
too confess, by being made a spectacle to the world, both to angels and to men (14).   810
Soon you too will confess: — but it is not yet time for you to hear of these things (15).

812

[3, 12]

Bearing your sins, you go down into the water; but the calling down of grace seals   824
your soul and does not permit that you afterwards be swallowed up by the fearsome
dragon. You go down dead in your sins, and you come up made alive in righteousness.   836

813

[3, 14]

And if your piety is unfeigned the Holy Spirit will come down upon you also, and   753
from on high a paternal voice will sound over you: not, "This is My Son (16)," but   755
"This is now become My son." The "is" belongs to Him alone, because "In the beginning   256
was the Word, and the Word was with God, and the Word was God (17)." To Him belongs
the "is", because always the Son of God He is. To you belongs the "is now become",   740
because you have sonship not by nature, but have received it by adoption.

814

[4, 4]

First let there be laid as a foundation in your soul the doctrine concerning God: that   157
there is one God alone, unbegotten, without beginning, unchangeable and immovable;   155
neither begotten of another nor having another to succeed to His life; who neither began   250
to live in time nor will ever cease to be; and that He is good and just. Therefore, should   156

ever you hear a heretic say that there is one who is just and another who is good (18),   460
you will immediately remember and will detect the poisoned arrow of heresy. . . . There
is, then, one only God, the Maker both of souls and of bodies; the Creator of heaven
and of earth is one, and the Maker of Angels and Archangels; the Creator of many, but
the Father before the ages of one only, — of one only, His only-begotten Son, our Lord
Jesus Christ, by whose agency He made all things, those which are visible and those   284
invisible.

815

[4, 5]

    This Father of our Lord Jesus Christ is not circumscribed in any place, nor is He   154
less than the heavens. . . . He knows beforehand the things that shall be, and is mightier
than all. He knows all, and does as He will. He is not subject to the consequences of   189
events, neither to astrological geniture (19), nor to chance, nor to fate. He is in all   158
things perfect, and possesses equally every absolute (20) of virtue, neither diminishing   153
nor decreasing, but remains ever the same and unchanging (21). And He has prepared   155
punishment for sinners and a crown for the righteous.

816

[4, 7]

    Believe also in the Son of God, the one and only, our Lord Jesus Christ, who is God   252
begotten of God, who is Life begotten of Life, who is Light begotten of Light, who is in
all things like unto the Begetter (22); and who did not come to be in time but was   256
before all the ages, eternally and incomprehensibly begotten of the Father. He is the   239
Wisdom of God, and His Power, and His Righteousness subsisting as a Person (23); and   261
He sits at the right of the Father through all the ages.

817

[4, 9]

    Believe that this only-begotten Son of God came down from heaven to earth on account   310
of our sins, and took humanity of a like condition (24) to ours, and was born of the Holy   781
Virgin and of the Holy Spirit; and was made man, not in appearance or phantasy, but in   311
truth. Neither did He pass through the Virgin as through a channel (25), but was truly
made flesh of her, and was truly nourished with her milk (26), and did truly eat as we eat,
and truly did drink as we drink. For if the incarnation was a phantasm, so too is   314
salvation a phantasm. The Christ was twofold: Man in what was seen, but God in what   332
was not seen. As Man, He truly ate as we do, for His flesh was of a condition like to   348
ours; and as God, He fed the five thousand with five loaves (27).

818

[4, 11]

    [Christ] descended into the subterranean regions so that He might ransom from there   390
the just. Now tell me, could you wish the living to rejoice in His grace, though most of
them are not holy, and not at the same time want those to regain their liberty who, from
Adam on, had been imprisoned for such a long time? Isaias the prophet proclaimed such
things about Him; and would you not want the King to go down and free His herald?
David was there, and Samuel, and all the prophets; and John, the same who, through
his messengers, said: "Are You the one who is to come, or shall we look for another (28)?"
Would you not want Him to go down to free such men as these (29)?

818a

[4, 12]

But He that descended into the subterranean regions came up again. And Jesus, who   84
was buried, truly rose again on the third day. If ever the Jews taunt you, meet the
challenge at once, and question them in this way: Did Jonas come forth from the whale
on the third day (30), and Christ — did He not then come forth from the earth on the
third day? Was a dead man raised to life by being touched with the bones of Eliseus (31),
and is it not much easier for the Maker of man to be raised by the power of the Father?

Well now, He truly rose, and having risen He was seen again by the disciples. Twelve
disciples were witnesses to His resurrection, and they did not bear witness with pleasing
words, but insisted upon the truth of the resurrection even in the face of torture and
death. Well, according to the Scriptures, "In the mouth of two witnesses or three every
word shall stand (32)." Twelve bear witness to the resurrection of Christ, and are you
still without faith in that resurrection?

818b

[4, 17]

Keep always in mind this seal (33), which I have until now but briefly summarized for
you in my discourse, but which, the Lord willing, shall after this be stated to the best of
my ability with the proofs from the Scriptures. In regard to the divine and holy mysteries   22
of the faith, not the least part may be handed on without the Holy Scriptures. Do not   100
be led astray by winning words and clever arguments. Even to me, who tell you these
things, do not give ready belief, unless you receive from the Holy Scriptures the proof of
the things which I announce. The salvation in which we believe is proved not from clever   10
reasoning, but from the Holy Scriptures (34).

818c

[4, 25]

While you maintain perfect chastity, do not be puffed up in vain conceit against those   984
who walk a humbler path in matrimony. As the Apostle says, "Let marriage be held in   983
honor, and let the marriage bed be undefiled (35)." And you who keep your chastity:
were you not born of those who had married? Because you have a possession of gold
do not on that account hold the silver in contempt. Let those also be of good cheer
who are married and use their marriage properly; who enter marriage lawfully, and not
out of wantonness and unbounded license; who recognize periods of continence so
that they may give themselves to prayer (36); who in the assemblies bring clean bodies as
well as clean garments into church; who have embarked upon the matrimonial estate for   968
the procreation of children, and not for the sake of indulgence.

818d

[4, 26]

And those who are once married — let them not hold in contempt those who have   979
accommodated themselves to a second marriage. Continence is a good and wonderful   968
thing; but still, it is permissible to enter upon a second marriage, lest the weak might
fall into fornication.

818e

[4, 32]

The Lord has given a redemption of repentance (37), so that our chief sins, or   836
rather, all our sins, may be cast off; and so that we may receive the seal of the Holy
Spirit, and may thereby be made heirs of eternal life.

819

[4, 34]

The process [of translating the Septuagint from the Hebrew text] was no invention 29
of words and contrivance of human wisdom (38). On the contrary, the translation was
effected by the Holy Spirit, by whom the Divine Scriptures were spoken. [35] Of these, 40
read the twenty-two books; but have nothing to do with the apocrypha. Study diligently
those only which we read publicly in the Church. Far wiser than you, and much more
pious, were the Apostles and the bishops of old, the rulers of the Church who handed
down these books. You, therefore, being a child of the Church — infringe not on its 41
statutes. Of the Old Testament, as we have said, study the twenty-two books; and if
you happen to be desirous of learning, strive to remember them by name as I recite
them. Of the Law, the first five are the books of Moses: Genesis, Exodus, Leviticus,
Numbers, and Deuteronomy. Next, Jesus the Son of Nave; and the Book of Judges
together with Ruth, counted as the seventh.

Of the others, the historical books, the first and second Books of Kingdoms are
counted by the Hebrews as one book; and as one book also, the third and the fourth.
Likewise, with them, the first and second Books of Paralipomenon are accounted as one
book; and the first and second of Esdras are reckoned as one. The twelfth book is
Esther. And these are the historical books.

Those, however, which are written in verses are five: Job, the Book of Psalms, Proverbs,
Ecclesiastes, and the Song of Songs, which is the seventeenth book. After these there are
the five prophetic books: of the twelve prophets, there is one book; of Isaias, one; of
Jeremias, one, along with Baruch, Lamentations, and the Letter; next, Ezechiel; and
the Book of Daniel is the twenty-second book of the Old Testament. 42

[36] In the New Testament there are four only Gospels. The others are falsely
written and harmful. The Manicheans have written a Gospel according to Thomas, which,
being touched on the surface with the fragrance of an evangelic title, corrupts the souls
of the simple. Receive also the Acts of the Twelve Apostles; and in addition to these
the seven Catholic Epistles of James, Peter, John, and Jude; and, as a seal upon all,
the last work of the Disciples, the fourteen Epistles of Paul. Let all the rest be put
outside as foreign. And whatever books are not read in the churches, do not read even
by yourself, as you have already heard me say. So much for these matters.

820

[5, 10]

As a noun the word *faith* is but one; yet, its meaning is twofold. There is the one 552
kind, dogmatic faith, involving assent of the soul to something or other; and it is
profitable to the soul, as the Lord says: "Whoever hears My words, and believes Him
who sent Me, has everlasting life, and will not come to the judgment (39)." . . . Do
not doubt whether it is possible: for He that on this sacred Golgotha saved the robber
after only one hour of believing, the same will save you, if you believe. 556

[11] But there is a second kind of faith, which is given by Christ as a kind of
grace. "For to one there is given through the Spirit a word of wisdom; but to another
a word of knowledge according to the same Spirit; and to another faith, in the same
Spirit; and to another, gifts of healing (40)." This faith, then, which is given as a gift
from the Spirit, is not solely doctrinal, but also, it performs works beyond the power
of man. For whosoever has this faith shall say to the mountain, "Remove yourself
yonder from this place," and it shall remove itself (41). For whenever anyone says
this according to faith, and believes that it will happen, and does not doubt in his heart,
then will he be given the grace (42).

821

[6, 2]

Of God we cannot say all that ought be said, — for that is known to Him alone,   174
but only as much as our human nature has grasped, only as much as our weakness is   188
able to bear. We do not explain what God is; rather, we confess quite candidly that   175
we have not a precise knowledge concerning Him. In those matters which concern God,
to confess our ignorance is already great knowledge.

822

[6, 6]

What about this? Someone may say, "Is it not written that 'The Angels of the little   172
ones always behold the face of My Father who is in heaven' (43)?" But the Angels see
God not as He is, but insofar as they themselves are capable. It is Jesus Himself who
says, "Not that anyone has seen the Father, except Him that is from God — He has
seen the Father (44)." The Angels, then, behold as much as they are able, and the   488
Archangels, as much as is their capacity; and the Thrones and Dominations, more
than the others mentioned, yet less than His true dignity. Only the Holy Spirit,
with the Son, can behold Him properly.

822a

[6, 7]

For the sake of devotion this alone is enough: to know that we have a God; a   157
God who is one, a living God, existing always; a God like unto Himself; who has   156
none other for a father; than whom there is none mightier, none to thrust Him out   158
of His kingdom; who in name is manifold; who is all-powerful, and uniform in   151
substance (45). For all that He is called Good, and Just, and Almighty, and Sabaoth,
He is not diverse and various. Rather, being one and the same, He sends forth the
multitudinous operations of the Godhead; not exceeding in this and deficient in that,
but in all things He is like unto Himself. He is not great in loving-kindness only, and
little in wisdom; but in wisdom and loving-kindness, He is of equal power. He is not
seeing in part, and in part devoid of sight; but He is all eye, and all ear, and all mind.
He is not like us, apprehending in part, and in part not knowing. Such a statement
were blasphemous, and unworthy of the divine substance. He knows beforehand the   189
things that shall be. He is holy, almighty, excelling all in goodness, greater than all,
and wiser than all. Of Him we are able to declare neither beginning, nor form, nor
appearance.

822b

[6, 11]

Whence came the polytheistic error of the Greeks? God has no body: whence,   152
then, the adulteries alleged among those whom the Greeks call gods? I will say nothing
of the transformation of Zeus into a swan. I am ashamed to mention his transformation
into a bull; for bellowings (46) are unworthy of a god. The god of the Greeks has been
found an adulterer, and they are not ashamed! But if he is an adulterer, let him not be
called a god. They tell also of deaths, and falls, and thunderstrokes of their gods.

Do you see from how great a height and how low they are fallen? Was it without   370
reason, then, that the Son of God came down from heaven? Was it not that He might   372
heal so great a wound? Was not the reason the Son came, that the Father might be
known again? You have learned what moved the Only-begotten to come down from the
righthand throne: the Father was despised, and the Son must correct the error; for He   363

through whom all things were made must make of all things an offering for the Master of all.

822c

[6, 14]

[Simon Magus] so deceived the City of Rome that Claudius erected a statue of him, and wrote beneath it in the language of the Romans *Simoni Deo Sancto,* which is translated *To the Holy God Simon.* [15] While the error was extending itself Peter and   431
Paul arrived, a noble pair and the rulers of the Church; and they set the error aright. When the reputed god Simon was about to show himself off, they showed him for a corpse. Simon promised to rise aloft to the heavens, and came riding in the air in a chariot of the demons. The servants of God fell on their knees and, displaying that agreement of which Jesus said, "If two from among you shall agree about anything at all for which they ask, it shall be done for them (47)," they launched the weapon of their like-mindedness in prayer against the Magus, and struck him down to earth.

It was marvellous enough, and yet, no marvel at all: for Peter was there, he that   435
carries about the keys of heaven (48). And it was nothing to marvel at: for Paul was there, he that was caught up into the third heaven and into paradise, and heard unspeakable words which it is not lawful for a man to utter (49). And they brought the reputed god down from sky to earth, to be taken away to the regions below the earth (50).

823

[7, 5]

In a metaphorical sense (51), God is the Father of many; but by nature and in truth,   252
He is the Father of one only, the only-begotten Son, our Lord Jesus Christ. He did not   302
attain to Fatherhood in time, but is ever the Father of the Only-begotten. He was not at   256
a prior time without a son, becoming afterwards by a change of purpose a father. Rather, before every substance and before every intelligence, before times and before all ages, God has the paternal dignity.

824

[10, 19]

Many, My beloved, are the true witnesses to Christ. The Father bears witness from   236
heaven to His Son (52). The Holy Spirit bears witness, coming down bodily in the form of a dove (53). The Archangel Gabriel bears witness, bringing good tidings to Mary (54).   780
The Virgin Mother of God (55) bears witness (56). . . . The holy wood of the cross bears   125
witness, seen among us to the present day, and now almost filling the whole world by means of those who in faith take away from here portions of it.

825

[11, 10]

The Father begot the Son, not as among men the mind begets a word. With us, the   265
mind is substantially existent; but a word, when spoken, is dispersed in the air and comes to an end. We know, however, that Christ was begotten not as an uttered word, but as a Word substantially existent and living — not spoken by the lips and dispersed, but begotten of the Father eternally and inexpressibly, and in substance.

826

[11, 18]
    Whoever sees the Son, sees the Father (57): for the Son is like the Begetter in all   252
respects (58). . . . The Father, having begotten the Son, remained Father, and did not   261
become other than He was. He begot Wisdom, but did not Himself become unwise.
He begot Power, and was not weakened. He begot God, but lost not His own divinity.
He neither lost anything of Himself by diminution or change; nor is there anything
lacking in Him that was begotten. He that begot is perfect; and perfect is He, the   257
Begotten. He that begot is God; and God is He that was begotten.

827

[12, 1]
    Companions of purity and disciples of chastity, with lips full of purity we raise our
hymn to the God born of a virgin (59). . . . For neither is it holy to worship the mere   323
man, nor is it pious to say that He is God only, without the manhood. If Christ is God,   342
as indeed He is, but took not human nature upon Him, then our estate is as strangers to
salvation. Let us, then, worship Him as God, and believe that He also was become man.
Neither does it profit us to speak of the man without the Godhead; nor is there salvation
in refusing to confess the manhood together with the Godhead. Let us confess the
presence (60) of the King and Physician; for Jesus the King, when about to become our
Physician, girded Himself around with the apron of humanity; and He healed that which   314
was sick.

828

[12, 14]
    Well then, the proof of our weakness having been demonstrated (61), — the Savior   347
took upon Himself that which man required. Since man required to hear from one of
countenance like his own, the Savior took upon Himself a condition like ours (62), so   373
that we might be the more easily instructed. [15] . . . Men abandoned God, and fashioned
images carved after the human form. Since an image of man was falsely worshipped as
God, God became truly man, so that the falsehood might be destroyed. . . . The Lord   375
took upon Himself from us a likeness with us, so that He might save mankind. He took   313
our likeness, so that He might give a greater grace to that which was lacking, — so that
sinful mankind might become partaker of God.

829

[13, 1]
    The crown (63) of the cross led into the light those who were blinded by ignorance,   375
loosed all those who were chained by their sins, and redeemed the totality of men.   376
[2] Do not wonder that the whole world is redeemed. It was no mere man, but the
only-begotten Son of God, who died on its behalf. Indeed, one man's sin, that of Adam,   611
had the power to bring death to the world. If by the transgression of one, death reigned   614
over the world (64), why should not life more fittingly reign by the righteousness of
one? If they were cast out of paradise because of the tree and the eating thereof, shall
not believers now enter more easily into paradise because of the tree of Jesus? If that
man first formed out of the earth ushered in universal death, shall not He that formed
him out of the earth bring in eternal life, since He Himself is Life? If Phinees in his zeal
slew the evil-doer, thereby staying the hand of God (65), shall not Jesus, who slew not
another, but gave Himself as a ransom, set aside the anger against mankind?

830

[13, 6]

[The Savior] did not give up His life by compulsion, nor were He put to death by a   350
butchery of His life, except it were voluntary. Hear what He says: "I have the power to
lay down My life, and I have the power to take it up again (66). Willingly do I yield
it to My enemies; for if I did not so will, it would not happen." Well then, He came of
set purpose to His passion, rejoicing at the noble deed, smiling at the crown, cheered by
the salvation of men. He was not ashamed of the cross, for it was effecting the salvation   334
of the world. Indeed, it was no common man who was suffering. It was God made man,
striving for the prize of His endurance.

831

[13, 33]

The Savior endured these things, and made peace through the blood of the cross for   375
things in heaven and things on earth (67). We were enemies of God through sin, and God
had appointed the sinner to die. It was necessary, then, that one of two things should
happen: either that God, in His truth, should destroy all men, or that in His loving-
kindness He should blot out the sentence. But behold the wisdom of God: He preserved
both the truth of His sentence, and the exercise of His loving-kindness. Christ bore our
sins in His body on the tree, so that by His death we might die to sin and live to   383
righteousness (68). He that died for us was of no small account. He was not literally a
sheep; nor was He merely man. Neither was He only an Angel. Indeed, He was God   385
made man.   334

The transgression of sinners was not so great as the righteousness of Him that died for
them. The sin which we committed was not so great as the righteousness worked by
Him who laid down His life for us, who laid it down when He pleased, and took it up   350
again when He pleased. Do you wish to know that He did not lay down His life by its
being violently wrested from Him, and that He did not give up the spirit unwillingly?
He cried to the Father saying, "Father, into your hands I commend My spirit (69); I
commend it, so that I may take it up again." And having said these things, He gave up
the spirit (70); but not for any great length of time, because He quickly rose again from
the dead.

832

[15, 11]

When formerly He was about to become man, and when God was expected to be born
of a Virgin, the devil attempted to anticipate events by craftily preparing among idolaters
fables of false gods begetting and begotten of women, so that the falsehood might come   1010
first, and the truth, as he supposed, might then be subjected to disbelief. And now, in
this same way, since the true Christ is to come a second time, the adversary makes use
of the expectations of the simple, and especially of those of the circumcision; and he
brings in a certain man who is a magician, and who is quite expert in sorceries and
enchantments of beguiling craftiness. This one shall seize for himself the power of the
Roman Empire, and shall falsely style himself Christ. By this name Christ he shall
deceive the Jews, who are expecting the Anointed (71); and he shall seduce the gentiles
by his magical illusions.

[12] This afore-mentioned Antichrist is to come when the times of the Roman Empire
shall have been fulfilled and the end of the world is drawing near. There shall rise up
together ten kings of the Romans, reigning in different parts, perhaps, but all reigning at
the same time. After these there shall be an eleventh, the Antichrist, who by the evil
craft of his magic shall seize upon the Roman power. Of the kings who reigned before
him, three shall he humble (72), and the remaining seven he shall have as subjects under

him. At first he shall feign mildness, — as if he were a learned and discreet person, — and sobriety and loving-kindness.

Having beguiled the Jews by the lying signs and wonders of his magical deceit, until they believe he is the expected Christ, he shall afterwards be characterized by all manner of wicked deeds of inhumanity and lawlessness, as if to outdo all the unjust and impious men who have gone before him. He shall display against all men, and especially against us Christians, a spirit that is murderous and most cruel, merciless and wily. For three years and six months only shall he be the perpetrator of such things; and then he shall be destroyed by the glorious second coming from heaven of the only-begotten Son of God, our Lord and Savior Jesus, the true Christ, who shall destroy him with the breath of His mouth (73), and shall deliver him over to the fire of Gehenna.

832a

[15, 22]

But what — lest a hostile power dare to counterfeit it — is the sign of His coming? 1010
"And then shall appear," He says, "the sign of the Son of Man in the heavens (74)." Christ's own true sign is the cross. The sign of a luminous cross shall go before the King, pointing out Him that was formerly crucified.

833

[16, 18]

Do you see how the Holy Spirit enlightens the saint? . . . [19] If perhaps, while 682
you have been sitting here, a thought concerning chastity or virginity has come to you, it is His teaching. Has it not often happened that a maiden, already come to the threshold of the bridal chamber, has fled away upon being taught by Him about virginity? Has not often a man, distinguished in the palace, scorned wealth and rank under the teaching of the Holy Spirit? Has not often a young man closed his eyes upon seeing beauty, and fled away from the sight, and escaped defilement? Do you ask how this comes about? The Holy Spirit taught the soul of this young man. In the world there are many ways to grow wealthy; yet, Christians live in poverty. Why? Because of the promptings of the Holy Spirit.

834

[16, 24]

The Father gives to the Son, and the Son shares with the Holy Spirit. For it is 283
Jesus Himself, not I, who says, "Everything is delivered to My by My Father (75);" 270
and of the Holy Spirit, He says, "When He, the Spirit of Truth, shall come," and so forth, "He shall glorify Me; for He shall receive of what is Mine, and shall announce it to you (76)." The Father through the Son with the Holy Spirit gives every gift. The gifts of the Father are not this, and those of the Son that, and of the Holy Spirit the other. For there is one salvation, one power, and one faith. There is one God, the Father; one Lord, His only-begotten Son; and one Holy Spirit, the Advocate; and it is enough for us to know these things. Do not inquire curiously into His nature or 239
substance. If it had been written, we would have said so; but since it is not written, let us not be reckless. It is sufficient for us, in regard to our salvation, to know that there is Father, Son, and Holy Spirit (77).

834a

[16, 26]

You see everywhere the type in the Old Testament, and in the New the same. In the 51 days of Moses, the Spirit was given by the laying on of hands; and by the laying on of hands, Peter gives the Spirit (78). On you also, who are about to be baptized, His grace will come. But how this shall be, I will not say; for I will not anticipate the proper time.   810

835

[17, 14]

    The water flows around on the outside, but the Spirit baptizes also the soul within,   800
and that completely. But why should you marvel at this? Take a material example,   752
small indeed and humble, but useful to the simpler sort of men: if fire, passing in
through a mass of iron, makes all of it fire, so that what was cold becomes burning and
what was black becomes bright, — if fire, which is a body, penetrates and works thus
unhampered in iron, which also is a body, why should you marvel that the Holy Spirit
enters into the inmost recesses of the soul?

835a

[17, 27]

    In the power of the same Holy Spirit, Peter, both the chief of the Apostles and the   430
keeper of the keys of the kingdom of heaven, in the name of Christ healed Aeneas the
paralytic at Lydda, which is now called Diospolis (79); and at Joppa he raised the
beneficent Tabitha from the dead (80).

836

[18, 1]

    The root of every good work is the hope of the resurrection; for the expectation   770
of a reward nerves the soul to good work. Every laborer is prepared to endure the   1011
toils if he looks forward to the reward of these toils. But they who labor without   583
reward — their soul is exhausted with their body. . . . He that believes his body will   584
remain for the resurrection is careful of his garment and does not soil it in fornication;   1013
but he that has no faith in the resurrection gives himself to fornication, and abuses his
own body as if it belonged to another. A great precept and teaching of the Holy
Catholic Church, therefore, is belief in the resurrection of the dead — great and most
necessary, but contradicted by many, although it is rendered credible by the truth.
Greeks contradict, Samaritans disbelieve, heretics mutilate. Contradiction is manifold,
but truth is uniform.

837

[18, 18]

    This body shall be raised, not remaining weak as it is now; but this same body shall   1013
be raised. By putting on incorruption it shall be altered, as iron blending with fire   1044
becomes fire — or rather, as the Lord who raises us knows. However it be, this body
shall be raised, but it shall not remain such as it is; rather, it shall abide as an eternal
body. It shall no longer require for its life such nourishment as now, nor shall it require
a ladder for its ascent; for it shall be made a spiritual body (81), a marvelous thing,
such as we have not the ability to describe. "Then shall the just," it is said, "shine
forth like the sun and the moon, and like the splendor of the firmament (82)."

    And knowing beforehand the disbelief of man, God has caused little worms in the
summer to emit beams of light from their bodies, so that from the things seen that
which is awaited might be believed. He that gives the part is able also to give the
whole (83); and He that made the worm radiant with light will much more be able
to make radiant a righteous man. [19] We shall be raised, then, all having eternal   1012

bodies, but not all with bodies alike. If a man is righteous, he shall receive a heavenly
body, so that he may be able to converse worthily with the angels. But if a man is
sinful, he shall receive an eternal body fitted to endure the penalties of sins, so that he
may burn in the eternal fire without ever being consumed.   1032
 And justly will God assign to those of either group their portion; for we do nothing   1034
without the body. We blaspheme with the mouth; with the mouth we pray. We
fornicate with the body; with the body we are chaste. We rob with the hand; with
the hand we bestow alms; and the rest in like manner. Since in all things the body has
been our agent, it too shall in the future share in the fruits of what has been done.

838

[18, 23]
 [The Church] is called Catholic (84), then, because it extends over the whole world,   421
from end to end of the earth; and because it teaches universally and infallibly each and
every doctrine which must come to the knowledge of men, concerning things visible and
invisible, heavenly and earthly; and because it brings every race of men into subjection   419
to godliness, governors and governed, learned and unlearned; and because it universally
treats and heals every class of sins, those committed with the soul and those with the
body; and it possesses within itself every conceivable form of virtue, in deeds and in
words and in the spiritual gifts of every description.

839

[18, 26]
 And if ever you are visiting in cities, do not inquire simply where the House of the   421
Lord is, – for the others, sects of the impious, attempt to call their dens the Houses of
the Lord, – nor ask merely where the Church is, but where is the Catholic Church. For
this is the name peculiar to this holy Church, the Mother of us all, which is the Spouse
of our Lord Jesus Christ, the only-begotten Son of God.

840

[19 (*Mystagogic* 1), 7]
 Indeed, those things too which are hung up at the idolatrous Panegyris (85), either
meat or bread or any other such things contaminated by the invoking of most abominable
demons, are to be included in the pomp of the devil. For just as the bread and the wine   860
of the Eucharist before the holy invocation (86) of the adorable Trinity were simple bread   863
and wine, but the invocation having been made, the bread becomes the Body of Christ and   856
the wine the Blood of Christ, so in the same way (87) such foods belonging to the pomp
of Satan, though in their own nature simple, become profane by the invoking of demons.

840a

[20 (*Mystagogic* 2), 4]
 After these things, you were led by the hand to the holy pool of divine Baptism, as   824
Christ was carried from the cross to this sepulchre here before us (88). And each of
you was asked if he believed in the name of the Father, and of the Son, and of the   826
Holy Spirit. And you confessed that saving confession, and descended three times into   825
the water, and again ascended; and in this there was suggested by a symbol the three
days of Christ's burial.

841

[21 (*Mystagogic* 3), 1]

And to you in like manner, after you had come up from the pool of the sacred   824
streams, there was given chrism, the antitype of that with which Christ was anointed: 841
and this is the Holy Spirit.   846

842

[21 (*Mystagogic* 3), 3]

But beware of supposing that this is ordinary ointment. For just as the Bread of the   863
Eucharist after the invocation (89) of the Holy Spirit is simple bread (90) no longer, but
the Body of Christ, so also this holy ointment is no longer plain ointment, nor, so to   840
speak, common, after the invocation. Rather, it is the gracious gift (91) of Christ; and
it is made fit for the imparting of His Godhead by the coming of the Holy Spirit (92).   842
This ointment is symbolically applied to your forehead and to your other senses; and
while your body is anointed with the visible ointment, your soul is sanctified by the   846
Holy and Lifecreating Spirit.

842a

[21 (*Mystagogic* 3), 4]

Just as Christ, after His Baptism and the coming upon Him of the Holy Spirit, went   846
forth and defeated the adversary, so also with you: after Holy Baptism and the Mystical
Chrism, having put on the panoply of the Holy Spirit, you are to withstand the power of
the adversary and defeat him, saying, "I am able to do all things in Christ, who strengthens
me (93)."

843

[22 (*Mystagogic* 4), 1]

This one teaching of the blessed Paul is enough to give you complete certainty about   878
the Divine Mysteries, by your having been deemed worthy of which, you have become
united in body and blood with Christ (94). For Paul proclaimed clearly that: "On the   852
night in which He was betrayed, our Lord Jesus Christ, taking bread and giving thanks,
broke it and gave it to His disciples, saying, 'Take, eat, This is My Body.' And taking
the cup and giving thanks, He said, 'Take, drink, This is My Blood (95).' " He Himself,
therefore, having declared and said of the Bread, "This is My Body," who will dare any   856
longer to doubt? And when He Himself has affirmed and said, "This is My Blood," who
can ever hesitate and say it is not His Blood?

844

[22 (*Mystagogic* 4), 2]

Once in Cana of Galilee He changed the water into wine (96), a thing related to   856
blood; and is His changing of wine into Blood not credible? When invited to an
ordinary marriage (97), with a miracle He performed that glorious deed. And is it not
much more to be confessed that He has bestowed His Body and His Blood upon the
wedding guests (98)?

845

[22 (*Mystagogic* 4), 3]

Let us, then, with full confidence, partake of the Body and Blood of Christ. For in   851
the figure of bread His Body is given to you, and in the figure of wine His Blood is   871

given to you, so that by partaking of the Body and Blood of Christ, you might become
united in body and blood with Him (99). For thus do we become Christ-bearers (100),
His Body and Blood being distributed through our members. And thus it is that we
become, according to the blessed Peter, sharers of the divine nature (101).

878

845a

[22 (*Mystagogic* 4), 4]
   Once when Christ was discoursing with the Jews, He said, "If you do not eat My
Flesh and drink My Blood, you do not have life in you (102)." Not hearing His words
in a spiritual way, they were scandalized and went away to the hinterlands (103),
believing that He had exhorted them to the eating of flesh.

870

846

[22 (*Mystagogic* 4), 6]
   Do not, therefore, regard the Bread and the Wine as simply that; for they are,
according to the Master's declaration, the Body and Blood of Christ. Even though the
senses suggest to you the other, let faith make you firm. Do not judge in this matter by
taste, but — be fully assured by the faith, not doubting that you have been deemed
worthy of the Body and Blood of Christ.

871
851
560

847

[22 (*Mystagogic* 4), 7]
   [David says:] "You have anointed my head with oil (104)." With oil He anointed
your head, your forehead, in the God-given sign of the cross (105), so that you may
become that which is engraved on the seal: A HOLY THING OF THE LORD (106).

842

798

848

[22 (*Mystagogic* 4), 9]
   Having learned these things, and being fully convinced that the apparent Bread is not
bread, even though it is sensible to the taste, but the Body of Christ; and that the
apparent Wine is not wine, even though the taste would have it so; and that of old
David spoke of this, when he sang, "And bread strengthens the heart of man, so much
so that his face is made cheerful with oil (107)," — strengthen your heart, partake of
that Bread as something spiritual, and put a cheerful face on your soul.

851

848a

[23 (*Mystagogic* 5), 1]
   By the loving-kindness of God you have, in our former meetings, heard enough about
Baptism, and Chrism, and of the reception of the Body and Blood of Christ. And now
it behooves us to pass on to what is next. Today we will set the crown in place on the
structure of your spiritual succour (108).

808

848b

[23 (*Mystagogic* 5), 2]
   You have noticed that the deacon gives the priest water with which to wash, as also
to the presbyters (109) who stand around the altar of God. He certainly did not give
it because of any lack of bodily cleanliness. That is not why. We had no bodily
uncleanness when first we came into the church. Rather, the washing is a symbol, that

796

you ought to be pure of all sinful and lawless deeds. Since the hands are a symbol of action, by washing them, it is clear, we represent the purity and blamelessness of our actions. Did you not hear the blessed David opening this very Mystery, and saying, "I will wash my hands among the innocent, and I will encircle Your altar, O Lord (110)?" The washing of hands, therefore, is a symbol of immunity from sin.

848c

[23 (*Mystagogic* 5), 3]

Then the deacon cries out: "Take note one of another and bid one another welcome (111)!" Do not suppose that this kiss is like those given by mutual friends in the market-place.   880 Such a kiss this is not. This kiss blends souls one with another, and woos for them forgetfulness of every injury. This kiss, then, is a sign of the intermingling of souls and of the banishment of every remembrance of injury. It was in this regard that Christ said: "If you are offering your gift at the altar, and while there you remember that your brother has something against you, leave your gift at the altar and go out first and be reconciled to your brother; and then come up and offer your gift (112)." The kiss, therefore, is reconciliation, and because of this it is holy. Just so, where the blessed Paul cried out, saying: "Bid one another welcome in a holy kiss (113);" and Peter, "In a kiss of charity (114)."

848d

[23 (*Mystagogic* 5), 4]

After this the priest cries out: "Your hearts aloft (115)!" For truly, in that most solemn hour it behooves us to have our hearts aloft with God, and not below, with the earth and earthly things. It is, then, as if the priest instructs us in that hour to dismiss all physical cares and domestic anxieties, and to have our hearts in heaven with the benevolent God. Then you answer: "We keep them with the Lord (116)," giving assent to it by the avowal which you make. Let no one come here, then, who could say with his mouth, "We keep them with the Lord," while he is pre-occupied with physical cares.

848e

[23 (*Mystagogic* 5), 5]

Then the priest says, "Let us give thanks to the Lord (117)." Surely we ought to give   374 thanks for His having called us, unworthy though we are, to so great a grace; for His having reconciled us when we were His enemies; for our having been deemed worthy of the adoption of sons (118) by the Spirit. Then you say, "Worthy and just (119);" for in giving thanks, we do a worthy thing, and just. But what He did in accounting us worthy of such great benefits was not merely just, but more than just.

849

[23 (*Mystagogic* 5), 6]

After this we make mention of the heavens and the earth and the sea, of the sun and   488 the moon, of the stars; and of all creation, rational and irrational, visible and invisible; of the Angels, Archangels, Virtues, Dominations, Principalities, Powers, Thrones, of the many-faced Cherubim, saying in effect with David, "Magnify the Lord with me (120)." We make mention also of the Seraphim (121), whom Isaias, in the Holy Spirit, saw standing around in a circle at the throne of God, with two of their wings veiling their face; with two, their feet; and with two, flying, while they exclaimed, "Holy, holy, holy Lord Sabaoth (122)." It is for this reason that we recite this theology handed down by the Seraphim: that we may be participants with the superterrestrial armies (123) in the singing of their hymn.

850

[23 (*Mystagogic* 5), 7]
    Then, having sanctified ourselves by these spiritual songs, we call upon the benevolent   863
God to send out the Holy Spirit upon the gifts which have been laid out (124): that He   856
may make the bread the Body of Christ, and the wine the Blood of Christ; for whatsoever   285
the Holy Spirit touches, that is santified and changed.

851

[23 (*Mystagogic* 5), 8]
    Then, upon the completion of the spiritual Sacrifice, the bloodless worship, over that   890
propitiatory victim (125) we call upon God for the common peace of the Churches, for   897
the welfare of the world, for kings, for soldiers and allies, for the sick, for the afflicted;
and in summary, we all pray and offer this Sacrifice for all who are in need.

852

[23 (*Mystagogic* 5), 9]
    Then we make mention also of those who have already fallen asleep: first, the patriarchs,   122
prophets, Apostles, and martyrs, that through their prayers and supplications God would
receive our petition; next, we make mention also of the holy fathers and bishops who   1001
have already fallen asleep, and, to put it simply, of all among us who have already fallen
asleep; for we believe that it will be of very great benefit to the souls of those for
whom the petition is carried up, while this holy and most solemn Sacrifice is laid out.

853

[23 (*Mystagogic* 5), 10]
    And I wish to persuade you by an illustration. For I know that there are many who   1001
are saying this: "If a soul departs from this world with sins (126), what does it profit
it to be remembered in the prayer?" Well, if a king were to banish certain persons who
had offended him, and those intervening for them were to plait a crown and offer it to
him on behalf of the ones who were being punished, would he not grant a remission of   897
their penalties? In the same way we too offer prayers to Him for those who have
fallen asleep, though they be sinners. We do not plait a crown, but offer up Christ who   895
has been sacrificed for our sins; and we thereby propitiate the benevolent God for them
as well as for ourselves.

853a

[23 (*Mystagogic* 5), 11]
    Then, after these things, we say that prayer which the Savior imparted to His own
disciples (127); and with a pure conscience we describe God as Father, saying: *"OUR
FATHER, WHO ART IN HEAVEN."* Oh, how great is the loving-kindness of God! On
those who have defected from Him, and who were in the extremities of wickedness, He
has bestowed such an amnesty for their wicked deeds and so great a sharing in grace that
they may even call Him Father. *OUR FATHER, WHO ART IN HEAVEN.* But they too   753
are a heaven who bear the likeness of the heavenly (128), in whom is God, dwelling and
walking about (129).

853b

[23 (*Mystagogic* 5), 12]

HALLOWED BE THY NAME:— which for all our saying or not saying, the name of God is by nature holy. But since it is sometimes profaned among sinners, according to the saying, "Through you My name is continually blasphemed among the gentiles (130)," we pray that among us the name of God may be hallowed: not that from not being holy it may come to be holy, but that it may become holy among us, by our being made holy and by our doing of deeds worthy of holiness.

853c

[23 (*Mystagogic* 5), 13]

THY KINGDOM COME. It is the privilege of a pure soul to say with holiness: 392
"THY KINGDOM COME." He that has heard Paul say, "Let not, therefore, sin reign in your mortal body (131)," and has cleansed himself in deed and in thought and in word will say to God, *"THY KINGDOM COME."*

853d

[23 (*Mystagogic* 5), 14]

THY WILL BE DONE ON EARTH AS IT IS IN HEAVEN. The divine and blessed   490
angels of God do the will of God, as David says when He sings, "Bless the Lord, all you His angels, you that are mighty in strength, doing the things He wills (132)." In effect, then, in so praying, you say, "As Your will is done in the angels, Master, so also let it be done on earth in me."

853e

[23 (*Mystagogic* 5), 15]

GIVE US THIS DAY OUR SUPERSUBSTANTIAL (133) BREAD. The bread which   878
is of the common sort is not supersubstantial. But the Bread which is holy, that Bread is supersubstantial, as if to say, directed toward the substance of the soul. This Bread does not go into the belly, to be cast out into the privy (134). Rather, it is distributed through your whole system, for the benefit of body and soul. And by the words *this day* [τὸ σήμερον] it is as if it were said *each day* [καθ᾽ ἡμέραν], as Paul says, "While it is still called *this day* (135)."

853f

[23 (*Mystagogic* 5), 16]

AND FORGIVE US OUR DEBTS, AS WE ALSO FORGIVE OUR DEBTORS. And we   632
have many sins; for we offend both in word and in thought, and we do much that is worthy of condemnation. And, as John says, "If we say that we have no sin, we lie (136)." We make a pact with God, entreating Him to forgive us our sins, just as we forgive our neighbors their debts. Considering then, what we receive and in return for what, let us neither delay nor postpone forgiving one another. The offenses committed against us are small and trivial and easily settled. But those which we have committed against God are great and require a loving-kindness such as is His alone. Beware therefore, lest, because of small and trivial sins against yourself, you might close off from yourself God's forgiveness of your most grievous sins.

853g

[23 (*Mystagogic* 5), 17]

AND LEAD US NOT, O LORD, INTO TEMPTATION. That we should pray not to be tempted at all — is this what the Lord teaches? How then is it written elsewhere, "A man untempted is a reprobate (137)"? And again, "Count it all joy, my brethren, when you fall into various temptations (138)." But wait — does not 'being led into temptation' really mean 'being submerged by temptation'? For temptation is like a winter torrent, something difficult through which to pass.

Those, therefore, who are not submerged in temptations, pass through, demonstrating that they are excellent swimmers, and are in no wise swept away by the temptations. But they who are not such, enter into them and are submerged. Such, for example, was Judas, who entered into the temptation provided by the love of money, and could not swim through it. He was submerged, and was strangled in body and in spirit. Peter entered into the temptation of the denial. But having entered, he was not submerged. Rather, he swam through it quite nobly, and was delivered from temptation.

Listen again, in another place, to a chorus of saints unscathed, giving thanks for their deliverance from temptation: "You have proved us, O God; you have tried us by fire as silver is tried in the fire. You brought us into the net. You laid afflictions on our backs. You set men upon our heads. We went through fire and water, and you led us out into a cool refreshing place (139)." You see, they speak frankly of their having come through without having been exhausted. "And you led us out," they say, "into a cool refreshing place." Their coming into a cool refreshing place is their having been delivered from temptation.

853h

[23 (*Mystagogic* 5), 18]

BUT DELIVER US FROM EVIL. If 'lead us not into temptation' meant not being tempted at all, He would not have said, *"But deliver us from evil."* *Evil* signifies the demon adversary, from whom we pray to be delivered. Then, after the prayer has been completed, you say, "Amen." Through this *Amen,* which signifies *So be it,* you set your seal upon the petitions of this divinely-taught prayer.

494

853i

[23 (*Mystagogic* 5), 19]

After this, the priest says, "Holy things to the holy." The offerings laid out are holy, having received the visitation of the Holy Spirit. And you are holy, having been deemed worthy of the Holy Spirit (140). The Holy Things, therefore, correspond to the holy persons. Then you say, "One is holy, one is Lord, Jesus Christ." For there is but One who is truly holy, holy by nature. We too are holy, but not by nature; rather, by participation and discipline and prayer.

285

853j

[23 (*Mystagogic* 5), 20]

After this you hear the singing which invites you with a divine melody to the Comm of the Holy Mysteries, and which says, "Taste and see that the Lord is good (141)." trust to the judgment of the bodily palate — no, but to unwavering faith. For they are urged to taste do not taste of bread and wine, but of the antitype, of the Body Blood of Christ (142).

853k

[23 (*Mystagogic* 5), 21]

In approaching, therefore, do not come up with your wrists apart or with your fingers   898
spread, but make of your left hand a throne for the right, since you are about to receive
into it a King. And having hollowed your palm, receive the Body of Christ, saying over
it the *Amen.* Then, after cautiously sanctifying your eyes by the touch of the Holy Body,   859
partake, being careful lest you lose anything of it. For whatever you might lose is clearly   878
a loss to you from one of your own members. Tell me: if someone gave you some grains
of gold, would you not hold them with all carefulness, lest you might lose something of
them and thereby suffer a loss? Will you not, therefore, be much more careful in keeping
watch over what is more precious than gold and gems, so that not a particle of it may
escape you?

853*l*

[23 (*Mystagogic* 5), 22]

Then, after you have communicated yourself of the Body of Christ, come forward also   898
to the cup of His Blood, not reaching out with your hands, but bowing; and in an   871
attitude of worship and reverence say the *Amen,* and sanctify yourself by partaking also
of the Blood of Christ. And while the moisture of it still adheres to your lips, touch it
with your hands and sanctify your eyes and forehead and the rest of your senses. Then,
while awaiting the prayer, give thanks to God, who has deemed you worthy of such great
Mysteries.

853m

[23 (*Mystagogic* 5), 23]

Keep these traditions inviolate, and preserve yourselves from offenses. Do not cut   875
yourselves off from Communion, do not deprive yourselves, through the pollution of sins,
of these Holy and Spiritual Mysteries. And may the God of peace sanctify you completely;
and may your body and soul and spirit be preserved intact at the coming of our Lord
Jesus Christ (143); to whom be glory, honor, and might: with Father, and Son, and Holy
Spirit, now and forever, and in the ages of ages. Amen.

1. The authenticity of the *monitum* (given here in its entirety) has been questioned, but it seems on insufficient
grounds. The difficulty which some have is that the *monitum* supposes a written copy, whereas the lectures
were given orally. It is an invented difficulty, however, because it is obvious that the lectures *were* written,
nd were in fact taken down in short-hand while Cyril was lecturing: so, he might well have given the *monitum*
 orally when first delivering the lectures, because he knew that some would write down what he was
 say; or he might have had the *monitum* written into the copy made at that time, or into a copy
ater date. Upon reading the lectures one cannot but be impressed by the fact that, short as the
 vocabulary and style are perfectly consistent with the rest of the *Procatechesis* and with the
heses. As for the five *Mystagogic Catecheses,* I seem to detect something of another style
erhaps to John, Cyril's successor, as their redactor. The content of the *monitum* is
Cyrillic authenticity; for he gives other warnings of the arcane discipline in various
 example, § 811, below)
ve have translated above: *for those about to be illuminated;* or we might
di. See § 407, above. All four of the terms mentioned by Clement of
 be found with some frequency in various grammatical constructions
ed to in the immediately preceding note.
easier translation would be: *Do not give them in their entirety,*
. . The stronger prohibition of our translation is demanded by
a colloquial usage in the Greek.
med to think of the catechumenate as an uninterrupted pre-
er, the state of those engaged in such. It is clear that Cyril
tuted in a group of those who have had only initial instructions,
more advanced and in fact quite proximate to Baptism are called not
r some period after Baptism and Confirmation, they are — we should like

to say neophytes, and perhaps that is what Cyril meant: but the word he uses is not νεόφυτοι, but νεοφώτιστοι, i.e., the *newly illumined;* or perhaps he is engaging in a little play on words, and to follow his example, we should say *neophotes.* Apparently their instructions continue in this period; or at least, the period is opened with a course of post-Baptismal instructions, the five mystagogic lectures. From this usage we can see the historical precedents of the recently promulgated revised discipline of Baptism, according to which the Baptismal ceremonies are performed intermittently at various stages in the course of instructions given to converts.

6. ὡς ἐπὶ Κυρίου.
7. Matt. 7:6.
8. Matt. 23:26.
9. Out of context the remark may seem obscure. But only recall that Cyril is addressing his catechumens in preparation for Baptism, and the great theological truths hidden in the remark begin to unfold. The Sacrament confers its grace *ex opere operato,* and all who receive the Sacrament do equally have their sins forgiven and receive the title to further grace; but their ultimate reception of actual graces and how they will respond to those graces will in some way depend upon their own dispositions.
10. Heb. 10:22.
11. John 3:5.
12. Luke 1:44.
13. Mark 10:38.
14. 1 Cor. 4:9.
15. Here again we have an indication of the *disciplina arcana.* See above, § 807.
16. Matt. 3:17.
17. John 1:1.
18. Cerdo taught that the God of the Old Testament is not the Father of our Lord Jesus Christ; that the God of the Old Testament is knowable and just, but the Father of the Lord is unknowable and good. Certain teaching's of Marcion were very similar to this particular point of Cerdo's doctrine. See Irenaeus, *Adversus Haereses* 1, 27 (on Cerdo) and 3, 25 (on Marcion).
19. The word used is simply γενέσει. But, like the word *nativity* in English, the Greek word is also a technical term meaning the horoscope plotted from the time of one's birth. We have used the less accurate *astrological geniture* because it is our impression that astrology is now so decrepit a subject that few readers would catch the point of the remark if the more accurate term *nativity* were employed.
20. Cyril's word is ἰδέαν: and he thereby attempts to baptize a Platonic term and concept. We might say: "possesses equally *the perfection* of every virtue."
21. Here there is quite clearly a verbal dependance upon Plato's *Phaedo* 78 C: ἀεὶ κατὰ ταῦτα [τὰ αὐτὰ] καὶ ὡσαύτως ἔχει [ἔχων] (Cyril's forms in brackets).
22. τὸν ὅμοιον κατὰ πάντα τῷ γεννήσαντι. This is a Homoian semi-Arian formula, the same as was proposed by Ursacius of Singidunum and Valens of Mursa at the Council of Rimini. (See Athanasius, *Letter Concerning the Councils of Rimini and Seleucia* 8). Yet, it can well be taken in an orthodox sense. Cyril is one of those pitiable souls, whose name was legion, whose language was too unorthodox for them to have made friends with the Catholic party, and whose thought was too orthodox for them to have been accepted beyond the pale.
23. τὴν δικαιοσύνην τὴν ἐνυπόστατον.
24. ὁμοιοπαθῆ. See Acts 14:15 (Greek text) and James 5:17.
25. In general the passage is against docetism; but this particular phrase is spoken against the gnostic Valentine, who, according to Irenaeus (*Adversus Haereses* 1, 7, 2), taught that God produced a son of mere animal nature, who passed through Mary like water through a tube, and upon whom the Savior descended only at His Baptism.
26. Though manuscript evidence is mostly against the clause *and was truly nourished with her milk,* it is restored to the text from Theodoret's quoting it.
27. Matt. 14:17-21.
28. Matt. 11:3.
29. This passage on the descent into hell — the hell of limbo — is a most engaging one, and through it we[?] a happy glimpse of Cyril, the beguiling master, busy at the task of molding the faith of his young c[?] He knows that on this particular point of Catholic doctrine he can find no direct scriptural suppor[?] wheedles his audience, "What would you have done? It is fitting, is it not?" For us, of course, t[?] is to the most ancient teachings of an infallible Church: but in this we have a charism which wa[?] available to Cyril.
30. Jonas 2:1-11.
31. 4 Kgs 13:21.
32. Deut. 19:15.
33. *I.e.,* the faith, or the creed as an embodiment of the faith.
34. The sentence is rather badly constructed in Greek, and in order to avoid suggesting some[?] not there we have been especially literal in our translation.
35. Heb. 13:4.
36. 1 Cor. 7:5.

37. Reading λύτρον μετανοίας. Others would read λουτροῦ μετάνοιαν = *repentance at Baptism;* or λουτρὸν μετανοίας = *a Baptism of repentance.* But whatever be the correct reading – and since the lectures were taken down in short-hand from Cyril's preaching, not even the guarantee of a correct reading could in this case be taken as a guarantee of what Cyril said – it is clear in the context that Baptism is what Cyril meant.

38. Immediately preceding this remark is the well-known Aristean account of the translating of the Septuagint, similar to that already given from among the writings of pseudo-Justin (§ 149a, above).

39. John 5:24.

40. 1 Cor. 12:8-9.

41. Mark 11:23.

42. *Ibid., loc. cit.*

43. Matt. 18:10.

44. John 6:46.

45. ὑπόστασιν. This is Cyril's normal and perhaps exclusive term for *substance.*

46. Probably there is a rather vulgar double-entendre here, μυκήματα being suggestive of μύκητες, which is translatable by the Latin *virgae.*

47. Matt. 18:19.

48. Matt. 16:19.

49. 2 Cor. 12:2-4.

50. The sources for this remarkable account are the *Clementine Recognitions* 3, 63-65; *Clementine Homilies* 1, 15 and 3, 58; and the *Apostolic Constitutions* 6, 7-9.

51. καταχρηστικῶς, catachresis being one of the species of metaphor.

52. Matt. 3:17; 17:5. Luke 3:22.

53. Matt. 3:16. Luke 3:22.

54. Luke 1:26-38.

55. θεοτόκος.

56. Luke 1:26-38.

57. John 14:9.

58. Here again we have the so-called semi-Arian (Homoian) formula; but as always in Cyril, its accompanying explanation is perfectly orthodox. See also above, § 816.

59. The language and metrical flow of this line is such that we easily suspect that Cyril is actually quoting a hymn.

60. παρουσίαν.

61. Cyril has been at pains to show that man cannot safely look upon the face of God.

62. τὸ ὁμοιοπαθές.

63. ὁ στέφανος. If *crown of the cross* seems an odd phrase, consider that we do yet speak often of the *crown of martyrdom.*

64. Rom. 5:17.

65. Num. 25:6-13.

66. John 10:18. The rest, appearing also to be a quotation, is in reality a rhetorical device. Cyril explains the quote, placing also its elaboration in the mouth of the Savior.

67. Col. 1:20.

68. 1 Pet. 2:24.

  Luke 23:46. The note to § 830, above, is equally applicable here.

   Matt. 27:50.

  εἰμμένον. Aquila, a Greek-speaking Jew, had abandoned the Septuagint in order to make a more ...lation of the Old Testament Scriptures. In the Septuagint translation, מָשִׁיחַ is rendered ...t out of hatred for the name of Christ, and so as not to have in the Scriptures a constant ...hristians, Aquila used a synonym, ὁ Ἠλειμμένος. Cyril in this place uses Aquila's term ...h, quite probably, was in his time in common use among the Greek-speaking Jews.

...ssage are a typical manifestation of the Homoian attitude: the ...ral, and their use betrays only an unholy inquisitiveness.

major is utterly fallacious.

86. τῆς ἐπικλήσεως. The same word is used above for the invocation of demons, and is used twice more below, once again for the invocation of demons.

87. τὸν αὐτὸν δὴ τρόπον. Here, however, the force of the particle δή is not that which lends strength and precision, but is the mere continuing δή, signifying that the comparison is being taken up again, after so many words interposing between this place and the ὥσπερ γὰρ which opened the sentence.

88. In lecture 18, paragraph 33, Cyril advised the *illuminandi* that after Easter, at which time they would be baptized, they were to come each day, beginning on the second day of the week; and after the assembly they should come into the Holy Place of the Resurrection. It was in this Chapel of the Resurrection, encompassing the tomb of Christ, that the *Mystagogic Lectures* were delivered. Note, then, the internal tie between the undisputed eighteenth lecture, and the mystagogic lectures, which some attribute not to Cyril but to his successor, John. As suggested before, we are presently inclined to the view that Cyril is the author of all the lectures, though John may perhaps have had a hand in the revision of the last five of the twenty-four.

89. τὴν ἐπίκλησιν.

90. ἄρτος λιτός.

91. We wonder if perhaps χάρισμα may not be a misreading of χρῖσμα.

92. Others punctuate the Greek so as to read something to this effect: *the gracious gift of Christ and of the Holy Spirit, it is made effectual by the presence of His Godhead.* Other translations attempt to make it clear that the Godhead present is that of the Holy Spirit. Our translation is of set purpose ambiguous, in the same way that the Greek is ambiguous, so that the Godhead spoken of may be either Christ's or that of the Holy Spirit; and ultimately, of course, it is one and the same Godhead; no matter to which of the Persons it be referred. Yet, it does seem evident to me that Cyril regarded the Chrism as being within Christ's dominion, and considered that it imparts Christ's Godhead, through the coming of the Holy Spirit upon the chrism. And this view is given some probability by the formula for the consecration of the Chrism given in the *Apostolic Constitutions* 7, 44: *Grant you now this also: that this ointment may be made effective in the one who is baptized, so that the sweet odor of your Christ may remain in him firm and stable; and so that, having died with Him, he may rise again and live with Him.*

93. Phil. 4:13.

94. σύσσωμοι καὶ σύναιμι τοῦ Χριστοῦ.

95. The Greek text, of course, as anyone familiar with ancient Greek will know, has no punctuation to correspond to what we call quotation marks. Yet, from the manner in which this matter is set forth, there can be no doubt that what we have enclosed in quotation marks is intended to be taken as direct quotation; although, as we shall see, only as a literary device. Since Cyril introduces the matter as a teaching of St. Paul, we might have expected the quoting to be from 1 Cor. 11:23-25. It is actually a composite of Paul in that place, and of Matt. 26:26-27, having some words found only in Paul, and some only in Matthew — and in some respects it corresponds to neither. It actually represents a kind of mean reading between Paul and Matthew.

The problem, then, is how Cyril can dare to preface such a hodge-podge with the remark that this is what Paul *proclaimed clearly,* as if these were the very words of Paul's Epistle. The solution to the problem is in the following nice piece of detective work: Our passage § 843 constitutes the opening lines of Cyril's lecture. But the heading to the lecture in the manuscripts indicates that it is to be a lecture on 1 Cor. 11:23. Well, Cyril prefaced his lecture by reading from that passage in St. Paul. Then he opened his lecture with the remark, as we have it above in our translation: *This one teaching of the blessed Paul, etc.* But then, instead of reading or quoting Paul again, He did what we have already seen him do in §§ 830 and 831 above: he paraphrased the Scripture he had already quoted, giving the same thing but now in different words by way of explanation; and he delivered the paraphrase, as he regularly does, as if it were really a part of the same Scripture he had already quoted rather precisely. But how does Matthew get into it? His own familiarity with Matthew 26:26 has caused him quite unwittingly to use certain of Matthew's phrases as his own, in attempting to paraphrase Paul.

96. John 2:1-10.

97. γάμον σωματικόν: literally, a *bodily marriage.*

98. τοῖς υἱοῖς τοῦ νυμφῶνος: literally, *the children of the bridal chamber.* The same phrase occurs in M 9:15.

99. σύσσωμος καὶ σύναιμος αὐτοῦ.

100. χριστοφόροι: literally, *Christophers,* which the Latin of the Maurists in fact renders *christiferi.*

101. 2 Pet. 1:4.

102. John 6:54.

103. εἰς τὰ ὀπίσω.

104. Ps. 22 [23]:5.

105. διὰ τὴν σφραγῖδα ἣν ἔχεις τοῦ θεοῦ: literally, *through [across] the seal which you have*

106. ἁγίασμα θεοῦ. These are the words which were engraved on the little seal of gold attach and hanging over the forehead of the high priest. See Ex. 28:36-38.

107. Ps. 103 [104]:15.

108. Chapter five of the *Mystagogic Catecheses* is devoted to an exposition of the Liturgy its many good things, we will translate the entire lecture, which comprises, then, §§

109. The ministers of the Liturgy here spoken of are ὁ διάκονος, ὁ ἱερεύς, and οἱ πρεσβύτεροι. The first is obvious enough; and the last are the priests concelebrating, for were they only attending they had not been given water for the *lavabo;* but what of ὁ ἱερεύς? The celebrant or principal-celebrant, of course: but is he priest or bishop, and if priest, would a different word have been used for bishop? We are beginning to suspect that not infrequently the term πρεσβύτερος, embracing both priests and bishops, is applied to them in view of their sacramental orders; and that ἱερεύς again embraces both priests and bishops, but is applied to them in view of their sacrifical function.

110. Ps. 25 [26]:6. The same psalm is recited at the *Lavabo* in the Roman Rite: *Lavabo inter innocentes manus meas: et circumdabo altare tuum, Domine.*

111. Ἀλλήλους ἀπολάβετε καὶ ἀλλήλους ἀσπαζώμεθα.

112. Matt. 5:23.

113. 1 Cor. 16:20.

114. 1 Pet. 3:15.

115. Ἄνω τὰς καρδίας = *Sursum corda* (Roman rite).

116. Ἔχομεν πρὸς τὸν κύριον = *Habemus ad Dominum* (Roman rite).

117. Εὐχαριστήσωμεν τῷ κυρίῳ = *Gratias agamus Domino [Deo nostro]* (Roman rite).

118. υἱοθεσίας, *i.e.,* of Baptism. The ambiguity of our translation, — whether we are deemed worthy by the Spirit, of being adopted; or whether we are deemed worthy, of being adopted by the Spirit, — simply preserves the ambiguity of the Greek.

119. Ἄξιον καὶ δίκαιον = *Dignum et justum [est]* (Roman rite).

120. Ps. 33 [34]:4.

121. Here then, with the mention of the Seraphim, we have a complete enumeration of the nine choirs of angels: μνημονεύομεν . . . ἀγγέλων, ἀρχαγγέλων, δυνάμεων, κυριοτήτων, ἀρχῶν, ἐξουσιῶν, θρόνων, τῶν χερουβὶμ τῶν πολυπροσώπων . . . καὶ τῶν σεραφίμ . . . . In regard to the many-faced Cherubim, see Ezech. 10:1-21.

122. Is. 6:2-3.

123. ταῖς στρατιαῖς, *armies, ranks, hosts,* or *companies,* is a fair translation of the word Sabaoth, occurring above, Σαβαώθ being merely a transliteration into Greek letters of the Hebrew צְבָאוֹת . In fact, στρατιὰ and δύναμις are the usual Septuagint equivalents of צָבָא

The Hebrew term is frequently quite broad, including not only the various choirs of angels, but the sun, moon, and stars as well, as the dwelling places of angels. In Late Latin, Zebaoth — the best of numerous spellings — becomes a proper name of God, and is frequently found in exorcisms calling upon His various names. The following, headed *Ad cognoscendum, si aliquis vexetur a spiritibus immundis,* is a fairly recent example: *In Nomine Pa+tris, & Fi+lij, & Spiritûs + sancti, Amen. + Hel + Heloim + Sother + Emmanuel + Zebaoth + Agla + Tetragramaton + Agyos + Otheos + Ischiros + Atanathos + Iehova + Ya + Adanày + Sadây + Hombusion + Messias + Ezerespeye + Increatus Pater, + Increatus Filius, + Increatus Spiritus + sanctus. Iesus + Christus vincit, + Christus regnat, + Christus imperat, + si diabolus ligavit, vel tentavit te,* N. *suo effectu, per sua opera Christus Filius Dei vivi, per suam misericordiam liberet te ab omnibus spiritibus immundis, qui venit de Coelo, & incarnatus est in utero beatissimae Virginis Mariae, causa humanae salutis, & eijciendi diabolum, & omnem malignum spiritum à te in profundum inferni & abyssi. Ecce Crucem + Domini, fugite partes adversae, vicit Leo de tribu Iuda, radix David, Alleluja, Alleluja, Alleluja.* The above is as given in the first edition of Abraham a Sancta Clara, *Judas der Ertzschelm, Der anderte Thail,* Salzburg, Melchoir Haan, 1689, pp. 188-189. have preserved the spelling errors of the first edition. *Atanathos* is constant in all the early editions that we have seen; *eijciendi* is corrected in some but preserved in others.

ἀκείμενα.

ς ἐκείνης τοῦ ἱλασμοῦ.

s add *or not with sins.*

att.

2:5 is the place actually quoted. See also Rom. 2:24, where the ewhat loosely quoted.

of the Lord.
to the mitre
So as not to miss
848a through 853m.
ed

e present context *sufficient;* and praying for bread this day,
for *our daily bread.* From what follows, however, it is
lerstanding of the term, and took it to mean what we can
ldings of the *Our Father* know a frequent variant,
g the same misunderstanding of the Greek.

nslating the term as *supersubstantial* in our text above; but if we
yril's remarks, we must take the word as he understood it, and
e τὸν ἄρτον ἐπιούσιον as supersubstantial Bread, *i.e.,* the Eucharist;
short passage as *supersubstantial.* The confusion over this term is
we remember that Cyril's view of ἐπιούσιος depends upon deriving it

from the word ἔπειμι, formed of ἐπὶ + εἰμί [*to be*], whereas our view depends upon deriving it from ἔπειμι, but formed of ἐπὶ + εἶμι [*to go*].

134. Matt. 15:17.

135. Heb. 3:13 — wherein it is written, "But console one another each day [καθ' ἑκάστην ἡμέραν], while it is still called 'this day' [τὸ σήμερον]."

136. 1 John 1:8.

137. While something of the same idea can be found in various places in Scripture, notably Sirach 34:9-10, and Romans 5:3-4, none of these places is alike enough to Cyril's line to permit us to suppose that he is offering a loose quotation of such a passage. It is generally supposed, and no doubt quite rightly, that Cyril's line is one of the numerous apocryphal sayings of Jesus, or one of his sayings recorded in an apocryphal source. In fact, the *Apostolic Constitutions* provides a defense of this view when it states in Bk. 2, Ch. 8: "The Scripture says, 'A man that is a reprobate is not tempted by God.' "

138. James 1:2.

139. Ps. 65 [66]:10-12.

140. *I.e.*, having been baptized. "Holy things to the holy," then, means: "The Eucharist for the baptized."

141. Ps. 33 [34]:9. The *Graduale simplex* of the Roman rite permits the substitution of this psalm for the otherwise prescribed Communion verse, in all Masses.

142. ἀλλὰ ἀντιτύπου σώματος καὶ αἵματος τοῦ Χριστοῦ. The term *antitype* may, in the present grammatical structure, be either a noun or an adjective. Our translation above takes it as a noun, to which the phrase *of the Body and Blood of Christ* is in apposition. Taken as an adjective, the translation will be: . . . *but of the antitypical Body and Blood of Christ.* In either event, the meaning is the same. Some will maintain that *antitype* must be here the adjectival usage, because of the absence of the article with Body and Blood, in the Greek.

I would not make much of this argument, because Cyril uses the article rather sparingly, frequently omitting it where normal Greek would express it. Those, however, who translate to this effect: *"For they who are urged to taste do not taste bread and wine, but the antitype of the Body and Blood of Christ,* and understand thereby that Cyril regards the Eucharist as but a figure of Christ's Body, not only have a very illogical remark to explain, but simply betray the fact that they do not understand what an antitype is. Let the reader remember than an *antitype* is the thing itself which is prefigured by a *type*. For example, the bread and wine of Melchisedech is a *type* of the Eucharist, while in the same figure the Body and Blood of Christ is the *antitype*. What Cyril says, then, in either of the translations given above, and indeed, even in the mis-translation, if it be logically analyzed, is simply this: *"We do not eat the type, which is bread and wine; rather, we eat the antitype, which is Christ's Body and Blood."*

143. 1 Thess. 5:23. Note here the threefold division of man, composing him of body, soul, and spirit: a view which Cyril seems not otherwise to have shared. In these same *Catechetical Lectures* 3, 4 (§ 810a, above), Cyril states that man is composed of twofold elements, body and soul. Men are not always consistent, however; and the present isolated instance of lack of consistency provides no solid argument against Cyril's authorship of the Mystagogic Lectures. Even if we refuse to allow him such an inconsistency, it still may be no more than an indication of Bishop John's having revised the *Mystagogica.*

ST. HILARY OF POITIERS [*ca. A. D.* 315 - *A. D.* 367/368]

St. Hilary, the Athanasius of the West, so-called because of his staunch support of Nicene doctrine against the Arians, was born of a wealthy pagan family in Poitiers. He received an excellent early education in philosophy and rhetoric; and after making a study of the Old and New Testament Scriptures, he was converted to the faith. Although he was married, the clergy and laity of his native city elected him their bishop in 350 A. D.

In 356 A. D. Hilary was exiled by Constantius to Phrygia in Asia Minor, because he had been organizing resistance against the metropolitan of Gaul, Saturninus of Arles, who had Arian tendencies. But he made so much mischief for the Arians of Asia Minor that he was sent back to his own see in 359 A. D., where he promptly obtained the excommunication of Saturninus.

That Arianism in the West crumbled so quickly after the death of Constantius († 361 A. D.) is due largely to the long-standing and strenuous efforts of Hilary. He died in 367 or 368 A. D., and was proclaimed a Doctor of the Church by Pius IX in 1851.

COMMENTARY ON THE GOSPEL OF MATTHEW [*ca. A. D.* 353-355]

The *Commentary on the Gospel of Matthew* dates from before Hilary's Phrygian exile in 356, and belongs most likely to the years 353-355 A. D. Jerome knew the work for a genuine work of Hilary, and its authenticity is not contested. It may be that Hilary re-worked his homilies into the present form; but it is not as such a collection of homilies. The *Commentary* hangs together as a single and unified work. The book is made up of thirty-three chapters; but it once had also a preface, of which now only a few sentences can be gleaned from John Cassian's *The Incarnation of the Lord: a Treatise on Nestorius,* where they are quoted. Moreover, the book appears to lack a conclusion. Although two volumes of Hilary's writings have appeared in the Vienna Corpus edition, the *Commentary on the Gospel of Matthew* is not among them. The Maurist edition, reprinted by Migne, remains, however inadequate, the standard edition (PL 9, 917-1076).

854

5:31]   *"It was said, moreover: 'Whoever dismisses his wife, let him give*   974
of dismissal (1).' " Advising equitable conduct toward others in all   975
rongly that such equity be maintained for the peace of the
he Law, but takes nothing away. Nor indeed, can progress be
the freedom of giving notice of dismissal through an
lic faith enjoins upon a husband not only a good will
vels against him a charge of collusion in regard to
r out of the necessity created by her separation;
ng a marital union except this: lest a man
us wife.

855a

f binding and loosing given to the Apostles:— In   900
ued by the terror of that greatest dread (2). And

now, out in front of that terror, He sets the irrevocable apostolic judgment, however
severe (3), so that those whom they shall bind on earth, that is, whomsoever they leave
bound in the knots of their sins; and those whom they loose, which is to say, those
who by their confession receive grace unto salvation:— these, in accord with the apostolic
sentence, are bound or loosed also in heaven.

1. The term *written notice of dismissal* is covered in Latin by a single technical term, *repudium,* as also in the
   Greek text of scripture, ἀποστάσιον.
2. *I.e.,* the possibility of losing salvation.
3. Literally, *the irrevocable judgment of apostolic severity.*

THE TRINITY [*inter A. D.* 356-359]

Jerome refers to the present work variously as *Adversum Arianos, Adversus
Arianos,* and *Contra Arianos.* John Cassian knew it as the *De Fide.* Correctly
titled, it is *De Trinitate;* and it was recognized as early as the sixth century as
Hilary's masterpiece. A quite lengthy treatise in twelve books, the entire work on
The Trinity seems to have been written during Hilary's Phrygian exile, *i.e.,* during
the years 356 to 359 A. D. Unfortunately, this work, like the preceding one, has
not yet appeared in the Vienna Corpus edition; and so, for this too, the Maurist
edition, reprinted by Migne (PL 10, 23-472), remains the standard text.

857

[1, 5]

While I was occupied in mind with these and many other problems, I chanced upon   140
those books which, according to a tradition of the religion of the Hebrews, were written
by Moses and the Prophets. In these books the Creator, God Himself, gives testimony
about Himself, in such words as these, contained therein: "I am who am (1)"; and
again, "This you shall say to the children of Israel, 'He that is, has sent me to you (2).' "
I was frankly amazed at such a clear definition of God, which expressed the incomprehensible knowledge of the divine nature in words most suited to human intelligence. For
by none of His characteristics can more be understood of God than by His existence.
That which of itself is, does not belong to those things which someday will cease to be,
nor to those which had a beginning. It is not possible for that which combines eternity
with the power of unending happiness, to ever not have been; nor is it possible for it
someday not to be: for all that is divine is liable neither to destruction nor to origination.
And since the eternity of God is in no way separable from Himself, He has, as an assurance
of His unending eternity, in a fitting manner revealed this one thing only: that He is.

858

[2, 1]

Believers have always found satisfaction in that utterance of God which, by the   826
testimony of the evangelist, was poured out into our ears along with the very power of
its own truth: "Going now, teach all nations, baptizing them in the name of the Father
and of the Son and of the Holy Spirit, teaching them to observe everything whatsoever I
have commanded you. And behold, I am with you all days, even to the consummation
of the world (3)." Indeed, what is there of the mystery (4) of human salvation that is
not contained therein? . . . He commanded them to baptize in the name of the Father,   234
and of the Son, and of the Holy Spirit: that is, in a confession of the Author, and of
the Only-begotten, and of the Gift. There is one Author of all; for God the Father,   278
from whom are all things, is one. And the Only-begotten, our Lord Jesus Christ,

through whom are all things, is one. And the Spirit, the Gift in all things, is one.

Everything, therefore, is arranged according to its own properties and merits: there is one Power, from whom are all things; one Offspring, through whom are all things; one Gift of perfect hope. Nor will anything be found lacking in that grand perfection in which there is, in Father and in Son and in Holy Spirit, infinity in the Eternal, form in the Likeness, and enjoyment in the Gift (5).

859

[2, 5]

For one to attempt to speak of God in terms more precise than He Himself has used (6): — to undertake such a thing is to embark upon the boundless, to dare the incomprehensible. He fixed the names of His nature: Father, Son, and Holy Spirit. Whatever is sought over and above this is beyond the meaning of words, beyond the limits of perception, beyond the embrace of understanding. It cannot be expressed, cannot be reached, cannot be grasped. The nature of the subject itself is such that it exhausts the meaning of words, its impenetrable light obscures our mental perception:— whatever is without limits exceeds the capacity of our understanding. But in the necessity of doing this, we beg the indulgence of Him who is all these things: and we shall venture, we shall seek, and we shall speak.

239

860

[2, 6]

The Father is He to whom all that exists owes its origin. He is in Christ; and through Christ He is the source of all things. Moreover, His existence is existence in itself, and He does not derive His existence from anywhere else. Rather, from Himself and in Himself He possesses the actuality of His being. He is infinite because He Himself is not contained in something else, and all else is within Him. He is always beyond location, because He is not contained; always before the ages, because time comes from Him. . . . God, however, is present everywhere; and everywhere He is totally present.

141

154

Thus, He transcends the realm of understanding. Outside of Him there is nothing, and it is eternally His characteristic that He shall always exist. This is the truth of the mystery of God, and of the impenetrable nature which this name *Father* expresses. God is invisible, unutterable, and infinite. In His presence, let a word about to be spoken remain silent; let a mind attempting to investigate, admit its weariness; let an understanding which attempts to comprehend admit its own limitation. Yet, He has, as we have said, in the word *Father* a name to indicate His nature; but He is Father as such. For He does not, as humans do, receive His Fatherhood from elsewhere. He Himself is unbegotten, eternal; and it is His property, eternally in Himself, that He shall always be.

156

173

861

[2, 7]

But I would rather sense these things about the Father than speak of them; for it does not escape me that all language is powerless to give expression to the attributes which are His. We must sense that He is invisible, incomprehensible, and eternal. Moreover, that He exists in Himself and of Himself, and that it is His very nature to be; that He is invisible, incomprehensible, and immortal: — in these words certainly there is an acknowledgement of His praiseworthiness, and an intimation of our thoughts, and some kind of a round-about expression of what we mean.

173
174

141

But speech will surrender to the reality of His nature, and words do not express the thing as it is. . . . Therefore, our confession of God fails because of the limitations of language; and whatever aptness there is in our words, we cannot give expression to God as He is, nor to how great He is. Perfect knowledge is this: to know God in such a way that you know you must not be ignorant of Him, while yet you cannot describe Him. We must believe in Him, we must apprehend Him, we must worship Him; and it is these acts which must stand in place of our describing Him.

861a

[2, 29]
 Concerning the Holy Spirit, however, I ought not remain silent, nor yet is it necessary to speak. Still, on account of those who do not know Him, it is not possible for me to be silent. However, it is not necessary to speak of Him who must be acknowledged, who is from the Father and the Son, His Sources. Indeed, it is my opinion that there ought   273
be no discussion about whether He exists. If He is given, if He is received, if He is retained, then obviously He exists. . . . [30] I think, however, that the reason why some remain in ignorance or doubt about this, is that they see this third name, that by which the Holy Spirit is named, applied frequently also to the Father and to the Son. But there need be no objection to this, for both Father and Son are spirit and holy.

862

[3, 4]
 He is, therefore, the perfect Son of the perfect Father, and the only-begotten Offspring   258
of the unbegotten God. The Son receives all from Him who has all, God from God, Spirit from Spirit, Light from Light. The Son says with confidence: "The Father is in Me, and I in the Father (7)." For, as the Father is Spirit, so also the Son is Spirit; and as the Father is God, so also the Son is God; as the Father is Light, so also the Son is Light.
 Those properties, therefore, which are in the Son, are from those properties in the Father. That is, from the whole Father the whole Son is born: not from elsewhere, because nothing is prior to the Son; not out of nothingness, because the Son is of God; not in part, because the fullness of the Godhead is in the Son; not in some respects, because He is in all a Son; but as He willed who had the power, and as He knows, who   255
begot the Son. That which is in the Father is in the Son also; that which is in the Unbegotten is in the Only-begotten also; One from the Other, and both are One; not One made up of Two, but One in the Other, because in the Both there is no otherness. The Father is in the Son, because the Son is from Him. The Son is in the Father, because His Sonship has no other source: the Only-begotten is in the Unbegotten, because the Only-begotten is from the Unbegotten.

863

[3, 11]
 The many of us, indeed, are the sons of God, but not in the way that He is Son. For   340
He is both truly and properly the Son by origin and not by adoption, in truth and not by the figure of a word, by birth and not by being made such.

864

[3, 42]
 Besides Moses and Isaias, listen now a third time, and to Jeremias, who teaches the same thing, when He says: "This is our God, and no other shall be compared to Him. He has found every mode of knowledge, and Has given it to Jacob, His servant, and to Israel, His beloved. Afterwards He was seen on earth, and dwelt among men (8)."
 . . . You have, therefore, a God who was seen on earth and who dwelt among men. I   236
ask, then, how you think these words are to be understood: "No one has ever seen God,

except the only-begotten Son, who is in the bosom of the Father (9)," since Jeremias announces a God who was seen on earth and who dwelt among men. Certainly the Father is not visible, except only to the Son.

Who, therefore, is He that has been seen on earth and who dwelt among men? Certainly He is our God, and He is God visible in human form and tangible. . . . This, therefore, is the One who makes covenant with Abraham, who speaks to Moses, who testifies to Israel, who abides in the Prophets, who is born through the Virgin and of the Holy Spirit, who affixes to the tree of His passion the powers opposed and inimical to us, who destroys   781 death in hell, who confirms the faith of our hope by His resurrection, and who destroys   582 by the glory of His body the corrupting of human flesh. . . . The Prophet does not permit God, the Son of God, to be compared to another god, for the reason that He is God.

865

[7, 4]

The Church, instituted by the Lord and confirmed by the Apostles, is one for all   401 men; but the frantic folly of the diverse impious sects has cut them off from her. It   420 cannot be denied that this tearing asunder of the faith has arisen from the defect of poor intelligence, which twists what is read (10) to conform to its opinion, instead of adjusting its opinion to the meaning of what is read. However, while individual parties fight among themselves, the Church stands revealed not only by her own doctrines, but by those also of her adversaries. And although they are all ranged against her, she confutes the most wicked error which they all share, by the very fact that she is alone and one.

All the heretics, therefore, come against the Church; but while all the heretics can conquer each other, they can win nothing for themselves. For their victory is the triumph of the Church over all of them. One heresy struggles against that teaching of another, which the faith of the Church has already condemned in the other heresy, — for there is nothing which the heretics hold in common, — and the result is that they affirm our faith while fighting among themselves.

866

[7, 14]

And first I ask, what new element could His birth have introduced into the nature of   252 the Son, so that He were not God? The judgment of human intelligence excludes the   257 possibility that anything could be born with a nature different from that of its origin. . . . What madness is it, I ask, to connect the birth of the only-begotten God to a nature inferior to that of God, when birth cannot be except according to the quality of nature, and when there will be no birth if the quality of nature shall not have been in the birth. The object of all their heat and fury is to prove that in regard to the Son of God, there is   251 no birth, but a creation; and that He subsists does not preserve for His nature that of His origin, but draws from what did not exist a nature foreign to that of God. . . . However, the Son of God did not begin, out of nothing, to be God, but was born God; nor was He anything else beforetimes. And thus, He that was born into God did not begin to be, nor develop into, what God is. Birth, then, maintains the nature from which it subsists, and the Son of God does not subsist as anything other than that which God is.

867

[7, 31]

Thus in God the Father and in God the Son you cannot count two Gods, because   281 both are one. Nor can you proclaim them as singular, because both are not one. The apostolic faith, therefore, does not have two Gods, because there are neither two Fathers nor two Sons. By confessing the Father, it confesses the Son. Believing in the Father, it believes also in the Son, because the name *father* has in itself the name *son*. For there is no father except through a son; and the meaning of son is demonstrative of a father, because there is no son except from a father. In the confession of one, therefore, there is not one, since Sonship completes the notion of Fatherhood, the birth of the Son being from the Father. . . . [32] Let him assign a different nature to each, who does not know that Father and Son are proclaimed as one. Let the heretics delete the declaration which the Son made about Himself in the Gospel: "I am in the Father, and the Father in Me (11)," so that they can proclaim either two gods, or a singularity. There are no indications of a plurality of natures in the propriety of one nature; nor does the truth of God from God lead to two gods; nor does the birth of God admit of a singular God; nor are They not one who are in Each Other.

868

[7, 37]
   When they were asking Him to show them the Father, He said, "He that has seen Me has seen also the Father (12)." . . . But it is not this carnal body which He has by reason of birth from the Virgin, which can be of avail for the contemplating in Him of the form and image of God; nor does the form of a man which He assumed manifest the nature of the incorporeal God. But God is recognized in Him — if, indeed, He be recog-   257
nized by anyone — by the power of His nature. And when God the Son is recognized, it permits also the recognition of the Father; for the Son is His image in such wise that   264
He does not differ from the Father in nature, but manifests Him as His Source. . . . He is the Living Image of the Living; and having been born of Him, He does not have a nature different from His; and because His nature is in no way different, He possesses the power of the Father's nature, from which He does not differ. The fact that He is the image leads to this: that God the Father is made manifest by the birth of God's only-begotten, who is Himself made manifest as the form and image of the invisible God. At the same time, He does not lose the likeness, the union of Nature (13), because He does not lack the power of that nature.

869

[8, 10]
   They are excluded from the promises of the Gospel, who have no faith in those   567
promises; and the crime of perverse understanding utterly destroys hope. That you believe what is unknown (14) deserves not so much pardon as it does a reward, because the greatest recompense of faith is to have hope in what you do not know. But it is madness of an absolutely wicked kind, either not to believe what is understood, or to corrupt the meaning of what ought to be believed.

870

[8, 14]
   When we speak of the reality of Christ's nature being in us, we would be speaking   850
foolishly and impiously — had we not learned it from Him. For He Himself says: "My Flesh is truly Food, and My Blood is truly Drink. He that eats My Flesh and drinks My Blood will remain in Me and I in him (15)." As to the reality of His Flesh and Blood,   851
there is no room left for doubt, because now, both by the declaration of the Lord Himself and by our own faith, it is truly Flesh and it is truly Blood (16). And These Elements bring it about, when taken and consumed, that we are in Christ and Christ is   878
in us. Is this not true? Let those who deny that Jesus Christ is true God be free to

find these things untrue. But He Himself is in us through the flesh and we are in Him, while that which we are with Him is in God.

871

[8, 19]

[The Son says:] "When that Advocate who proceeds from My Father will have come,   291
the Spirit of Truth whom I shall send you from the Father, He will Himself bear witness about Me (17)." The Advocate will come, and the Son will send Him from the Father; and He is the Spirit of Truth, who proceeds from the Father. . . . He that sends, manifests His power by the fact of His sending. . . . [20] Nor do I now calumniate 'freedom of understanding' in this matter, whether they think the Spirit Paraclete proceeds from the Father, or from the Son. For the Lord has not left this in uncertainty: and after having spoken those same words (18), He says this: "I have much besides to say to you, but you cannot bear it in your present condition. When that Spirit of Truth shall come, He will direct you into all truth. For He will not speak on His own, but whatever He will have heard, He will speak, and He will announce future events to you. He will do honor to Me, because He will receive from Me and will announce to you. Everything whatsoever that the Father has, is mine — for which reason I have said, 'He will receive from Me, and will announce to you (19).' "

He receives, therefore, from the Son, by whom also He is sent; and He proceeds from the Father. Now I ask you, is it the same to receive from the Son as it is to proceed from the Father? But even if it be believed that there is a difference between receiving from the Son and proceeding from the Father, certainly it will be admitted that to receive from the Son is one and the same as to receive from the Father (20).

872

[8, 21]

We are all spiritual men, if the Spirit of God is in us. But this Spirit of God is the   753
Spirit also of Christ. And since the Spirit of Christ is in us, the Spirit of Him also who   270
raised Christ from the dead is in us; and He that raised Christ from the dead will vivify   1011
our mortal bodies too, on account of His Spirit's dwelling in us (21). We are vivified, therefore, on account of the Spirit of Christ's dwelling in us through Him that raised Christ from the dead.

873

[9, 3]

A man is ignorant indeed — he does not even know his own life — if he is ignorant of   310
the fact that Christ Jesus is true God as well as true man. And it is equally perilous to deny Christ Jesus, whether as Spirit of God or as flesh of our body. . . . He Himself has been appointed Mediator in His own person for the salvation of the Church. And in that   387
very mystery of mediation between God and man, He is one and both; for by the fact of His union of natures, He has the reality of each nature equally; and this in such wise   324
that He lacks nothing in either, lest perhaps He might cease being God by reason of His birth as man, or lest, on the other hand, He might not be a man while remaining God. This, therefore, is the true faith which brings blessedness to men: to acknowledge Him as God and man, to confess Him as the Word and as flesh, neither forgetting His divinity in view of His humanity, nor ignoring His flesh because He is the Word.

874

[9, 14]
    He that empties Himself is not other than He who receives the form of a servant. To   323
have received cannot be the part of one who did not exist, because receiving belongs to   334
one who does in fact exist. Therefore, the emptying of the form is not the destruction
of the nature, because He that empties Himself does not lack selfness, and He that receives
does already abide (22). And since He is the self-same person, whether emptying or
receiving, there is something of a mystery in this: that He empties Himself and receives,
but without any annihilation, lest emptying Himself He no longer exist, and be not there
for receiving. Therefore the emptying makes possible this: that the form of a servant may
appear; but not that Christ, who was in the form of God, may cease to be Christ; for it
is none other than Christ who received the form of a servant. When He emptied Himself
so that He might become the Man-Christ while continuing to be the Spirit-Christ, the
assumption of a nature and the change of condition (23) in His body did not prevent His
divine nature from remaining. For He is one and the same Christ, both when changing His
condition and when assuming our nature.

874a

[10, 15]
    If the Man Jesus Christ . . . of His own accord took flesh of the Virgin, and also of   781
His own accord joined for Himself a soul to the body conceived through Himself, then   311
it is necessary that the nature of His sufferings were in accordance with a nature of soul   312
and body.   347

875

[10, 22]
    But just as [the Son of God] of His own accord took for Himself a body from the   781
Virgin, so also from Himself He took for Himself a soul — which, indeed, is never   311
bestowed by man through the origins of those who are being born. For if the Virgin   312
did not conceive the flesh except of God, it is far more necessary that the soul of that   508
body have no origin except from God. And since that Son of Man is at the same time   302
He that is the Son of God, because the whole Son of Man is the whole Son of God,
how ridiculous it would be for us to preach besides the Son of God who is the Word
made flesh, another — I know not whom — something like a prophet animated by the
Word of God! — when in fact the Lord Jesus Christ is both Son of Man and Son of God.

876

[10, 23]
    Therefore, the Man Jesus Christ, the only-begotten God, who through the flesh and   310
the Word is both Son of Man and Son of God, assumed true manhood according to the
likeness of our manhood, without ceasing to be Himself, that is God. In this humanity,   347
when a blow was struck Him, or wounds were inflicted upon Him, or when ropes bound
Him, or when a hanging raised Him, these things did indeed inflict upon Him the
force of suffering; but they did not carry with them the pain of suffering. . . . Certainly the Lord Jesus Christ suffered when He was struck, when He was hung, when He
was crucified, when He died. The suffering which beset the body of the Lord, while
it was really suffering, did not, however, carry with it the natural effect of suffering. It
was violent indeed in its function of punishment; but the power of the body received
upon itself the force of that violent punishment without the sense of pain. . . . How
should we, by the nature of the human body, judge of flesh conceived by the Spirit?

That flesh, or rather, that Bread, is from heaven; and that humanity is from God. Certainly He had a body capable of suffering, and He suffered; but He had not a nature capable of pain. That body is of a nature proper and peculiar to itself. On the mountain it was transfigured in heavenly glory. By its touch it put fevers to flight, and by its spittle it restored sight.

877

[12, 25]

[Jesus Christ], therefore, was, and is, because He is from Him who is ever what He   256 is. But to be from Him, that is to say, to be from the Father, is birth. And to be ever from Him who ever is, is eternity — eternity, indeed, not from Himself, but from the Eternal. From the Eternal, however, comes nothing other than what is eternal; for if that were not eternal, then neither were the Father eternal, who is the source of generation. Since it is proper to the one that He be always Father, and to the other that He be always Son, and since eternity is indicated in the name HE THAT IS, then it follows also   140 that for Him to whom it is proper to exist, it is proper also to exist eternally.

878

[12, 56]

In the fact that before times eternal Your Only-begotten was born of You, when   239 we put an end to every ambiguity of words and difficulty of understanding, there remains only this: He was born. So too, even if I do not grasp it in my understanding, I hold fast in my consciousness to the fact that Your Holy Spirit is from You through Him (24).   272

1. Ex. 3:14.
2. *Ibid., loc. cit.*
3. Matt. 28:19-20.
4. *de sacramento.*
5. *infinitas in aeterno, species in imagine, usus in munere.*
6. See above, § 857.
7. John 10:38.
8. Baruch 3, 36-38. Baruch was secretary to Jeremias, and is cited by the Fathers mostly under the name of Jeremias.
9. John 1:18.
10. *I.e.,* the Scriptures.
11. John 10:38.
12. John 14:9.
13. *non amittit naturae unitatem similitudinem.*
14. *ignorare quod credas.*
15. John 6:56-57.
16. *De veritate carnis et sanguinis non relictus est ambigendi locus. Nunc enim et ipsius Domini professiones et fide nostra vere caro est et vere sanguis est. Et haec accepta atque hausta id efficiunt, ut et nos in Christo et Christus in nobis sit.* Note, however, that Hilary is in no way one with those modern free-thinkers who hold that our faith is the cause of what they explain as the eucharistic presence. For Hilary, our faith, along with Christ's express declaration, is the cause of the indubitability of the Eucharistic Presence.
17. John 25:26.
18. *I.e.,* the quotation above, John 25:26.
19. John 16:12-15.
20. Hilary's predominant fault of wordiness is certainly in evidence in the present passage — and we have ended it somewhat before he did. The next point in the argument would seem obvious enough to one who has been following Hilary's train of thought: that if to receive from the Son is the same as to receive from the Father, since all that the Father has belongs to the Son — then to proceed from the Father is the same as to proceed from the Son, since the Father and the Son are one. Fortunately, however, — whether because of or in spite of his wordiness is now beside the point, — Hilary never quite arrives at such an indiscretion. Had he so ignored the internal operations of the Trinity by considering them as being no different from their external operations, he would have opened himself to a charge of modalism. I am not aware that anyone has ever suggested that there are modalist over-

tones in Hilary's writings; yet, it seems to me that he is quite often on the very brink of a modalist pronouncement, only to dissolve into repetitious words without ever slipping over the edge. Perhaps Hilary himself was aware of such a tendency in his thought, and deliberately used a rhetorical fault to avoid a theological one.

At any rate, it gives us something to ponder: the West's most ardent defender of the homoousion standing at the brink of Sabellianism, just at a time when the homoiousian party was objecting so strongly to the term homoousios, on the grounds that its use could all unwittingly lead to Sabellianism. Not a very nice prospect for historians. However, this must be noted too: the whole matter of the procession of the Holy Spirit seems somewhat muddled in the passage, and finally one is forced to wonder whether or not Hilary is confusing two very distinct notions, that of the eternal procession of the Holy Spirit, with His Pentecostal parousia?

21. Rom. 8:11.
22. *Already* is supplied for clarification. It is not in the Latin, which, unfortunately, possesses the same ambiguity which would be in the English, were the *already* stricken.
23. *demutatio habitus.*
24. *ex te per eum: i.e., ex Patri per Filium,* which is taken to be equivalent to *ex Patri Filioque.*

ENCYCLICAL LETTER ON THE COUNCILS [*A. D.* 358/359]

The present work was written in the midst of Hilary's Phrygian exile, towards the end of the year 358 or in 359 A. D. By this time Arianism had descended to what must be its logical outcome: Anomoianism or Eunomianism, whose watch-word was 'The Father and the Son are unlike in all things.' With this radical Arianism to combat, Hilary, like Athanasius, is ready to regard the so-called semi-Arians, the homoiousian party, as potential allies. In attempting to reconcile the catholic party (homoousians) and the semi-Arian party (homoiousians), Hilary, again like Athanasius, is prepared to admit that with many of the so-called semi-Arians we really have no quarrel: for by their term homoiousios they mean precisely what we mean by homoousios. Of course, He is aware that this is not true of all adherents of the homoiousion, and he is not sacrificing principle. But in those cases where the quarrel is purely over a term and not over an entity, he sees no reason why there should not be a reconciliation. The present treatise, written at the request of certain Western bishops who desired a fuller information in regard to the theology of the Eastern bishops, makes this point clear.

The work is extant in its entirety in its Latin original. Generally standing after the *De Trinitate* in the manuscripts, the *Encyclical* has sometimes been taken as a thirteenth book of the former treatise. Jerome, however, already knew it as a separate writing, the *Liber de synodis;* and it is, in fact, an encyclical letter to all the bishops of Gaul.

Unfortunately a definitive edition has not yet appeared in the Vienna Corpus, and we must for the present be content with the Maurist edition, reprinted by Migne (PL 10, 479-546).

879

[59]
Since it was taught that the Son does not, like all other things, subsist from God's will,   254
lest He seem to have His existence only from the Father's will and not from His very   255
nature, it seemed that an occasion was thereby given to heretics to attribute to God the Father a necessity of begetting from Himself the Son, as if He had brought forth the Son by a law of nature and in spite of Himself. But God the Father has no such status of being acted upon. In the indescribable and perfect birth of the Son, it is not will alone that begot the Son, nor is the Father's essence changed or forced by a command of the natural law. Neither was any substance searched out for His begetting, nor is there any diversity of nature between the Begetter and the Begotten, nor does the unique name

Father come in time. Rather, before all times, the Father, out of the essence of His nature, with a volition unaffected from without, gave to the Son a birth which conveyed the essence of His nature (1).

880

[60]

To declare the Son incapable of being born is impiety of the worst sort, for then God were not one; and the nature of the one unborn God demands that one God be acknowledged. Since, therefore, God is one, it is not possible that there be two incapable of being born; and God is one — although both the Father is God and the Son of God is God — for the very reason that the quality of being unborn can pertain only when there is but one. The Son, however, is God, for the very reason that He derives His birth from that essence which is incapable of being born. Our holy faith refuses, therefore, to acknowledge a Son incapable of being born, so that it can acknowledge one God, there being in fact one God incapable of being born; and so that it can include the only-begotten nature, begotten of the unborn essence, in the one name of the unborn God. For the head of all things is the Son, while the head of the Son is God. By this position, and by this confession, all things are referred to one God, since the universe takes its beginning from Him to whom God Himself is the beginning (2).

250
257

881

[71]

It is not to be denied, beloved brethren, that the substance of the Father and the Son is one; yet, it is not to be acknowledged without explanation. That there be one substance results from the quality of the begotten nature, and not from any division, or union, or communion (3). In regard to the one substance, it is possible to speak reverently, and it is possible to maintain a reverent silence. There is birth; there is likeness. Why should we suspiciously view a word as a calumny (4), when we do not differ in our understanding of the facts? Let us believe and declare that there is one substance, but by reason of a quality of nature, and not so as to imply irreverently a union (5). Let there be one by reason of likeness, and not by reason of singularity.

258

1. The Second Council of Sirmium (*A. D.* 351) attached 27 anathemas to the Fourth Formula of Antioch, and promulgated its work as the First Creed of Sirmium. The present passage (§ 879) is Hilary's explanation of the 25th anathema, which reads: *If any man say that the Son was born against the will of the Father: let him be anathema. For the Father was not forced against His own will, nor was the Father led by any natural necessity, so as to beget the Son when He did not will it. Rather, as soon as He willed, without reference to time and unaffected from without, He begot the Only-begotten of Himself, and manifested Him.*
2. The present passage (§ 880) is Hilary's explanation of the 26th anathema (see the note immediately preceding): *If any man say that the Son is incapable of being born and without a beginning, in such a way as to say that there are two without beginning and two incapable of being born and two who were not born, thus making two Gods: let him be anathema. For the head which is the beginning of all, is Christ; and the head which is the beginning of Christ, is God: and thus do we refer the universe, through Christ, to One who is Himself incapable of a beginning, and who is the beginning of all.*
3. Were the unity of substance from division, each would have a part; were it from union, there would be but one Person; were it by communion, there would be a sharing in a substance prior to both.
4. He refers to the argument of homoousios *vs.* homoiousios.
5. For clarity of understanding, supply after *union* the phrase *of Persons*.

COMMENTARIES ON THE PSALMS [*ca. A. D.* 365]

Jerome states that Hilary's *Commentaries on the Psalms* is a translation of Origen.

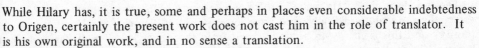

While Hilary has, it is true, some and perhaps in places even considerable indebtedness to Origen, certainly the present work does not cast him in the role of translator. It is his own original work, and in no sense a translation.

If Hilary wrote commentaries on all the psalms, which remains a distinct possibility, they have not all come down to us. Jerome's manuscript contained commentaries or homilies on only forty-seven, Psalms 1-2, 51-62, and 118-150, the numbering being that of the Vulgate and Septuagint. Our present corpus has the same forty-seven known to Jerome, with nine additional: on Psalms 13-14, and 63-69. That we are not yet complete, we know: for in his treatment of Psalm 59, Hilary refers to his previous treatment, already written and not now extant, of Psalm 44.

There are other psalms commented under the name of Hilary, but probably spurious, notably psalms 9 and 91; and still others, certainly spurious, such as those on Psalms 15, 31, and 41. Zingerle found several others which he labels as either badly transmitted or spurious. We are left with a work presently consisting of a prologue and authentic commentaries on fifty-six of the Psalms: 1, 2, 13, 14, 51 through 59, and 118 through 150, and the knowledge that at least one other, on Psalm 44, is lost.

The Maurist edition, reprinted by Migne (PL 9, 231-890), is now superseded by the critical edition of A. Zingerle in the Vienna Corpus (CSEL), Vol. 22, Vienna 1891.

882

[*Prologue,* 15]

And this is the reason why the Law of the Old Testament is reckoned as consisting of   41
twenty-two books: so that they may correspond to the number of letters (1). And they are so reckoned, according to the traditions of the ancients, so that of Moses there be five books; of Jesus Nave, a sixth; of Judges and Ruth, a seventh; the first and second of Kingdoms, in an eighth; the third and fourth, in a ninth; two of Paralipomenon be the tenth; the Words of Days of Esdras, in the eleventh; the Book of Psalms, in the twelfth; the Proverbs of Solomon, Ecclesiastes, and the Canticle of Canticles, in the thirteenth, fourteenth, and fifteenth; the twelve prophets constitute the sixteenth; then Isaias, and Jeremias along with the Lamentation and the Letter, and Daniel, and Ezechiel, and Job, and Esther, bringing the number of the books to twenty-two. It is to be noted also that by adding to these Tobias and Judith, there are twenty-four books, corresponding to the number of letters used by the Greeks.

883

[*On Ps. 1:* § 18 (13)]

"And all things whatsoever He does," it says, "shall be directed well." Never again   522
will His gift and His statutes be disrupted, as they were in the case of Adam, who by his sin of transgressing the Law lost the blessedness of having been made immortal. But now, through the redemption wrought by the tree of life, that is, by the Lord's passion, we   1044
shall ourselves be like the tree of life (2); and all that is in us will be eternal and we will have for eternity a sense of blessedness. For they shall prosper in all they do, being no longer uncertain by reason of change nor by nature infirm, when incorruption will swallow up corruption, and eternity will swallow up weakness, and the form of God will swallow up the form of earthly flesh.

884

[*On Ps. 2:* § 15]

[God] created man, not that He might Himself profit in any way by man's service,   465 but because He is good. He made him for the sharing of His own happiness, and He perfected a rational animal, alive and conscious, for the utilizing of His benefits in eternity; and this is clearly to be understood from the things He Himself has said. For He says: "And now, Israel, what does the Lord your God require of you, except that you fear the Lord your God, and that you walk in all His ways, and love Him, and that you serve the Lord your God with your whole heart and with your whole soul and with your whole strength, and that you keep the commandments of the Lord God, and His ceremonies which I enjoin upon you, so that it may be well with you (3)?"

885

[*On Ps. 2:* § 41]

[God] will repair what has been shattered, but not by mending it with something else.   1044
Rather, out of the old and very same material of its origin He will impart to it an   1013
appearance of beauty pleasing to Himself; and the resurrection of corruptible bodies in the glory of incorruption will not take away their nature by the utter destruction thereof, but will work only a qualitative change of condition. For it is not another body that will be resurrected, but the same body in another condition, as the Apostle says: "It is sown in corruption, it will rise in incorruption; it is sown in ignominy, it will rise in glory; it is sown in weakness, it will rise in strength; it is sown an animal body, it will rise a spiritual one (4)." There will, therefore, be a change, but this does not mean an annihilation. And if that which was, rises up as that which it was not, it has not lost its original material (5) but has perfected it unto glory.

886

[*On Ps. 2:* § 49 (48)]

[God's] anger, through which they shall perish from the just path, is not capricious.   991
Let no one, because judgment is delayed, tickle himself with flattery in respect to   995
deserved punishment; for His wrath is kindled suddenly. For the avenger hell captures   996
us straightway; and if so we have lived, we shall fall away from the body and perish suddenly from the right path. Our witnesses to this are the rich man and the poor one of the Gospel, one of whom the angels placed among the seats of the blessed and in the folds of Abraham's toga, while the other was received straightway into the region of punishment. And there the punishment of the dead overtook him immediately, even while his brothers remained in the land of the living (6). There is nothing here about delay or postponement. The day of judgment betokens an eternal measuring out either of happiness or of punishment. A time of death is set eventually for every man, and at judgment each man is relegated to Abraham or to punishment.

886a

[*On Ps. 51 [52]:* § 16]

It is said, "I will raise up the tabernacle of David, which has fallen (7)": — which   311
refers to that holy and venerable body and temple of God, born of the Virgin; in which   781
he that shall believe will dwell as a companion of the flesh of the Lord. But every
unbeliever, because he has not believed in this corporal kinship, that is, in the tabernacle   568
of God, will be plucked out and expelled as unworthy of a dwelling place in this spiritual tabernacle. It is understood that this is what the Lord means when He says, "I am the true vine; you are the branches; My Father is the farmer. Every branch not remaining in Me nor bearing fruit will be rooted out. And every branch remaining in Me, My Father will cleanse so that it can bear better fruit (8)." . . . The Son of God born of the Virgin did not first become the Son of God when He became Son of Man; but already being the Son of God, He then became the Son of Man, so that the Son of God might

be also the Son of Man. He took upon Himself the nature of all flesh and having in this
way become the true vine, He holds in Himself the racial strain of every branch.   313

887

[On Ps. 51 [52]: § 23]

There is hope of mercy in time and in eternity; but there is confession in time only,   991
and not in eternity. There is no confession of sins in any time except in this present   996
life. By his own will each man is permitted and has throughout life the freedom to choose
confession. But when we die we loose life and along with it the right to exercise our
will. For then a law already set down unto rest or unto punishment sustains, in accord
with its past exercise, the will of those withdrawing from the body. The prophet shows
that from that time on the will is no longer free but necessary, when he says: "In
those days I have no will (9)." For when freedom of will is at an end, the action of the
will — if such it can still be called — is also at an end.

888

[On Ps. 52 [53]: § 2]

"A fool says in his heart: 'There is no God (10).';" for if he wished to state this   130
with spoken words, it would be enough to convict him, in the judgment of common
consent, of being a fool. Who can ponder carefully, and not know that God exists?
But it happens frequently that although the necessity of truth compel us to an acknowledg-
ment of God, our pleasurable vices may yet persuade us that God does not exist; and
in our hearts we speak, on the counsel of wickedness, that which we would believe,
though it be in opposition to the faith.

889

[On Ps. 53 [54]: § 12]

We have declared repeatedly and without cease that it was the only-begotten Son of   381
God who was crucified, and that He was condemned to death: He that is eternal by
reason of the nature which is His by His birth from the eternal Father; and it must be
understood that He underwent the passion not from any natural necessity, but for the
sake of the mystery of man's salvation; and that His submitting to the passion was not   350
from His being compelled thereto, but of His own will. . . . God suffered, therefore,
because He voluntarily submitted Himself to the passion.   334
Yet, while He accepted upon Himself the natural forces of the assaults of those   347
sufferings, which of necessity inflict pain upon those undergoing them, He did not,
however, abandon the power of His nature so as to feel pain. [13] . . . He offered   374
Himself, therefore, to the death of the accursed, so that He might break the curse of the
Law. He offered Himself as a victim voluntarily to God the Father, so that by means
of a voluntary victim the curse which was consequent upon the discontinuance of the
required victim might be dissolved.
Mention is made of this sacrifice in another place in the Psalms: "A victim and an
oblation you did not desire, but you have perfected a body for me (11)": — that is,
by offering to God the Father, who refused the sacrifices of the Law, the pleasing victim
of the body which had been received. The blessed Apostle makes mention thus of this
sacrifice: "For this He did all in a single time, offering Himself to God as a victim (12),"
thereby redeeming the total salvation of the human race by the sacrifice of this holy and
perfect victim.

889a

[*On Ps. 64 [65]*: § 5]

"Blessed is he whom you have chosen and have taken up, that he may dwell in your   770
tabernacles (13)." Indeed, all flesh will come, which is to say, we will be gathered
together from every race of men: but whoever will be chosen, he is blessed. For many,
according to the Gospel, are called, but few are chosen (14). The elect are distinguished
in their wedding garment, splendid in the pure and perfect body of the new birth.
Election, therefore, is not a thing of haphazard judgment. It is a distinction made by
selection based on merit. Blessed, then, is he whom God elects: blessed for the reason
that he is worthy of election. And it is given us to know in what respect the blessed
shall be elect, this being clear from what follows: "He shall dwell in your tabernacles."

890

[*On Ps. 68 [69]*: § 23]

The Lord, accepting our sins and in pain for us, has been smitten in order that   347
soundness might be restored to us through the resurrection from the dead of Him that   376
was smitten even to the weakness of the cross and death. . . . [God] did not spare that   313
first Adam, he of the slime of the earth, whom after the fault He ejected from paradise
lest he might attain the tree of life and remain in punishment for eternity, so that when
the second Adam, He of heaven, had taken the nature of his body and had likewise been
smitten unto death, He might recall him again to eternal life, but now without an eternity
of punishment. Thus, then, have they persecuted Him that was smitten by God, adding
the pain of persecution to the pain of His wounds. For, according to the prophet, He felt
pain on our behalf (15): and it is in this respect that He has been accounted as being in
pain.

891

[*On Ps. 118 [119]*: *Heth*, 7]

Since David knew the saying in the Law, that no one might look upon the face of   170
God and live (16), and since from the Beatitudes in the Gospel there is no doubt that all   1041
the pure in heart shall see God (17), he spoke the eagerness of his desire after the fashion
of perfect modesty, when he said: "I make my supplication before your face in my whole
heart (18)." He knows that it is impossible for him at the present time to see what neither
eye has seen, nor ear heard, nor has it entered into the heart of man (19). He knows that
the glory of God is invisible to carnal eyes.

892

[*On Ps. 118 [119]*: *Nun*, 20]

To persevere in faith is certainly a gift from God; but the first stirring of faith has   656
its beginning in us. Our will must be such that, properly and of itself, it wills. God
will give the increase after a beginning has been made. Our weakness is such that we
cannot of ourselves carry through to completion; but the reward of growing to com-   671
pletion is in view of a beginning made in the will.

892a

[*On Ps. 118 [119]*: *Ain*, 10]

Human weakness is imbecillic if it expects to achieve anything by itself. The duty of   656
such a nature is simply this: to make a beginning with the will, so as to attach itself to
the service of God (20). Divine mercy is such that it aids those who are willing,

strengthens those who are beginning, and assists those who are attempting. The beginning, however, is our part, that He may bring to perfection.

893

[On Ps. 118 [119]: Koph, 8]

God is not contained within physical limits, nor is the immensity of divine power limited by boundaries or places. He is everywhere, and His totality is everywhere. He is not in part anywhere, but in all things, He is all (21). . . . Nothing is wanting to God; He lacks nothing. He is everywhere, like a soul in a body (22), which is diffused through all the members and is not absent from any individual parts whatever.

154

894

[On Ps. 129 [130]: § 3]

First it must be remembered that God is incorporeal. He does not consist of certain parts and distinct members, making up one body. For we read in the Gospel that God is spirit (23): invisible, therefore, and an eternal nature, immeasurable and self-sufficient. It is also written that a spirit does not have flesh and bones (24). For of these the members of a body consist, and of these the substance of God has no need. God, however, who is everywhere and in all things, is all-hearing, all-seeing, all-doing, and all-assisting. . . . The power of God, therefore, which is equal and inseparable, has the names of functions and members. Thus the power by which He sees is called eyes; the power by which He hears is called ears; the power by which He does things is called hands; the power by which He is present is called feet: and so on, through the various functions of His power.

152
154
175

895

[On Ps. 129 [130]: § 7]

We recall that there are many spiritual powers, to whom the name *angels* is given, or *presidents of Churches*. There are, according to John, angels of the Churches in Asia (25). And there were, as Moses bears witness, when the sons of Adam were separated, bounds appointed for the peoples according to the number of the angels (26). And, as the Lord teaches, there are for little children, angels who see God daily (27). There are, as Raphael told Tobias, angels assisting before the majesty of God, and carrying to God the prayers of suppliants (28). Mention is made of all this, because you might wish to understand these angels as the eyes, or the ears, or the hands, or the feet of God. Let us not have this as an opinion, the import of which is improbable (29), especially since it is written: "For they are ministering spirits, sent for service, for the sake of those who will inherit salvation (30)." It is not the nature of God, but the weakness of men, which requires their service. For they are sent for the sake of those who will inherit salvation. God is not unaware of anything that we do; but in our weakness we are impoverished for a minister of spiritual intercession in the matter of beseeching and propitiating.

483
493
492

896

[On Ps. 138 [139]: § 17]

The Father is greater than the Son: but this is said in respect to generation — as a father is to a son — and not of classification. The Son is, and He comes forth from Him. The possession of a paternal designation is permissive of a distinction; but there is no distinction as to nature. The God born of God is not dissimilar in substance to the One who bore Him. He is not able, therefore, to be made equal to Him from whom He is. For although the One remains in the Other through the uniform and similar glory of the

259
252
257
281

same nature, nevertheless, because the Father begot, it is clear that it is not possible for the Son to be made equal to Him from whom He was begotten (31).

896a

[*On Ps. 148:* § 3]

By a statement addressed to the intellect, and not without perfect doctrinal reasoning, 460 the prophet exhorts all the celestial powers to give praise. He avoids the first error of human ignorance, according to which the present state of the world assembled itself together by fortuitous and tumultuous circumstances, and was thus established in order by disorder: — indeed, they are venturesome who so believe! Others suppose that this world itself is God, who agitates Himself and moves, and by a measured calculation sets a bound to the course of the annual seasons. . . . [The prophet] excludes every ignorant error, when he says: "For the Lord spoke and they were made; He commanded, and they were created (32)."

1. *I.e.,* the number of letters in the Hebrew alphabet.
2. Hilary explains immediately after our present selection breaks off, that we shall be like the tree of life because we shall be planted in a garden where we shall never die.
3. Deut. 10:12-13.
4. 1 Cor. 15:42-44.
5. *non amisit originem.*
6. *in supernis:* Ordinarily the term would mean *in the heavenly regions,* as distinguished from being in any lower regions, whether terrestrial or infernal. Hilary clearly intends the term to mean *in the terrestrial regions,* as distinguished from being in the infernal. Literally, of course, it means *in the upper regions;* and if Hilary wishes to distinguish *in supernis* only from *in infernis,* making it synonymous with *in terrenis,* we can but smile and concede that what is up depends largely upon one's vantage point.
7. Amos 9:11.
8. John 15:1-2. Whereas the Vulgate writes *ut fructum plus afferat,* Hilary writes *ut fructum ampliorem ferat.* Whether or not *plus* and *ampliorem* are in this instance precisely equivalent may be disputed: but it is afterall of little consequence whether the branch is to bear *more* fruit, or *better* fruit, or *bigger* fruit. The point that interests us is the use, in both forms of the clause, of a verb in the subjunctive mood. In classic usage the subjunctive conveys the *may* concept, while *can* would require some form of the verb *posse,* in the indicative. In post-classical Latin, however, the distinction between the concepts of *may* and *can* is frequently ignored, — just as this same distinction is now rapidly disappearing in spoken English, — the subjunctive being used for either; and when the distinction is desired, it must be gotten from the context. In the present instance, although English editions of the Scriptures generally are quite scrupulous in rendering the subjunctive by *may,* it seems to us that the sense of the passage, both in Scripture and in the Hilarian context, demands *can.*
9. Hilary quotes the prophet's line as *Non est mihi in diebus illis voluntas.* The Maurist editors, at a loss to find such a verse in the Scriptures, suggested that it might be a corrupted reading of Malachias 1:10 — *Non est mihi voluntas in nobis.* However, we need not look so far afield. The line is in Ecclesiastes 12:1, although if we look for it in the Vulgate we will not recognize it: for Jerome renders it *Non mihi placent.* The solution to the mystery of what went wrong in the translating is simple enough, if we compare the Hebrew with the Septuagint.

   The Hebrew text, unpointed, reads: אֵין־לִי בָהֶם חֵפֶץ׃ . Jerome read the last word as חֵפֶץ meaning *pleasure.* The line might have been rendered quite literally *Non-est-mihi in-illis satisfactio;* but Jerome put it into good idiomatic Latin, *Non mihi placent.* The Septuagint translators, however, took the last word of the Hebrew as חֵפֶץ , meaning θέλημα *(voluntas);* and they rendered the line Οὐκ ἔστιν μοι ἐν αὐτοῖς θέλημα: and since the word ἡμέραι stands only two verses above as an antecedent for the pronoun αὐτοῖς, Hilary quotes the line in a form which is a quite literal translation of the Septuagint, only supplying the antecedent to the pronoun: *Non est mihi in diebus illis voluntas.* It need scarcely be pointed out that Hilary's quotation, in its Scriptural context, is not to his point.
10. Ps. 52 [53]:2.
11. Ps. 39 [40]:7. Hilary's reading reflects a variant of the Septuagint text, common to the three great codices, Vaticanus, Sinaiticus, and Alexandrinus: σῶμα (body) in place of ὠτία (ears).
12. Heb. 7:27.
13. Ps. 64 [65]:5.
14. Matt. 22:14.
15. Is. 53:4.
16. Exod. 3:6.

17. Matt. 5:8.
18. Ps. 118 [119]:58.
19. Is. 64:4. 1 Cor. 2:9.
20. *aggregare se in familiam Dei.* It seems to me that there are at least four other translations of this phrase, all of which, however, are directed toward the same idea as that expressed above, though each has its own slightly different flavor: *to join the army of God; to become a servant in God's household; to become a member of the family of God's household;* or *to acquire for oneself the friendship of God.*
21. *in omnibus omnis est.* That Hilary is, in his *Commentaries on the Psalms,* dependent in some degree upon Origen, is acknowledged. The terminology here is certainly Origenist, but the concept seems to be otherwise. Origen regularly speaks of God's being all in all as something which belongs to the future, in the time of the apokatastasis. (See above, § 468). Origen's idea seems to be that God will be all in all, when we are somehow assimilated into God. His use of such terminology opens him to a suspicion of pantheistic tendencies, much after the fashion of the modern mystic, Teilhard de Chardin, who is in many respects an Origenist, with this important difference: the errors of Origen are presented by Origen himself only as speculative possibilities, whereas Teilhard presents them as sound doctrine. Be that as it may, that God will be all in all seems to mean for Hilary only that the immense and indivisible God is everywhere, not by a division into parts, but by His totality being in every place.
22. *modo animae corporalis:* literally, *in the manner of a corporeal soul.*
23. John 4:24.
24. Luke 24:39.
25. Apoc. 1:20.
26. Deut. 32:8 [Septuagint].
27. Matt. 18:10.
28. Tob. 12:12-15.
29. It has ever been our view that when he encounters an ambiguous statement, it is the duty of the translator to preserve the ambiguity, so as not to eliminate any of the possible interpretations. The present passage is as taxing as any ever uttered by the Sybil: *habeamus non improbabilis intelligentiae auctoritatem.* This may be rendered: *Let us not accept this opinion, of improbable import;* or again: *Let us accept this opinion, not of improbable import.* The reader will duly note that a momentary stroke of brilliance has enabled us to translate the line in such a way as to preserve the ambiguity, thereby rendering him a noble service: *Let us not have this as an opinion* — what kind of an opinion? an opinion — *the import of which is improbable;* or, *Let us not have this as an opinion* — why? because it is one *the import of which is improbable.* It is obvious from the context, of course, that the latter is the meaning which Hilary attaches to his remark: he urges us to abandon such an opinion, should the possibility of such a thing have occurred to us.
30. Heb. 1:14.
31. Hilary clearly states that their inequality is only in the fact that one is Father and the other is Son, a relationship which, afterall, is meaningful, and cannot be ignored. At the same time, he does point out that there can be no distinction in their nature as God. If he seems at pains to stress, in this particular passage, an inequality, he has not suddenly deserted us for the Arian camp, but is only somewhat hard-pressed to explain the Gospel passages, John 5:19 and 14:28.
32. Ps. 148:5 [Septuagint].

PSEUDO-TERTULLIAN

POEM AGAINST THE MARCIONITES [*ante A. D.* 325]

The *Poem against the Marcionites,* first published in 1564 as *Adversus Marcionem libri quinque,* is found in the text tradition of Tertullian's works. It is dependent upon Tertullian's *Against Marcion,* but is certainly not from his pen. The work consists of five books, totaling in all 1302 hexameters. Formerly it was much argued whether it belonged to the pre-Nicene or post-Nicene era. The use of the term *Light of Light* was taken as evidence of its post-Nicene origin; but in fact several examples of the pre-Nicene use of this term can be cited. Some still hold that its anonymous author made use of Commodianus, which would prevent its being dated before the fifth century.

The latest scholarship, however, has evinced better reasons for its pre-Nicene authorship, and probably in Gaul. For the present we will be content to regard it as the work of an anonymous poet of Gaul, writing before the year 325 A. D.; and because the work is preserved as if a work of Tertullian, we shall know him as Pseudo-Tertullian. And we must note at the same time that all that can be said with absolute certainty of its authorship is that Tertullian did not write it.

The text given by Migne (PL 2, 1053-1090) is now superseded by the edition of R. Willems in the edition of Tertullian's works in the *Corpus Christianorum,* Vol. 2, Turnhout 1954, pp. 1421-1454.

897

[3, 276]

In this chair in which he himself had sat, Peter,   432
[277] In mighty Rome, commanded Linus, the first elected, to sit down.
[278] After him, Cletus too accepted the flock of the fold.
[279] As his successor, Anacletus was elected by lot.
[280] Clement follows him, well-known to apostolic men.
[281] After him Evaristus ruled the flock (1) without crime.
[282] Alexander, sixth in succession, commends the fold to Sixtus (2).
[283] After his illustrious times were completed, he passed it on to
[284] Telesphorus. He was excellent, a faithful martyr.
[285] After him, learned (3) of the law and a sure teacher,
. . .
[293] Hyginus, in the ninth place, now accepted the chair.
[294] Then Pius, after him, whose blood-brother was Hermas,
[295] An angelic shepherd, because he spoke the words delivered to him (4);
[296] And Anicetus accepted his lot in pious (5) succession.

1. *gregem* is conjectured in place of *legem.*
2. *Sextus Alexander Sixto commendat ovile.*
3. *doctus* is conjectured in place of *socius.*
4. The reference is to Hermas' authorship of the apocryphal apocalypse known as *The Shepherd.*
5. *Atque pio suscepit Anicetus ordine sortem.* The neat pun herein prevents our believing that *pio* is bad Latin for *a Pio.* Were this latter possible emendation to be made by some humorless person, the translation would be: *and Anicetus accepted his lot in succession from Pius.*

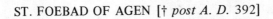

ST. FOEBAD OF AGEN [† *post A. D.* 392]

AGAINST THE ARIANS [*A. D.* 357/358]

St. Phoebadius or Foebad was bishop of Agennum, the present day Agen in the Guyenne. A strenuous opponent of Arianism, as soon as the Second Creed of Sirmium became known in Gaul, he wrote his *Liber contra Arianos* and sent it around as an encyclical letter to his fellow-bishops in Gaul. As a result, the Gallic bishops rejected the second Sirmian creed in a synod held about Easter in the year 358. At Rimini in 359, however, Foebad, like the unfortunate old Ossius of Cordoba, was so broken by force and intrigue, that he signed a formula of Arian tendency, the Fourth Creed of Sirmium.

In the year 392 Jerome wrote of Foebad: "He lives even to the present day, in decrepit old age."

A. Wilmart seems to have had in mind to edit a new edition of Foebad, as early as 1908; but I am unable to discover that it ever appeared. If I do not err, the text printed by Migne (PL 20, 13-20) is still the standard.

898

[22]

Therefore, as we have said, that rule is to be held which confesses that the Son is in the   238
Father, and the Father is in the Son; which acknowledges the arrangement of the Godhead by observing that there is one substance in two Persons. Therefore the Father is God, and the Son is God, because God the Son is in God the Father. And if this be a scandal to anyone, let him hear from us that the Spirit is from God: for He that has in the Son a Second Person has also a Third in the Holy Spirit. It is in this regard that the Lord says: "I shall ask of My Father, and He will give you another Advocate (1)." Thus, the Spirit is another from the Son, just as the Son is from the Father. Thus, in the Spirit there is a Third Person, just as in the Son there is a Second.

All, however, are one God. The Three are One. This we believe, this we hold, because   102
this we have received from the Prophets, this do the Gospels tell us, this the Apostles   231
handed down, this the martyrs confessed by their suffering. In this we adhere to the faith even with our faculties of mind — against which even if an angel of heaven pronounce, let him be anathema (2).

1. John 14:16.
2. Gal. 1:8.

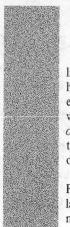

ST. GREGORY OF ELVIRA [† *post A. D.* 392]
THE ORTHODOX FAITH [*A. D.* 360/361]

Jerome speaks high praise of Gregory, Bishop of Elvira, who was apparently still living, already in ripe old age, in the year 392 A. D., when Jerome included him in his treatise *De viris illustribus.* He remarks that Gregory is the author of a work entitled *De fide:* but whether or not he is the author of the presently considered work entitled *De fide* is a question that has long puzzled scholars. The *De fide orthodoxa contra Arianos* has been variously attributed, to Gregory of Nazianz, to Ambrose of Milan, to Vigilius of Thapsus, to Foebad of Agen — and to Gregory of Elvira.

It is no longer possible to hold for Gregory of Nazianz, Ambrose, or Vigilius; and Foebad is regarded as a rather less likely author than Gregory of Elvira, whom the latest scholarship is inclined to favor. The work may be dated rather closely. It makes use of Foebad's encyclical *Against the Arians,* written in 357 or 358 A. D.; and it reflects the situation immediately subsequent to the close of the Council of Rimini, in 359 A. D. We may, then, regard it as a work of the year 360 or 361 A. D.

The edition planned fifty years ago by A. Wilmart seems never to have appeared; and the text printed by Migne (PL 20, 31-50) remains the standard.

899

[6]

What is the Son of Him that is the Father? Another the same. For it is on this account   282
that He is designated *Word:* because He proceeds properly from the mouth of the Divinity,   260
and the Father neither does nor commands anything without Him. He is called *Power,*
because He is truly from God and is always with God, and every power of the Father
subsists in Him. He is given the name *Wisdom,* because coming forth from the heart of the   261
Father, He imparts the secrets of heaven to believers.

He is designated *Right Hand,* because through Him all the divine works are brought to
perfection. He is called *Arm,* because all things are embraced by Him. He is given the name
Pearl, because there is nothing more precious than this. He is called *Treasure House,* by which
it is acknowledged that in Him are stored all the wealth and riches of the heavenly
kingdoms. He is called *Net,* because through Him and in Him the diverse multitudes of
peoples are gathered from the sea of the world, through the water of Baptism and into the
Church, where a distinction is made between the good and the wicked. He is designated
Plow, because it is by being submitted to the sign of His cross that hard hearts receive the
necessary preparation for fruition.

He is named *Fountain of Living Water,* because it is from Him that thirsty hearts are
refreshed by the grace of heavenly water. He is called *Rock,* because He is the strength
of believers, retaining the hardness of unbelief. He is called *Corner Stone,* because He
contains both parts of the Testament, Old and New, in Himself, and as Mediator joins them
as one. He is called *Lamb,* so as to demonstrate the innocence of Christ and His passion.
He is called *Man,* because He deigned to be born according to the flesh for the sake of us
men. He is called *Calf,* because of the suffering He bore on behalf of our salvation.

He is called *Eagle,* because after His venerable resurrection He flew like the winged king
to the throne of His Father. He is called *Lion,* because He Himself is the King of Kings,
who by His strength overcame death and the power of the devil (1).

He is the *Way,* because the ascent is through Him; the *Truth,* because He knows no lie.
He is the *Life,* because He vivifies the whole world. You see, therefore, through these
words, the meanings and explanations of the divine arrangements and operations. But is
God Himself not yet properly defined? Well then, God the Father is immeasurable,   156
eternal, incomprehensible, and inconceivable. His Son and our Lord is also God, just as   154
much as the Father is. And He is from no other source than the Father, because He

says: "I came forth from the Father," that is, Light from Light.   257

1. *zabulum = diabolum.* St. Foebad of Agen uses the adjective forms *zabolicum, zabolica,* and *zabolicae* in the first chapter of his *Against the Arians.*

HOMILIES ON THE BOOKS OF SACRED SCRIPTURE [*ca. A. D.* 365/385]

The twenty *Homilies on the Books of Sacred Scripture* were first published at Paris in 1900 in an edition by Batiffol, who was minded to attribute the work to Origen. Others voiced the opinion, however, that the homilies ought be attributed not to Origen but to Novatian. Further research has shown, however, that they bespeak a Trinitarian theology of such a character as to date them in the second half of the fourth century, thereby excluding the authorship of either Origen or Novatian. There is general agreement at the present time that the work may be attributed to Gregory of Elvira; and Weyman, who originated the opinion favoring Novatian's authorship, later changed his mind and accepted the view favoring Gregory. Pierre Batiffol's text of 1900 was reprinted by Adalbert Hamman in 1958 in his *Supplementum* to Migne (PLS 1, 1, 358-472).

900

[1]
     God is all eye, because He sees all; all ear, because He hears all; all mouth, because   175
He is all Word; all tongue, because He speaks all; all foot, because He is everywhere;
all hand, because He operates everywhere; all arm, because He embraces all and governs
all. And whatever you would say of Him, you will be naming the doing of His works and   173
the arrangements of His mysteries; but you will not be able to explain Him quantitatively
or qualitatively. That is how a concept about God is formed, while He is said to be
inconceivable.

901

[2]
     The tree of the cross, however, clearly represents an image which to some seems as   381
hard and rough as wood, because on it the Lord was hung so that our sins, which came   370
to us from the tree of transgression, might be punished by being affixed — again, it is
through the same Man (1) — to the tree of the cross. . . . To others it stands for shade
and refreshment, because believers are protected from the heat and rigor of persecution,
and there refreshed.

902

[6]
     The lion is the king of beasts. And therefore our Savior, who . . . is . . . the King of
Kings, is called a lion because of His power, the strength by which He conquered the
devil in death (2). But why is He called here (3) the whelp of a lion, when elsewhere
He is called the conqueror from the tribe of Juda (4)? It is for this reason that He is
called a whelp: so as to show that it refers not to the Father, but to the Son of God.
For when both a lion and the whelp of a lion are named, both the Father and the Son   258
are indicated. Their nature is not divided, but distinct Persons are manifested. For just   252
as a lion is born of a lion, so too it is said that God proceeds from God, and Light from
Light. And just as there is no change of nature when a lion is born of a lion, and a
single origin is manifested, so also God is born of God, and cannot be other than God.

903

[14]

For no one conquers unless he shall have believed that the Father and the Son and   282
the Holy Spirit are of equal power and do not differ in strength. Behold by what
sign (5) the army of Gedeon conquered its enemies, and by which even we who believe
in Christ are accustomed to defeat every wicked device of the adverse power.

1. *rursus per eumdem hominem.* It was a man who originated sin, by eating the forbidden fruit of the tree of
   the knowledge of good and evil; and it is the same, a Man, who expiates that sin, through his hanging on the
   tree.
2. The marks of omission in this sentence, which do not disturb the sense, indicate undecipherable words in the
   manuscript.
3. Gen. 49:9.
4. Apoc. 5:5.
5. *sacramento.* Gregory has already explained that Gedeon, in defeating the enemy, took with him three
   hundred men divided into three companies. Three hundred is expressed by the Greek letter Tau [T], itself
   signifying the cross. The three companies signify the Trinity; and the *sacramentum* is the cross of Christ,
   by which sign we too defeat our enemy, Satan.

MARIUS VICTORINUS [*fl. A. D.* 355]

Marius Victorinus was born in Africa about the year 300 **A. D.** He distinguished
himself in the secular estate as an orator in Rome, and was converted to the faith
about the year 355 A. D. Jerome remarks concerning his doctrinal writings that they
are very obscure and can be understood only by the learned; and of his commentaries
on the Epistles, that they prove "the learned orator can never have studied theology."
The date of his death is unknown.

AGAINST ARIUS [*ca. A. D.* 356/361]

The *Adversus Arium* is Marius Victorinus' reply to a letter of an Arian friend,
Candidus. The division of the work into four books must remain for the sake of
time-honored tradition: but it is the work of a later hand and not of the author.
The letter of Candidus, which called forth the present work and which consisted
largely of Candidus' quoting of two other letters translated into Latin, a letter of
Arius himself to Eusebius of Nicomedia, and another of the same Eusebius to
Paulinus of Tyre, is still extant and is printed in Migne, PL 8, 1035-1040. Marius'
reply, the *Adversus Arium,* treats of Trinitarian theology in general, of the
homoousion, of the relationship of the Word to the Father, and of the Person of
the Holy Spirit.

Schmid attempts to date the work in 357 A. D., Monceaux at the end of 359
A. D. It will be safer to regard it as a work written between 356 and 361 A. D.
The *editio princeps* appeared in 1528 at Basle. A critical edition still lacking, the

standard text is that of Gallandus' edition of 1772, reprinted by Migne, PL 8, 1039-1138.

904

[1, 13]

To live, then, is Christ; and to understand is the Spirit. Therefore the Spirit receives   237
from Christ, Christ Himself is from the Father — and in this way the Spirit too is from   272
the Father. [14] All, therefore, are one, but from the Father.

905

[1, 45]

The followers of Marcellus and Photinus . . . say that there is God, and the Logos, and   321
the Spirit. The Son, however, who is a man born of Mary, is a fourth one, whom the   311
Logos assumed. And they say that the Logos rules as an administrator in this man, who
was prepared as a dwelling for Him. Thus do they destroy the Trinity. If, however, the
Trinity is to remain, there is one who is man and Logos: which Logos we have already
demonstrated above to be the Son. That the Logos was made flesh, however, does not
mean that the Logos was corrupted and turned into flesh. Rather, the Logos through
whom all things are effected, was effected in all things and was made flesh (1), so that
when He would be in the flesh He might, according to the passivities of the flesh, redeem
all mankind by His passion and death. For if He was not Himself the man born of Mary,
why did He empty Himself? And what does *receiving the form of a servant* (2) mean?
And what, again, does *and the Logos was made flesh* (3) mean?

906

[3, 3]

The whole man, therefore, was assumed, and having been assumed was also made   314
free. For in Him all things were universal: universal flesh, and a universal soul. And   383
on the cross they have been offered and purified through the saving God, the Logos,   386
the universal of all universals: through whom all things were made, who is Jesus
Christ, God, our Lord and Savior. Amen.

907

[4, 33]

For men of faith, these things are sufficiently proved: that the Logos existed before   302
He was made flesh, and that in the flesh He was the same Son: — He that was begotten
before the ages; He that ascended into heaven after He descended, He that is for us the   285
Bread of Heaven. . . . And really, that the Holy Spirit, in some other way, is Jesus
Christ Himself, hidden, interior, conversing with souls, teaching these things and   272
imparting understanding, and begotten of the Father through Christ, and in Christ. To   276
be sure, we have expounded in many books on whether Christ be the only-begotten
Son; and it is clear enough that we have proved it with the aid of many examples.

Here, then, is how, and how it is to be understood, that God the Father is homoousios   237
with the Son, and the Son, because He is Life, is homoousios with the Father, while,   257
because Christ Himself is Understanding, the Holy Spirit too is understood to be   268
homoousios: It is because the Spirit has been received by having been joined to the   281
Father and the Son, that the Son is the same as the Holy Spirit, in that way, indeed,
in which the Son is the same as the Father — that is, in just such a way as that by which   238
the Father and the Son, although they are one, have each their own existence, so that
the Father exists, and the Son likewise, but both are of one and the same substance: —

and so it is with Christ and the Holy Spirit. Although both are one, Christ yet exists with His own existence, and the Holy Spirit with His own. But both are of one substance, out of which all, that is, the whole Trinity, is one; and the Father is joined with the Son, and the Son with the Holy Spirit, all in the same way (4).

And this is a Trinity by reason of the Father's having been joined with the Holy Spirit through Christ, each one, however, having His own individual existence; and there is this homoousion, since all of them have from eternity one and the same like substance. This is our salvation, this our liberation, this the full salvation of every man: — that this be his faith in God the Father almighty, as also in Jesus Christ the Son, and as also in the Holy Spirit. Amen.

1. *sed Logos, per quem effecta sunt omnia, et omnia effectus, et caro factus est.* There is a play on words here, of a sort, the second *omnia* being the adverbial usage, *totally,* or *in every respect, i.e., in all things.*
2. Phil. 2:7.
3. John 1:14.
4. Marius has a difficult way of describing the Trinity, and the present statement seems to pinpoint the problem. He views the Trinity as three entities coming together to form a being of one substance. Perhaps Bardenhewer's old remark is not too harsh: *It was no loss to the Theology of the East that Victorinus' doctrine of the Trinity was utterly disregarded.*

THE GENERATION OF THE DIVINE WORD [*ca. A. D.* 356/361]

The present work is, like that treated immediately above, a reply of Marius to Candidus, in the course of their friendly doctrinal interchange. It was called forth by the Arian Candidus' work entitled *De generatione divina,* which has likewise survived and is printed in Migne, PL 8, 1013-1020, immediately before the present work of reply. *The Generation of the Divine Word* represents Marius' first reply to Candidus, and belongs chronologically before the *Adversus Arium,* already treated; but, like the latter, it can best be dated only between the years 356 and 361 A. D. A third doctrinal work of Marius Victorinus, written afterwards as a kind of appendix to the *Adversus Arium,* is entitled *De ὁμοουσίῳ recipiendo* (Migne, PL 8, 1137-1140). This latter work had its *editio princeps* at Basle in 1528, along with the *Adversus Arium.* The *editio princeps* of *The Generation of the Divine Word* was also at Basle, but twenty years later, in 1548. Like the other two works, a critical edition is still lacking, and the standard text is that of Gallandus, Paris 1772, reprinted in Migne: PL 8, 1019-1040.

908

[28]

Because no name worthy of God can be found, we give a name to Him from those   175
things which we do know, while bearing in mind that we cannot give to God a name or appellation that is proper to Him. That is how we say, "God lives," or "God understands." Hence, from our own actions, we give a name to the actions of God, considering them as being His in a supereminent way; not such as He really is, but as an approach to what He   180
really is: oudè óntòs hypárchontos, allà óntos mikroû hypárchontos (1). It is likewise   177
in this way that we impose substance, existence, and other such concepts, upon God. And we speak in a certain way of His ousía or essence, in hinting at what really pertains to Him and at what His being really is, by the consideration of created substance.

1. Victorinus was afraid we might not understand his Latin *neque tantum existente, sed quasi existente,* so he repeats the same thought for us in Greek: οὐδὲ ὄντως ὑπάρχοντος, ἀλλὰ ὄντος μικροῦ ὑπάρχοντος: — which might be rendered: *Not really as He is, but something less than He really is.*

FIRST COUNCIL OF CONSTANTINOPLE [*A. D.* 381]

Arianism had declined sharply in the West after the death of Constantius in 361 A. D.; and in 364 A. D., after the short reigns of Julian and Jovian, the empire was again shared by co-Emperors, Valentinian and Valens. In the West, Valentinian's policies favored orthodoxy, and in his empire Arianism was soon a negligible factor. In the East, however, Valens was himself an ardent Arian, and his policies constituted a virtual persecution of the orthodox faith. With his death, however, in 378 A. D., and the accession of Theodosius in 379 A. D., Arianism began its sudden decline in the East.

The purpose of the Council of Constantinople in 381 A. D. was to reassert the faith of Nicaea, to decide who was rightful Bishop of Constantinople, and to bring about a unity in the Church in the face of the numerous and disastrous divisions caused by the fragmentation of Arianism.

The idea of another general and plenary council had been contemplated in 378 and 379 A. D., but was abandoned in 380, when it was seen that such a council could only arouse political interests after the re-alignment of provinces forced upon Theodosius in that year by Gratian, who had succeeded Valentinian in the Western Empire in 375 A. D. Under the apprehension that a plenary council at this time could only result in further mutual mistrust between East and West, it was decided that Constantinople should be entirely an Eastern council. It was, then, an ecumenical council neither in its conception, nor in its convocation, nor in its sessions. No Latin bishops were present when the Council met, in answer to Theodosius' convocation, in May of 381 A. D.; and Rome had no official representation in the Council, although Ascholius of Thessalonica, who arrived late, apparently brought with him private instructions from Pope Damasus to oppose Gregory of Nazianz, whom Damasus distrusted.

The number of bishops present at the Council is given in the earliest accounts as one hundred and fifty. The list of signatories to the Council has only one hundred and forty-eight names, of which ten are priests and one a lector. It is, of course, easily admitted that the number one hundred and fifty is a round number and an approximation. However, the list of signatories, arranged as it is by provinces, seems to be the work of a later reviser, so that it may very well be that the round number of the earliest traditions is really more accurate than the nicer list of signatories.

Thirty-six bishops of the Pneumatomachian party arrived at Constantinople for the Council, but were refused admittance when they would not accept the Nicene Creed. They left the city before the opening session.

The Council opened under the presidency of Meletius of Antioch. He died during the proceedings, and was succeeded in the presidency by Gregory of Nazianz. The first business of the Council was to declare the disorderly consecration of the interloper Maximus invalid, and to confirm Gregory of Nazianz as Bishop of Constantinople, in which see he had already been installed by Theodosius about a year earlier. Gregory of Nazianz had long ago been consecrated as Bishop of Sasima, a See which he never wanted, never accepted, and never entered. He called Sasima a wretched and bewitched place; and after his consecration he remained in Nazianz as a kind of auxiliary bishop to his father. Now, however, his enemies seized upon the fact of his consecration as Bishop of Sasima to oppose his transfer to Constantinople. The canons of numerous earlier councils, including Nicaea, forbade a bishop to transfer from one diocese to another. This also was, if not the reason, at least the pretext for Damasus' opposition to Gregory; and so set upon by his enemies and distrusted by Rome, Gregory resigned before the Council closed, and went back, not to his own See, but to his home in Nazianz.

The recognition of First Constantinople as an Ecumenical Council seems to have been an accomplished fact in the East when, at the Council of Chalcedon in 451

A. D., appeals were made to First Constantinople as to an Ecumenical Council. And even at Chalcedon these appeals were not challenged by papal representatives. In the West, its recognition as an Ecumenical Council came about gradually. Finally, by Gregory the Great, Constantinople was accepted as ecumenical in its dogmatic aspects, although its canons were still rejected.

A doctrinal tome drawn up by the Council is not extant, although it is supposed by some that its contents may yet be summarized in an Arabic collection of twenty-three anathemas, attributed to the Council. These twenty-three anathemas, however, are identical to those found in the celebrated *Tome of Damasus* (see below, pp. 402-406); and the precise relationship between the Arabic collection and the work of Damasus is not yet established. The most important part of the authentic *Acts* of the Council are its four canons. Before turning to the canons, however, we shall treat first and briefly of the so-called *Nicene-Constantinopolitan Creed*.

THE SO-CALLED NICENE-CONSTANTINOPOLITAN CREED [*A. D.* 363/374]

The Council of Constantinople of 381 A. D. insisted mightily upon adherence to the Creed of Nicaea. Among the *Acts* of Constantinople there is to be found a creed which is in fact identical to our own familiar liturgical creed, except that ours has now the addition of the *Filioque*. This Creed, the liturgical creed without the *Filioque*, has until recent times been referred to as the Nicene-Constantinopolitan Creed, under the misapprehension that it is an elaboration of the Nicene Creed made at the Council of Constantinople.

The so-called Nicene-Constantinopolitan Creed was first attributed to the Council of Constantinople by the Council of Chalcedon, in 451 A. D. It is provable, however, that this Creed actually pre-dates the Council of Constantinople by at least seven years, and probably by about twenty years. It was recited in its entirety by Epiphanius of Salamis in his *Ancoratus*, written in 374 A. D. It obviously depends ultimately upon the Creed of Nicaea; but so also does the Baptismal Creed of Jerusalem. And it is quite probable that the Baptismal Creed of Jerusalem is the intermediate step between the Nicene Creed and the so-called Nicene-Constantinopolitan. It may be taken as a certainty that the latter is directly an elaboration made upon the Baptismal Creed of Jerusalem, probably soon after the Council of Alexandria of 362 A. D.

But how did this Creed come to be included in the *Acts* of Constantinople? When Gregory of Nazianz resigned the See of Constantinople during the Council in 381 A. D., the Fathers of the Council fixed upon Nectarius, a venerable old man who had been a senator and was now a praetor, to succeed Gregory in the now vacant See of Constantinople. It was soon discovered, however, that Nectarius had never been baptized. He was hastily instructed, and was rushed along from neophyte to bishop, a thing which was obviously as much an infringement of the ancient canons as was Gregory's transfer from Sasima; but now Gregory's enemies, previously so zealous for the scrupulous observance of all the canons, did not seem to notice the infraction. In any case, by way of explaining how the so-called Nicene-Constantinopolitan Creed comes to be present in the *Acts* of the Council, it has been suggested in a purely hypothetical manner, that it was this elaboration of the Baptismal Creed of Jerusalem that Nectarius recited during the Council when he was baptized.

The text of the Creed in question is found in Mansi, Vol. 3, 565-566. Hefele-Leclercq's style of Greek letters is easier to read than Mansi's ligatured Greek, and he gives also the text of the Baptismal Creed of Jerusalem: *Histoire des Conciles*, 2, 1, Paris 1908, pp. 13-15.

910a

We believe in one God, the Father Almighty, the Maker of heaven and of earth and   157
of all things visible and invisible. And in one Lord Jesus Christ, the Son of God, the   158
Only-begotten, begotten of the Father before all the ages. Light of Light; true God   460,252
of true God; begotten, not made; of the same substance as the Father; through   257
whom all things were made; who for us men and for our salvation came down from   284
heaven and took flesh of the Holy Spirit and of Mary the Virgin and was made man.   370,302
He was crucified for us in the time of Pontius Pilate and suffered and was buried;   781
and rose up on the third day, according to the Scriptures; and ascended into heaven,   347,391
and is seated at the right of the Father, and will come again in glory to judge the   392
living and the dead; of whose kingdom there will be no end. And in the Holy Spirit,   1043
the Lord, the Giver of life, who is proceeding from the Father, who together with the   266,269
Father and the Son is adored and glorified, who spoke through the prophets. In one   268
holy, catholic, and apostolic Church; we confess one Baptism for the remission of   21,418
sins; and we await the resurrection of the dead and a life of the age to come. Amen.   836,1011

THE CANONS [*A. D.* 381]

The *Acts* of Constantinople preserve seven canons, of which, however, only the first four are authentic. Canons 5 and 6 belong to a Council of Constantinople of 382 A. D., a fact which makes it easy to see how they could have become attached to the canons of 381 A. D. Canon 7 is an extract of a letter from the Church of Constantinople to Martyrius, Bishop of Antioch, dating from the middle of the fifth century.

The text of the canons, in Greek and in the Latin versions of Dionysius and Isidore, is found in Mansi, Vol. 3, 557-574. The Priscan version, which knows only the four authentic canons, is also found in Mansi, Vol. 6, 1174-1176. The Greek text, along with valuable commentary, is to be found in Hefele-Leclercq, *Histoire des Conciles,* 2, 1, Paris 1908, pp. 20-40.

910b

[Canon 1]

    The Creed (1) of the three hundred and eighteen Fathers who were assembled at   452
Nicaea in Bithynia is not to be set aside, but is to remain in force; and every heresy
is to be anathematized, and especially that of the Eunomians or Anomoians (2), and
that of the Arians or Eudoxians (3), and that of the semi-Arians or Pneumatomachians (4),
and that of the Sabellians (5), and that of the Marcellians (6), and that of the
Photinians (7), and that of the Apollinarists (8).

910c

[Canon 2]

    Bishops outside their diocese are not to be set over Churches beyond their confines,   899
nor are they to disturb the Churches; but, according to the canons, the Bishop of
Alexandria is to have charge only over Egypt; the bishops of the East are to rule only
the East, while keeping intact the prerogatives of the Church of Antioch, in accord with
the canons of Nicaea (9); and the bishops of the diocese of Asia shall rule only throughout Asia; and those of Pontus, only over Pontus; and those of Thrace shall have charge
only over Thrace. Bishops are not to go outside of their diocese to ordain or for any
other acts of ecclesiastical administration, except they be invited. If the rule prescribed

for the dioceses be observed, it will be clear that in every province affairs are to be managed by the synod of the province, in accord with the decisions of Nicaea (10). The Churches of God among the barbarian tribes must be administered in accord with the custom observed since the times of the Fathers (11).

910d

[Canon 3]

The Bishop of Constantinople shall have the primacy of honor after the Bishop of Rome, because his city is New Rome (12).

435
899

910e

[Canon 4]

In regard to Maximus the Cynic and the disorders which took place in Constantinople on account of him (13), we declare that Maximus neither is nor ever was a bishop, and that a cleric of whatsoever rank ordained by him is not ordained at all, since all things undertaken in his behalf and by him are invalid.

960

1. τὴν πίστιν.
2. Eunomius was the leader of the Anomoian party, the radical Arians who held that the Father and the Son are *unlike* in all things.
3. Eudoxius was the leader of the party formerly known as Acacians, followers of Acacius of Caesarea, who had made the very unsatisfactory compromise between ὁμοούσιος and ὁμοιούσιος, by holding simply that the Son is ὅμοιος τῷ πατρί – *like the Father*. They are known also as Homoians.
4. In an earlier period the term semi-Arian is synonymous with Homoiousian. But by the time of Constantinople many of the homoiousians had agreed to a homoousian formula in respect to the relationship between Father and Son; but now they have become Macedonians, followers of the error of Macedonius, a former Bishop of Constantinople; and they deny that the Holy Spirit is homoousios with the Father and the Son. The terms Macedonian and Pneumatomachian, the latter meaning *a defamer of the Holy Spirit,* are synonymous with each other, and in this period, with the term *semi-Arian.*
5. The followers of Sabellius, a monarchian modalist, who held that the Son and the Holy Spirit are not Persons at all, but modes or emanations from the Father.
6. The followers of Marcellus, Bishop of Ancyra, who also taught a variety of Modalism, a modified form of Sabellianism, or who at least was reputed to have been the teacher of a doctrine of such character.
7. The Photinians are the followers of the doctrines of Photinus, Bishop of Sirmium, who was exiled as a heretic in 351 A. D., when earlier excommunications leveled against him were found ineffective. His errors, too, were modalist in nature, very much akin to the errors of Sabellius and of Paul of Samosata.
8. The Apollinarists were followers of Apollinaris the Younger, Bishop of Laodicea. He is reputed to have taught various Christological errors. As with Marcellus of Ancyra, considerable further study into his doctrines is needed in our own times.
9. Canon 6 of Nicaea, § 651*l,* above.
10. Canon 5 of Nicaea, § 651k, above.
11. The custom referred to is that by which Churches among the barbarians remained subject to the bishop of the place from which missionaries had first come to establish such a Church. For example, the Church in Georgia was subject to the Church in Antioch, because some fifty-five years before the Council of Constantinople, Eustathius of Antioch, at the request of King Miraeus of Georgia, had gone into that land with an entourage of priests and deacons; and while there he had ordained a certain John to be first Bishop of Georgia.
12. It was, of course, Constantine himself who had moved the seat of his government from Rome to Byzantium, which city he then re-named in his own honor. He seems himself to have referred to his newly named Constantinople also as *New Rome.* If the previous canon made no mention of prerogatives, patriarchal in nature, of the Bishop of Rome, certainly it is because the Council was concerning itself only with the East. As noted in the introduction to the present section, First Constantinople was not intended to be an Ecumenical Council, and was purely Eastern in its convocation and in its sessions.

However, it is also a fact that by the time of First Constantinople there was a certain amount of jealousy of Rome among the Bishops of the East. The present canon claims only a primacy of honor, and after that of Rome. Nevertheless, the reasoning behind the canon is political in nature, and suggests in some way that ecclesiastical authority can be gained or lost with empires. Certainly this is a canon which Rome must look upon with a jaundiced eye. Moreover, the canon is prejudicial to Alexandria and Antioch, which by the sixth canon of Nicaea were ranked in second and third place after Rome. Of course, Rome, when it recognized Constantinople as an Ecumenical Council, accepted only its dogmatic pronouncement that the Creed of Nicaea must remain, and otherwise rejected the canons. The 28th Canon of Chalcedon, which affirmed the 3rd Canon of Constantinople and declared that it meant the Bishop of New Rome held an honor equal to that of the Bishop of Old Rome was likewise rejected in Old Rome.

When in 869 A. D., the 21st Canon of the Eighth Ecumenical Council, the Fourth Ecumenical Council of Constantinople, again reiterated the list of those sees which by that time were patriarchal in the proper sense, and again placed Constantinople immediately after Rome and ahead of Alexandria, Antioch, and Jerusalem, the papal legates made no objection. This was the first time Rome had accepted in theory that Constantinople was second to Rome. This same canon, however, treated the matter in a much different context, and was directed to protecting Rome and the other Patriarchates from civil encroachments. But even though Rome accepted in theory in 869 A. D. that the Bishop of Constantinople was second in honor to the Bishop of Rome, it was not until the Fourth Council of the Lateran in 1215 A. D. that the second place was ever actually given to a Bishop of Constantinople, — and then it was given to the Latin Patriarch of Constantinople! Only in 1439 A. D., at the Council of Florence, was second place of honor given to the Greek Patriarch of Constantinople.

13. Maximus had arrived in Constantinople at about the same time as Gregory of Nazianz. He ingratiated himself with Gregory, presenting himself as a cynic philosopher and as a convert to the faith. But he was even then secretly plotting with Peter of Alexandria to have himself established as Bishop of Constantinople. Peter sent bishops up from Alexandria, who arrived in Constantinople at night, and proceeded in the company of some sailors to Gregory's church, where they immediately began to consecrate Maximus. However, some of Gregory's clergy noted the presence of people in the church at such an early hour, investigated, and gave the alarm. The entire populace of the neighborhood, both Arian and orthodox, rushed into the church and expelled the interlopers in the midst of the ceremony. The Egyptian bishops along with Maximus then repaired to the home of a flute player, where they completed the ceremony! The people were so outraged by this conduct that Maximus was expelled from the city. He attempted to gain the support of Theodosius, who, though it is Gregory who tells it to us, "spurned him like a dog."

Certainly the canon is restrained, then, when it speaks of disorders in connection with such a blasphemous outrage as was Maximus' consecration. The canon pronounces his consecration invalid, and therefore equally invalid, any ordinations he may have performed. First Constantinople is too early for us to expect any clear distinction between what is invalid and what is valid but illicit: yet, the disorders of this miserable affair were so great that the Fathers of Constantinople, in view of the extremely rigid laws of the early Church in respect to jurisdiction, very probably did quite right in proclaiming Maximus' orders invalid, and not merely wrongly gotten. Certainly the Church can make laws pertinent not only to the licit but also to the valid administration of the Sacraments. The Church today, for example, requires jurisdiction for a valid administration of the Sacrament of Penance. It is not too strong, I think, to say that the Church in the fourth century required jurisdiction for the valid administration of Holy Orders.

ST. DAMASUS I, POPE [*regn. A. D. 366-384*]

Pope St. Damasus I is remembered as having commissioned Jerome's translations of the Scriptures, and for having changed the liturgical language of the Roman Church from Greek to Latin. He interested himself in adorning the tombs of the martyrs, and composed numerous metrical epitaphs, generally referred to as epigrams, and had them engraved on marble slabs by the skilled calligrapher, Furius Dionysius Philocalus. At the present time fifty-nine such epigrams are accepted as authentic.

Among Damasus' literary remains besides the epigrams there are some ten letters and synodal encyclicals, the most important of which, no doubt, is the so-called *Fides* or *Tomus Damasi.*

THE TOME OF DAMASUS [*A. D.* 382]

St. Ambrose of Milan was instrumental in having a council meet in Rome, hoping to obtain the re-instatement of Maximus in Constantinople and of Paulinus in Antioch. His ends were thwarted before ever the council met. Nevertheless, the Council was convoked by the Emperor Gratian, and the principal metropolitans of the West assembled around Damasus for the Council of Rome, in 382 A. D. The document which is variously called the *Tomus Damasi,* the *Fides Damasi,* the *Confessio fidei catholicae Damasi,* and the *Epistula Damasi ad Paulinum Antiochenum episcopum,* is in fact an instrument of this Council of Rome. We have already noted that an Arabic collection of twenty-three anathemas, which some have supposed is a summation of the doctrinal tome drawn up by the Council of Constantinople of 381 A. D., is in fact virtually identical to *The Tome of Damasus.* St. Ambrose of Milan was present in the Council of Rome; and it is not unlikely that the actual drawing up of *The Tome of Damasus* is a work which devolved upon Ambrose.

The text of *The Tome of Damasus* can be found in Mansi, Vol. 3, 481-484 and 486-490; or in Migne, PL 13, 357-364; or with P. Galtier's comments, in *Recherches de science religieuse,* Vol. 26, Paris 1936, pp. 385-418, and 563-578; or in C. H. Turner, *Ecclesiae occidentalis monumenta iuris antiquissima,* Vol. 1, Fasc. 2, part 1, p. 284 *ff.*

910f

[1]

We anathematize those who do not freely proclaim that the Holy Spirit is of one power and substance with the Father and the Son.

268

910g

[2]

We anathematize those also who follow the error of Sabellius in saying that the same one is both Father and Son.

293

910h

[3]

We anathematize Arius and Eunomius, who, with equal impiety although in different words, declare that the Son and the Holy Spirit are creatures.

292

910i

[4]
    We anathematize the Macedonians, who, coming as offspring of the Arians, have changed   292
their name but not their faithlessness.

910j

[9]
    Those also who have moved from one church to another we continue to regard as   899
estranged from our communion until they return to the city in which they were first
established. But if someone has been ordained in the place of another who is yet alive
but has moved away from his place, let him that deserted his own city be without the
priestly dignity until his successor rests in the Lord.

910k

[16]
    If anyone does not say that the Holy Spirit is truly and properly of the Father, just   268
as the Son, of the divine substance and true God: — he is a heretic.   266

910l

[17]
    If anyone does not say that the Holy Spirit can do all things, knows all, and is   267
everywhere, just as the Son and the Father: he is a heretic.

910m

[18]
    If anyone says that the Holy Spirit is a creature, or that He was made by the Son: 266
he is a heretic.

910n

[19]
    If anyone does not say that the Father made all things, that is, the visible and the   283
invisible, through the Son and the Holy Spirit: he is a heretic.

910o

[20]
    If anyone does not say of the Father, Son, and Holy Spirit, that there is one godhead,   237
strength, majesty, and power, one glory and dominion, one reign, and one will and truth:
he is a heretic.

910p

[21]
    If anyone does not say that there are three Persons of Father, and of Son, and of   238
the Holy Spirit, equal, always living, embracing all things visible and invisible, ruling all,   282
judging all, giving life to all, making all, and saving all: he is a heretic.

910q

[22]

If anyone does not say that the Holy Spirit, just as the Son and the Father, is to be   266
adored by every creature: he is a heretic.

910r

[24]

But if anyone takes thought and says the Father is God, and His Son is God, and the   157
Holy Spirit is God, so as to speak of gods; and thus he calls them God not by reason
of the one godhead and power which we believe and know belongs to Father and Son
and Holy Spirit; or, if he detracts from the Son or Holy Spirit in such wise that he   257
thinks the Father only is to be called God, and in this way believes that God is one: 268
he is in every respect a heretic, or rather, a Jew, because they gave and attached the
name of *gods* both to the angels and to all the holy ones of God. It is not the name
of *gods,* however, but of *God,* which, in respect to the Father and the Son and the
Holy Spirit, and in view of their one and equal divinity, is revealed and declared to us,
so that we might believe; for we are baptized only in the Father and the Son and the   234
Holy Spirit, and not in the names of Archangels or Angels, as are the heretics, or Jews,
or even demented pagans. This, then, is the salvation of Christians: that believing in   758
the Trinity, that is, in the Father and in the Son and in the Holy Spirit, and baptized
in it, we believe without doubt that there is one only true godhead and power, the same
in majesty and substance.

THE DECREE OF DAMASUS [*A. D.* 382]

Belonging also to the Acts of the Council of Rome of 382 A. D. is a decree of
which three parts are extant. The first part of this decree (§ 910s, *below*) has long
been known as the *Decree of Damasus,* and concerns the Holy Spirit and the sevenfold gifts. The second part of the decree (§ 910t, *below*) is more familiarly known
as the opening part of the *Gelasian Decree,* in regard to the canon of Scripture:
De libris recipiendis vel non recipiendis. It is now commonly held that the part of
the *Gelasian Decree* dealing with the accepted canon of Scripture is an authentic
work of the Council of Rome of 382 A. D., and that Gelasius edited it again at the
end of the fifth century, adding to it the catalog of the rejected books, the apocrypha.
It is now almost universally accepted that these parts one and two of the *Decree of
Damasus* are authentic parts of the *Acts* of the Council of Rome of 382 A. D.

In regard to the third part of the *Decree of Damasus* (§ 910u, *below),* opinion is
still divided. C. H. Turner's work failed to convince everyone, and while little has
been written on the subject in most recent years, it must be pointed out that some
still prefer to regard this part three as pertaining peculiarly to the *Gelasian Decree,*
and in no way to the *Decree of Damasus.* We ourselves are satisfied by its manuscript attributions to Damasus, and by what seems to be strong internal evidence in
favor of authenticity. Certainly, the explicit statement that Rome's primacy is not
based upon conciliar concession from other Churches would seem to be Damasus'
answer to Canon 3 of First Constantinople. If it is not his answer, it is certainly
the answer he ought to have made! Further, there is good reason to believe that
certain of the instruments of the Council of Rome of 382 A. D. were sent off to
the Council then meeting in Constantinople; and if anything at all was sent at this
time from Rome to Constantinople, something like part three of the *Decree of
Damasus* ought to have been sent there.

N. B. Canon 1 of the Council of Constantinople of 382 A. D., preserved

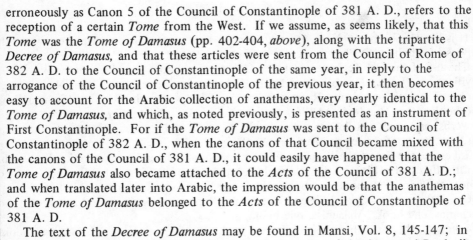

erroneously as Canon 5 of the Council of Constantinople of 381 A. D., refers to the reception of a certain *Tome* from the West. If we assume, as seems likely, that this *Tome* was the *Tome of Damasus* (pp. 402-404, *above*), along with the tripartite *Decree of Damasus*, and that these articles were sent from the Council of Rome of 382 A. D. to the Council of Constantinople of the same year, in reply to the arrogance of the Council of Constantinople of the previous year, it then becomes easy to account for the Arabic collection of anathemas, very nearly identical to the *Tome of Damasus*, and which, as noted previously, is presented as an instrument of First Constantinople. For if the *Tome of Damasus* was sent to the Council of Constantinople of 382 A. D., when the canons of that Council became mixed with the canons of the Council of 381 A. D., it could easily have happened that the *Tome of Damasus* also became attached to the *Acts* of the Council of 381 A. D.; and when translated later into Arabic, the impression would be that the anathemas of the *Tome of Damasus* belonged to the *Acts* of the Council of Constantinople of 381 A. D.

The text of the *Decree of Damasus* may be found in Mansi, Vol. 8, 145-147; in Migne, PL 19, 787-793; with C. H. Turner's "Latin Lists of the Canonical Books," in *The Journal of Theological Studies,* Vol. 1, (1900), p. 556 *ff.;* and in Hefele-Leclercq, *Histoire des Conciles,* 2, 1, Paris 1908, pp. 56-58 (reprint of the text established by Turner).

910s

[1]
It is decreed: We must treat first of the sevenfold Spirit who reposes in Christ:— the   548
Spirit of Wisdom: *"Christ, the power of God and the wisdom of God* (1)"; the Spirit of Understanding: *"I will give you understanding and will instruct you in the way in which you shall go* (2)"; the Spirit of Counsel: *"And His name shall be called 'Angel of Great Counsel'* (3);" the Spirit of Power: as above, *"the power of God and the wisdom of God* (4)"; the Spirit of Knowledge: *"on account of the eminence of the knowledge of the Apostle, Christ Jesus* (5)"; the Spirit of Truth: *"I am the way, the life, and the truth* (6)"; the Spirit of Fear: *"The fear of the Lord is the beginning of wisdom* (7)."

The arrangement of the names of Christ, however, is manifold: *Lord,* because He is   260
Spirit; *Word,* because He is God; *Son,* because He is the only-begotten Son of the Father;   781
Man, because He was born of the Virgin; *Priest,* because He offered Himself as a sacrifice;   382
Shepherd, because He is a guardian; *Worm,* because He rose again; *Mountain,* because He is strong; *Way,* because there is a straight path through Him to life; *Lamb,* because   380
He suffered; *Corner-Stone,* because instruction is His (8); *Teacher,* because He demonstrates how to live; *Sun,* because He is the illuminator; *Truth,* because He is   373
from the Father; *Life,* because He is the creator; *Bread,* because He is flesh; *Samaritan,* because He is the merciful protector (9); *Christ,* because He is anointed; *Jesus,* because He is the Savior; *God,* because He is of God; *Angel,* because He was sent; *Bridegroom,* because He is a mediator (10); *Vine,* because we are redeemed by His blood; *Lion,* because He is king; *Rock,* because He is firm; *Flower,* because He is the chosen one; *Prophet,* because He has revealed what is to come.   270

The Holy Spirit is not of the Father only, or the Spirit of the Son only, but He is the Spirit of the Father and the Son. For it is written: "If anyone loves the world, the Spirit of the Father is not in him (11)"; and again it is written: "If anyone, however, does not have the Spirit of Christ, he is none of His (12)." When the Father and the Son are named in this way, the Holy Spirit is understood, of whom the Son Himself   269
says in the Gospel, that the Holy Spirit "proceeds from the Father (13)," and that "He shall receive of mine and shall announce it to you (14)."

910t

[2]

It is likewise decreed: Now, indeed, we must treat of the divine Scriptures: what the universal Catholic (15) Church accepts and what she must shun.

The list of the Old Testament begins: Genesis, one book; Exodus, one book;   41
Leviticus, one book; Numbers, one book; Deuteronomy, one book; Jesus Nave, one book; of Judges, one book; Ruth, one book; of Kings, four books; Paralipomenon, two books; One Hundred and Fifty Psalms, one book; of Solomon, three books: Proverbs, one book; Ecclesiastes, one book; Canticle of Canticles, one book; likewise, Wisdom, one book; Ecclesiasticus, one book.

Likewise, the list of the Prophets: Isaias, one book; Jeremias, one book, along with Cinoth, that is, his Lamentations; Ezechiel, one book; Daniel, one book; Osee, one book; Amos, one book; Micheas, one book; Joel, one book; Abdias, one book; Jonas, one book; Nahum, one book; Habacuc, one book; Sophonias, one book; Aggeus, one book; Zacharias, one book; Malachias, one book.

Likewise, the list of histories: Job, one book; Tobias, one book; Esdras, two books; Esther, one book; Judith, one book; of Maccabees, two books.

Likewise, the list of the Scriptures of the New and Eternal Testament, which the holy   42
and Catholic Church receives: of the Gospels, one book according to Matthew, one book according to Mark, one book according to Luke, one book according to John. The Epistles of the Apostle Paul, fourteen in number: one to the Romans, two to the Corinthians, one to the Ephesians, two to the Thessalonians, one to the Galatians, one to the Philippians, one to the Colossians, two to Timothy, one to Titus, one to Philemon, one to the Hebrews.

Likewise, one book of the Apocalypse of John. And the Acts of the Apostles, one book.

Likewise, the canonical Epistles, seven in number: of the Apostle Peter, two Epistles; of the Apostle James, one Epistle; of the Apostle John, one Epistle; of the other John, a Presbyter, two Epistles; of the Apostle Jude the Zealot, one Epistle. Thus concludes the canon of the New Testament.

910u

[3]

Likewise it is decreed: After the announcement of all these prophetic and evangelic   433
as well as apostolic writings which we have listed above as Scriptures, on which, by the grace of God, the Catholic Church is founded, we have considered that it ought to be announced that although all the Catholic Churches spread abroad through the world   420
comprise but one bridal chamber of Christ, nevertheless, the holy Roman Church has been placed at the forefront not by the conciliar decisions of other Churches, but has received the primacy by the evangelic voice of our Lord and Savior, who says: "You are Peter,   430
and upon this rock I will build My Church, and the gates of hell will not prevail against it; and I will give to you the keys of the kingdom of heaven, and whatever you shall have bound on earth will be bound in heaven, and whatever you shall have loosed on earth shall be loosed in heaven (16)."

In addition to this, there is also the companionship of the vessel of election, the most blessed Apostle Paul, who contended and was crowned with a glorious death along with Peter in the City of Rome in the time of the Caesar Nero — not at a different time, as   431
the heretics prattle, but at one and the same time and on one and the same day: and they equally consecrated the above-mentioned holy Roman Church to Christ the Lord; and by their own presence and by their venerable triumph they set it at the forefront over the others of all the cities of the whole world.

The first see, therefore, is that of Peter the Apostle, that of the Roman Church, which   432
has neither stain nor blemish nor anything like it. The second see, however, is that at

Alexandria, consecrated in behalf of blessed Peter by Mark, his disciple and an evangelist, who was sent to Egypt by the Apostle Peter, where he preached the word of truth and finished his glorious martyrdom. The third honorable see, indeed, is that at Antioch, which belonged to the most blessed Apostle Peter, where first he dwelt before he came to Rome, and where the name *Christians* (17) was first applied, as to a new people.

1. 1 Cor. 1:24.
2. Ps. 31 [32]:8.
3. Is. 9:6 [Septuagint].
4. 1 Cor. 1:24.
5. Phil. 3:8.
6. John 14:6.
7. Ps. 110 [111]:10; Prov. 9:10.
8. *Lapis angularis, quia instructio.* There is a confusion of ideas in this phrase. *Instructio* means both *instruction* and *construction* with reference to *doctrine* and to *building.* It is the same kind of a semantic problem that one finds in the riddle: *Why is a dog like a tree? Because he has a rough bark.* Obviously, this makes the phrase virtually untranslatable.
9. No doubt the reference is to the parable of the good Samaritan. Here there is token of another interesting linguistic phenomenon. The Savior chose a Samaritan for the role of the merciful person in the parable, because Samaritans were so commonly regarded as absolutely despicable people. But through the frequent reciting of the parable, the term *Samaritan* quickly took on the connotation which it has even today: a friend to his fellow men.
10. *Sponsus, quia mediator.* Here we suspect there is a problem much like that mentioned in footnote 8 above: a confusion of ideas. The word *Sponsus,* is, in its first meaning, indicative of a betrothed person, a *Bridegroom;* but it can also mean a *bail bondsman,* one who goes surety for another.
11. 1 John 2:15.
12. Rom. 8:9.
13. John 15:26.
14. John 16:14.
15. The tautology of *universalis catholica ecclesia* indicates that the word *Catholic* is no longer a common adjective, but has become a proper adjective or noun, more important as an appellation than for the meaning it ought to convey.
16. Matt. 16:18-19.
17. Acts 11:26.

INDEX OF SCRIPTURAL REFERENCES AND CITATIONS

The reference numbers are to the consecutive numbering of the text passages rather than to pages, whether the Scripture reference be pertinent to the passage itself or to its accompanying notes. Passages which require Septuagint consultation are marked *Sept.;* and in these, the numbering is that of the Septuagint.

DOCTRINAL INDEX

In the following index points of doctrine are numbered consecutively. After each statement of doctrine appear the numbers of the passages in the body of the book which have some bearing upon the particular doctrinal statement. The passage itself will usually be found to be an affirmation of the doctrinal statement; but in some instances it will be found to be in contradiction to it. In the latter case, the passage number is enclosed in parentheses. The Fathers and early Christian Writers do not agree with each other with a precise mathematical unanimity, nor could it be expected that they would. And in any case, we must stress that a particular patristic text is in no instance to be regarded as a "proof" of a particular doctrine. Dogmas are not "proved" by patristic statements, but by the infallible teaching instruments of the Church. The value of the Fathers and Writers is this: that in the aggregate, they demonstrate what the Church believes and teaches; and again, in the aggregate, they provide a witness to the content of Tradition, that Tradition which is itself a vehicle of revelation.

NATURAL RELIGION

1. The concept of religion:
   631 635
2. Man has a natural tendency toward religion [see also 130].
   270 275

REVEALED RELIGION
REVELATION

10. Revelation deserves the assent of reason [see also 558].
    173 354a 455 562 818b
11. In the present order revelation is for us a moral necessity.
    334 629
13. Miracles provide an external criterion of revelation [see also 82].
    133b
14. Miracles do not of themselves, however, suffice to confirm the truth of doctrine.
    638
15. Prophecy affords another external criterion of revelation [see also 81].
    57 61 175 276a 530 626

SACRED SCRIPTURE
INSPIRATION

20. The Sacred Scriptures, written under the inspiration of the Holy Spirit, have God for their author [see also 50].
    22 26b 122b 123 126 149 185 203 328b 390a 400 404 447a 468a 483 577
21. Inspiration consists in the action of God's using the intellect and will of the sacred writer, after the fashion of an instrument.
    122b 149 162 163 175 179 388 910a
22. The primary object of such inspiration is the things which concern salvation.
    149 818b
23. Nevertheless, inspiration extends to all parts of Sacred Scripture, and in some sense, even to the words themselves.
    483
25. No error can be found in the Sacred Scriptures.
    22 138 203 390a 400 480
27. Bearing in mind that every assertion made by the sacred writer is true, according to the meaning which he wished to express and did express, the presence of apparent errors in Scripture in regard to history and the sciences can be explained.
    138
29. Some of the Fathers believed that the Septuagint version was made under inspiration.
    149a 819
30. In regard to the several senses of Scripture:
    447a 469 480

CANONICITY

40. The sole criterion of canonicity is Catholic Tradition, which has its basis in Apostolic Tradition.
    341 745s 819
41. The Tridentine canon of the Old Testament is founded in Catholic Tradition.
    190 484 745t 791 819 882 910t
42. So also is the Tridentine canon of the New Testament founded in Catholic Tradition.
    94 95 211 268 341 439-440 479a? 503 538 652 652b 653 656 745t 791 819 910t

THE OLD LAW

50. God is the author of the Law, both the Old and the New [see also 20].
    185 230 276a 410a 421a 445 680
51. The purpose of the Old Law was to prepare for the coming of Christ [see also 300].
    61 134b 188 303a 834a
52. The Old Law, therefore, is abrogated by the revelation of the New Law.
    45 46 96 133a 134a

THE GOSPEL

60. Gospel: meaning of the word: the single and fourfold gospel.
    5 7a 9 20 31 57 60 61 81a 112 128 195 208 215 238 288 427
61. The authenticity and historicity of the four Gospels was acknowledged in Christian antiquity.
    129 141 143 199a 208 214 215 268 339 341 439-400 474 503 538
62. The witnesses who affirm the genuinity of the four Gospels are worthy of belief.
    (201) 212 (261) 264
63. The four Gospels contain true histories.
    60 195 264 268 519 619 666
64. The authenticity and historicity of the Gospel of Matthew:
    1 5 7a 10 95 143 167 208 214 339 341 439-440 503 538
65. The authenticity and historicity of the Gospel of Mark:
    13 24 31 95 208 214 268 339 341 439-440 503 538 651bb 652
66. The authenticity and historicity of the Gospel of Luke:
    1 63 143 195 208 214 217 268 339 341 439-440 503 538
67. The Gospel of John is also authentic and historic, although it takes a spiritual approach to history.
    182 208 214 264 268 339 341 439-440 503 538
68. The genuinity of the four Gospels is confirmed from the apocryphal gospels.
    474
69. The genuinity of the four Gospels is confirmed also from the manner in which the heretics of antiquity made use of them.
    195 214 339 340 341 474

DIVINE ORIGIN OF CHRISTIANITY

80. Jesus Christ came into the world as a divine legate [see also 302 and 310].
    47 51 54b 290 405 520
81. The predictions of the Prophets fulfilled in Christ prove His mission divine [see also 15 and 300].
    61 122 125 127 222 468a 638
82. The divine character of Christ's mission is proved also by His miracles [see also 13].
    109 122 189 618 619
83. Christ's predictions of the future, which have been fulfilled, prove His mission divine.
    116 654
84. The resurrection of Christ is proved by arguments that are certain.
    13 47 51 63 129 665 818a
85. The wonderful spread of Christianity along with its continued endurance serve to prove its divine origin [see also 404 and 405]. 274 279 282 320a 369 555-556 621
86. The virtues of Christians, when compared to the vices of the pagans, argue to the divine origin of Christianity and its teachings.
    97 112 186 271 273 274 280 281 283 285
87. The change in moral values which comes with conversion argues to the divine origin of Christianity and its teachings.
    118 263 276 369 621 661a
88. Martyrdom is a testimony to the truth of the Christian religion.
    11 63 144 243 285 640
89. The internal character of Christian doctrine argues to its divine origin.
    118 192 276a 405

TRADITION

100. Sacred Tradition is a true source of revelation.
  192 198 242 291 295 371 (818b)
101. Sacred Tradition completes Sacred Scripture through its authentic interpretation thereof.
  242 291 443
102. Apostolic Tradition has always been acknowledged as the rule of faith.
  74 94 190a 191 192 209 210 211 212 213 257 264 293 296 298 329 341 394 443 445 785 898
103. There was a progressive revelation until the death of the Apostles.
  239
104. Since the death of the Apostles it has not been possible for the body of revelation to be either augmented or diminished.
  2 213 226 242 288 289 293 785
105. Nevertheless, the proposition that there is a certain progress in dogma is not to be in every sense rejected.
  226 328a 371 444
107. As private teachers, the Fathers can err.
  190a

RELIGION AND CULT

120. Among the acts of religion there is prayer [see also 712].
  26a 55 79 281b 557a
121. The saints in heaven are worthy objects of worship, which worship, however, is not the same as that given to God.
  81 572
122. There is a communion of saints, by which the souls of the just dead, knowing us and our needs, pray for us.
  852
123. Christian tradition bears witness to the honoring of relics.
  70 81
125. The cross of our Lord is to be held in honor, whether it be a question of its actual relics, or images of it, or the sign of the cross made by the motion of the hand.
  367 751a 824

THE ONE GOD
EXISTENCE OF GOD

130. The existence of God is able to be known with certainty by the natural light of reason.
  197 228 269 270 275 287 331 334 416 455 645 662 888
131. Man is able to arrive at a knowledge of God from a consideration of the order in the visible world.
  152 172 198 228 269 332 515 624 662 746 747
132. Man is able to arrive at a knowledge of God from a consideration of the government of providence.
  110 172 269
133. Man is able to arrive at a knowledge of God from the dictates of conscience.
  411
134. Positive revelation is not necessary in order to arrive at a natural knowledge of God.
  (227) 269
135. There is a certain natural knowledge of God's existence innate in men [see also 2].
  130 270 332 403 425 662
137. The existence of God is provable a posteriori.
  334

ESSENCE OF GOD

140. The essence of God is existence itself, whence His proper name, Yahweh.
  729 786 857 877
141. God is existence, of Himself and independently.
  754 860 861

ATTRIBUTES OF GOD

150. The divine attributes are really the same as the divine substance.
  192a 199b 229
151. God is utterly simple and admits of no composition whatever.
  199b 321 424 451 754 756 786 822a
152. God is spirit.
  111 152 164 277 374 451 452 822b 894

153. God has every perfection in an infinite degree.
   229 423 815
154. God is immeasurable and is present everywhere.
   85 177 234a 424 608 754 815 860 893 894 899
155. God is completely unchangeable.
   111 132 814 815
156. God is eternal.
   110 152 161 164 206 321 331 608 628 814 822a 860 899
157. God is one and unique.
   45 191 194 196 199a 203 205 274a 275 290 322 328a 331 397 445 515 608
   608a 625 651f 814 822a 910a 910r
158. God is all-powerful.
   111 171 194 205 323 325 328a 402 424 628 651f 815 822a 910a

KNOWLEDGE ABOUT GOD

170. No creature can of its unaided nature see God.
   236 270 451 452 747 891
171. In regard to seeing God with bodily eyes:
   452 645
172. A creature can be elevated to the sight of God, as in fact is done for the angels and for the blessed.
   236 822
173. God is incomprehensible and inexpressible.
   164 205 234a 270 450 603 668 747 756 786 860 861 900
174. We cannot, properly speaking, know the essence of God.
   130 270 416 623 821 861
175. We do arrive at some knowledge of God, through various concepts which describe Him.
   192a 199b 331 423 424 455 603 786 821 894 900 908
176. The concepts we employ in arriving at a descriptive knowledge of God are at best extremely faulty.
   760a
177. The concepts we employ in arriving at a descriptive knowledge of God are faulty because they cannot be understood of God in the same way in which they are understood of creatures.
   270 623 754 760a 908
178. We attempt to arrive at some knowledge of the perfections of God from a consideration of His creatures, by the *way of negation*.
   110 423
179. We attempt to arrive at some knowledge of the perfections of God from a consideration of His creatures, by the *way of causality*.
   110 455
180. We attempt to arrive at some knowledge of the perfections of God from a consideration of His creatures, by the *way of eminence*.
   110 450 674 908

GOD'S OWN KNOWLEDGE

188. God has perfect knowledge of Himself.
   205 270 821
189. God knows all things, not only of the present but even of the future, as with a single intuitive act.
   166 177 202 397 429 471 815 822a
190. God's foreknowledge is not the cause of future events.
   471 663
191. God knows all future events, even those which shall come about through man's exercise of free will.
   116
192. God's foreknowledge of events in no way destroys or detracts from man's exercise of free will.
   663
193. In regard to God's foreknowledge of evil:
   471 663
194. God knows even the outcome of future conditional events.
   471
195. The providence of God is extended to all His creatures.
   202

PREDESTINATION AND REPROBATION

200. God desires the salvation of all men.
   93b 389
202. In regard to the predestination of the saints:
   28 28a 37a 80a 435
210. In regard to reprobation, or predestination to damnation:
   466

THE TRIUNE GOD

THE TRINITY

230. That God is triune is clear in the Tradition of the Church even in the pre-Nicene era.
20 23 28 40 47a 80 108 112 113 117 126 128 164 165 180 191 235 256 307 371
376 377 394a 394b 394c 408 445 452 470 479 546 557 596 608 608a 611 681 701
792a

231. In their struggle against Arianism the later Fathers appeal to the pre-Nicene trinitarian tradition.
757 782 792a 898

232. The Fathers believed that they could find in the Old Testament certain hints of the Trinity, the beginnings
of a progressive revelation even in this regard.
180 194 377 405 789

233. The Fathers did especially find evidence of the beginning of the progressive revelation of the Trinity in
Genesis 1:26.
31 235 361

234. The Trinity is expressed in the formula of Baptism [*see also* 826].
784 789 858 910r

235. The Joannine comma cited:
378 557

236. In regard to the theophanies:
127 182 290 824 864

237. Although Father, Son, and Holy Spirit are one, they are yet distinct.
(91) 164 179 371 376 596 611 768 778 779 904 907 910o

238. Father, Son, and Holy Spirit are distinct in such a way that in the unity of one nature there are three
Persons.
371 376 378 782 789 898 907 910p

239. The Most Holy Trinity is a mystery.
204 668 779 816 834 859 878

PERSONS OF THE TRINITY

250. Only the Father does not proceed.
479 608 634 679 814 880

251. The Son was not made.
164 442 470 675 756 761 764 765 866

252. The Son was truly born of the Father.
153 373 374 391 540 608 651f 668 674 760 765 816 823 826 866 896 902 910a

253. The generation of the Son from the Father is not free.
153 775

254. Although the generation of the Son from the Father is not free, neither is it forced.
775 879

255. Neither free nor yet forced, the generation of the Son from the Father is voluntary and natural.
470 608 862 879

256. The Son is co-eternal with the Father.
130 137? 153 182 189 200 205 391 393 401 442 470 608 609 611 651f 668 676
679 760 761 813 816 823 877

257. The Son is consubstantial (*homoousios*) with the Father.
153 277 (376) 392 398 409 540 608 651f 755 756 761 765 767 767a 768 769 783
787 792a 826 866 868 880 896 899 907 910a 910r

258. Between Father and Son there is an identity of nature and a distinction of Persons.
374 375 376 409 536 636 862 881 902

259. In some way, the Father is greater than the Son.
256 374 376 608 636 679 896

260. *Word (Verbum* or *Logos)* is the proper name of the Son.
45 205 290 608 632 632a 770 787 899 910s

261. The Son is called *Wisdom of the Father.*
137 165 182 373 460 540 674 764b 787 816 826 899

262. The Son is called *Word (Sermo) of the Father.*
371 373 375 379 632 632a

263. The Son is called *Splendor of the Father.*
18 756 768 770

264. The Son is called *Image of the Father.*
536 611 674 746 764b 768 769 787 868

265. The Son proceeds from the Father by an intellectual generation.
137 179 182 200 277 373 398 470 610 632 754 825

266. The Holy Spirit is God.
377 680 779 784a 910a 910k 910m 910q

267. That the Holy Spirit is God is proved by His operation.
780 910*l*

268. The Holy Spirit is consubstantial *(homoousios)* with the Father and the Son.
611 783 784 784a 907 910a 910f 910k 910r

269. The Holy Spirit proceeds from the Father.
     164 910a 910s
270. The Holy Spirit is Spirit also of the Son.
     378 388 683 783 784a 834 872 910s
271. The Holy Spirit is called *Image of the Son*.
     228a 611
272. The Holy Spirit proceeds from the Father through the Son *(a Patre per filium)*.
     372 479 611 878 904 907
273. The Holy Spirit proceeds from the Father and the Son *(a Patre Filioque)*.
     375? 861a
275. The Holy Spirit is not a Son.
     778
276. Neither is the procession of the Holy Spirit a generation.
     (907)?
277. The Holy Spirit is Holiness itself.
     611
278. The Holy Spirit is the Gift of God.
     858

RELATIONS AND APPROPRIATIONS

281. The Divine Persons are distinguished among themselves only by their relations one to another.
     867 896 907
282. Because the Divine Persons are distinguished among themselves only by their relations one to another, they are co-equal as to perfection.
     779 899 903 910p
283. Their external operations are common to the three Divine Persons.
     235 769 779 782 784 834 910n
284. Creation is a work appropriated to the Word.
     98 130 153 156 164 179 194 234 235 277 290 371 391 394 398 401 479 608 651f
     748 761 764 764a 767a 814 910a
285. Sanctification is a work appropriated to the Holy Spirit.
     371 389 449 611 810b 850 853i 907

THE MISSION OF THE DIVINE PERSONS

290. The Son is sent by the Father.
     182 376 394 398
291. The Holy Spirit is sent by the Son.
     290 871
292. Arian doctrine in regard to the Son:
     321 608a 648 648a 648b 650 650a 651 651a 777 910h 910i
293. Sabellian doctrine:
     371 376 608a 651 768 782 910g

THE INCARNATE WORD
TRUE DIVINITY

300. Jesus Christ and His divine mission were predicted in the Old Testament [*see also* 51 *and* 81].
     31 35 45 57 122 122a 127 133a 141 277 290 390 394 398 445 468a 638 664
301. That Jesus Christ is true God is witnessed to by pre-Nicene tradition.
     18 31 35 37a 42 45 52 69 81 98 101 112 113 117 131 136 137 160 189 191 218
     222 248 277 350 377 399 401 405 406 445 468a 596 617 632 634 651a 692
302. The only Son of God is incarnate, and He is Jesus Christ [*see also* 80].
     43 45 62 69 (91) 98 112a 117 127 136 141 191 214 218 290 328a 371 377 393
     398 401 632 651f 788 823 875 907 910a

TRUE HUMANITY

310. The Son of God took a true human nature, not merely the appearance thereof.
     39 51 62 63 63a 189 217a 343 353 357 394 405 426 445 604 680 767a 794 817
     873 876
311. Christ has a true body, formed of the substance of Mary.
     51 62 112 136 277 290 353 371 389 398 611ii 711 759 817 874a 875 886a 905
312. Christ has a rational soul.
     394 460 461 874a 875
313. Since He is of the race of Adam, Christ is consubstantial *(homoousios)* with ourselves.
     217a 239 353 394 398 604 762 788 794 828 886a 890

314. What were not assumed were not healed: whatever part of human nature the Son of God had not taken upon Himself would not have been affected by His work of salvation.
    221 794 817 827 906

THE UNION OF NATURES, HUMAN AND DIVINE

321. The Word was not changed into nor inextricably mixed with a human nature.
    379 394 (634) 905
322. The Word assumed a human nature, so that now He has two natures, each distinct.
    39 189 353 379 453 482 605
323. Though distinct, the two natures of the Word are in some way united.
    221 277 460 759 773 827 874
324. The union of the two natures in the Incarnate Word is a personal union.
    379 393 873
329. This union was made in conception and is inseparable.
    218
330. In Christ there are two wills.
    790
331. The two wills in Christ are never contrarily opposed to each other.
    790
332. In Christ there are two operations: one divine, the other human.
    277 379 759 771 773 794 817
333. In regard to theandric operation:
    771
334. In Christ there is a true communication of idioms.
    460 (482) 759 771 795 830 831 874 889

CONSEQUENCES OF THE UNION OF NATURES

340. The man Jesus Christ is not the adoptive but the natural Son of God.
    788 863
341. Christ is utterly filled with grace and is holy in every respect.
    682
342. The man Christ is to be adored.
    81 762 795 827
344. Christ was free of original sin.
    611ii
345. Christ was free of personal sin.
    350 357 394 482 684
346. Christ was unable to sin.
    461
347. Christ had a body capable of suffering.
    31 45 63 66 124 214 221 371 389 426 445 520 651f 772 773 794 828 874a 876 889 890 910a
348. Christ had a body subject to human infirmities.
    379 771 772 817
349. Christ had a body subject to human passions.
    131 136 379 (426)
350. Christ freely suffered and died.
    830 831 889
351. Whether there was any ignorance in Christ:
    204 774

NECESSITY OF THE INCARNATION

360. If Adam had not sinned the Incarnation would not have taken place.
    254 492 765
361. God could certainly have effected the redemption of the human race in some other way than through the Incarnation.
    767
362. The Incarnation, therefore, is a free gift of God.
    99 127
363. Although the Incarnation is a free gift of God, there is yet a certain sense in which it may be said that the Incarnation was necessary.
    31 612 751 767 822b

PURPOSE OF THE INCARNATION

370. The purpose of the Incarnation and Passion of Christ is the effecting of man's salvation.
    12 26 40 45 66 74 75 99 108 112 127 131 389 405a 508 651f 771 822b 901 910a

371. The Incarnation and Passion was not intended, however, to effect the salvation of the fallen angels.
356
372. It was intended, however, that the Incarnation and Passion should serve as a manifestation of God's love of men.
98 248 822b
373. Christ desired to serve as an example for men, to show us how to live.
201 398 401 409a 409b 508 632 634 669 828 910s
374. Christ desired to redeem us from sin and from the servitude in which we were held by the devil.
31 69 89 130 133b 221 249 370 399 405 436a 492 498 669 680 684 691 848e 889
375. Christ desired to return to men the gifts of grace and immortality.
33 127 345 634 711 751 752 767 828 829 831
376. Christ desired to lead men back to the pristine state lost through the sin of Adam.
223 255 394 399 405 563 612 703 767 829 890

THE CARRYING THROUGH OF THAT PURPOSE

380. Christ effected redemption by means of a true sacrifice.
18 33 76 80 492 498 664 669 673 751 794 910s
381. Christ offered that true sacrifice on the cross to God.
406 889 901
382. In that true sacrifice, Christ was both Priest and Victim.
581 910s
383. Christ effected redemption by means of a true vicarious satisfaction.
62 140 436a 482 552 565 664 673 691 751 767 831 906
384. The true vicarious satisfaction by which Christ effected redemption was paid out not to the devil, but to God.
(508)
385. The satisfaction which Christ made is superabundant.
492 831
386. The satisfaction which Christ made is universal.
12 224 498 (508) 664 669 751 767 906
387. Christ became Mediator between God and man.
199a 405 691 701 766 769 873
388. Graces are dispensed through Christ and because of the satisfaction He made.
7 18 61 405
389. The graces won by Christ were dispensed even to those who found their justification in the period of the Old Law.
45 57 61
390. The soul of Christ descended into the lower regions.
238 259 818
391. Christ ascended into heaven in His human nature.
191 259 371 651f 680 910a
392. Christ will come again to judge the living and the dead.
31 33 101 125 191 290 328a 371 552 599a 647 651f 853c 910a

THE CHURCH
FOUNDATION

400. In a certain sense the Church may be said to have existed from the beginning of the world.
82 105 435
401. Jesus Christ founded a society, with Himself its Head, which is to last forever and which is called His Church.
20 29a 38b 105 217a 289 555-556 571 865
402. This Church which Jesus Christ founded serves to continue His own life on earth.
62 256
403. In the Acts of the Apostles, St. Luke recites an authentic history of the primitive Church.
217 268 538
404. From the earliest times the Church spread throughout the whole world [see also 85].
6 7 11 38 77 79 81a 93 97a 112 144 144a 187 191 192 215 257 268 405 652a
405. From the earliest times and even in its initial spread, the Church showed that it was a single unified body.
43 47a 58a 62 77 84 93 188 192 281
406. From earliest times the Church was hierarchically constituted and showed itself as such.
9 19 20 21 25 38a 43a 44 47a 49 50 56 58a 65 413 427 438 571 599a

PROPERTIES AND NOTES

410. The Church is a monarchical society.
546 546a 573 (576b) (599a)

411. The Church is an independent society.
     759a
412. The Church is a visible society.
     97a 281
413. As a society, the Church consists of twofold elements, visible and invisible, called body and soul.
     97a
414. On earth, the Church is mixed in its membership, having both good and wicked within its fold.
     (435)
415. Heretics and schismatics, in the teaching of the Fathers, are not members of the Church.
     213 237 241 257 295a 298 308 587 589 591 593 597 601c 602 602a
416. There is but one true Church of Christ.
     408 435 573 589 680
417. Outside the one true Church of Christ there is no salvation.
     56 226 537 557 597a 637
418. The true Church of Christ can be recognized by certain notes.
     587 910a
419. Sanctity of its foundations and members belongs only to the true Church of Christ.
     226 838
420. Unity of faith and government belongs only to the true Church of Christ.
     1b 6 7 56 93 188 192 213 241 257 292 293 295 296 328a 329 435 555-556 576b
     587 588a 589a 865 910u
421. Catholicity belongs only to the true Church of Christ.
     65 79 80a 81a 435 555-556 575 587 680 838 839
422. Apostolicity belongs only to the true Church of Christ.
     80a 210 213 237 292 293 296 297 298 329 341 589 680
423. In any individual Church these notes are discoverable through its union with the successor of Peter.
     574a 587 654a

THE PRIMACY

430. Among the Apostles, Peter received from Christ the primacy of jurisdiction in the Church.
     381 387 436 479a 489 555-556 571 587 592a 693a 706 810 835a 910u
431. Peter came to Rome and died there.
     11 106a 106b 297 341 368a 439-440 611gg 647a 651aa 651cc 651dd 652b 822c 910u
432. Peter established his See at Rome, and made the Bishop of Rome his successor in the primacy.
     54 188 208 210 211 296 575 602a 651aa 702a 897 910u
433. The Roman Pontiffs have always laid claim to the primacy of jurisdiction.
     10a 21 25 27 28a 29 190a 592a 601a 601b 602a 860a 910u
434. From earliest times the Roman Church has been regarded as the center of unity.
     52 53 106c 107 187 210 211 575 580
435. From earliest times it was acknowledged that supreme power over the whole Church belonged to the
     Bishop of Rome as successor of Peter.
     82a 107 (190a) 211 265 573 (592a) (599a) (601a) (601b) (602) (602a) 702a 702b
     702c 806a 822c 910d
436. The title *Pope* is of quite early origin, but was not until later restricted in usage to the Bishop of Rome.
     568a 570b 651

THE EPISCOPATE

440. Bishops are not less than the legitimate successors of the Apostles.
     20 21 48 49 56 65 188 209 212 237 242 257 296 341 438 602
441. Although the bishops are the successors of the Apostles, the transmission of jurisdiction was made in
     various ways in the primitive churches.
     9 575 588 745g
442. In regard to the College of Bishops:
     576b 588a 599b

INFALLIBILITY

450. The Church is infallible in transmitting the teachings of Christ.
     213 295
451. The Roman Pontiff enjoys infallibility when he teaches *ex cathedra*.
     294 580
452. Bishops gathered in an ecumenical council have always been acknowledged as infallible judges of the faith.
     785 792 910b

CREATION
IN GENERAL

460. God created all things.
  13a 14 85 98 110 112 117 152 154 171 178 191 194 199a 205 328a 397 402 409 445 459 608 651f 681 748 814 896a 910a
461. It was out of nothing *(ex nihilo)* that God created all things.
  85 111 114 129 150 171 178 179 194 199 275 290 323 324 325 326 327 328 363 398 445 628 687 748 750 754 761
462. God alone can create.
  178 764 764a
463. God creates freely.
  168 196 205 235 391 397 748
465. God creates because He is good.
  168 231 462 884
466. God creates so that His perfections may be manifested and acknowledged.
  7 171 179 275 643
467. It is the Trinity that creates.
  235
468. The material world is not eternal.
  154 178 179 206 207 322 325 391 397 447 454? 761
469. God is not the author of evil [*see also* 638].
  324 398

ANGELS

480. There exist angels created by God.
  17 63b 83 113 156 164 165 228a 320 448 643 667
481. In regard to the time of the creation of the angels:
  83 156 448
482. The angels possess by nature a certain excellence.
  18
483. In regard to the spiritual nature of the angels:
  278 354 646 667 895
484. Angels are not everywhere.
  278 781
486. The angels were created free.
  63b 142 156 244
488. The angels are divided into various ranks or choirs.
  83 427 612 822 849
489. The angels are elevated to the supernatural order.
  278
490. Many angels, having attained eternal blessedness, are already confirmed in goodness.
  853d
491. Many angels, having fallen into grave sin, have hastened to eternal damnation.
  191 356 446a 567
492. The good angels are ministers of God and assist men in the business of working out their salvation.
  83 89 228a 446 448 895
493. There are guardian angels assigned to individuals, nations, societies, etc.
  89 430 475 895
494. The devil and the other wicked angels are able to harm men.
  69 87 112a 258 278 286 446 475 751a 853h

MAN

500. Man is composed of body and soul.
  147 159 170
501. The human soul is incorporeal.
  252 346 346a 349 355
502. The human soul is immortal.
  (132)? (133)? 157 168 169 206 249 252 349 683
503. In a man there is but one soul only.
  170 467?
504. In regard to the trichotomy:
  133 148
505. Man is free.
  123 142 156 184 244 335 446 622 667
506. The human soul is created by God.
  683
507. The soul is not pre-existent to the body.
  (466) 611hh

508. The soul does not spring up through the procreative process.
(446)? 875
509. Whether God created man immediately:
250 360 361 611hh 687
512. Man is created in the image of God.
156 159 361 746

FIRST MAN

520. Before the fall our first parents were endowed with certain gifts of nature not owed to them: original justice, . . . [see also 610].
225 253 567 612
521. . . . immunity from concupiscence, . . .
224
522. . . . and immunity from the necessity of dying.
184 566 749 750 883

DIVINE WATCHFULNESS

530. God preserves all things.
171 206 207 458 563

VIRTUES
IN GENERAL

540. The concept of virtue:
641
541. There are certain infused virtues: faith, hope, and charity.
72
548. In regard to the gifts of the Holy Spirit:
910s

FAITH

552. Faith is intellectual assent.
62 417 820
553. The intellectual assent of faith is free.
245 417
554. The free intellectual assent of faith is firm.
13a 62 418
555. Faith is a supernatural act.
418 419
556. In regard to the *faith of miracles,* which is a charism:
820
557. The motive of faith is not the rational evidence of the object proposed for belief.
417
558. The intrinsic motive of faith is the authority of God revealing.
162 173 175 359a 417 562
559. A sure knowledge of its having been divinely revealed is a prerequisite to faith in any proposed object.
417 627 629 643a
560. Faith is more certain than any natural knowledge.
173 417 418 846
561. Faith is not opposed to reason.
173
563. Faith sometimes precedes reason, and elevates it to a more perfect mode of knowledge.
418 433
564. Reason is able to demonstrate the basis of faith.
344 627
565. When reason has been illuminated by the light of faith, it can perfect our knowledge of divine things.
433
566. Faith must be universal, extending to every revealed truth.
298
567. There is always some obscurity about faith, precisely because it is those things which are not seen that are believed through faith.
417 869
568. For those who are of sufficient intellectual maturity, faith is of absolute necessity for justification and salvation.
289 417 886a

HOPE

582. Hope is founded in faith, and for that reason is most certain.
301a 419 864
583. The principal motive of hope is the goodness of God, from whom a reward is expected.
836
584. A secondary motive for hope is our own merits.
836

CHARITY

590. Charity establishes a true friendship between God and man.
26 433
591. Charity is the most excellent of all the virtues.
242 419
592. Charity is the root and perfection of all other virtues.
26
595. Charity supposes faith and is founded on it.
433

SIN

ORIGINAL SIN

610. Our first parents, having fallen into grave sin, lost their original justice [see also 520].
225 286 567
611. Death is an effect of Adam's sin.
183 345 395 566 567 612 749 750 829
612. Through his sin, Adam lost other free gifts.
183 225 703
613. But in spite of his fall, Adam kept free will.
244 349 398
614. The sin of Adam was passed on to all men.
224 224a 255 286 345 486 496 501 586 612 683 684 698 703 763 829
615. Original sin is transmitted by a father in the natural process of procreation.
586

PERSONAL SIN

632. There are sins which are entirely internal.
119 166 239 273 352 853f
633. Sins are distinguished as mortal and venial.
497 611s
636. Without free consent there can be no sin.
123 244 335
637. Ignorance of gravity can be a mitigating factor in regard to the guilt of sin.
611n 611w 611x 611cc
638. God is not the author of sin, but only permits it [see also 469].
471
639. Sin results in the death of the soul.
184

ACTUAL GRACE

NECESSITY OF GRACE

650. Grace is absolutely necessary for the performance of any good work ordered to salvation.
220 348 558
656. Grace is necessary even for the beginning of faith and conversion.
114 808 (892) (892a)
657. Without grace a man cannot for very long resist concupiscence and grave temptation.
436 548

PERSEVERANCE

671. The just man cannot persevere for very long without the help of grace.
485 892
672. Final perseverance is a great gift of God.
79a 557a

NATURE OF GRACE

680. Even if in a less proper sense, creation, free will, and the preaching of the gospel may be termed *graces*.
114 287
681. Protection from sinning, along with the other external favors of providence directed toward salvation, also pertains to grace.
59 186
682. Grace is an internal movement.
833
683. Actual grace consists both in the enlightening of the intellect, . . .
430 548
684. . . . and in the inspiring of the will.
53 430 548

NOMENCLATURE

690. Grace so cooperates *(gratia co-operans)* with the human will that a man can do nothing that is good without God's doing it along with him.
436 465 485
695. There is a kind of grace called *sufficient grace,* which truly suffices for the producing of its effect, but which does not actually produce it.
244 247 622
696. There is another kind of grace called *efficacious grace,* which effectively moves the will.
348 558

GRACE AND FREEDOM

700. Grace does not destroy free will.
244 436 446 704
701. Because grace does not destroy free will, with equal graces one person may succeed while yet another fails.
247

GRACE AS A GIFT

711. Grace is freely given: *i. e.,* it is gratuitous.
(808)?
712. It is proper that we pray for grace.
507a
713. It is possible to win the graces of conversion and final perseverance with prayers of supplication.
699

DISTRIBUTION OF GRACE

724. To no one, not even to infidels, does God deny grace sufficient for faith and for salvation.
12 622

HABITUAL GRACE

THE SUPERNATURAL ORDER

740. Among the gifts which God has bestowed upon His creatures, some are natural and some are supernatural.
253 699 813

JUSTIFICATION

750. In justification, the permanent supernatural gift of habitual grace is infused.
251 253 449
751. In justification, sins are truly blotted out.
146 407
752. In justification man is renewed internally.
32 36 219 548 607 835
753. In justification man receives within himself the indwelling Holy Spirit.
36 158 159 219 251 449 607 683 770 780 813 853a 872
754. In justification man becomes a sharer of the divine nature.
40 412 613 770 780 787 788
755. In justification man becomes the adoptive son of God.
407 766 770 788 813
756. In justification man becomes an heir of the heavenly kingdom.
607
757. In justification man becomes a friend of God.
433
758. It is by faith that a man is justified.
16 48 57 173 245 310a 428 481 910r
759. Man is not justified by works.
16 (176) 699
760. Although it is by faith and not by works that a man is justified, works too are necessary for his justification.
15 16 428 481 564
761. Habitual or sanctifying grace is lost through mortal sin.
158 683 770

MERIT

770. The just man can have true merit.
68 123 246 311 836 889a
771. The just can merit eternal life.
173 176 396 564
775. Besides the promise of God and the state of grace, another condition of meriting is free will.
123 156

MARY

779. Mary is truly the Mother of God, . . .
42 223 256a 710a 711
780. . . . the *deipara* or *theotókos.*
680 788 824
781. Mary conceived as a virgin *(virgo ante partum).*
42 112 122a 127 134a 141 191 222 223 224 277 328a 330 358 359 371 380 389 394 398 408 495 633 634 711 788 817 864 874a 875 886a 910a 910s
782. Mary was a virgin during the birth *(in partu).*
(359) 710a
783. Mary remained a virgin after the birth of Christ *(virgo post partum).*
(380) 767a
784. Mary is the New Eve, the co-operatrix in the mystery of the redemption.
141 224 358
786. Mary was conceived immaculate, *i.e.,* without original sin.
719

SACRAMENTS

IN GENERAL

790. Sacraments are outward signs which confer the very grace they signify.
181 303 590 601b
792. Among the sacramental rites, the imposition of hands signifies in a special way the conferring of grace [*see also* 906, 958 *and* 959].
304 362 568b 569 595 601b 611v
795. Circumcision was a sacrament of the Old Law, prefiguring Baptism.
134
796. The Sacraments confer grace more abundantly upon a better disposed recipient.
809 848b
798. The Sacraments of Baptism, Confirmation and Holy Orders imprint an indelible spiritual character.
712 808 847

799. Because Baptism, Confirmation and Holy Orders confer an indelible spiritual character, they are never to be repeated.
    308 314 592a 593 651n
800. The Sacraments confer grace from the power, present in the rite, of the Holy Spirit.
    303 607 683 835
803. The validity of the Sacraments does not depend upon the faith of their minister [*see also* 830 *and* 962].
    (308) (592) (594) (596) (599b) (601a) (601c) (602)
807. For a licit and fruitful reception of the Sacraments on the part of an adult, certain dispositions are necessary.
    504
808. The Fathers knew all of our seven Sacraments.
    299 362 848a
809. In regard to the washing of feet *(lotio pedum):*
    611y 690
810. The Fathers are witness to the fact that there was, especially in regard to the Sacraments, a rule of secrecy *(disciplina arcana).*
    274 394i 807 811 834a
811. Besides the Sacraments there are certain sacred things or rites called Sacramentals, which also are of value for sanctification.
    394i

BAPTISM

820. Baptism is a true Sacrament, instituted by Christ.
    4 34 126 299 302 329 362 491 681 690
821. The Baptism of John was not a Sacrament.
    305 690
822. The remote matter of Baptism is natural water.
    4 92 126 302 303 367 394i 810a
823. The proximate matter of Baptism is the washing in water.
    4 126 307 394i 810a
824. There is witness to the washing having been done by immersion, by infusion, and by aspersion.
    4 34 92 304 394i 547 590 812 840a 841
825. The triple washing is not of necessity: but it is a usage of greatest antiquity.
    4 367 394i 840a
826. In the form of Baptism it is essential that there be a distinct expression of God as One and Three.
    4 126 219 307 394i 500 597 601d 647c 651y 745d 840a 858
827. Baptism conferred in the name of Jesus, lacking the trinitarian formula, is held to be invalid.
    500 597
828. In regard to the minister of solemn Baptism:
    65 310 394i 594 601 601c
829. Any man, using the requisite matter and form and having the intention of baptizing, can validly confer Baptism; but he does so licitly only when he does so in a case of necessity.
    310 366 611u
830. Even heretics can baptize validly [*see also* 803].
    (308) (591) (592a) (593) (599b) (600) (601a) 601d (602a) 647c
831. Baptism is necessary for all in respect to salvation, whether they be infant or adult.
    92 135a 302 306 310 (310a) 496 501 586 601? 752a 810a 811
833. In the case of infants or adults, martyrdom can take the place of actual Baptism in water.
    309 493 597a 598 811
834. A fit subject for Baptism is any person not yet baptized.
    126 201 585
835. The Church has always acknowledged that even infants are capable of receiving Baptism.
    201 394i 496 501 585
836. The effect of Baptism is spiritual regeneration, which consists in the remission of every sin with the punishment due it, and the infusion of first grace.
    34 87 92 93b 126 181 187a 220 302 304 312 362 394i 407 491 493 501 548 594 597a 613 683 812 818e 910a

CONFIRMATION

840. Confirmation is a true Sacrament.
    174 304 362 390 547 592 595 698 725 842
841. The remote matter of Confirmation is blessed oil (chrism).
    174 304 394i 698 841
842. The proximate matter of Confirmation is the anointing made with chrism on the forehead, in the form of a cross.
    174 299 304 394i 592 745q 842 847
843. In regard to the ordinary minister of Confirmation:
    394i 595 601c 611ee

845. There is an obligation, however less strict, of receiving Confirmation.
       547 592 611ee
846. The effect of Confirmation is the more abundant pouring out of the graces and gifts of the Holy Spirit.
       362 745q 841 842 842a

EUCHARIST

Real Presence

849. The Sacrament of the Eucharist was instituted by Christ in memory of His passion and death.
       135 708 725
850. In the words recounted by John (6:48ff), Christ promised that He would give Himself, His own flesh and blood, in a real sense, as food and drink.
       408 491 559 870
851. Christ is really present in the Eucharist under the appearances of bread and wine.
       54a 56 64 128 187 187a 234 249 362 367 394i 410 490 707 708 845 846 848 853j 870
852. The truth of the Real Presence is evident from the words of institution.
       128 232 240 300a 689 707 843
853. Some Fathers occasionally referred to the Eucharist as a sign or figure of the body of Christ, . . .
       337 343 394i 504
854. . . . and even of His Mystical Body, the Church.
       589a
855. The presence of Christ in the Eucharist does not depend upon the faith and dispositions of the recipient.
       (504)? (707)?
856. The bread and wine, through the words of consecration, are changed into the Body and Blood of Christ.
       128 249 802 840 843 844 850
857. In the Eucharist Christ is really present, but in a spiritual manner.
       410
858. Christ is present in the Eucharist, entirely in each of the two species.
       318
859. Christ is present in the Eucharist, entirely in every particle of each of the two species.
       367 490 707 853k
860. The matter of the Eucharist is bread and wine.
       6 128 129 187 249 394i 581 582 671 707 802 840
861. A small amount of water is to be added to the wine before the consecration.
       128 129 240 249 410 583
862. The Fathers regarded the form of the Eucharist as consisting either of the words of Christ, . . .
       128
863. . . . or of the epiclesis; . . .
       234 840 842 850
864. . . . or, less precisely, they refer to it as the *prayer* or *blessing*.
       128 504 802
865. The Eucharist is a permanent Sacrament.
       301 318
866. The minister of the confecting of the Eucharist is a priest.
       65 (366) 647e 671
867. In offering the Sacrifice of the Mass, the priest functions as another Christ.
       584

Communion

868. In regard to the minister of the distribution of the Eucharist:
       128 129 394i 552a
870. In a broad sense, eating of the Eucharist is a necessity for the soul.
       845a
871. In the ancient Church it was generally the custom that Communion was taken under both species.
       6 7 128 187 394i 436a 552a 845 846 853l
872. Examples of Communion under only one species, however, are not totally lacking.
       318
873. It was the practice of the early Church that the faithful received the Eucharist daily.
       301 436a 559
874. Only the baptized may receive the Eucharist.
       6 128
875. For a licit and fruitful reception of the Eucharist it is necessary to be in the state of grace.
       7 8 368 504 551 552a 569 853m
877. The Eucharist was so instituted that it might be received in the manner of food, for the refreshment of the soul.
       7 187 362 394i 408 410 436a 707
878. Through Communion the just become, in a certain sense, concorporeal and consanguineal with Christ.
       249 843 845 853e 853k 870

879. The Eucharist is a pledge of resurrection and of life eternal.
43 234 249 436a 559
880. The Eucharist both signifies and assures the unity of the Church.
6 56 848c

The Mass

890. The Mass is a true sacrifice.
21 232 233 320 382 552a 584 851
891. The Mass is a re-enactment of the sacrifice of the cross.
582
892. The sacrifice of the Mass was prefigured in the sacrifices of the Old Law.
135 233
893. The sacrifice of the Mass was prefigured in a special way in the sacrifice of Melchisedech.
581 671
894. The Mass was announced beforehand in the prophecy of Malachias.
8 135 232
895. Christ is the Victim offered in the sacrifice of the Mass.
853.
897. The Mass is a sacrifice offered for adoration, thanksgiving, propitiation, and supplication.
232 367 851 853

Liturgy and Law

898. There were liturgical regulations even in the early Church; . . .
19 19a 394e 651x 651z 671 745k 745*l* 745r 853k 853*l*
899. . . . and other regulations, seemingly arbitrary, but really prompted by prudence, in view of the necessities of good order.
611o 611p 611z 647b 647f 647i 651g 651h 651i 651j 651k 651*l* 651m 651o 651u
651v 651w 702a 745m 745n 745o 745p 910c 910d 910j

PENANCE

900. The Church has received from Christ the power of remitting or of refusing to remit sins.
387 584a 602 611e 611f 611i 637 855a
901. This power extends to all and every sin committed after Baptism.
59 385 (386) 561 577 578
902. Adultery, murder, and apostasy or heresy were regarded as more grave than other sins.
81c 93a 383 385 568 576a 576b 611k 611q 611bb 611cc 611dd
904. In the ancient Church public penance was imposed for the more grievous public crimes.
315 385 568 568b 569 578 611a 611*l* 611m 651q 651r 651s 651t 745b
905. Less grave sins were remitted without public penance.
485a 497
906. Reconciliation was made through the imposition of hands, ordinarily administered by the bishop.
386 568b 569 570 611s 647c 651n 745c 752a
907. There are indications that forgiveness through public penitential acts was granted only once to any one penitent; . . .
81b 86 87 314 315 386a 497 611r
908. . . . but there are indications also, and even clear statements, that the private reception of sacramental forgiveness was repeatable.
314 317 485a 497 561 637 685
909. In regard to private absolution, granted in the imminent danger of death:
570 576 651s 752a
910. Repentance is a true virtue, by which a man detests and grieves for his sin, and intends to repair what was, in a certain sense, an injury done to God.
27 86a 315
911. Repentance is necessary in order to obtain the forgiveness of sins.
90 103 315 386 611n
912. Contrition, which is sorrow for sin motivated by perfect charity, always and immediately by its very nature justifies.
26 434 493
914. Attrition, which is sorrow for sin motivated by the fear of punishment, is a good act and suffices, in respect to sorrow, for the obtaining of absolution.
434
916. Some kind of confession, not made to God only, but external, is required for the remission of sins.
3 8 26a 37 192b 193 315 316 477 485a 493 551 569 570 685
918. For absolution, there is required a distinct accusation of sins.
485a 494 553
919. A declaration of sins joined to penance:
485a 493

920. Confession was made privately to a priest.
    485a 493 553 685
921. With confession made privately, the priest was obligated not to make public knowledge the sins confessed.
    685
923. There remains after absolution the necessity of making the satisfaction demanded by God's justice.
    313 315 584a
925. The minister of the Sacrament of Penance is a priest only; . . .
    73? 315 394a 551 553 578
926. . . . but a deacon might, in case of necessity, be the minister of reconciliation, . . .
    611s
927. . . . and Cyprian of Carthage seems to have allowed in such cases that confession even might be made to a deacon, but whether or not with absolution given by the deacon is not clear.
    570
928. Penance is necessary for all who have fallen into grave sin after Baptism.
    314 561
929. Venial sins can be remitted by charity, by prayer, and by good works.
    493 563 564 707

Indulgences

935. Something of the canonical penance could be remitted through the intercession of the martyrs.
    387a 570
936. There exists in the Church a treasury of merits, from which indulgences can be applied to sinners in respect to the punishments due their sins.
    552

SACRAMENT OF THE ILL

940. Extreme Unction, the Sacrament of the Ill, is a true Sacrament, the effect of which is to blot out the remains of sin and to strengthen both soul and body.
    493 698

HOLY ORDERS

951. In the Church the clergy constitute a rank distinct from the laity.
    19 48 49 50 300 366 438 477a 611aa 651g 745h 753
952. Episcopate, priesthood, and diaconate constitute the major orders.
    43a 44 47a 49 50 58a 70a 394c 413 427 546a 611j 611k 745m
953. Bishops are constituted in an order superior to that of priests.
    19 43b 394c 546c
954. Deacons are the helpers of bishops and priests in the sacred functions.
    9 19 20 43a 48 84 128 394c 546a
955. Subdeacons were the helpers of deacons; and they are constituted in a rank established later by the Church.
    70a 394h 546a 745j 745m
956. Besides Subdiaconate there were other orders also, called minor orders.
    70a 300 394g 546a 570a 745i 745m
957. In the ancient Church women were able to be consecrated to God in a special way, as deaconesses or widows; but they received no order in the proper sense, and were not ordained.
    70a 300 394f 413 477a 546a 651y 745f
958. The matter of orders is the imposition of hands.
    394a 394d 588
959. The form of orders is the prayer which is conjoined to the imposition of hands.
    394a 394b 394c
960. The minister of orders is the bishop only.
    394a 394b 394c 601c 753 910e
961. The minister of episcopal consecration is a bishop, and from earliest times three bishops were regularly required.
    394a 651j
962. Even heretics can validly ordain; . . .
    (592) 651n
963. . . . but valid Baptism is a necessary prerequisite to a valid reception of orders.
    651y
964. In the Church it was already the custom in antiquity to impose celibacy on clerics in major orders or at least to prohibit their marrying a second time.
    299 366 381 611t 647g
965. The effects of the reception of orders are the augmenting of grace, the imprinting of a character, and the conferring of spiritual power.
    237 394a
966. The Church can establish impediments to the reception of the Sacrament of Orders.
    651g 651h 651o 651p

MATRIMONY

968. The ends of matrimony are the begetting of offspring, the mutual help of the spouses, and the providing of a remedy against concupiscence.
433a 507 818c 818d
969. From earliest times the Church has regarded abortion as a most grievous crime, . . .
1a 396a
970. . . . and contraception, too, as a grievous sin against the ends of marriage.
396a
972. Christian marriage is a true Sacrament.
67 320 384 420a 420b 505
974. Matrimony effects a bond which is completely indissoluble.
86 119 320 420 506 507 611b 611d 642 854
975. The indissoluble bond of Matrimony cannot be broken, not even on account of adultery on the part of one of the spouses.
86 (342) 507 611c 642 854
976. The Pauline Privilege case:
506? 611d
977. The Sacrament of Matrimony effects an exclusive bond.
167 186 271 281a
979. In regard to second marriages:
88 119 167 366 382 477a 506 611u 651n 745a 818d
980. The Church is competent to establish matrimonial impediments.
320 384 611g 611h 611i 647d 647h 745e
982. A vow of chastity is an impediment to subsequent marriage.
568
983. Matrimony is good and lawful, a holy estate; . . .
818c
984. . . . but it is surpassed in dignity by celibacy and virginity.
67 433a 516a 576a 818c

ESCHATOLOGY

DEATH

990. Death is the separation of the soul from the body.
252 345 349a 683
991. After death there is no longer any possibility of meriting or demeriting.
103 560 561 576 578 693 886 887

PARTICULAR JUDGMENT

995. The soul undergoes the particular judgment as soon as it leaves the body.
(646) 886
996. Even before the general judgment souls are already in blessedness or in torment.
132 (259)? (351)? 352 446 (646) 721 886 887

PURGATORY

1000. A place of purgation exists, where those souls of whom further expiation is required undergo temporary punishment.
352 646?
1001. The souls of the dead detained in purgatory can be aided by the suffrages of the living.
187 187a 367 382 852 853

END OF THE WORLD

1010. Various signs will precede the end of the world.
10 832 832a
1011. The dead will rise, . . .
10 13 13a 51 54 74 112 147 155 157 169 173 190a 249 250 252 259 272 276
301a 328a 345 363 364 446 680 681 687 721 836 872 910a
1012. . . . not the just dead only, but all the dead.
(63)? (64)? 124 191 290 365 395 646 647 694 837
1013. The dead will rise in their same bodies.
104 120 155 345 365 395 446 468 686 836 837 885
1014. Origenism, in regard to the final apokatastasis:
456 457 463 464 467a 468

1015. Origenism, in regard to spiritual fire:
   463 464
1016. Millenarianism or chiliasm was admitted by some Fathers, . . .
   138a 260 261 338 447? 647 658
1017. . . . but was rejected by others.
   138a 263? 658

GENERAL JUDGMENT

1020. After the end of the world there will take place the general judgment.
   74 155 364 396 579 694

HELL AND PUNISHMENT

1030. Those who die in mortal sin are thrust into hell.
   41 317   579
1032. In hell, besides the pain of loss in the deprivation of God, there is also the pain of sense, through true
   corporeal fire.
   41 78 98a 100 106 115 121 124 166 176 273 276 284 317 346 396 437 560 646
   837
1033. The fire of hell torments both the souls of the damned and the demons.
   124 356 579 646
1034. The punishment of the damned is eternal.
   41 78 100 102 106 115 121 124 176 191 239 273 276 284 290 317 396 437 446
   560 579 646 837
1035. Although it is eternal, the punishment of the damned is not of equal severity for all.
   697
1036. In regard to the mitigation of punishment:
   273 396 560

HEAVEN AND BLESSEDNESS

1040. The object of blessedness is God only.
   53a
1041. Perfect blessedness in heaven consists in seeing and loving God.
   236 301a 579 891
1042. The blessed are not able any more to sin.
   693
1043. Blessedness is eternal and cannot be lost.
   102 176 191 239 276 284 290 396 468 579 693 910a
1044. The bodies of the blessed will be glorious and immortal.
   166 338 395 468 837 883   885
1045. In regard to accidental blessedness:
   78 176 579
1046. There will be various degrees of blessedness, in respect to merits.
   696

GENERAL INDEX

Numerical references are to page numbers in the text. Numbers followed by an *n* are to footnotes on the page indicated by the number. Numbers preceded by *DI* are to propositions so numbered in the Doctrinal Index, pp. 413–432 above.

"The Fathers were enlightened theologians who illumined and defended Catholic dogma. For the most part, they were also zealous pastors who preached it and applied it to the needs of souls. As preachers, they were the first to give systematic form to apostolic preaching; for this, as St. Augustine affirms, they fulfilled a task in the development of the Church which the Apostles had fulfilled for its birth: 'Talibus post Apostolos sancta Ecclesia plantatoribus, rigatoribus, aedificatoribus, nutritoribus crevit" (*Contra Iulianum Pelagianum - de originali peccato*, II, 10, 37; PL 44, 700).

"As pastors, the Fathers felt the need to adapt the gospel message to contemporary thought, and with the food of the true Faith, to nourish both themselves and the People of God. The result was that for them catechesis, theology, Sacred Scripture, liturgy, spiritual and pastoral life were all joined up together in a vital unity; their works did not speak only to the intellect but to the whole man, embracing intellect, will and emotions."

— Pope Paul VI

THE FAITH OF THE EARLY FATHERS

is but one title among scores of publications in the **POPULAR LITURGICAL LIBRARY.** There are whole sections in this library catalog devoted to:

> **THE MASS LITURGY**
> **THE SACRAMENTS**
> **SACRED SONG**
> **THE LITURGY OF THE HOURS**
> **SACRED SCRIPTURE**
> **FAMILY LIFE**
> **LITURGICAL YEAR**
> **PARISH SERVICE AIDS**
> **CARDS AND PLAQUES**
> **PERIODICALS**
> **RECORDINGS**

We would be pleased to send you a free copy of our **POPULAR LITURGICAL LIBRARY** descriptive catalog.

Address: The Liturgical Press, Saint John's Abbey, Collegeville, Minnesota 56321.